THE OXFORD HISTORY OF ANGLICANISM

General Editor: Rowan Strong

The Oxford History of Anglicanism, Volume I
Reformation and Identity, c.1520–1662
Edited by Anthony Milton

The Oxford History of Anglicanism, Volume II
Establishment and Empire, 1662–1829
Edited by Jeremy Gregory

The Oxford History of Anglicanism, Volume III
Partisan Anglicanism and its Global Expansion, 1829–c.1914
Edited by Rowan Strong

The Oxford History of Anglicanism, Volume IV
Global Western Anglicanism, c.1910–present
Edited by Jeremy Morris

The Oxford History of Anglicanism, Volume V
Global Anglicanism, c.1910–2000
Edited by William L. Sachs

The Oxford History of Anglicanism, Volume II

Establishment and Empire, 1662–1829

Edited by
JEREMY GREGORY

OXFORD
UNIVERSITY PRESS

Great Clarendon Street, Oxford, OX2 6DP,
United Kingdom

Oxford University Press is a department of the University of Oxford.
It furthers the University's objective of excellence in research, scholarship,
and education by publishing worldwide. Oxford is a registered trade mark of
Oxford University Press in the UK and in certain other countries

First Edition published in 2017

Impression: 1

Published in the United States of America by Oxford University Press
198 Madison Avenue, New York, NY 10016, United States of America

British Library Cataloguing in Publication Data
Data available

Library of Congress Control Number: 2016942494

ISBN 978-0-19-964463-6

Printed and bound by
CPI Group (UK) Ltd, Croydon, CR0 4YY

For John Walsh and in memory of Garry Bennett

Acknowledgements

This has been an extremely interesting project with which to be involved and I am grateful to my fellow editors in the series, Anthony Milton, Jeremy Morris, Bill Sachs, and Rowan Strong for their friendship and encouragement. I would especially like to thank Rowan Strong who, as General Editor of the series, steered us safely to completion and who gave very useful comments on the chapters which follow.

I would like to thank the contributors who rose to the challenge of writing for the volume and who responded cheerfully to editorial requests. In particular, I would like to thank Tim Grass who took on the major task of finalizing the chapters for submission to Oxford University Press. Tim's skills as a copy-editor are legendary and his attention to detail, his courtesy, and his shrewd judgement, are hugely appreciated both by me and by the contributors. I would like to thank the University of Manchester and the University of Nottingham for financial and other support.

At OUP, I am very grateful to Karen Raith, Senior Assistant Commissioning Editor, who oversaw the publication of the volume. Saraswathi Ethiraju provided excellent support throughout the production process and Joanna North gave an eagle-eyed final copy-edit.

My own work on the Church of England in the long eighteenth century was kindled by being taught as an undergraduate by John Walsh (and the late Colin Matthew) on the fabled Oxford University History Final Honours Special Subject 'Church, State, and English Society, 1829–1854' which stimulated me to ask what the Anglican Church was like before 1829. I was supervised for my DPhil by John Walsh and the late G. V. Bennett, both of them pupils of Norman Sykes who is often regarded as the key figure in the study of evidenced-based analysis of the Church of England in the years covered by this book. Many of the other contributors to this volume have either been taught by John or Garry, have benefited from their sage counsel, or have learnt from and been inspired by their publications. For these reasons we dedicate this volume to them.

Contents

PART III. ANGLICAN IDENTITIES

List of Figures

List of Contributors

Gareth Atkins is Fellow and Director of Studies in History at Magdalene College, Cambridge, and a Postdoctoral Fellow on the ERC-funded Bible and Antiquity in Nineteenth-Century Culture Project at the Centre for Research in Arts, Social Sciences and Humanities (CRASSH), also in Cambridge. He works on religious culture and politics in eighteenth- and nineteenth-century Britain, ranging from maritime religion to Protestant and Catholic constructions of heroes (and villains) from history. His edited book, *Making and Remaking Saints in Nineteenth-Century Britain*, was published by Manchester University Press in 2016. He has published widely on Anglican Evangelicalism and is currently completing a monograph, *Converting Britannia: Anglican Evangelicals and British Public Life, c.1770–c.1840*. His new project uses the reception of King David to explore debates about masculinity, sexuality, the Bible, archaeology, and empire in nineteenth-century culture.

Toby Barnard, FBA, MRIA (Hon.) is Emeritus Fellow of Hertford College, Oxford. His most recent book is *Brought to Book: Print in Ireland, 1680–1784* (Dublin, 2017). He also edited (with W. G. Neely) *The Clergy of the Church of Ireland, 1000–2000: Messengers, Watchmen and Stewards* (Dublin, 2006).

James B. Bell is Distinguished Fellow, Rothermere American Institute at the University of Oxford. His research has focused on the political, religious, and cultural history of the Church of England during the seventeenth and eighteenth centuries in England and in early America. He is the author of *The Imperial History of the King's Church in Early America, 1607–1783* (Basingstoke, 2004), *A War of Religion: Dissenters, Anglicans and the American Revolution* (Basingstoke, 2008), *Empire, Religion and Revolution in Early Virginia, 1607–1786* (Basingstoke, 2013), and *Anglicans, Dissenters and Radical Change in Early New England, 1686–1786* (Basingstoke, 2017), and has compiled the database of the 1,281 colonial American clergy of the Church of England at <http://www.jamesbbell.com>.

J. C. D. Clark was educated at Cambridge, where he was a Fellow of Peterhouse, and moved to Oxford, where he was a Fellow of All Souls College. At the University of Chicago he was a Visiting Professor at the Committee on Social Thought, and is currently Hall Distinguished Professor of British History at the University of Kansas. His research addresses British history in the long eighteenth century, and has argued especially for the reintegration of politics, political thought, and religion. His best known works are *English Society 1660–1832* and *The Language of Liberty 1660–1832*; his book on the thought of Thomas Paine is forthcoming, and he is completing a study of the Enlightenment.

Tony Claydon is Professor of Early Modern History at Bangor University. His research has centred on the culture, politics, and religion of the late Stuart period in England, particularly the propaganda of William III, the European identities of England, and concepts and experiences of time. Beyond numerous articles on these topics, he is author of *William III and the Godly Revolution* (Cambridge, 1996) and *Europe and the Making of England 1660–1760* (Cambridge, 2007).

Elizabeth Elbourne is an Associate Professor in the Department of History and Classical Studies, McGill University. Scholarship includes *Sex, Power and Slavery* (Athens, OH, 2014), co-edited with Gwyn Campbell, and *Blood Ground: Colonialism, Missions and the Contest for Christianity in Britain and the Eastern Cape, 1799–1853* (Montreal and Kingston, 2003). She was co-editor of the *Journal of British Studies* with Brian Cowan from 2010 to 2015.

William Gibson is Professor of Ecclesiastical History and Director of the Oxford Centre for Methodism and Church History at Oxford Brookes University. His research focuses on the religious history of England from 1660 to 1900. He is editor of *The Oxford Handbook of the British Sermon 1689–1901* (Oxford, 2012). His most recent books include *Britain 1660–1851: The Making of the Nation* (London, 2013) and (with Joanne Begiato) *Sex and the Church in the Eighteenth Century* (London, 2017).

Jeremy Gregory is Pro-Vice-Chancellor for the Faculty of Arts and Professor of the History of Christianity at the University of Nottingham. His research and publications have shaped and contributed to the debates concerning the role of the Church of England in particular, and religion in general, in English social, cultural, political, and intellectual history from the mid-seventeenth to the mid-nineteenth centuries. He is the author of *Restoration, Reformation, and Reform, 1660–1828: Archbishops of Canterbury and their Diocese* (Oxford, 2000).

Joseph Hardwick is Senior Lecturer in British History at Northumbria University. He is the author of *An Anglican British World: The Church of England and the Expansion of the Settler Empire, c.1790–1860* (Manchester, 2014), and currently researches the history of special acts of worship in the British Empire.

Clare Haynes is Senior Research Associate on the Leverhulme-funded project *The Medieval Parish Churches of Norwich: City, Community and Architecture* at the University of East Anglia. She is the author of *Pictures and Popery: Art and Religion in England, 1660–1760* (Aldershot, 2006) and has completed a book manuscript provisionally entitled *In the Idol's Shadow: Art in the Church* *of England 1660–1839.* In addition to her research on art and religion, other interests include graphic satire, the history of collecting, and antiquarianism.

Robert G. Ingram is Associate Professor of History at Ohio University and director of the George Washington Forum on American Ideas, Politics and Institutions. He is the author of *Religion, Reform and Modernity in the Eighteenth Century: Thomas Secker and the Church of England* (Woodbridge, 2007) and co-editor of *God in the Enlightenment* (New York, 2016) and *Between Sovereignty and Anarchy* (Charlottesville, VA, 2015).

W. M. Jacob was Principal of Lincoln Theological College, and Archdeacon of Charing Cross in London Diocese. He has published extensively about religious history in England and Wales in the eighteenth and nineteenth centuries.

David Manning received his PhD in history from Clare College, Cambridge, after completing a dissertation entitled 'Blasphemy in England, *c.*1660–1730' (2009). He is now an Honorary Visiting Fellow at the University of Leicester and pursues wide-ranging research interests in the history of Christian thought and culture in early modern Britain and the British Atlantic world, *c.*1500–*c.*1800. He edited and contributed to *Reformation & Renaissance Review*, Special Issue: *The Church of England as 'Primitive Christianity Restored'?* (2011). His other publications include 'Reformation and the Wickedness of Port Royal, Jamaica, 1655–*c.*1692', in Crawford Gribben and Scott Spurlock (eds.), *Puritans and Catholics in the Trans-Atlantic World, 1600–1800* (Basingstoke, 2015). David's forthcoming work engages with divine illumination, practical divinity, speechlessness, and blasphemy.

Louis P. Nelson is Professor of Architectural History and the Associate Provost for Outreach at the University of Virginia. He is a specialist in the built environments of the early modern Atlantic world, with published work on the American South, the Caribbean, and West Africa. Nelson has produced two book-length monographs and three edited collections of essays, served two terms as Senior Co-Editor of *Buildings and Landscapes*—the leading English-language venue for scholarship on vernacular architecture—and penned numerous articles. His early work on colonial religious architecture is best realized in his monograph *The Beauty of Holiness: Anglicanism and Architecture in Colonial South Carolina* (Chapel Hill, NC, 2008), winner of the 2010 SESAH Best Book of the Year Prize. His latest monograph, *Architecture and Empire in Jamaica*, has recently been released from Yale University Press.

Daniel O'Connor is an Anglican priest and has served in England, India, and Scotland. He is an Honorary Research Fellow of Edinburgh University. His early research was on devotional literature, later on anti-colonial missionaries. He was responsible for the tercentennial history of the United Society for the

Propagation of the Gospel, and more recently published *The Chaplains of the East India Company 1601–1858* (New York, 2012) and contributed to *The Oxford Handbook of Anglican Studies* (Oxford, 2016).

Alasdair Raffe is a Chancellor's Fellow in History at the University of Edinburgh. He is a historian of Scotland in the seventeenth and eighteenth centuries, with interests in religion, politics, and ideas. He is the author of *The Culture of Controversy: Religious Arguments in Scotland, 1660–1714* (Woodbridge, 2012) and *Scotland in Revolution, 1685–1690* (Edinburgh, forthcoming).

Mark Smith is Associate Professor of History at the University of Oxford. His research interests include the history of the parish, local responses to religion, and the Anglophone Evangelical tradition. He is the author of *Religion in Industrial Society* (Oxford, 1994). He is also the editor of *Doing the Duty of the Parish* (Winchester, 2004) and *British Evangelical Identities Past and Present* (Milton Keynes, 2008) and with Stephen Taylor of *Evangelicalism in the Church of England c.1790–c.1900* (Woodbridge, 2004).

Bryan D. Spinks is Bishop F. Percy Goddard Professor of Liturgical Studies and Pastoral Theology at Yale Divinity School. His research interests include East Syrian rites, Reformed rites, issues in theology and liturgy, and worship in a post-modern age. He is the author of *The Worship Mall: Contemporary Responses to Contemporary Culture* (London, 2010) and *Do This in Remembrance of Me: The Eucharist from the Early Church to the Present Day* (Norwich, 2013). He co-edited, with Teresa Berger, *Liturgy's Imagined Past/s: Methodologies and Materials in the Writing of Liturgical History Today* (Collegeville, MN, 2016).

Grant Tapsell is Fellow and Tutor in History at Lady Margaret Hall, Oxford. His research interests focus on political and religious affairs across the British Isles, c.1640–c.1689, and he is currently researching the career of Archbishop William Sancroft. He is the author of *The Personal Rule of Charles II, 1681–85* (Woodbridge, 2007) and (with George Southcombe) *Restoration Politics, Religion, and Culture: Britain and Ireland, 1660–1714* (Basingstoke, 2010). He has edited or co-edited three collections of essays, including *festschriften* for Clive Holmes and John Morrill and *The Later Stuart Church, 1660–1714* (Manchester, 2012).

Nicholas Temperley is Emeritus Professor of Music at the University of Illinois in Urbana-Champaign; he holds a PhD in music from Cambridge University. As a musicologist he has specialized in English music from the sixteenth to the nineteenth century. He has published *The Music of the English Parish Church*, 2 vols. (Cambridge, 1979) and *The Hymn Tune Index: A Census of English-Language Hymn Tunes in Printed Sources from 1535 to 1820*, 4 vols. (Oxford, 1998; online at hymntune.library.illinois.edu). His critical edition of Sternhold and Hopkins's *Whole Book of Psalms* (1562), co-edited with Beth Quitslund, will shortly be published.

David R. Wilson holds a PhD from the University of Manchester and teaches courses in church history, theology, and ethics at Portland Seminary of George Fox University and Warner Pacific College in Portland, Oregon. He is the author of *Church and Chapel in Industrializing Society: Anglican Ministry and Methodism in Shropshire, 1760–1785* (New York, 2017), and is a contributor to the *Oxford Encyclopedia of Biblical Interpretation* (Oxford, 2013), *Dissent and the Bible in Britain, c.1650–1950* (Oxford, 2013), and *Making and Remaking Saints in Nineteenth-Century Britain* (Manchester, 2016). He also co-edited *Holy Imagination: Thinking about Social Holiness* (Lexington, KY, 2015). His research has explored gender and ecclesiology within Anglicanism and Methodism in the long eighteenth century, and he is currently working on a book project focused on the Church, justice, and the margins of society.

Paula Yates is the Dean of St Padarn's Institute, the Church in Wales's innovative new theological college. She teaches Christian history, specializing in the history of Anglicanism and setting Welsh Anglicanism into its wider context. Her research interests are in interdenominational relationships in the eighteenth and nineteenth centuries; the interaction between Christianity and politics in Britain and the role played by schooling in both those areas, particularly in Wales. She has published a number of articles on aspects of Welsh Anglicanism.

B. W. Young is University Lecturer and Charles Stuart Tutor in History, Christ Church, Oxford. He is the author of *Religion and Enlightenment in Eighteenth-Century England* (Oxford, 1998), and *The Victorian Eighteenth Century* (Oxford, 2007). He is completing a study of relations between Christians and unbelievers in eighteenth-century England.

Natalie A. Zacek is Senior Lecturer in American History at the University of Manchester. Her monograph, *Settler Society in the English Leeward Islands, 1670–1776* (Cambridge, 2010), won the Royal Historical Society's Gladstone Prize. She is currently at work on a study of thoroughbred horse-racing in the nineteenth-century United States.

Series Introduction

Rowan Strong

Even Henry VIII at his autocratic best could hardly have imagined that his Church of England would, nearly five centuries after he had replaced papal authority with his own, become a global Christian communion encompassing people and languages far beyond the English. Formally, Henry asserted his royal power over the national Church on a more global scale—on the imperial theory that 'this realm of England is an empire' asserted the Act in Restraint of Appeals (to Rome) in 1533. Yet this was sixteenth-century imperial theory serving a national end. England was an empire and therefore King Henry was an emperor, that is, a ruler who was the paramount earthly authority and consequently superior to the papacy. So Henry's Church of England was always a national project, meant first and foremost to be the Church of the English—all the English—who would, if necessary, be compelled to come in. That national politico-religious agenda—a Church of all the English with the monarchy as its supreme head—formed the thrust of the policy of all but one of the succeeding Tudor monarchs. However, that royal agenda of the inclusion of all the English lay at the heart of the problem of this national ecclesiastical project.

At no time since Henry VIII ushered in his religious revolution did all the English wish to be part of this Church of England, though for over two centuries the monarchy and the English ruling classes attempted to encourage, cajole, or compel everyone in England to at least attend their parish church on Sunday. In Henry's reign, religious dissent from this monarchical Church was disparate and small, partly because Henry ensured it was dangerous. So some advanced Evangelicals (as early Protestants were called), such as Robert Barnes and William Tyndale, were executed by the regime in the early years of the religious revolution. Later, some prominent conservatives influenced by Catholic reform, such as Bishop John Fisher, Sir Thomas More, and some members of particular observant religious orders, followed their Evangelical enemies to the scaffold or the block. As the Protestant Reformation unfolded, and Catholic reform began to gather definition, from the reign of Edward VI onwards, those among the English who dissented from, or who were dissatisfied with, this national Church began to increase in numbers. Even those within it argued among themselves as to what the Church of England stood for.

Consequently, the Church of England, and its later global Anglican expansion, was always a contested identity throughout its history. It was contested both by its own adherents and by its leadership. This series looks at the history of that contestation and how it contributed to an evolving religious identity eventually known as Anglican. The major question it seeks to address is: what were the characteristics, carriers, shapers, and expressions of an Anglican identity in the various historical periods and geographic locations investigated by the volumes in the series? The series proposes that Anglicanism was not a version of Christianity that emerged entire and distinct by the end of the so-called Elizabethan Settlement. Rather, the disputed and developing identity of the Church developed from Henry VIII's religious revolution began to be worked out in the various countries of the British Isles from the early sixteenth century, went into a transatlantic environment in the seventeenth century, and then evolved in an increasing global context from the eighteenth century onwards. The series proposes that the answer to 'what is an Anglican?' was always debated. Moreover, Anglican identity over time experienced change and contradiction as well as continuities. Carriers of this developing identity included formal ecclesiastical dimensions such as clergy, Prayer Books, theology, universities, and theological colleges. Also among such formal carriers of Anglican identity was the English (then the British) state, so this series also investigates ways in which that state connection influenced Anglicanism. But the evolution of Anglicanism was also maintained, changed, and expressed in various cultural dimensions, such as architecture, art, and music. In addition, the series pays attention to how Anglicanism interacted with national identities, helping to form some, and being shaped itself by others. Each volume in the series devotes some explicit attention to these formal dimensions, by setting out the various Anglican identities expressed in their historical periods by theology, liturgy, architecture, religious experience and the practice of piety, and its interactions with wider society and politics.

A word needs to be said about the use of the term 'Anglicanism' to cover a religious identity whose origins lie in the sixteenth century when the name was not known. While recognizing the anachronism of the term Anglicanism, it is the 'least-worst' appellation to describe this religious phenomenon throughout the centuries of its existence. It is a fallacy that there was no use of the term Anglicanism to describe the Church of England and its global offshoots before John Henry Newman and the Oxford Movement in the 1830s. Newman and his Tractarian *confreres* certainly gave wider publicity to the name by using it to describe the separate Catholic culture of their Church. However, its usage predates the Tractarians because French Catholic writers were using it in the eighteenth century. It has become acceptable scholarly usage to describe this version of Christianity for the centuries prior to the nineteenth, notwithstanding its admittedly anachronistic nature.[1] Into the nineteenth century

---

[1] John Spurr, *The Restoration Church of England* (New Haven, CT, 1991), pp. xiii–xiv; John Walsh, Colin Haydon, and Stephen Taylor (eds.), *The Church of England c.1689–c.1833* (Cambridge, 1993), ch. 1; J. C. D. Clark, *English Society 1660–1832* (Cambridge, 2000 edn.), p. 256; Nigel Voak,

contemporaries used the terms 'Church of England' or 'Churchmen' to encompass their Church, even in countries and colonies beyond England. However, these names are not acceptable or understood today with their formerly inclusive meaning. The latter is objectionable on gender terms; and the former, while used by Anglicans in a variety of different lands and cultures, only leads to confusion when addressing the Church of England beyond England itself. Consequently, it has long been recognized in the scholarly literature that there is a need for some term that enshrines both the Church of England in England, its presence beyond that nation, and for that denomination over its entire historical existence. The most commonly adopted term is Anglicanism, and has been used by a number of recent scholars for periods prior to the nineteenth century.[2] A less Anglo-centric term—'Episcopal' or 'Episcopalianism'—is widely used in some parts of the world for the same ecclesiastical phenomenon—Scotland, North America, and Brazil. However, that term does not figure as widely as Anglican or Anglicanism in the historical literature, so it is the predominant usage in this series.

Consequently, Anglicanism is understood in this series as originating as a mixed and ambiguous ecclesiastical identity, largely as a result of its foundation by the Tudor monarchs of the sixteenth century who were determined to embrace the whole of the English nation within their national Church. It is, consequently, a religious community that brings together aspects of ecclesiastical identity that other Western Churches have separated. From an English Church that was predominantly Reformed Protestant in the sixteenth century, emerging Anglicanism developed a liturgical and episcopal identity alongside its Protestant emphasis on the Bible as the sole criterion for religious truth. The series therefore views Anglicanism as a Church in tension. Developing within Anglicanism over centuries was a creative but also divisive tension between Protestantism and Catholicism, between the Bible and tradition, between the Christian past and contemporary thought and society, that has meant Anglicanism has not only been a contested, but also at times an inconsistent Christian identity.

Within England itself, the Tudor project of a Church for the English nation became increasingly unrealistic as that Church encompassed people who were not English, or people who thought of themselves less as English than as different nationalities. But it has proved to have a surprisingly long life for the English themselves. The series demonstrates various ways in which the

---

Richard Hooker, and Reformed Theology: A Study of Reason, Will, and Grace (Oxford, 2003), pp. 1–5; Patricia U. Bonomi, *Under the Cope of Heaven: Religion, Society, and Politics in Colonial America* (Oxford, 2003 edn.), pp. 40–61.

[2] John Frederick Woolverton, *Colonial Anglicanism in North America* (Detroit, 1984); Thomas Bartlett, 'Ireland and the British Empire', in P. J. Marshall (ed.), *The Oxford History of the British Empire: The Eighteenth Century* (Oxford, 1998), p. 270.

Church over the centuries attempted to enforce, encourage, or cling to its national identity in England, with some degree of success, not least in retaining an enduring cultural appeal for some English who were only loosely connected to its institutional life, or barely to its theological or religious claims. Even today English cathedrals often attract audiences to daily Evensong that otherwise would not be there.

But for those in England and beyond for whom their Church was more central, contestation, and the evolution of identity it prompted, was probably inevitable in a Church that, after its first two supreme heads, was deliberately re-founded by Elizabeth I to be ambiguous enough in certain key areas to give a Church for all the English a pragmatic chance of being accomplished. But this was a loaded gun. A basically Protestant Church, aligned with the Swiss Reformation, but with sufficient traditional aspects to irritate convinced Protestants at home (though less so major European Reformers); but insufficiently Catholic to pull in reformed Catholics for whom papal authority was non-negotiable, simply pleased no one for quite a while. It was neither Catholic fish nor properly Protestant fowl, at least according to those English that wanted the Church of England to conform completely to the worship and polity of Geneva, by the later sixteenth century the pre-eminent centre of international Protestantism. Even Elizabeth's bishops were not entirely comfortable with the Church they led, and some of them tried to push the boundaries towards a properly Reformed Church modelled on that of the New Testament. Until, that is, they realized Elizabeth was having none of it, and made it clear she would not deviate beyond the Church and worship enacted by Parliament in 1558–9. In her mind, though probably in no one else's, those years constituted 'the settlement' of religion. When her archbishop of Canterbury, Edmund Grindal, refused to suppress the so-called 'prophesyings' of local clergy meeting for what would now be termed professional development, the queen simply suspended him for the rest of his life and put his functions into the hands of an appointed committee. Royal Supremacy was an undoubted component of the Church of England's identity, and Elizabeth and her successors for many years were not about to let anyone forget it, be they bishops or religiously interfering Members of Parliament.

The fact that Elizabeth emulated the long reigns of her father and grandfather, and not the short ones of her half brother and half sister, meant that her Church of England had time to put down local roots, notwithstanding the 'Anglican' puritans who sought to remake it in Geneva's image; or the zealous Catholic mission priests who hoped to dismantle it by taking Catholics out of it completely.

Where the English went their Church was bound to follow, though this intensified the unhappy situation of Ireland where the English had for centuries sought political domination undergirded by settlement. The consequence of legally establishing a Protestant Church of Ireland was to add religious difference to the centuries-old colonial condition of that island, whose Gaelic-speaking population remained stubbornly Catholic, in part because the Catholic Church was not English. Generally, the Irish wanted no part of this Church, aside from a small percentage of Irish who stood to gain from alliance with the prevailing Protestant power.

The following century saw the contest for the Church of England become more militant and polarized, until the English went to war to settle the issue among themselves. Perhaps the most surprising development was the emergence of a group of Anglicans who began to publicly advocate for the conservative aspects of the Church of England, a group that coalesced and became another sort of Anglican to the usual sort of Calvinist. This new variety of Anglican was particularly encouraged by specific royal patronage under the first two Stuart kings, James I and Charles I. These new contestants for the identity of the Church have been called by various names—Arminians, Laudians, avant-garde conformists—partly because they were not tightly defined but represented various agendas. Some sought, with the support of Charles I (the first Supreme Governor to be born into the Church of England), to bolster the independence and wealth of the Church; others, to oppose the Church's Calvinist theology and particularly the doctrine of predestination; others, to redress the lack of attention given to the sacraments and sacramental grace compared with the fervour for preaching among the more devout. But all were more or less agreed that the worship of the Church and the performance of the liturgy were woeful and needed to be better ordered, and churches should be more beautiful as aids to devotion and the fundamental significance of the sacraments.

But whether their agenda was liturgical, theological, or sacramental, to their puritan opponents this new Anglicanism looked like Catholicism, and that was the Antichrist from whose idolatrous and superstitious clutches the Protestant Reformation had released the English into true Christianity. They were not prepared to hand over the Church of England to a Catholic fifth-column. But while James I was cautious in his support for these avant-garde Anglicans, liking their support for divine-right monarchy but not their anti-Calvinism, his aesthetic, devout, and imperious son was markedly less so. The religious ball was in the royal court, particularly when Charles pulled off, in the 1630s, a decade of ruling without calling a Parliament, thereby silencing that body's uncomfortable and intolerable demands for royal accountability and religious reform.

The export in 1637 of Charles's particular version of the Church of England to his other kingdom of Scotland, in the form of a Scottish Prayer Book, not only stoked the fires of Scottish Presbyterian nationalism, but also released the pent-up energies of those within the Church of England who wanted an end to what they saw as royal absolutism and religious renovation by would-be papists. The rapid result of this intensification of political and religious contestation was the outbreak in 1642 of years of civil war in the royal Supreme Governor's three kingdoms. The internal Anglican quarrel, part of wider political differences, ended with the demise of the revolution begun by Henry VIII—the legal abolition of the Church of England, sealed in 1645 in the blood of the beheaded archbishop of Canterbury, William Laud; and followed by that of his Church's head, Charles I, in 1649. For the first time in its legal existence the Church of England (and the Church of Ireland) no longer officially existed.

Then an unexpected thing happened—some people continued to worship and practise their devotional lives according to the use of the defunct Church of England, demonstrating that its identity, though contested, was by this time a genuine reality in the lives of at least some of the English. They did this despite it being illegal, though the republican regime under Oliver Cromwell was not particularly zealous in its proscription of such activities. However, the diarist John Evelyn was present one Christmas Day when a covert congregation in London was dispersed by soldiers while keeping the holy day (proscribed by the regime) by gathering for Holy Communion according to the Book of Common Prayer.[3] Evelyn and others worshipped this way, and numbers of clergy used as much of the Prayer Book as they could in the parishes, notwithstanding that their leaders, the bishops, did little to set an example or to ensure the continuation of their illegal order. Anglican identity through worship and the ordering of the week and the year according to the Prayer Book and the Calendar of the Church of England was now being maintained, not by the state, but at the clerical and lay grassroots.

When Charles II landed in Dover in 1660 as the recognized king of England, after the rapid demise of the republican regime with its non-episcopal quasi-congregationalist Church following the death in 1658 of Lord Protector Oliver Cromwell, one outcome was the restoration of the legal monopoly of the Church of England. What that legal restoration did not do was to restore the spirituality, devotion, practice, and belief of the Church of England, because these had been ongoing in the period of the Church's official demise. Nevertheless, the legislation that brought back the establishment of the Church of England did newly define some ingredients of Anglican identity.

Before the Commonwealth the Church of England had not made ordination by bishops a non-negotiable aspect of Anglicanism. While it was certainly normal, there were exceptions made for some ministers who had been ordained in non-episcopal Churches elsewhere to minister in the Church of England without re-ordination. Now all clergy in the Church had to be episcopally ordained, with the sole exception of those clergy who came from Churches with a long historic tradition of episcopacy—the Roman Catholic,

---

[3] William Bray (ed.), *Diary and Correspondence of John Evelyn FRS* (1878, 4 vols.), I, p. 341 (25 Dec. 1657).

Orthodox, and the Church of Sweden. So from 1660 episcopacy became a basic characteristic of Anglicanism. The result was the expulsion of hundreds of clergy who would not conform to the requirement and to that of using only the Book of Common Prayer in worship. These dissenting clergy and laity, most of whom came from the previous Calvinist and puritan groups, now became permanent Nonconformists outside the Church of England. In 1662 a slightly revised Book of Common Prayer was passed by Parliament as the only authorized liturgy for the Church therefore reinforcing liturgical worship as a fundamental criterion of Anglican identity. Parliament again passed an Act of Uniformity and various other acts against Nonconformist worship. Uniformity was restored as an aspect of Anglicanism. So also was the royal supremacy.

However, while episcopacy has remained virtually unquestioned, and uniform liturgical worship remained uncontested within Anglicanism until the late twentieth century, the same could not be said for the other dimensions of the 1662 resettlement of Anglicanism—legal establishment, the royal supremacy, and uniformity. These identifiers were to be victims of the global success of Anglicanism from the eighteenth century, as the Church of England expanded; first across the Atlantic into North American colonies, and then globally within and beyond the British Empire. The first to go was legal establishment when the Americans successfully ushered in their republic after their War of Independence with Britain and some Anglicans remained in the new state. No longer could these Anglicans be subject to the British crown, or be legally privileged in a country in which they were a decided minority, when the Americans had gone to so much trouble to jettison these things. So an Anglicanism—known after the Scottish precedent as Episcopalianism—came into existence for the first time in history without monarchical headship, but rather as a voluntary association. Even within the British Empire these legal and political aspects of Anglicanism, so much a part of its foundation in the sixteenth century, were in trouble by the 1840s. It was then that the bishop of a very new colony, almost as far away from England as you could get, started acting as though the monarchy and establishment were Anglican optional extras. Inspired by the United States precedent, Bishop Augustus Selwyn began unilaterally calling synods of his clergy just four years after New Zealand had been annexed in 1840 as a crown colony, and a few years later he was leading his Church into a constitution which made authoritative synods of laymen, clergy, and bishops. Voluntaryism was catching on in international Anglicanism.

Contestation and evolution continued to be a part of Anglicanism. One of its most enduring characteristics, the sole use of an authorized liturgical form for public worship, began to be challenged by two mutually hostile internal parties—Evangelicals and Anglo-Catholics. In some dioceses the latter succumbed to the temptation to use the Roman missal with the permission of sympathetic diocesan bishops. In contrast, encouraged by the global ambitions of the wealthy diocese of Sydney, some of the former had *de facto* abandoned the use of an authorized Prayer Book entirely. Into this recent Anglican contest has been thrown issues of human sexuality which have conflicted wider society, particularly in the West, but which have been accentuated for Anglicans by questions of how varieties of human sexuality conform or do not conform to the authority of Scripture. So these historical forces have not ceased to play their part within the dynamic of Anglican identity. The post-colonial era following the retraction of the British Empire has brought further criticism, from Anglicans themselves, about the extent to which their denomination was complicit in British imperialism, and that therefore their identity suffers from being an imperial construct. For such Anglican critics, necessary deconstruction has to occur which allows English markers of identity, even as basic as liturgical worship or episcopacy, to be questioned or even relinquished.

Since the nineteenth century and the effective end of the royal supremacy—whether that was exercised by the monarch or the British Parliament—emerging global Anglicanism was increasingly beset into the twenty-first century by the issue of authority. There has been no effective replacement for the royal supremacy, in part because of Anglicanism's historical origins in anti-papal national royalism. Beyond the purely diocesan level, the Anglican Communion struggled to find an operative replacement for the authority of the royal supremacy. Various attempts at authority by moral consensus, all bedevilled by anxiety that something akin to a centralized (i.e. papal) authority was being constructed, were tried. But all such central organizations of an emerging international communion were saddled with the original limitations imposed by Archbishop Longley when he agreed to call the first Lambeth Conference of diocesan bishops in 1867. By repudiating any real global authority, and opting for the consultative label of 'conference' rather than 'synod', Longley found a way to bring opposing parties of Anglicans together. But the emerging Anglican Communion, with its so-called 'Instruments of Unity'—be they the Anglican Consultative Council, or Primates' Meeting—tried to emulate Longley and both avoid the devil—papal centralism—and the deep blue sea—myriad manifestations that belied the claim to unity. True to its origins, Anglicanism perhaps remained more comfortable with its various national existences, than with its international one.

However, the history of Anglicanism is not merely the tracing of the evolution of a now global form of Western Christianity, important though that may be to tens of millions of contemporary Anglican adherents. As part of the historical turn to religion in recent academic interest, in the past two decades there has been a great increase of interest in the history and development of both the Church of England and its global offshoots. Scholars have investigated a plethora of facets of these religious phenomena, from the institutional to the popular, from formal theological belief and worship to informal, more diffusive faith. Other historians have looked at seminal

Anglican figures and movements. As well as specifically religious history, other historians have been recapturing the pivotal importance of Anglicanism in wider social and political contexts.

There has been a general historiographical revision which might broadly be described as moving the Church of England (and religion generally) from the margins to the centre of major economic social, political, and cultural development in English, British, imperial, and global history from the sixteenth to the twentieth centuries. The Church of England, Anglicanism, and religion more generally are now seen to be seminal dimensions of these various historical periods. So, for example, the significance of religion in the British Empire has now been recognized by a number of important scholars.[4] However, the major religious denomination in that empire, the Church of England, has been only sparsely studied compared to Nonconformity and is just now beginning to be critically examined.[5] Belatedly religion is moving up the scale of historical importance in British, imperial, and global history, but it still lags behind the significance and attention that it has received from historians of England. There have been various studies of the Church of England in its national context, but these have not always been integrated into wider British and global studies.[6]

A number of studies of historical Anglicanism have focused on the narrative of the institutional and theological history of Anglicanism, either as the Church of England or as an Anglican Communion. These include Stephen Neil's now very dated *Anglicanism*, originally published in 1958. More recently, there have been William L. Sachs's *The Transformation of Anglicanism: From State Church to Global Communion* (1993), and Kevin Ward's *A History of Global Anglicanism* (2006). However, these scholarly histories are single-volume histories that inevitably provide insufficient depth to do justice to the breadth of scholarship on their subject. Anglicanism is now a subject of such complexity as both an institutional Church and a religious culture that sufficient justice cannot be done to it in a single-volume historical treatment.

But there is now sufficient international historical interest and extant scholarship to make an extensive, analytical investigation into the history of Anglicanism a feasible intellectual project. In undertaking such a challenge the

---

[4] Andrew Porter, *Religion versus Empire? British Protestant Missionaries and Overseas Expansion, 1700–1914* (Manchester, 2004); Catherine Hall, *Civilising Subjects: Metropole and Colony in the English Imagination 1830–1867* (Chicago, 2002); Jeffrey Cox, *The British Missionary Enterprise since 1700* (Abingdon, 2008).

[5] Rowan Strong, *Anglicanism and the British Empire 1700–c.1850* (Oxford, 2007); Steven S. Maughan, *Mighty England Do Good: Culture, Faith, Empire, and World in the Foreign Missions of the Church of England, 1850–1915* (Grand Rapids, MI, 2014).

[6] Nancy L. Rhoden, *Revolutionary Anglicanism: The Colonial Church of England Clergy during the American Revolution* (Basingstoke, 2007); Rowan Strong, *Episcopalianism in Nineteenth-Century Scotland: Religious Responses to a Modernizing Society* (Oxford, 2000); Bruce Kaye (ed.), *Anglicanism in Australia* (Melbourne, 2002).

scholars who embarked on the project back in 2012 understand that not only was Anglicanism a religious identity shaped by theological and ecclesiastical understandings, but Anglicans were also formed by non-religious forces such as social class, politics, gender, and economics. Anglicanism has, therefore, been an expression of the Christianity of diverse social groups situated in the differing contexts of the past five centuries—monarchs, political elites, and lower orders; landowners and landless; slave-owners and slaves; missionaries, settlers, and indigenous peoples; colonizers and colonized—and by their enemies and opponents, both within and without their Church.

1

Introduction

Jeremy Gregory

The two 'E-word' coordinates of this second volume in *The Oxford History of Anglicanism*—'Establishment' and 'Empire'—denote what were arguably the most significant factors affecting the Anglican Church between 1662 and 1829. There are, of course, a large number of other issues which have been seen to shape and constrain both the condition of the Church of England and its role and position in the wider world between these dates and which could have been name-checked in the volume's title. These include the pressures caused, particularly from the second half of the eighteenth century, by population growth, urbanization, and industrialization, which have often been regarded as overwhelming the structures and resources of the Anglican Church, principally in England and Wales, in unprecedented ways.[1] Equally, the title might have signposted what have been considered as new stresses put on Anglicanism by two other 'E-words'—'Enlightenment' and 'Evangelicalism'—both of which have conventionally been seen to have stood largely outside the Anglican Church and as critical reactions against it. But, whatever the merits of these views, which will be explored in some of the chapters that follow, it is certainly the case that demographic, economic, intellectual, and rival religious developments affected other periods in the history of Anglicanism and so cannot be seen as especially characteristic of, or as features specific to, this era. And while it could be rightly observed that 'Establishment' and 'Empire' were both themes which had their parts to play in other centuries of the Church's history, there is a strong case to be made, as the various contributions to this volume show, that these two (sometimes converging, sometimes opposing) factors moulded the nature and reach of Anglicanism during the long eighteenth century in fundamental, and sometimes novel and unique, ways. What

---

[1] A. D. Gilbert, *Religion and Society in Industrial England: Church, Chapel, and Social Change, 1740–1914* (London, 1976); Peter Virgin, *The Church in an Age of Negligence: Ecclesiastical Structures and the Problems of Church Reform, 1700–1840* (Cambridge, 1989).

were the consequences for the Anglican Church of its establishment status, and
how was it affected by being the established Church of an emerging global
power? In turn, Anglicanism influenced understandings and experience of both
'Establishment' and 'Empire' during the period covered in this volume.

It is worth noting right at the start that in histories of the Anglican Church
the period with which this volume deals has usually been deemed its most
lifeless and least interesting. Compared to both the initial century of the
Church's story, covered in the first volume of this series, and developments
in the period after 1830, covered in the third volume, the period between 1662
and 1829 remained remarkably under-studied until fairly recently. The general picture was of a Church which had failed to live up to the ideals and
energy of both its predecessor and successor. Its bishops were often sharply
castigated for neglecting their diocesan duties and acting largely as political
pawns; its clergy were routinely criticized for lacking pastoral concern and
were stereotyped either as 'fox-hunting parsons' or as woefully poor curates,
either aping, or bowing to, the mores of the local aristocratic and gentry elites.
These stock caricatures built on some of the Nonconformist and Methodist
critiques of the Church which had been articulated in the period itself. This
framework for understanding the history of the Church in the long eighteenth
century was firmly cemented within Anglican circles in the Victorian era as
Evangelical and Tractarian perspectives on the Church in the preceding
century agreed in essence on its shortcomings. Apart from the researches of
the scholar-cleric Norman Sykes from the 1920s to the 1950s, in particular his
Church and State in England in the Eighteenth Century (1934) which demonstrated that the Church was more efficient as an organization and its clergy
more hard-working as individuals than had previously been recognized,[2] the
'minor industry' of biographies of bishops published in the mid-century,
written by historians who themselves were ordained members of the Church
of England,[3] and the editing of primary sources such as visitation returns,[4]
detailing some aspects of the Church in the localities, which provided evidence
for a more positive point of view, the Victorian understanding of the later

---

[2] Norman Sykes, *Church and State in England in the Eighteenth Century* (Cambridge, 1934).

[3] G. V. Bennett, *The Tory Crisis in Church and State, 1688–1730: The Career of Francis
Atterbury, Bishop of Rochester* (Oxford, 1975), p. vii; G. V. Bennett, *White Kennet, 1660–1728,
Bishop of Peterborough* (London, 1957); Edward Carpenter, *Thomas Sherlock, 1678–1761*
(London, 1936); E. Carpenter, *Thomas Tenison, Archbishop of Canterbury: His Life and Times*
(London, 1948); W. M. Marshall, *George Hooper, 1640–1727: Bishop of Bath and Wells*
(Milborne Port, 1976); A. Tindal Hart, *The Life and Times of John Sharp, Archbishop of York*
(London, 1949); C. E. Whiting, *Nathaniel Lord Crewe, Bishop of Durham (1674–1721) and his
Diocese* (London, 1940). Note also the biographies by Sykes: *Edmund Gibson, Bishop of London,
1669–1748: A Study in Politics and Religion in the Eighteenth Century* (Oxford, 1926); *William
Wake, Archbishop of Canterbury, 1657–1737*, 2 vols. (Cambridge, 1957).

[4] E.g. S. L. Ollard and P. C. Walker (eds.), *Archbishop Herring's Visitation Returns, 1743*,
Yorkshire Archaeological Society: Record Series, 71, 72, 75, 77, 79, 5 vols. (Leeds, 1928–31).

Stuart and Hanoverian Church remained extremely durable until the late twentieth century, leading Mark Goldie to note as late as 2003 that it was 'overcast by what must be the longest shadow in modern historiography'.[5] The prevailing negative tone was expertly analysed by John Walsh and Stephen Taylor in the extended introduction to their seminal collection of essays published in 1993 which also showcased the broadly revisionist turn which has characterized much of the writing on the Church from the 1980s.[6] Rather than dwelling on the failures and shortcomings of the Anglican Church, modern scholars have highlighted its successes and strengths. They have argued that, rather than being an incompetent institution, the Church had begun to reform itself long before the administrative restructuring and theological changes of the period after 1830. The criticisms of earlier historians can be shown to be based on the biased opinions of the Church's opponents or the result of anachronistic expectations, judging the Church by late nineteenth-century standards.

The current volume builds on the work of the Walsh, Haydon, and Taylor collection, which has helped to stimulate more in-depth research on specific issues and topics. But it seeks to go beyond it in offering a much more comprehensive regional coverage of the Church and extending the geographical range to include the fortunes of the Anglican Church outside England (including not only Wales, Ireland, and Scotland, but, as the title indicates, Anglicanism overseas as well). It also includes a number of thematic chapters, allowing an assessment of continuity and change. While the volume cannot pretend to be a complete account of all aspects of the history of Anglicanism, nevertheless it is intended to be an authoritative summary of current research. If there is one single message that the volume seeks to convey it is that the Anglican Church was far more vital to the life of the period than is often maintained, and its history should be of interest to more than just those concerned with religion. Throughout the era covered by the volume, the Church was central to political, social, intellectual, and cultural matters, and for that reason it is timely to draw together a comprehensive study of Anglicanism between these dates.

* * *

The reasons for selecting 'Establishment' as the first 'E-word' coordinate should be uncontentious and this choice has dictated the chronological parameters of what follows. Between 1662 and 1829, the Anglican Church was established by law as the official state Church in England (as it was in Wales and Ireland, as well as in parts of the British Empire). While this was also the case, at least for England, Wales, and Ireland, and some places

---

[5] Mark Goldie, 'Voluntary Anglicans', *Historical Journal*, 46 (2003): 977–90, at p. 988.

[6] John Walsh and Stephen Taylor, 'Introduction: The Church and Anglicanism in the Long Eighteenth Century', in John Walsh, Colin Haydon, and Stephen Taylor (eds.), *The Church of England, c.1689–c.1833: From Toleration to Tractarianism* (Cambridge, 1993), pp. 1–64.

overseas, both before and after these dates, nevertheless, during our period the Anglican establishment was, through various key pieces of legislation, supported by the civil authority arguably much more overtly and with greater consequences than it had been before or would be afterwards, so much so that during this period the Church of England was frequently referred to simply as 'the Established Church'. The Restoration of 1660 had restored not only the monarchy but also the Church of England as the Established Church of the nation with special rights and privileges (such as allowing twenty-six of its bishops to sit in the House of Lords). The crucial law upholding the Anglican establishment was passed in May 1662 when 'An Act for the Uniformity of Public Prayers and Administration of Sacraments, and other Rites and Ceremonies, and for establishing the Form of making, ordaining and consecrating Bishops, Priests and Deacons in the Church of England' set the overarching framework for the Anglican establishment for more than 160 years. The Act, 'in regard that nothing conduceth more to the settling of the peace of this nation . . . nor to the honour of our religion and the propagation thereof, than a universal agreement in the public worship of almighty God', defined more clearly than ever before what it meant to be an Anglican, and mandated that all religious services had to adopt the forms of prayer and worship as set out in the 1662 revised Book of Common Prayer.[7] The Act also required clergy to read publicly from, and declare their 'unfeigned assent and consent to all and everything' in, the amended Prayer Book by 24 August (St Bartholomew's Day).[8] In addition, the Act demanded that in future all those wanting to be ordained into the Church of England had to subscribe to it, and that those clergy who had not been episcopally ordained had to be re-ordained. As a consequence, nearly a thousand clergy were ejected from their livings and the issue of loyalty to the Prayer Book became a crucial division between Anglicans and Nonconformists from then on. In Nonconformist circles, this was remembered as 'Black Bartholomew', viewed as the decisive event in defining the difference between 'the Church' and 'Dissent'. It has indeed recently been claimed that the Act of Uniformity and its consequences 'comprise perhaps the single most significant episode in post-Reformation English religious history'.[9] For the Nonconformist minister Philip Henry, it caused a disastrous divide between true 'godly' ministry and 'the Church'.[10] Henry emphasized the pain this gave to those who were forced into Nonconformity, many of whom, like him, would have wanted to remain within a national state Church were it not for what they regarded as unnecessary and even 'popish'

---

[7] J. P. Kenyon (ed.), *The Stuart Constitution, 1603–1688* (Cambridge, 1986 edn.), pp. 378–82.

[8] Ian Green, *The Re-establishment of the Church of England, 1660–1663* (Oxford, 1978), pp. 145–7.

[9] N. H. Keeble (ed.), *'Settling the Peace of the Church': 1662 Revisited* (Oxford and New York, 2014), back cover.

[10] Quoted in R. Greaves, 'Henry, Philip (1631–1696)', *ODNB*, <http://www.oxforddnb.com>, accessed 10 Aug. 2016.

impositions, such as having to be re-ordained and being forced to read the Prayer Book in services.[11]

The Act of Uniformity and the revised Book of Common Prayer were the twin pillars of the Anglican establishment during the long eighteenth century. As a consequence of its establishment status, the century and a half after 1662 has claims to be regarded as the golden age of the Prayer Book. During this period it structured English religious (and to a certain extent social) life in ways in which arguably it did not before or since.[12] It was also a time when both at home, and, as we will see, perhaps even more abroad, adherence to the Prayer Book can justifiably be considered to have been the defining mark of affiliation to the Church and the unequivocal badge of Anglicanism. The mindset articulated by both the Act of Uniformity and the Prayer Book was dominated by the memory of the civil war and the ways in which religious diversity and experimentation were considered to have led to political and social anarchy. The revised Prayer Book incorporated special forms of prayer which were not technically part of it, but which, until 1859, were included in it for the annual thanksgiving days of 30 January (to remember the death of Charles I in 1649); 29 May (the thanksgiving for the restoration of Charles II in 1660); and 5 November (the thanksgiving for the failure of the Gunpowder Plot in 1605—and by coincidence the day of William III's landing at Torbay in 1688, which meant that by a special Act of Parliament in 1689 insertions were made which thanked Providence for William, and which could be used at the 5 November service that year); as well as the annual thanksgiving service for the accession of the current monarch. The memory of what happened when the world had been turned upside-down formed the habits of mind and actions of Church of England clergy from the late seventeenth to the early nineteenth centuries, making them suspicious of groups or movements which it was feared might undermine the Church's position. The reminiscence of the Great Rebellion, when the Church had been overthrown, the archbishop of Canterbury executed, and Anglican clergy harried in their parishes, became deeply fixed in Anglican consciousness, and the fear that there might be another civil war often determined their responses to events.

The Anglican establishment created in 1662 therefore shaped political and social, as well as religious, life until the early nineteenth century, and this was reinforced by subsequent legislation. Even before the 1662 Act, and in antici-pation of what would follow, the Corporation Act of 1661 required all members of municipal corporations to affirm that they had taken Holy Communion according to the rites of the Prayer Book within the year. The Conventicle Acts

---

[11] G. F. Nuttall, 'The First Nonconformists', in G. F. Nuttall and O. Chadwick (eds.), *From Uniformity to Unity, 1662–1962* (London, 1962), pp. 149–87.

[12] Jeremy Gregory, '"For all sorts and conditions of men": The Social Life of the Book of Common Prayer during the Long Eighteenth Century: or, Bringing the History of Religion and Social History Together', *Social History*, 34 (2009): 29–55.

of 1664 and 1670 declared illegal all meetings in private houses of more than five persons (other than the household) for worship not according to that prescribed in the Prayer Book, and the Five Mile Act of 1665 prohibited Nonconformist minsters from preaching, teaching, or coming within five miles of a town or parish where they had previously officiated unless they had taken the oath of non-resistance. For Nonconformists, these laws, which defined the nature of the Anglican religious establishment during the Restoration, contributed to what was traditionally summed up as 'the Great Persecution',[13] when non-Anglicans might be imprisoned, stoned, molested, and harried for their religious convictions. Yet persecution, and the reasons for it, might be more complex than it appears. Mark Goldie has described the Anglican 'theory of religious intolerance' highlighting the theological imperatives which led churchmen to suppress those perceived to be heretics. He has convincingly demonstrated the importance of the Fathers, especially St Augustine, in fuelling such a mentality and in a view of religious Dissent as 'schism' which clergy had a duty to quash. He has argued that it was these theological arguments, and not merely political or social imperatives, which sustained the defence of religious intolerance.[14] Against accusations of persecution, Anglicans could maintain that coercion provided an opportunity for a reconsideration of religious views on the part of the persecuted. Moreover, persecution was not the only tactic or strategy used to try to win Nonconformists back to the Church; there were also the softer tools of persuasion and pastoral care. The passing of the Test Acts in 1673 and 1678, by obliging office-holders and MPs to conform to the Anglican Church, further enshrined the Church of England at the heart of the political establishment, helping to create what has been seen by J. C. D. Clark as a 'confessional state' whereby the Established Church dominated the English polity and society, sustaining and privileging not only a Protestant, but more specifically an Anglican, constitution.[15] There were further attempts to make the Anglican establishment even more impregnable. During the High Church and Tory revival under Queen Anne, the Occasional Conformity Act of 1711 sought to stop Dissenters from taking the sacrament to qualify for office and

---

[13] G. R. Cragg, *Puritanism in the Period of the Great Persecution, 1660–1688* (Cambridge, 1957).

[14] Mark Goldie, 'The Theory of Religious Intolerance in Restoration England', in Ole Peter Grell, Jonathan Israel, and Nicholas Tyacke (eds.), *From Persecution to Toleration: The Glorious Revolution and Religion in England* (Oxford, 1991), pp. 331–68.

[15] J. C. D. Clark, 'England's Ancien Regime as a Confessional State', *Albion*, 21 (1989): 450–74; J. C. D. Clark, 'Great Britain and Ireland', in Stewart J. Brown and Timothy Tackett (eds.), *The Cambridge History of Christianity*, vol. VII: *Enlightenment, Reawakening and Revolution, 1660–1815* (Cambridge, 2006), pp. 54–71. For the full statement, see J. C. D. Clark, *English Society, 1660–1832: Religion, Ideology, and Politics during the Ancien Regime* (2nd edn., Cambridge, 2000); see also G. F. A. Best, 'The Protestant Constitution and its Supporters, 1800–1829', *Transactions of the Royal Historical Society*, 5th series, 8 (1958): 107–27.

the Schism Act of 1714 forbade Dissenters from teaching or running schools. The latter was seen as a particularly bold move for the emasculation and de-energizing of Dissent by outlawing the academies which were crucial for nurturing Dissent and where Nonconformists could receive the equivalent of a university education. However, both these Acts were repealed in 1719 as part of George I's concessions to Protestant Dissenters. Apart from the various Roman Catholic 'relief' Acts from the 1770s, and the extension of toleration to Socinians in 1813, this remained the legal framework of the Anglican political establishment until the repeal of the Test and Corporation Acts in 1828, which allowed non-Anglican Protestants to hold political office, and the eventual granting of Roman Catholic Emancipation in 1829. This had been delayed by George III's refusal to break the oath he had made at his coronation to 'maintaine the laws of God, the true profession of the Gospell and the Protestant reformed religion established by law'.[16]

Clark's understanding of the Anglican 'confessional state' between 1662 and 1829 has been influential in stressing the centrality of the Church of England to political and social life in the context of a historiography which had tended to minimize the political significance of the Anglican establishment, and for taking seriously the religious and theological arguments which were articulated in its defence in preference to the conventional concentration on the secular, this-worldly, and financial privileges gained by the Church from its establishment status, an interpretation in which the political involvement of bishops, particularly after 1714, was viewed simply as voting-fodder for the government of the day. However, some parts of Clark's argument have been controversial.[17] His concentration on the 'orthodox political theology' favoured by a select group of 'Hutchinsonian' clergy has risked making Anglican political ideology seem rather obscure; nevertheless, his robust contention, albeit to a certain extent anticipated by a number of previous historians, that English political life was dominated by the traditional pillars of the crown, the Church, and the aristocracy, has been noteworthy in reminding historians of the Church's extensive political clout. But how far the legislative position of the Church meant that England should be seen as a 'confessional state' can be debated. Clearly sections of the English population did not conform to it, even though some Dissenters, through the practice of occasional conformity, made themselves eligible for public office. Yet the wide-ranging nature of the Church's legal position did have a profound impact on its political and social role, ensuring that the state, the English universities, the army, and the civil service were Anglican strongholds, and in the regions clergy were often justices of the

---

[16] W. C. Costin and J. Steven Watson (eds.), *The Law and Working of the Constitution: Documents, 1660–1914*, vol. I: *1660–1783* (London, 1952), pp. 57–9.

[17] See J. A. Phillips, 'The Social Calculus: Deference and Defiance in Later Georgian England', *Albion*, 21 (1989): 426–49.

peace, responsible for the administration of local government. Perhaps a more accurate description of the Church's situation is not as a central plank of a confessional state so much as an Anglican hegemony which was buttressed by its establishment status.

Although its place was contested, the Church effectively dominated society and politics and sought to marginalize those who challenged its role. Many churchmen believed that the interests of Church and state were in fact inseparable. Between 1662 and 1829 the theory of the Anglican establishment maintained that there was an interdependence of Church and state whereby 'the Church upheld the natural hierarchy of mutual obligations which were thought to provide social cohesion, and the State protected the legal establishment as the appropriate agent of benevolence and public morality'.[18] As a consequence, enemies of the state were also seen as enemies of the Church. A good indication of this attitude can be seen in the Church's response to the Jacobite rebellions of 1715 and 1745, when the Church's hierarchy, and the vast bulk of its clergy, vigorously supported the Hanoverian regime.[19] Although there were by the late eighteenth century challenges to the principle of establishment,[20] the theory (and to a large extent the practice) remained very resilient, and was trumpeted more loudly than ever in the face of increased political and social radicalism in the late eighteenth and nineteenth centuries. Again, the Church was a staunch defender of the government during the French Revolution, believing that the threat to the state would also be destructive to the Church and to true religion generally.[21] In many ways, then, the more than 160 years covered by this volume have claims to be the heyday of the Church of England, when its influence on English politics and society was more pronounced and entrenched than before or since.

It has sometimes been argued that the force of the Act of Uniformity and the strength of the Anglican establishment were in effect undermined by the so-called 'Toleration Act' of 1689 which granted religious freedoms to non-Anglicans.[22] Even before this, the Anglican religious establishment was compromised by the royal declarations of indulgence of 1672, 1687, and 1688, which allowed Dissenters some freedom in religious matters and which can be seen as Charles II and James II giving a personal lead on religious toleration (although there were those who suspected that the Catholic James's declarations were really just a way to promote Roman Catholicism). But the 1689 Act did

---

[18] E. R. Norman, *Church and Society in England, 1770–1970: An Historical Study* (Oxford, 1976), p. 19.

[19] Jonathan Oates, *York and the Jacobite Rebellion of 1745*, Borthwick Paper 107 (York, 2005); Jonathan Oates, *The Last Battle on English Soil, Preston 1715* (London, 2015).

[20] G. F. A. Best, *Temporal Pillars: Queen Anne's Bounty, the Ecclesiastical Commissioners and the Church of England* (Cambridge, 1964), pp. 35–45.

[21] Robert Hole, *Pulpits, Politics and Public Order in England, 1760–1832* (Cambridge, 1989).

[22] Grell et al. (eds.), *From Persecution to Toleration*.

not advocate toleration in anything like a twenty-first-century understanding of the term, and its intent is better summed up in its proper title: 'An act for exempting their majesties' protestant subjects, dissenting from the Church of England, from the penalties of certain laws'.[23] The Act did not envisage any form of toleration for Roman Catholics or Unitarians, let alone those of non-Christian faiths. Freedom of worship was only granted to Protestant Dissenters, who, moreover, could legally only worship in registered meeting-houses with the door open and if the minister subscribed to the Thirty-Nine Articles of the Church (a set of doctrinal statements defining the position of the Church originally written in the sixteenth century and from 1682 append-ed to the Prayer Book), except those concerning baptism and church govern-ment. In the period leading up to the Act, 'toleration' was often seen as second best to 'comprehension'.[24] A comprehension, it was argued by its supporters in the 1670s and 1680s, would have taken away most of the conditions to which clergy were required to subscribe, thereby bringing over the majority of moderate Dissenting ministers and their lay supporters to the Church. In this case, 'toleration' would be given to those hardline groups who continued outside the bounds of the Church. Thus, rather than being a basic human right, 'toleration' in the late seventeenth century was originally designed for those who could not be accommodated within a comprehensive Church of England establishment.

Nor did the Act seek to alter the Test and Corporation Acts privileging Anglicans in the political sphere. Rather than seeing the 'Toleration Act' in a Whiggish light, ushering in a period of religious freedom and pluralism and putting Nonconformity on a virtually equal footing with the Established Church, we should note that its impact was much less revolutionary. Not only did certain High Churchmen bemoan the impact of the Act over their control of the religious life of their parishioners, and seek to repeal or modify it, there was also considerable discussion of what it actually implied. Ralph Stevens has shown how Anglican clergy were actually deeply divided about its meaning and argues that it 'settled next to nothing about the relationship between the Church and Dissent', observing that some Anglicans believed that 'Toleration had never been intended to allow Dissent to establish itself as a permanent feature.' He emphasizes the sheer vagueness and ambiguity of the 1689 legislation and the ways in which the 'new religious dispensation was a drawn out process of experimentation, debate and contest rather than a transformative constitutional moment'.[25]

[23] Andrew Browning (ed.), *English Historical Documents*, vol. I: *1660–1783* (London, 1966), pp. 400–3.

[24] John Spurr, 'The Church of England, Comprehension and the Toleration Act of 1689', *English Historical Review*, 104 (1989): 927–46.

[25] Ralph Stevens, 'Anglican Responses to the Toleration Act, c.1689–1714', PhD thesis, University of Cambridge, 2015, pp. 25, 157, 4 respectively.

Nevertheless, it would be misleading to downplay the ways that the Church of England prided itself on its moderate and reasonable behaviour towards its rivals, and clergy often noted the 1689 Act as evidence of this. Whatever the reality on the ground, the self-perception of the Church contrasted with the assumed persecutory nature of 'popery'. While 'toleration' did not undermine the establishment status of the Church it did help to shape both its own understanding and to constrain its behaviour. Whatever the kind of 'toleration' which existed, it was 'toleration within establishment', with all the limitations implied by that formulation. But conversely, at least after 1689, establishment itself was increasingly understood in the context of toleration.[26] So, no matter what its intentions, the 'Toleration Act' became significant for the self-definition of the Church as one which was charitable and enlightened (at least compared with its competitors and rivals) and in which the outright persecution of Dissent was seen to be a hallmark of popery.[27] Although evidence can be found after 1689 of mobs stoning and harrying Dissenters, and pulling down their meeting-houses, Anglican clergy at least had to work within a framework where they persuaded rather than intimidated Nonconformists back into the fold. In general, Anglican clergy do seem to have treated Protestant Dissenters with respect after 1689 and some clergymen saw both Anglicans and Nonconformists as their parishioners, a lingering suggestion of the view that the Established Church had a responsibility for the whole nation. What was increasingly of more concern was the apparently growing section of the population who did not attend any form of religious worship (the 'Toleration Act' was widely suspected of having encouraged them to attend no place of worship at all), and in order to combat this, clergy might combine with Dissenting ministers. This shared pastoral endeavour can be witnessed in Anglicans working with Dissenters in the Societies for the Reformation of Manners and in educational projects such as the setting up of charity schools.

Something similar, in terms of a coexistence between different religious groups, and shedding light on the nature of the Anglican establishment, is the fact that individuals not uncommonly held dual or even multiple religious affiliation, attending a variety of denominations, which indicates that religious affiliation was not exclusive and that lines between different groups could in fact be blurred. This was particularly the case for relations between Anglicans and Methodists, for which in many ways it is more accurate, at least up until Wesley's death in 1791, to view Methodism as a subset of Anglicanism.[28] But it

---

[26] Jeremy Gregory, 'Persecution, Toleration, Competition, and Indifference: The Church of England and its Rivals in the Long Eighteenth Century', in C. D'Haussey (ed.), *Quand religions et confessions se regardent* (Paris, 1998), pp. 45–60.

[27] William Gibson, *The Church of England, 1688–1832: Unity and Accord* (London, 2001).

[28] David Wilson, 'Church and Chapel: Parish Ministry and Methodism in Madeley, c.1760–1785, with Special Reference to the Ministry of John Fletcher', PhD thesis, University of Manchester, 2010.

is also true of relations between Anglicans and Nonconformists even in the years between 1660 and 1689, when it was not unusual for people to attend both the parish church and a Nonconformist meeting. And apart from the existence of 'occasional conformists' and 'occasional dissenters', who might to varying degrees attend both the parish church and Nonconformist places of worship, there is evidence of parishioners who regularly attended a range of worshipping sites which makes it difficult to speak of clear-cut differences between denominations. In 1786, for instance, the incumbent of St Alphege's, Canterbury, noted that 'many . . . go to the Cathedral in the morning, to the Presbyterian meeting in the afternoon, and to the Methodist meeting at night'.[29] How far did these men and women actually see themselves first as 'Anglicans', then 'Presbyterians', and then 'Methodists' at different times of day, or were these labels almost indifferent to them and did they just enjoy participating in a variety of religious experiences? It is certainly useful for what it tells us of the nature of the Anglican establishment and contrasts with the church/chapel divide familiar from the period after 1830.[30]

But whatever its consequences for the relationship between Anglicans and Dissenters, the 'Toleration Act' did not offer any form of toleration to Roman Catholicism and anti-popery remained the key ideological determinant of the Established Church. Twenty-five years ago, Linda Colley argued persuasively for the vital importance of Protestantism and anti-Catholicism for forging a sense of British national identity in the period after 1707.[31] Some scholars have queried the role of an overarching Protestantism in uniting the British nation, noting that there were differences between Protestants as well as a shared anti-popery.[32] Nevertheless, a common Protestantism was something members of the Church of England could agree on with Protestant Dissenters, apart from those occasions, such as under James II, when some Protestant Dissenters and Roman Catholics could join in support of the king's attempt to dismantle the Anglican establishment.[33] There was, however, a huge distinction between an atavistic fear of 'popery' (which usually assumed some foreign 'other') and the ways in which Anglicans might relate to their own Roman Catholic neighbours.[34] There is evidence, particularly from the eighteenth century, of

---

[29] Quoted in Jeremy Gregory, *Restoration, Reformation, and Reform, 1660–1828: Archbishops of Canterbury and their Diocese* (Oxford, 2000), p. 228.

[30] Gilbert, *Religion and Society*.

[31] Linda Colley, *Britons: Forging the Nation, 1707–1837* (New Haven, CT, 1992).

[32] Tony Claydon and Ian McBride, 'The Trials of the Chosen People: Recent Interpretations of Protestantism and National Identity in Britain and Ireland', in Tony Claydon and Ian McBride (eds.), *Protestantism and National Identity in Britain and Ireland, c.1650–c.1850* (Cambridge, 1998), pp. 3–29.

[33] Scott Sowerby, *Making Toleration: The Repealers and the Glorious Revolution* (Cambridge, MA, 2013).

[34] Colin Haydon, *Anti-Catholicism in Eighteenth-Century England, c.1714–18: A Political and Social Study* (Manchester, 1993), pp. 11–13.

harmonious relations between members of the Church and local Roman Catholics. The ways in which Catholics could be integrated into their communities were sometimes surprising, even contributing to the upkeep of parish churches. Catholics might also take on the role of churchwarden and their wives were often churched in the parish church, indicative of the ways in which the Established Church was the national church and could have a function even for those who ought to have had nothing to do with it.[35]

In concluding this section on 'Establishment', it has often been claimed that in spite of, and actually because of, the Church's established status, this was a nadir in the history of the Church. The Church's massively privileged position and its entanglement in the politics of the day have been seen as detrimental to its pastoral and religious mission. How far this was the case will be considered later in this chapter, but it is worth noting here what has been considered one of the consequences for the Anglican Church of the particularities of its establishment status during the long eighteenth century.

*   *   *

The second coordinate of this volume is 'Empire'. The period witnessed the growth of Britain's imperial reach, ranging from North America, Canada, and the Caribbean to India, Africa, and, from the late eighteenth century, Australia and New Zealand.[36] This brought new opportunities for the Anglican Church for dramatically extending its sphere of activity overseas as well as challenges of planting the Church in unusual and often unpromising and inhospitable locations. The extension of Anglicanism outside England goes back to Ireland in the sixteenth century and Virginia in the early seventeenth century. Although the expansion of empire from the late seventeenth to the early nineteenth centuries and the widening of the Anglican fold did not go hand in hand straightforwardly, since parts of the empire, and particularly the north-eastern American colonies, were puritan strongholds, where Anglicanism was regarded with suspicion, nevertheless other parts of the empire were regions where the Anglican Church was, or became, the religious establishment.[37] In these places, the empire helped to spread Anglican identity and the Anglican Church could itself be an instrument of empire-building by forging

---

[35] Marie B. Rowlands (ed.), *English Catholics of Parish and Town, 1558–1778* (London, 1999).

[36] *Oxford History of the British Empire*, general editor, W. R. Louis: vol. I, Nicholas Canny (ed.), *The Origins of Empire* (Oxford, 1998); vol. II, P. J. Marshall (ed.), *The Eighteenth Century* (Oxford, 1998); and volumes in the Companion Series, Norman Etherington (ed.), *Missions and Empire* (Oxford, 2005); Stephen Foster (ed.), *British North America in the Seventeenth and Eighteenth Centuries* (Oxford, 2013).

[37] Eliga H. Gould, 'Prelude: The Christianising of British America', in Etherington (ed.), *Missions*, pp. 19–39; Jeremy Gregory, ' "Establishment" and "Dissent" in British North America: Organizing Religion in the New World', in Foster (ed.), *British North America*, pp. 136–9; Evan Haefeli, 'Toleration and Empire: The Origins of American Religious Pluralism', in Foster (ed.), *British North America*, pp. 103–35.

ties of loyalty and affection between the metropole and the colonies. There were also colonies, such as those in New England, where the Anglican Church gradually took root, although it was never established.[38] Yet the relationship between religion and empire was complex and there were tensions over whether it was Protestantism generally, or Anglicanism more specifically, which should be promoted by Britain in its empire. There were also sometimes debates about how far religious legislation enacted for England should or could be enforced overseas. Theoretically Virginia's religious establishment was Anglican throughout the entire length of the colonial period and on occasion the powers that be even sought to deny that the 1689 'Toleration Act' had any force in the colony. Similarly, metropolitan New York had a Church of England establishment and in 1766 the colonial government sought an opinion to determine whether the English Act of Uniformity applied in the colonies, refusing to charter a Presbyterian congregation as late as 1775.[39]

Having 'Empire' as one of the coordinating themes of the volume is worth underscoring because until very recently historians of the Anglican Church have concentrated their attention almost totally on the Church within England. The history of Anglican Churches outside England was barely noted in Victorian histories of the Church, and early studies of the fortunes of the Anglican Church in various outposts of the British Empire were written from the perspective of nineteenth- and early twentieth-century clergy who, while noting the sometimes heroic activities of their forebears, also highlighted their failure to make much headway in planting Anglicanism overseas, through a combination of lack of resources and proper organizational structures (including for the most part the lack of a bishop) and a want of true missionary zeal and properly dedicated clergy, all of which would only be rectified during the nineteenth century.[40] Moreover, these researches were usually seen as a contribution to the history of that specific region or area and were seldom integrated into a broader study of imperial Anglicanism. Only in the twentieth century did historians begin to examine the interrelationships between Anglicanism at home and abroad. Carl Bridenbaugh's *Mitre and Sceptre*, published in 1962, dwelt on the negative ways in which Congregationalists in New England viewed eighteenth-century Anglican expansion in North America as part of a British popish plot to subdue the colonies.[41] More recently, Stephen Taylor, James Bell, Robert Ingram, and Rowan Strong, among others, have explored the more positive trans-oceanic Anglican links and the ways by which, despite the huge problems of distance

---

[38] Jeremy Gregory, 'Refashioning Puritan New England: The Church of England in British North America, c.1680–c.1770', *Transactions of the Royal Historical Society*, 6th series, 20 (2010): 85–112.

[39] Gregory, '"Establishment" and "Dissent"', pp. 148, 157.

[40] Edward L Bond, *Spreading the Gospel in Colonial Virginia: Sermons and Devotional Writings* (Lanham, MD, 2004).

[41] Carl Bridenbaugh, *Mitre and Sceptre: Transatlantic Faiths, Ideas, Personalities, and Politics, 1689–1775* (London, 1962).

and communication, the different Anglican worlds could be connected.[42] William Bulman has incorporated the Anglican experience in North Africa into his study of England and its empire between 1648 and 1715 and has illuminated the impact on those clergy who travelled between them.[43]

The emerging British Empire gave the Anglican Church in the century and a half after the Restoration the chance of operating on a much broader canvas, and the prospect of bringing Anglicanism to a far wider world, than had been dreamt of in the first century of the Reformation. It has often been (rightly) claimed that the Church of England in the first part of the seventeenth century had been rather slow at conceiving British colonies as either a mission field or for enlarging the territories under its charge.[44] 'A prayer for all conditions of men', a new prayer written in 1662 for the Prayer Book's Morning Service, wished for 'thy saving health unto all nations', which was a foreshadowing of Anglican missionary aspirations. The revised Prayer Book also included a new baptism service 'for those of riper years', added in part because it was anticipated that it 'may be always useful for the baptizing of Natives in our Plantations and others converted to the Faith'.[45] The prayers for those at sea (including daily prayers, prayers for defeating enemies, a thanksgiving for victory, prayers for use during and after storms, and for burial at sea) reflected the ways in which England had by now become a maritime power, which was central to the growth of its empire.[46] The religious rhetoric in the charters issued for a number of colonies after the Restoration stressed the ambition of converting the Amerindians to Christianity, and the Church itself participated in this discourse and aspiration. The later Stuart period also saw the founding of two organizations which would have a tremendous impact on the Church's activities across the world: the Society for the Propagation of Christian Knowledge (SPCK) in 1698 and, even more pertinently, the Society for the Propagation of the Gospel in Foreign Parts (SPG) in 1701.[47] This was

---

[42] James B. Bell, *The Imperial Origins of the King's Church in Early America, 1607–1783* (Basingstoke, 2004); Stephen Taylor, 'Whigs, Bishops and America: The Politics of Church Reform in Mid-Eighteenth-Century England', *Historical Journal*, 36 (1993): 331–56; Robert G. Ingram, *Religion, Reform and Modernity in the Eighteenth Century: Thomas Secker and the Church of England* (Woodbridge, 2007); Rowan Strong, *Anglicanism and the British Empire, c.1700–1850* (Oxford, 2006).

[43] William J. Bulman, *Anglican Enlightenment: Orientalism, Religion and Politics in England and Its Empire, 1648–1715* (Cambridge, 2015).

[44] Hans Jacob Cnattingius, *Bishops and Societies: A Study of Anglican Colonial Missionary Expansion, 1698–1850* (London, 1952), pp. 1–12.

[45] Brian Cummings (ed.), *The Book of Common Prayer: The Texts of 1549, 1559, and 1662* (Oxford, 2011), p. 211.

[46] See N. A. M. Rodger, *The Command of the Ocean: A Naval History of Britain*, vol. II: *1649–1815* (London, 2003).

[47] C. F. Pascoe, *Two Hundred Years of the S.P.G.: An Historical Account of the Society for the Propagation of the Gospel in Foreign Parts, 1701–1900*, 2 vols. (London, 1901); H. P. Thompson, *Into All Lands: The History of the Society for the Propagation of the Gospel in Foreign Parts*

established by royal charter, with its threefold mission to Native Americans,[48] African American slaves,[49] and European settlers, and was instrumental in coordinating overseas Anglican activity by dispatching missionaries, books (particularly copies of the Book of Common Prayer), catechists, and school-masters to those colonies where the Church was not established. Clergy sent over were also accompanied by a rudimentary starter-kit for planting Anglicanism abroad, complete with a silver communion cup and patens, a pulpit cloth and cushion, and a carpet and linens for the communion table. These initiatives provided the framework for the Church's global endeavour in the next two centuries and beyond, and in so doing represented a significant new departure in the history of Anglicanism.

For virtually the entire period covered by this volume, the vast majority of the overseas colonies where Anglicanism reached were devoid of bishops and the institutional structures and ecclesiastical apparatus so crucial to the func-tioning of the Anglican Church in England. This, together with a shortage of clergy, meant that the particular signifier of Anglican identity in the colonial world became the Book of Common Prayer. This was the Church's official liturgical manual and without it Anglicanism could not be transplanted. In disseminating a distinctively Anglican piety in the empire, the Prayer Book was arguably even more important than the King James Version of the Bible, which by the late seventeenth century was the favoured translation of British Protestant Dissenters as well as the Church. Time and again Anglican clergy and missionaries wrote back to England for more copies of the Prayer Book, believing that access to it would play the key role in spreading the faith. In these circumstances, the essential step was to ensure that copies of the Prayer Book were available, for without them efforts to carry out the Anglican liturgy would come to nothing as it was virtually impossible to procure copies of the Prayer Book overseas.[50] The use of the Prayer Book may have been the single unifying denominator of global Anglicanism when virtually everything else about Anglican worship may have differed from the ideal type of service envisaged in Old England. In some instances, Anglican congregations abroad,

---

(London, 1951); Daniel O'Connor and others, *Three Centuries of Mission: The United Society for the Propagation of the Gospel, 1701–2000* (London, 2000); Andrew Porter, *Religion versus Empire? Protestant Missionaries and Overseas Expansion, 1700–1914* (Manchester, 2004), pp. 16–28. For the global development of the Christian Churches more generally in this period, see David Hempton, *The Church in the Long Eighteenth Century* (London, 2011).

[48] Laura M. Stevens, *The Poor Indians: British Missionaries, Native Americans, and Colonial Sensibility* (Philadelphia, PA, 2004).

[49] Travis Gleason, *Mastering Christianity: Missionary Anglicanism and Slavery in the Atlantic World* (Oxford, 2012).

[50] Jeremy Gregory, 'Transatlantic Anglicanism, c.1680–c.1770: Transplanting, Translating and Transforming the Church of England', in Jeremy Gregory and Hugh McLeod (eds.), *International Religious Networks*, Studies in Church History, Subsidia 14 (Woodbridge, 2012), pp. 127–43, esp. pp. 134–7.

in the absence of clergy, held services in private houses led by a layperson who read to them from the Prayer Book. This meant that members of the Anglican community, wherever they were in the world, when participating in a service would use identical words and formulations. This had a crucial function in creating an imagined Anglican global community and may have been the most compelling, and perhaps the only, tie binding together Anglicans living thousands of miles away from each other in the knowledge that co-religionists throughout the world were hearing the same readings from the same version of the Bible on the same day. And, through the prayers said for the monarchs and royal family, this was a weekly reminder of the relationship between the colonial Anglican congregations and their monarchs in the mother country, helping to fashion an emotional bond between congregations and their Supreme Governor.[51]

A crucial question to ask is how far the global increase of the Anglican Church changed the nature of Anglicanism: how far did the act of transplanting Anglicanism overseas enable Anglicanism to remain as it had been at home, or how far did its migration transform and alter it? Expanding Anglicanism throughout large parts of the empire (by 1776, for example, it had become the most pervasive religious denomination in British North America, as well as the second largest denomination in the American colonies) clearly resulted in locating it in very different contexts. In this, it thereby in some measure anticipated the world-wide Anglican Communion of subsequent centuries. What was disseminated was in part a uniform Anglicanism—the Prayer Book was the only approved handbook used across the Anglican world—but there were also huge variations, and in some cases Anglicans abroad lacked both the clergy and the churches central to Anglican worship in England. In these circumstances, the laity often had more involvement in specifically religious matters in the colonies than they did in the home country, with significant consequences for the nature of Anglicanism in disparate parts of the world both then and in subsequent centuries. A striking change in global Anglicanism occurred as a result of the American War of Independence. The Book of Common Prayer, with its prayers for the royal family, became anathema, and Anglicanism was viewed as an arm of empire. The Protestant Episcopal Church of the United States of America was founded in the years after 1784, acquiring its own bishops and a revised Prayer Book to reflect the changed political position, and formally breaking away from the Church of England in 1789.

---

[51] Jeremy Gregory, 'The Hanoverians and the Colonial Churches', in Andreas Gestrich and Michael Schaich (eds.), *The Hanoverian Succession: Dynastic Politics and Monarchical Culture* (Farnham, 2015), pp. 107–28, esp. pp. 117–19. See also Lauren F. Winner, *A Cheerful and Comfortable Faith: Anglican Religious Practice in the Elite Households of Eighteenth-Century Virginia* (New Haven, CT and London, 2010), pp. 190–2.

But if empire (and its break-up) might make a difference to the types of Anglicanism experienced in the British colonies, it arguably also altered Anglicanism at home, since, through the activities of organizations such as the SPG, people were made aware of their co-religionists abroad. It has sometimes been asked whether ordinary men and women in eighteenth-century Britain knew much about, or even cared for, the empire.[52] Modern scholarly research has tended to emphasize the myriad ways in which they were apprised about, and even experienced, empire. In this the Church of England had a role, by disseminating information about the Church's colonial projects to the metropolis, and through an annual fundraising sermon in London and the abstracts of annual proceedings published under the auspices of the SPG.[53] By these means, men and women in Britain and Ireland were informed about the colonial Anglican cause and could contribute to the Society's work in transmitting over and financially sustaining Church of England clergy in the colonies, helping to pay towards church-building, giving funds for catechists and schoolmasters, and shipping bibles, Books of Common Prayer, and other religious tracts and pamphlets, across the ocean. How far this changed the mental horizons and religious world-view of eighteenth-century Anglicans in Britain is hard to judge, but they were certainly frequently told about their global co-religionists.

* * *

The twin themes of 'Establishment' and 'Empire' have often been viewed as potentially damaging to the Church of England between 1662 and 1829. Precisely because it was so entwined with the English state (with the unity of the Church often disfigured by party politics),[54] and because it was in many cases seemingly caught up in economic and political reasons for imperial expansion rather than religious ones, commentators, both in the period itself and more particularly Victorian Evangelical and Tractarian critics of 'the Hanoverian Church', portrayed this as a bleak period in the Church's history. The pastoral ills most flagged up for adverse comment include pluralism, which meant that clergy were frequently non-resident in their parishes; the issue of tithes, which led to disputes between clergy and those who were not members of the Established Church, and antagonism from parishioners who

---

[52] Peter J. Marshall, 'Who Cared about the Thirteen Colonies? Some Evidence from Philanthropy', *Journal of Imperial and Commonwealth History*, 27 (1999): 52–67.

[53] Jeremy Gregory, 'The Anglican Society for the Propagation of the Gospel in Foreign Parts: Anniversary Sermons and Abstracts of Proceedings', in Alexander Schunka and Markus Friedrich (eds.), *Reporting Christian Missions: Communication, Culture of Knowledge and Regular Publication in a Cross-Confessional Perspective* (Wiesbaden, forthcoming 2017).

[54] W. A. Speck, *Tory and Whig: The Struggle in the Constituencies, 1701–1715* (London, 1970); Jeffery S. Chamberlain, *Accommodating High Churchmen: The Clergy of Sussex, 1700–45* (Urbana and Chicago, IL, 1997).

resented clergy gaining from improvements in agricultural production; the increasing gentrification of clergy which supposedly distanced clergy from the majority of their parishioners; and a generally slothful attitude to pastoral work which left parishioners un-catered for, and in some interpretations made them open to the attractions of Methodism.[55] During the last thirty years or so, there has emerged what might be called a revisionist school of historians whose detailed work, particularly on what the Church was doing at the local and diocesan level, has modified and in some cases reversed the more negative opinions of some of their predecessors.[56] The Church is now seen as having been more pastorally dynamic than conventional interpretations allowed, which has raised questions about the relationship between Methodism, Evangelicalism, and 'mainstream' Anglicanism. Importantly, too, this revisionist view has begun to influence some historians writing outside the confines of 'Church history'. Carolyn Steedman's pathbreaking *Master and Servant: Love and Labour in the English Industrial Age* (2007) was the first major study by a leading social historian to take seriously the revisionist approaches to the eighteenth-century Church; the master of the title and the hero of the book is a late eighteenth-century Church of England cleric, whose charitable attitude to his unmarried pregnant servant, and then to her daughter, made him a model of the clerical professional.[57] Scholars have also uncovered much more about the religious views of the laity. William Jacob's study of lay piety was a landmark project,[58] as was the publication of the diary of the Sussex shopkeeper Thomas Turner, which gave a vivid portrayal of how religion and the Church were central to his life.[59]

This rehabilitation of the Anglican Church has also led scholars to engage with the relationship been Anglicanism and a third 'E-word': 'Enlightenment'. Amongst the most commonly used period-labels for the eighteenth century as a whole have been 'The Enlightenment' or 'The Age of Reason', where 'the enlightenment' and 'reason' were deemed to have been on the wining offensive against 'religion'. One of the most influential interpretations of the century has been Peter Gay's two-volume blockbuster, *The Enlightenment: An Interpretation*,

---

[55] Deryck Lovegrove, *Established Church, Sectarian People: Itinerancy and the Transformation of English Dissent, 1780–1830* (Cambridge, 1988).

[56] Walsh et al. (eds.), *Church of England*; Mark Smith, *Religion in Industrial Society: Oldham and Saddleworth, 1740–1865* (Oxford, 1994); Judith Jago, *Aspects of the Georgian Church: Visitation Studies of the Diocese of York, 1761–1776* (Cranberry, NJ, 1996); Gregory, *Restoration, Reformation, and Reform*; Jeremy Gregory and Jeffery S. Chamberlain (eds.), *The National Church in Local Perspective: The Church of England and the Regions, 1660–1800* (Woodbridge, 2003); W. M. Jacob, *The Clerical Profession in the Long Eighteenth Century, 1680–1840* (Oxford, 2007); Ingram, *Religion, Reform and Modernity*.

[57] Carolyn Steedman, *Master and Servant: Love and Labour in the English Industrial Age* (Cambridge, 2007).

[58] W. M. Jacob, *Lay People and Religion in the Early Eighteenth Century* (Cambridge, 1996).

[59] *The Diary of Thomas Turner, 1754–1765*, ed. David Vaisey (Oxford, 1984).

whose subtitles, *The Birth of Modern Paganism* (1967) and *The Science of Freedom* (1970), captured what were conventionally regarded as the dominant traits of the age. In this scenario, the Enlightenment was viewed as a modernizing attack on religion *tout court* (seeing all forms of religion as no better than backward-looking superstition) and on institutionalized churches and clergy more particularly, where Voltaire's cry, *écrasez L'Infame*, could be taken as representing the spirit of the century. In this interpretation, the salient characteristic of the period was the birth of secularization, where in all walks of life—political, intellectual, social, cultural, and economic—religious priorities were on the wane.[60] Not only did the Enlightenment constitute an attack on religion and churches, but in eighteenth-century Methodist and nineteenth-century Evangelical and Tractarian critiques, the Anglican Church itself was seen to have succumbed to the cult of rationality which was judged to have led to the downgrading of spirituality and faith. The Anglican Church was thus seen both as an enemy of the Enlightenment and as a body which had embraced its anti-religious values.[61]

One of the most significant historiographical developments during the past thirty years has been to complicate what might be meant by 'the Enlightenment'. Rather than seeing it as an essentially anti-religious force, scholars have broadened their understanding and have suggested that there were other models than the French version of the Enlightenment. In 1981, Roy Porter, whose vast number of publications often celebrated the standard account of the Enlightenment and who revelled in the anti-religious and a-religious voices of the age, in a prescient essay on 'The Enlightenment in England' nevertheless recognized the part played by Anglican clergy in the Enlightenment enterprise, where reason and piety could go hand in hand.[62] Porter's emphasis on the alliance between the Church and the Enlightenment was mirrored and developed in a number of studies such as John Gascoigne's *Cambridge in the Age of Enlightenment* (1989) and Brian Young's *Religion and Enlightenment in Eighteenth-Century England* (1998).[63] More recently scholars have argued that the Enlightenment was not necessarily anti-religious at all, and the relationship between 'religious' and 'enlightenment' concerns is now one of the most fruitful areas of research. Jane Shaw's *Miracles in Enlightenment England* (2006), for

[60] Peter Gay, *The Enlightenment: An Interpretation*, 2 vols. (London, 1967, 1970).

[61] Leslie Stephen, *A History of English Thought in the Eighteenth Century*, 2 vols. (London, 1876); G. R. Cragg, *The Church and the Age of Reason* (London, 1960).

[62] Roy Porter, 'The Enlightenment in England', in Roy Porter and Mikuláš Teich (eds.), *The Enlightenment in National Context* (Cambridge, 1981), pp. 1–18; contrast this with his *Enlightenment: Britain and the Creation of the Modern World* (London, 2000).

[63] John Gascoigne, *Cambridge in the Age of Enlightenment: Science, Religion and Politics from the Restoration to the French Revolution* (Cambridge, 1989); B. W. Young, *Religion and Enlightenment in Eighteenth-Century England: Theological Debate from Locke to Burke* (Oxford, 1998); see also Knud Haakonssen (ed.), *Enlightenment and Religion: Rational Dissent in Eighteenth-Century Britain* (Cambridge, 1996).

example, has demonstrated how a large range of commentators were able to balance 'religious enthusiasm' with 'reason', and her reading incorporates elements of the supernatural into an Enlightenment world-view which clearly challenges conventional paradigms of an Enlightenment hostile to religious sensibilities.[64] William Bulman's *Anglican Enlightenment* (2015) has now positioned the Anglican Church in the late seventeenth and early eighteenth centuries in the vanguard of Enlightenment thought, deploying it in defence of, rather than against, the Church establishment.[65] Clearly the relationship between Anglicanism and Enlightenment is much more complex than older versions allowed.

Finally, there is a fourth 'E-word' we should note in relation to the Anglican Church during the long eighteenth century: Evangelicalism. Conventionally, Evangelicalism and Evangelicals have been seen as standing largely outside mainstream Anglicanism and they have been regarded as representing a substantial, if not damning, critique of the Established Church from 1662 onwards. 'The Evangelical Revival' voiced many of the criticisms of the functioning of the Anglican Church which then became the basis of its negative historiography.[66] Methodism from the late 1730s, and then the broader revival both within and outside the Church from the late eighteenth century, stressed the need for religious renewal to counter what was viewed as a lifeless and somnolent Church. However, research has now queried the model of a wholesale Evangelical attack on the Established Church. Scholarship on the Wesleys and early Methodism, for instance, has re-emphasized the Anglican context of their movement, seeing the brothers, and in particular Charles, as building on earlier Anglican initiatives and wanting to reinvigorate the Church from within rather than aiming to set up an independent movement outside it.[67] The Methodist societies, as John Walsh and Henry Rack have shown,[68] drew on the Anglican-sponsored religious societies which are frequently given credit for nourishing parish piety in the late seventeenth century, where the more religiously committed of the parish could find a spiritual outlet and which could be regarded as an optional addition to, rather than a subversion of, parish Anglicanism. How far, we might ask, was 'Evangelicalism' broadly conceived as something reserved for the Church's opponents, and how far

---

[64] Jane Shaw, *Miracles in Enlightenment England* (New Haven, CT and London, 2006), pp. 3–5, 14–15, 18, 28, 42–4.

[65] Bulman, *Anglican Enlightenment*; see also William J. Bulman and Robert G. Ingram (eds.), *God in the Enlightenment* (Oxford, 2016).

[66] G. M. Ditchfield, *The Evangelical Revival* (London, 1998); see Anthony Armstrong, *The Church of England, the Methodists and Society, 1700–1850* (London, 1973).

[67] Gareth Lloyd, *Charles Wesley and the Struggle for Methodist Identity* (Oxford, 2007).

[68] John Walsh, 'Religious Societies: Methodist and Evangelical, 1738–1800', in W. J. Sheils and Diana Wood (eds.), *Voluntary Religion*, Studies in Church History 23 (Oxford, 1986), pp. 279–302; H. D. Rack, 'Religious Societies and the Origins of Methodism', *Journal of Ecclesiastical History*, 38 (1987): 582–95.

were religious revival and renewal, and pastoral innovation, matters in which the Church itself engaged? The general picture of the entire chronological span from 1662 to 1829 as a lifeless time for the Church has sometimes been more nuanced and specific episodes have found approval for their concern with pastoral issues. The Restoration Church itself (despite its reputation in Dissenting circles for persecution) is sometimes noted for its pastoral vigour, with elements of religious revival being discerned during the 1670s and 1680s. The dominant Anglican innovations of the late seventeenth and early eighteenth centuries—the SPCK and the SPG, as well as the Societies for the Reformation of Manners—indicate the Church's willingness to effect religious and social change in ways which could be seen as 'Evangelical'. Much of this enterprise has been studied afresh by Brent Sirota.[69] He emphasizes the voluntary, associational, entrepreneurial, and lay features of these initiatives and, although some clergy remained suspicious that the Church might lose control over this type of Anglican revival, he concludes that this activity led to 'an age of benevolence' which, as exemplified by the work of the SPG, encouraged English men and women to feel compassion for people round the world, thereby anticipating Victorian and modern global humanitarian concerns. In a neat twist on conventional understanding, Sirota suggests that this Anglican Evangelical activity can actually be seen as secularization in its true sense: the taking of Anglicanism out of the churches into the world, led by the laity instead of just by clergy. This Anglican laicization of religion, Sirota more provocatively proposes, could actually be seen as 'an alternative sacralisation' of civil society.[70]

The generally negative opinion of the history of Anglicanism from 1662 to 1829 has viewed it as both a victim of, and a contributor to, secularization. Modern research is now beginning to reverse this view and to see how the role of the Anglican Church helped make religion central to this period. The history of Anglicanism in this era was clearly shaped by 'Establishment' and 'Empire', but it was also more involved in 'Enlightenment' and 'Evangelicalism' than previous histories have assumed. While these four 'E-words' often had separate, and sometimes competing, trajectories, as this volume indicates, Anglicanism during the long eighteenth century could also hold them together in distinctive ways.

---

[69] Brent Sirota, *The Christian Monitors: The Church of England and the Age of Benevolence, 1680–1730* (New Haven, CT and London, 2014).

[70] Sirota, *The Christian Monitors*, p. 258.

Part I

Defining Anglicanism

2

The Church of England, 1662–1714

Grant Tapsell

The church of England has but one miracle, which is that it subsists.

(George Savile, marquis of Halifax, *c*.1680–*c*.1691)[1]

For many of Halifax's less sardonic contemporaries the re-establishment of the Church of England after the puritan revolution was so marvellous as to be genuinely heaven-sent. Less than a month after the 'great ejection' of Nonconforming ministers on St Bartholomew's Day 1662, the bishop of Exeter, Seth Ward, rejoiced in the 'Rout' that they had suffered, and trusted 'that God will be pleased to improve the present advantage to a p[er]fect settlem[en]t next to the miraculous restitution' of the Church.[2] It was telling that Ward recognized that 'settlement' did not automatically follow on from 'restitution', but rather was a work in progress. The tumultuous shifts of fortune across the later Stuart period would ensure that hopes for providential deliverance were repeatedly voiced by friends of the Established Church, notably during the reign of the Catholic James II: 'God I doubt not will preserve this Church w[hi]ch he so miraculously restored, though probably he will put the members of it to hard tryalls.'[3] Nor would the Revolution of 1688–9 usher in religious peace and unity: 'the Churchmen and the Dissenters will never be friends and forgive each other: for both would be uppermost and will admit of no equality'.[4] Recreating a legally privileged national Church was not viewed complacently by churchmen as a secure and permanent achievement. This was especially the

---

[1] 'Miscellanys', in Mark N. Brown (ed.), *The Works of George Savile, Marquis of Halifax*, 3 vols. (Oxford, 1989), III, p. 70. On the issue of dating the comment, see Brown (ed.), *Works of George Savile*, pp. 6–8.

[2] Bishop of Exeter to [?Gilbert Sheldon, bishop of London], 20 Sept. 1662, Bodleian Library [Bodl.], MS Tanner 48, f. 45.

[3] Sir Charles Cottrell to his daughter, [?May/June 1686], British Library [BL], Add. MS 72516, f. 30.

[4] Francis Lane to Sir William Trumbull, 26 Dec. 1689, *Report on the Manuscripts of the Marquess of Downshire, vol. I*, part 1 (London, 1924), p. 329.

case because it was recognized that the civil wars and Interregnum had entrenched passionate religious divisions to an unprecedented degree, and 'a long and great separation from the Church' made it difficult to win loyalties back.[5] God's mercy to the realm of England was felt to be qualified, limited, and something that needed regularly to be earned anew.

Since the later Stuart Church's moment of legal re-creation involved the ejection of much of the old puritan wing of the pre-war Church of England, and since a further crisis would be triggered by 'non-jurors' refusing to recognize the right of William and Mary to the throne after the Revolution of 1688–9, schismatic division was undoubtedly one major theme that runs through the later Stuart era.[6] It needs, though, to be placed in the balance with more constructive impulses within the Church, even if the physical restoration of the fabric of the Church was in many places a lengthy business. The scale of the damage that had been inflicted on 'the tidy physical world of Anglican religious experience' by a combination of radical puritan zeal and the broader breakdown of systems of administration and governance was immense.[7] At a parochial level, in 1664 the churchwardens of Coldwaltham in Sussex recorded in typically spare prose: 'Our church was gone to decay, but is now in repayring.'[8] Just as it had been for Seth Ward when considering the political position of the Church, the emphasis here was on a process that was far from complete. Even in the cathedrals, the great 'mother churches' of the kingdom, it often took until *c.*1680 physically to restore the full gamut of luxurious liturgical equipment, and financial problems dogged several chapters for even longer.[9] Monotonous complaints about tight-fisted patrons and parishioners litter the record. The bishop of Lichfield and Coventry, John Hacket, grumbled in 1665 that the rebuilding of his cathedral 'never went faster on, and never did monies come slower in', while the churchwardens of Dewsbury in Yorkshire criticized local Dissenters for failing to pay for the upkeep of the church clock, and presented four men 'who are noe Lovers of the Church and begrudge every penny that is layd out upon it'.[10] Despite all these problems and delays,

---

[5] J. Wickham Legg, *English Church Life from the Restoration to the Tractarian Movement* (London, 1914), p. 9; John Swinfen MP, 11 Mar. 1668, quoted in Caroline Robbins (ed.), *The Diary of John Milward* (Cambridge, 1938), p. 217.

[6] John Spurr, 'Schism and the Restoration Church', *Journal of Ecclesiastical History*, 41 (1990): 408–24.

[7] R. A. Beddard, 'Sheldon and Anglican Recovery', *Historical Journal*, 19 (1976): 1005–17 (p. 1015); Julie Spraggon, *Puritan Iconoclasm during the English Civil War* (Woodbridge, 2003).

[8] Hilda Johnstone (ed.), *Churchwardens' Presentments (17th Century): Part 1. Archdeaconry of Chichester*, Sussex Record Society 49 (Lewes, 1948), p. 133.

[9] Grant Tapsell, 'Introduction: The Later Stuart Church in Context', in Grant Tapsell (ed.), *The Later Stuart Church, 1660–1714* (Manchester, 2012), pp. 1–17 (p. 10), and the sources given in nn. 71–2.

[10] Bishop of Lichfield and Coventry to archbishop of Canterbury, 5 Aug. 1665, MS Tanner 45, f. 17; John Addy, *The Archdeacon and Ecclesiastical Discipline in Yorkshire 1598–1714: Clergy and the Churchwardens*, St Anthony's Hall Publications 24 (York, 1963), p. 26.

in the last four decades of the seventeenth century a 'beauty of holiness' gradually became the fashionable norm within English church buildings (especially in London) to an extent that would have astonished Archbishop Laud amidst his acrimonious attempts to change the face of English worship in the 1630s.[11] If the later Stuart Church was often buffeted by external threats, and locked in internecine polemical warfare, it was also boosted by phases of renewal that found expression in both physical fabric and devotional activity.[12]

In the rest of this chapter the focus will remain on the fundamental tensions within the restored Church. Should the narrow and exclusive 'settlement' of 1660–2 be defended at all costs, or was it imperative to modify its harsher edges to accommodate scrupulous Nonconformists? Was the later Stuart Church the perfect evolution of the English Reformation, or a perversion of its heritage, rightly understood? Did the Church fundamentally fail the Christian commonwealth of England, whether through arrogant clericalism, pallid parish worship, or separation from the wider European Reformed world; or did it actually prove an improbably successful and integrative national Church after the extreme disruptions and discontinuities imposed during the civil wars and Interregnum? It should be obvious that by focusing on different issues, places, or points in time, historians can readily construct very different images of the Church's 'success' or 'failure'.[13] Overall, two approaches will be adopted in successive sections of this chapter: a descriptive account of events and issues, and a definitional analysis of what, ultimately, 'the Church of England'—its character and compass— meant in this period.

DESCRIBING THE CHURCH: FORM AND CONTEXT

The re-established Church of England developed within a Petri dish of festering political affairs. Although the period after 1660 used to be presented as one characterized by a secularizing spirit and a gradual 'growth of political stability' after the cataclysm of the civil wars, the bulk of recent scholarship has instead exposed the chronic instability that was at the heart of the Restoration

---

[11] Kenneth Fincham and Nicholas Tyacke, *Altars Restored: The Changing Face of English Religious Worship, 1547–c.1700* (Oxford, 2007), ch. 8.

[12] Terry Friedman, *The Eighteenth-Century Church in Britain* (New Haven, CT and London, 2011); Brent S. Sirota, *The Christian Monitors: The Church of England and the Age of Benevolence, 1680–1730* (New Haven, CT, 2014).

[13] Jeremy Gregory, 'The Making of a Protestant Nation: "Success" and "Failure" in England's Long Reformation', in Nicholas Tyacke (ed.), *England's Long Reformation 1500–1800* (London, 1998), pp. 307–34.

experience.[14] Religious disputes were the most significant part of this volatility in the wake of what many felt had been a botched and traumatic rebirth for the Church between 1660 and 1662.[15] This had led to a narrow religious establishment, not an integrative institution dedicated to wider goals of 'healing and settling'. Persecution became a key part of Restoration society; the 'comprehension' of nonconforming Protestants an enduring hope for those who deplored new realities.[16] Before turning to deeper questions of identity in the next section of this chapter, it is necessary first to sketch a threefold descriptive outline of the 'body' of the Church that developed between 1662 and 1714: its statutory 'bones'; the competing 'organs' directing its activity; and the 'diet' of issues that simultaneously sustained and poisoned its existence.

The 1662 Act of Uniformity (14 Car. II, c. 4) provided the legislative copingstone for the later Stuart Church as a national institution.[17] Its framers sought to protect 'the Reformed Religion of the Church of England' from the influence of the distressingly large number of the king's subjects who followed 'theire owne sensualitie', and lived 'without knowledge and due feare of God'. Nothing, they argued, would be more conducive to God pouring out his blessings on the realm than 'Common Prayers due useing of the Sacraments and often preaching of the Gospell with Devotion of the Hearers'.[18] To that end, all ministers of the Church would have to swear their 'unfeigned assent and consent' to all sections of the Book of Common Prayer, even though it had not been revised along the lines demanded by Presbyterians.[19] As a result, the pursuit of 'uniformity' would prove to be one of the most divisive issues of the age. The Act was part of a wave of repressive statutes—the Corporation Act (1661), the Quaker Act (1662), the first Conventicles Act (1664), the Five Mile Act (1665)—together misleadingly labelled 'the Clarendon code', after Charles II's Lord Chancellor, Edward Hyde, earl of Clarendon, who

---

[14] Contrast J. H. Plumb, *The Growth of Political Stability in England 1675–1725* (London, 1967) and Jonathan Scott, *England's Troubles: Seventeenth-Century English Political Instability in European Context* (Cambridge, 2000).

[15] Gary S. De Krey, 'Between Revolutions: Re-appraising the Restoration in Britain', *History Compass*, 6 (2008): 738–73, esp. pp. 748–53, 'The Importance of Religion'.

[16] Mark Goldie, *Roger Morrice and the Puritan Whigs* (Woodbridge, 2007), ch. 6.

[17] For a summary of the provisions of the relevant legislation, see Geoffrey Holmes, *The Making of a Great Power: Late Stuart and Early Georgian Britain 1660–1722* (London, 1993), pp. 454–5, 457–9.

[18] *The Statutes of the Realm, printed by command of his Majesty King George the Third, Vol. V* ([London], 1819), p. 364. For context, see Paul Seaward, *The Cavalier Parliament and the Reconstruction of the Old Regime, 1661–1667* (Cambridge, 1989), ch. 7; Andrew Swatland, *The House of Lords in the Reign of Charles II* (Cambridge, 1996), ch. 9; Ronald Hutton, *The Restoration: A Political and Religious History of England and Wales 1658–1667* (Oxford, 1985), pp. 171–80.

[19] Jeremy Gregory, 'The Prayer Book and the Parish Church: From the Restoration to the Oxford Movement', in Charles Hefling and Cynthia Shattuck (eds.), *The Oxford Guide to the Book of Common Prayer: A Worldwide Survey* (Oxford, 2006), pp. 93–105 (pp. 93–4).

actually pursued a more nuanced approach to the politics of religion, often to the chagrin of his more intolerant allies.[20] Further iterations of these penal laws would be provided by the second Conventicles Act (1670), and the first and second Test Acts (1673, 1678). Repetitions and elaborations of statutory requirements in early modern England were invariably a sign of evasion and anxiety, and the religious legislation of the Restoration was no exception. The second Conventicles Act tellingly included a new clause financially to punish magistrates who failed to execute its terms; the second Test Act began by openly acknowledging that previous 'divers good laws ... made for preventing the increase and danger of popery in this kingdom ... have not had the desired effects'.[21] Such phrasing suggests the complexities of local government and the variety of local attitudes towards Nonconformists of many kinds.[22] Nevertheless, although the repressive religious legislation of the age was never wholly successful in crushing the resolve of those outside the national Church, it sustained a chimerical vision that somehow, sometime, the Church of England would include all of the king's subjects. In other words, it underpinned a mindset that abhorred any notion of pluralistic toleration, or even qualified relief for the scrupulous.[23] The basic premises of such legislation during the 1660s and 1670s would recur during the last, Tory-dominated, years of Queen Anne's reign with the Occasional Conformity Act (1711) and the Schism Act (1714). At the end of the period, as at the beginning, proving conformity was a vital qualification for office-holding: a crucial and contested issue, not least because of the immense range of offices that could be held by individuals far down the social hierarchy.[24]

The 1689 Toleration Act (1 William and Mary, c. 18) stands within a very different strand of public affairs.[25] Reciting the list of statutes that together created a 'confessional state' in later Stuart England should not obscure the extent to which this was a partisan achievement by one faction or party triumphing over others. It was a matter of contingency, not of inevitability, that hardline advocates of religious intolerance regularly imposed their views,

[20] For Clarendon's pursuit of 'moderation' in the religious settlement, see Paul Seaward, 'Hyde, Edward (1609–1674)', *ODNB*.

[21] J. P. Kenyon (ed.), *The Stuart Constitution 1603–1688: Documents and Commentary* (Cambridge, 1986 edn.), pp. 359, 386.

[22] Anthony Fletcher, 'The Enforcement of the Conventicle Acts 1664–1679', in W. J. Sheils (ed.), *Persecution and Toleration*, Studies in Church History 21 (Oxford, 1984), pp. 235–46; Grant Tapsell, *The Personal Rule of Charles II* (Woodbridge, 2007), pp. 74–8.

[23] Mark Goldie, 'The Theory of Religious Intolerance in Restoration England', in Ole Peter Grell, Jonathan Israel, and Nicholas Tyacke (eds.), *From Persecution to Toleration: The Glorious Revolution and Religion in England* (Oxford, 1991), pp. 331–68.

[24] Mark Goldie, 'The Unacknowledged Republic: Officeholding in Early Modern England', in Tim Harris (ed.), *The Politics of the Excluded, c.1500–1850* (Basingstoke, 2001), pp. 153–94.

[25] John Spurr, 'The Church of England, Comprehension and the Toleration Act of 1689', *English Historical Review*, 104 (1989): 927–46.

and this tended to reflect successful exploitation of divisions within both the royal court and Parliament. By contrast, between 1662 and 1689 there were numerous unsuccessful attempts to draft and pass legislation that might reshape the Church in ways that could 'comprehend' a significant number of Nonconformists, primarily Presbyterians.[26] Compared to such efforts, the Toleration Act was actually a disappointing and limited affair, all that was left in the wake of further failed efforts at 'comprehension'. The grudging nature of its full title is telling: 'an Act for exempting their Majesties' Protestant subjects, dissenting from the Church of England, from the penalties of certain laws'. Nevertheless, its effects were enormous. The Church of England remained the Established Church, but lost its full claims to be the national Church.[27] What seemed to intolerant churchmen to be a terrifying number of Dissenting meeting-houses and educational academies sprang up across the country during the 1690s and 1700s.[28] At a personal level, individuals felt that a distinct era of persecution was over: a Presbyterian clergyman, Roger Morrice, recorded in February 1689 that after the passage of the Toleration Act he could walk through Westminster Hall, at the very centre of public affairs, without fear for the first time since 1662.[29]

Debates about religious legislation raised the crucial question of who rightfully controlled the Church. The later Stuart era saw developments of many earlier tensions resulting from the peculiarly bifurcated nature of the magisterial English Reformation.[30] The Church of England was simultaneously a royal Church, governed from the throne by successive Supreme Governors, and an institution shaped by parliamentary statutes. In the long shadow of the regicide, a huge amount of post-1662 clerical ink and lung-power went into emphasizing how much the restored Church supported the monarchy.[31] Even at the start of the Catholic James II's reign, many contemporaries clung to the declaration the king made to his first Privy Council meeting that he would protect the Church. Yet many observers viewed the commitment of the later Stuarts to the Established Church with well-founded

---

[26] Gary S. De Krey, 'The First Restoration Crisis: Conscience and Coercion in London, 1667–73', *Albion*, 25 (1993): 565–80; Henry Horwitz, 'Protestant Reconciliation in the Exclusion Crisis', *Journal of Ecclesiastical History*, 15 (1964): 201–17.

[27] W. M. Jacob, *Lay People and Religion in the Early Eighteenth Century* (Cambridge, 1996), p. 15.

[28] Around 3,900 licences for meeting-houses were granted between 1689 and 1710: Holmes, *Making of a Great Power*, p. 353; for academies, see the *Dissenting Academies Online* project, <http://www.english.qmul.ac.uk/drwilliams/academies.html>, accessed 1 Aug. 2014.

[29] Goldie, *Roger Morrice*, p. 55.

[30] Jacqueline Rose, *Godly Kingship in Restoration England: The Politics of the Royal Supremacy, 1660–1688* (Cambridge, 2011).

[31] Notably in sermons preached on 30 Jan., the anniversary of the regicide: Andrew Lacey, *The Cult of King Charles the Martyr* (Woodbridge, 2003), chs. 5–6.

scepticism. A particular local low point may be discerned in Radnorshire during June 1685, when a rector, Charles Lloyd, preached a funeral sermon and whilst 'praying for the King as Defender of the Faith, added [these words] *as yett*'.[32] Although after the Revolution of 1688–9 Queen Mary would provide an Anglican buffer between the Church and her Dutch Reformed husband until her death in 1694, thereafter many fretted about a Supreme Governor so unversed in, and unsympathetic towards, the traditions of the Church of England.

If the Supreme Governor could not always be trusted, where could churchmen turn for support? Archbishop Sheldon proved an adept parliamentary manager, vigorously lobbying the rest of the episcopate in the House of Lords to vote with him, and cajoling lay peers and MPs.[33] Reliance on Parliament, though, created as many problems as it solved. At a tactical level, parliamentary majorities could come and go, with a sizeable number of MPs and peers ill-disposed to clerical pretensions on the basis of long memories. When a bill to have James's children educated as Protestants under the control of bishops was discussed in 1677, Sir Thomas Littleton noted bitterly that the measure would be counter-productive, since 'we have had a sort of clergy ever since Archbishop Laud's time too much addicted to Popery'.[34] At the level of principle, reliance on Parliament undermined the Church's intrinsic self-regard, and left it vulnerable to Roman Catholic critiques that it was a mere human creation. As one clerical polemicist, and future bishop, Laurence Womock, fretted in 1679: 'We are allready upbraided for a p[ar]liamentary Religion.'[35] 'Faith by statute' thus created both political and ideological problems for defenders of the restored Church of England.

Such uncertainties about support from secular authorities left some clerics hoping that the Church could defend itself through the more active presence of the clergy's own bicameral representative body, Convocation. Having fallen into desuetude between the Restoration and the Revolution, agitation for its recall mounted during the 1690s, and William III was obliged to acquiesce in order to secure in government the services of leading Tory grandees.[36] Convocation proved to be a theatre in which clerical actors from different wings of

---

[32] Bishop of St David's to archbishop of Canterbury, 27 June 1685 (my emphasis), MS Tanner 31, f. 123.

[33] John Spurr, 'Sheldon, Gilbert (1598–1677)', *ODNB*. Beddard has wisely cautioned against exaggerating Sheldon's influence in isolation from other power-brokers: 'Sheldon and Anglican Recovery', p. 1011.

[34] Quoted in Basil D. Henning (ed.), *The House of Commons 1660–1690*, 3 vols. (London, 1983), II, p. 751.

[35] Laurence Womock to [George Thorp], 18 Mar. 1678/9, MS Tanner 39, f. 214. Womock became bishop of St David's in 1683.

[36] Norman Sykes, *From Sheldon to Secker: Aspects of English Church History, 1660–1768* (Cambridge, 1959), pp. 43–4; G. V. Bennett, *The Tory Crisis in Church and State, 1688–1730: The Career of Francis Atterbury, Bishop of Rochester* (Oxford, 1975); Grant Tapsell, 'Laurence Hyde

the Church could engage in vitriolic verbal combat, much of which spun out into lengthy published exchanges that did nothing to cool the fevered electoral world maintained by the Triennial Act (1694).[37] The fact that early Enlightenment England featured numerous assaults on 'priestcraft' owed much to the continuing prominence of preachers and polemicists in public life.[38] This would reach a crescendo in the years immediately after Henry Sacheverell's notorious sermon of 5 November 1709 on the 'perils of false brethren'. His supporters could angrily contrast his politically motivated prosecution by a Whig ministry with the favour shown to Benjamin Hoadly, 'an icon of heterodox whiggery', whose views on conditional obedience to secular authorities and robust defence of 'revolution principles' infuriated Tory High Churchmen.[39] Mobs ransacked Dissenting meeting-houses, and such symbols of Whig fiscal-military state-building as the Bank of England, while at least 575 editions of sermons, tracts, and broadsheets concerning Sacheverell were published in the twelve months after his incendiary pulpit performance.[40] Both individually and collectively, clergy were crucial figures in maintaining a vehement and contentious politics of religion into the reign of Anne and beyond.

Nevertheless, it is important to balance such a focus on the clergy with the deeper realities of lay power that did so much to influence the Church of England at national and local level.[41] Nationally, a Parliament of lay landowners prevented the re-creation of a powerful High Commission that had proved such a valuable enforcement mechanism for Laudian ecclesiastical

---

and the Politics of Religion in Later Stuart England', *English Historical Review*, 125 (2010): 1414–48 (pp. 1443–5).

[37] Geoffrey Holmes and W. A. Speck, *The Divided Society: Parties and Politics in England, 1694–1716* (London, 1967); W. A. Speck, *Tory and Whig: The Struggle in the Constituencies, 1701–1715* (London, 1970).

[38] Justin A. I. Champion, *The Pillars of Priestcraft Shaken: The Church of England and its Enemies, 1660–1730* (Cambridge, 1992); Mark Goldie, 'Priestcraft and the Birth of Whiggism', in Nicholas T. Phillipson and Quentin Skinner (eds.), *Political Discourse in Early Modern Britain* (Cambridge, 1993), pp. 209–31.

[39] For a good example of the close attention which Tories in the localities paid to the Sacheverell case, see John Addy et al. (eds.), *The Diary of Henry Prescott, LL.B., Deputy Registrar of Chester Diocese*, 3 vols., Record Society of Lancashire and Cheshire, 127, 132–3 (Gloucester, 1987–97), I, pp. 270–9. For the contrast with Hoadly, and the descriptive quotation, see Andrew Starkie, *The Church of England and the Bangorian Controversy, 1716–1721* (Woodbridge, 2007), pp. 50–1.

[40] Geoffrey Holmes, *The Trial of Doctor Sacheverell* (London, 1973), esp. ch. 7; Geoffrey Holmes, *British Politics in the Age of Anne* (rev. edn., London, 1987), p. xix. See also Mark Knights (ed.), *Faction Displayed: Reconsidering the Impeachment of Dr Henry Sacheverell* (Chichester, 2012).

[41] The best short account is now John Spurr, 'The Lay Church of England', in Tapsell (ed.), *Later Stuart Church*. See also Jacob, *Lay People*, and a brilliant local study of Wiltshire, Donald A. Spaeth, *The Church in an Age of Danger: Parsons and Parishioners, 1660–1740* (Cambridge, 2000).

policy during the 1630s. Although bishops were readmitted to the House of Lords, their support of Danby's ministry during the 1670s left them wide open to anti-clerical assault as politicians, rather than as spiritual leaders, a charge that would recur in the more complex political divisions of the post-Revolution world.[42] Locally, lay patrons maintained a fierce grip on appointments to livings and the layout of parish churches within their spheres of influence, their proprietary language—'my seate' (i.e. pew), 'my 2 new parsons', 'my [parish] church'—an accurate reflection of the legal and social realities into the eighteenth century.[43] Much of Sheldon's early Restoration success in rebuilding the institution of the Church came from shrewdly yoking together ideas of clerical and lay hierarchy after the chronic instability of the 1640s and 1650s. As Ronald Hutton has acutely observed, in effect Sheldon reworked James VI and I's celebrated aphorism for a new age: 'no bishops, no gentlemen'.[44]

It would be misleading, though, to present the later Stuart era straightforwardly in terms of elite control of a submissive and wholly deferential populace. Congregations throughout the land proved ready, in a variety of ways, to shape and influence their own religious lives, and to expect clergy to assist them. Although it is hard to gauge how commonplace such activity was, some parishes presented mass petitions for or against a particular clergyman being appointed to the local living.[45] Others shifted their priorities and interests as the period went on. William Sampson was rector of Clayworth in Nottinghamshire from 1676 to 1714, and in 1701 offered an account of how he had been told that in the immediate post-Restoration years the 'over-joyd' local people treated perambulating the bounds of the parish as a great novelty, charitably giving entertainments over three days. As he glumly went on, this 'hot Fit' of loyalty soon faded, and 'charity began to wax cold', leaving all 'on ye Parsons shoulders ... & was expected as a Right'.[46] Such Eeyore-ish pessimism

---

[42] Mark Goldie, 'Danby, the Bishops and the Whigs', in Tim Harris, Paul Seaward, and Mark Goldie (eds.), *The Politics of Religion in Restoration England* (Oxford, 1990), pp. 75–105.

[43] D. R. Hainsworth and Cherry Walker (eds.), *The Correspondence of Lord Fitzwilliam of Milton and Francis Guybon, his Steward 1697–1709*, Northamptonshire Record Society 31 (Northampton, 1990), pp. 218, 172; Raymond A. Anselment (ed.), *The Remembrances of Elizabeth Freke 1671–1714*, Camden Society, 5th ser., 18 (London, 2001), pp. 111, 122; D. R. Hainsworth, *Stewards, Lords and People: The Estate Steward and his World in Later Stuart England* (Cambridge, 1992), p. 177.

[44] Hutton, *Restoration*, p. 176.

[45] Doreen Slatter (ed.), *The Diary of Thomas Naish* (Devizes, 1965), p. 27; Andrew Cambers (ed.), *The Life of John Rastrick 1650–1727*, Camden Society, 5th ser., 36 (London, 2010), p. 85; Hainsworth, *Stewards, Lords and People*, p. 178; Samuel S. Thomas, *Creating Communities in Restoration England: Parish and Congregation in Oliver Heywood's Halifax* (Leiden, 2013), ch. 4. I am grateful to Dr Andrew Foster for introducing me to the last of these works, and for much other valuable advice.

[46] Henry Gill and Everard L. Guilford (eds.), *The Rector's Book of Clayworth, Notts.* (Nottingham, 1910), p. 143.

was commonplace among many clergy, though it should be contrasted with improving clerical incomes over the period: at the upper end of the spectrum, some clerics became able to ape the life-style of local gentlemen; at the lower end Queen Anne's Bounty raised many out of very poor economic circumstances.[47] Whatever their financial position, clergymen who did not live up to the expectations of their parishioners—whether because of moral turpitude, laziness, or liturgical views that were out of step with lay preferences—could find themselves in very difficult positions, not least through presentments to Church courts. The laity were thus not mere passive recipients of sermons, sacraments, or sentences from the Church courts.

Lying beneath these broad questions of authority and control lay a vast welter of political events that cannot be discussed here in any detail.[48] In bare schematic terms, though, it is possible to describe three broad phases of anxious national debate that were particularly meaningful for the development of the Church of England.

First, during the 1660s a lingering hangover from the civil wars concerned ongoing fears about puritans' political disobedience. A number of plots and small-scale revolts facilitated hostile commentators' efforts to maintain a connection between puritan religiosity and political disobedience.[49] Links between the disaffected across the Stuarts' three kingdoms provoked particular anxiety in governing circles: the destabilizing impact of Scottish and Irish events on English politics in the early 1640s had not been forgotten. The lived reality of the 'great ejection' was also powerful. Many of those clergy who had conformed in 1662 had done so reluctantly, and diaries like those of Ralph Josselin reveal troubled souls who were never again comfortable in their ministry.[50] Others who had not conformed, like Richard Baxter, maintained hopes that a reformulation of the Church would one day accommodate Presbyterians.[51] Less striking, but no less historically significant, was the difficulty that clergy would experience in recovering their rights, incomes, and status at a local level. Although there were very considerable continuities

---

[47] Zachary Cawdrey to Archbishop Sancroft, 24 Oct. 1682, MS Tanner 35, f. 117; Ian M. Green, 'The First Five Years of Queen Anne's Bounty', in Rosemary O'Day and Felicity Heal (eds.), *Princes and Paupers in the English Church, 1500–1800* (Leicester, 1981), pp. 231–54.

[48] The best overall account of the period is now Tim Harris, *Restoration: Charles II and his Kingdoms, 1660–1685* (London, 2005); Tim Harris, *Revolution: The Great Crisis of the British Monarchy, 1685–1720* (London, 2006); an older survey text, Holmes, *Making of a Great Power*, remains valuable.

[49] George Southcombe and Grant Tapsell, *Restoration Politics, Religion and Culture: Britain and Ireland, 1660–1714* (Basingstoke, 2010), pp. 21–3; Matthew Neufeld, *The Civil Wars after 1660: Public Remembering in Late Stuart England* (Woodbridge, 2013), intro. and ch. 1.

[50] Alan Macfarlane (ed.), *The Diary of Ralph Josselin 1616–1683* (Oxford, 1976).

[51] Michael P. Winship, 'Defining Puritanism in Restoration England: Richard Baxter and Others Respond to *A Friendly Debate*', *Historical Journal*, 54 (2011): 689–715; N. H. Keeble, 'Baxter, Richard (1615–1691)', *ODNB*.

of clerical personnel and popular Anglicanism across the 1640–60 period,[52] this did not mean that all laymen were delighted to see clerical power fully rebuilt.[53]

Secondly, during the 1670s and 1680s the primary focus within the politics of religion was the renewal of the early Stuart nightmare prospect famously labelled by Andrew Marvell 'popery and arbitrary government'.[54] Two issues in particular combined to inflame religious passions: the knowledge that the heir to the throne, James, duke of York, was a Catholic, and the extent to which Louis XIV's increasing bellicosity in Europe appeared to anxious English observers like the Presbyterian intelligencer and ejected clergyman Roger Morrice to indicate coordinated efforts to 'extirpate the Northren heresie'.[55] In some quarters this would stimulate calls for the 'comprehension' of as many Protestants as possible within the Church of England as a means of bolstering national unity in the face of threats to the very existence of Protestant England. Others, however, believed passionately that the best way to safeguard the long-term future of the Church of England was to persecute Dissenters into obedience. Since it was their over-scrupulous consciences that had divided the nation, polemicists like Roger L'Estrange vigorously presented Dissenters as puppets of the papacy and its malign agenda for England.[56] Alternatively, Dissenters could see their persecutors as a popish fifth column, only too ready to further a process of re-Catholicization in their own twisted religious interests, or for shallow material gain.[57]

A third phase of national debate came after the Revolution of 1688–9 had 'cauterised the national fear' of popery:[58] the 1690s and 1700s witnessed a renewed emphasis on England's relationship with Europe in the context of unprecedented fiscal-military commitments. Restraining Louis XIV's France may have been about defeating Catholic universal monarchy, yet many feared

---

[52] Kenneth Fincham and Stephen Taylor, 'Episcopalian Conformity and Nonconformity, 1646–1660', in Jason McElligott and David L. Smith (eds.), *Royalists and Royalism during the Interregnum* (Manchester, 2010), pp. 18–43; Kenneth Fincham and Stephen Taylor, 'Vital Statistics: Episcopal Ordination and Ordinands in England, 1646–60', *English Historical Review*, 126 (2011): 319–44; Kenneth Fincham and Stephen Taylor, 'The Restoration of the Church of England: Ordination, Re-ordination and Conformity', in Stephen Taylor and Grant Tapsell (eds.), *The Nature of the English Revolution Revisited: Essays in Honour of John Morrill* (Woodbridge, 2013), pp. 197–232; Judith Maltby, 'Suffering and Surviving: The Civil Wars, the Commonwealth and the Formation of "Anglicanism"', in Christopher Durston and Judith Maltby (eds.), *Religion in Revolutionary England* (Manchester, 2006), pp. 158–80.

[53] For a droll local case study, see Clive Holmes, *Seventeenth-Century Lincolnshire* (Lincoln, 1980), pp. 224–6.

[54] Nigel Smith, *Andrew Marvell: The Chameleon* (New Haven, CT and London, 2010), ch. 12.

[55] Mark Goldie (gen. ed.), *The Entring Book of Roger Morrice, 1677–91*, 7 vols. (Woodbridge, 2007–9), III, pp. 45, 151, 198–9, 245, 252; IV, pp. 180, 443–4.

[56] Mark Goldie, 'Roger L'Estrange's *Observator* and the Exorcism of the Plot', in Anne Dunan-Page and Beth Lynch (eds.), *Roger L'Estrange and the Making of Restoration Culture* (Aldershot, 2008), pp. 67–88.

[57] Tapsell, *Personal Rule*, pp. 126–31.   [58] Goldie, *Roger Morrice*, p. 21.

that its consequences at home would entrench William as a neo-Cromwellian warlord who cared little for the Church of England.[59] Contemporary events thus inflamed long-standing debates about the relationship of the Church of England to foreign Protestant Churches. Many Dissenters, and some within the Established Church, looked beyond England for theological and ecclesiological inspiration.[60] Others viewed such a vision as tantamount to undermining the royal supremacy and episcopal hierarchy of the Church—two of the key characteristics thought by some writers positively to differentiate English Reformation developments from more chaotic changes on the continent.[61] Although Anne's reign would to some extent ameliorate the fears of those clergy who enunciated an essentially insular view of the Church of England, both William's ecclesiastical patronage and the prospect of the Hanoverian succession helped to fuel an aggressive discourse of the 'Church in danger'.[62] This rhetoric was at the heart of post-revolutionary Church politics with developing use of 'High' and 'Low' Church as pejorative labels. The former connoted those hostile to nonconformity and passionately committed to the ceremonies of the Church re-established in 1662; the latter those who were more interested in pragmatic dialogue with Dissenters, and who stressed 'reasonable' religion rather than minute concern with liturgical and ecclesiological norms.[63] Rancorous partisan activity within the Church was matched by vehement external criticism from those non-jurors who indefatigably emphasized their own purity of principle compared to the more malleable consciences of those who shook off their allegiance to James II after 1688.[64] Such writing formed just one part of a culture of public debate in the post-Revolution era that was further fuelled by the final lapsing of the Licensing Act in 1695.[65]

[59] Charles-Edouard Levillain, 'Cromwell Redivivus? William III as Military Dictator: Myth and Reality', in Esther Mijers and David Onnekink (eds.), *Redefining William III: The Impact of the King-Stadholder in International Context* (Aldershot, 2007), pp. 159–76; Jonathan I. Israel, 'William III and Toleration', in Grell et al. (eds.), *From Persecution to Toleration*, pp. 129–70.

[60] Tony Claydon, 'The Church of England and the Churches of Europe, 1660–1714', in Tapsell (ed.), *Later Stuart Church*, pp. 173–92.

[61] John Spurr, *The Restoration Church of England, 1646–1689* (New Haven, CT and London), ch. 3, esp. p. 132.

[62] G. V. Bennett, 'William III and the Episcopate', in G. V. Bennett and J. D. Walsh (eds.), *Essays in Modern English Church History in Memory of Norman Sykes* (London, 1966), pp. 104–31; Bennett, *Tory Crisis*, part 1; Craig Rose, *England in the 1690s: Revolution, Religion and War* (Oxford, 1999), pp. 171–8.

[63] For further discussion of parties and partisanship, see, in this volume, the chapter by J. C. D. Clark.

[64] John Findon, 'The Nonjurors and the Church of England 1689–1716', DPhil thesis, University of Oxford, 1979.

[65] For the clergy as polemicists, see Grant Tapsell, 'Pastors, Preachers and Politicians: The Clergy of the Later Stuart Church', in Tapsell (ed.), *Later Stuart Church*, pp. 79–83; Mark Knights, *The Devil in Disguise: Deception, Delusion, and Fanaticism in the Early English Enlightenment* (Oxford, 2011), ch. 5.

By 1714 the Church of England had thus experienced a half-century of re-establishment that had not created religious uniformity. The narrow 'settlement' of 1662 and the Revolution of 1688–9 both proved deeply divisive. Nevertheless, the Established Church remained a crucial part of national and local affairs. What remains is to examine further the character of that institution, in terms of polemical definitions and quotidian activity.

DEFINING THE CHURCH: THE STRUGGLE FOR IDENTITY

What exactly was 'the Church of England' between 1662 and 1714? Unsurprisingly, the answers offered by contemporaries were very various indeed, even setting aside external criticisms by Roman Catholics and Protestant Nonconformists. At one end of the spectrum, after a period travelling widely abroad during the Interregnum, Dr Isaac Basire preached in Westminster Abbey in November 1661 that the Church of England was 'the most perfect under Heaven'.[66] Men as different as the disciplinarian archbishop of Canterbury Gilbert Sheldon and the self-consciously 'moderate' MP Sir John Holland could piously refer to the Church as 'our mother'.[67] If some spoke with reverence or affection, others conceptualized the Church in more matter-of-fact, even clinical, ways. In his 1672 declaration of indulgence, Charles II coolly referred to it as 'the basis, rule and standard of the general and public worship of God'.[68] As the political nation fractured into increasingly bitter rival camps, some Whig 'Low' Churchmen professed loyalty to an idealized hope of what might be, of the Church of England 'as *shall be* established by law' (1689), or as it 'OUGHT to be by law established' (1705).[69] For 'High' Churchmen, both lay and clerical, this was profoundly disturbing talk that left 'the Church in danger'.[70] In their eyes, 'Low Church is no Church' (1710).[71] Overall, it is easy to agree with the anti-clerical conformist layman William Lawrence when he wrote in 1675 that 'there are as many Sects and Separations

[66] Esmond S. de Beer (ed.), *The Diary of John Evelyn*, 6 vols. (Oxford, 1955), III, p. 303 (10 Nov. 1661).

[67] [Gilbert Sheldon to 'Sir'], after 6 Mar. 1664, Bodl., MS Add. C 308, f. 20; Caroline Robbins (ed.), *The Diary of John Milward, September 1666 to May 1668* (Cambridge, 1938), p. 325. For Holland, see John Miller, 'A Moderate in the First Age of Party: The Dilemmas of Sir John Holland, 1675–85', *English Historical Review*, 114 (1999): 844–74.

[68] Kenyon, *Stuart Constitution*, p. 382.

[69] Rose, *England in the 1690s*, p. 164 (Rose's emphasis); Eveline Cruickshanks, Stuart Handley, and D. W. Hayton (eds.), *The House of Commons 1690–1715*, 5 vols. (Cambridge, 2002), II, p. 62.

[70] Bennett, *Tory Crisis*; George Every, *The High Church Party 1688–1718* (London, 1956).

[71] Cruickshanks et al. (eds.), *House of Commons*, II, p. 373.

in the English Church as there are points in the Compass'.[72] This was not a matter of indifference for Lawrence, however facetious, and even satirical, his tone could sometimes be. The national Church in which he worshipped was under grave threat: 'I feare the Church of England thus crucify'd between the papist and the many-headed puritan, is but short-liv'd: these are the two Theeves that endeavor to rob it of its Glory.'[73] Such language emphasizes some of the continuities for the Church with earlier periods, redolent as it is with assumptions about charting a course between the perceived extremes of Rome and Geneva.[74]

Defining the Church was not necessarily merely a matter of political name-calling or abstract commentary. It could also be an explicit and powerful tool in public debate. Two brief case studies will make the point, both taken from the central 1670s, but very different in their nature and purpose. The first comprises the exceptionally lengthy and bitter exchanges in the House of Lords on 12 May 1675, when Anthony Ashley Cooper, earl of Shaftesbury, a leading critic of government in Church and state, asked what was meant by 'the Protestant religion'.[75] The context was the controversy surrounding the oath of non-resistance introduced at the behest of Charles II's Lord Treasurer, Thomas Osborne, earl of Danby, for all office-holders, privy councillors, JPs, MPs, and peers: 'I do swear that I will not endeavour to alter the Protestant religion, or the government of either Church or State.'[76] Intended in part to bolster the king's dubious Protestant credentials, the wording of the oath prompted revealing comments on all sides. According to Shaftesbury, 'it is a far different thing to believe, or to be fully persuaded of the doctrine of our Church, and to swear never to endeavour to alter [it]; which last must be utterly unlawful, unless you place infallibility either in the Church or yourself; you being otherwise obliged to alter, whenever a clearer or better light comes to you'. In the opinion of several bishops present, the answer to defining the Protestant religion was easy: Shaftesbury merely needed to consult the Thirty-Nine Articles, the liturgy, the catechism, the homilies, and the canons. This prompted a gleeful series of no doubt pre-planned comments from him, pointing out apparent discrepancies between what had been agreed regarding doctrine in the Elizabethan Settlement and what seemed to be being preached

---

[72] G. E. Aylmer (ed.), *The Diary of William Lawrence* (Beaminster, 1961), p. 30.

[73] Aylmer (ed.), *Diary of William Lawrence*, p. 30.

[74] Anthony Milton, *Catholic and Reformed: Roman and Protestant Churches in English Protestant Thought, 1600–1640* (Cambridge, 1994).

[75] Unless otherwise noted, quotations from this debate are drawn from K. H. D. Haley, *The First Earl of Shaftesbury* (Oxford, 1968), ch. 18, esp. pp. 378–9, and Goldie, 'Danby, the Bishops and the Whigs', pp. 82–3. I am grateful to Robin Eagles for drawing my attention to this great parliamentary occasion.

[76] Andrew Browning, *Thomas Osborne, Earl of Danby and Duke of Leeds 1632–1712*, 3 vols. (Glasgow, 1944–51), I, pp. 152–5, 164–5; III, pp. 122–5.

in contemporary England; the fact that the liturgy then in use had only been agreed thirteen years previously; and, by contrast, that the canons were simply 'the old Popish canons'. The bishops' apparently immovable foundations for the Church were in fact shifting sands. Everything they had pointed to was either too new, or else too old and insufficiently revised, for men to swear never to alter.

The second case study, the Compton Census of 1676, gives some sense of how religious identities were refined and understood in the localities. Although named after the bishop of London who did much to administer it, the census was really set in train by the earl of Danby as part of a wider effort to convince Charles II that his subjects were overwhelmingly conformist members of the Church of England.[77] Statistical proof of this could then serve a political purpose: to dissuade the king from continuing to support indulgence policies towards those outside the Church of England, on the basis that they were numerically insignificant. But who counted as 'conformist'? Slack drafting of written instructions to the lesser clergy and churchwardens left multiple ambiguities.[78] Asking for numbers of 'popish recusants' and 'other Dissenters' only advanced the matter so far. What of 'church papists', Catholics who were careful to attend their parish churches in order to avoid recusancy charges? What of those Protestants, like the Lancashire Presbyterian Roger Lowe, who were more or less enthusiastic members of local congregations, but whose primary religious activity lay outside the parish church in Dissenting meeting-houses or private homes?[79] Was being a conformist merely a matter of physical attendance in a church building, or did it require some more active proof of commitment?[80] In particular, when written instructions for the census referred to those who 'either obstinately refuse or wholly absent themselves from the Communion of the Church of England at such times as by Law they are required', what exactly did 'Communion' mean?[81] Thoughtful incumbents were not slow to see the problems. As the vicar of St Lawrence in Thanet noted, if being in communion meant 'joineing in the publique worship with the Congregation in hearing the praiers of the Church in the parish Church on

---

[77] This and other points of interpretation are drawn from Anne Whiteman's magisterial introduction to her *The Compton Census of 1676: A Critical Edition*, with the assistance of Mary Clapinson (Oxford, 1986).

[78] Not least whether children and women should be counted, or even whether only male householders should be enumerated: Whiteman (ed.), *Compton Census*, pp. xxx–xxxi, xxxiii–xxxvi.

[79] William L. Sachse (ed.), *The Diary of Roger Lowe, of Ashton-in-Makerfield, Lancashire, 1663–74* (London, 1938); John D. Ramsbottom, 'Presbyterians and "Partial Conformity" in the Restoration Church of England', *Journal of Ecclesiastical History*, 43 (1992): 249–70.

[80] For the extent to which churchwardens would continue to grapple with this question, see Margaret Spufford, 'The Importance of Religion in the Sixteenth and Seventeenth Centuries', in Margaret Spufford (ed.), *The World of Rural Dissenters 1520–1725* (Cambridge, 1995), pp. 1–102 (p. 12).

[81] Whiteman (ed.), *Compton Census*, p. xxix.

the Lords day', then only about sixty of 1,200 local residents were wholly absent. On the other hand, if communion actually referred to taking the sacrament, only around 200 did so once a year, and fewer than 100 were canonically obedient by receiving three times a year. As he despairingly added, few 'will be induced to receive the Communion by any arguments or perswasions'.[82] Another Kentish clergyman, the rector of Frittenden, elaborated on the complexities of parish life in slightly different terms. Setting out the variety of Nonconformists, he also referred to thirty or forty local 'Newtralists' who were 'between Presbiterians and Conformists', as well as eleven or twelve men who were 'Licentious or such as profess no kind of Religion'.[83] Such descriptions are highly revealing, not least of the assumptions of those doing the labelling. They make all attempts to count heads on confessional criteria fraught with risk: it will never be possible to state precisely what proportion of the population were members of the Church of England in this period, in the sense of having a positive inner commitment to its liturgy and teachings.[84]

Taken together, these case studies demonstrate that religious identities in the Church remained after 1662 various, contested, and built from three crucial components. First, there were differing conceptions of the historical development of the Church of England. The Church's long and convoluted gestation under the Tudors and early Stuarts offered great opportunities for arguing the necessity of further changes under the veil of returning to a past point in time. Shaftesbury variously claimed to wish 'to restore the liturgy to what it was in Queen Elizabeth's days', or emphasized how 'glorious' the Edwardian reformation had been, juxtaposing the tenor of reform at that time with the 'preiest ridden' medieval England that preceded it, and which might yet be recreated by neo-Laudian clericalists.[85] In making such arguments, Shaftesbury stood against another interpretation of the Church, a Laudian, or neo-Laudian, one which sought to argue that the restored Church represented a seamless continuity with that of the Elizabethan period, marginalizing critics as heirs to the violent puritan incendiaries of earlier eras.[86] A telling instance of such historical identity formation can be seen in later

---

[82] Whiteman (ed.), *Compton Census*, pp. xxxviii–xxxix.

[83] Whiteman (ed.), *Compton Census*, pp. xxxviii–xxxix.

[84] Margaret Spufford's highly sensitive account of problems of evidence—'Can we Count the "Godly" and the "Conformable" in the Seventeenth Century?', *Journal of Ecclesiastical History*, 36 (1985): 428–38—is much to be preferred to Clive Field's round figures and caveats—'Counting Religion in England and Wales: The Long Eighteenth Century, c.1680–c.1840', *Journal of Ecclesiastical History*, 63 (2012): 693–720.

[85] John Spurr, 'Shaftesbury and the Politics of Religion', in John Spurr (ed.), *Anthony Ashley Cooper, First Earl of Shaftesbury 1621–1683* (Aldershot, 2011), pp. 127–52 (pp. 135–6, 138–41, 145, 147–8).

[86] Calvin Lane, *The Laudians and the Elizabethan Church: History, Conformity and Religious Identity in Post-Reformation England* (London, 2013), esp. pp. 181, 183, 185; Anthony Milton,

Stuart memories of past archbishops of Canterbury. Gilbert Sheldon wished to be buried next to his fiercely anti-puritan predecessor, John Whitgift, whilst William Cade, a minor canon of Canterbury Cathedral, gave his son the idiosyncratic first name 'Laud'.[87] By contrast, Nonconformists and Low Churchmen could look back on George Abbot's primacy as the last era of sound Calvinistical government in the Church before the great Laudian perversion.[88] In the wake of the Revolution of 1688–9, Roger Morrice raged that the bishops had been 'open betrayers of themselves and the Nationall interest...for 80 yeares last past'.[89] If men of many different stamps fought to lay claim to the apostolic heritage of the Church,[90] they thus divided most sharply over the nature of its relatively recent history.

A second key component of religious identity developed naturally from the first: was the current establishment of the Church of England a fixed and final point, or a staging post in an ongoing process of development? Shaftesbury was not the only contemporary to note the malleability of religious labels. In the tense year 1685, Sir Thomas Meres MP observed that 'time and use changed the nature of words', and this extended to 'Protestant' as much as it did to 'knave'.[91] Reflections on change and instability would lead to much soul-searching arising from the narrow foundations of the 1662 settlement, the Toleration Act, and developing cultures of occasional conformity thereafter. Perhaps the most acutely affected group proved to be clergymen with puritanical leanings: should they stay within the Church after 1662 in order to do as much good as they could, or leave to maintain a purity of principle? Ralph Josselin and Isaac Archer offer well-documented examples of the former approach,[92] John Rastrick an intriguing instance of the latter. Although ordained deacon in 1671 and priest in 1673, Rastrick was always tortured by aspects of ceremonial conformity, and attracted to works of what he described as 'English Practicall Divinity', notably those of Richard

---

Laudian and Royalist Polemic in Seventeenth-Century England: The Career and Writings of Peter Heylyn (Manchester, 2007).

[87] Beddard, 'Sheldon and Anglican Recovery', p. 1017; Jeremy Gregory, 'Canterbury and the *Ancien Régime*: The Dean and Chapter, 1660–1828', in Patrick Collinson, Nigel Ramsay, and Margaret Sparks (eds.), *A History of Canterbury Cathedral* (Oxford, 1995), pp. 204–55 (p. 217). Cade had married Laud's niece. John Spurr presents a picture of Laud's name more effectively being used by critics than admirers: '"A Special Kindness for Dead Bishops": The Church, History, and Testimony in Seventeenth-Century Protestantism', *Huntington Library Quarterly*, 68 (2005): 313–34 (pp. 331–2).

[88] Lane, *Laudians and the Elizabethan Church*, pp. 88, 183. For Roger Morrice's approving emphasis on the 'Abbotists', see Goldie (gen. ed.), *Entring Book*, I, pp. 176, 281, 293; III, p. 204.

[89] Goldie (gen. ed.), *Entring Book*, IV, p. 476.

[90] Jean-Louis Quantin, *The Church of England and Christian Antiquity: The Construction of a Confessional Identity in the Seventeenth Century* (Oxford, 2009).

[91] Goldie (gen. ed.), *Entring Book*, III, p. 9.

[92] Macfarlane (ed.), *Diary of Ralph Josselin*; Matthew Storey (ed.), *Two East Anglian Diaries, 1641–1729* (Woodbridge, 1994), pp. 41–200.

Baxter.[93] After years of deepening conflict with his flock, who were antagon-
ized by what they viewed as excessively rigorous policing of parish morality,
Rastrick eventually decided that 'the Cause of Conformity was not of
God', and left the Church of England in 1687 to become a Nonconformist
minister.[94] In his lengthy and fascinating account of his decision-making at
that time, written *c.*1713, Rastrick explained that he had learned from reading
Baxter that although the English had reformed 'Religion' (i.e. doctrine), 'and
<in part our> Worship', ecclesiology was untouched: 'the form of Church
Government had never been reformed at all'.[95] Tellingly, Rastrick was careful
to distinguish between different parts of the Church he left. What he described
as 'the Learned sound and Pious Part of the Church of England' were worthy of
respect because they 'understand and Expound the Terms of Conformity . . .
with a Latitude, and assert the necessity of a favourable Construction', unlike
another, savagely inflexible, group who 'by the letter of Conformity understood and expounded in the most strict and rigid Sense that can be'.[96]

Edmund Bohun provides a good example of such strictness and rigidity in a
lay churchman.[97] Despite, or because of, a puritan upbringing, he grew up to
be an exceptionally abrasive and intolerant Suffolk JP during the 1670s and
1680s, given both to fulminating against 'the Puritane Party', and lambasting
those who 'under the pretext of prudence and moderation in ecclesiastical
affairs, are ruining both church and state'. Such men included the rector of
Wrentham, who Bohun (characteristically) told to his face that he was the
kind of man who would read the Qur'an if necessary in order to keep his
position. This outburst was triggered by the rector's admission that he had
'fallen in with the church' after the Restoration for the sake of peace, despite
his earlier compliance with the Cromwellian Church, and still showed 'forbearance towards the wandering sheep of the parish', in the form of a
congregational group.[98] What Josselin described as the 'hot partie' would
only be spurred to greater hostility against the Nonconformists by the Toleration Act and the growth of the practice of 'occasional conformity' to qualify
individuals for public office.[99] Such ill will would come to be focused on those
Low Church bishops who were seen as selling out to politically well-connected
Dissenters. Looking back on his two decades as bishop of Salisbury from the

---

[93] Cambers (ed.), *Life of John Rastrick*, pp. 78, 83, 50–1, 64–5.

[94] Cambers (ed.), *Life of John Rastrick*, pp. 91, 93–6, 104 (quotation), 105–6, 107–12.

[95] Cambers (ed.), *Life of John Rastrick*, pp. 100–1.

[96] Cambers (ed.), *Life of John Rastrick*, pp. 110–11.

[97] Roger Morrice would frequently rail against the 'hierarchists' whom he felt facilitated
popery by dividing the Protestant interest: Goldie (gen. ed.), *Entring Book*, via index (vol. VII),
s.v. 'hierarchists'.

[98] S. Wilton Rix (ed.), *The Diary and Autobiography of Edmund Bohun* (Beccles, 1853),
pp. 37, 28–9.

[99] Macfarlane (ed.), *Diary of Ralph Josselin*, p. 498.

vantage point of the latter part of Anne's reign, Gilbert Burnet mournfully noted that 'tho...I kept an open table to all the Clergy, yet nothing could mollify their aversion to a man that was for tolleration and for treating the Dissenters with gentlenes'.[100] Burnet and others of his stamp would found and support various societies for the 'reformation of manners', which cumulatively created a space for dialogue and cooperation between Nonconformists and those sympathetic to them within the national Church.[101] Such inclusive efforts proved highly controversial. Although Bishop William Lloyd enthusiastically dispatched 2,000 copies of an account of the various societies into his diocese of Worcester in spring 1700, the Tory archdeacon of Carlisle, William Nicolson, was one of many clergy who were deeply suspicious of the whole enterprise: 'Separate Societies and *Councils of Reformation* have always been reckoned necessary implements towards the subverting of an Establishment.'[102] Indeed the whole rhetoric of 'further reformation' was acutely politicized, with critics harking back endlessly to the destructive forces unleashed by calls for 'root and branch' reform of the Church in the 1640s.

The third key component of religious identity to place alongside understandings of the past and hopes for the future was the nature of the lived experience of religion in contemporary parishes. The beliefs and character of local clerics must have been a major influence on lay perspectives: negligent or morally corrupt clergy could be hounded by their parishioners through the Church courts; meek and charitable figures who confined themselves to spiritual rather than social and political affairs could attract tremendous loyalty and gifts from their parishioners.[103] In particular, congregations were 'discriminating lay audiences' for sermons in 'a culture saturated by preaching'.[104] Although certain notoriously inflammatory and divisive sermons on political subjects may have attracted the most attention from modern scholars, the capacity of many others to exert a positive influence at the parochial level

---

[100] H. C. Foxcroft (ed.), *A Supplement to Burnet's History of my own Time: Derived from his original Memoirs, his Autobiography, his Letters to Admiral Herbert, and his private Meditations, all hitherto unpublished* (Oxford, 1902), p. 499. For an extended case study of the opposition Burnet faced in his diocese from High Church clergy, see Tapsell, 'Pastors, Preachers and Politicians', pp. 88–91.

[101] For useful overviews, see Rose, *England in the 1690s*, pp. 205–9; Sirota, *Christian Monitors*, ch. 3.

[102] David Robertson (ed.), *Diary of Francis Evans, Secretary to Bishop Lloyd, 1699–1706*, Worcestershire Historical Society 15 (Oxford, 1903), pp. 15–18; William Nicolson to William Wotton (and three others), 26 Feb. 1699/1700, in John Nichols (ed.), *Letters on Various Subjects, Literary, Political and Ecclesiastical, to and from William Nicolson, D.D.*, 2 vols. (London, 1809), I, p. 154.

[103] Barry Till, *The Church Courts 1660–1720: The Revival of Procedure*, Borthwick Paper 109 (York, 2006); Spaeth, *Church in an Age of Danger*, ch. 3; H. J. Morehouse (ed.), *Extracts from the Diary of the Rev. Robert Meeke* (London, 1874), pp. 44–5.

[104] John Spurr, *The Laity and Preaching in Post-Reformation England*, Friends of Dr Williams's Library, 66th Lecture (London, 2013), pp. 4, 7.

should not be underestimated: in 1708, for instance, Anne Clavering made peace with a neighbour, having heard a sermon on the subject by Bishop Burnet.[105] On the other hand, the intolerant contempt displayed at a parochial level by High Churchmen towards 'our Comprehensive Friends'—those sympathetic towards reintegrating Dissenters into the Established Church—sustained bitterness and conflict into the early decades of the eighteenth century.[106] Moments of crisis would particularly expose the partisan fault lines within the Church of England. Morrice anatomized this with particular care at the time of James II's first declaration of indulgence in April 1687. He believed that this policy would affect the different wings of the Church in contrasting ways: the hierarchists' congregations would be unchanged, 'for their hearers will never come to the Dissenters', while the congregations of 'the most Religious, and most Practicall Preachers' would plummet, as they had been artificially buoyed since 1662 by the attendance of those who, without legal penalties, would have attended Dissenting worship, but had made do with the least worst option available.[107] By the 1690s anti-clerical authors could sneer that the petty small-mindedness of clerics meant that to all intents and purposes 'the name Church signifieth only a Self-interested Party'.[108]

Returning to the theme of communion, however, offers a different concluding sense of the contemporary Church as a site of negotiation between numerous clerical and lay agendas.[109] For some laymen, like the persecuting Suffolk JP Edmund Bohun in 1677, an emphasis on the importance of communion served a partisan point: puritanically minded clerics pursued popularity in the pulpit, arrogantly claiming the status of prophets. 'Hence sermons or prophesyings are extolled to the skies, sacraments and prayers are neglected. Knowledge we have: devotion, reverence, charity we have lost.'[110] From the pinnacle of the hierarchy, Archbishop William Sancroft in the 1680s vigorously championed the goal of weekly communion in cathedrals as an example to the whole Church.[111] Yet his archiepiscopal counterpart at York, John Dolben, repeated some clerics' fears that this would be 'call'd an in[n]ovation', despite the rubrics of the Church.[112] Other bishops, notably Morley of Winchester, proved suspicious of efforts by some of their parochial clergy to enforce weekly communion at a local level for fear of its divisive

---

[105] Spurr, *Laity and Preaching*, p. 9.

[106] Jeffrey S. Chamberlain, *Accommodating High Churchmen: The Clergy of Sussex, 1700–1745* (Urbana and Chicago, IL, 1997), esp. pp. 46–7.

[107] Goldie (gen. ed.), *Entring Book*, IV, pp. 8–9.

[108] William Stephens, quoted in Rose, *England in the 1690s*, p. 178.

[109] Arnold Hunt, 'The Lord's Supper in Early Modern England', *Past & Present*, 161 (1998): 39–83; Spufford, 'Importance of Religion', pp. 86–101.

[110] Rix (ed.), *Diary and Autobiography of Edmund Bohun*, p. 32.

[111] Tapsell, *Personal Rule of Charles II*, p. 126 and the sources in n. 16; R. A. P. J. Beddard, 'Sancroft, William (1617–1693)', *ODNB*.

[112] Archbishop of York to archbishop of Canterbury, 20 Oct. [1683], MS Tanner 34, f. 185.

potential: 'it may grow to a schisme in the orthodoxe and conformable party of ye Church'.[113] Those in favour of weekly communion of course argued precisely the opposite. Laying emphasis on 'primitive' apostolic practice, clerics like the curate of Holdenhurst in Dorset claimed that 'there is no other effectual expedient to retreive the peace and wellfare of our church, and to render her adversaries better affected to her'.[114]

Was this true? As the earlier discussion of the Compton Census has already emphasized, crucial sources of evidence generated specifically to anatomize the Stuarts' subjects by religious criteria nevertheless prove on examination to be highly ambiguous. Take the Wiltshire parish of Somerset Magna in 1673. No fewer than fourteen of its inhabitants were prosecuted in the bishop of Salisbury's court that year for failing to take communion. As with many court cases, however, interpreting events is difficult: the defendants countered that it was their clergyman's conformity to the Church of England that ought to be in doubt, not their own, and that he was abusing the ecclesiastical courts as a means of harassing his local enemies. Similarly, did the forty-six inhabitants of Fugglestone in the same county deserve to be labelled 'Churchmen, but negligent' for failing to take communion in 1682? They, and others like them in many parishes across England and Wales, may have refused to take communion not because of dissatisfaction with the restored Church of England per se, but because their reverence for the eucharist prevented them from accepting it at the hands of unfit ministers, or if they felt themselves to be unworthy. Many laymen may actually have felt that they were involved in communion simply by watching its administration. Many clerics may have lacked a sensitive appreciation of the fact that the members of their congregations understood the character of the Church of England's worship in different ways to themselves: 'parishioners conformed and yet did not conform. They remained committed to the Church, and to the community which it represented, without accepting every aspect of the Anglican liturgy.'[115]

CONCLUSION: STRENGTH IN DIVERSITY?

The later Stuarts' subjects evidently possessed very varied views on the nature and quality of the Church of England they experienced in their daily lives. In

---

[113] Bishop of Winchester to [?bishop of London], 2 July 1684, MS Tanner 32, f. 80.

[114] John Foster to bishop of Winchester, 23 June 1684, MS Tanner 32, f. 106; Eamon Duffy, 'Primitive Christianity Revived: Religious Renewal in Augustan England', in Derek Baker (ed.), *Renaissance and Renewal in Christian History*, Studies in Church History 14 (Oxford, 1977), pp. 287–300.

[115] For the foregoing examples, and an excellent discussion of this theme, see Spaeth, *Church in an Age of Danger*, pp. 174–93; see also Thomas, *Creating Communities*, pp. 114–19.

1667 an elderly resident of Great Ellingham in Norfolk unfavourably compared the current situation with 'the glory of our Church of England, and the flourishinge state of the kingdome about 40 yeers since (w[hi]ch I well knew)'.[116] By contrast, after a visitation tour of Cornwall in 1671, the bishop of Exeter was able to inform Sheldon with some complacency that 'I do not think there hath bene a more sober or learned Clergy in mans memory and upo[n] the best inquiry…I do not finde any reason to complain of the contempt of the Clergy heer, unles it be fro[m] Fanaticks.'[117] Such comments illustrate the importance of perspective. Viewed from the vantage point of relatively recent memories of the civil wars and Interregnum, the flourishing state of the later Stuart Church was remarkable, symbolized par excellence by the magnificence of Wren's St Paul's Cathedral, whose structure was completed in 1708 and which dominated a metropolitan skyline replete with church steeples rebuilt after the Great Fire.[118] On the other hand, some would continue to hark back to a pre-civil wars' lost world in which the Established Church had included nearly all of the monarch's subjects. Disestablishment and destruction in the 1640s and 1650s, and the divisions formalized by the Act of Uniformity (1662), put paid to that forever.

The messy realities of the later Stuart Church thus resist easy concluding simplifications, especially singular defining labels, or confident depictions of dominance by one of the 'more or less disparate interests' that made up its 'coalition'.[119] We can, however, say that historiographical perspectives on its developing nature have shifted markedly. Scholars writing from the 1960s to the 1980s tended to emphasize the extent to which the 1680s were the Church's 'golden decade', and 'the high point of Anglican endeavour in the entire seventeenth century', to which the Revolution of 1688–9 dealt a devastating blow: 'the magnificent monolith of Anglican unity was shattered for ever'.[120] Such comments implicitly privileged one particular section of the Church, its disciplinarian, ceremonialist, 'Sancroftian' side, which was indeed fatally undermined by the consequences of Williamite invasion.[121] Clerics from a different wing of the Church, that which espoused ideas of ecclesiastical moderation and charity towards Nonconformists, naturally viewed the 1690s and 1700s in much more positive terms, not least through enthusiasm for the

---

[116] Mr Saltmarsh to William Sancroft, [8 Feb. 1667], MS Tanner 45, f. 276.

[117] Bishop of Exeter to archbishop of Canterbury, 21 Sept. 1671, MS Add. C 305, f. 231, Bodl.

[118] Derek Keene, Arthur Burns, and Andrew Saint (eds.), *St Paul's: The Cathedral Church of London 604–2004* (New Haven, CT and London, 2004), chs. 19–20. Perhaps the most striking image of church spires and the London skyline can be found in Canaletto's *The City of London from the terrace of Richmond House, Whitehall* (c.1747), in Keene et al. (eds.), *St Paul's*, p. 198.

[119] Nicholas Tyacke, 'From Laudians to Latitudinarians: A Shifting Balance of Theological Forces', in Tapsell (ed.), *Later Stuart Church*, pp. 46–67 (p. 46).

[120] Geoffrey Holmes, *Augustan England: Professions, State and Society, 1680–1730* (London, 1982), pp. 87, 84; Findon, 'Nonjurors and the Church of England', p. 38.

[121] Here the extensive work of Bennett and Beddard has been particularly influential.

various Societies for the Reformation of Manners. Rather than praising or vilifying particular segments of the Church of England, several scholars have emphasized the strength accruing to the Church from its accommodation of different viewpoints, and the extent to which this led to overall pastoral success into the eighteenth century.[122] It is nevertheless telling that uncertainty remains about whether the Church attained an unprecedented degree of homogeneity in that pastoral activity, or whether it is better to emphasize the scope for local choice and innovation within the Church at a parish level.[123]

In conclusion, though, it is best to return to Halifax's aphorism at the head of this chapter with a renewed sense of the scale of the threats faced by the Church of England in this period. Well-wishers in 1659 had feared that the age and ill health of the few surviving bishops meant that the apostolic succession would be broken and therefore the Church of England was about to 'expire'.[124] Some Catholic observers would eagerly anticipate the Church of England's death after the birth of a male heir to James II in June 1688.[125] During the 'rage of party' in Anne's reign, rival High and Low Church partisans foretold the demise of what they valued in the Church according to how the political winds blew.[126] All of these terminal visions proved precipitate. Even as the last Stuart monarch was increasingly plagued with ill health, the Church of which she was Supreme Governor retained a vigorous and privileged position in English society. Its evolution would continue far beyond Anne's last breath, as the following chapters will make clear.

SELECT BIBLIOGRAPHY

Aston, T. H. (gen. ed.), *The History of the University of Oxford*, 8 vols. (Oxford, 1984–2000), IV, pp. 803–954; V, pp. 9–98.

Beddard, R. A., 'The Restoration Church', in J. R. Jones (ed.), *The Restored Monarchy 1660–1688* (London, 1979), pp. 155–75.

---

[122] Spurr, *Restoration Church*, esp. pp. 164–5; Jacob, *Lay People*, pp. 6–7.

[123] Jeremy Gregory and Jeffrey S. Chamberlain, 'National and Local Perspectives on the Church of England in the Long Eighteenth Century', in Jeremy Gregory and Jeffrey S. Chamberlain (eds.), *The National Church in Local Perspective: The Church of England and the Regions, 1660–1800* (Woodbridge, 2003), pp. 1–28 (pp. 26–7); Spaeth, *Church in an Age of Danger*, esp. pp. 4–5.

[124] Bosher, *Making of the Restoration Settlement*, p. 97.

[125] Steve Pincus, 'The European Catholic Context of the Revolution of 1688–89: Gallicanism, Innocent XI, and Catholic Opposition', in Allan I. Macinnes and Arthur H. Williamson (eds.), *Shaping the Stuart World 1603–1714: The Atlantic Connection* (Leiden, 2006), pp. 79–114 (p. 100 n. 109).

[126] For a visual instance, see W. A. Speck, *The Birth of Britain: A New Nation 1700–1710* (Oxford, 1994), p. 189.

Bennett, G. V., 'Conflict in the Church', in Geoffrey Holmes (ed.), *Britain after the Glorious Revolution 1689–1714* (London, 1969), pp. 155–75.

Bennett, G. V., *The Tory Crisis in Church and State, 1688–1730: The Career of Francis Atterbury, Bishop of Rochester* (Oxford, 1975).

Champion, J. A. I., *The Pillars of Priestcraft Shaken: The Church of England and its Enemies 1660–1730* (Cambridge, 1992).

Every, George, *The High Church Party, 1688–1718* (London, 1956).

Fincham, Kenneth and Nicholas Tyacke, *Altars Restored: The Changing Face of English Religious Worship, 1547–c.1700* (Oxford, 2007), ch. 8.

Findon, John, 'The Nonjurors and the Church of England 1689–1716', DPhil thesis, University of Oxford, 1979.

Goldie, Mark, *Roger Morrice and the Puritan Whigs* (Woodbridge, 2007).

Goldie, Mark, 'The Theory of Religious Intolerance in Restoration England', in Ole Peter Grell, Jonathan Israel, and Nicholas Tyacke (eds.), *From Persecution to Toleration: The Glorious Revolution and Religion in England* (Oxford, 1991), pp. 331–68.

Gregory, Jeremy and Jeffrey S. Chamberlain (eds.), *The National Church in Local Perspective: The Church of England and the Regions, 1660–1800* (Woodbridge, 2003).

Hampton, Stephen, *Anti-Arminians: The Anglican Reformed Tradition from Charles II to George I* (Oxford, 2008).

Holmes, Geoffrey, *Augustan England: Professions, State and Society, 1680–1730* (London, 1982).

Holmes, Geoffrey, *The Trial of Doctor Sacheverell* (London, 1973).

Pruett, John H., *The Parish Clergy under the Later Stuarts: The Leicestershire Experience* (Urbana and Chicago, IL, 1978).

Rose, Jacqueline, *Godly Kingship in Restoration England* (Cambridge, 2011).

Seaward, Paul, *The Cavalier House of Commons and the Reconstruction of the Old Regime, 1661–1667* (Cambridge, 1989), ch. 7.

Sirota, Brent S., *The Christian Monitors: The Church of England and the Age of Benevolence, 1680–1730* (New Haven, CT, 2014).

Spaeth, Donald A., *The Church in an Age of Danger: Parsons and Parishioners, 1660–1740* (Cambridge, 2000).

Spurr, John, 'The Church of England, Comprehension and the Toleration Act of 1689', *English Historical Review*, 104 (1989): 927–46.

Spurr, John, 'Religion in Restoration England', in Lionel K. J. Glassey (ed.), *The Reigns of Charles II and James VII & II* (London, 1997), pp. 90–124.

Spurr, John, *The Restoration Church of England, 1646–1689* (New Haven, CT, 1991).

Sykes, Norman, *From Sheldon to Secker: Aspects of English Church History 1660–1768* (Cambridge, 1959).

Tapsell, Grant (ed.), *The Later Stuart Church, 1660–1714* (Manchester, 2012).

Till, Barry, *The Church Courts 1660–1720: The Revival of Procedure*, Borthwick Paper 109 (York, 2006).

Walsh, John, Colin Haydon, and Stephen Taylor (eds.), *The Church of England c.1689–c.1833: From Toleration to Tractarianism* (Cambridge, 1993).

Whiteman, Anne (ed.), with the assistance of Mary Clapinson, *The Compton Census of 1676: A Critical Edition* (Oxford, 1986).

3

The Church of England, 1714–1783

Robert G. Ingram

'My last gave you an account of the Death of our good Lord, and the circumstances of it; To this I am now to add that the Bishop of Lincoln kissed the King's hand for the Archbishopric yesterday.'[1] So Archbishop Thomas Tenison's chaplain, Edmund Gibson, announced Tenison's death and William Wake's succession to the see of Canterbury in late December 1715. From one perspective, Tenison's passing might seem to mark the end of a long, divisive era in the nation's religious and political history. This chapter argues that it did not; rather, subsequent Church leaders confronted many of the same challenges that had confronted Tenison and other late Stuart churchmen and they confronted them in Tenisonian ways. To understand the eighteenth-century Church of England, then, requires starting with Tenison and the world from which he emerged.[2]

Thomas Tenison had served as archbishop of Canterbury under Queen Anne (r. 1702–14), the last of the Stuarts, the royal family whose members had been usurped not once but twice during the religio-political revolutions of the seventeenth century. Anne came to the throne in 1702 hoping to heal the wounds opened up by England's 'troubles'. The seventeenth century had been especially brutal for the Church of England. The institution had nearly been destroyed in the 1650s, during England's stretch of 'unkingship' and religious disestablishment. Even after the monarchy's restoration and the Church's re-establishment in 1660, the memory of those years remained fresh and reminded churchmen what might happen if religious Dissenters got their way. The Test and Corporation Acts (1661, 1673) disbarred Protestant Dissenters from public office, hoping to prevent a return of the religious and political anarchy of the mid-century. Yet the Glorious Revolution (1688–9),

---

[1] Gibson to William Nicholson, 17 Dec. 1715, Bodleian Library (Bodl.), Add. MS A269, p. 51.
[2] Cf. Grant Tapsell, 'Introduction: The Later Stuart Church in Context', in Grant Tapsell (ed.), *The Later Stuart Church, 1660–1714* (Manchester, 2012), pp. 1–17.

itself a response to the 'thoroughgoing project of Catholic modernization' of James II's reign, had ushered in a new kind of religious settlement, one which had at its core the Toleration Act (1689), a piece of legislation which allowed the Church to retain its establishment status while at the same time depriving the institution of its functional monopoly on public worship and legally confirming and condoning England's religious pluralism.[3]

Tenison's challenge was to reconcile the Church of England to the post-revolutionary state. Edmund Gibson reckoned that Tenison, the son of a royalist and a Williamite appointee in 1694, had mostly succeeded. As Gibson explained, 'many others have more state politicks but he had the true Christian Policy; great goodness, and Integrity improved by long Experience and a natural Sedateness and Steadiness of Temper; and a general knowledge of men and of things. Had it not pleased God to raise up such an one to steer, in the storm times that we have had (for these last 20 years) the Church in all human probability must have been shipwrecked over and over.'[4]

Like the monarchs he served, Tenison's world-view had been forged in the crucible of the seventeenth century's internecine religio-political wars and he had moved into Lambeth Palace determined to effect peace between Church and state. No one doubted his commitment to reforming and revitalizing the Church. He had a well-deserved reputation as a model parish priest in central London parishes like St Martin-in-the-Fields; he had long supported voluntary religious societies like the Society for the Promotion of Christian Knowledge (SPCK) and the Society for the Promotion of the Gospel in Foreign Parts (SPG); an energetic bishop of Lincoln and archbishop of Canterbury, he had worked to improve both clerical quality and Church discipline; and he had written powerfully against both popery and anti-Trinitarianism. But Tenison's political sympathies were those of a resolute Whig: he had been actively involved in the seven bishops' resistance to James II's promulgation of the declaration of indulgence in 1688; he had worked with Archbishop John Tillotson and others in 1689 to get a comprehension bill passed; he had no truck with non-jurors; he zealously promoted the Hanoverian succession; and he saw the Whigs as the only sure guarantors of a Protestant England. However, the Church–Whig alliance he tried to forge sat poorly with the lower clergy, who themselves were mostly Tory and who did not, like their archbishop, reckon that the Protestant Church of England might only be safe when those most committed to the Protestant succession—the Whigs—controlled both Church and state. Perhaps not surprisingly, then, even during

---

[3] Steven Pincus, *1688: The First Modern Revolution* (New Haven, CT, 2009), p. 178; William J. Bulman, 'Enlightenment and Religious Politics in Restoration England', *History Compass*, 10 (2012): 752–64; G. V. Bennett, *The Tory Crisis in Church and State, 1688–1730: The Career of Francis Atterbury, Bishop of Rochester* (Oxford, 1975), pp. 3–22.

[4] Gibson to Nicholson, 3 Dec. 1715, MS A269, pp. 48–9.

the spells of Whig supremacy during Anne's reign, Tenison could do little to quell the Tory cries of 'Church in danger', or to prevent a crisis like that which attended Henry Sacheverell's *Perils of False Brethren* sermon in 1709 and his subsequent trial and acquittal. Despite Tenison's own Whig irenicism, then, he died in December 1715, having helped to improve Church–Whig relations, but having failed 'to prevent the church ... from becoming the battlefield of political faction'.[5]

The new monarch from Hanover, George I (r. 1714–27), and his archbishop of Canterbury, William Wake, however, aimed to usher in a new era, one in which religio-political strife would no longer bedevil the nation. Indeed, the new Hanoverian regime hoped to draw a line under the past once and for all. It failed, or at least it did not succeed quickly, for the memory of the seventeenth-century troubles haunted the eighteenth century.[6] Indeed, the policies pursued in Church and state after 1689 aimed to prevent a return to revolution. This, though, is hardly registered in the historiography of the Church of England, an institution which played such a great part in the nation's tumultuous post-Revolution history.

Almost from the outset, historians of the Established Church between 1714 and 1783 were more intent on explaining where they themselves came from rather than how things were during the eighteenth century. Nineteenth-century religious historians—especially those writing in Evangelical or Anglo-Catholic veins—certainly seemed incapable of thinking about the Church of the previous century in anything but presentist terms, routinely comparing it unfavourably to the religious institutions of their own day.[7] On their view, the eighteenth century was at best a fallow period in the Church's history, sandwiched between the more robust—and revolutionary—seventeenth and nineteenth centuries. At worst, it was a time during which the Church was beset by corruption and pastoral neglect, led by undistinguished bishops who were themselves slaves to their masters, the Whig politicians, and when the religious temperament was decidedly latitudinarian, which was to say mostly moribund. 'The bishop, rector, or vicar of the Established Church in the eighteenth century is a by-word in English ecclesiastical history', J. H. Froude (1818–94) insisted; while Mark Pattison (1813–84) reckoned that '[t]he genuine Anglican omits that

[5] Edward Carpenter, *Thomas Tenison, Archbishop of Canterbury: His Life and Times* (London, 1948); G. V. Bennett, *To the Church of England*, ed. Geoffrey Rowell (Worthing, 1988), pp. 99–110; Geoffrey Holmes, *Religion and Party in Late Stuart England* (London, 1975).

[6] Matthew Neufeld, *The Civil Wars after 1660* (Woodbridge, 2013); J. G. A. Pocock, 'Within the Margins: The Definitions of Orthodoxy', in Roger D. Lund (ed.), *The Margins of Orthodoxy: Heterodox Writing and Cultural Response, 1660–1750* (Cambridge, 1995), p. 38; George Watson, 'The Augustan Civil War', *Review of English Studies*, 36 (1985): 321–37.

[7] B. W. Young, *The Victorian Eighteenth Century: An Intellectual History* (Oxford, 2007), pp. 70–147; William Gibson, *The Church of England, 1688–1832: Unity and Accord* (London, 2001), pp. 4–27.

period from the history of the Church altogether. In constructing his *Catena Patrum* he closes his list with Waterland or Brett, and leaps at once to 1833, when the *Tracts for the Times* commenced.'[8] Even John Overton (1835–1903), a High Church historian who acknowledged that the history of the eighteenth century was not 'a blank page in English Church history', nevertheless reckoned of the period that 'a lover of the English Church cannot study it without a blush. It is a period of lethargy instead of activity, of worldliness instead of spirituality, of self-seeking instead of self-denial, of grossness instead of refinement.'[9] Nineteenth-century historians of all stripes seemed to agree that things somehow had gone wrong during the eighteenth century, things which were somehow put right during the nineteenth: the eighteenth-century Church of England had, put another way, been a barrier to progress, rather than an agent of it.

Modern ecclesiastical historians have been more optimistic about the eighteenth-century Established Church, yet theirs has been a project more about negating than about constructing.[10] Or, as Mark Goldie acidly put it, their 'starting point is, as it were, a Hogarth cartoon of a corpulent curate and a snoozing congregation': the revisionist project, at its most reductive, has been to refute that cartoon.[11] Norman Sykes (1897–1961) is widely acknowledged to have inaugurated serious scholarly reconsideration of the eighteenth-century Church.[12] He judged the Georgian Church by Georgian standards rather than by Victorian ones, an approach since taken by others. Viewed this way, the eighteenth-century Church looked rather less problem-ridden than earlier historians might have thought. Parochial clergy did their jobs more conscientiously, were paid less poorly, held fewer livings in plurality, and were non-resident less often than previously reckoned.[13] So too their clerical

---

[8] J. A. Froude, *Short Studies on Great Subjects: 2nd Series* (New York, 1872), p. 257; Mark Pattison, 'Tendencies of Religious Thought in England, 1688–1750', in Henry Nettleship (ed.), *Essays by the late Mark Pattison, sometime Rector of Lincoln College, Oxford*, 2 vols. (Oxford, 1889), II, p. 43.

[9] John H. Overton and Frederic Relton, *The English Church from the Accession of George I to the End of the Eighteenth Century (1714–1800)* (London, 1906), p. 1.

[10] B. W. Young, 'Religious History and the Eighteenth-Century Historian', *Historical Journal*, 43 (2000): 849–69; John Walsh and Stephen Taylor, 'Introduction: The Church and Anglicanism in the "Long" Eighteenth Century', in John Walsh, Colin Haydon, and Stephen Taylor (eds.), *The Church of England c.1689–c.1833: From Toleration to Tractarianism* (Cambridge, 1993), pp. 1–64.

[11] Mark Goldie, 'Voluntary Anglicans', *Historical Journal*, 46 (2003): 977–90.

[12] Norman Sykes, *From Sheldon to Secker: Aspects of English Church History 1660–1768* (Cambridge, 1959); Norman Sykes, *William Wake, Archbishop of Canterbury, 1657–1737*, 2 vols. (Cambridge, 1957); Norman Sykes, *Church and State in England in the XVIIIth Century* (Cambridge, 1934); Norman Sykes, *Edmund Gibson, Bishop of London, 1669–1748: A Study in Politics & Religion in the Eighteenth Century* (Oxford, 1926).

[13] W. M. Jacob, *The Clerical Profession in the Long Eighteenth Century, 1680–1840* (Oxford, 2007); Jeremy Gregory and Jeffrey S. Chamberlain (eds.), *The National Church in Local Perspective: The Church of England and the Regions, 1660–1800* (Woodbridge, 2003).

leaders, the bishops, were slightly less beholden to the state and, at times, more vigorous defenders of the Established Church's rights and privileges than some might have supposed during the nineteenth century.[14] And, finally, the Church was less intellectually sterile or derivative than it might once have seemed.[15]

Yet revisionist scholarship has failed to explain why the Established Church was important to the nation's history. One answer, surely, is that the Church of England's history between the Hanoverian succession and the end of the American Revolution highlights the flaws inherent since the sixteenth century in Protestantism generally and in the Church of England more particularly. More to the point, the religio-political questions which began bedevilling the English nation during the 1530s remained live ones during the eighteenth century. What sort of Church should the Church of England be? What should the relation of Church to state be? What should constitute the Church's doctrinal orthodoxy? Whom should the Church comprehend? What were the bounds of toleration? These questions had not been solved at the Glorious Revolution, so that the story of the eighteenth-century Church of England is the concluding chapter in the story of England's long Reformation.[16] And what ultimately brought that particular story to a close was not Enlightenment secularism but the changes catalysed by empire and war and the fear of relapse into seventeenth-century-like religious violence.[17] This chapter sketches the lineaments of that story primarily from the vantage point of the eighteenth-century episcopal bench and, especially, from the view of the archbishops of Canterbury, who from their perches in Lambeth Palace, led the Established Church of England.

William Wake (1657–1737, archbishop of Canterbury 1715–37) succeeded Thomas Tenison as archbishop late in 1715, having already made a name for himself as a champion of the Whigs. Like Tenison, he came from a family committed to the royalist cause during the mid-seventeenth century, but Wake himself was no slavish follower of the Stuarts. Indeed, during James II's reign, he had publicly defended the Church of England against the king's

---

[14] Robert G. Ingram, *Religion, Reform and Modernity in the Eighteenth Century* (Woodbridge, 2007); Jeremy Gregory, *Restoration, Reformation and Reform, 1660–1832* (Oxford, 2000); Stephen J. C. Taylor, 'Church and State in England in the Mid-Eighteenth Century: The Newcastle Years, 1747–62', PhD thesis, University of Cambridge, 1987.

[15] J. G. A. Pocock, *Barbarism and Religion*, vol. V: *Religion: The First Triumph* (Cambridge, 2011); B. W. Young, *Religion and Enlightenment in Eighteenth-Century England* (Oxford, 1998); J. A. I. Champion, *The Pillars of Priestcraft Shaken: The Church of England and its Enemies, 1660–1730* (Cambridge, 1992).

[16] William J. Bulman and Robert G. Ingram, 'Religion, Enlightenment, and the Paradox of Innovation', in Donald A. Yerxa (ed.), *Religion and Innovation: Antagonists or Partners?* (London, 2015), pp. 100–12.

[17] William J. Bulman, *Anglican Enlightenment: Orientalism, Religion and Politics in England and its Empire, 1648–1715* (Cambridge, 2015).

Catholicizing policies, with no less a figure than Gilbert Burnet reckoning him the era's leading pro-Church polemicist.[18] After the Glorious Revolution, Wake's *Rights, Powers and Privileges of the English Convocation* (1700) also had upended Francis Atterbury's argument that Convocation and Parliament were like bodies, both independent of the monarchs who summoned them to meet: Wake showed that Atterbury had fundamentally misunderstood English history and that there was no constitutional or legal precedent for any independent clerical assembly. Convocation sat by the grace of the monarch.[19] This Erastian argument successfully undermined Tory High Church claims regarding Convocation, but many of Wake's allies thought he had put his case too baldly. Yet Wake, perhaps inadvertently, was on to something, for his archiepiscopate demonstrated that in its partnership with the state, the English Church was what it had ever been since Henry VIII's reign, the junior partner.

The deeply anti-clerical Stanhope–Sunderland ministry posed a particular challenge for Wake. For while both he and George I's political ministers were Whigs, Wake was always a distinctive member of the Church–Whig species. He was not, for instance, instinctively anti-non-juror, and, indeed, had previously declined livings—including two bishoprics—because they had been vacated by non-juring clergy. Stanhope and Sunderland, by contrast, were anti-clerical Whigs who looked upon Tories and High Churchmen, and much more upon non-jurors, as anathema. Their legislative agenda, not surprisingly, was pro-Dissent and anti-clerical.[20] It made for an uneasy relationship between them and the archbishop.

In spring 1716, for instance, they supported the Close Vestries Bill, which sought not just to address acknowledged abuses in London's select vestries, but to replace those vestries with elected bodies—which might even include Dissenters—independent of the clergy. The bill made it through the Commons but was defeated in the Lords, Wake himself speaking strongly against it. Undeterred, Stanhope introduced into the Lords late in 1718 a bill to repeal the Occasional Conformity and Schism Acts (1711, 1713): the former had prevented Protestant Dissenters from communicating occasionally in the Church of England solely to qualify for public office, while the latter had banned religious Nonconformists from running schools. Getting rid of both had been one of George I's domestic priorities from his reign's outset. The ministry introduced the repeal bill—formally called the Bill for Strengthening the Protestant Interest—as the Bangorian controversy raged. Benjamin Hoadly's 31 March 1717 court sermon had ignited the controversy, and Stanhope and

---

[18] Gilbert Burnet, *Bishop Burnet's History of His Own Time*, 6 vols. (Oxford, 1823), III, p. 99.

[19] Bennett, *Tory Crisis*, pp. 48–62.

[20] G. M. Townend, 'Religious Radicalism and Conservatism in the Whig Party under George I: The Repeal of the Occasional Conformity and Schism Acts', *Parliamentary History*, 7 (1988): 24–44.

Sunderland had timed the sermon's delivery and publication to coincide with their repeal effort. The controversy itself centred on Hoadly's anti-sacerdotalist argument that Christ had 'left behind Him, no visible, humane Authority; no Viceregents, who can be said properly to supply his Place; no Interpreters, upon whom his Subjects are absolutely to depend; no Judges over the Consciences or Religion of his People'.[21] By implication the Church of England enjoyed its establishment not by right but by the grace of the state. And, furthermore, the Established Church's ecclesiology, liturgy, and doctrines were themselves not inherently superior to those of other Protestant Churches. There was, then, no rationale for the Test and Corporation Acts. This was incendiary stuff from a sitting bishop, and his sermon unleashed a flood of mostly unfavourable responses. A committee of Convocation's lower house unanimously condemned it for having given 'great and grievous Offence, by certain Doctrines and Positions' in it, while most of the bishops, including Wake, also rejected its argument.[22] So much did the Church's response frighten the Stanhope–Sunderland ministry that the king prorogued Convocation in 1717, and it would not be until the 1850s that the state would again allow it to conduct substantive business.[23]

If Hoadly's sermon united the episcopal bench in opposition, the Bill for Strengthening the Protestant Interest divided them. Wake sided with fourteen other bishops who opposed its passage, while Edmund Gibson (1669–1748), then bishop of Lincoln, was numbered among the eleven other bishops, including Hoadly, who supported rolling back the Occasional Conformity and Schism Acts. Gibson's reasoning highlighted what he saw as the Church's post-Stuart dependence upon the Whigs. '[A]ll my political reasonings proceed upon these two positions', he explained to a fellow bishop, 'that there is no way to preserve the Church but by preserving the present establishment in the state; and that there is a far greater probability that the Tories will be able to destroy our present establishment in the state than [that] the Dissenters will be able to destroy our establishment in the Church.'[24] His was a Tenisonian approach, no doubt developed while serving as the old archbishop's domestic chaplain. With the parliamentary backing of bishops like Gibson, the repeal bill eventually passed into law in early 1719, and by the time of its passage

---

[21] Benjamin Hoadly, *The Nature of the Kingdom, or Church, of Christ: A Sermon preach'd before the King, at the Royal chapel at St. James's, on Sunday March 31, 1717* (London, 1717), p. 11; cf. Stephen Taylor, 'The Clergy at the Courts of George I and George II', in Michael Schaich (ed.), *Monarchy and Religion: The Transformation of Royal Culture in Eighteenth-Century Europe* (Oxford, 2007), pp. 129–51; Andrew Starkie, *The Church of England and the Bangorian Controversy, 1716–1721* (Woodbridge, 2007); William Gibson, *Enlightenment Prelate: Benjamin Hoadly, 1676–1761* (Cambridge, 2004), pp. 147–98.

[22] *A Report of the Committee of the Lower House of Convocation . . .* (London, 1717), p. 3.

[23] Sykes, *From Sheldon to Secker*, pp. 36–67.

[24] Gibson to Nicholson, 3 Dec. 1717, MS A269, p. 72.

Wake was an isolated figure, one who by the mid-1720s rarely appeared at Parliament but kept close to Lambeth Palace, where he pursued his scholarship and kept up an interesting, but ultimately inconsequential, flow of correspondence with continental Protestants.[25] Instead, it was his former protégé, Gibson, who would serve as the chief ecclesiastical adviser to the Whig governments led by Robert Walpole because, for a time at least, he, unlike Wake, could balance being a Whig and a churchman. Wake had, in the end, proved more loyal to the Church than to the Whigs; Gibson seemed not to see a conflict between the two.

Perhaps for that reason, Gibson willingly took up the role as Walpole's 'church minister'.[26] 'He must be pope, and would as willingly be our pope as anybody's', Walpole concluded with typical bluntness.[27] Walpole had tapped Gibson because he thought the bishop of London could help in his effort to neutralize religion as a contentious political issue. For Walpole had served as one of the Whig managers of Sacheverell's trial, which, along with the tepid clerical support of the Hanoverian succession and Bishop Francis Atterbury's involvement in a Jacobite plot in 1722, had taught him that the English Church needed to be declawed as a political force. He hoped that Gibson could help him do just that by promoting a Church–Whig alliance. That alliance required reciprocal obligations in return for reciprocal benefits. The Church had to do what it could to encourage religious calm and allegiance to the state, and its leaders had to support the Whig ministry's legislative programme in Parliament. The Whig-led state, in return, obliged itself to promote a certain kind of churchman and to shield the Church from hostile legislation in Parliament. This is not to endorse the hoary view that the bishops were but 'voting fodder' in the Lords, or that the state almost effortlessly controlled the Church. It is, though, to recognize that when the state's needs conflicted with those of the Church, those of the state won out with unrelenting regularity. The Church–Whig alliance existed to minimize those conflicts.

Patronage and legislation were the two chief tools in forging and sustaining that alliance. The state had in its gift twenty-six bishoprics and twenty-five deaneries but only a small percentage of the nearly 10,000 parish livings in English and Wales. It was Gibson's job to vet candidates for open posts in the state's gift to ensure their theological and political acceptability. 'When Promotions were vacant and my opinion was ask'd, I gave it him freely and did not only consider the affection that the persons were known to bear to the

---

[25] Sykes, *Wake*, II.

[26] Stephen Taylor, '"Dr. Codex" and the Whig "Pope": Edmund Gibson, Bishop of Lincoln and London, 1716–1748', in Richard W. Davis (ed.), *Lords of Parliament: Studies, 1714–1914* (Stanford, CA, 1995), pp. 9–27.

[27] Walpole to Newcastle, 6 Sept. 1723, British Library [BL], Add. MS 32686, f. 312.

Constitution of the Church (which I thought my self obliged to attend to in the first place) but also their affection to [Walpole] and his administration', Gibson explained.[28] In choosing candidates, then, Gibson favoured those who were reliable Walpolean Whigs. He also privileged theological orthodoxy over theological heterodoxy. So, for instance, when someone like Thomas Rundle, the administration's choice for the vacant bishopric of Gloucester in 1733–4, was rumoured to be an Arian, Gibson successfully opposed him. Surely the bishops, 'on account of their dutiful behaviour to the Court, might hope for some regard to their inclination and good liking, in the choice of every new member for the Bench', Gibson implored Walpole.[29] For the nomination, he reported, 'has given very great offence to the clergy; and I may truly add, that the uneasiness is general, among the Whig as well as the Tory part of them'.[30] The prospect of a Christologically heterodox cleric was too much for Gibson and most of his fellow bishops, who combined to oppose Rundle's candidacy for Gloucester. '[T]he general sense of the Bishops and Clergy, will not permit me to concur or acquiesce in it', Gibson informed Walpole, before adding tellingly that the episcopate's obeisance to the state had earned it the right to have its wishes heeded on Church matters. 'The Bishops, on account of their dutiful behaviour to the Court, might hope for some regard to their inclination and good liking in the choice of every new member of the Bench', he protested.[31] In this instance, Walpole acceded to the wishes of Gibson and the bishops, but, in retrospect, the Rundle affair marked the beginning of the end of Gibson's 'papacy'.

By August 1736, Gibson had joined Wake as a sidelined ecclesiastical minister. Like Wake, he focused on his diocese, but he was no longer the government's principal adviser on ecclesiastical appointments. He fell out with Walpole because the prime minister had failed to uphold his side of the Church–Whig alliance and Gibson had objected. While Gibson had been tasked with helping to identify orthodox churchmen who were also clubbable Whigs for vacant Church positions, Walpole was to block anti-clerical measures in Parliament. This he had mostly done during the 1730s, including short-circuiting the Tithe Bill (1731), the Church Rates and Repairs Bill (1733), and the Ecclesiastical Courts Bills (1733, 1734). But in 1736, he let through the Mortmain and Quakers Tithe Bills, neither of which had actually been put forward by his ministry. The Mortmain Bill made it more difficult for charities to receive donations of large tracts of land, while the Quakers Tithe Bill softened the legal threats facing the Quakers, who refused to pay tithes on

[28] Gibson to Francis Hare, 4 Aug. 1736, University of St Andrews Library [SAL], Gibson MS 5312.

[29] Gibson to Walpole, [December 1733], SAL, Gibson MS 5285.

[30] Gibson to Walpole, [December 1733], SAL, Gibson MS 5285a.

[31] Gibson to Walpole, 18 Dec. 1734, Cambridge University Library, Cholmondeley MSS Ch (H) 2106; cf. Taylor, '"Dr. Codex" and the Whig "Pope"'; Taylor, 'The Bishops at Westminster'.

the grounds that it was immoral to salary ministers of the gospel.[32] While the Mortmain Bill passed into law, the Quakers Tithe Bill did not, thanks largely to the concerted episcopal opposition which Gibson led. He and the bishops opposed the bill because they thought that it would further complicate the already sensitive clerical task of tithe collection; that it affronted their property rights; that it would eventually lead to the abolition of all tithes; and that it undermined the Church's independence by imposing restrictions on the ecclesiastical courts which normally heard tithe disputes. In the end, Walpole let the bill die, but he also cut Gibson loose. 'As I have no Credit, no Service will be expected of me', Gibson concluded stoically.[33]

While Gibson's withdrawal changed the character of the Church–Whig alliance, it did not wound it fatally. After 1736, first Walpole and then the Pelhamite ministries of the 1740s and 1750s cultivated the partnership. What was missing after Gibson's fall, though, was a clear Church leader with whom the state could deal. Walpole had a chance to choose a more amenable clerical partner when in 1737 he picked Wake's successor as archbishop of Canterbury. He settled on John Potter, a former Dissenter who had been a formidable High Church polemical divine. In *The Discourse on Church Government* (1707), he had argued for the Church's autonomy and for a sacerdotal priesthood, while during the Bangorian controversy he had publicly attacked Hoadly's Erastianism. To his unquestioned orthodoxy Potter allied an unswerving commitment to the Whigs, and he had two decades' experience on the episcopal bench. He seemed, then, like Gibson's natural successor. But he was at heart a scholar and non-confrontational at that, something anti-clerical Whigs close to Walpole thought exploitable. As Lord Hervey explained it to the prime minister, 'Potter is a man of great learning, of as little doubted probity... [H]is character will support you in sending him to Lambeth; and his capacity is not so good, nor his temper so bad, as to make you apprehend any great danger in his being there.'[34] Hervey proved right, for while Potter was universally reckoned a decent, if slightly officious, man, neither he nor his immediate successors—Thomas Herring (1693–1757, archbishop of Canterbury 1747–57) and Matthew Hutton (1693–1758, archbishop 1757–8)—had Gibson's vision, political skill, or dynamism. Yet they too led a Church facing challenges that stemmed both from its sixteenth-century origins and from the post-revolutionary settlement.

Heterodoxy topped the list of clerical worries. Admittedly heterodoxy had been a perennial Christian complaint, but it is also clear that those living

---

[32] Stephen Taylor, 'Sir Robert Walpole, the Church of England and the Quakers Tithe Bill of 1736', *Historical Journal*, 28 (1985): 51–77; T. F. J. Kendrick, 'Sir Robert Walpole, the Old Whigs and the Bishops, 1733–1736', *Historical Journal*, 11 (1968): 421–55.

[33] Gibson to Hare, 4 Aug. 1736, Gibson MS 5312.

[34] John Hervey, *Some Materials towards memoirs of the Reign of King George II*, ed. Romney Sedgwick, 3 vols. (London, 1931), II, p. 547.

during the first half of the eighteenth century thought it was a particular problem of the age. Most have chalked up heterodoxy's rise to the ineluctable process of secularization, in which the enlightened shed older, benighted truths; this surely accounts for the disproportionate scholarly attention paid to the minority (freethinkers, deists, and the like) rather than to the majority (the orthodox).[35] Affixing labels to eighteenth-century English polemical divines is a fraught matter, not least because most labels—'deism', 'atheism', 'infidel', and the like—were terms of abuse, not self-description. 'Orthodoxy', though, was simultaneously self-descriptive and abusive; and it entailed an acceptance of the Nicene Creed (and perhaps the Athanasian one, as well); of episcopal ecclesiology; and of the necessity of the Church's legal establishment defended by penal laws. For those living during the eighteenth century, to be 'heterdox' was, most fundamentally, to be not-orthodox, and most of the bishops reckoned that Thomas Rundle was heterodox.

There were, then, reasons—beyond his heretical Christology—why the bishops found the Arian Thomas Rundle's possible promotion to the bench so objectionable. To begin with, most at the time reckoned that theological heterodoxy and political radicalism correlated.[36] In addition, heterodoxy's rise provided further evidence of the Reformation's failure. The Reformation was a religious movement meant to ground truth on something solid, irrefutable, and irrefragable, *sola scriptura*. Rather than revealing or recovering truth, though, the Reformation unexpectedly and wholly unintentionally generated competing truth-claims. In the name of truth, it disturbed the peace, pitting person against person, Church against Church, nation against nation in violent struggle over what was truth or, perhaps more accurately, over who or what had the power to determine or to assert truth.[37] In the wake of the seventeenth-century English religio-political wars, people sought again to establish truth on a firm and permanent basis. A few proposed rationalistic metaphysics as that foundation. Most, though, would subsequently retain the language of 'reason' while simultaneously abandoning that metaphysical project, as reason only catalysed the production of more and more truth-claims. Instead, far more tried to ground truth in history, since it had been recorded and was thus recoverable. The terrain on which the eighteenth-century orthodox and heterodox mostly sparred was that of history. And they, like their forebears, reached no easy consensus.[38]

---

[35] Champion, *Pillars of Priestcraft*, best anatomizes the heterodox mind; Young, *Religion and Enlightenment*, is the best treatment of orthodoxy.

[36] J. C. D. Clark, *English Society, 1660–1832: Religion, Ideology and Politics during the Ancien Regime* (Cambridge, 2000).

[37] Brad S. Gregory, *The Unintended Reformation: How a Religious Revolution Secularized Society* (Cambridge, MA, 2012).

[38] Robert G. Ingram, *Reformation Without End: Religion, Politics and the Past in Post-Revolutionary England* (forthcoming); Bulman, *Anglican Enlightenment*; Dmitri Levitin, *Ancient Wisdom in the Age of the New Science* (Cambridge, 2015).

In the mid-eighteenth-century phase of the conflict, the orthodox won. Or, as Mark Pattison rightly noted long ago, by the 1750s, 'the Deists ceased to be'.[39] A number of reasons explain this. Firstly, contemporaries thought that the orthodox proved more persuasive. Secondly, freethinkers, deists, and other heterodox figures had an intellectual programme that was about dissolution rather than construction, about proving a set of beliefs false rather than reaffirming older truths or demonstrating or illuminating previously unperceived ones. Finally, the orthodox trounced the heterodox during the mid-eighteenth century because they effectively combined persuasion with suasion. One sign of orthodoxy's cultural power was that one of its bitterest critics, Matthew Tindal (*c.*1657–1733), never once published a work with his name on it, despite the fact that he held offices that gave him financial security. For all his bluster and bile, Tindal clearly worried about what would happen if he dropped the veil of anonymity and publicly acknowledged his authorship of heterodox works like *The Rights of the Christian Church* (1706) or *Christianity as Old as the Creation* (1733). If Tindal, a lawyer with a secure income, felt pressured, even more so did heterodox polemical divines within the Established Church. Perhaps the clearest instance of this was Conyers Middleton (1683–1750).[40] During the 1730s, Middleton had developed a reputation as 'the most acute controvertist of the Age'.[41] His chief sin was casting aspersions on orthodoxy's most distinguished contemporary defender, the Cambridge don Daniel Waterland. For this, he was harried and punished, for one of his acknowledged intellectual merit and production would normally have landed plum ecclesiastical preferment. Middleton was blocked even from a relatively minor position like the vacant mastership of the Charterhouse. When he met with a sympathetic Robert Walpole in 1737, Walpole informed him that Edmund Gibson and Thomas Sherlock, then bishop of Salisbury, had lobbied against him and that Walpole was not—perhaps especially after the Quakers Tithe Bill fiasco the previous year—willing to offend the bench. When Middleton subsequently confronted Sherlock, the bishop stood firm:

> He put [Middleton] in Mind, how very obnoxious he had made himself to the whole body of the Clergy by taking Part in the Cause of Infidelity, against Dr Waterland, who had wrote in Defence of Christianity: that He himself, and all the World knew that the King referred the Promotion of Clergy to Bp Gibson and himself; that if one who had made himself so justly obnoxious to the clergy, and the believing Part of the Kingdom was to be promoted to such a Piece of Preferment in the City of London, the Odium thereof must necessarily fall on him.[42]

---

[39] Pattison, 'Tendencies', p. 49.

[40] Robert G. Ingram, 'Conyers Middleton's *Cicero*: Enlightenment, Scholarship and Polemic', in William Altman (ed.), *Brill's Companion to the Reception of Cicero* (Leiden, 2015), pp. 95–123.

[41] Richard Hurd to John Potter, 27 Jan. 1743, in Sarah Brewer (ed.), *The Early Letters of Bishop Richard Hurd, 1739–1762* (Woodbridge, 1995), p. 95.

[42] William Cole's account of Conyers Middleton, n.d., Add. MS 5833, f. 233, BL.

Middleton later appealed directly to John Potter to remove the semi-official episcopal block on his preferment to higher office; Potter refused, insisting that 'there was nothing contained [in Middleton's anti-Waterland tracts], from which one could infer the author's belief in the Christian religion'.[43] In the end, Middleton rose no higher than the Cambridge librarian's office he had held since the 1720s and died a deeply embittered man. But a message had been sent to the clergy that heterodox polemical divinity was a career-killer.

If heterodoxy posed a major challenge to the mid-eighteenth-century Church of England, so too did Methodism. The movement originated in Oxford during the late 1730s, following George Whitefield's 'new birth' in 1735 and John Wesley's conversion at a religious meeting in Fetter Lane in 1738. There, Wesley reported, 'I felt my Heart strangely warm'd. I felt I did trust in Christ, Christ alone for Salvation: And an Assurance was given me, That he had taken away *my* sins, even *mine*, and saved *me* from the Law of Sin and Death.'[44] Afterwards, Wesley, Whitefield, and others began preaching campaigns, both in Britain and North America, that drew huge crowds, though perhaps not huge membership. By 1767, there were no more than 24,000 Methodists in England.

Methodism's emergence was part of a larger, transatlantic Evangelical revival that stretched from Moravia to Massachusetts.[45] Yet the English located Methodism not within its international, but within its national contexts. In particular, they understood Methodism against the backdrop of the previous century's religio-political troubles. Firstly, there was the question of whether Methodism was a separatist movement.[46] Wesley always insisted that he only sought to work within the Church of England to help revitalize the institution through a preaching ministry that emphasized conversion and personal salvation; others saw it as an extra-establishment movement. Fears of schism were not mollified when Whitefield justified preaching at a non-licensed chapel by explaining, 'I hope Your Lordship's candour will overlook a little Irregularity, since I fear that in these dregs of time, these last days wherein we live, we must be Obliged to be Irregular or in short we must do no good at all.'[47] In addition to worrying about schism, many at the time questioned Methodist 'enthusiasm', a cardinal sin in the eighteenth-century mind.[48]

---

[43] Middleton to Potter, [Oct.] 1740, BL, Add. MS 32457, fos. 155–8.

[44] John Wesley, *An Extract of . . . John Wesley's Journal, from February 1, 1737–8* (Bristol, 1740), p. 30.

[45] G. M. Ditchfield, *The Evangelical Revival* (London, 1998).

[46] Jeremy Gregory, '"In the Church I will live and die": John Wesley, the Church of England and Methodism', in William Gibson and Robert G. Ingram (eds.), *Religious Identities in Britain, 1660–1800* (Aldershot, 2005), pp. 147–78.

[47] Whitefield to Zachary Pearce, 16 Feb. 1756, Westminster Abbey Library and Muniment Room, Muniment 64774.

[48] J. G. A. Pocock, 'Enthusiasm: The Antiself of Enlightenment', *Huntington Library Quarterly*, 60 (1998): 7–28.

A 1747 complaint from a Cornish delegation to the bishop of Exeter, George Lavington, captures the worries that Methodist enthusiasm aroused in Church and state. 'A set of people who stile themselves Methodist have infus'd their enthusiastick notions into the minds of vast numbers of the meaner sort of people', they complained to Lavington. When the commission of peace tried to get the Methodists to quit their field preaching in Cornwall, though, they responded 'that they did not differ from the Church of England as by law Established'. Yet the Methodists' routine harangues against the Established Church's clergy led the commissioners to conclude that the Methodists were actually 'endeavouring to undermine the Church, that they may be at full liberty to effect their schemes, whatever they are'.[49] Even a decade after Methodism's emergence, then, local political leaders looked at the Methodists as enthusiasts and schismatics bent upon destroying the Established Church.

In the printed literature of the period, polemical divines made clear the connection between Methodism and the seventeenth-century religio-political 'troubles'.[50] George Lavington took three volumes to show how Methodist practices were 'but an humble Imitation of the most fanatical Deceivers in the most corrupt Communion in the Christian World', while William Hogarth's famous print, *Credulity, Superstition and Fanaticism*, satirized Whitefield and Wesley, portraying a cross-eyed preacher—meant to be Whitefield—as a disguised Jesuit whose wig covered a tonsured head and whose cassock hid a harlequin's costume.[51] Others at the time, though, likened the Methodists not to papists but to Protestant schismatics. So, for instance, there were pamphlets on 'Quakero-Methodism' and on the ways in which George Fox and George Whitefield resembled one another in 'their Pretences to Inspiration, to every intimate Familiarity with the Deity, and the Power of working Miracles'.[52] Still others argued that '[t]hey, who now go under the name Methodists were, in the days of our Forefathers, called Precisians', who would later rename themselves 'Puritans' and then 'Independents'.[53] The most charitably inclined orthodox reckoned that Methodism was simply a well-intentioned movement

[49] John Derbyshire Birkhead and Mr Tremayne to George Lavington, 23 May 1747, Lambeth Palace Library [LPL], Secker Papers 8, fos. 4–5.

[50] Clive Field, 'Anti-Methodist Publications of the Eighteenth Century: A Revised Bibliography', *Bulletin of the John Rylands Library*, 73 (1991): 159–280; Clive Field, 'Anti-Methodist Publications of the Eighteenth Century: A Supplemental Bibliography', *Wesley and Methodist Studies*, 6 (2014): 154–86.

[51] George Lavington, *The Enthusiasm of Methodists and Papists compared*, 3 vols. (London, 1749), I, p. 30; Bernd Krysmanski, 'We See a Ghost: Hogarth's Satire on Methodists and Connoisseurs', *Art Bulletin*, 80 (1998): 292–310.

[52] James Bate, *Quakero-Methodism; or, a Confutation of the First Principles of the Quakers and Methodists* (London, 1739); Zachary Grey, *The Quaker and the Methodist Compared: In an Abstract of George Fox's Journal* (London, 1740), preface.

[53] William Warburton, *The Doctrine of Grace: Or, the Office and Operations of the Holy Spirit vindicated from the Insults of Infidelity, and the Abuses of Fanaticism* (London, 1763), pp. 136, 137.

that had gone off the rails. 'They all set out at first I believe with a very good intention but have run into Indiscretions and Extravagancies', Thomas Secker, then bishop of Oxford, reckoned in 1739. Nonetheless, 'some of them, particularly Mr Whitefield, seem blown up with a vanity which I fear hath and will lead them into mighty wrong behaviour'.[54]

Two decades after first encountering Methodists in the diocese of Oxford, Thomas Secker (1693–1768, archbishop of Canterbury 1758–68) moved into Lambeth Palace.[55] He was the greatest archbishop of Canterbury since Thomas Tenison, the person he took as his role model. Secker, his own domestic chaplain attested, 'used to declare that of all his predecessors none discharged the Duties and conducted the business of his see with more Judgment and ability than Dr Tenison'.[56] What distinguished Secker from his predecessors since Tenison was not just evident political skill and energy but the alliance of those with a coherent reforming vision. It was, to be clear, a vision, not an enumerated agenda. Such reforms that might emerge would be restorative, rather than transformative, which is to say that they would revive or resuscitate ancient beliefs or practices in order to fix a current problem, to help the institution navigate its way forward, or to make the institution somehow truer to itself. As Secker himself explained it, 'I am far from being insensible that our Ecclesiastical Establishment needs to be reformed and improved. And I am far from being against all Efforts at Amendment.'[57] Nonetheless, his vision of what could and should be amended was informed, and delimited, by past practices and beliefs. 'We must always endeavour not only to maintain the form of the ancient system, but also to restore its strength, as far as divine and human allow', he counselled, praising 'those means [by which] the doctors in the first centuries flourished, and the same means are entrusted to us. There is no other way to be respected, and if other ways forward exist, we would not serve the interest of men or attain to eternal life by following them.'[58] Where pastoral care was concerned, for instance, this meant not the sort of structural reforms enacted during the nineteenth century, but a revival of past institutions—like the rural dean—and, more importantly, a rekindling of the apostolic spirit of the primitive Church.[59]

[54] Secker to George Secker, 11 Sept. [1739], LPL, MS 1719, f. 15.

[55] Ingram, *Religion, Reform and Modernity*, anatomizes Secker's orthodox Church reform initiative.

[56] MS A269, p. 105 (undated, on the back flyleaf of a bound volume of letters).

[57] Secker to Theophilus Alexander, 4 Dec. 1762, LPL, Secker Papers 7, fos. 150–1.

[58] Thomas Secker, *Oratorio*, in *The Records of Convocation (Canterbury 1509–1852)*, ed. Gerald Bray (Woodbridge, 2006), pp. 361, 366.

[59] Arthur Burns, 'English "Church Reform" Revisited, 1780–1840', in Arthur Burns and Joanna Innes (eds.), *Rethinking the Age of Reform: Britain, 1780–1850* (Cambridge, 2003), pp. 136–82.

Secker's outsider's perspective surely shaped his thinking about the institution, for he was brought up a Dissenter and trained originally to be a medical doctor before converting to the Established Church in his late twenties and taking clerical orders when he was almost thirty. He came to the priesthood knowing how the Church's Protestant confessional competitors thought and, evidently, with a keen sense of the threat that they posed to the Church of England. After only eleven years as a parish priest, first in Durham and then in the prestigious London parish of St James's, Westminster, he was translated to the vacant see of Bristol in late 1734. Three things recommended him for promotion then and later, when he was translated to Oxford in 1737 and to Canterbury in 1758: his theological outlook, his political sentiments, and his political connections. He was unswervingly orthodox, reliably Whig, and possessed of powerful patrons, including two of the leading Pelhamite Whig ministers, the duke of Newcastle and the earl of Hardwicke.

The Pelhams, who had served under Walpole, had learned from his mistakes. '[N]ot the least alteration will be made in the Ecclesiastical System', William Warburton confidently predicted in 1750. 'The present Ministers were bred up under and act entirely on the maxims of the last. And one of the principal of his [*sic*] was not to stir what is at rest.' Indeed, on his deathbed, Walpole regretted that his own political fall in 1742 had resulted from his 'neglect of his own maxim'.[60] Secker himself had shown an independent voting streak, especially early in his episcopal career. In addition to joining Gibson in opposition to the Quakers Tithe Bill, he voted against the ministry in the Spirituous Liquors Bill (1743) and the Bill for Disarming the Scottish Highlands (1748), and secured revisions to Hardwicke's Marriage Act (1753) to allay clerical concerns. Though a staunch parliamentary Whig, then, he was not a servile one; and yet, when the Whigs really needed his support—as during the Stamp Act repeal efforts of 1766—they could count on Secker to rally the bishops in support of the ministry.[61]

None of this, though, enabled Secker to achieve any of his orthodox reform objectives if those objectives conflicted with the imperatives of the state. His inability to secure a colonial episcopate exemplifies this most clearly.[62] Church leaders since William Laud had argued that practical necessity required an

---

[60] Warburton to Doddridge, 11 June 1750, HM 20438, Huntington Library; cf. Clyve Jones, 'The House of Lords and the Fall of Walpole', in Stephen Taylor, Richard Connors, Clyve Jones, and Philip Lawson (eds.), *Hanoverian Britain and Empire: Essays in Memory of Philip Lawson* (Woodbridge, 1998), pp. 102–36.

[61] William Lowe, 'Archbishop Secker, the Bench of Bishops, and the Repeal of the Stamp Act', *Historical Magazine of the Protestant Episcopal Church*, 46 (1977): 429–42.

[62] Stephen Taylor, 'Whigs, Bishops and America: The Politics of Church Reform in Mid-Eighteenth-Century England', *Historical Journal*, 36 (1993): 331–56; James B. Bell, *A War of Religion: Dissenters, Anglicans and the American Revolution* (Basingstoke, 2008), esp. pp. 81–122; cf. Jeremy Gregory, 'Refashioning Puritan New England: The Church of England in British North America, *c*.1680–*c*.1770', *Transactions of the Royal Historical Society*, 6th series, 20 (2010): 85–112.

American episcopate. As things stood during the eighteenth century, super-vising the colonial Church fell to the bishops of London, an arrangement that most everyone recognized was untenable: as one bishop of London freely admitted, 'for a Bishop to live at one end of the world, and his Church at the other, must make the office very uncomfortable to the Bishop, and in great measure useless to the people'.[63] Yet there was also an ecclesiological impera-tive for a colonial bishop. The orthodox believed that the Church of England was the most primitive—and hence the most pure—Church in the world and that episcopacy was the most primitively pure ecclesiology.[64] As one of Secker's North American correspondents insisted, 'as the Practice of the primitive church was a faithful Comment on the Laws of Christ, and his Apostles, relating to the Government of the Church; so it is not so difficult a Matter to discover what that Practice was': on his reading, not surprisingly, 'Episcopal Government obtained very early in the Church'.[65] Not to have a bishop on the ground in America was, in practice, not to have an episcopal Church—properly understood—on the ground there either.[66]

Yet neither necessity nor theology mattered to the politicians. For one thing, America was a tinderbox by the late 1760s. Winning the Seven Years War both won the English a huge North American empire and burdened it with new problems of governance at home and abroad. So, it was especially problematic when colonial opponents of episcopacy raised the spectre of a revival of religio-political strife: Secker got cast as a latter-day Laudian innovator, and non-Anglican British North Americans styled themselves as heirs to the anti-tyrannical Puritans of the previous century.[67] This clearly unnerved the politicians, for as Secker himself explained in 1767, 'the Ministry were intirely averse to sending Bishops to America at Present', not least because 'as America seemed on the point of Rebellion & Independency, the Ministry were deter-mined to retain every hold on America . . . This hold would be lost if a Bp should be sent.'[68] This, in turn, points to a deeper structural challenge for the eighteenth-century Church: while the seventeenth-century confessional mindset and its imperatives remained alive and well in North America, the pressures of empire and war were slowly de-confessionalizing English politics. The empire, put another way, was fracturing intellectually and culturally as

---

[63] Thomas Sherlock to Doddridge, 11 May 1751, in William Stevens Perry (ed.), *Historical Collections relating to the American Colonial Church*, vol. I: *Virginia* (New York, 1969), p. 373.

[64] Norman Sykes, *Old Priest, New Presbyter: Episcopacy and Presbyterianism since the Refor-mation with special relation to the Churches of England and Scotland* (Cambridge, 1956).

[65] Thomas Bradbury Chandler, *An Appeal to the Public, in behalf of the Church of England in America* (2nd edn., London, 1769), pp. 7, 9.

[66] Peter Doll, 'The Idea of the Primitive Church in High Church Ecclesiology from Samuel Johnson to J. H. Hobart', *Anglican and Episcopal History*, 65 (1996): 16–43.

[67] Bell, *War of Religion*, pp. 91–106.

[68] *Extracts from the Itineraries and other Miscellanies of Ezra Stiles*, ed. Franklin B. Dexter (New Haven, CT, 1916), p. 254.

parts of the nation's historical memory faded to irrelevance in the mother country. Consider, for instance, the divergent responses to the Quebec Act (1774), passed by Parliament to reorganize the former French government in Canada. Among the Act's provisions was one which allowed Roman Catholics to practise their religion unmolested. Even High Church Anglican clerical defenders of the measure understood the provision in prudential terms. As one explained, 'the Popish religion is no more than tolerated within that dominion; which was one of the conditions on which the country surrendered itself to the crown of Great Britain; and . . . a proper foundation is laid for the establishment of the Protestant religion, which is meant to take place'.[69] Protestant Dissenters in North America, though, saw something more sinister afoot. 'Now when such favour is shewn to the bloody religion of Rome', the Congregational minister Ebenezer Baldwin contended, 'it argues either for a favourable disposition in the parliament towards that religion; or that it is done, in order to carry out some other favourite scheme.'[70] That 'scheme'—robbing the English of their religious and political liberties in the name of 'popery and arbitrary government'—was one which would have been familiar to most English people during the 1670s. That it was neither recognized nor relevant to the metropolitan English during the 1770s suggests that an era in the mother country's—and in its established Church's—history had passed.[71] With the American Revolution, the English Reformation drew to a close.

SELECT BIBLIOGRAPHY

Bennett, G. V., *The Tory Crisis in Church and State, 1688–1730: The Career of Francis Atterbury, Bishop of Rochester* (Oxford, 1975).

Bulman, William J. and Robert G. Ingram, 'Religion, Enlightenment, and the Paradox of Innovation', in Donald A. Yerxa (ed.), *Religion and Innovation: Antagonists or Partners?* (London, 2015), pp. 100–12.

Champion, J. A. I., *The Pillars of Priestcraft Shaken: The Church of England and its Enemies, 1660–1730* (Cambridge, 1992).

Gibson, William, *The Church of England, 1688–1832: Unity and Accord* (London, 2001).

Gregory, Jeremy, 'Refashioning Puritan New England: The Church of England in British North America c.1680–c.1770', *Transactions of the Royal Historical Society*, 6th series, 20 (2010): 85–112.

---

[69] Thomas Bradbury Chandler, 'A Friendly Address' (1774), in Gordon Wood (ed.), *The American Revolution: Writings from the Pamphlet Debate, 1773–1776* (New York, 2015), p. 285.

[70] Ebenezer Baldwin, 'Stating the Heavy Grievances' (1774), in Wood (ed.), *The American Revolution*, p. 265.

[71] Eric Nelson, *The Royalist Revolution: Monarchy and the American Founding* (Cambridge, MA, 2014), esp. pp. 29–107.

Gregory, Jeremy, *Restoration, Reformation and Reform, 1660–1828: Archbishops of Canterbury and their Diocese* (Oxford, 2000).

Gregory, Jeremy and Jeffrey S. Chamberlain (eds.), *The National Church in Local Perspective: The Church of England and the Regions, 1660–1800* (Woodbridge, 2003).

Holmes, Geoffrey S., *The Trial of Doctor Sacheverell* (London, 1973).

Ingram, Robert G., *Religion, Reform and Modernity in the Eighteenth Century: Thomas Secker and the Church of England* (Woodbridge, 2007).

Jacob, W. M., *The Clerical Profession in the Long Eighteenth Century, 1680–1840* (Oxford, 2007).

Pocock, J. G. A., *Barbarism and Religion*, vol. V: *Religion: The First Triumph* (Cambridge, 2010).

Sirota, Brent, *The Christian Monitors: The Church of England and the Age of Benevolence, 1680–1730* (New Haven, CT, 2014).

Sykes, Norman, *Church and State in England in the XVIIIth Century* (Cambridge, 1934).

Sykes, Norman, *From Sheldon to Secker: Aspects of English Church History 1660–1768* (Cambridge, 1959).

Taylor, Stephen J. C., 'Church and State in England in the Mid-Eighteenth Century: The Newcastle Years, 1747–62', PhD thesis, University of Cambridge, 1987.

Walsh, John, Colin Haydon, and Stephen Taylor (eds.), *The Church of England, c.1689–c.1833: From Toleration to Tractarianism* (Cambridge, 1993).

Young, B. W., *Religion and Enlightenment in Eighteenth-Century England* (Oxford, 1998).

Young, B. W., *The Victorian Eighteenth Century: An Intellectual History* (Oxford, 2007).

4

The Anglican Churches, 1783–1829

Mark Smith

The years from 1783 to 1829 were in many respects tumultuous ones for the Anglican Church. The recognition of American independence in 1783 and the consecration by Scottish Episcopalians of Samuel Seabury as bishop of Connecticut the following year saw the effective creation, on the foundations of the colonial Church, of the first Anglican province beyond the jurisdiction of the crown. The precedent for the creation of episcopal sees outside the British Isles having been set, Seabury's consecration was rapidly followed not only by those of further bishops in the United States but also in Nova Scotia in 1787, Calcutta from 1814, and the West Indies, beginning with Barbados and Jamaica in 1824.[1] In Scotland, the failure of the main Stuart line by the deaths of Charles Edward Stuart in 1788 and his brother Cardinal Henry in 1807 removed the major obstacles to political accommodation with the British crown which resulted in a repeal of the penal laws in 1792 and a gradual reconciliation of the non-juring and 'qualifying' branches of the Church. In Ireland the reverberations of successive revolutions in America and France were felt even more strongly, promoting a coalescence of the political interests of the Church of Ireland's main rivals, the Roman Catholics and the Presbyterians. This resulted first in the attempted revolution of 1798, and then in the Acts of Union of 1800 which created not just the United Kingdom but also the United Church of England and Ireland, and finally in the political tensions which undermined the exclusively Protestant basis of the British constitution in 1829. In England and Wales, events were less dramatic and establishment more secure but the emergence of new rivals, the impact of revolution abroad, and increasingly urgent calls for reform ensured that this would be a period of change for the Established Church

---

[1] W. M. Jacob, *The Making of the Anglican Church Worldwide* (London, 1997), pp. 62–93; William L. Sachs, *The Transformation of Anglicanism: From State Church to Global Communion* (Cambridge, 1993), pp. 57–69.

even on its home ground. It is with these developments that this chapter is principally concerned.

ESTABLISHMENT

The dates which frame this chapter, 1783—the recognition of American independence—and 1829—the emancipation of Roman Catholics within the United Kingdom—point to the character of the Anglican Church as an established Church and a central part of the constitution of the United Kingdom and, by extension, of its empire. The establishment character of the Church can be viewed at a number of levels in late Hanoverian society. Most obviously the Church, its clergy, and laity retained a central place in the main governing institutions of the British state, especially the two houses of Parliament. Twenty-six bishops sat in the House of Lords, comprising some 10 per cent of its active membership—a role which required a significant commitment from these leading churchmen in an age of regular parliamentary sessions. The Act of Union of 1707 had diluted the virtual Anglican monopoly in the House of Commons by the addition of forty-five solidly Presbyterian Scottish MPs and, whatever might be contended for England and Wales, the new nation of Great Britain represented by that Parliament could not be regarded as a purely Anglican confessional state. This new dispensation was reinforced by the terms of the coronation oath, which required the monarch to maintain 'the Protestant Reformed Religion established by law': in the context of union this implied in England and Wales the support of Anglicanism against all comers, including Presbyterians, and in Scotland the support of Presbyterianism against all comers, including Anglicans. Nonetheless, the Anglican ascendancy in Parliament remained assured at the start of this period, essentially unthreatened by the Scots and the handful of Nonconformists from south of the border who found their way into the House of Commons. This was a key condition for the persistence of the view that the English state and Church were two sides of the same coin so that Parliament could be seen as the 'lay synod' of the Church of England and a vital reassurance to a Church which, given the suspension of Convocation from 1717, lacked any other collective decision-making body. Equally, as Jonathan Clark has pointed out, in an age in which much constitutional and political discourse was conceived and conducted in the language of religion, Anglican political theology, whether High Church or Latitudinarian in flavour, retained a vital function as a key ideological prop of the establishment in England and Wales.[2]

---

[2] J. C. D. Clark, *English Society 1660–1832: Religion, Ideology and Politics during the Ancien Regime* (Cambridge, 2000), pp. 256–84.

The central role of the Church in the establishment was equally prominent at more local levels. Bishops and the higher clergy, for example, could be significant figures in the county community. Perhaps the grandest of them all (and certainly the most wealthy after the archbishop of Canterbury), the bishop of Durham, still retained palatine jurisdiction in the county. Describing the advent of William Van Mildert, the new bishop, Elizabeth Varley notes:

> His triumphal entry into the diocese on 14th July 1826 was a masterpiece of traditional pageantry from the crossing over Croft-on-Tees bridge into County Durham, greeted by 'about forty other carriages besides a large cavalcade of horsemen, and some hundreds of people on foot', to the final arrival at Auckland castle escorted by an honour guard of 'about 30 or 40 horsemen' who 'preceded us to the Castle Gate and there drew up on each side in rank and file while we passed through them into the Castle Court'.[3]

It was an occasion which amply symbolized the close integration of Church and state. Other bishops and cathedral clergy played a similar if less magni-fied role in their own jurisdictions. Even more fundamental and far more pervasive, however, was the establishment of the Church at local or parish level. Here, for the vast majority of the population of England and Wales, the structures of the Church were woven most closely into the textures of everyday life.

The character of the majority of Anglican parishes was powerfully shaped by the Church's mainstream soteriology. This was a conditional understanding of justification in which people became Christians by baptism but were thereafter required to qualify for their final justification by fulfilling their obligations—a sincere attempt to obey the law of Christ—in other words, the practice of holiness and good works. In this context it was the role of the Church first to ensure that as many parishioners as possible had been baptized and then to assist them in fulfilling the conditions of their final salvation. This approach, though challenged by the emerging Evangelical movement, was common to High Churchmen and latitudinarians alike. It saw the clerical task as partly sacramental, to make available the means of grace that fuelled progress to heaven; partly educative, to ensure that the conditions of salvation were properly understood; and partly pastoral, to enforce, by preaching, conversa-tion, and example, the practice of Christian virtues, especially charity and good works according to the respective stations of parishioners. In the case of the gentry and other parish elites, their Christian duties were not simply a private affair, concerned only with their own salvation but also, like those of the parish clergy, exemplary, to be done in the sight of, and for the benefit of, the commu-nity at large. Such duties included not only church-going—their presence being

---

[3] E. A. Varley, *The Last of the Prince Bishops: William Van Mildert and the High Church Movement of the Early Nineteenth Century* (Cambridge, 1992), p. 108.

emphasized by the prominence of their pews in the parish church—but also a range of other activities, from the support of local charities to the administration of the 'civil' functions of the parish, especially in poor relief and the maintenance of the order on which communal harmony depended. Indeed, by the turn of the century clergy themselves were increasingly joining the gentry on the magistrates' bench with the same objects in mind. For the generality of the parish, it was very widely agreed that the most urgent task of the Church lay in explaining their duty to them, and so both clerical handbooks and episcopal visitations placed considerable emphasis on the catechetical ministry of the clergy. It was also the main topic of parish preaching, hence the moral cast often associated with the Hanoverian pulpit. A review of the surviving manuscript sermons of James Woodforde, for example, reveals an emphasis on the avoidance of conflict and its contributory causes, such as bickering, gossip, and slander, and the practice of social virtues, such as fair dealing, justice, generosity, and hospitality.[4] A soteriology that taught parishioners that perseverance in ordinary holiness and a set of duties that constituted good neighbourliness was a condition of their salvation was, of course, also ideally suited to the promotion of communal harmony of the sort desired by the state and recognized as such by legislators.[5]

The Church in both theory and practice thus occupied a crucial position within the body politic of England and Wales. However, by 1783 it faced significant problems in fulfilling its assigned tasks of teaching the faith and maintaining social and political cohesion via the effective working of the parish system. Some of its deficiencies—like non-residence and pluralism or the closely related issue of the poverty of many benefices—were of long standing in the Church but rendered newly urgent by social and economic change in the second half of the eighteenth century. Certainly these problems were sufficiently prominent to deserve attention. Peter Virgin has estimated on a sample of six counties that the percentage of parishes with resident incumbents around the start of the period may have been as low as 40 per cent and that approximately 36 per cent of clergy with benefices were pluralists.[6] However, the bare statistics tell only part of the story. Much pluralism was relatively local in nature with a single clergyman holding two benefices in the same neighbourhood or at least the same county. Non-residence, too, was a

---

[4] Mark Smith, 'The Hanoverian Parish: Towards a New Agenda', *Past & Present*, 216 (2012): 79–105.

[5] G. M. Ditchfield, 'Ecclesiastical Legislation during the Ministry of the Younger Pitt, 1783–1801', *Parliamentary History*, 19 (2000): 64–80; J. Innes, 'Parliament and Church Reform: Off and On the Agenda', in Gordon Pentland and Michael T. Davies (eds.), *Liberty, Property and Popular Politics: England and Scotland, 1688–1815. Essays in Honour of H. T. Dickinson* (Edinburgh, 2015), pp. 39–57.

[6] Peter Virgin, *The Church in an Age of Negligence: Ecclesiastical Structure and Problems of Church Reform, 1700–1830* (Cambridge, 1989), pp. 193–4.

complex issue, with sickness or the lack of a suitable parsonage accounting for a significant proportion of instances. This did not mean that the bulk of parishes suffered from pastoral neglect, since in some cases where the parsonage was unfit the incumbent lived nearby and performed all the regular parish duties himself. Even in cases where the incumbent lived at a distance or was too sick or insufficiently inclined to do the work, the vast majority of benefices received attention by arrangements with the clergy of neighbouring parishes or else were served by resident curates.[7] Even if the pastoral consequences were minor, however, an institution that routinely used paid substitutes to perform a key part of its core tasks was to become increasingly anomalous in an age of economical reform. In analysing the causes of pluralism, the balance between poverty and cupidity is difficult to assess, but it is amply clear that, despite several decades of activity by Queen Anne's Bounty, there were far too many benefices in the Church with an income too small to support a clergyman in respectable circumstances, with over a thousand yielding less than £50 p.a. as late as 1810.[8] It was clearly difficult to insist on resident incumbencies under such circumstances and the issue of clerical incomes was to provoke considerable discussion from the 1790s, especially given the controversies often provoked by its major component, tithes on agricultural produce.[9]

Other problems were essentially new, the direct products of social and economic changes and the demographic and religious shifts which accompanied them. First to emerge was the challenge to the Anglican establishment posed by the rapid growth of Nonconformist denominations, especially those created or energized by the Evangelical Revivals of the eighteenth century. This challenge operated at a national level where newly assertive Nonconformists sought to erode the special position accorded to the Anglican Church in the constitution and upheld by restrictive legislation like the Test and Corporation Acts. It also operated locally where Anglican clergy were alarmed by the use of the liberties granted by the Toleration Act by itinerant Evangelical preachers, who were able to penetrate their parishes almost at will and to offer an alternative to both the teaching and the authority of the establishment. These concerns gained additional force when war with France engendered the fear of subversion at home, both placing additional weight on the role of the establishment and raising concern about itinerants suspected of sinister political purposes. Similarly, the shift in the centre of gravity of the population as industrial towns, especially in the north and Midlands, began to enjoy a

---

[7] For some of the complexities of non-residence and pluralism, see Mark Smith (ed.), *Doing the Duty of the Parish: Surveys of the Church in Hampshire, 1810* (Winchester, 2004).

[8] Virgin, *Age of Negligence*, p. 68.

[9] Eric J. Evans, 'Some Reasons for the Growth of Anti-Clericalism in England', *Past & Present*, 66 (1975): 84–109.

disproportionate share of the demographic growth of the later Hanoverian period posed a new set of challenges for a Church whose parish system had evolved to match the population distribution of medieval England with only minor changes since then. By the turn of the century the question of how to promote the subdivision of unwieldy parishes and provide additional churches in populous places was increasingly beginning to occupy the minds of thoughtful churchmen and to engage the attention of leading politicians.

In Ireland the situation was, in some respects, even worse. Never particularly well endowed with parish churches, and with damage caused by political violence as late as the United Irishmen's abortive revolution in 1798, the Church struggled to maintain a reasonable physical presence across the island even in relation to the 10 per cent of the population which associated with Irish Anglicanism. Despite several decades of attempts to improve the infrastructure of the Church with support from the Irish Parliament from 1786, a partial survey of the Church conducted in 1808 revealed that almost a quarter of the parishes lacked a church building in good repair and almost three-quarters lacked a decent parsonage. Given these conditions it is hardly surprising that, surveyed in the previous year, almost half the clergy were habitually non-resident.[10]

REFORM

The parliamentary reform of the Church of England is principally associated with the formation of the Ecclesiastical Commission in 1834. However, the possibility of using legislation to address acknowledged problems with the functioning of the establishment was already on the table during the administration of William Pitt and his successors, gathering pace especially under Spencer Perceval and Lord Liverpool.[11] It was Pitt's government in the 1780s which addressed the claims of exiled loyalist clergy after the recognition of American independence, provided a landed endowment for the Church in Canada, and facilitated the first wave of colonial bishops. High on Prime Minister William Pitt's domestic agenda was fiscal consolidation and administrative reform and it is probably in a similar vein that he at first approached the issues of the Church, beginning in the early 1790s with an investigation into whether the heat might be taken out of growing tensions between the

---

[10] Stewart J. Brown, *The National Churches of England, Ireland and Scotland, 1801–1846* (Oxford, 2001), pp. 21–2.

[11] The best accounts of the proposals for legislative church reform in the last two decades of the eighteenth century can be found in Ditchfield, 'Ecclesiastical Legislation', and Innes, 'Parliament and Church Reform'.

Church and its Nonconformist rivals by finding an alternative to tithe as a way of financing the parochial ministry. Although this initiative was displaced by new priorities following the outbreak of war with France in 1793, religious issues remained significant in this period. The prospect of union with Ireland raised in a more acute form the issue of the place of non-Anglicans within the constitutional settlement of the United Kingdom. The rise of Evangelical Dissent (reinforced by the gradual separation of the main body of Wesleyan Methodists from the Church after 1795) highlighted the issue of the pastoral effectiveness of the Anglican parish system. Despite the granting of formal religious toleration to Roman Catholics in 1791, the constitutional issues remained unresolved and indeed the firm defence of the Protestant nature of the constitution by the king eventually forced Pitt's resignation. The concerns about pastoral effectiveness came to focus on the residence of the clergy and the welfare of the curates who served the benefices of the non-residents. A Stipendiary Curates Act of 1796 raised the maximum stipend for curates to £75,[12] and although episcopal concern about the Erastian implications of parliamentary action remained strong, the issue of residence became more acute at the turn of the century with a surge in activity by informers under the Henrician statutes which allowed lay prosecutions for non-residence.[13]

An attempt to tackle these issues emerged in the form of an 'Ecclesiastical Plan', apparently first developed by Pitt and his cousin Lord Grenville with Pitt's main ecclesiastical adviser George Pretyman, bishop of Lincoln, and then further developed with a wider circle of leading figures in the Church, including Samuel Horsley, bishop of Rochester, legal expert Sir William Scott, and ultimately the archbishop of Canterbury. In its most developed form this was a highly ambitious scheme which included more effective powers for the bishops in relation to their clergy, bodies of trustees in dioceses which would be empowered to unite or subdivide benefices in order to render them more efficient, and provisions to raise the minimum value of livings in the Church to £70 p.a. funded, if necessary, by the state. The scheme provoked a series of objections, especially from ecclesiastical lawyers and clergy concerned about the independence of the Church, and may have proved impossible to implement. It was in any case effectively killed by Pitt's departure from office in 1801. Nevertheless, the issue of the prosecution campaign remained an urgent one and produced, under Pitt's successor Addington, the first significant ecclesiastical measure of the new century, the Non-residence Act of 1803.[14] The prime mover of the legislation was Scott, and conceived as it was to deal with vexatious prosecutions it was designed rather to clarify the proper

---

[12] 36 Geo III c. 83.   [13] Innes, 'Parliament and Church Reform', p. 41.
[14] 43 Geo III c. 84.

grounds for non-residence than to diminish the practice. Nonetheless, the Act did require bishops to ensure that clergy had good reason for absence, either because they fell into an exempt category or because they could show sufficient grounds for the bishop to issue a licence. From 1805, bishops were required to submit annual returns to Parliament showing both the scale of and reasons for non-residence, a development which prompted episcopal activity in the dioceses and also provided additional material for reform-oriented conversations at the centre.

Framed essentially as a defence of the clergy, Scott's non-residence legislation had a fairly smooth passage through Parliament. When he moved on to a second target for reform—the decent remuneration of the curates who substituted for non-resident clergy—the reaction proved to be rather different. The central proposal that incumbents should be required to pay their curates a minimum salary related to the value of the living could easily be represented as an attack on property rights which, if admitted in the case of clerical property, could potentially be extended by future Parliaments to other kinds of property. It thus failed to find favour either with concerned churchmen who feared the intrusion of Parliament into the fabric of the Church or with a landowning House of Commons concerned about the sanctity of property. After two failed attempts at legislation in 1803 and 1804 Scott admitted defeat and withdrew from the fray. At this point the initiative in legislative attempts to reform the Church passed to a new group of men. These included rising stars among conservative Anglicans, such as Addington (ennobled as Viscount Sidmouth in 1805) and Jenkinson (Lord Liverpool from December 1808). However, among its key players were also men who had Evangelical affinities, especially Spencer Perceval, successively attorney general, chancellor of the Exchequer, and prime minister (1809–12), Dudley Ryder, earl of Harrowby, whose younger brother Henry was the first Evangelical to sit on the episcopal bench, and Nicholas Vansittart, who became chancellor of the Exchequer when Liverpool succeeded Perceval in 1812. Perceval began by picking up the threads of Scott's attempts to improve both clerical residence and the lot of curates. In 1805 he introduced a bill which would have allowed bishops to require residence on livings worth less than £400 a year and to ensure that curates were paid at least £200 on the rest, only to see it lost in the Lords. Introducing a similar measure the following year he faced opposition concerted in Oxford University as well as in Parliament and this time lost on the second reading in the Commons. Finally, in 1808, he introduced from the government benches a new measure, which in the case of livings worth over £400 would have required non-residents to pay their curates 20 per cent of the value of the living in question up to a maximum of £250, but with the same object of securing an effective clerical presence in every parish as it was staffed by men who would be enabled both to live respectably among their neighbours and to set an example in the duties of charity and hospitality.[15] As he explained in the pamphlet he wrote in defence of his bill:

> I have no difficulty in saying, that I wish there was not a single parish in the kingdom without a resident officiating Minister with a salary of at least two hundred and fifty pounds per annum; I believe that such an improvement in the state of Church property would be the greatest blessing that could be conferred upon the religion, the morals, the industry, the happiness, and all the best interests of the people.[16]

Unfortunately for Perceval the bill ran into opposition, partly from conservatives who continued to worry about the parliamentary invasion of property rights, prompting hysterical accusations of Jacobinism,[17] and who may have been further alarmed by Perceval's assertion that the holding of clerical property was contingent on the performance or proper provision for the associated duties.[18] It was also attacked by Whiggishly inclined opposition politicians and churchmen like Sydney Smith, whose assault contained what Geoffrey Best described as 'his usual mix of wit, common sense and unfairness'.[19] The bill passed the Commons but was lost on its final reading in the Lords, where it was opposed by an episcopal phalanx headed by the archbishop of Canterbury. Progress was stalled until 1813 when, the baton having been passed to Lord Harrowby, he succeeded in passing the bill fortified by appeals to the memory of Perceval and by the publication of returns to Parliament on the incomes of curates serving in the place of non-residents. It was a more modest measure than those proposed by Perceval, with a minimum stipend for smaller parishes of only £80, or the value of the benefice if lower, but it was much less easy to oppose and began to establish the principle that the use of clerical property might be subject to legislative control to ensure that it was employed for its proper purposes.[20]

The defeat of his proposals to improve the position of curates did not deter Perceval from other efforts to improve the position of the Anglican establishment. In 1808, for example, he began a series of annual grants to the Church of Ireland (£50,000 in the first year, then £60,000 p.a. from 1809–16, £30,000 p.a.

---

[15] Denis Gray, *Spencer Perceval: The Evangelical Prime Minister, 1762–1812* (Manchester, 1963), pp. 22–4.

[16] S. Perceval, *A Letter to the Rev. Dr. Mansel on the Subject of the Curates Bill* (London, 1808), p. 27.

[17] Gray, *Spencer Perceval*, pp. 23–4.   [18] Perceval, *Letter to Mansel*, pp. 15–16.

[19] G. F. A. Best, *Temporal Pillars: Queen Anne's Bounty, the Ecclesiastical Commissioners, and the Church of England* (Cambridge, 1964), p. 206; Mark Smith, 'St Paul's and its Parishes, 1750–1870', in Derek Keene, Arthur Burns, and Andrew Saint (eds.), *St Paul's: The Cathedral Church of London, 604–2004* (New Haven, CT and London, 2004), pp. 372–80 (pp. 373–4).

[20] The Act was 53 Geo III c. 149. See Virgin, *Age of Negligence*, pp. 221–41. For the significance of the argument about the special nature of clerical property, see Best, *Temporal Pillars*, pp. 207–9.

from 1817–21, and £10,000 p.a. from 1822–3).[21] These were funnelled by the Board of First Fruits and could be used for a variety of purposes including church building, the endowment of parishes by the purchase of glebes, and the repair or building of glebe houses. Deployed in such a way as to promote supplementation from local donors, this cash injection had significant effects. According to one estimate, between 1808 and 1829, 633 churches and 550 glebe houses were built or rebuilt and 193 glebes purchased.[22] A combination of these improvements with a legislative tightening of the residence rules in 1808 produced an increase in rates of residence from around 46 per cent in 1806 to over 65 per cent in 1819.[23] In England and Wales support was provided on an even more generous scale. In 1809 Perceval began a series of grants from public funds channelled via Queen Anne's Bounty with the intention first of raising all poor livings to a minimum of £50 per annum and ultimately of ensuring that no benefice yielded less than £150. If this fell short of his desire that every Anglican clergyman with a cure of souls should have an income of £250, it was nonetheless an ambitious policy in the midst of a lengthy and expensive war to which no end was in sight, and a further confirmation of the value placed by the state on an efficient Church establishment. The grants ran at £100,000 per annum and were continued under the premiership of Lord Liverpool until 1820, thus amounting to £1.1 million in total.[24] The money was used imaginatively, with an eye to raising at least partly matching benefactions from local sources and giving priority to parishes with larger populations. Use was also made for the first time of an Enabling Act of 1803 which freed Queen Anne's Bounty to permit the spending of its benefactions on parsonages.[25] Peter Virgin has calculated that the use of the parliamentary grants together with the Bounty's own funds produced a reduction in the number of benefices yielding less than £50 of 72 per cent (from 1,061 to 297) between 1810 and 1830, while the number worth between £100 and £150 increased 32 per cent (from 1,211 to 1,602) in the same period, despite the effects of an agricultural depression which hit clerical incomes.[26]

One more area remained where the government might come to the aid of the establishment—the provision of sufficient churches to accommodate the growing population of early nineteenth-century England. Perhaps too, Parliament might facilitate amendments to the parish system so that it could more appropriately match the changed geographical distribution of that population, especially its concentration in towns and cities. Concern about the inadequacy of accommodation and its probable consequences in handing the initiative to

[21] Alan Acheson, *A History of the Church of Ireland, 1691–1996* (Dublin, 1997), pp. 111–12; Brown, *National Churches*, pp. 65–6.

[22] Acheson, *Church of Ireland*, p. 112.   [23] Brown, *National Churches*, p. 65.

[24] Brown, *National Churches*, pp. 64–5.   [25] 43 Geo III c. 107.

[26] Virgin, *Age of Negligence*, pp. 67–8.

the Dissenters was evident among concerned Anglican laymen already in 1810, when Sidmouth opened a discussion on the subject in the House of Lords. He moved successfully that the house should collect information about accommodation in parishes where the population appeared to be greater than 1,000, and the results were printed as a House of Lords Sessional Paper in 1811.[27] It was a point of reference for Lord Harrowby's reintroduction of the Curates Bill in 1812, and Perceval had been preparing to address the issue of church provision prior to his assassination.[28] With the war and its associated expenses reaching a climax, no legislative steps could at first be taken.[29] This left space for the generation of a campaign by concerned Anglicans and ultimately, in 1818, of independent initiatives which ran in parallel with parliamentary action. Much of the activity was coordinated by the London-based High Church group known as the Hackney Phalanx, led in practice by two parish clergymen, Henry Handley Norris and John James Watson, and amongst its lay associates by John James's wealthy brother, Joshua Watson.[30] Well connected both in Church and government circles, the Phalanx began to bring its considerable weight to bear, drawing up memorials for the prime minister, seeking support throughout the establishment, and energizing episcopal support. A wider pamphlet campaign, the most effective product of which was Richard Yates's *The Church in Danger*,[31] helped both to maintain pressure on Parliament and to raise public awareness of the issue. Following a public meeting in May 1817, a deputation secured the consent of the archbishop of Canterbury for a new organization, eventually named the Incorporated Church Building Society (ICBS). Its purpose was to collect subscriptions in order to make grants in support of church building and it came into operation in 1818.

In the same year, armed not just with Yates's analysis but with a further set of returns to the House of Lords just published,[32] the Evangelical chancellor of the Exchequer, Nicholas Vansittart, supported by Lord Harrowby and the prime minister, set out the government's own plan for church extension.[33] A million

---

[27] Hansard's Parl. Debs. (1st ser.), 17, cols. 770–1 (19 June 1810); House of Lords Sessional Papers 1810–11, vol. XLVI, paper 48.

[28] *Substance of the Speech of the Earl of Harrowby on moving for the Recommitment of a Bill for the Better Support and Maintenance of Stipendiary Curates* (London, 1812), pp. 1–2; M. H. Port, *Six Hundred New Churches: The Church Building Commission 1818–1856* (Reading, 2006 edn.), pp. 24–5.

[29] Port, *Six Hundred New Churches*, p. 25.

[30] For a brief anatomy of the Phalanx, see Clive Dewey, *The Passing of Barchester* (London, 1991).

[31] Richard Yates, *The Church in Danger: A Statement of the Cause, and of the probable Means of averting that Danger, attempted in a Letter to the Earl of Liverpool* (London, 1815).

[32] House of Commons Sessional Papers 1818, vol. XVIII, paper 5.

[33] *Substance of the Speech delivered by the Chancellor of the Exchequer...On proposing a Grant of One Million for providing Additional Places of Worship in England* (London, 1818).

pounds of public money (supplemented by a further half a million in 1824) was to be provided, administered by a body of commissioners, to build new churches in populous districts, and the commissioners could assign ecclesiastical districts or parishes to the new churches (provided that the patron and the bishop consented). A supplementary Act of 1819 allowed the commissioners also to assign ecclesiastical districts to existing chapels of ease. Despite the complexities of ecclesiastical rights with which they were faced, the commissioners made good headway, and by the time of their first report (in 1821) had already provided for eighty-five new churches with almost 150,000 seats, one-third of which were free of pew-rents. Dozens of new districts were also assigned, and thus the first steps were taken in breaking up the rigidity of the parish system and paving the way for the vast expansion of the Victorian period.[34]

The early success of the Church Building Commissioners rested, at least in part, on a substantial voluntary effort within the Church itself. There were gifts of sites, and financial subscriptions from individuals, local committees, and diocesan church building societies, as well as from the national ICBS, and W. R. Ward has estimated that during the 1820s private and local contributions exceeded those of the government by approximately three to one.[35] The creation of the ICBS and more local church building societies were representative of a much wider phenomenon—an upsurge of voluntary activity within the Church. Some of the earliest examples of this were in the field of education. Sunday schools took off in the late eighteenth century, following publicity in the *Gloucester Journal* and the *Gentleman's Magazine* and proved to be a successful way of extending the Church's mission to a youthful expanding population, especially in the towns.[36] Early Sunday schools were often pan-denominational and by virtue of that feature of their constitution subject to controversy. More palatable to many churchmen were exclusively Anglican parish schools, and in 1811 a group principally from the High Church Hackney Phalanx founded the National Society for the Education of the Poor in the Principles of the Established Church in England and Wales. The society raised funds to support the building of primary schools and was backed, like the ICBS, by local and diocesan organizations often created at the instance of the bishop. Some existing parish charity schools came under the umbrella of the new society, but there were many new foundations and by 1824 it was estimated that there were around 400,000 pupils in 3,054 schools in connection with the society.[37]

---

[34] Port, *Six Hundred New Churches*.

[35] W. R. Ward, *Religion and Society in England, 1790–1850* (London, 1972), p. 110.

[36] Thomas Walter Laqueur, *Religion and Respectability: Sunday Schools and Working Class Culture 1780–1850* (New Haven, CT and London, 1976).

[37] R. A. Soloway, *Prelates and People: Ecclesiastical Social Thought in England 1783–1852* (London, 1969), pp. 358–79; W. M. Jacob, *The Clerical Profession in the Long Eighteenth Century, 1680–1840* (Oxford, 2007), pp. 250–3.

A further aspect of self-generated church reform, especially in the 1820s, was the beginning of a rejuvenation of the structures of the diocese itself sufficiently pervasive for Arthur Burns to describe it as a diocesan revival. Some bishops, like Kaye at Lincoln and the Sumner brothers at Llandaff and Chester, began to conduct more effective visitations with charges that reflected analysis of statistics collected in advance from printed visitation queries. They thus exercised increased superintendence of their clergy and laid the basis for policy initiatives. Similar renewed activity was evident from the bishops' principal lieutenants in their dioceses, the archdeacons, with a particular focus on improving the upkeep of parish churches and issues of clergy discipline. This process reinforced a revival of a further level of superintendence, that carried out by the rural deans, whose office seems to have been restored in a series of dioceses beginning in Wales and the south-west between 1811 and 1825. These developments also facilitated more effective communication between bishops and their clergy at large, as rural deans could convey clerical opinion in both directions.[38] As these innovations demonstrate, while the leaders of the Church could be resistant to change when (as in the case of the Stipendiary Curates Bills) they thought issues of principle were at stake, they also had the capacity to respond with some energy to the problems with which they were faced.

In Ireland, this new energy issued in what was to become perhaps the first significant attempt by the Established Church actively to convert the bulk of the population to Anglican Protestantism, in what became known as the New or Second Reformation. The first moves in this direction came from Church of Ireland Evangelicals, with a series of initiatives to distribute the Bible more widely within Irish society and in the language most appropriate to the local population. The most important of these was the foundation of the Hibernian Bible Society in 1808, which by the end of the 1820s had distributed over 200,000 bibles, some in English and some in Gaelic. Its work was complemented by the London Hibernian Society, which from 1814 concentrated on the promotion of Scripture-based education. At first High Churchmen were suspicious of these developments, not least because the Bible Society in particular was open to the Dissenters, who were seen as significant rivals to the establishment, especially in Ulster. However, by the early 1820s, with a resurgent Catholic political interest threatening the position of the establishment, many High Churchmen concluded that more vigorous action was required. This period saw a confluence of mainly Evangelically inspired voluntary action with an emphasis on more vigorous pastoral activity on the part of the mainstream Anglican clergy in an attempt to win the mainly Catholic Irish for the establishment. There was early excitement about the

---

[38] Arthur Burns, *The Diocesan Revival in the Church of England, c.1800–1870* (Oxford, 1999).

potential of this movement, with some individual clergy recording significant local success and Protestant gentry providing support. However, the movement ultimately produced a reaction among the leaders of Catholic society, who responded both with aggressive tactics, using crowds to break up Bible Society meetings, and with a propaganda offensive which claimed that those who had conformed to Protestantism had done so only because they had been bribed. More importantly it produced a renewal of Catholic pastoral activity designed to match that of the establishment. As a consequence the New Reformation began to run out of steam in the late 1820s and early optimism faded.[39]

The Anglican Churches of the late Hanoverian period have often been characterized as unable or unwilling to face up to the emergent challenges of the new century and requiring both the spiritual renewal brought by the Tractarians and the radical surgery of parliamentary reform in the 1830s before they could even begin to make progress. However, the efforts of supporters of the Established Church within Parliament and the activity of clergy and laymen outside it are testimony both to a determination to make the establishment work and to a capacity to make it work better, which deserves further exploration by historians.

REVOLUTION

The Anglican Churches of the British Isles faced revolutionary developments in their constitutional position at the end of the 1820s. Their sister Church in North America, however, had to face that situation from the outset as they entered the uncharted waters of the new republic. An immediate issue was the trend towards abandoning religious establishments in favour of a free market in religion which began early in the post-revolutionary period, even in states like Virginia where Anglicans had generally supported the Revolution. Moreover, alongside supporters of the patriot position the Church had also produced many of the most significant spokesmen for the loyalist cause in the 1770s and early 1780s. As a consequence it lost many of its most active ministers, suffered significant losses of physical assets like church buildings during the Revolution, and subsequently found it difficult to shake off anti-patriotic associations in the popular mind. Mark Noll concludes that the 'Episcopal church experienced such severe trauma in the Revolutionary decades that its continued existence as a major Protestant tradition was in

---

[39] Brown, *National Churches*, pp. 93–136; see also David Hempton and Myrtle Hill, *Evangelical Protestantism in Ulster Society, 1740–1890* (London, 1992), pp. 47–61.

doubt'.[40] Indeed, given that the Anglican ordination service required all candidates to take an oath of allegiance to the king, even the continuation of the basic ministry of the Church beyond the current generation could not be taken for granted. The Church that faced these new conditions was itself far from united, with major divisions emerging from the start between the broadly latitudinarian tradition of the southern and middle states and the High Church tradition represented particularly strongly in the minority Anglican Churches of New England. These contrasting traditions issued in different approaches to solving the conundrum of representing Anglicanism beyond the territories of the British crown.

One solution was represented by Samuel Seabury who, nominated as their bishop by the clergy of Connecticut in 1783, immediately proceeded to England to seek consecration from the English episcopate. Although treated sympathetically by the archbishop of Canterbury, Seabury's mission ran into a roadblock created by the Pitt administration's caution, in the context of continuing war with France and its allies, about doing anything that would alienate American opinion. They did promote legislation which on a temporary basis would allow the ordination of subjects of a foreign power without the oath of allegiance.[41] However, especially given the antipathy of pre-revolutionary America to the presence of a bishop, they were not prepared to countenance Seabury's consecration by the Church of England. In 1784, he went north to be consecrated by the Scottish Episcopal Church, emphasizing that his was a purely spiritual episcopacy after a primitive fashion, with no secular powers or pretensions.[42] The alternative approach, associated more with the latitudinarian tradition, aimed at the creation of a new version of Anglicanism more suited to emerging American conditions. In 1785 a General Convention of what now called itself the 'Protestant Episcopal Church in the United States of America' met in Philadelphia with both lay and clerical delegates from seven states (none from High Church New England), which called for election of bishops by a mix of lay and clerical state delegates. After negotiations with the English episcopate now given a fair wind by the government, which in 1786 passed legislation to make the temporary dispensation from the oath of allegiance permanent,[43] two more bishops (William White and Samuel Provoost) were consecrated at Lambeth in 1787. After something of a standoff with Seabury, a compromise was reached between the two models in 1789, when a separate House of Bishops was added to the General Convention as an accommodation to the High Church ideal of episcopal

[40] Mark A. Noll, *America's God: From Jonathan Edwards to Abraham Lincoln* (Oxford, 2002), p. 120.

[41] 24 Geo III c. 35.

[42] Peter M. Doll, *Revolution, Religion, and National Identity: Imperial Anglicanism in British North America, 1745–1795* (London, 2000), pp. 221–7.

[43] 26 Geo III c. 84.

government, and agreement was reached on a constitution for the new Church, canon law, and a revised Prayer Book. This was a considerable achievement for a body whose continued existence had looked precarious only a few years before, and the Church began to grow in numbers around the turn of the century.[44] However, although the Church developed its own Evangelical wing,[45] it was unable to match the flexibility and enterprise of the Baptists, the Methodists, and the new Evangelical denominations which emerged in the wake of the revivals of the early nineteenth century, and thus began to lose ground in relative terms. The American bishops did, however, provide a precedent for the establishment of a bishop with spiritual rather than spiritual and secular powers in Canada, with the consecration of Charles Inglis as bishop of Nova Scotia in 1787 and the provisions of the Constitutional Act of 1791 which endowed, rather than established, Anglicanism in Upper Canada.[46]

If Anglicans in the United States were adopting revolutionary constitutional arrangements after 1783, revolutionary methodologies at a more local level were increasingly to be found in the Anglican established Churches of the British Isles. This was especially the case in the activity of those Evangelicals who remained within those Churches after the departure of the bulk of the Methodists—a move delayed in the case of the Welsh Calvinistic Methodists until as late as 1811. At the local level Evangelical theology challenged the accepted soteriology of the Church, placing a premium on conversion which was foreign to mainstream Anglicanism. While Anglican Evangelicals gradually moved away from the more confrontational approaches of the first generation (especially concerning itinerancy and preaching across parish boundaries), they nonetheless developed a new set of methods to bring the gospel to bear on their own parishioners. These included informal meetings in unconsecrated premises, tract and bible distribution, and systematic programmes of parochial visitation, often enlisting the services of the laity to make these practicable. Such innovations were encouraged by some High Churchmen like Thomas Burgess, bishop successively of St David's and Salisbury, and especially by the first Evangelical bishops like Henry Ryder (younger brother of Lord Harrowby) and John Bird Sumner, consecrated as bishop of Chester in 1828, who drew on the pastoral theology of the leading Church of Scotland divine Thomas Chalmers in advocating what became known as the 'Aggressive approach' in parish ministry.[47] If the pastoral innovations introduced by Evangelicals had potentially revolutionary

---

[44] Robert T. Handy, *A History of the Churches in the United States and Canada* (Oxford, 1976), pp. 145–8.

[45] For an early exponent, see G. F. A. Best, 'Church Parties and Charities: Three American Visitors to England, 1823–4', *English Historical Review*, 78 (1963): 243–62.

[46] Doll, *Revolution, Religion, and National Identity*, pp. 229–41.

[47] Henry Ryder, *A Charge delivered to the Clergy of the Diocese of Lichfield and Coventry at the Second Visitation of that Diocese* (Stafford, 1828), pp. 46–50; John Bird Sumner, *A Charge*

consequences for the Church's ministry at parish level, this was even more true of their new approach to voluntary organization. The older form of voluntary action, still the default position of those agencies originated or dominated by High Churchmen, operated with the grain of the traditional territorial and authority structures of the Church. When bodies like the SPCK or the National Society set up local organizations, they began with networks of diocesan committees under the control of the bishop. Indeed, according to Herbert Marsh, one of the most tenacious defenders of the High Church position, it was one of the chief advantages of this plan that 'it invigorates the principle of diocesan government'.[48] It was thus congruent with the diocesan reform initiatives discussed earlier. The many organizations led by Anglican Evangelicals were different in character. Some, like the British and Foreign Bible Society, were interdenominational, involving cooperation on the basis of shared gospel principles with the very Dissenters who were threatening the constitutional position of the establishment. But even those organizations which, like the Church Missionary Society, were exclusively Anglican in membership nonetheless represented a revolutionary development in Anglicanism. This was both because they cut across the traditional territorial jurisdictions of the Church and because they were largely governed, if not led, by the laity, giving votes not only to the socially prominent but also to their ordinary subscribers, both male and female. This new model of voluntary autonomous Anglicanism, effectively free from any effective ecclesiastical authority, brought with it a new dynamism but, as its High Church critics were only too aware, it tended at the same time to subvert the *ancien régime* in the Established Church.[49]

The sensitivity of conservative churchmen to Evangelical voluntarism was magnified by the simultaneous threat to the *ancien régime* constitutional position of the Church. The threat came from two directions: an increasingly assertive nonconformity and a Catholic community whose claims were given new force and new urgency by the union with Ireland. When attempts to repeal the Test and Corporation Acts, which imposed civil disabilities on Dissenters, began in earnest in the 1780s, Pitt's government held firm in its determination to support this element of the constitution while at the same time resisting demands to tighten restrictions even further. Consequently, the

---

delivered to the Clergy of the Diocese of Chester at the Primary Visitation (London, 1829), pp. 23–39. For Chalmers and his influence, see Stewart J. Brown, *Thomas Chalmers and the Godly Commonwealth in Scotland* (Oxford, 1982).

[48] Herbert Marsh, *The National Religion the Foundation of National Education: A Sermon preached in the Cathedral Church of St Paul, London, on Thursday, June 13, 1811* (London, 1811), p. 45.

[49] For a further exploration of this kind of development and the High Church reaction to it, see Mark Smith, 'Henry Ryder and the Bath CMS: Evangelical and High Church Controversy in the Later Hanoverian Church', *Journal of Ecclesiastical History*, 62 (2011): 726–43.

only significant legislative action before the turn of the century was the Relief Act in 1791 which effectively extended the provisions of the Toleration Act to Roman Catholic places of worship—a case of giving legal effect to the *de facto* toleration that had been in place for many years.[50] The situation was fundamentally changed by the union with Ireland, which convinced many British politicians, including Pitt, that constitutional change was inevitable—to the extent that he felt it necessary to resign when the king rejected his proposals for political concessions to the Catholics in 1801. Even after George III ceased to be an effective force in politics after 1807 there seemed little immediate prospect of Catholic Emancipation and powerful arguments were made, both by established figures like Lord Eldon and by rising stars such as Robert Peel, in defence of the essentially Protestant nature of the constitution, its foundational status for British liberties, and the inability of Catholics who were considered to owe allegiance to a foreign power to give effective securities for their behaviour once emancipated.[51] For Dissenters too there was at first little progress towards meeting their aspirations for full civil rights. In 1811 there was even a brief threat that their position might be worsened when Lord Sidmouth, alarmed by what he thought were radical agitators masquerading as Dissenting preachers, proposed legislation which would have imposed significant controls on the itinerant preaching that was the spearhead of Nonconformist growth.[52] Sidmouth was ultimately thwarted by an effective lobbying campaign which undermined the support of his government colleagues and in 1812 a Relief Act relaxed rather than tightened controls by repealing two elements of the Clarendon Code, the Five Mile Act and the Conventicle Act.[53] Thereafter the political situation began gradually to change. The evident loyalty of the vast majority of both Nonconformists and Catholics through the long war with Napoleon made assertions of the danger of admitting them to the franchise increasingly implausible. Even under Liverpool it was becoming difficult to form a government on the basis of an Anglican or even Protestant platform. The Prime Minister treated it as an open question in Cabinet and emancipation motions began to achieve majorities in the Commons as early as 1813. By the later 1820s there was an increasingly powerful Dissenting lobby conscious of the growing numbers and respectability of the people it represented and energized by a range of issues, including resentment at the large-scale Anglican church-building efforts of the period, some of

---

[50] Ditchfield, *Ecclesiastical Legislation*, pp. 74–8.

[51] For an interpretation which stresses the strength of the conservative position and the suddenness of its collapse, see Clark, *English Society 1660–1832*, pp. 501–47.

[52] Deryck W. Lovegrove, *Established Church, Sectarian People: Itinerancy and the Transformation of English Dissent, 1780–1830* (Cambridge, 1998).

[53] David Hempton, *The Religion of the People: Methodism and Popular Religion c.1750–1900* (London, 1996), pp. 109–15.

which were funded by compulsory church rates levied on churchmen and Dissenters alike.[54] The Catholics too were increasingly well organized, especially after the foundation of Daniel O'Connell's Catholic Association in 1823, which received support from Catholic Ireland to the extent that attempts at suppression in 1825 threatened to plunge the country into a state of civil war. By 1828 an increasingly fragile Tory party led by Wellington and Peel after Liverpool's stroke in 1827 concluded that the existing constitutional position was no longer defensible. They put up only feeble resistance to a Whig motion to repeal the Test and Corporation Acts, which passed later that year, partly because the increasing likelihood of Catholic emancipation made it impossible to maintain restrictions on the political participation of Protestants. The following year, with O'Connell forcing the government's hand by successfully contesting the County Clare by-election, Peel agreed not merely to accept but to pilot a measure granting Catholic emancipation through the Commons, which despite a popular petitioning campaign against it reached the statute book in April 1829.[55]

The years between 1783 and 1829 were transformative for the Anglican Churches. The changes to their constitutional position—complete in America and gaining momentum in the rest of the Anglican world—meant that the nature and even the fact of their established position would be increasingly contested in the years to come. The impact of Evangelical Revival challenged the soteriological consensus that had dominated the Church since the beginning of the eighteenth century and pointed to a new trend towards diversity within Anglican thought and practice that would become even more prominent with the resurgence of High Church and liberal Anglicanism from the 1830s. At the same time, the Church had proved itself resilient and capable of constructive reform to meet the emergent challenges of the new century. It had surmounted what was perhaps an existential threat in the American context, moved back into the mainstream of Scottish religious life, and made the most of state aid to refurbish and extend its infrastructure in England, Wales, and Ireland. The beginnings of a new colonial episcopate and a resurgence of Anglican voluntarism provided models for expansion overseas and innovative responses to new challenges at home. If the Anglican Churches were thereby developing new muscles it was just as well, for in the colder climate of the Victorian period, with state support hard to come by, they would need to rely on their own resources if they were to survive and grow.

---

[54] Ward, *Religion and Society*, pp. 110–15.

[55] Frank O'Gorman, *The Long Eighteenth Century: British Political and Social History 1688–1832* (London, 1997), pp. 351–9.

SELECT BIBLIOGRAPHY

Acheson, Alan, *A History of the Church of Ireland, 1691–1996* (Dublin, 1997).

Best, G. F. A., *Temporal Pillars: Queen Anne's Bounty, the Ecclesiastical Commissioners, and the Church of England* (Cambridge, 1964).

Brown, Stewart J., *The National Churches of England, Ireland, and Scotland, 1801–1846* (Oxford, 2001).

Burns, Arthur, *The Diocesan Revival in the Church of England, c.1800–1870* (Oxford, 1999).

Ditchfield, G. M., *The Evangelical Revival* (London, 1998).

Doll, Peter M., *Revolution, Religion, and National Identity: Imperial Anglicanism in British North America, 1745–1795* (London, 2000).

Jacob, W. M., *The Clerical Profession in the Long Eighteenth Century, 1680–1840* (Oxford, 2007).

Jacob, W. M., *The Making of the Anglican Church Worldwide* (London, 1997).

Nockles, Peter B., *The Oxford Movement in Context: Anglican High Churchmanship, 1760–1857* (Cambridge, 1994).

Virgin, Peter, *The Church in an Age of Negligence: Ecclesiastical Structure and Problems of Church Reform, 1700–1830* (Cambridge, 1989).

Wolffe, John, *The Expansion of Evangelicalism* (Nottingham, 2006).

Part II

Regional Anglicanisms

5

England

W. M. Jacob

INTRODUCTION

England changed radically during the 167 years of our period. The unprecedented population growth, urban and industrial development, and development of a market economy and an empire all impacted on religious life. However, there were a number of constants in English, and especially Anglican, religious life. Most obviously, there was a constant awareness of the threat of death and of divine judgement on individuals and on the nation, for shortcomings in terms of heterodoxy and sin. The agents of judgement on the nation were thought to be hostile foreign powers, most often Roman Catholic, Revolutionary, and Napoleonic France, but also the weather, and sickness in people and animals. Throughout the period the memory of the danger and disorder of the civil wars overhung people's imaginations. This framed religious, political, intellectual, and social thought and life for the whole period. A concern to be right with God was central to most people's lives, public and private. Satirists might lampoon gluttonous clergymen, canting priests and over-enthusiastic Dissenters, but never faith itself.[1]

Some fears were justified. Britain was at war with France for sixty-five of these years, there were seven Jacobite risings or scares of risings, and the Counter-Reformation gained ground on the continent until the 1750s. However, anxieties about growing numbers of Dissenters, who might disrupt the settlement achieved in 1662 and renew the disorder of the 1640s, did not become well founded until the 1780s: reports of heterodoxy, atheism, impiety, immorality, and wickedness have always alarmed the devout, and there were successive waves of activity to suppress vice and turn people from sin.

---

[1] Vic Gatrell, *City of Laughter: Sex and Satire in Eighteenth-Century London* (London, 2006), p. 144.

CONTEXT

The Church of England met the religious aspirations of most English people across the social spectrum, and most of them engaged with its spiritual, moral, and pastoral disciplines. Religion framed people's lives and much of their personal, political, economic, and social activity. Citizenship and Anglicanism were coterminous. Baptism was the evidence of one's identity in society, as a citizen and parishioner. The Church was ever-present to people, including overseas: in the army or navy, the 'factories' of the Levant and the East India Company, and India and the colonies.

The Church of England was expressed locally in the parish, a territorial unit with a unitary spiritual and civil governance. Each parish was independent, governed by its vestry, elected by householders, chaired by the parish priest, assisted by elected lay officers, and supervised in matters ecclesiastical and moral by the bishop and his officers, and in administration and finance by magistrates. However, this model of Church and society was difficult to sustain in the later eighteenth century as a result of population growth, especially in towns and the new mining and manufacturing settlements located in previously under-populated, geographically large parishes, remote from parish churches and existing chapelries, particularly in the north and the West Midlands. Furthermore, a growing minority of Dissenters from the doctrines and ordering of the Church ceased to regard Church and state as coterminous.

Sacred and secular were inseparable in this period. Churches were the focus of communal life. As the largest assembly places in towns as well as villages, elections to vestries, and of mayors in boroughs, were often in churches. Village and town fairs, often on the church's patron saint's day, usually began with morning prayer and a sermon in church. Friendly and other societies liked a church service and sermon for their annual festivals. Mayors and councillors in boroughs attended church in state on Sundays, festivals, and red-letter saints' days, preceded by maces and sword. Seating layouts were designed to reflect the parish social hierarchy. In towns, the 'better sort' sat in the galleries, their servants ranged behind them, with the mayor, flanked by aldermen, councillors, and their wives, seated opposite the reading desks of the incumbent and the parish clerk, level with the pulpit. In towns people rented seats in church. To avoid disputes over the allocation of seats, churchwardens sometimes auctioned the seats, as at Boston in Lincolnshire, to allow people to position themselves in terms of social rank.[2] In villages, pews were seldom rented but often allocated to particular properties. Everywhere, free seating was provided for the poor, usually on benches in the centre of the church.

[2] Vestry Minute Book, 1705–74, LAO Boston 10/1, Lincolnshire Archives.

Often women and men, especially single people, were seated on opposite sides of a church. The proliferation of proprietary chapels in growing towns in the later eighteenth and early nineteenth centuries, which were commercial enterprises financing a clergyman from the pew-rents, suggests that people of the middling and better sorts were committed church attenders.

When designing or redesigning urban town centres, or a new development, the parish church, or a new church, was often the focal point for the street layout. Borough corporations, as at Doncaster, paid for the organ and the organist's salary.[3] He directed public and private musical events in the town, and for the local gentry and aristocracy, as did Charles Burney at King's Lynn and across Norfolk.[4] Town and village churches usually had groups of singers, often trained by peripatetic singing teachers, to lead psalm-singing and canticles at church services and to sing an anthem.[5] From the early nineteenth century small orchestras often accompanied the singing, or barrel organs were acquired.

The church was where members of communities met. The Prayer Book required public notices, announcements, and banns of marriage to be read during Sunday morning services. Baptisms, marriages, and churching of women often took place in the context of these services, as did public penances. Children and servants were rehearsed in their knowledge of the Prayer Book catechism at evening prayer on Sunday afternoons. Distribution of parochial charities, comprising money payments, loaves of bread, or clothes to poor people, often happened after Sunday morning services. Non-attendance at their parish church excluded people from their community. Certainly during the earlier part of our period excommunication by order of the consistory court for particularly heinous or persistent moral offences, impacted on a person's whole life, including social and commercial life.

Canon law required churchwardens to maintain the parish church's fabric, and look after the churchyard: statute law required parish vestries, through their officers—overseers of the poor, surveyors of the highways, and constables, supervised by justices of the peace—to maintain law and order, highways, and bridges, and to provide for the poor and destitute. Officers, with the vestry's consent, raised rates on occupiers of property to fund these responsibilities. Parish officers needed to be familiar with parish boundaries to know from whom to levy rates, the limits of their roads, and the poor people for whom they were responsible. People needed to know in which church they

[3] St George's, Doncaster, Erection of the Gallery and Organ Loft, 1736–9, DAD P1/3/C2/13, Doncaster Archives.

[4] Peter Marchbanks, '"A First Rate Man": The Life and Work of Dr Charles Burney', unpublished paper delivered to Norfolk Archaeological and Historical Research Group, April 2015.

[5] W. M. Jacob, *The Clerical Profession in the Long Eighteenth Century 1680–1840* (Oxford, 2006), pp. 188–91.

should be baptized, married, and buried, to which incumbent they must pay tithe, and where they could claim poor relief and charity. Until parishes were accurately mapped, therefore, a Rogationtide procession to 'beat the bounds' of the parish was essential, as at Chute in Wiltshire in 1785 (where it was noted that 'a gospel was read' at seven points along the route), to remind people of parish boundaries, as well as to pray for good yields for their crops.[6]

REGIONALISM

There is evidence of regional variations in patterns of Sunday worship. North and west of a line from Portland Bill to the Tees, especially in upland areas, two services were likely in parishes, but in rural parishes to the east of the line one was more usual.[7] Church attendance varied regionally, particularly where there were significant numbers of Dissenters, for example Roman Catholics in Lancashire, and Protestant Dissenters in Essex, Buckinghamshire, and Wiltshire. Where Methodism flourished, there seems to have been no significant impact on church attendance for most of our period.

Patterns of patronage varied between dioceses and counties. Canterbury diocese had a much higher than average number of livings held by ecclesiastical patrons and the archbishop. In some counties, such as Sussex, Wiltshire, and Cambridgeshire, a small group of party-orientated magnates presented to a majority of livings, and so there may have been more non-local clergy appointed, sympathetic to their patron's cause.[8] However, whether patronage influenced the political or theological complexion of a county or diocese is difficult to gauge, for clergy often long outlived the patron who presented them, and anyway, once appointed they might vote as they liked. It was unlikely that a bishop or a group of politically motivated magnates could make much difference to the ecclesiastical or political complexion of the clergy in a diocese or a county. Where gentry families held a high proportion of patronage, for example in Norfolk, more local men may have been presented. In dioceses remote from Oxford and Cambridge, there were fewer graduates among the clergy.[9] Advances in agriculture in the later eighteenth and nineteenth centuries, for example in Norfolk and Lincolnshire, may have meant

[6] Steven Hobbs (ed.), *Gleanings from Wiltshire Parish Registers*, Wiltshire Record Society 63 (Chippenham, 2010), p. 65.

[7] F. C. Mather, 'Georgian Churchmanship Reconsidered: Some Variations in Anglican Public Worship 1714–1830', *Journal of Ecclesiastical History*, 36 (1985): 255–83.

[8] Jacob, *Clerical Profession*, pp. 80–6; W. M. Jacob, *Laypeople and Religion in the Early Eighteenth Century* (Cambridge, 1996), pp. 22–8.

[9] Sara Slinn, 'Non-Graduate Entrants to the Anglican Clerical Profession 1780–1839: Routes to Ordination', PhD thesis, University of Nottingham, 2014; Jacob, *Clerical Profession*, pp. 38–9.

that in some regions more clergy became more affluent and identified with gentry than in other areas. In the 1830s, in West Yorkshire at least, fewer local men were presented to livings.[10]

However, significant regional variations were reduced by developments in communications, notably with the spread of newspapers and provincial printing and the distribution of chapbooks; and in transport, with the growth of the canal network as well as improvements in road transport. There was significant internal migration, even amongst the poorer sort. In the 1680s, nineteen families in Myddle in Shropshire had at least one son or daughter who had lived in London.[11] In the 1770s, people migrated from Coalbrookdale in Shropshire to work in west London market gardens. Servants moved between their masters' estates and London, and men moved about via service in the army and navy. Poor law records show that paupers were surprisingly mobile. James Woodforde, a Somerset man who ministered in Norfolk, never mentioned difficulties with understanding dialect. Bishops and archdeacons were seldom local men, and there is much evidence that they implemented in their dioceses policies agreed at national bishops' meetings.

Towns even to the south and east of a line from the Tees to the Exe were for most of the period usually small in area, and often in population, and to the north and west of that line they were often quite far apart. Except for major cities like London, Norwich, and Bristol, towns abutted the countryside and included farms. They included more people of the middling sort: professional people, such as apothecaries, surgeons, attorneys, merchants, and shopkeepers, as well as local clergy and their families. Often county gentry had local town houses, providing opportunities for genteel, Jane Austen-ish society, and a congregation for weekday services and monthly Holy Communion.

THE INTELLECTUAL CONTEXT

Heaven, hell, Providence, and divine judgement impinged on every aspect of life. Poverty, piety, wealth, and worship intersected in society and in people's lives. Concern about their afterlife significantly influenced people's conduct of earthly affairs. The rich were regarded as exercising stewardship on behalf of God, and the poor had reasonable expectations that the rich would provide for them, for God expected his gifts to be used charitably, not selfishly. Being right with God was important for people, but that did not necessarily mean they

[10] Philip Rycroft, 'Church, Chapel and Community in Craven 1764–1851', DPhil thesis, University of Oxford, 1988, pp. 109–10.

[11] David G. Hey, *The English Rural Community: Myddle under the Tudors and Stuarts* (Leicester, 1974), p. 192.

deferred to their 'betters' or even to clergy. The Bible and the Prayer Book read in church and at home, and sermons, reminded the rich of their responsibilities and the poor of their expectations. God, people believed, could and might intervene to punish or reward in this life individuals or, more worryingly, the nation. The godly therefore had a responsibility for the ungodly, whose impiety and immorality might incur divine wrath on the nation, in the form of defeat in war, invasion, and the imposition of oppressive, absolutist government.

The boundary between the ordinary and the extraordinary, the natural and the supernatural, was a constant talking point. Almanacs (including *Old Moore's*) continued to be sold in vast numbers, as did chapbook 'prophecies'. People were interested in predictions of marriage partners, as well as Judgement Day. They experienced visions and detected warnings and judgements. Educated and urbane people like John Wesley believed in witchcraft. Spas such as Bath and Buxton were holy wells where people had sought cures since time immemorial.[12] Reactions to the London earthquakes of 1750 and the Lisbon earthquake of 1755 showed that ideas about Providence and divine wrath were alive and well. Thomas Sherlock, bishop of London, published a letter to his clergy and people in March 1750 claiming that the recent shocks were a divine warning to Londoners to examine their shortcomings; it was reprinted several times. Many educated people, however, were keen to test the plausibility of the relationship between the natural world and apparently miraculous events.[13]

The clergy, both in the universities and the parishes, were a major element in the intelligentsia, as classicists, theologians, philosophers, literary scholars, and historians, and also in the sciences, especially botany, zoology, and geology. In England the Enlightenment was a predominantly Christian, Anglican, and clerical phenomenon. Devout Anglicans pioneered new thinking in the natural sciences, regarding themselves as investigating and exploring a God-made world.[14]

The great majority of English clergy, whether Whig or Tory in their political sympathies, were probably orthodox in their theological views, with high doctrines of the Church, the apostolic succession, and the sacraments. They, and laypeople, bought the large numbers of books and pamphlets in defence of orthodox doctrine written against alleged 'atheists', 'deists', and 'Socinians'. However, such pejorative terms were always applied by opponents: the accused never adopted them, regarding themselves as Protestant Christians seeking to explore the intellectual implications of their faith. Successive government ministries from the 1720s endeavoured to avoid public debate about

---

[12] Jacob, *Laypeople and Religion*, pp. 112–20.
[13] Jane Shaw, *Miracles in Enlightenment England* (New Haven, CT and London, 2006).
[14] B. W. Young, *Religion and Enlightenment in Eighteenth-Century England: Theological Debate from Locke to Burke* (Oxford, 1998).

theological issues, for fear of raising the cry 'the Church in danger'. Even in 1771, when Francis Blackburne and Theophilus Lindsey petitioned Parliament to remove the requirement for all clergy (and some lay office-holders) to subscribe to the Thirty-Nine Articles, the ultimate test of orthodoxy, only 250 people signed it, of whom 200 were clergy. That was an insignificant representation of the clergy of the Church.[15]

LAYPEOPLE

The Canons of 1604 and the Prayer Book required daily morning and evening prayer in churches, with sermons on Sundays. In towns and large villages this generally happened, but the smaller the population, the less likelihood there was of two Sunday services plus the daily services.[16] The evidence for church attendance is patchy and anecdotal, for there was no requirement to record it. On a Wednesday afternoon in April 1759, a visitor at St James's, Piccadilly, in London noted 'a large congregation', and at Bath on a Thursday morning in 1767 a visitor described the abbey as 'quite full'.[17] In villages clergy often commented on the difficulty of gathering a weekday congregation because of people's working patterns, but James Woodforde at Weston Longville on Sundays in the 1780s and 1790s noted 'good congregations'.[18] Often the largest congregation was on a Sunday afternoon. Holy Communion was celebrated monthly in towns, but usually quarterly in villages, but sometimes in both cases with two or three celebrations around Easter. In Clayworth in Nottinghamshire at Easter 1688, the rector noted that 190 people out of an adult population of 202 received communion.[19] However, large numbers of people seem to have been deterred from receiving communion except at Easter by expectations that extensive personal preparation was required, and fears of their unworthiness and consequent divine punishment. Not everyone attended church all the time. It was often noted that people caring for farm animals or young children, or gathering in the harvest, especially where the parish church or chapelry was far distant,

---

[15] G. M. Ditchfield, 'Feathers Tavern Petitioners (act. 1771–1774)', *ODNB*.

[16] At least south and east of a line from Portland Bill to the Tees: see section on 'Regionalism' earlier in this chapter.

[17] Gavin Hannah (ed.), *The Deserted Village: The Diary of an Oxfordshire Rector, James Newton of Nuneham Courtney 1736–1767* (Gloucester, 1992), p. 26; Brigitte Mitchell and Hubert Penrose (eds.), *Letters from Bath 1766–1767: The Revd John Penrose* (Gloucester, 1983), p. 38.

[18] *The Diary of James Woodforde, 11, 1785–1787*, ed. Roy Winstanley and Peter Jameson (n.p., 1999), pp. 206, 249, 253, 257.

[19] *The Rector's Book of Clayworth, Nottinghamshire*, ed. Harry Gill and Everard L. Guilford (Nottingham, 1910), pp. 80, 86.

might be unable to attend.[20] Some people might attend one service in church, and another at a Dissenting meeting-house. Failure to attend church frequently was not necessarily evidence of irreligion among the poorer sort, as can be seen by the enduring importance of religion for British soldiers and sailors.[21]

Monarchs set an example of daily attendance at morning and evening prayer. Many aristocratic and gentry houses had chapels, where daily prayers, attended by the household (including servants) were conducted by the chaplain, often a local incumbent and tutor to the children, and friend and confidant of the family. The many low-cost devotional books providing forms of family prayers and sold in large numbers suggest that daily family prayers were common. Some employers provided chaplains and chapels to conduct daily prayers for their workforce, for example at Crowley's Ironworks in County Durham in the early eighteenth century, and the East India Company in Poplar and their 'factories' in India.[22] But daily prayers probably declined with the development of factory processes in manufacturing and changing work patterns.[23]

Devotional and theological books were the staple product of publishers throughout the period, and formed the greatest proportion of booksellers' stocks. Vast numbers of devotional books for laypeople, such as *The Whole Duty of Man*, intended for the 'meanest reader', went through many editions. People prepared carefully, using devotional books, to receive Holy Communion. Diaries and letters show people of all sorts making notes on sermons they heard. Printed collections of sermons, sold in vast quantities, stocked the libraries of the gentry, and regularly featured in the *Gentleman's Magazine*, the most widely read periodical of the age. People read them aloud to one another, and discussed them.[24] Many town churches had libraries attached, as at Wisbech in Cambridgeshire and Reigate in Surrey, and surviving lending registers show laypeople, including women, as borrowers, as well as clergy.[25]

[20] Mark Smith (ed.), *Doing the Duty of the Parish: Surveys of the Church in Hampshire 1810*, Hampshire Record Series 17 (Winchester, 2004), p. li.

[21] Michael Snape, *The Redcoat and Religion: The Forgotten History of the British Soldier from the Age of Marlborough to the Eve of the First World War* (London, 2005); Richard Blake, *Evangelicals and the Royal Navy 1775–1815: Blue Lights and Psalm Singers* (Woodbridge, 2008).

[22] *The Law Book of the Crowley Iron Works*, ed. M. W. Flinn, Surtees Society 167 (Durham, 1952), p. 163.

[23] W. M. Jacob, '"Conscientious Attention to Publick and Family Worship of God": Religious Practice in Eighteenth-Century English Households', in John Doran, Charlotte Methuen, and Alexandra Walsham (eds.), *Religion and the Household*, Studies in Church History 50 (Woodbridge, 2014), pp. 307–17.

[24] *The Diary of Thomas Turner 1754–1765*, ed. David Vaisey (Oxford, 1984).

[25] W. M. Jacob, 'Libraries for the Parish: Individual Donors and Charitable Societies', in Giles Mandelbrote and K. A. Manley (eds.), *The Cambridge History of Libraries in Britain and Ireland*, vol. II: *1640–1850* (Cambridge, 2006), pp. 65–82.

Vestries (or borough corporations) oversaw the repair and updating of churches. Much work was done, especially after the depredations and neglect of the civil war, which left most churches in some towns, for example Colchester and Lincoln, in ruins. After the Fire of London destroyed many City churches in 1666, most of them and St Paul's were rebuilt from the proceeds of a tax on coal (which was used by everyone) imported into London. Their vestries funded the furnishing of their rebuilt churches in very splendid style. Many new churches were built at the expense of borough corporations or church ratepayers to provide accommodation for growing populations, as in Liverpool, Leeds, Manchester, and Sunderland. Individuals or groups of laity provided new chapels in geographically extensive parishes and proprietary chapels in populous places with rich parishioners or visitors, such as Bath or Hampstead. Laypeople, as vestries and borough corporations, funded impressive new reredoses and altars and altar rails for existing churches, for example at Holy Trinity, Hull; St Mary Redcliffe, Bristol; and Wigan; often individuals provided expensive fabrics for altar coverings and hangings for pulpits, and donated vast quantities of silver chalices, patens, flagons, and alms dishes for use in Holy Communion services, suggesting that people valued the sacraments highly.[26]

The laity largely paid for the clergy by paying tithes on the produce of the land, or rents for pews in churches, and (in towns) often making grants from borough funds to augment the vicar's stipend and pay for curates. There were, of course, disputes, sometimes vitriolic and long-standing, sometimes with major landowners, about paying tithes. These were in theory a tenth part of the produce of the land and of people's labour, but were often a negotiated cash payment based on long-standing local custom, revision of which might involve complex negotiations. However, given the scale of tithe payments across the nation, there were relatively few disputes. Even Dissenters mostly paid tithes (and church rates, so they contributed towards the upkeep of the parish church and incumbent as well as their own ministers and meeting-houses) without significant objection until the 1820s.[27] Many laypeople made generous donations to Queen Anne's Bounty, funded from ancient taxes on the clergy, to augment the endowments of the poorest livings, and

---

[26] K. J. Allison (ed.), *A History of the County of York East Riding*, vol. I: *The City of Kingston upon Hull* (London, 1969), p. 292; M. J. H. Liversedge, *William Hogarth's Bristol Altarpiece* (Bristol, 1980), pp. 8–9; George T. O. Bridgeman, *The History of the Church and Manor of Wigan in the County of Lancashire*, 4 vols., Chetham Society, new series, 15–18 (Manchester, 1889), III, pp. 620–5; Grantham Parish Church Charity Boards, in the Ringing Chamber; Anon., *The Treasury: An Exhibition of Church Plate in Nottinghamshire* (Newark, 1981).

[27] For tithes, see Daniel Cummins, 'The Social Significance of Tithes in Eighteenth-Century England', *English Historical Review*, 128 (2013): 1129–54; Jacob, *Laypeople and Religion*, pp. 36–9.

to augment endowments for paying clergy of parishes or chapelries in which they had an interest.[28]

One of the most significant roles laity played in relation to the Church was as patrons of livings, in presenting clergy to a bishop to be instituted as incumbent. Patronage was the universal means of recruiting people to posts, in the armed forces and the civil service as well as in the Church. Most patrons were laypeople, whether as individuals in their own right, as ministers advising the crown, as borough corporations, or, sometimes, as inhabitants or ratepayers electing their incumbent. Many laypeople took great care in exercising patronage. They were aware of their responsibilities before God to appoint good and suitable people who would exercise spiritual and pastoral care and teach the Christian faith. Often they nominated people they knew personally, or who were reliably recommended by someone they trusted. Sometimes they made enquiries to reassure themselves about the person. Sometimes patrons got it wrong, and appointments were disastrous, but that was not necessarily for lack of care. Generally people had high expectations of clergy in terms of prayer, preaching and pastoral attentiveness, and charitableness, and complained about them if they did not get what they required. They expected a return on their tithe contributions.

Laypeople worked closely with clergy to promote the work of the Church, by establishing societies, whether for the 'reformation of manners', to abate what was feared to be a rising tide of vice and profanity in the late seventeenth century, or 'religious societies' for deepening the faith of laypeople, especially young men. Laypeople played a major part in founding, funding, and managing the great national societies, the Society for the Promotion of Christian Knowledge (SPCK) in 1698 and the Society for the Propagation of the Gospel (SPG) in 1701, and later the Church Missionary Society (CMS). Lay supporters of the SPCK established schools for poor children, financed leaflets to instruct people about the Christian faith and encourage their devotional lives, to be distributed at cost to clergy for giving to parishioners and for chaplains to distribute to soldiers and sailors in the armed forces, and funded missionary work in India. Laypeople raised funds for the SPG and recruited, selected, and managed chaplains and missionaries for the North American colonies. Laymen were active in managing the CMS in the early nineteenth century. They were also prominent in the national Corporation of the Sons of the Clergy, and in diocesan and county charities to support clergy widows and children.

---

[28] G. F. A. Best, *Temporal Pillars: Queen Anne's Bounty, the Ecclesiastical Commissioners and the Church of England* (Cambridge, 1964); Ian Green, 'The First Five Years of Queen Anne's Bounty', in Rosemary O'Day and Felicity Heal (eds.), *Princes and Paupers in the English Church 1500–1800* (Leicester, 1981), pp. 231–54.

WOMEN

Women were very active in the life of the Church, among other roles as authors of devotional works and convenors of devotional groups. Examples include Lady Betty Hastings at Ledsham in Yorkshire, whose sister-in-law, the countess of Huntingdon, formed her own connexion of societies, and theological writers such as Elinor James, Elizabeth Bowdler, Henrietta Maria Bowdler, and most notably Hannah More and Sarah Trimmer.[29] Women were occasionally elected as churchwardens. They were particularly prominent as philanthropists, endowing schools for poor children and charities to support poor people, funding the building of new churches, and repairing and beautifying existing ones. Lady Ann Bland largely paid for St Ann's, Manchester, in 1709 and Lady Betty Hastings contributed significantly to building Holy Trinity, Leeds, in 1727. Many women gave large quantities of silver for use at Holy Communion; for example, Lady Frances Leake in 1705 gave silver chalices, patens, flagons, alms dishes, and candlesticks, weighing 700 ounces, to Newark parish church, for use at celebrations of Holy Communion. They were generous contributors to Queen Anne's Bounty to augment endowments of livings. Women as patrons presented clergy to bishops to institute them to livings.[30]

BISHOPS

Bishops exercised their oversight of the Church along lines initiated by Archbishops Sancroft, Tenison, and Sharp in the 1680s and 1690s to reform the Church of England administratively and pastorally. The intent was to align it more closely with the 'primitive Church' of the first four centuries, making it a more effective means of administering grace and saving souls, and to restore Dissenters and backsliders to the Church. Drawing on methods adopted by the Counter-Reformation and Pietism in the continental Reformed Churches, they enforced the Canons of 1604 to improve the standard and efficiency of the clergy and formalized selection procedures for ordination candidates to ensure that, if at all possible, only devout and able men were ordained. University colleges, of which many bishops had been fellows or heads, were essentially the Church's seminaries, where sons of the aristocracy and gentry

[29] Paula McDowell, 'James, Elinor (1644/5–1719)'; Emma Major, 'Bowdler, Elizabeth (*d.* 1797)'; M. Clare Loughlin-Chow, 'Bowdler, Henrietta Maria (1750–1830)'; and Barbara Brandon Schnorrenbery, 'Trimmer, Sarah (1741–1810)', all *ODNB*; Anne Stott, *Hannah More: The First Victorian* (Oxford, 2003); W. K. Lowther Clarke, *Eighteenth-Century Piety* (London, 1944).

[30] Howe Church, Norfolk, inscription on brass plate on north wall of chancel; C. E. Medhurst, *The Life and Work of Lady Elizabeth Hastings* (Leeds, 1914), p. 59.

were also educated; these institutions adapted themselves as centres for enlightened Christian learning and developed systems to assist students' spiritual development. Bishops reinforced the regulations regarding clergy holding benefices in plurality and employing curates, to limit the risk of absentee incumbents neglecting pastoral care and oversight in their parishes. To provide mutual support and encouragement, and to promote professional development for clergy, they urged them to meet in rural deaneries to consult together about developing their spiritual lives, and their teaching and pastoral ministries.[31] To assist this Gilbert Burnet, bishop of Salisbury, published his *Discourse of the Pastoral Care* in 1692 as a handbook for clergy in their parishes. Bishops regularly published their visitation charges, offering advice on pastoral strategies and care. Burnet persuaded Queen Anne to establish Queen Anne's Bounty, which, over time, improved clergy incomes significantly and reduced the financial necessity of holding benefices in plurality.

Most bishops were able men, many of them scholars, and experienced administrators, having been incumbents of large London or Westminster parishes, heads of university colleges, deans of cathedrals, or archdeacons. Although membership of the House of Lords required their presence in London from December to May annually, travel in the country in those months was in any case difficult, and they were kept in touch with diocesan affairs by their chancellors, archdeacons, secretaries, and chaplains. In their dioceses in the summer and autumn they conducted ordinations, and visitations and confirmations at major centres around their diocese, normally on a three-yearly cycle. All clergy and churchwardens, and anyone else holding a bishop's licence, including schoolmasters and midwives, were summoned to their local centre for the bishop's officials to check their letters of orders and licences against the registers, and to check parishes' inventories of land and church furnishings owned by the parish. Elderly and infirm bishops commissioned younger bishops to ordain and confirm on their behalf, and chancellors deputized for them at visitations.

In 1707 William Wake as bishop of Lincoln began to overhaul episcopal visitations, shifting the emphasis from a judicial process, requiring churchwardens to report on oath shortcomings in their parishes, to a more pastoral, supervisory model, requiring clergy to complete a questionnaire about their parishes. This enabled bishops to compile a compendium to inform themselves (and modern researchers) about parishes and to trace trends and changes over

---

[31] See, for example, *The Diary of Francis Evans, Secretary to Bishop Lloyd, 1699–1706*, ed. David Robertson, Worcestershire Historical Society (Oxford, 1903); Jeremy Gregory, 'Standards of Admission to the Ministry of the Church of England in the Eighteenth Century', in Theo Clemens and Wim Janse (eds.), *The Pastor Bonus: Papers read at the British–Dutch Colloquium at Utrecht, 18–21 September 2002*, Dutch Review of History 83 (Leiden, 2004), pp. 283–95.

time. They borrowed and adapted each other's questionnaires. When, following the example of Bishop Porteus of London in 1790, they issued them well before the visitation, asking clergy to return them in advance, they were able to speak knowledgeably in their visitation charges about their dioceses and to discuss current local issues, as well as comment on current theological debates.[32] Bishops might follow up with incumbents matters noted in questionnaire answers that caused them concern.[33] Visitations, during which a bishop stayed with the aristocracy and gentry, enabled him to familiarize himself with and be aware of current economic, social, and political issues in the diocese. They were also opportunities to meet clergy over dinner after the visitation and to be seen by churchwardens.

Bishops carefully checked the credentials of ordination candidates and of applicants for licences or institution to a living. They took seriously their responsibility for the spiritual welfare of their clergy and parishes, and the rights, privileges, and endowments of their office, not least for the benefit of their successors. Bishops seldom had many livings in their gift, and while often appointing family members or people they knew well, they did not risk their souls, or reputations, by appointing people they knew to be incompetent. Bishops themselves were sometimes pluralists, holding (with permission) *in commendam* a deanery, parish, or headship of a college, but only if the diocese's endowments were meagre, as with Bristol, Oxford, or Rochester, or because the legal fees for becoming a bishop and the costs of fitting up see houses, acquiring a coach, and paying staff involved considerable initial outlay before they began to receive the see's revenues.

Bishops took disciplinary action against clergy relatively rarely. Usually they endeavoured to resolve disputes or disciplinary matters informally by mutual consent. However, if an incumbent declined to admit an offence, it could be difficult. Bishops were reluctant to risk scandal by bringing an offender into the consistory court, or to bring shame and homelessness upon a married incumbent's family. Also legal expenses, which bishops had to bear themselves, might be enormous. Some cases dragged on for many years.[34]

---

[32] For example, *The Speculum of Archbishop Thomas Secker*, ed. Jeremy Gregory, Church of England Record Society 2 (Woodbridge, 1995); *The Diary of Henry Prescott, LL.B., Deputy Registrar of Chester Diocese*, vol. II: *1711–1719*, ed. John Addy and Peter McNiven, Record Society of Lancashire and Cheshire 132 (n.p., 1994); Smith (ed.), *Doing the Duty*.

[33] A. P. Jenkins (ed.), *The Correspondence of Thomas Secker, Bishop of Oxford 1737–58*, Oxfordshire Record Society 37 ([Oxford], 1991).

[34] Francis Knight, 'Ministering to the Ministers: The Disciplining of Recalcitrant Clergy in the Diocese of Lincoln, 1830–1845', in W. J. Sheils and Diana Wood (eds.), *The Ministry: Clerical and Lay*, Studies in Church History 26 (Oxford, 1989), pp. 357–66; R. B. Outhwaite, *Scandal in the Church: Dr Edward Drax Free 1764–1843* (London, 1997).

CLERGY

Clergy were well integrated into their local contexts.[35] Their role was to be pastors of their parishes, administering the sacraments, teaching by means of sermons and catechizing, and ensuring their parishioners lived godly lives in preparation for divine judgement. They were socially representative of a wide range of English society, mostly recruited from the sons of the urban trading and professional classes who, via local grammar schools (which provided a basic education in the classics) gained entry to university colleges, where they were educated alongside the lay elites. In both schools and colleges there was spiritual formation in terms of attendance at daily prayers and hearing weekly sermons. Classics, and mathematics at Cambridge, gave an intellectual foundation for studying divinity at postgraduate level. However, because of the expense of an extra two years' study for the MA degree, probably the majority of clergy studied divinity independently, often with an incumbent who took a number of ordination candidates to teach and provide experience in pastoral ministry. Some colleges had strong regional links, for example Devon, Lincolnshire, and northern grammar schools, with Exeter, Lincoln, and the Queen's Colleges, Oxford, respectively, and St John's and Caius and Corpus Christi Colleges, Cambridge, with Yorkshire and Norfolk respectively. Clergy often returned to be ordained in the region from which they came, so perhaps ensuring support networks amongst people with whom they had long-standing relationships, including the gentry. A significant proportion of clergy did not complete their degrees or (especially in the north) did not go to university but continued at grammar schools, where divinity was taught, sometimes supporting themselves by teaching. Bishops, at least from the later eighteenth century, offered syllabuses of reading for ordination candidates who did not go to or continue at university, which provided the basics for the examinations preceding ordination as deacon.[36] Clergy had to undertake further study and examination before being ordained priest.

Most clergy on being ordained as deacons undertook an apprenticeship with an experienced parish priest, as a curate. 'Curate' was an omnibus term, used to designate a 'perpetual curate' of a benefice, the tithes and glebe of which had been donated to a monastery prior to the Reformation to provide a priest to serve the parish, and which after the Reformation were acquired by a layperson who appointed a priest and paid him a salary from the income; and to describe a priest, often a neighbouring incumbent, who looked after a parish for a non-resident or infirm incumbent. To become an incumbent, a curate had to secure a patron to present him to a parish. Bishops, as we have noted, had little patronage; members of colleges, especially fellows, might be elected

---

[35] For clergy in this period, see Jacob, *Clerical Profession*.
[36] Slinn, 'Non-Graduate Entrants', pp. 192–252.

to a college living. Otherwise much patronage was, as we have noted, exercised by laypeople. Sometimes it took a long time for a curate, looking after an absentee incumbent's parish and always at risk from the incumbent deciding to take up residence or dying (when he would be given notice), to secure a living. Some clergy had a sense of being in limbo for many years, and others felt fobbed off by prospective patrons.[37]

Much clerical non-residence was because parishes lacked a parsonage house or sufficient endowments to build one, or because it was unsatisfactory, or because their wife disliked the isolation and loneliness of living in a village. Clergy often lived in nearby market towns within walking distance of their parishes, and visited them frequently. They could thus attend daily prayers in the town church, have the company of other clergy, and use the library, and they and their wives and daughters could participate in the social, literary, and musical activities of polite urban society.

Incumbents' incomes, derived from cultivating or renting out the glebe land with which the parish was endowed and collecting the money at which tithe was valued or from selling the produce collected in tithe, are difficult to estimate. However, contemporaries in the late seventeenth century reckoned that many livings were poor, placing clergy on the level of small farmers, although their outgoings, especially in terms of charitable support for parishioners, and social expectations were considerably higher. Over the eighteenth century grants from Queen Anne's Bounty gradually resulted in significantly improved incomes for clergy in the poorest livings. Agricultural improvement, especially when land was 'enclosed' in the later eighteenth and early nineteenth centuries, very significantly increased the incomes of clergy in some regions, notably Norfolk and Lincolnshire, which moved some clergy into the social range of minor gentry. Some rebuilt their parsonage houses on a grander scale, and adopted gentry lifestyles, and more sons of the gentry and aristocracy sought ordination.[38] In regions where this happened, clergy might become distanced and alienated from their communities.[39]

Clergy holding two (or occasionally more) livings in plurality could only live in one of them. This was no problem if parishes were near to one another, for they could easily serve both. If parishes were far apart, they employed a neighbouring incumbent to look after the parish as curate, as noted earlier. Sometimes they spent part of the year in each parish. This did not necessarily

[37] *The Journal of the Rev. William Bagshaw Stevens*, ed. Georgina Galbraith (Oxford, 1965), p. 27; *The Diary of the Revd William Jones, 1777–1821*, ed. O. F. Christie (London, 1929), pp. 83–4, 106.

[38] Jeremy Gregory, '"A Just and Sufficient Maintenance": Some Defences of the Clerical Establishment in the Eighteenth Century', in W. J. Sheils and Diana Wood (eds.), *The Church and Wealth*, Studies in Church History 24 (Oxford, 1987), pp. 321–32.

[39] Jacob, *Clerical Profession*, pp. 139–41; Robert Lee, *Rural Society and the Anglican Clergy 1815–1914* (Woodbridge, 2006), pp. 122–3.

imply that clergy were lax in looking after a parish, but it was an efficient means of ensuring that most clergy had sufficient income to support their families and meet their parishioners' expectations of charity.

There was no career structure for clergy: opportunities for preferment as a prebendary, dean, or archdeacon were few, so, unless they could secure a much better-endowed living, they often remained a lifetime in a parish. Moving was expensive. Legal fees for the necessary documentation were considerable, and much expenditure might be required on the new parsonage house, which they were responsible for providing and maintaining, and to improve the glebe land. This may account for clerical 'dynasties' in which sons who were ordained succeeded fathers, if patrons were cooperative. It also avoided the tragedy that befell clergy families if an incumbent died leaving a wife and children, and especially unmarried daughters, for they lost their income and home.[40] Charities for clergy widows and children were very necessary.

Clergy wives may have helped to bridge the gap between clergy and parishioners, and helped men to feel more comfortable with clergy, and less suspicious of their possible malign influence on their wives. Wives helped to integrate clergy with local society, providing a model of a well-regulated household; they may also have assisted in many aspects of pastoral ministry, and may have been soul-mates and supporters in what was often a rather isolated role.[41] Many 'blue stockings' were clergy daughters, notably Jane Austen. However, some wives may have seriously disadvantaged their husband's ministries, for example by declining to live in what they considered an unhealthy parish.

Bishops, as we have seen, encouraged clergy to be proactive in their pastoral ministries, regularly visiting people at home to exhort them to attend church, to receive communion, to teach their children and servants the catechism, to be charitable to the poor and needy, to reconcile themselves with those with whom they were in dispute, to admonish them for neglecting their duties towards God and their neighbours, and to pray for them in sickness and at death. The evidence as to how far they fulfilled these duties is limited, but diaries and letters suggest that some clergy performed some of them; perhaps most clergy performed most of them. Many clergy, especially in towns, formed religious societies for young men to meet for prayer, to learn to sing at church services, and to undertake charitable works; they also provided and taught in schools for poor children to learn the catechism and to read and sometimes to

[40] *Diary of William Jones*, ed. Christie, p. 106; Nigel Surry (ed.), 'Your affectionat and loving sister': The Correspondence of Barbara Kerrich and Elizabeth Postlethwaite, 1733–1751 (Guist, Norfolk, 2000), pp. 106–13.

[41] Jack Ayres (ed.), *Paupers and Pigkillers: The Diary of William Holland, a Somerset Parson, 1799–1810* (Gloucester, 1984), p. 282.

write and 'reckon'; distributed improving pamphlets to their parishioners and provided lending libraries and book clubs for parishioners; and established thrift clubs and savings banks.[42] In the later eighteenth century, with lay-people, they set up Sunday schools for children who had to work during the week to learn the catechism and to read.[43]

There is little evidence of complaints from laypeople about clerical indifference to their duties. Mostly clergy seem to have had good relationships at the parish level, but poorer parishioners may have been alienated from clergy as members of the propertied classes and employers. To what extent their involvement with local economies, cultivating their glebe and needing to know about local economic conditions in order to collect their tithe, helped or hindered their relationships with parishioners is unclear. Sometimes relationships with parishioners were tense, not merely in relation to tithe collection. Clerical diaries suggest that parishioners did not necessarily defer to clergy. Better-off tithe payers might get drunk at tithe dinners and behave badly towards the incumbent. People might be abusive towards clergy who did not do what they wanted, for example refusing to baptize a child at home, or not giving as much as was expected to a poor person.[44]

Bishops and laypeople had high expectations that clergy, assisted by the parish clerk, would conduct liturgy well; this included being audible and making sense of it. Singing was sometimes a bone of contention. From the 1730s bishops and clergy began to resist singers sitting together, especially in galleries, claiming that they monopolized music rather than leading it. Thomas Sherlock as bishop of Salisbury instructed his archdeacons to support clergy in suppressing anthem-singing, which resulted in numerous quarrels between clergy and singers. In Exeter diocese during the 1730s a standard clause was inserted in faculties for galleries barring their use by singers. From time to time, there could be major clashes between clergy and singers.[45]

Diaries suggest that people were unenthusiastic about attending services without a sermon. Preparing sermons was therefore an important clerical activity. Archbishop Tillotson's sermons provided a model, and in some cases the source, for very many sermons. Diary-keeping clergy record giving significant amounts of time to sermon preparation but, once prepared, surviving collections of manuscript sermons show that they were preached many times. Sometimes clergy indexed them for future use according to subject

[42] Jacob, *Clerical Profession*, pp. 173–267.   [43] Jacob, *Clerical Profession*, pp. 246–50.

[44] *Diary of a Country Parson: James Woodforde, 1758–1803*, ed. John Beresford, 5 vols. (Oxford, 1926–31), I, p. 212.

[45] Donald A. Spaeth, *The Church in an Age of Danger: Parsons and Parishioners 1660–1740* (Cambridge, 2000), pp. 235–40; Ken Baddeley, 'Trouble in the Gallery', in Christopher Turner (ed.), *Georgian Psalmody*, vol. I: *The Gallery Tradition* (Corby Glen, 1997), pp. 17, 24; *Journal of a Somerset Rector: John Skinner, A.M., Antiquary, 1772–1839*, ed. Howard Coombs and Arthur N. Bax (London, 1930), pp. 8, 15, 238.

matter and biblical texts. John Longe, vicar of Coddenham in Suffolk, listed thirty-seven sermons he wrote within two years of his ordination but thereafter he only added twenty-seven more to his catalogue in twenty-eight years, although he may also have used his father's sermons, which he inherited in 1806.[46] Clergy seem to have aimed to preach sermons that were accessible for their congregations and related to their personal and spiritual lives. Mostly clergy seem to have avoided preaching about current theological controversies. Even people involved in current theological controversies might not preach about them, but focused on their congregations' pastoral needs.

Church courts with jurisdiction over people's spiritual and moral behaviour (including marriage), as well as over clergy and maintenance of churches, continued to be active in many dioceses, and were much used by laypeople throughout the eighteenth and early nineteenth centuries. Their inquisitorial process assisted in resolving communally divisive conflicts and restoring peace in communities. Most cases were brought by laypeople against fellow laity, rather than representing the enforcement of ecclesiastical discipline. Women in particular used them to defend themselves against defamation, sexual slander, and gossip. In London their matrimonial jurisdiction was much in demand for granting judicial separations.[47] Surprisingly, perhaps, people were willing to accept the courts' severest penalty, public penance, to be performed in their parish church during Sunday morning service; this often achieved the reconciliation of a person with the community. In 1764 the vicar of St Mary's, Nottingham, noted that 'many publick penances' had been performed in his church. However, the vicar of Radcliffe-on-Trent commented that men seldom did penance for fornication or fathering a child out of wedlock, adding: 'I cannot tell why they are excused, or what it may cost them.'[48]

Maintaining peace in a parish was an important part of a clergyman's role, so that parishioners might live 'in love and charity' with one another. This, as well as their significantly improving incomes, may have been why in some counties during the second half of the eighteenth century clergy were nominated in large numbers to serve as magistrates. Surviving justices' notebooks recording their activities suggest that, whether sitting alone or in petty sessions, they were more concerned with resolving disputes between neighbours than punishing crimes. This may indicate that, until the rapid rise in the

---

[46] *The Diary of John Longe (1765–1834), Vicar of Coddenham*, ed. Michael Stone, Suffolk Records Society 51 (Woodbridge, 2008), p. 171.

[47] For ecclesiastical courts, see Anne Tarver, *Church Court Records: An Introduction for Family and Local Historians* (Chichester, 1995); Jacob, *Laypeople and Religion*, pp. 77–92; Susan Waddams, *Sexual Slander in the Nineteenth Century: Defamation in the Ecclesiastical Courts* (Toronto, 2000).

[48] Howard Fisher (ed.), *Church Life in Georgian Nottinghamshire: Archbishop Drummond's Parish Visitation Returns, 1764*, Thoroton Society of Nottinghamshire 46 ([Nottingham], 2012), pp. 125, 137.

crime rate after the Napoleonic Wars, being a magistrate was not obviously incompatible with the role of a priest.[49]

ANTI-CLERICALISM

After the teething troubles of re-establishing Anglicanism following the Restoration, especially in predominantly puritan areas and parishes, there is little evidence of anti-clericalism in England. There is plenty of evidence of antipathy towards individual clergy, and irritation, jealousy and sometimes animosity, and criticism, especially in relation to tithes, their supposed wealth and pluralism, their involvement in the magistracy, and over baptisms and burials, but little general hostility towards clergy.[50] Clergy were often satirized in public prints, but so were most public figures. Satirists conveyed amusement rather than condemnation.[51] There is little evidence of sustained intellectual attacks on Christianity in general or the Church and its clergy in particular.

There was a symbiotic relationship between clergy and laity, religiously in terms of a culture of faith and the mediation of divine grace, judgement, and forgiveness through the offices of the Prayer Book and pastoral words and care; and socially and economically through the close integration of clergy into the community and economies of their parishes. Inevitably there were tensions and conflicts of interest, for clergy, if they were effective, were by their calling and education slightly distanced from people of all sorts, but conflicts seldom seriously disrupted community life.

DISSENT

Memories of the 1640s and 1650s, when the religious world was turned upside down, deeply influenced the attitudes and mindsets of people throughout our period. In 1660 the restored king and his ministers and the restored bishops sought an inclusive Church and state, including everyone in the community

---

[49] W. M. Jacob, ' "...In love and charity with your neighbours": Ecclesiastical Courts and Justices of the Peace in England in the Eighteenth Century', in Kate Cooper and Jeremy Gregory (eds.), *Retribution, Repentance, and Reconciliation*, Studies in Church History 40 (Woodbridge, 2004), pp. 205–17.

[50] Spaeth, *Church in an Age of Danger*; Frances Knight, 'Did Anticlericalism Exist in the English Countryside in the Early Nineteenth Century?', in Nigel Aston and Matthew Cragoe (eds.), *Anticlericalism in Britain c.1500–1914* (Stroud, 2000), pp. 159–78.

[51] John Miller, *Religion in the Popular Prints 1600–1832* (Cambridge, 1986), pp. 45–8; Gatrell, *City of Laughter*, p. 144.

of citizens and faithful. While restored Anglicanism exercised a powerful attraction, especially among the gentry, it was not accepted by everyone. In many communities there were some who rejected episcopacy and the modestly revised Elizabethan Prayer Book of the restored Church as inadequately reformed, and so were considered 'Dissenters' from the Established Church. Because theological opinions informed political theories, and Dissenters' forebears had overturned the monarchy and the Church, their alternative meetings might be suspected of being subversive and potentially disloyal: in excluding themselves from the Church, they were excluded from rights of citizenship, and legislation was passed to encourage their conformity.

Dissenters included Roman Catholics, who were particularly suspect as fifth columnists of a hostile foreign power, France, especially after the flight there of James II in 1688. In the wake of Jacobite plots and the risings in 1715 and 1745 they were prosecuted. Their numbers were relatively small except in London and Lancashire, and there was often friendly social intercourse, between Roman Catholic and Anglican gentry at least, especially after the arrival of French émigrés in the 1790s.

Some Anglicans declined to swear allegiance to William and Mary, and later to George I, and as 'non-jurors' separated themselves to a greater or lesser extent from the Established Church. They too were regarded as politically suspect, although most attended their parish churches regularly. There was a significant undercurrent among Anglicans, especially in gentry and aristocratic circles, of Jacobite sympathies until after 1745, even though 'James III' was adamant about not becoming an Anglican.[52]

In the post-Restoration period Protestant Dissenters—imprecisely labelled as Presbyterians, Independents, or Baptists by their opponents—in strongly Puritan regions such as Wiltshire resisted the legislation to encourage them to conform to the restored Church and might be harshly dealt with, but most magistrates were reluctant to prosecute their neighbours, and the laws were only sporadically enforced.[53] After James II's flight in 1689, following further unsuccessful attempts to achieve a 'comprehension' including Trinitarian Protestant Dissenters, they were granted toleration of worship in their own licensed meeting-houses. To be legally married, all Dissenters, whether Roman Catholic or Protestant, had to be married in their parish church, and most were buried in the parish churchyard, in both cases according to the rites of the Church of England.

---

[52] Edward Gregg, 'The Exiled Stuarts: Martyrs for the Faith', in Michael Schaich (ed.), *Monarchy and Religion: The Transformation of Royal Culture in Eighteenth-Century Europe* (Oxford, 2007), p. 196.

[53] Spaeth, *Church in an Age of Danger*; George Southcombe, 'Dissent and the Restoration Church of England', in Grant Tapsell (ed.), *The Later Stuart Church 1660–1714* (Manchester, 2013), pp. 195–216.

Although perhaps only about 6.2 per cent of the population were Dissenters,[54] their regional concentrations—London, Essex, Wiltshire, Buckinghamshire, and Cumbria, especially in towns, where they often built large and splendid meeting-houses—made them seem numerous and threatening. Most Dissenters and their ministers, apart from some Quakers, were on good terms with incumbents, paying tithes and church rates, even renting a pew in the parish church and sometimes accepting election as churchwardens. High Churchmen, however, particularly disliked Dissenters attending their parish church as well as a meeting-house, claiming that they did so merely to qualify for civic offices, in which they would seek to undermine the Church. From time to time in the early eighteenth century, especially in towns, High Churchmen fomented popular riots against Dissenters, claiming that the 'Church was in danger'.[55] Quakers and Dissenters were, however, politically well organized through the Board of Dissenting Deputies; they monitored and lobbied against Anglican attempts at encroachment, notably in relation to the creation of a diocese in the North American colonies, and politicians were unwilling to alienate them.

'THE CHURCH IN DANGER'

Anxiety that the Church and state were 'in danger' permeated the period. The threat was perceived as emanating from Roman Catholics, Protestant Dissenters, freethinkers, atheists, and Socinians, and later from radicals and Revolutionary and Napoleonic France. These were seen as agents of divine punishment for the nation's evil ways, which were manifested in drunkenness, debauchery, licentiousness, profanity, Sabbath-breaking, and heterodox beliefs. In response the orthodox sought to ensure that the nation was right with God. As divine Providence had ensured the restoration of Church and king and saved the nation from judgement in the form of James II's suspected plans for absolutist and popish rule, so the nation must live worthily of this divine intervention. Three times a year the Prayer Book provided special liturgies— on the anniversaries of Charles I's execution and Charles II's restoration, and (on 5 November) of Parliament's preservation from Roman Catholic terrorists in 1605 and William III's landing which provoked James II's flight in 1688—as part of which sermons were required to remind people of their divine deliverance and to call them to respond by godly living. To ensure that people would live worthily, as we have seen, the bishops implemented administrative

---

[54] M. R. Watts, *The Dissenters: From the Reformation to the French Revolution* (Oxford, 1978), p. 270.

[55] Geoffrey Holmes, *The Trial of Doctor Sacheverell* (London, 1973).

reform in the Church, and they and leading laypeople sought to combat heterodoxy and reform the nation's morals. In successive theological controversies they sought to protect and defend the truth of the Church's teaching and to ensure that divine judgement would not again be provoked.[56]

Similarly, the (mostly lay) initiatives to 'reform manners' in the late seventeenth and early eighteenth centuries and to 'suppress vice' in the late eighteenth and early nineteenth centuries were intended to make England a worthy recipient of divine mercies. Societies for the Reformation of Manners (often sponsored by supporters of the SPCK and mostly in larger towns), which aimed to seek out and prosecute prostitutes and their customers, sodomites, gamblers, drunkards, and Sunday traders, were intended to remedy the shortcomings of the ecclesiastical courts in purifying the nation in response to God's providential intervention, and so to ensure that battles against the French would be won. William Wilberforce's Society for the Suppression of Vice, and numerous similar societies, were likewise intended to purify the nation as a fit instrument to resist godless Revolutionary and Napoleonic France. In thanksgiving in 1818 Parliament voted £1 million to build new churches in populous places lacking sufficient church accommodation.

THE EVANGELICAL REVIVAL

During the 1730s a number of (mostly High Church) clergy and laypeople independently experienced spontaneous personal conversion, which had the effect of 'renewing' their faith and leading them to want to share this experience with others for the renewal of the Church. The laity were often members of parish religious societies seeking a deeper and more intense experience of God than the communal expression of faith that parish churches offered, and to live more intensely Christian lives, over against what they regarded as the average churchperson's conventional faith and practice, and the lures of false teaching, especially 'Deism'. Many had met, or read the writings of, continental Protestant refugees from the forces of the Counter-Reformation, in particular Moravians, who had established communities in England and the North American colonies, and German Pietists, especially from the new university at Halle. Some people rediscovered puritan Calvinist authors of the previous century, while others, notably John Wesley, remained Arminians. Much emphasis was placed on separation from 'worldly' activities, which

---

[56] For example, Robert G. Ingram, '"The Clergy Who Affect to Call Themselves Orthodox": Thomas Secker and the Defence of Anglican Orthodoxy, 1758–68', in Kate Cooper and Jeremy Gregory (eds.), *Discipline and Diversity*, Studies in Church History 43 (Woodbridge, 2007), pp. 342–53.

often put the converted at odds with parish churches' involvement with communal celebrations; they frequently criticized unconverted clergy as worldly time-servers.

Some clergy who experienced evangelical renewal formed clerical societies, not based on deaneries as late seventeenth-century bishops had urged, but on common spiritual experiences, to support one another in developing evangelistic parochial ministries and renewing the Church. They preached to convert people, held 'cottage lectures' in people's homes to help them to know Christ personally, sought every opportunity to make pastoral and evangelistic contacts with people, visited the healthy as well as the sick, sought to protect their converts from the temptations surrounding them, and gathered groups from their congregations to deepen their spiritual lives. Some felt impelled to preach and establish groups or congregations in their unconverted neighbours' parishes. From the late 1730s some established 'circuits' for preaching, and societies, including Samuel Walker in Cornwall, the layman Benjamin Ingham in Yorkshire, William Grimshaw around Haworth, and John Berridge in Bedfordshire.

John Wesley and George Whitefield as unbeneficed clergy regarded all the British Isles and North American colonies as their evangelistic field, in which they sought to renew the Church, preaching to people they thought parish clergy were neglecting. This novel phenomenon of 'field preaching' in the open air attracted unprecedented numbers of people. They took over parish religious societies, and attracted young people who had learned to read and write at parish charity schools, and women, away from the communal and family solidarity of traditional expressions of religion. Their intensification of devotional life and the opportunities their meetings provided for singing new worship songs to new tunes, just when bishops were expressing alarm about singing groups in parish churches, aroused anxieties and suspicions. With his High Church sympathies, his societies, and his capacity to draw crowds, amidst the long-standing insecurity of the Hanoverian regime Wesley was suspected of being a Jacobite agent. Unsurprisingly, the perceived exclusiveness of the societies of Wesley and Whitefield and their followers' claims to spiritual superiority also aroused hostility, attracting the attention of mobs in the 1740s. The activities of Methodists and Evangelicals revived fears of the religious divisiveness of the previous century.

Evangelicals, especially with the patronage of the countess of Huntingdon, attracted numbers of the aristocracy and gentry and successful businessmen into their congregations and networks. By the end of the eighteenth century Evangelicals were well established in the universities and armed forces, and influenced social and political issues in Parliament, including the abolition of the slave trade and the drawing up of a new East India Company charter permitting missionary work in India. They also developed a network of clergy, recruiting, coaching, funding, and training ordination candidates. At the initiative of Charles Simeon, from the 1820s they established a trust to acquire patronage of parishes, providing livings for Evangelical clergy and ensuring a continuing Evangelical tradition in those parishes. This strategy, along with annual conferences for Evangelical clergy held at Islington parish church, contributed significantly to establishing Evangelicalism as the first coherent 'party' in the Church of England.

Until the 1790s Wesley's societies' coverage of England was varied. He made little headway in Lancashire, perhaps because of the significant Roman Catholic presence there, nor in Dorset, where Dissent was strong, nor in Norfolk. Membership of his societies fluctuated: members were rapidly gained and lost.[57] The evidence of visitation returns suggests most clergy did not regard his society members in their parishes as Dissenters: they often noted Methodists to be frequent attenders at Holy Communion and other church services. In some places there was very close interaction between Methodism and the parish church.[58] Even in the 1820s, after the great expansion of Wesleyan Methodism and its various breakaway groups, some Methodists continued to attend parish churches.

From the 1770s the Evangelical Revival began to influence 'old' Dissent—Baptists, Independents (later Congregationalists), and Presbyterians—but there is little evidence at the local level of animosity between church and chapel until the 1820s. In Lancashire there was considerable cooperation, at least between Evangelical parish churches and Dissenters.[59] In West Yorkshire the evidence suggests that chapels, whether Dissenting or Methodist, were only built where population growth had outstripped the available seating in churches, or where people felt Anglican pastoral care was inadequate. Chapels, it seems, provided additional foci for community.[60] The conflict model of local relations between the Church of England and Nonconformist churches only developed in the 1830s.

REFORM AND RENEWAL

From 1689 initiatives for change in the Church, such as the episcopal reinvigoration of processes for supervision and pastoral oversight of clergy and

---

[57] Robert Schofield, 'Methodist Spiritual Conditions in Georgian Northern England', *Journal of Ecclesiastical History*, 63 (2014): 780–802.

[58] David Wilson, 'Church and Chapel: Methodism as Church Extension', in Geordan Hammond and Peter Forsaith (eds.), *Religion, Gender, and Industry: Exploring Church and Methodism in a Local Setting* (Cambridge, 2011), pp. 53–76.

[59] Mark Smith, *Religion in Industrial Society: Oldham and Saddleworth, 1740–1845* (Oxford, 1994), pp. 227–41.

[60] Rycroft, 'Church, Chapel and Community', pp. 225–30.

parishes and the establishment of para-church bodies like the SPCK and SPG, were achieved without legislation. However, the increasing pace of change in society during the later eighteenth century, including population growth and the development of water- and steam-powered mills and factories requiring people to live close to sources of power and raw materials (especially iron and coal), mostly in previously under-populated areas, outflanked the Church's historic parochial pattern of pastoral care. Geographically extensive parishes in the West Midlands, Lancashire, Yorkshire, and the north-east acquired new settlements, remote from the parish church or chapel and from clergy ministrations. Mostly populated by factory or mill workers, people of the poorer sort, such settlements contributed to the emergence of a stratified, class society.

The rebellion in the North American colonies, encouraged by New England Congregationalists, echoed for many churchmen the evils of disorder experienced in the civil war. The ensuing defeat and the loss of the thirteen colonies provoked a crisis of confidence in Britain, with calls for spiritual and moral renewal and questions about the Church's response to the challenges of urban, industrial, and population growth. This coincided with growing Methodist independence, the Evangelical Revival's revitalization of Dissent, and the emergence of 'rational Dissent' associated with Joseph Priestley, mostly consisting of small but rich and highly articulate congregations. The identification of some Dissenters, especially Baptists, with radical politics in the 1790s as the French Revolution got underway, along with the perceived growth of Dissent, raised new alarms of 'the Church in danger'. The first public proposal for reform was Richard Watson's *Letter to the Archbishop of Canterbury* in 1783, which proposed equalizing the incomes of the bishops and appropriating those of deans and chapters to augment incomes of poor parishes. Legislative intervention in the Residence Act of 1802, responding to suspicions that clergy neglected their duties by not living in their parishes, required bishops to make annual returns about clergy residence to the Privy Council. More positively, in 1809 Spencer Perceval, the prime minister, secured a parliamentary grant of £100,000 to Queen Anne's Bounty, subsequently renewed annually, for grants to augment the endowments of poor livings so that poor clergy would only need one living to support them and their families.

In the 1790s and 1800s, while the population grew, numbers of ordination candidates declined, from 3,360 in the 1780s to 2,921 in the 1790s and 2,381 in the 1800s, recovering to 3,488 in the 1810s.[61] From the 1770s bishops had renewed their efforts to improve the educational standards of ordination candidates by issuing reading lists for those only having Bachelor's degrees, and by seeking to improve educational provision for non-graduate candidates

---

[61] Slinn, 'Non-Graduate Entrants', p. 41.

through the approval of some grammar schools for training clergy, for example St Bees, Bampton, and Ravenstonedale in Chester diocese. This may have contributed to the decline in numbers of ordination candidates. In 1817 Bishop Law of Chester established a college for non-graduate candidates at St Bees in Cumbria. Some bishops in the 1820s attempted to adopt a policy of only accepting graduates for ordination, perhaps reflecting the universities' increase in recruitment in the 1810s, but recruitment of graduates failed to keep pace with population growth.[62]

Laypeople responded with initiatives similar to those of a century before, by establishing new voluntary bodies and seeking to reinvigorate the Church's infrastructure. The challenge of providing elementary education for working children in an industrializing society was met by establishing Sunday schools, which taught the catechism and reading and writing. Anxieties about responding to the moral state of the nation were focused by the initiative of William Wilberforce and Bishop Porteus of London to secure in 1787 a Royal Proclamation for the Encouragement of Piety and Virtue, and for the Preventing and Punishing of Vice, Profaneness and Immorality, to be read in churches four times a year. It resulted in numerous local societies to suppress crime and immorality, and (in 1803) in the Society for the Suppression of Vice.

Amongst Evangelicals Wilberforce and Hannah More were pre-eminent. Wilberforce became almost the conscience of the nation, leading the campaigns against immorality and vice, and for the abolition of slavery. His extensively read *A practical view of the prevailing religious system of professed Christians in the higher and middle classes of this country contrasted with real Christianity* became the Evangelical movement's manifesto. Hannah More's publications about education, especially for women, and her extensive writing about popular morality in the Cheap Repository Tracts made her a household name. Their influence and that of other rich and aristocratic Evangelicals penetrated much of early nineteenth-century social and political life.[63] Such Evangelicals established the Church Missionary Society and ensured that it became possible for missionaries to work in India.

There was a similar pattern of influence amongst High Churchmen. William Stevens, a wealthy London businessman, wrote widely read popular theological books and applied his business acumen to managing leading Church societies, including the Society for the Relief of Poor Widows and Children of Clergymen, the Corporation of the Sons of the Clergy, the SPG, and Queen Anne's Bounty. An informal ginger group of High Churchmen emerged, known as the Hackney Phalanx. They included Joshua Watson, a wealthy London wine merchant and friend of Stevens; lawyers, including John

---

[62] Slinn, 'Non-Graduate Entrants', pp. 117–64.

[63] See John Wolffe, 'The Clapham Sect (act. 1792–1815)'; S. J. Skedd, 'More, Hannah (1745–1833)'; John Wolffe, 'Wilberforce, William (1759–1833)', all *ODNB*.

Richardson and James Park; and a number of clergy. These included James Watson, who became Archbishop Manners-Sutton's key adviser; Henry Handley Norris, who was chief adviser on patronage to the earl of Liverpool (prime minister from 1812 until 1827); William Van Mildert, subsequently bishop of Durham; and Christopher Wordsworth, subsequently master of Trinity College, Cambridge.

In 1811 they established the National Society for Promoting the Education of the Poor in the Principles of the Established Church, to coordinate initiatives, in partnership with parishes, for day schools to teach children of the poor the catechism, reading and writing, and good Anglican citizenship. Watson masterminded the Society's highly successful fundraising, and reinvigorated the SPCK to produce reading material for newly literate children. Rivingtons, the High Church publishers, produced books and the *British Critic* for the middling and better sorts. Watson transformed the administration of Queen Anne's Bounty, and turned the SPG into a highly effective missionary agency.[64]

The Hackney Phalanx had close links with Lord Liverpool's ministries, and secured the appointment of a succession of reforming High Church bishops, as well as lobbying the government to create and fund new dioceses in India, Canada, and Australia, to which they secured the appointment of competent High Churchmen. Watson was largely instrumental in founding the Church Building Society in 1817 to build new churches in populous parishes, and influenced Lord Liverpool to set up the Church Building Commission in 1818 with a parliamentary grant of £1 million and a supplementary grant of £500,000 in 1824. Further large sums were raised by Watson from voluntary sources over the next twenty years for church building in London. They encouraged the establishment of diocesan auxiliary committees to raise local funds for all these societies. By 1833 over two hundred new churches had been built by the Commission and an estimated £6 million had been spent on building and renovating churches.[65] Phalanx members were prominent in the foundations of King's College London and Durham University. Oxford and Cambridge also experienced a revival, and revised their teaching and examination systems; as we have noted, their recruitment revived.

Bishops appointed under the Phalanx's influence reviewed their diocesan administration. When John Fisher moved from Exeter to Salisbury in 1811 he revived the office of rural dean, which had continued in Exeter throughout the

---

[64] Robert M. Andrews, *Lay Activism and the High Church Movement of the Late Eighteenth Century: The Life and Thought of William Stevens 1732-1807* (Leiden, 2015); Mark Smith, 'Hackney Phalanx (act. 1800-1830)', *ODNB*; Peter B. Nockles, 'Watson, Joshua (1771-1855)', *ODNB*; A. B. Webster, *Joshua Watson: The Story of a Layman 1771-1855* (London, 1954); Colin Podmore, *Aspects of Anglican Identity* (London, 2005).

[65] J. H. Overton, *The English Church in the Nineteenth Century, 1800-1833* (London, 1894), p. 153; M. H. Port, *Six Hundred New Churches: A Study of the Church Building Commission, 1818-1856, and its Church Building Activities* (London, 1961).

eighteenth century, to support and monitor clergy on behalf of the bishop and archdeacons. Other bishops followed this example and Porteus's example of issuing visitation questionnaires well in advance to gather statistics about changes in their dioceses. In some dioceses archidiaconal visitations had been neglected in the late eighteenth and early nineteenth centuries, but were revived in the 1820s.[66]

Parochial ministry was in many places revitalized, especially in response to the distress of the poor in the face of rising food prices during the French Revolutionary and Napoleonic Wars. Henry Ryder, the Evangelical vicar of Lutterworth, provided free soup for 160 poor families every Friday, and organized a subscription to buy in large quantities of bacon and rice to sell at a discount to the poor.[67] High Churchmen adopted many Evangelical pastoral strategies.

The new energy in the Church after 1815 was paralleled by a rapid growth in Dissenting and Methodist congregations. A new radicalism emerged amongst some Dissenters, focused on what was regarded as 'old corruption', calling for probity, frugality, economy, and financial rectitude in the Church, drawing attention to allegedly rich and idle bishops, dignitaries, and clergy, compared with poor and hardworking incumbents and curates. A focus of such suspicions and attacks was the attempts by the dean and chapter of Durham to secure the full value of the tithe on lead due from rich quarry owners. *The Times* and the *Edinburgh Review* publicized these attacks, provoking some clergy to formidable defences of their rights. Dissenters in some towns resisted paying church rates towards building or repairing churches.

The agitation in 1828 for the repeal of the Test and Corporation Acts, to place Dissenters on an equal footing as citizens with Anglicans, seems to have arisen suddenly, but High Church Tory politicians did not regard their repeal as contentious, or as a threat to the Church. However, their repeal paved the way for Roman Catholic emancipation in 1829, which was strongly opposed by conservative clergy and laymen. The relative ease with which this legislation passed through Parliament aroused anxieties among churchmen that the sense of England as a 'confessional state' was disappearing and that Parliament could no longer be relied on to assist in reinvigorating the Church, for the House of Commons was no longer a lay Anglican assembly, and Dissenters could influence ecclesiastical legislation.[68] This provoked new fears amongst High Church clergy and laity of 'the Church in danger' from parliamentary

---

[66] Arthur Burns, *The Diocesan Revival in the Church of England, c.1800–1870* (Oxford, 1999), pp. 76–91.

[67] Henry Ryder, 'A Charge Delivered to the Clergy of the Diocese of Gloucester in the Year 1816', ed. Mark Smith, in Mark Smith and Stephen Taylor (eds.), *Evangelicalism in the Church of England, c.1790–1900*, Church of England Record Society 12 (Woodbridge, 2004), p. 56.

[68] Boyd Hilton, *A Mad, Bad and Dangerous People? England 1783–1846* (Oxford 2006), p. 390.

'interference' in the Church led by Protestant Dissenters and Roman Catholics, which would be ignited in the 1830s.

Much had been achieved by the Church to keep pace with social changes, but the still-medieval administrative structure and financial arrangements of the Church required radical legislative intervention to equip it to minister in a changing society. However, with a House of Commons that was no longer strictly Anglican, and increasing Nonconformist hostility and a new and a divisive party spirit within the Church, troubled waters lay ahead.

SELECT BIBLIOGRAPHY

Elliott-Binns, L. E., *The Early Evangelicals: A Religious and Social Study* (London, 1953).

Gregory, Jeremy, *Restoration, Reformation and Reform 1660–1828: Archbishops of Canterbury and their Diocese* (Oxford, 2000).

Gregory, Jeremy and Jeffrey S. Chamberlain (eds.), *The National Church in Local Perspective: The Church of England and the Regions, 1660–1800* (Woodbridge, 2003).

Jacob, W. M., *The Clerical Profession in the Long Eighteenth Century, 1680–1840* (Oxford, 2007).

Jacob, W. M., *Laypeople and Religion in the Early Eighteenth Century* (Cambridge, 1996).

Smith, Mark, 'The Hanoverian Parish: Towards a New Agenda', *Past & Present*, 216 (2012): 79–105.

Smith, Mark, *Religion in Industrial Society: Oldham and Saddleworth, 1740–1865* (Oxford, 1994).

Snape, M. F., *The Church in Industrialising Society: The Lancashire Parish of Whalley in the Eighteenth Century* (Woodbridge, 2003).

Spaeth, Donald A., *The Church in an Age of Danger: Parsons and Parishioners 1660–1740* (Cambridge, 2000).

Tapsell, Grant (ed.), *The Later Stuart Church, 1660–1714* (Manchester, 2012).

Walsh, John, Colin Haydon, and Stephen Taylor (eds.), *The Church of England c.1689–c.1833: From Toleration to Tractarianism* (Cambridge, 1993).

6

Wales

Paula Yates

History, it is said, is written by the victors, and in Wales the winner of the religio-political wars of the nineteenth and early twentieth century was non-conformity. As a consequence, the developing historiography of post-Reformation Christianity in Wales presented it very largely from a point of view hostile to Anglicanism. Attitudes to Anglicanism in Wales were also coloured from the second quarter of the nineteenth century by a developing Welsh nationalism, strongly linked to chapel culture, which by the time of the final battles for disestablishment early in the twentieth century had decisively identified Anglicanism in Wales as an 'alien Church', a phrase which was widely used in the run-up to disestablishment, to the anguish of Anglican leaders.[1] According to this narrative, the Welsh Anglican Church before disestablishment was an organ of English imperialism, which sought to impose English culture and the English language on a conquered nation. Although the language in which this narrative is perpetuated has been greatly softened by the influence of ecumenism and secularization, it still has power, especially in those parts of Wales where Welsh culture and language is strongest. Compared with nonconformity, Anglicanism in Wales has attracted little attention from historians until recently and the revisionist historiography which has, to some extent at least, rehabilitated the eighteenth-century Church of England is only beginning to be applied to the Established Church in Wales.[2]

---

[1] For example, T. J. Jones (of Gelligaer), *The Church in Wales not Alien: A Reply to Mr J. W. Willis Bund* (Cardiff, 1906).

[2] Significant contributions to the development of a more balanced view of Anglicanism in Wales have been made by authors such as Eryn White, in, for example, 'The Established Church, Dissent and the Welsh Language, *c.*1660–1811', in Geraint Jenkins (ed.), *The Welsh Language before the Industrial Revolution* (Cardiff, 1997), pp. 235–87; David Ceri Jones, *A Glorious Work in the World: Welsh Methodism and the International Evangelical Revival 1735–1750* (Cardiff, 2004). A broader revisionist discussion can be found in Glanmor Williams, William Jacob, Nigel Yates, and Frances Knight, *The Welsh Church from Reformation to Disestablishment, 1603–1920* (Cardiff, 2007).

In this short chapter it is not possible to write a comprehensive history of Anglicanism in Wales during the century and a half covered by this volume. Instead, the chapter focuses particularly on those aspects of Anglicanism where our modern understanding has been most clearly shaped by Nonconformist and nationalist agendas in the nineteenth and twentieth centuries. It will consider particularly Welsh Anglicanism's identity in relation to England and what, if anything, distinguished Anglicanism in Wales from that in England. It will discuss the Welsh Church's relationship to Wales, to the Welsh language, and to Dissent. It will maintain that, far from being 'alien', the Church of England in Wales was solidly indigenous, as far as the vast majority of both clergy and laypeople were concerned, throughout this period. It will trace the tendency, as the eighteenth century progressed, of Welsh Anglican gentry families to pursue upward mobility by sending their sons to English schools and spending more time and effort engaging with the English establishment; and it will discuss how that process contributed to anti-establishment feeling towards the end of the century. It will assert the interconnectedness of radical politics, the second Evangelical Revival from the 1780s, and the early stirrings of Welsh nationalism, and it will suggest that by the end of our period the process was irrevocably under way which would rob Welsh Anglicanism of its Welsh identity from the 1840s.

WELSH DISTINCTIVENESS

In many ways it is impossible to separate Wales from England in our period, whether politically, ecclesiastically, or legally. It was not until the last quarter of the nineteenth century that the first separate legislation (the Welsh Sunday Closing Act of 1881) was enacted, reflecting the developing pressure at that time to see Wales as having an identity, or identities, which differed from England's. Ecclesiastically, the Welsh dioceses were part of the province of Canterbury and the borders of the dioceses of St Davids and St Asaph crossed political boundaries to include parts of Herefordshire and Shropshire. In terms of law, England and Wales had shared the same legal system since the second quarter of the sixteenth century although it was not until a tidying up exercise in 1746 that Wales, together with Berwick-upon-Tweed, was formally defined in the Wales and Berwick Act as being included in the term 'England'.

Nevertheless, Wales did have its own individuality, though this was in no sense nationalistic or separatist but rather historic. The Welsh were proud of their Celtic past and, as we shall see, this period saw a great reawakening of interest in that past. Wales had its own language, though without the nationalist connotations that it has today, and it had its own particular characteristics. Chief amongst these was its poverty, both socially and ecclesiastically. Until the later part of our period the economy of Wales was very largely rural, with only a limited amount of industry, centring mainly on the small-scale exploitation of mineral resources. Patterns of settlement were still largely based on the medieval *tref* or farmstead system, rather than on the usual English clustering in villages. Towns were very small and few and far between. By the middle of the eighteenth century, Wrexham was the largest town in Wales, with a population of fewer than seven thousand.[3] Consequently, Welsh society was fairly polarized between the noble and gentry families on the one hand and the poor on the other, with very few of the middling sorts who increasingly influenced the rather more urban English society in the eighteenth century. Of course this picture changed dramatically, and very rapidly, in parts of Wales, mainly the south-east, towards the end of the period, with the coming of the Industrial Revolution, but for most of Wales it remained much the same throughout the long eighteenth century. The incumbent of Llanfawr, Merionethshire, in 1818 differed only in degree from many of his fellow clergy when he reported that the parish was 'in so ruinous a state, it would be necessary to feed and clothe the children before they could attend school and they at present live by begging'.[4] Very similar accounts are to be found in reports from across Wales.

Ecclesiastically, at least in the early part of the period, both dioceses and parishes in Wales were among the poorest in the country. In the course of the century the two northern dioceses of St Asaph and Bangor received augmentations to the episcopal income which moved them into the mid-range of dioceses,[5] but the two southern dioceses of St Davids and Llandaff remained very poor. Even into the 1820s Llandaff had no episcopal residence and its bishop, Edward Copleston, was said to spend more than the income of the diocese just on donations and subscriptions as part of his episcopal costs. It is perhaps not surprising that Welsh clerics, even from gentry families, could hardly afford to be bishops in south Wales and most southern bishops chose to move on when another diocese was offered. Parish incomes were similarly low. In 1736, 83.9 per cent of parishes in Llandaff diocese and 91.5 per cent in St Davids were officially classed as impoverished, being worth less than £50. In that year 22.5 per cent of parishes in Llandaff and 37.8 per cent in St Davids were worth less than £10. Comparable figures for the northern dioceses were 13.7 per cent of parishes in Bangor worth less than £10 and 49.7 per cent worth less than £50, with 9.9 per cent of parishes in St Asaph worth less than

---

[3] Williams et al., *Welsh Church*, p. 69.

[4] Parliamentary Papers 1819, IX, *Digest of Parochial Returns made to the Select Committee inquiring into the Education of the Poor, 1818* (London, 1819–21), p. 1242.

[5] D. R. Hirschberg, 'Episcopal Incomes and Expenses 1660–*c*.1760', in Rosemary O'Day and Felicity Heal (eds.), *Princes and Paupers in the English Church 1500–1800* (Leicester, 1981), pp. 211–30 (pp. 213–16).

£10 and 67.9 per cent worth less than £50.[6] Many clergy, especially in the south, were of relatively humble origins and could not afford to attend university. Instead, they were educated in grammar schools, or Dissenting academies, which provided well-regarded education and were not viewed with suspicion until towards the end of the eighteenth century. This strengthened the affinity of these clergy with their congregations, though it lowered their reputation with their English and better educated brethren.

All this affected Welsh relations with the rest of the country in two important ways. Firstly, it meant that many people of ability left Wales to pursue careers in England and maintained their Welsh identity in doing so, creating significant Welsh populations in English cities, particularly London, where various Welsh Societies provided leadership both for charitable giving to Wales and for some influential cultural developments, such as *eisteddfodau*, of which more later. Secondly, the inhabitants of Wales were seen by their wealthier compatriots as being in need of both physical and (especially) spiritual nourishment. As in other remote parts of the country, the Welsh enjoyed a number of medieval religious survivals, which were seen as super-stitious. These included visits to holy wells and other places, vigils for the dead, and celebrations associated with religious festivals. The Evangelical leaders of the 1730s preached against these but there is some evidence that their prede-cessors, both clerical and lay, had been prepared to tolerate them and even to participate.[7] Anglican leaders were less tolerant of *mabsantau* (wakes, patron-al festivals) and *anterliwtau* (interludes, quasi-theatrical performances), many of which were seen as threatening public morality. Whether because of the preaching or for more complex social reasons, these traditions were dying out in the 1730s, but William Bulkely of Brynddu could still note in his diary entry for 27 July 1740 that the church was very poorly attended 'occasioned by the old superstition of persons of all sexes and ages going to Llaneilian to visit an old dry skull, scrapeing of an old stone, and playing other Jugling tricks'.[8] These customs were often seen as a product of ignorance, and initiatives to bring religious education to the Welsh poor are a repeated feature of this period, frequently led by Welsh Anglican clerics and the wealthier laypeople, and using Anglican networks, especially in England, to raise the necessary funding. The nature of these initiatives was strongly affected by attitudes to Dissent as they developed through the century. There was a good deal of cooperation between denominations in the early part of the period but an

---

[6] Ian Green, 'The First Years of Queen Anne's Bounty', in O'Day and Heal (eds.), *Princes and Paupers*, pp. 231–54 (pp. 243–4).

[7] G. Nesta Evans, *Religion and Politics in Mid-Eighteenth-Century Anglesey* (Cardiff, 1953), pp. 28–35.

[8] Evans, *Religion and Politics*, p. 57.

increasing tendency from the end of the eighteenth century, especially in the somewhat wealthier north, for Anglican and Dissenting schools to be a focus for denominational competition.

EFFECTS OF THE RESTORATION AND
THE GLORIOUS REVOLUTION ON WALES

The relatively low levels of Dissent in Wales after the Restoration may well have contributed to generally peaceful relations between Dissenters and the Established Church. Some at least of those who felt themselves driven into Dissent at the Restoration held beliefs not hugely different from some of their Anglican counterparts.[9] There was some persecution of Quakers in St Asaph diocese in the 1660s, and Dissent was disapproved of by bishops. In practice, however, there was generally little active hostility between Anglicans and Dissenters, except in times of political uncertainty, until the latter decades of the eighteenth century, when the situation changed significantly. Jacob points out that in practice it was not always easy to distinguish Dissenters clearly because of the practice of attending both the Dissenting meeting-house and the parish church. This practice, and the spirit of cooperation which attended it, extended to cases of Dissenters preaching in parish churches, though it is not clear how common that was.[10]

The charitable attitudes to Wales both of the English and of the Welsh expatriate community in England were largely free, at least until the final decades of the eighteenth century, from the political complexity of similar attitudes to Ireland and to the rural, highland areas of Scotland. As well as having a different political relationship to England from other Celtic areas, Wales was crucially free, unlike Ireland and the Jacobite Highlands, from any suspicions of harbouring Roman Catholicism. With only one or two exceptions, the Welsh gentry were securely Protestant and indeed securely Anglican. This meant that the use of the Welsh language was not seen by the authorities as a cover for political dissent and it was allowed to flourish. This contrasted strongly with similar initiatives in Ireland and the Gaelic-speaking areas of Scotland, where the indigenous language was firmly, though not always successfully, suppressed.[11]

---

[9] D. Densil Morgan, *Wales and the Word: Historical Perspectives on Welsh Identity and Religion* (Cardiff, 2008), p. 96.

[10] Williams et al., *Welsh Church*, pp. 71–2.

[11] Paula Yates, 'The Established Church and Rural Elementary Schooling: The Welsh Dioceses 1780–1830', PhD thesis, University of Wales, Lampeter, 2007, pp. 57–61.

Acceptance of the Welsh language was reinforced by the fact that, in the somewhat anxious period following the Restoration of the monarchy and the reinstatement of the Established Church, appointees to Welsh parishes were predominantly Welsh, and Welsh-speaking.[12] Guy sees this as a deliberate policy 'in an endeavour to re-establish the Church of England in the affections of the people'.[13] It may, however, have had a detrimental effect on the intellectual quality of some of the clergy. Although Jesus College, Oxford, was set up by Queen Elizabeth and liberally endowed by Hugh Price of Brecon, to educate Welsh clergy, it was the case that, particularly in the poorest areas of the south, candidates for ordained ministry were drawn mainly from farming families who could not afford to send their sons to university without the financial support of a charity or benefactor. Bishop Lloyd of St Asaph (bishop 1680–92) defended the practice of ordaining those with no university degree on the grounds of limited choice: 'as most of the people understand nothing but Welsh, we cannot supply the cures with other than Welshmen'.[14]

This expectation that parochial clergy would be Welsh, and Welsh-speaking where that was needed, continued throughout our period. Although only English bishops were appointed to Welsh sees between 1727 and 1870, they were keen to ensure that Welsh-language services were provided in Welsh-speaking areas and frowned on the use of English in services out of deference to a few prominent families. In 1710 Bishop Fleetwood of St Asaph pointed out the foolishness of doing so, as these families 'understand the British [i.e. Welsh] perfectly well, as being their native tongue'.[15] It was recognized that books of religion and devotion had to be made available in Welsh, and many were translated from the English, frequently by Welsh Anglican clergy.[16] In 1814 Bishop Majendie of Bangor used his charge to recommend three such books to his clergy, all recently written in, or translated into, Welsh by clerics in the diocese.[17] The books, he said, would 'form a very useful addition to the few printed Welsh books now remaining'. One was a book of original sermons 'on the nature and benefit of Prayer, in general, and more especially of the Liturgy of our Church', by John Jones, archdeacon of Merioneth, who was a founder member and secretary of a group of clergy in the diocese of Bangor

---

[12] See especially John R. Guy, 'The Significance of Indigenous Clergy in the Welsh Church at the Restoration', in Stuart Mews (ed.), *Religion and National Identity*, Studies in Church History 18 (Oxford, 1982), pp. 335–44.

[13] Guy, 'The Significance of Indigenous Clergy', p. 342.

[14] A. Tindal Hart, *William Lloyd 1627–1717: Bishop, Politician, Author and Prophet* (London, 1952), p. 64.

[15] William Fleetwood, *The Bishop of St Asaph's Charge to the Clergy of that Diocese in 1710* (London, 1712), p. 12.

[16] White, 'The Established Church, Dissent and the Welsh Language', p. 245.

[17] Henry William Majendie, *A Charge to the Clergy of the diocese of Bangor, in the month of August, 1814* (Chester, 1814), p. 29.

that published tracts in Welsh.[18] Apart from Jones's book of sermons, the others were 'a volume of sermons part original and part translated, from approved English Divines, for the use of the pulpit' by the Revd Dr Williams, prebendary of Penmynydd and rector of Llanbedrog, and a volume of translated 'discourses' by the Revd R. Lloyd, rector of Llanegrad with Llanallgo.

Whether because of the Welsh character of the clergy and services or for some other reason, the Restoration of the Established Church seems to have been relatively easy in Wales. There was a smattering of Dissenting congregations and a number of eminent Dissenting ministers, some of whom founded very successful Dissenting academies. In many cases these provided an education to rival any provided by Anglican grammar or free schools in Wales; some Anglican clergy for the poorer parts of Wales continued to be educated in them until the early nineteenth century, when episcopal efforts to tighten up, faced with growing denominational divides, included limiting the schools from which ordinands could be drawn and (finally) founding St Davids College, Lampeter, in 1822. Nevertheless, Dissenters were not numerous in Wales (about 6 per cent of the population) until the last quarter of the eighteenth century, a significantly lower percentage of the population than was the case for England and Wales as a whole.[19]

The perceived freedom of Wales from dangerous political dissent survived the uncertainties of the Glorious Revolution of 1688–9, despite the fact that Wales was known to harbour Jacobite sympathizers. Popular royalism in Wales was manifested between about 1709 and 1715 in demonstrations and occasional attacks on Dissenting meeting-houses.[20] A number of gentry families, and some larger magnates, were indeed loyal to the Stuarts, but they were saved from the strongest accusations of disloyalty because their sympathy was on royalist rather than religious grounds and was more theoretical than practical.[21] Jacobitism was strongest in the north-east of Wales, where the Circle of the White Rose was founded in 1710 by a number of local worthies, including Sir Watkin Williams-Wynn of Wynnstay.[22] Although

---

[18] T. I. Ellis, 'John Jones (1775–1834)', *Dictionary of Welsh Biography*, <http://yba.llgc.org.uk/en/s-JONE-JOH-1775.html>, accessed 5 Aug. 2016.

[19] Geraint Jenkins, 'The Established Church and Dissent in Eighteenth-Century Cardiganshire', in Geraint Jenkins and Ieuan Gwynedd Jones (eds.), *Cardiganshire County History*, vol. III: *Cardiganshire in Modern Times* (Cardiff, 1998), pp. 453–77; Geraint Jenkins, *Protestant Dissenters in Wales, 1639–1689* (Cardiff, 1992), p. 52; Geraint Jenkins, *The Foundations of Modern Wales 1642–1780* (Oxford, 1993), pp. 381–4; Philip Jenkins, 'Church, Nation and Language: The Welsh Church, 1660–1800', in Jeremy Gregory and Jeffrey S. Chamberlain (eds.), *The National Church in Local Perspective: The Church of England and the Regions, 1660–1800* (Woodbridge, 2003), pp. 265–84 (pp. 269–71).

[20] Jenkins, 'Church, Nation and Language', p. 275.

[21] Craig D. Wood, 'The Welsh Response to the Glorious Revolution of 1688', *Journal of Welsh Religious History*, new series, 1 (2001): 21–39 (p. 24).

[22] Wood, 'The Welsh Response to the Glorious Revolution of 1688', p. 22.

Williams-Wynn corresponded regularly with members of the Stuart cause in France, neither he nor any other Welsh royalist lent concrete support to either of the Jacobite uprisings.

THE EVANGELICAL REVIVAL OF THE 1730s

The great Evangelical or Pietist movement which swept across Protestant Europe from the 1720s began to influence Wales at about the same time as it was influencing the Wesleys and others in the rest of the country. By contrast with English Methodism, in Wales it settled into a predominantly Calvinist form. As in other parts of the country it had earlier roots. There were already those who showed some of the characteristics which we would now categorize as Evangelical but who did not necessarily identify themselves with the Methodists. Griffith Jones, rector of Llanddowror, was one such. As a young man he had considered missionary work in India but stayed instead to work, first with the Society for the Promotion of Christian Knowledge (SPCK) and later through his own networks, to bring the gospel to the ignorant in his own country. He sparred with his bishop over his willingness to preach outside his own parish and in the open air but he found the extremes of Methodism unnecessary and irritating. Though a father figure to the early Methodist leaders, Jones felt that they risked alienating the largely Anglican sources of funding for his Welsh circulating schools, by means of which he hoped to bring the Bible, the catechism, and the Book of Common Prayer to the people of Wales. Tradition has it that Daniel Rowland was converted in 1735 while listening to Griffith Jones's preaching, and Howel Harris sought advice from Jones on many occasions. Rowland and Harris, one clerical and one lay, were probably the two most important of the early leaders of Welsh Methodism, along with others, particularly William Williams, Pantycelyn, named in the Welsh fashion from the name of his farm at Llanfair-ar-y-Bryn, near Llandovery, whose hymns drove the revival forward. Rowland and Harris were very different personalities and their relationship was never easy. They fell out finally in 1752 over doctrine, differences of style, and the potential for scandal of Harris's behaviour with Madame Sydney Griffith.

David Ceri Jones has demonstrated that the Great Awakening in Wales must be understood as part of a strongly international Evangelical movement.[23] It must also be understood, in Wales as in England, primarily as a reform movement within Anglicanism. Its prominent figures were mainly Anglican clergy, though a number of gentry families joined the societies and the

[23] Jones, *Glorious Work.*

movement also had some support from aristocratic families like that of Sir John Phillips of Picton Castle, who was a friend of the Wesleys. Harris chose Anglican clergy as leaders when he organized his followers into societies. They were identified by non-Methodists within the Anglican Church as Anglicans, though with a particular set of views and habits. There seem to have been initial interactions between Harris and some Dissenting groups,[24] but generally the Evangelical Revival of the first half of the century had little influence on the older Dissenting congregations in Wales.

With few exceptions the Dissenting congregations of Wales, mainly *Annibynwyr* (Independents) but also including Baptists and Quakers, were not drawn to the emotionalism of the Evangelical Revival. The independent Philip Pugh did not approve of the preaching style of Daniel Rowland and warned him to

> Apply the Balm of Gilead, the Blood of Christ, to their spiritual wounds... If you go on preaching the law in this manner you will kill half the people in the country, for you thunder out the curses of the law, and preach in such a terrific manner that no one can stand before you.[25]

The fact that the Great Awakening had had only limited impact probably helped to perpetuate the identification of Methodism as 'a renewal movement within the established church; spiritually renewing it rather than constitutionally reforming it'.[26] In Cardiganshire, where Methodism was strong, very few clerics identified Methodists as Dissenters in the visitation returns of 1799, and only seven Methodist meeting-houses had been registered as Dissenting chapels by 1811.[27] Attitudes in north Wales were rather different by the end of the century, as will be seen.

By mid-century, therefore, Anglicanism in Wales was leading a fairly peaceful existence. The Jacobite rebellions had passed Wales by and left it largely unscathed. Clergy and leading lay people were generally on good terms with their few Dissenting neighbours. Methodism was moderately, but not alarmingly, successful in the south and had made only limited inroads in the north. The increased social polarization which was to mark the second half of the century was only just beginning, and though life was often hard it was generally fairly settled.

It is, however, the case that, although the leaders were mainly Anglican clergy, most exhorters (lay preachers) and superintendents (leaders of societies) in Wales up to 1750 were farmers, schoolmasters, carpenters, blacksmiths, and

---

[24] Williams et al., *Welsh Church*, p. 167.

[25] W. R. Ward, *The Protestant Evangelical Awakening* (Cambridge, 1992), p. 321.

[26] Williams et al., *Welsh Church*, p. 168.

[27] Jenkins, 'The Established Church and Dissent in Eighteenth-Century Cardiganshire', p. 469.

butchers, with a smattering of others of the middling sort.[28] These too were mainly Anglican but the seeds were there for the growth of anti-establishment feeling in the nineteenth century. From the early period there were some amongst the Methodist societies who wanted to separate from the Anglican Church, and an unsuccessful move seems to have been made to ordain Methodist ministers to celebrate Holy Communion at the first Welsh Methodist Association meeting in 1743.[29] In fact, ordinations did not take place until 1811, and the Welsh Calvinistic Methodist Church was not formally constituted until 1823.

It is not clear how extensive the Great Awakening was in its first phase in Wales. The fervour and faith of its leaders is not in doubt but, after a brief initial period of excitement and success, the revival became harder to sustain. It is difficult to estimate numbers but in south Cardiganshire, for example, one of Methodism's strongest areas, it has been estimated that there were thirteen societies, with a maximum of 200 members, in 1745.[30] Differences of background and tradition caused disagreement. Those who had joined the societies from a less committed Anglican position, both in England and Wales, could not understand the loyalty to the Established Church of most of the Methodist leaders.[31] In Wales, Harris and Rowland became increasingly divided until their split around 1752. The revival left the Dissenting congregations largely untouched and their numbers remained relatively small; in 1763 there were only about twenty-two ministers in the diocese of Llandaff, several of whom were over 60. Only three were under 45.[32] Within Anglicanism, Methodism was unable to extend itself to any great extent into north Wales until Thomas Charles moved to Bala and began to preach for the Methodists in the 1780s.

ANGLICANISM AND ITS CELTIC PAST

Welsh Anglicans were proud of their Celtic identity, both for the antiquity of its Christian inheritance—traditionally it was claimed that Christianity had been brought to Britain by Joseph of Arimathea—and for its apparent freedom from papal influence. Their Celtic ancestors, it was felt, had inherited an original faith directly from one of the followers of Jesus, and only later had it been corrupted by the activities of missionaries from Rome. This narrative

---

[28] Williams et al., *Welsh Church*, p. 170.

[29] Yates, 'The Established Church and Rural Elementary Schooling', p. 82.

[30] Jenkins, 'The Established Church and Dissent in Eighteenth-Century Cardiganshire', p. 462.

[31] Jones, *Glorious Work*, pp. 144–6.

[32] John R. Guy (ed.), *The Diocese of Llandaff in 1763*, South Wales Record Society Publications 7 (Cardiff, 1991), p. 175.

was developed as part of a determined effort to sell Protestantism to the conservative Welsh and continued both to reflect and to feed anti-Catholic feeling throughout our period. It first appeared in the preface to the Welsh New Testament of 1567 and continued to be perpetuated in a number of works, including the widely read *Drych y Pryf Oesoedd* (*Mirror of the First Ages*) by the Anglican cleric Theophilus Evans. Evans held a succession of parishes in Breconshire, including Llanynys, Llangamarch, and Llanfaes. The first edition was published before Evans's ordination in 1718, and between the first and second editions of this work (1716 and 1740) Evans somewhat enlarged the claims of Wales and the Welsh Church to antique purity and influence, possibly to bolster the authority of traditional Anglicanism against an *arriviste* Welsh Methodism which drew its identity less from Welsh tradition than from European Protestant radicalism.[33] Even bishops from outside Wales could be happy to stress this Celtic identity when they took up appointments in Welsh sees. In the aftermath of the Jacobite rising of 1714, Richard Reynolds, during his brief tenure of the see of Bangor, had time to hold a visitation of the diocese in 1722 and took the opportunity, in his charge, to address his clergy as 'descendants ... of those Holy Men of Bangor who ... withstood the Acts as well as the arms of the Romans and could never be brought to yield up the liberties of their Churches ... to any Foreign Power whatsoever'.[34]

This identification with Wales's Celtic inheritance also found its way to the Welsh community in London. In the heyday of societies, Bishop John Evans of Bangor was not only an early member of the SPCK but also, with Lord Lisburne the leading Cardiganshire magnate, founded the Most Honourable and Loyal Society of Antient Britons in London in 1715.[35] There followed a plethora of Welsh societies in London, with inextricably overlapping memberships, of which the best known are probably the Honourable Society of Cymmrodorion and the Gwneddigion.[36] These were societies for those who had successfully left Wales to seek their fortune, as well as many of those Welsh worthies whose way of life included the London season. Their zeal for the preservation of Welsh culture and heritage was matched by their enthusiasm for the delights of the table and the cellar. These societies came into their own in the later eighteenth century when Enlightenment ideas and

---

[33] Eryn White, 'The Eighteenth-Century Evangelical Revival and Welsh Identity', in Mark Smith (ed.), *British Evangelical Identities Past and Present*, vol. I: *Aspects of the History and Sociology of Evangelicalism in Britain and Ireland* (Milton Keynes, 2008), pp. 85–96 (pp. 91–4).

[34] Richard Reynolds, *A Charge delivered to the Clergy of Bangor, at the Primary Visitation ... May 30th, 1722* (London, 1722), p. 6.

[35] E. D. Evans, 'John Evans, Bishop of Bangor 1702–16', *Transactions of the Honourable Society of Cymmrodorion*, new series, 7 (2001): 44–65 (p. 59).

[36] For a full account of these societies, see Emrys Jones (ed.), *The Welsh in London 1500–2000* (Cardiff, 2001).

the Romantic Movement provided a receptive context for the revival, or reinvention, of ancient customs. The Ancient Order of Druids held its first meeting in Poland Street, Soho, in November 1781; the modern *eisteddfod* movement began in 1789, and the first *Gorsedd* ceremony was directed by Iolo Morgannwg on Primrose Hill in June 1792.[37] The *eisteddfod* movement soon spread within Wales, led by a mixture of enthusiastic Anglicans, both clerical and lay, and some leaders of old Dissent. The *Gorsedd* ceremony was included in the first formal *eisteddfod*, which took place in Carmarthen in 1819, under the auspices of Bishop Burgess of St Davids and Archdeacon Thomas Beynon of Carmarthen. The contribution of Anglicans, mainly clergy, to Welsh culture and learning in this period was considerable, not only through the London societies and the Welsh *eisteddfodau* but also through the translation of religious and other works into Welsh and the publication of many antiquarian local histories in the last quarter of the eighteenth and the first quarter of the nineteenth centuries.[38]

In this period, therefore, Welsh Anglicans, both clerical and lay, identified closely with Wales. It was a time in which a strong Welsh identity could be combined with a strong English identity without any sense of tension between the two. The British, as the educated Welsh often called themselves, were simply the purest and most ancient of the English, and no incompatibility was seen between Welsh and English identity. Even during the anti-establishment pamphlet wars of the early nineteenth century, there was no hint of political nationalism. Welsh cultural nationalism was not seen as leading to Welsh separatism, but rather as contributing to a multi-cultural British state.[39]

THE RISE OF RADICALISM

From the 1770s, the establishment in England and Wales saw itself as increasingly under threat from dangerous political radicalism. In the course of the last quarter of the century, unrest in France escalated into the French Revolution and its ensuing bloodbath. Thomas Paine's *Rights of Man*, defending the Revolution, was published and very widely read. In Wales, as elsewhere in the country, many Anglicans found it hard to distinguish between political and religious radicalism and they associated the growth in religious Dissent

[37] Jones (ed.), *The Welsh in London*, pp. 76–7; see also D. Jones (ed.), *The Letters of Edward Williams, 'Iolo Morgannwg'*, 3 vols. (Cardiff, 2007).

[38] Nigel Yates, *Eighteenth-Century Britain: Religion and Politics 1714–1815* (Harlow, 2008), pp. 123–4.

[39] Marion Löffler with Bethan Jenkins, *Political Pamphlets and Sermons from Wales 1790–1806* (Cardiff, 2014), pp. 9–11, 62.

with that in political dissent. How accurate this was is hard to say, but there is no doubt that political feelings were expressed in religious terms and language which barely distinguished between Church and state was used on both sides.[40] For example, David Jones, writing in 1790 as 'a Welsh Freeholder', warned Bishop Samuel Horsley of St Davids that his (Jones's) cause would 'prove destructive to slavish establishments and tyrannical hierarchies ... [and would] restore to [the people] civil and religious freedom'.[41] In response a clergyman of the diocese accused the 'Welsh Freeholder' of being both heretical and seditious.[42] Some twenty-five years later, but still more than a decade before the first fruits of this radical movement, the Reform Act of 1832, Bishop William Majendie of Bangor referred in his visitation charge to 'blasphemous and seditious tracts, industriously circulated, gratis, among the lower orders, and from the poison of which not even the seclusion of this Principality, and the peculiarity of its language, has entirely protected us'.[43] In fact Löffler has suggested that the pamphlet war in Wales, though contributing to the wider pamphlet debates across the country, began later and continued energetically for some years after that in the rest of the country had largely died down.[44] Majendie may have had some reason to feel threatened; the pamphlet war seems to have been accompanied by direct action and in the same year he referred to two occasions when churches had been 'most audaciously violated by pre-occupation of a number of persons not in Communion with us ... to the exclusion of their own rector or licensed minister'.[45]

The mixing of politics and religion produces a heady cocktail and under the twin influences of the second Evangelical Revival and political radicalism the numbers of Dissenting worshippers grew rapidly between about 1790 and 1830. Fiery preaching has a tendency to radicalize, and pro-Anglican Methodists found their position increasingly unsustainable. Thomas Charles, the most prominent figure in Welsh Methodism at the end of the century, found himself forced to defend the Methodists against accusations of disloyalty and schismatic tendencies.[46] In this period Anglican attitudes to both Methodism and Dissent were clearly hardening, though the intensity of this varied considerably, both from individual to individual and from area to area.[47] There is some evidence that hostility to Dissent, and the tendency to categorize

---

[40] Löffler and Jenkins, *Political Pamphlets and Sermons*, pp. 11–12.

[41] A Welsh Freeholder, *A Letter to the Revd Samuel Lord Bishop of St Davids on the Charge he lately delivered to the Clergy of his Diocese* (London, 1790), p. 12.

[42] *An Answer to a letter from a Welsh Freeholder ... by a clergyman of the Diocese of St Davids* (London, 1790).

[43] Henry William Majendie, *A Charge delivered to the Clergy of the diocese of Bangor, in the Month of September, 1817* (Bangor, 1817), p. 7.

[44] Löffler and Jenkins, *Pamphlets and Sermons*, p. 10.

[45] Majendie, *Charge 1817*, p. 25.

[46] Thomas Charles, *The Welsh Methodists Vindicated* (Chester, 1802).

[47] Williams et al., *Welsh Church*, pp. 210–12.

Methodists as Dissenters, was significantly greater in the wealthier diocese of Bangor than in the diocese of St Davids, and it has been suggested that this may have been because the clergy of Bangor diocese were by and large better off and better educated, so that hostility to, and fear of, Dissent in a period of political radicalism were reinforced by differences in social status between most clergy and most Dissenting and Methodist congregations.[48]

As in the rest of the country, one of the responses to political and religious radicalism was increased fervour in the provision of schools. Bishops' charges clearly reveal a belief that the poor could be educated into both religious orthodoxy and political loyalty. Clergy were exhorted to set up Sunday schools and many did so, on strictly Anglican principles. The circulating schools of Griffith Jones, referred to earlier, were revived in the early nineteenth century with a thoroughly Anglican organization. These had been continued after his death by his friend and collaborator, Madame Bridget Bevan, but the network of schools collapsed when her will, leaving most of her fortune to them, was contested by her family and spent thirty years in Chancery. The Bevan charity, which ran the schools after the case was finally settled in 1804, had a constitution which ensured their Anglican character and put them firmly under the control of the bishop in each diocese. The National Society, founded in 1812, was turned to for funding by many Welsh clergy. It was under the influence of the National Society that, for the first time, preference began to be given to teaching schools through the medium of English. Up to that time the language used in schools seems to have depended mainly on whether the teacher could speak Welsh, but the National Society prescribed the books which could be used in schools and insisted on the use of English, perhaps reflecting a new perception that Welsh, like the other Celtic languages, could provide cover for radical political propaganda. Though the use of Welsh in schools probably did not end immediately, this move was just part of a growing tendency for Anglicanism in Wales to be identifiable by its radical opponents as more English than Welsh.

WELSH ANGLICANISM AND ENGLISH IDENTITY

Across England and Wales in the eighteenth century, while the bishops and clergy may be seen as the protectors of Anglican identity, the carriers of Anglican identity were as much the prominent laypeople, the nobility and gentry, as the clergy. Whilst the need for Welsh language services meant that the clerical body remained predominantly Welsh, and Welsh-speaking, during

---

[48] Yates, 'The Established Church and Rural Elementary Schooling', p. 279.

this period, the century saw the gentry families becoming increasingly Anglicized. Jacob has identified a tendency for estates to pass to heirs based outside Wales as landed families failed to produce male heirs.[49] Social ambition prompted gentry families, in both Wales and Scotland, to send their sons to schools in England, and to colleges other than Jesus, the Welsh college. It is not clear that this process caused them to lose their Welsh entirely—the business of the London Welsh societies was conducted in Welsh—but by the end of the eighteenth century the wealthier Welsh families spoke a form of Welsh very different from the colloquial Welsh dialects spoken by the people. This wider gulf which had developed over the eighteenth century between the gentry and the poor, together with the heady social changes associated with industrialization and urbanization, helped to encourage the radicalism of the last thirty years of our period and to lend the anti-establishment feeling in Wales an anti-English character which found its outlet in the growing nationalism of the later nineteenth century.

The association of Englishness with the powerful in Welsh society was given further credence from another source. The urbanization and industrialization of the south-east brought with it an influx of workers from other parts of Wales and from England. The Anglican Church, fettered by the legal requirements of establishment, was unable to respond quickly to this sudden vast expansion of the population. It was only natural that these workers should become identified with the more nimble Nonconformist groups, who could set up new causes wherever the need was seen. Along with the workers came wealthy English industrialists, men like Richard Crawshay of the Cyfarthfa works (Moloch the Iron King), who were more likely to associate themselves with the establishment and to expect the ministrations of the Church to be received through the medium of English.[50] These twin trends, the Anglicization of the more prosperous indigenous Welsh families and the arrival of wealthy English mine owners in the industrial south-east, did not at the time give rise to separatist anti-English feeling. Nevertheless they put in place a linguistic, social, and religious fault line which echoed the anti-establishment contours of political radicalism. As Welsh nationalist feeling began to grow from the 1840s this fault line was to split open, leaving the largely indigenous Welsh clergy stranded with the rich and powerful lay leadership in Wales on the English side of a chasm which was as much socio-economic and political as it was religious.

---

[49] Williams et al., *Welsh Church*, p. 69.

[50] Chris Evans, *The Labyrinth of Flames: Work and Social Conflict in Early Industrial Merthyr Tydfil*, Studies in Welsh History 7 (Cardiff, 1993), pp. 131–3.

CONCLUSION

The Anglican Church in Wales in the long eighteenth century was subject to the same economic, political, and religious pressures as the rest of the Church of England and it responded in very similar ways. Its poverty may have worsened some of the problems of pluralism and non-residence. The need for Welsh-speaking clergy may have led to lower educational standards in some parts. The appointment of non-Welsh bishops annoyed some of its clergy and damaged its reputation with future generations. However, throughout most of our period, it was firmly rooted in the culture which it served. With some exceptions it was broadly tolerant both of Dissent and of Methodism, until the upsurge of political and religious radicalism in the last quarter of the eighteenth century. The growing Englishness of its most influential lay members, as well as many of its senior clergy, contributed to the nature of anti-establishment feeling in Wales in this period and laid the foundations for the later identification of the Anglican Church with England and nonconformity with Wales and Welsh nationalism.

SELECT BIBLIOGRAPHY

Evans, Chris, *The Labyrinth of Flames: Work and Social Conflict in Early Industrial Merthyr Tydfil*, Studies in Welsh History 7 (Cardiff, 1993).

Guy, John R., 'The Significance of Indigenous Clergy in the Welsh Church at the Restoration', in Stuart Mews (ed.), *Religion and National Identity*, Studies in Church History 18 (Oxford, 1982), pp. 335–44.

Jenkins, Geraint H., *The Foundations of Modern Wales 1642–1780* (Oxford, 1993).

Jones, Emrys (ed.), *The Welsh in London 1500–2000* (Cardiff, 2001).

Löffler, Marion with Bethan Jenkins, *Political Pamphlets and Sermons from Wales 1790–1806* (Cardiff, 2014).

Morgan, D. Densil, *Wales and the Word: Historical Perspectives on Welsh Identity and Religion* (Cardiff, 2008).

Morgans, John I. and Peter C. Noble, *Our Holy Ground: The Welsh Christian Experience* (Talybont, 2016).

White, Eryn, '"A Poor Benighted Church": Church and Society in Mid-Eighteenth-Century Wales', in R. R. Davies and Geraint H. Jenkins (eds.), *From Medieval to Modern Wales* (Cardiff, 2004), pp. 123–41.

Williams, Glanmor, William Jacob, Nigel Yates, and Frances Knight, *The Welsh Church from Reformation to Disestablishment, 1603–1920* (Cardiff, 2007).

Yates, Paula, 'The Established Church and Rural Elementary Schooling: The Welsh Dioceses 1780–1830', PhD thesis, University of Wales, Lampeter, 2007.

7

Ireland

Toby Barnard

In outward forms and structures, Ireland had an established Church that resembled England's. As Archbishop William King of Dublin observed (to his counterpart of Canterbury), 'it has been the design of the kings of England ever since the conquest to conform the government of Ireland to that of England both in spirituals and temporals'.[1] Parliamentary statutes enacted in Ireland but modelled on English prototypes established its governance and doctrines. The most comprehensive laws were passed in 1560 (Acts of Uniformity and Supremacy) and 1662. The Church of Ireland possessed dioceses, some of which had been united, ruled by twenty-two bishops with seats in the upper house of the local legislature in Dublin, until it was abolished in 1800. At least notionally, there were cathedrals as the administrative and spiritual centres of most dioceses. The entire island was enmeshed in a network of parishes.[2] It possessed the church fabrics that survived from before the sixteenth-century Reformations, although often these were ruinous or in inconvenient locations. Moreover, the Established Church enjoyed legal privileges, again akin to those of the Church of England. From 1703, with the passage of a Test Act (modelled on the English measure), until 1829, full citizenship and entry into many official positions and professions other than medicine were allowed only to those certified as having taken communion according to the Church of Ireland rite at least once in the year.[3]

---

[1] Archbishop William King to Archbishop William Wake, 12 Sept. 1717, copy in Dublin, Representative Church Body Library [RCB], form-book of Bishop Thomas Fletcher, 1744, M/31.
[2] Charles Doherty, 'The Idea of the Parish', in Elizabeth Fitzpatrick and Raymond Gillespie (eds.), *The Parish in Medieval and Early Modern Ireland* (Dublin, 2006), pp. 21–32; K. W. Nicholls, 'Rectory, Vicarage and Parish in the Western Irish Dioceses', *Journal of the Royal Society of Antiquaries of Ireland*, 101 (1971): 53–84.
[3] Toby Barnard, *A New Anatomy of Ireland: The Irish Protestants, 1649–1770* (New Haven, CT and London, 2003), p. 167; Michael Mulcahy (ed.), *Calendar of Kinsale Documents, Vol. 7* (Kinsale, 1998), p. 42.

The doctrines and practices of the Irish Church generally reproduced those of the Church of England (Book of Common Prayer, translations of the Bible, canons, Thirty-Nine Articles, and preferred catechisms). Yet variations occurred, especially in the canons adopted by the Irish Convocation in 1634. The tendency of these was towards an unabashed Calvinism, in a bid to distinguish itself clearly from the ceremonial and doctrines of Catholicism.[4] Otherwise, conformity to English norms was further assisted by the shared language of instruction (English), a common stock of theology in which its clergy were grounded, the adoption of forms of prayer (both routine and occasional) that had originated in England,[5] and a regular importation of English (with occasional Scots and Welsh) to fill bishoprics and other high-ranking dignities. Moreover, if a Calvinistic emphasis on the preaching of the word was marked, it did not preclude sacramentalism. The centrality of the administration of communion, encouraged by followers of Archbishop Laud who had come to Ireland, persisted into the eighteenth century.[6] After 1820, Richard Mant, arriving from England as a bishop, introduced the preoccupations of the Hackney Phalanx.[7]

Not all the derivatives from the Church of England were welcome. They could generate resentments about humiliating subordination to English priorities which paralleled the incipient patriotism in the secular sphere. The Church of Ireland was also blighted by several of the same flaws as its English counterpart: embarrassing disparities in clerical incomes, a parochial system which no longer corresponded to the distribution of the population, inadequate buildings and revenues, and uneven standards of education and attentiveness among the clergy. As in England, therefore, considerable energies had to be expended on tackling these problems. Both strenuous individuals and collectives (Convocation or ad hoc associations of would-be reformers) addressed them.

There was, however, one vital difference between the positions of the Church of Ireland and the Church of England. Although by the 1660s Protestants in England splintered into conformists and Dissenters, Protestantism had been adopted—nominally at least—by the bulk of the population. The percentage of Catholics had dwindled, maybe to five. The situation in Ireland was very different. Attempts had been made to introduce Protestantism as an essential in the drive to bring Ireland into obedience to the Tudor monarchy. Political, more than spiritual, imperatives lay behind these efforts, causing them to be resisted from dislike of English ambitions and intrusions. The decades between

[4] Alan Ford, 'The Church of Ireland, 1558–1634: A Puritan Church?', in Alan Ford, James McGuire, and Kenneth Milne (eds.), *As by Law Established: The Church of Ireland since the Reformation* (Dublin, 1995), pp. 52–68.

[5] *Letters written by His Excellency Hugh Boulter, D.D., Lord Primate of All Ireland*, 2 vols. (Oxford, 1769), I, pp. 208, 212, 218, 221, 222.

[6] F. R. Bolton, *The Caroline Tradition of the Church of Ireland* (London, 1958).

[7] Nigel Yates, *The Religious Condition of Ireland, 1770–1850* (Oxford, 2006), pp. 96–8.

the 1530s and 1690s were regularly punctuated by uprisings demonstrating Irish attachment to Catholicism: English conquest was conflated with the forcible imposition of Protestantism. The more fiercely that any extension of English authority into the whole island was resisted, the more urgent was thought the need to implant an English-style religion in place of Catholicism. The latter, gaining fresh dynamism with the Counter-Reformation, was seen as a device by which England's Catholic enemies, notably Spain and France, might increase their influence within Ireland and through it their ability to embarrass England. Uprisings were suppressed; bit by bit the secular authority of the English state in Ireland was strengthened. With these apparent successes came a slow but perceptible entrenchment of a Protestant Church. From the redoubts of English settlement—Dublin, ports, and the enclave of the Pale around Dublin—it began to spread into remoter regions largely peopled by the Irish Catholics.

The Church of Ireland was conceived as a vital agent of Anglicization. But this role may have hampered its work. It needs also to be considered how far Anglicization and Anglicanism were synonymous. There were ways in which leaders of the Church of Ireland sought to adapt it to local conditions. If this then meant some weakening of the Church's Anglicizing mission, did it also dilute the Anglicanism? Moreover, whatever the formal ordinances and directives which governed the conduct of Church of Ireland clergy, individuals may have deviated from them.

The two most protracted bids either to modify or throw off completely English power in Ireland—in the 1640s and between 1688 and 1692—saw seizures of the ancient buildings and their return to Catholic worship, and violence against personnel of the Church of Ireland. Such episodes deepened the existing antipathies between Catholics and Protestants, inducing in the latter a wariness which sometimes took the form of aggression rather than defensiveness. One consequence after 1692 was the enactment of a series of laws which discriminated against Catholics (and Protestant Nonconformists) and enlarged the privileges already enjoyed by the Church of Ireland and its communicant members. These discriminations, culminating in the Test Act of 1703, copied measures taken earlier in England. Where Ireland differed was in the proportions of beneficiaries and victims of the laws.

Estimates vary, but by the close of the seventeenth century adherents of the Church of Ireland amounted to between 10 and 20 per cent of the total population. The Established Church had been further weakened by the defection of Protestants to Dissenting congregations. The divisions which had beset Protestantism in England and Wales spread into Ireland. Soldiers and settlers arriving during the 1640s and 1650s introduced the religious views of the Independents, Baptists, and Quakers. Meanwhile Presbyterianism, which had been imported mainly by Scots who were colonizing north-eastern Ulster from the 1620s, grew. Its vitality was strengthened by campaigning Scottish troops and then by more immigrants. The Church of Ireland, particularly in the north but also in Dublin and a few larger towns, found itself competing with tenacious and vigorous Protestant nonconformity as well as with the Catholicism to which most adhered.[8]

How best to respond to these challenges preoccupied the more reflective within the Church of Ireland. From the first engagement of Protestants with Ireland in the sixteenth century, two approaches had been proposed, sometimes as alternatives, sometimes as complements. Coercion was one option, with the English faith of Protestantism imposed in the wake of military victories and—if necessary—through the same violent methods and with draconian penalties for non-compliance. The gentler method was persuasion. Fervent evangelization by preaching ministers would bring the unfortunate natives of Ireland from ignorance and superstition to the light of the gospel. Disagreement among the proponents of the rival schemes hampered any systematic application of either approach. Official policy tended to veer unpredictably from the one to the other. In addition, the lack of a consistent and sustained campaign combined with other weaknesses. The numbers and calibre of the ministers who would undertake the labour were seriously deficient. To improve the supply and preparedness of evangelists, a university was established—Trinity College, Dublin—in 1592. Under dynamic provosts, it took seriously its function as the seminary for a Protestant Ireland, particularly between the 1660s and 1690s. But it remained small: between 1685 and 1750, on average seventy-eight newcomers matriculated each year.[9] Among the graduates, only a minority was destined for ordination. Nor could the Church of Ireland dictate what was taught either to the impressionable young or to the intending ordinands. Only in 1791 did the archbishops and bishops agree on what candidates for the diaconate and the priesthood should know.[10]

Efforts to achieve ideological cohesiveness among the clergy through collaboration and discussion were strongest in the later seventeenth century. The shock of the fragmentation of the Irish Protestant interest and the renewed vitality of Catholicism, reaching a new peak of confidence with the accession of the Catholic James VII and II in 1685, may explain why interested members of Trinity College formed themselves into a discussion club. Some from the group became bishops during the 1690s. In their dioceses, they introduced measures intended to raise clerical standards and to infuse the laity with scriptural ideals; they joined in collective endeavours to combat immorality. After 1713, with Convocation suspended, the possibility of coordinated and comprehensive campaigns dwindled.

---

[8] Barnard, *New Anatomy*, pp. 1–20.

[9] David Hannigan, 'The University of Dublin, 1685–1750: A Study of Matriculation Records', MA thesis, St Patrick's College, Maynooth, 1995, pp. 8, 24.

[10] Alex Erck, miscellaneous notebook [*c*.1782–1825], pp. 365–6, RCB, MS 103.

For the most part, these initiatives were aimed at the converted, not designed to make converts. They reflected an introspectiveness which—arguably—beset the Church of Ireland. The ultimate objective of turning Ireland into a Protestant nation comparable with England had not been abandoned, but, for the time being, it was postponed. For most, servicing their own was paramount—the more urgent owing to the resilience and magnetism of Protestant Dissent, the incursions of Methodism from the 1740s, and the apparent growth in irreligion as manifest in non-attendance at worship and vicious, even blasphemous behaviour. Towards the end of the eighteenth century, the greater assertiveness of the Catholics, and the shock of insurrection in 1798 followed quickly by statutory Union of Ireland with Great Britain, goaded the Church of Ireland into renewed evangelism.[11]

Advocates of persuasion were dismayed and sometimes disillusioned by the small headway that had been made. Leniency, it seemed, had been met with uprisings during the 1640s, between 1689 and 1691, and in 1798, in which the persons and property of the Church of Ireland had been targeted. In consequence, during the 1690s, restrictive laws multiplied. The immediate aim was to disable Irish Catholicism from again threatening to topple the Protestant dominance—an incipient Ascendancy. The religious, social, and economic leaders of Catholicism were to be weakened or even extinguished. Looking further into the future, it could be that Catholics, bereft of their leaders, would move in droves towards Protestantism. Yet little was done by the Church of Ireland actively to encourage the migration. It is true that a form of prayer was devised for those who wished publicly to recant the errors of Catholicism and embrace Anglicanism.[12] When used, it endowed the action with solemnity and publicity. In the cathedral at Armagh, there were five public renunciations of popery between 1750 and 1758.[13] But such conversions arose from the decisions of individuals, not from mass movements.

If the Church of Ireland was to take its message into Irish Catholic communities, practical obstacles had to be surmounted. A principal impediment was language. Until well into the eighteenth century, the first language of most Catholics in Ireland was Irish, although bilingualism was growing. It was acknowledged, therefore, that Church of Ireland evangelism required clergy

---

[11] Donald H. Akenson, *The Church of Ireland: Ecclesiastical Reform and Revolution, 1800–1885* (New Haven, CT and London, 1971); Joseph Liechty, 'Irish Evangelicalism, Trinity College Dublin, and the Mission of the Church of Ireland at the End of the Eighteenth Century', PhD thesis, St Patrick's College, Maynooth, 1987; Yates, *Religious Condition of Ireland*.

[12] *The Book of Common Prayer* (Dublin, 1716), pp. [381–8]; form-book of Bishop Fletcher, fos. 23, 34.

[13] L. A. Clarkson, 'Armagh, 1770: Portrait of an Urban Community', in David Harkness and Mary O'Dowd (eds.), *The Town in Ireland*, Historical Studies 13 (Belfast, 1981), p. 88; cf. Edward Parkinson, 'The Vestry Books of the Parish of Down', *Ulster Journal of Archaeology*, 14 (1908), pp. 146, 147.

fluent in the Irish language and armed with written and printed aids. But the acknowledgement was neither universal nor uncontroversial. After 1714, the interest of clerics in the Irish vernacular was largely diverted away from proselytizing and into historical and antiquarian studies.[14] The general failure of schemes to print, teach, and preach in the Irish language contrasts with the fruitful adoption of Welsh by Protestants.[15]

In the earliest phases of the Protestant Reformation in Ireland, leaders had been sought in England. Gradually the supply from within Ireland increased, thanks to the settlement of more newcomers from Britain who were already conforming Anglicans when they disembarked. Yet suspicions persisted among the English authorities that neither the Established Church nor the law courts in Ireland could be entrusted to the Irish-born and -reared. A reluctance to appoint the Irish to bishoprics was deepened when the few who were elevated, such as William King, bishop of Derry (1691-1703), and the elder Edward Synge, archbishop of Tuam (1716-41), emerged as fluent champions of Irish interests. They exercised a disproportionate influence in the poorly attended Irish House of Lords.[16] The primacy (the archbishopric of Armagh) was habitually reserved for an English cleric. Late in the century, Charles Agar, an awkward and effective defender of Church of Ireland interests, progressed no further than Cashel, although he was rewarded with a lay peerage at the Act of Union.[17] Instead of Agar, William Stuart, a son of Lord Bute, became primate in 1800.

This discriminatory policy was rudely reminiscent of the essentially sub-ordinate position of Ireland, including its Established Church. Within the Church itself it could cause resentment and bring friction between the paro-chial incumbents, overwhelmingly of Irish provenance, and their diocesans, so often imported from Britain. It remains to be established whether or not education in Ireland gave its beneficiaries a markedly different outlook from their English superiors. Trinity College offered further study to those aiming at ordination. Both the linguistic requirements (Greek and Hebrew) and the texts to be studied had much in common with the staples current in England. How the reading was then interpreted and applied depended heavily, not just on the assiduity of the student, but on discussion with tutors and peers. Further

---

[14] T. C. Barnard, 'Scholars and Antiquarians: The Clergy and Learning, 1600-2000', in T. C. Barnard and W. G. Neely (eds.), *The Clergy of the Church of Ireland, 1000-2000: Messengers, Watchmen and Stewards* (Dublin, 2006), pp. 231-58.

[15] T. C. Barnard, 'Protestants and the Irish Language, c.1675-1725', *Journal of Ecclesiastical History*, 44 (1993): 243-72, reprinted in T. C. Barnard, *Irish Protestant Ascents and Descents, 1641-1770* (Dublin, 2004), pp. 170-207; James Kelly, 'Irish Protestants and the Irish Language in the Eighteenth Century', in James Kelly and Ciarán Mac Murchaidh (eds.), *Irish and English: Essays on the Irish Linguistic and Cultural Frontier, 1600-1900* (Dublin, 2012), pp. 189-217.

[16] Patrick McNally, '"Irish and English Interests": National Conflict within the Church of Ireland Episcopate in the Reign of George I', *Irish Historical Studies*, 29 (1995): 295-314.

[17] A. P. W. Malcomson, *Archbishop Charles Agar: Churchmanship and Politics in Ireland, 1760-1810* (Dublin, 2002).

variations, hard to retrieve, were introduced when, in the final stages of preparation, the novice clergy were closely overseen by a bishop. Some overseers, impatient with the formalities, were lax in their examinations.[18] Mindful of obligations to patrons, kinsfolk, and neighbours, bishops could be indulgent, accepting for ordination candidates whom colleagues had rejected as inadequately qualified or temperamentally unfit.[19] These foibles militated against standardization in doctrinal teaching and pastoral dutifulness. Yet, even Francis Hervey, the 'earl bishop' of Derry (1768–1803), sometimes treated 'as a byword for eccentricity and absenteeism, insisted on minimum qualifications in ordinands. The canonical requirement was a competent knowledge of Latin, together with a grasp of the Thirty-Nine Articles and the canons. To these, Hervey added familiarity with the first four centuries of Christian history.[20] Elsewhere, knowledge of Greek was regarded as a *sine qua non*.[21]

A powerful vein of anti-clericalism continued. Indeed a more visible parochial clergy, supported by tithes, to which all regardless of denomination were liable, exacting other fees, and living in some style, could exacerbate hostility. The stark confessional imbalance may have bred deeper and stronger resentments than in England. Moreover, the ecclesiastical parish was loaded with multifarious administrative and regulatory duties, several of which—the upkeep of roads, the relief of the poor and aged, schooling—involved additional mulcts.[22] Understandably there was frequent non-compliance.

The first to resist the payment of tithes, as lacking divine sanction, were the Quakers. Even nominal adherents of the Church of Ireland disliked the regular payments. When, in the 1730s, the bishops promoted a bill to clarify and extend the liability of landowners and farmers to tithes, it aroused angry opposition. It was bitterest in the lower house of the Dublin Parliament, technically the sole preserve of members of the Established Church.[23] More

---

[18] Revd Robert Howard to William Howard, undated [between 1720 and 1726], Dublin, National Library of Ireland [NLI], MS 12149.

[19] Bishop Richard Tennison to Bishop William Smythe, 7 Feb. 1695[6], 17 July 1796, NLI, PC 436; Bishop Francis Hutchinson to William Smythe, 28 Aug. 1733, and Revd James Smythe to William Smythe, 30 Apr. 1734, NLI, PC 449; Thomas Williams to Sir J. Caldwell, 13 Oct. 1750, Manchester, John Rylands Library [JRL], B 3/10/398; A. T. Hamilton to Lord Abercorn, 5 Oct. 1781, Belfast, Public Record Office of Northern Ireland [PRONI], D 623/A/44, 137; cf. Archbishop William King to Richard Baldwin, 18 Sept. 1723, Trinity College, Dublin [TCD], MS 2537/15–16.

[20] Bishop Francis Hervey to Sir James Caldwell, 8 Apr. 1769, 7 May 1769, 7 Feb. 1775, JRL, B/3/17/23, 24, 29; cf. Bishop Henry Maule to William Smythe, 16 Feb. 1748 [or 1746], PC 449; Erck, notebook, p. 365.

[21] Revd James Smythe to William Smythe, 20 Oct. 1741, 10 Nov. 1741, 'Sunday night' [1741], PC 449.

[22] Rowena Dudley, 'The Dublin Parishes and the Poor, 1660–1740', *Archivium Hibernicum*, 53 (1999): 80–94.

[23] David Hayton, 'Select Document: The Division in the Irish House of Commons on the "tithe of agistment", 18 Mar. 1736, and Swift's "Character . . . of the Legion Club"', *Irish Historical Studies*, 38 (2012): 304–21.

systematic opposition to the annual collections developed in some Presbyterian and Catholic communities, so that efforts to collect outstanding moneys with force became flashpoints for violence. Localized trouble spread through areas of Ulster and Munster in the 1760s and again during the 1780s in Munster. The latter unrest prompted the bishop of Cloyne, Richard Woodward (arrived from England), to formulate justifications for the levy which went beyond tithes themselves and incorporated them into the fabric of Protestant rule in Ireland. The concept of a Protestant, or more accurately Church of Ireland, ascendancy was formulated. In practice, this had existed since the 1690s, but Woodward's was a public and published (and provocative) apologia.[24] The payment by all of tithes remained a grievance onto which in the 1820s bold Catholics fastened in a sustained campaign for reform.

With clergy superabundant (between 1806 and 1826, the total of clergy rose from 1,253 to 1,977), even when buildings and other resources were wanting, it was possible for an effective ministry to be practised, so fulfilling the mission of the Church of Ireland.[25] Some of the newly ordained eked out a living as a tutor or taught in schools; many never climbed above the first rung of a curacy on the clerical ladder.[26] A distinct caste of clergy was of course fundamental to the theory and government of that Church, as of the Church of England. In return for their legal privileges, Church of Ireland clerics were expected to uphold the political order embodied in the Hanoverian state in Ireland. As beneficiaries of the Church of Ireland ascendancy, with its near monopoly over most of the remunerative and prestigious aspects of public and social life, they should justify and defend the system. And many of them did. Preaching on days of prescribed celebration and thanksgiving, and before congregations headed by the viceroy or members of the two houses of the Dublin Parliament, clerics expatiated on the benefits of British rule over Ireland, in which Anglicanism was integral.[27] Published clerical defences included both sermons and tracts. Indeed, clerics were compulsive authors, of verse and satire as much as of philippics on moral and material

---

[24] Richard Woodward, *The Present State of the Church of Ireland* (Dublin, 1787); cf. James Kelly, 'Defending the Established Order: Richard Woodward, Bishop of Cloyne (1726–94)', in James Kelly, John McCafferty, and Charles Ivor McGrath (eds.), *People, Politics and Power: Essays in Irish History in Honour of James I. McGuire* (Dublin, 2009), pp. 143–74.

[25] Akenson, *Church of Ireland*, p. 127.

[26] Benjamin Barrington to Sir Arthur Acheson, 11 Nov. 1758, PRONI, D 1606/1/20A.

[27] T. C. Barnard, 'The Uses of 23 October 1641 and Irish Protestant Celebrations', *English Historical Review*, 106 (1991): 889–920, reprinted in Barnard, *Irish Protestant Ascents and Descents*, pp. 111–42; S. J. Connolly, 'The Church of Ireland and the Royal Martyr: Regicide and Revolution in Anglican Political Thought, *c.*1660–*c.*1745', *Journal of Ecclesiastical History*, 54 (2003): 484–506; Robert Eccleshall, 'The Political Ideas of Anglican Ireland in the 1690s', in D. George Boyce, Robert Eccleshall, and Vincent Geoghegan (eds.), *Political Discourse in Seventeenth- and Eighteenth-Century Ireland* (Basingstoke and New York, 2001), pp. 62–80; Suzanne Forbes, '"Publick and solemn acknowledgements": Occasional Days of State-Appointed Worship in Ireland, 1689–1702', *Irish Historical Studies*, 38 (2013): 559–78.

improvement.[28] Clergymen, if polished and articulate, passed muster in polite society, but the very same attributes may have distanced them from parishioners drawn from the middling and laborious sorts, as most Church of Ireland congregations were.

The linkage of the secular and sacred arms of British rule in Ireland, reinforced by the manner in which the bishops were appointed (with English interests apparently uppermost), involved the clergy in the general animosity. Auxiliaries or infantry of an Anglicizing campaign, some stood at the forefront of hostility in the seventeenth century, during the 1780s, in 1798, and again during the 1820s and 1830s. Legislative Union of Ireland and Great Britain in 1800 promised complete congruity of the Church of England and of Ireland. It remained only an aspiration. With the Dublin Parliament abolished, Irish episcopal representation in the House of Lords at Westminster was reduced to four. Since the bishops were chosen in rotation and served for only one session, the chances of their exercising great influence were slight.[29] The steady freeing of Catholics from legal disabilities, with Emancipation in 1829, emboldened them. Church of Ireland protests had not halted a generosity arising more from British imperial commitments than from sensitivity to injustices towards Ireland.

The Church of Ireland, dreading eventual disestablishment (which happened in 1869), acted to meet the Catholic challenge. Denied much political backing, the Church was obliged to rely on its own, not inconsiderable, resources. Direction was given by Primate Stuart, an Anglo-Scot, and the Anglo-Irish Charles Broderick, archbishop of Cashel (both sons of peers). The Board of First Fruits, with its revenues—granted originally by Queen Anne—supplemented by Parliament, financed the building of glebe houses for the clergy and churches. Between 1787 and 1832, the number of churches rose by 30 per cent to 1,293, and that of glebe houses from 354 to 829.[30] Thomas Lewis O'Beirne, a convert from Catholicism, and after 1795 successively bishop of Ossory and Meath, was conspicuous in these activities. So, too, were individual incumbents, such as Daniel Beaufort at Collon, County Louth.[31] These improvements allowed an insistence on clerical residence and reduced pluralism.

The Church of Ireland recognized an urgent need to educate the young and impressionable, if they were to be retained within the Church. Efforts were

---

[28] T. C. Barnard, 'Outlooks and Activities of the Church of Ireland Clergy in the Time of Swift', in K. Juhas, Hermann J. Real, and Sandra Simon (eds.), *Reading Swift: Papers from the Sixth Münster Symposium on Jonathan Swift* (Munich, 2013), pp. 303–21.

[29] G. C. Bolton, *The Passing of the Irish Act of Union* (Oxford, 1966), p. 198; Malcomson, *Agar*, pp. 542–3, 559–614.

[30] Akenson, *Church of Ireland*, pp. 71–144; Stewart J. Brown, *The National Churches of England, Ireland and Scotland, 1801–1846* (Oxford, 2001); Yates, *Religious Condition of Ireland*.

[31] C. C. Ellison, *The Hopeful Traveller: The Life and Times of Daniel Augustus Beaufort, LL.D., 1739–1831* (Kilkenny, 1987); M. C. Gallagher, 'Bishop Thomas Lewis O'Beirne and his Church Building Programme in the Diocese of Meath, 1798–1823', PhD thesis, National University of Ireland, 2009.

systematized through the Hibernian Bible Society (founded in 1808) and the Kildare Place Society (1811). Faith was placed in subsidizing the supply of bibles and other religious tracts, and was backed by evangelistic preaching. The schemes won the support of landowners like Lord Farnham, eager to have tractable tenants. But the campaigns—sometimes termed a 'Second Reformation'—were opposed as proselytism and provoked Catholic ripostes. Again the demand for and collection of tithes proved a flashpoint. Furthermore, with the formation in 1822 of a Catholic Association, momentum for the dismantling of the rickety Church of Ireland confessional state accelerated.[32]

How far the vigour and health of the Anglican interest in Ireland relied on the ministrations of its clergy can be questioned. The patchy and diffuse exertions that have been described hardly solidified that interest. Enquiries across the island, notably in 1731, confirmed impressions that the hold of Catholicism on the majority had not been loosened.[33] Indeed, the confessional demography of Ireland changed little during the eighteenth century. In addition, rapid population growth increased dramatically the absolute numbers of Catholics and emphasized the disparities between the status of the minority and of the majority. The Church of Ireland retained those born and raised as members. Inertia and pragmatism assisted this stability. Until the 1780s, conformity (or at least certification of yearly communion) was the best guarantor of a share in the limited spoils of Ireland. Thereafter, the enlargement of the British Empire and the informal and then statutory lifting of religious tests ended this advantage in regard to military, naval, and civil appointments enjoyed by members of the Church of Ireland.

Turning to the laity, can a distinctive Church of Ireland but discernibly Anglican piety be detected among them? Frustratingly, direct comment comes chiefly from the clergy. Many lamented what they saw as the stubborn, even irredeemable sinfulness of the nation, the tenacity with which both Catholics and Protestant Dissenters resisted Anglican ministrations, the absence of so many from worship, and the backsliding and freethinking of nominal members of their congregations. Others were cheered by a Church from which the most blatant abuses had been expunged, with services regularly and decently conducted, fabrics beautified, promising initiatives in education and charity, and greater administrative order.

Practice among regular worshippers varied between urban and rural parishes. In the latter, services were irregular and the celebration of communion only quarterly. Inadequate churches, awkward of access, deterred even the faithful.

---

[32] Irene Whelan, *The Bible War in Ireland: The 'Second Reformation' and the Polarization of Protestant-Catholic Relations in Ireland, 1800–1840* (Dublin and Madison, WI, 2005).

[33] S. J. Connolly, *Religion, Law and Power: The Making of Protestant Ireland 1660–1760* (Oxford, 1992), p. 146; M.-L. Legg (ed.), *The Census of Elphin, 1749* (Dublin, 2004).

On occasion, worshippers arrived for services but the clergyman did not.[34] By contrast, in Dublin in 1719, when a majority of the inhabitants were—at least nominally—members of the Established Church, most parish churches saw the sacrament given monthly. At St Patrick's Cathedral, Holy Communion was celebrated every Sunday. 'For the convenience of servants', one church provided morning prayer at 7 a.m. Several others had prayers at six in the evening.[35] Divergence between town and country is clear in visitation returns of the 1730s, which include parts of the city of Derry and its remoter hinterland in County Donegal. In Derry itself there was monthly communion. At the principal festivals of the year, 500 communicants are recorded. In the countryside, communion services four times each year were the norm.[36]

The public-spirited were drawn into the work of the parish. Yet, willingness to take on the often irksome duties as churchwardens, sidesmen, overseers, and members of select vestries cannot automatically be equated with religious commitment.[37] Private beliefs resist recovery. Devotional reading through which understanding was to be nurtured closely resembled that of Anglicans in England. The Bible, in a multiplicity of formats and at varying prices, was the book most commonly found in private houses. It was left to expositors and readers to make parallels between the trials and deliverances narrated in Scripture and those endured by Irish Protestants. The Gospels were supplemented by printed catechisms, lives of saints, the holy, penitents, and those turned from the errors of popery, superstition, and unbelief. Some Church of Ireland clergymen published their own catechisms.[38] Others compiled manuscript guides.[39] All communicated the fundamentals familiar in England.[40] Providing cheap bibles and catechisms became a practical act to which earnest clergy and laypeople attended. Supplies were augmented especially after the Bible Societies had been established early in the nineteenth century.

---

[34] M.-L. Legg (ed.), *The Diary of Nicholas Peacock 1740–51* (Dublin, 2005), p. 140.

[35] Anon., *An Address to Absenters from the Publick Worship of God* (Dublin, 1719 edn.).

[36] Visitation, diocese of Derry, c.1733, RCB, GS 2/7/3/34.

[37] T. C. Barnard, 'Churchwardens' Accounts and the Confessional State in Ireland, c.1660–1800', in V. Hitchman and A. Foster (eds.), *Views from the Parish: Churchwardens' Accounts, c.1500–c.1800* (Cambridge, 2015), pp. 109–20; Rowena Dudley, 'The Dublin Parish, 1660–1730', and T. C. Barnard, 'The Eighteenth-Century Parish', in Fitzpatrick and Gillespie (eds.), *The Parish in Medieval and Early Modern Ireland*, pp. 277–96, 297–324; Rowena Dudley, 'Dublin's Parishes, 1660–1729: The Church of Ireland Parishes and their Role in the Civic Administration of the City', PhD thesis, Trinity College, Dublin, 1995.

[38] Board Book, Incorporated Society, 1761–75, p. 55, *s.d.* 2 May 1764, TCD, MS 5225; Roll and accounts, Ardbraccan charter school, 'goods delivered at Ardbraccan', 1769–98, TCD, MS 5997; Roll and accounts, Ballycastle charter school, 'goods delivered at Ballycastle, 1770–97', TCD, MS 5609; James Pelletreau, *An Abridgement of the Sacred History* (Dublin, 1760); James Pelletreau, *A Short Catechetical Explanation of the Principles of Natural and Revealed Religion* (Dublin, 1764).

[39] Revd Robert Hazlett, Catechism paraphrase, c.1770–1780, PRONI, D 668/E/28.

[40] Ian Green, ' "The Necessary Knowledge of the Principles of Religion": Catechisms and Catechizing in Ireland, c.1560–1800', in Ford et al. (eds.), *As by Law Established*, pp. 69–88.

By the 1770s, printed copies of hymns and psalms were provided, geared sometimes to particular congregations (as in Derry and Drogheda).[41] Printed sermons, including earlier classics and topical discourses, multiplied. Many were distributed free or at low prices, thanks to generous subsidies. However, some were purchased and then read within the household. Sometimes the reading was aloud, to guide the young and servants. They also formed the focus of private devotion.[42] A few had been preached originally in Ireland. A defence of *A Gentleman's Religion* by the future Archbishop Synge proved so popular in England as well as Ireland that it went through eight editions between 1693 and 1778.[43] But the pious authors most frequently noted on Irish shelves were stalwarts of the Church of England, with John Tillotson a recent favourite.[44] Improving and exhortatory reading was not confined to English and Irish Anglicans, as the popularity of Richard Baxter, Augustine, Francis de Sales, and Fénelon's *Telemachus* showed.[45]

Local exemplars brought to the notice of Irish readers in the seventeenth century were generally bishops. Their lives seldom included dramatic acts of sacrifice and heroism. Celebration of that sort, implicitly or explicitly describing the dangers to which the Church of Ireland minority in a Catholic land had been subjected, was channelled into annual celebrations of the deliverances on 23 October (from a planned massacre in 1641) and on 4 and 5 November (from successive Catholic plots, most lately with William of Orange as the Protestants' saviour). Addresses occasioned by these commemorations, typically anti-Catholic in tone and content, continued to be published until the 1770s.[46]

Strenuous bishops were not especially gripping exemplars to put before a miscreant laity. In the mid-eighteenth century, when a Dublin minister was held up for admiration, it was primarily as an example to younger clergy.[47] Lay

---

[41] *A Collection of Psalms and Hymns proper for Christian Worship* (Londonderry, 1788); *Psalms Selected for the Use of St. Peter's Church, Drogheda* (Drogheda, 1777).

[42] H. F. Berry, 'Notes from the Diary of a Dublin Lady in the Reign of George II', *Journal of the Royal Society of Antiquaries of Ireland*, 5th series, 8 (1898), pp. 143–4; Noel Ross (ed.), 'The Diary of Marianne Fortescue, 1797–1800', *County Louth Archaeological and Historical Journal*, 24 (1998–9): 222–44, 357–79.

[43] Lady Llanover (ed.), *The Autobiography and Correspondence of Mary Granville, Mrs Delany*, 6 vols. (London, 1861–2), III, p. 87.

[44] For contradictory views on Tillotson's popularity, see *Seasonable Advice to the Publick concerning a Book of Memoirs lately published* (Dublin, 1748); *An Answer to Seasonable Advice to the Publick* (Dublin, 1748).

[45] Raymond Gillespie, *Devoted People: Belief and Religion in Early Modern Ireland* (Manchester, 1997).

[46] Barnard, 'The Uses of 23 October 1641'; James Kelly, '"The Glorious and Immortal Memory": Commemoration and Protestant Identity in Ireland 1660–1800', *Proceedings of the Royal Irish Academy*, sect. C, 94 (1994): 25–52.

[47] Matthew West, *The Blessedness of Death: A Sermon preached at the Funeral of the Revd. John Clements Chaigneau* (Dublin, 1776).

paragons were rare. An exception was James Bonnell. Of a family driven from continental Europe by Catholic persecution, he had risen high in the Dublin administration but died young in 1699. Bonnell's grieving widow pressed to have his conspicuous piety publicized. The *Life*, heavily subsidized, entered many Irish homes. Yet, it remained a lonely example of the genre, and its impact is impossible to gauge.[48] Bonnell did offer an early instance of practical piety rather than quietism. In this, he pointed the way to the fusion of classical and Christian humanism which underlay the civic activism strong among Church of Ireland laypeople later in the eighteenth century. These traits were not peculiar to Ireland. Indeed, as in so much else in the Church of Ireland— its liturgy, teaching, literature, and preoccupations—the dependence on England was heavy. In Ireland, however, the disjunction between the legal favours lavished on the Established Church and its numerical strength was more, and embarrassingly, glaring. In order to justify these privileges and to still criticism, the Church of Ireland needed to be seen at the fore of attempts to alleviate Irish ills and to reach beyond its own adherents. Arguably the often precocious schemes of economic, medical, and educational amelioration were the answers. Members of the Church of Ireland were not alone in these ventures, but, thanks to their unusual advantages of power and money, they were well placed to act.[49] Some did.

SELECT BIBLIOGRAPHY

Akenson, Donald H., *The Church of Ireland: Ecclesiastical Reform and Revolution, 1800–1885* (New Haven, CT and London, 1971).

Barnard, Toby, 'Fabrics of Faith: The Material Worlds of Catholic Ireland and Protestant Ireland, 1500–1800', in Raghnall Ó Floinn (ed.), *Franciscan Faith: Sacred Art in Ireland, AD 1600–1750* (Dublin, 2011), pp. 31–41.

Barnard, Toby, *A New Anatomy of Ireland: The Irish Protestants, 1649–1770* (New Haven, CT and London, 2003).

Barnard, T. C. and W. G. Neely (eds.), *The Clergy of the Church of Ireland, 1000–2000: Messengers, Watchmen and Stewards* (Dublin, 2006).

Connolly, S. J., *Religion, Law and Power: The Making of Protestant Ireland, 1660–1760* (Oxford, 1992).

Fauske, Christopher (ed.), *Archbishop William King and the Anglican Irish Context, 1688–1729* (Dublin, 2004).

---

[48] William Hamilton, *The Life and Character of James Bonnell Esq* (Dublin, 1703); Toby Barnard, 'Print and Confession in Eighteenth-Century Ireland', in Caroline Archer and Lisa Peters (eds.), *Religion and the Book Trade* (Newcastle upon Tyne, 2015), pp. 99–129.

[49] Cf. Colm Lennon, 'Confraternities in Ireland: A Long View', in Colm Lennon (ed.), *Confraternities and Sodalities in Ireland: Charity, Devotion and Sociability* (Dublin, 2012), pp. 23–4.

Fauske, Christopher, *A Political Biography of William King* (London, 2011).

Ford, Alan, James McGuire, and Kenneth Milne (eds.), *As by Law Established: The Church of Ireland since the Reformation* (Dublin, 1995).

Gillespie, Raymond, *Devoted People: Belief and Religion in Early Modern Ireland* (Manchester, 1997).

Gillespie, Raymond and R. Ó Gallachóir (eds.), *Preaching in Belfast, 1747–72: A Selection of the Sermons of James Saurin* (Dublin, 2015).

Gillespie, Raymond and W. G. Neely (eds.), *The Laity and the Church of Ireland, 1000–2000: All Sorts and Conditions* (Dublin, 2002).

Hayton, D. W., *The Anglo-Irish Experience, 1680–1730: Religion, Identity and Patriotism* (Woodbridge, 2012).

Hayton, D. W., 'Parliament and the Established Church: Reform and Reaction', in D. W. Hayton, James Kelly, and John Bergin (eds.), *The Eighteenth-Century Composite State: Representative Institutions in Ireland and Europe, 1689–1800* (Basingstoke, 2010), pp. 78–106.

James, Francis Godwin, *North Country Bishop: A Biography of William Nicolson* (New Haven, CT and London, 1956).

Kelly, James, 'Defending the Established Order: Richard Woodward, Bishop of Cloyne (1726–94)', in James Kelly, John McCafferty, and Charles Ivor McGrath (eds.), *People, Politics and Power: Essays in Irish History in Honour of James I. McGuire* (Dublin, 2009), pp. 143–74.

Leighton, C. D. A., 'The Enlightened Religion of Robert Clayton', *Studia Hibernica*, 29 (1995–7): 157–84.

McNally, Patrick, '"Irish and English Interests": National Conflict within the Church of Ireland Episcopate in the Reign of George I', *Irish Historical Studies*, 29 (1995): 295–314.

Milne, Kenneth, *The Irish Charter Schools, 1730–1830* (Dublin, 1997).

O'Regan, Philip, *Archbishop William King (1650–1729) and the Constitution in Church and State* (Dublin, 2000).

Whelan, Irene, *The Bible War in Ireland: The 'Second Reformation' and the Polarization of Protestant–Catholic Relations in Ireland, 1800–1840* (Dublin and Madison, WI, 2005).

Yates, Nigel, *The Religious Condition of Ireland, 1770–1850* (Oxford, 2006).

8

Scotland

Alasdair Raffe

For most of our period, the Episcopal Church in Scotland was not 'Anglican', and its relationship to the Church of England was ambiguous. After the Restoration of the monarchy, Charles II re-established bishops in England, Ireland, and Scotland, hoping that greater religious uniformity would ensure political peace. But the Scottish Church differed in important ways from the Churches of England and Ireland. The Scottish Church retained practices and structures deriving from the Presbyterian system, notably the parochial kirk session with its lay elders and the district-level presbytery. For some years after 1662, a majority of the clergy lacked episcopal orders. In line with sixteenth- and early seventeenth-century practice, few entering the ministry in the Restoration period were ordained deacons before becoming presbyters. More often than not, indeed, conformists saw episcopacy itself as a thing indifferent, well suited to royal power, but not necessarily the system of government specified by God. Church services were based on extemporary prayer and lengthy preaching rather than a formal liturgy. And Presbyterian Dissent gravely undermined the Church, especially in southern and western Scotland. When at the Revolution of 1688–90 a weak Church, led by uncompromisingly Jacobite bishops, faced a resurgent Presbyterianism allied with William of Orange's chief supporters, established episcopacy could not survive.[1]

Considering the trials they faced during the Restoration period, it is unsurprising that the Scottish prelates wished their Church were more closely allied to the Church of England. The southern establishment is 'in all respects, the best constituted Church in the world', the Scottish bishops addressed their English counterparts in 1680. Nevertheless, the Scots wrote later that year,

---

[1] Alasdair Raffe, 'The Restoration, the Revolution and the Failure of Episcopacy in Scotland', in Tim Harris and Stephen Taylor (eds.), *The Final Crisis of the Stuart Monarchy* (Woodbridge, 2013), pp. 87–108; Walter R. Foster, *Bishop and Presbytery: The Church of Scotland, 1661–1688* (London, 1958); Gordon Donaldson, 'Scottish Ordinations in the Restoration Period', *Scottish Historical Review*, 33 (1954): 169–75.

'the happines of a perfect union betwixt the two sister Churches in this island is, through the unhappines and distraction of the tymes, denyed us'.[2] Leading Scottish Episcopalians would have liked the worship and constitution of their Church to be remodelled after the Anglican pattern. But Charles II and James VII feared a reprise of the Prayer Book riots and Bishops' Wars of the 1637–40 period, and sought to avoid the unrest that reforms might have provoked.[3] Moreover, the restored monarchy had more authority over the Church of Scotland than in the Church of England, and to have brought the northern Church into alignment with the southern would have weakened the crown's considerable discretion in religious policy.

After the Revolution of 1688–90, the Jacobitism of most Episcopalian clergy and many laypeople further complicated their attitudes towards the Church of England. Strictly speaking, the Scots' sister Church was now the group of English non-jurors that had split from the much larger body of Anglicans who recognized William and Mary as monarchs. It was only the participation of Scottish bishops that allowed for the continuation of an English non-juring episcopate, through the canonical consecration of new Jacobite bishops in 1713.[4] When in the late eighteenth century this English succession failed, the Scottish bishops retained links with the remaining non-juring clergy south of the border.[5] Even in the reign of Queen Anne, to whom some moderate Jacobites gave allegiance, Bishop Alexander Rose of Edinburgh declined to give a clear answer when asked if the Scottish bishops were in communion with the Church of England.[6] By this time, many Scottish Episcopalians used the English Book of Common Prayer, and had adopted robust doctrines of episcopacy.[7] Nevertheless, Jacobitism made impossible a formal union with the Church of England.

There were, however, Episcopalians who accepted William, Anne, and the Hanoverian monarchs. Under an Act of the Scottish Parliament of 1695, Episcopalian ministers who swore the allegiance oath and signed the assurance that William was monarch *de jure* were entitled to retain parish churches they had held since the Revolution.[8] About 116 complied; they were not required to cooperate with the Presbyterian Church courts. But most of these Episcopalians

---

[2] W. N. Clarke (ed.), *A Collection of Letters addressed by Prelates and Individuals of High Rank in Scotland and by two Bishops of Sodor and Man to Sancroft Archbishop of Canterbury* (Edinburgh, 1848), pp. 8, 14.

[3] Clarke (ed.), *A Collection of Letters*, pp. 67, 86, 92–3; Raffe, 'Restoration'.

[4] Henry Broxap, *The Later Non-Jurors* (Cambridge, 1924), pp. 11, 349.

[5] George Grub, *An Ecclesiastical History of Scotland*, 4 vols. (Edinburgh, 1861), IV, pp. 89–90.

[6] John Skinner, *An Ecclesiastical History of Scotland*, 2 vols. (London, 1788), II, p. 615.

[7] Alasdair Raffe, 'Presbyterians and Episcopalians: The Formation of Confessional Cultures in Scotland, 1660–1715', *English Historical Review*, 125 (2010): 570–98.

[8] *Records of the Parliaments of Scotland to 1707*, ed. Keith M. Brown and others, 1695/5/186, <http://www.rps.ac.uk/>, accessed 2 Sept. 2013.

had died or been removed from their parishes by 1716.[9] Statutory toleration for Episcopalian worship in meeting-houses was first granted by the British Parliament in 1712. The Act required that clergy qualify by swearing the oaths (now including an abjuration of the Pretender), submit their letters of orders to the local justices of the peace, and pray for the monarch and royal family by name.[10] 'Qualified' chapels began to open where there was a desire for worship according to the 1662 Book of Common Prayer, and (as in Edinburgh) where the congregation was partially English. At first, there was some cooperation between qualified clergy and non-jurors, but the Jacobitism of the latter increasingly deterred Episcopalians loyal to the Hanoverian monarchs. A change to the law in 1746 (as clarified in 1748) allowed toleration only to clergy ordained by an English or Irish bishop.[11] These ministers did not subject themselves to the Scottish bishops, and while in Scotland they were free from English or Irish episcopal oversight. There were no regular arrangements for laypeople to be confirmed by a bishop. The qualified chapels were few in number: there were twenty-four at the start of the nineteenth century.[12] But as we shall see, these congregations helped to determine that the future of the Scottish Episcopal Church lay in closer conformity with the Church of England.

The majority of Scottish Episcopalians who remained outwith the protection of the law were subject to only intermittent harassment and prosecution. The authorities' actions against them peaked after the Jacobite risings of 1715 and 1745. The 1712 Toleration Act had threatened ministers with a fine of twenty pounds sterling for failing to pray publicly for the queen, and with three years' deprivation from ministerial office for a second offence.[13] From 1719, ministers who preached to congregations when unqualified or failed to pray for the king were liable to six months' imprisonment, during which time their meeting-houses were to be shut. This statute defined an episcopal congregation as nine persons in addition to members of the minister's household.[14] The more severe penal law of 1746 imposed transportation for unqualified ministers convicted twice, redefined a congregation as five persons other than the household, and specified fines and imprisonment for lay worshippers.[15] Only in 1792 were the penalties relaxed—to the levels set in 1712. Episcopalian ministers were again asked to qualify themselves by swearing the allegiance, assurance, and abjuration.[16] The great majority of Episcopalian clergy had abandoned their association with the exiled royal family after the death of Prince Charles Edward Stuart in 1788. But they saw the abjuration oath as incompatible

---

[9] Tristram N. Clarke, 'The Scottish Episcopalians, 1688–1720', PhD thesis, University of Edinburgh, 1987, pp. 130–2, 384–5.

[10] 10 Ann. c. 7.   [11] 19 Geo. II c. 38; 21 Geo. III c. 34.

[12] John Skinner, *Annals of Scottish Episcopacy, from the Year 1788 to the Year 1816* (Edinburgh, 1818), pp. 419–20; Patrick Jones, 'The Qualified Episcopal Chapels of the North-East of Scotland, 1689–1898', *Northern Scotland*, 20 (2000): 47–69.

[13] 10 Ann. c. 7.   [14] 5 Geo. I c. 29.   [15] 19 Geo. II c. 38.   [16] 32 Geo. III c. 63.

with their former Jacobite principles and refused to swear it. The clergy remained in breach of the law, and yet they enjoyed the informal toleration that had gradually developed from the 1760s.[17]

Though many Episcopalians remained principled Jacobites until 1788, in reality the Church became increasingly independent of the Stuarts from the 1720s. After the death in 1704 of Archbishop Arthur Ross of St Andrews, his metropolitan see was not filled, though Bishop Alexander Rose of Edinburgh claimed vicariate authority in the province of St Andrews. Mindful of the power of 'James VIII' over episcopal nominations, which the exiled king considered it 'impracticable' to exercise, the consecrations of the 1700s and 1710s created mere 'college' bishops, men without dioceses or formal power to govern the Church. When Rose, the last surviving pre-Revolution bishop, died in 1720, the clergy of the Edinburgh area elected John Fullarton to the see, and the other bishops gave him the title of 'primus' of the episcopal college.[18] Rose's death encouraged calls for bishops to exercise authority over specified districts (somewhat modified from the traditional dioceses). Though some ministers and (more often) laymen continued to defer to James's prerogatives, others insisted that a district's clergy should elect its bishop. On the other hand, the so-called 'college party' continued to consecrate bishops without assigning them territorial jurisdiction. In 1727, the bishops of the 'diocesan party' met as a synod and attempted to resolve the dispute with a set of canons creating elected diocesan bishops. These canons were then unacceptable to the college bishops, but the principles of territorial episcopacy and elections by the clergy were reiterated in an agreement of 1731 and canons of 1743.[19] Thus the consequences of the sudden disestablishment of episcopacy in 1689—a reform sought neither by the bishops nor by their king—were worked out over several decades. From the debates between the college party and their 'diocesan' opponents emerged a self-governing, non-established Episcopal Church. When in 1784 legal restrictions hindered English bishops from consecrating Samuel Seabury as the first bishop of the American Episcopal Church, the Scots were free to perform the rite.[20] Moreover, the Scottish Church's autonomy, its escape from early modern patterns of Erastian interference, helped to gain it the admiration of English High Churchmen and Tractarians.[21]

---

[17] Skinner, *Annals of Scottish Episcopacy*, pp. 245–7; F. C. Mather, 'Church, Parliament and Penal Laws: Some Anglo-Scottish Interactions in the Eighteenth Century', *English Historical Review*, 92 (1977): 540–72; Grub, *Ecclesiastical History*, IV, pp. 86–7.

[18] Grub, *Ecclesiastical History*, III, pp. 346–57, 381–4; Anthony Aufrere (ed.), *The Lockhart Papers*, 2 vols. (London, 1817), II, p. 39 (quotation).

[19] Grub, *Ecclesiastical History*, III, pp. 385–7, 395–9, IV, pp. 1–17.

[20] Gavin White, 'The Consecration of Bishop Seabury', *Scottish Historical Review*, 63 (1984): 37–49.

[21] Peter Nockles, '"Our Brethren of the North": The Scottish Episcopal Church and the Oxford Movement', *Journal of Ecclesiastical History*, 47 (1996): 655–82.

The disestablishment of Scottish episcopacy made structural change inevitable. And the removal of close governmental control over the Episcopalians was a prerequisite for the other major controversy of the early eighteenth century: the debate about liturgical usages.[22] As we have noted, the Restoration Church of Scotland had no liturgy. In Anne's reign, many Episcopalians adopted the 1662 Book of Common Prayer, to secure English sympathy for their cause, and out of a desire for more formal worship.[23] Though copies of the Scottish Prayer Book of 1637 were scarce, ministers were aware that its communion service had restored traditional prayers present in the 1549 Prayer Book but absent in subsequent English Prayer Books. Influenced by English non-jurors, notably Jeremy Collier and Thomas Brett, a party of 'usagers' favoured the saying of prayers of invocation and oblation in the consecration of the eucharist, the mixing of water with the communion wine, and prayers for the faithful departed.[24] As with the debates about ecclesiastical structures, the Scottish bishops were divided. Opponents of the usages complained that their advocates lacked the authority to introduce them to the Church's worship.[25] But no individual's authority was sufficient to resolve the dispute, and it required negotiation to achieve a compromise. The concordat signed in July 1724 between the leading usager Bishop James Gadderar and his episcopal brethren allowed for the invocation and oblation, which were sanctioned by the 1637 book, but prevented Gadderar from promoting the other usages.[26]

The communion office of 1637 was reprinted in a series of editions from 1722 (known as 'wee bookies'), and its use became more widespread. The scholarship of Thomas Rattray, bishop of Dunkeld and editor of the posthumous *Ancient Liturgy of the Church of Jerusalem* (1744), helped ensure that the concordat of 1724 did not end the Episcopalians' interest in primitive liturgical forms. Indeed, the communion office's various editors gradually reordered the prayers so that the service resembled one published by the English non-jurors in 1718. Though qualified chapels and some other Episcopalians preferred the 1662 service, the revised communion office of 1764 became widely used in the Scottish Episcopal Church, especially in the north.[27] The office had resulted from a process of liturgical experimentation and evolution, which could scarcely

---

[22] See also, in this volume, Chapter 14 by Bryan D. Spinks.

[23] Tristram Clarke, 'Politics and Prayer Books: The Book of Common Prayer in Scotland, c.1705–1714', *Edinburgh Bibliographical Society Transactions*, 6 (1993): 57–70.

[24] Charles Hefling, 'Scotland: Episcopalians and Non-Jurors', in Charles Hefling and Cynthia Shattuck (eds.), *The Oxford Guide to the Book of Common Prayer: A Worldwide Survey* (Oxford, 2006), pp. 166–75; Kieran German, 'Aberdeen, Aberdeenshire and Jacobitism in the North-East of Scotland, 1688–1750', PhD thesis, University of Aberdeen, 2010, pp. 83–6.

[25] E.g. Bishops John Fullarton, Arthur Millar, Andrew Cant, and David Freebairn to Alexander Robertson, 9 Mar. 1723, CH12/12/11, National Records of Scotland, Edinburgh.

[26] Grub, *Ecclesiastical History*, III, pp. 394–5.

[27] John Dowden, *The Scottish Communion Office 1764* (Oxford, 1922 edn.), pp. 63–79; Hefling, 'Scotland', pp. 172–3.

have happened in the Established Church of England. Again, disestablishment had set the Scottish Church on a distinctive course.

While the Scottish Episcopalians made structural and liturgical reforms, their Church shrank. The penal laws deterred worshippers, the commitment of laypeople to Jacobitism waned, and the rise of Presbyterian Moderatism attracted many to the Established Church. There were perhaps 150 clergy in communion with the Scottish bishops in 1745.[28] In 1800, the primus Bishop John Skinner estimated that the Episcopal Church (excluding qualified congregations) had a membership of around 11,000 regularly attending adults. The largest communities were in Edinburgh and the north-east. There were now fifty presbyters, overseen by six bishops.[29] The latter combined their episcopal responsibilities with a congregational ministry; often a bishop's meeting-house was outside his diocese. Robert Forbes, a minister in South Leith, was elected bishop of the northerly diocese of Ross and Caithness in 1762. Though he set out for a visitation tour, the distance between his home and diocese, together with the official harassment resulting from his Jacobitism, complicated his activities as bishop.[30]

After transferring their allegiance from the Stuarts to the Hanoverians in 1788, the Scottish Episcopalians were able to lobby for the repeal of the penal laws. As we have noted, the Relief Act of 1792 had little practical effect. But it was symbolic of the Church's gradual rehabilitation; by the time of George IV's visit to Scotland in 1822, Scottish Episcopalians were known for their loyalty to the crown.[31] The changes of 1788 and 1792 also initiated attempts to confront three remaining anomalies in the Church's position: the continued lack of official doctrinal standards for Episcopalians, the status of the qualified congregations, and the related debates about the Scottish communion office.

The Relief Act of 1792 required clergy to approve the Church of England's Thirty-Nine Articles in order to receive full legal protection.[32] When the bill was before Parliament, the chancellor Lord Thurlow had requested that it include some measure of the Episcopalians' doctrinal views. Declaring assent to the Thirty-Nine Articles was the obvious test; parliamentarians recalled the equivalent requirement in the Act of 1689 granting toleration to English

---

[28] Grub, *Ecclesiastical History*, IV, p. 32.

[29] Rowan Strong, *Alexander Forbes of Brechin: The First Tractarian Bishop* (Oxford, 1995), pp. 12–13.

[30] J. B. Craven (ed.), *Journals of the Episcopal Visitations of the Right Rev. Robert Forbes* (London, 1886).

[31] Rowan Strong, 'The Reconstruction of Episcopalian Identity in Scotland: The Renunciation of the Stuart Allegiance in 1788', *Records of the Scottish Church History Society*, 33 (2003): 143–64 (pp. 160–1).

[32] 32 Geo. III c. 63.

Dissenters.[33] Representing the Episcopalians, Bishop Skinner argued that, while his brethren generally accepted the Thirty-Nine Articles, they would object to signing them as the articles of the Church of England, 'since the Scottish Episcopal Church was no part of the Church of England, and could not...be included in it'.[34] In 1803, Skinner explained that Episcopalian clergy, as members of a disestablished Church, would not give an account of their doctrinal views before civil magistrates.[35] In fact, the Scots' reservations about the Articles were more substantial than this, and included hostility to potential Calvinistic readings of the seventeenth article, and concern that the twenty-fifth article's criticism of Catholic sacraments denigrated confirmation.[36]

Nevertheless, there were at least two reasons for the Church formally to accept the Thirty-Nine Articles. One was its lack of a confession of faith, aside from the historic creeds. This made the Episcopalians vulnerable to criticism, and potentially allowed them to harbour theological innovation. The second was that it was hoped that adopting the Articles would encourage qualified chapels to unite with the Scottish Episcopal Church. This consideration had a particular influence on the synod at Laurencekirk in October 1804, which saw the Church declare its approval of the Thirty-Nine Articles. Bishop Skinner, a leading proponent of the reform, was shortly before the meeting persuaded to abandon a preamble addressing the clergy's doubts about the Articles. Aside from the doctrinal issues already mentioned, the preamble explained that articles 35, 36, and 37, concerning the homilies, episcopal consecration, and the civil magistrate, 'are all peculiar to the religious establishment of England'.[37] It was politically wise to suppress this document; even though it was not adopted, Evangelicals later questioned how fully the Episcopal Church accepted the Thirty-Nine Articles.[38] But the preamble well illustrated the Episcopalians' self-image as an independent, non-established Church, residing in a part of the United Kingdom in which the Church of England had no legal status.

By providing a 'public testimony' of the Scottish Church's 'agreement in doctrine and discipline with the united Church of England and Ireland', the adoption of the Thirty-Nine Articles was a crucial step towards uniting the qualified chapels with the other Episcopalians.[39] A qualified congregation in

---

[33] Skinner, *Annals of Scottish Episcopacy*, p. 214; Mather, 'Church, Parliament and Penal Laws', p. 563.

[34] Skinner, *Annals of Scottish Episcopacy*, p. 215.

[35] John Skinner, *Primitive Truth and Order Vindicated from Modern Misrepresentation* (Aberdeen, 1803), p. 479.

[36] Skinner, *Annals of Scottish Episcopacy*, pp. 539–41.

[37] Skinner, *Annals of Scottish Episcopacy*, pp. 251–2, 330–51, 539–43 (quotation at p. 542).

[38] Nockles, '"Our Brethren of the North"', pp. 677–8.

[39] Skinner, *Annals of Scottish Episcopacy*, pp. 348–9.

Banff had joined itself to the diocese of Aberdeen after the Relief Act of 1792. But it was the Laurencekirk synod that prompted the important Edinburgh Anglican Daniel Sandford to unite his congregation to the Scottish Episcopal Church in November 1804. After legal advice was received that the provision in the 1792 statute preventing the Scottish clergy from receiving preferment in the Church of England did not apply to Scots in English orders, other qualified congregations formally joined the Scottish Church. In March 1806, Bishop Skinner could inform the archbishop of Canterbury that thirteen of the twenty-four qualified chapels were now subject to the Scottish bishops. In the previous month, Sandford had been consecrated as bishop of Edinburgh. Understandably pleased with the progress of Episcopalian integration, Skinner described Sandford's elevation as a sign of 'increasing union and communion' between the 'sister' Churches in Scotland and England.[40]

Nevertheless, liturgical variety remained an occasional source of tension within the Church. Most of the former qualified chapels used the Book of Common Prayer for all services; many erstwhile non-jurors preferred the Scottish office for communion. The Church's official position was that articles 20 and 34 of the Thirty-Nine Articles justified the use in Scotland of a distinctive office.[41] But this argument did not necessarily explain why the Church allowed *both* forms of service. According to Alexander Grant, minister of the English congregation in Dundee, '[t]wo different Liturgies in the same church, instead of unity would introduce division, and produce confusion, where all must allow the necessity of preserving order'. Grant insisted that the Scottish office did not differ from the Prayer Book simply in verbal points, and that it contained erroneous beliefs and practices, notably prayers for the dead and the mixed cup. For Grant, these matters made it unthinkable that he should unite with the Scottish Church.[42] Though his objections were overstated, Grant highlighted one of the Church's problems. Bishop Skinner encouraged clergy to continue using the Scottish office, but others who prioritized unity with England or held Evangelical views saw the non-jurors' liturgical tradition as faulty.[43]

Pressures towards more complete communion with the Church of England shaped another early nineteenth-century liturgical debate: that concerning precise conformity with the Prayer Book's text and rubrics. In the non-juring tradition, which Bishop Skinner defended, it was common for clergy to

---

[40] Skinner, *Annals of Scottish Episcopacy*, pp. 242–5, 358–9, 388–90, 404–18, 419–20 (quotations at pp. 408–9); Eleanor Harris, 'Reconciliation and Revival: Bishop Daniel Sandford of Edinburgh, 1766–1830', *Records of the Scottish Church History Society*, 42 (2013): 35–73.

[41] *The Code of Canons of the Episcopal Church in Scotland* (Aberdeen, 1811), pp. 18–19.

[42] Alexander Grant, *An Apology for Continuing in the Communion of the Church of England* (Dundee, 1805), p. 4 (quotation).

[43] Skinner, *Annals of Scottish Episcopacy*, pp. 433–5, 444; Christopher Knight, 'The Anglicising of Scottish Episcopalianism', *Records of the Scottish Church History Society*, 23 (1987–9): 361–77.

introduce small verbal alterations in daily worship. By contrast, George Gleig, who was elected coadjutor bishop of Brechin in 1808, urged his clergy to stick rigidly to the Prayer Book's words. This disagreement encouraged the adoption by a synod at Aberdeen in 1811 of canons more detailed than any since 1636.[44] Though canon 15 authorized the Scottish communion office, canon 16 required clergy to use the Prayer Book's precise words in morning and evening prayer, except where the Church's non-established status led the bishop to allow alterations. When the canons were revised in 1828, even this justification for verbal variety was omitted.[45]

From 1788 to the end of our period, the various changes in the Scottish Church's status brought it into closer alignment with the Church of England. Another sign of the 1811 canons' tendency to promote Anglican norms was the recommendation, in an appendix, that clergy wear the surplice.[46] The integration of formerly non-juring and qualified congregations had catalysed an Anglicizing process, which continued through the nineteenth century.[47] But at the same time, the Scottish Church was aware of its status as a branch of the universal catholic Church, characterized by Episcopalian order and mildly Protestant doctrine. This understanding of an international Church, which lay behind Samuel Seabury's consecration, was further developed in 1825 with the elevation to the episcopate of Matthew Luscombe to serve as missionary bishop to Anglicans in continental Europe. Preaching at Luscombe's consecration, the English priest Walter Farquhar Hook asserted the 'catholicism of the Church of England and the other branches of the episcopal Church', among which he included the Scottish and American Churches.[48] Luscombe's appointment was to address problems among continental Anglicans—a lack of episcopal oversight and difficulties in obtaining ordination and confirmation—that had recently characterized the Scottish qualified congregations. Though his office was to prove a temporary expedient, it suggests that at the end of the period, even while the Scottish Episcopalians emulated their English brethren, their recent past offered lessons for the future of international Anglicanism.[49]

---

[44] Skinner, *Annals of Scottish Episcopacy*, pp. 483–507.

[45] *Code of Canons*, pp. 18–19; *The Code of Canons of the Protestant Episcopal Church in Scotland* (Edinburgh, 1828), pp. 51–2.

[46] *Code of Canons* (1811), appendix, pp. 5–6.

[47] Knight, 'Anglicising of Scottish Episcopalianism'.

[48] Walter Farquhar Hook, *An Attempt to Demonstrate the Catholicism of the Church of England and the other Branches of the Episcopal Church* (London, 1825).

[49] Gregory K. Cameron, 'Locating the Anglican Communion in the History of Anglicanism', in Ian S. Markham, J. Barney Hawkins IV, Justyn Terry, and Leslie Nunez Steffensen (eds.), *The Wiley-Blackwell Companion to the Anglican Communion* (Chichester, 2013), pp. 3–14 (p. 11).

SELECT BIBLIOGRAPHY

Clarke, Tristram N., 'The Scottish Episcopalians, 1688–1720', PhD thesis, University of Edinburgh, 1987.

Foster, Walter R., *Bishop and Presbytery: The Church of Scotland, 1661–1688* (London, 1958).

Grub, George, *An Ecclesiastical History of Scotland*, 4 vols. (Edinburgh, 1861).

Hefling, Charles, 'Scotland: Episcopalians and Non-Jurors', in Charles Hefling and Cynthia Shattuck (eds.), *The Oxford Guide to the Book of Common Prayer: A Worldwide Survey* (Oxford, 2006), pp. 166–75.

Knight, Christopher, 'The Anglicising of Scottish Episcopalianism', *Records of the Scottish Church History Society*, 23 (1987–9): 361–77.

Nockles, Peter, '"Our Brethren of the North": The Scottish Episcopal Church and the Oxford Movement', *Journal of Ecclesiastical History*, 47 (1996): 655–82.

Raffe, Alasdair, 'Presbyterians and Episcopalians: The Formation of Confessional Cultures in Scotland, 1660–1715', *English Historical Review*, 125 (2010): 570–98.

Raffe, Alasdair, 'The Restoration, the Revolution and the Failure of Episcopacy in Scotland', in Tim Harris and Stephen Taylor (eds.), *The Final Crisis of the Stuart Monarchy* (Woodbridge, 2013), pp. 87–108.

Strong, Rowan, 'The Reconstruction of Episcopalian Identity in Scotland: The Renunciation of the Stuart Allegiance in 1788', *Records of the Scottish Church History Society*, 33 (2003): 143–64.

9

North America

James B. Bell

The account of English colonization and the accompanying extension of the Church of England to North America in the seventeenth and early eighteenth centuries was in large part shaped by a continuation of Old World political and diplomatic conflicts in the New World, particularly clashes between Spain and France. The first effort at colonization at Jamestown, Virginia, was delegated to, and under the sponsorship of, the merchant adventurers of the Virginia Company of London in 1607, and the second at St John's, Newfoundland, eighty years later was arranged by the Board of Trade and Plantations. England's forays in the region began during the age of exploration and discovery and were driven by a concern to counter France's position and power in diplomatic, military, and political affairs. Relations between these two European powers in the Western hemisphere moved through several wars and stages of resolution at peace conferences at Utrecht in 1713, Aix-la-Chapelle in 1748, and Paris in 1763.

For more than four centuries after Bishop White Kennett's 1706 publication of *An Account of the Society for the Propagation of the Gospel* an array of historians have presented in different styles, manners, and perspectives accounts of the extension of the Church of England to early America.[1] Interest in the subject accelerated particularly in America during the nineteenth and twentieth centuries, with a primary focus on its development as a distinctive denomination and the controversies with non-Anglicans over the nature and establishment of episcopacy and the role of the missionaries of the Society for

---

[1] White Kennett, *An Account of the Society for the Propagation of the Gospel in Foreign Parts* (London, 1706); *Bibliothecanae Primordia: An Attempt towards laying the Foundation of an American Library, in several Books, Papers, and Writings, humbly given to the Society for the Propagation of the Gospel in Foreign Parts* (London, 1713); *The Lets and Impediments in Planting and Propagating the Gospel of Christ: A Sermon Preach'd before the Society for the Propagating of the Gospel at their Anniversary Meeting in the Parish-Church of St. Mary-le-Bow, 15th of February, 1711/12* (London, 1712).

the Propagation of the Gospel.[2] More recently attention has shifted to recognition of the Church as a component of the unwritten constitution of England and Great Britain and as a vital element of imperial policy, administration, and philanthropy during the seventeenth and eighteenth centuries. This chapter reflects on the place of the Church during the period between 1660 and 1829 in the context of contemporary transatlantic imperial political, religious, and cultural affairs in England and the five varied geographical regions of English and British America.

THE AMERICAN COLONIES: 1662–1783

In the Virginia colony the first meeting of the provincial legislature at Jamestown in 1619 established the Church of England, more than a decade after settlement and after the arrival at irregular intervals of half a dozen men to serve as ministers. By 1624 the company was bankrupt, and the next year the province was created as a royal jurisdiction by James I. During the next five decades the Church made marginal progress in the sparsely settled colony with a string of ministers. All of the men arrived independently, not under the auspices of an English prelate or state agency, perhaps attracted by the opportunity to receive on arrival a head grant of fifty acres of land for each member of his family or party. By 1660 the legislature had created fifty-four parishes in the counties, but there were only eight church buildings and eight ministers for a thin population of 22,020 persons. In New England a handful of ministers arrived individually between about 1622 and 1660 but without regularly performing services or gaining any right to grants of land.[3] They too were without formal supervision by an English Church official guided by a defined imperial policy for the kingdom's overseas territorial interests.

England's North American presence during the years between 1660 and 1700 was without uniformity, varying in law and organization in New England, the Middle, Chesapeake, and Southern colonies. Over the half-century following 1660, English interest in the New World began and included the introduction of stronger royal government and economic policies and the Anglican Church. The administrative affairs of the overseas territories were in the hands of the members and bureaucrats of the Board of Trade and Plantations at Whitehall. But in England the attention of Archbishop Gilbert

---

[2] Included among the group are the publications of James S. M. Anderson, Francis Lister Hawks, Ernest Hawkins, William Stevens Perry, William W. Manross, Raymond W. Albright, John F. Woolverton, Alfred Lyon Cross, Carl Bridenbaugh, Patricia U. Bonomi, and Frederick V. Mills, Sr.

[3] James B. Bell, *Anglicans, Dissenters and Radical Change in Early New England, 1686–1786* (Basingstoke, 2017).

Sheldon of Canterbury to the overseas Church was overshadowed and driven by the essential role which he played in leading the political process for the re-establishment in 1662 of the Church and the Book of Common Prayer. Unexpectedly, the situation for the Church in North America would be transformed by a letter in 1661 from Roger Green, a graduate of St Catharine's College, Cambridge, and minister at West Parish in Nansemond County, Virginia, between 1653 and 1671, to Sheldon (then bishop of London) under the pen name 'R.G.', reporting on the state of the Church and its twelve ministers in the colony.[4] His letter was published in London the following year with the title *Virginia's Cure*, and he pointedly declared that after more than half a century the Church was struggling with several deficiencies: the parishes lacked church buildings or glebes, and only about one-fifth of the congregations had ministers. He noted that at churches with an incumbent there was usually only one service on Sunday, and sometimes not at all if the weather was either too hot or too cold. His letter was not given further administrative attention for fifteen years until Sheldon, in 1676, asked Henry Compton, bishop of London, to present the details of the Church's circumstances in the American colonies of Virginia and Maryland, as reported by Green and John Yeo, for consideration at the next meeting of the Privy Council's Committee on Trade and Plantations.[5] As chief officers of state, both prelates were *ex officio* members of the committee. Compton, in his report, highlighted several basic shortcomings in the administration of the overseas Church, including the denial of the crown's right of patronage and presentation of all clergymen to parishes, a procedure that was neither asserted nor acknowledged by the colonial governors as the chief royal officials or the legislatures; the inadequate and precarious salaries of the ministers; the keeping of some parishes vacant to save the payment of a parson's salary; the retention of lay readers rather than the appointment of ordained ministers, to save the difference in salary; and the appropriation by the vestries of 'sole management of church affairs and [their] exercising an arbitrary power over the Ministers'.[6] The next year the crown delegated to Compton official

---

[4] James B. Bell, *The Imperial Origins of the King's Church in Early America, 1607–1783* (Basingstoke, 2004), pp. 12–13; Roger Green, *Virginia's Cure: or An Advisive Narrative Concerning Virginia. Discovering the True Ground of that Churches Unhappiness and the only true Remedy. As it was presented to the Right Reverend Father in God Guilbert Lord Bishop of London, September 2, 1661. Now publish'd to further the Welfare of that and the like Plantations* (London, 1662).

[5] Bell, *Imperial Origins*, pp. 12–14; *Calendar of State Papers, Colonial Series, 1675–1676* (London, 1893), pp. 435–6; *Calendar of State Papers, Colonial Series, 1677–1680* (London, 1896), pp. 121–2.

[6] The document is conveniently reprinted in E. T. Corwin (ed.), *Ecclesiastical Records, State of New York*, 7 vols. (Albany, NY, 1901–16), I, pp. 693–4; cf. Darrett Bruce Rutman and Anita H. Rutman, *A Place in Time: Middlesex County, Virginia, 1650–1750* (New York, 1986), pp. 56–7, 125–7.

jurisdiction and responsibility for the administration and supervision of the Church in the American settlements and the Caribbean Islands. Gradually over the next two decades the Church overseas was shaped in part by a coalition in London which included the Board of Trade and Plantations and the bishop of London, and in part by the provincial proprietor, the royal governor, or the legislature in the colonies. During the 1660s, twelve men served Virginia's parishes, increasing to nineteen in the 1670s, and thirty-three in the 1680s.[7] Presumably it was with the approval of the Board of Trade that the first Anglican ministers were appointed to serve in other colonies, including Boston (1686), Charleston (1688), and Philadelphia (1695). By 1680 the situation had dramatically improved in Virginia, with thirty-eight parishes served by thirty-four men.[8] Compton's experience, political sagacity, and standing with the government at home, and also his attentive interest in the overseas regions, shaped the accomplishments and destiny of the Church in North America until the Declaration of Independence. Among his successors in that episcopal office before the outbreak of the War for Independence only Edmund Gibson matched Compton's interest for a time, until his clash with the government leaders over the Quaker Bill in 1736.

Without any prospect of Parliament approving the creation of an American diocese or colonial bishop, Compton pressed for a detailed revision of the royal instructions issued to colonial governors in 1679 by the Privy Council. These charged the officials with several ecclesiastical duties: to ensure that the Book of Common Prayer was read each Sunday, that Holy Communion was celebrated according to the rites of the Church of England, and that no clergyman should be inducted into a benefice without a certificate from the bishop of London.[9] At Compton's prompting, a clause was added to the governors' instructions, directing them to oversee that laws were enacted in their colonies for the punishment of blasphemy, profanity, adultery, polygamy, profanation of the Sabbath, and other crimes against common morality. The instructions also required that the laws be enforced by the civil courts upon testimony furnished by the churchwardens. Whenever new members of the provincial councils were to be appointed, their names were submitted to the bishop of London for any objections he might have to their religious principles.[10] Under the evolving circumstances, the Board of Trade referred all colonial laws touching on religion or religious questions to Compton for

[7] James B. Bell, *Empire, Religion and Revolution in Early Virginia, 1607–1783* (Basingstoke, 2013), p. 60.

[8] Bell, *Imperial Origins*, pp. 11–13; Bell, *Empire, Religion and Revolution*, pp. 44, 111–12.

[9] Leonard Woods Labaree (ed.), *Royal Instructions to British Colonial Governors, 1670–1776*, 2 vols. (New Haven, CT, 1935), II, pp. 482–5.

[10] *Calendar of State Papers, Colonial Series, 1710–1711* (London, 1924), p. 560; *Journal of the Commissioners of Trade and Plantations, preserved in the Public Record Office: From February 1708/9 to March 1714/5* (London, 1925), pp. 284, 378.

review, since they may have encroached on his ecclesiastical jurisdiction, just as all statutes were sent to the crown's attorneys for any objection 'in point of law'.

Religious and civil leaders varied in the degree to which they welcomed the appearance of the Church of England in early America. Opposition was strongest in Massachusetts and Connecticut, accepted in the diverse religious community of New York, vastly outnumbered by Presbyterians and Dutch Reform ministers and churches in New Jersey and Pennsylvania and by Presbyterians in North and South Carolina. The establishment of the Anglican Church in six of the colonies was the result of the political persuasion and force of the royal governors and the approval of the colonial legislatures, usually after prolonged and acrimonious partisan objections. Establishment of the Church occurred in Virginia in 1619, in Maryland in 1692, in the lower four counties of New York the next year, in South Carolina in 1706, in Georgia in 1752, and in North Carolina in 1765. In Maryland, after fifteen years of toleration of the arbitrary government of the proprietor, Lord Baltimore, and directing him to establish the Church of England, his rule was suspended in 1691 and the colony came under royal control. The following year the province's Assembly passed the Church Act that established the Church. For the next decade the statute was disputed by legal officials and Dissenters in Annapolis and London before taking effect.[11]

Between 1675 and 1701 Church affairs in London were transformed for the extension and administration of the Church of England overseas. The authority and responsibility of the Board of Trade and Plantations for religious affairs in the imperial territories was gradually reduced and the role of the bishop of London and the recently chartered Society for the Promotion of Christian Knowledge (SPCK) and the Society for the Propagation of the Gospel in Foreign Parts (SPG) increased. It was a transformation that may have been directly attributable to the political activity and role of bishop of London Henry Compton on behalf of the advancement of William and Mary to the throne in 1689. Compton had become exasperated during the 1680s and 1690s with the annual effort to plead for the approval of the Board of Trade for the crown to pay the annual salaries of the increasing number of ministers serving congregations in Virginia. His first step was to appoint a secretary, Thomas Bray, to aid with the recruitment of men to serve the Church in the plantations.

The bishop of London's political and ecclesiastical manoeuvring dramatic-ally shifted the interests and responsibility of imperial Church affairs from the hands of a government agency at Whitehall to new philanthropic societies supervised by the Church's highest leaders. Organizations were funded not by

---

[11] Bell, *Imperial Origins*, pp. 26, 27, 28.

the money bills of Parliament but by private patronage and the annual dues of members including bishops, clergy, and well-disposed men and women. This represented a convergence of politics, stewardship, and philanthropy for the extension and administration of the Church of England to the nation's overseas imperial territories for the remainder of the eighteenth and throughout the nineteenth centuries.

Immediately in the New England, Middle and Southern colonies, the SPG became the driving force for providing missionaries to serve congregations in the regions and the payment of their salaries until the close of the War for Independence in 1783. Compton reserved for himself and his successors the supervision of the Church in Virginia and Maryland, where the Church was established and the clergymen's salaries set and paid by the provincial legislatures. A situation that provided a differing course of administration and supervision existed in the two Chesapeake colonies with the largest concentration of congregations and ministers in early America and the largest number of blacks and slaves.

In addition to the SPG's role for the appointment and support of missionaries to posts in the colonies under its supervision was its defining evangelization effort to indigenous peoples, blacks, and slaves in the regions, particularly in New York and South Carolina. This significant and extensive programme has been examined, analysed, and described by Glasson and Strong.[12]

Virginia and Maryland were not included in the SPG's jurisdiction in America and little is known of the efforts to bring the Christian message to the blacks and slaves in the two colonies. It is estimated that the population of blacks and slaves in Virginia in 1750 stood at about 150,000 and in Maryland at about 52,000 persons. Several of the men reported to bishop of London Edmund Gibson from time to time that they had received and distributed to the masters of plantations in their congregations his several *Pastoral Letters* regarding the evangelization of the peoples.[13] Yet it remains unclear the number of the ministers in Virginia who observed this practice or the number of blacks, men, women, and children that may have been affected by the evangelization efforts or were allowed to attend services.

Professor Otto Lohrenz has noted that in the 1787 Census of Virginia eighty-one Anglican ministers reported that they owned a total number of 1,824 slaves, or an average of 22.52 slaves per clergyman.[14] The distribution

---

[12] Travis Glasson, *Mastering Christianity: Missionary Anglicanism and Slavery in the Atlantic World* (New York, 2012); Rowan Strong, 'Continuity and Change in Anglican Missionary Theology: Dr Thomas Bray and the 1920 World Missionary Conference', *Journal of Postcolonial Theory and Theology*, 2 (2011): 1–17.

[13] Fulham Palace Papers, VI, fol. 253; XII, fos. 134–5, 140–1, 163–4, 180–1, 186, 209–10, 237–8, Lambeth Palace Library, London.

[14] I am grateful to Professor Otto Lohrenz for sharing with me the details of his research.

Table 9.1. Numbers of slaves owned by ministers,
1787 Census of Virginia

Number of slaves	Number of ministers
1–5	6
6–10	13
11–20	24
21–30	16
31–40	15
41–50	2
51–60	3
68	1
103	1

among the men ranged from a few to a gradual increase to many persons per minister. The range of ownership among the ministers is shown in Table 9.1.

In the absence of a resident colonial bishop, Compton attempted to establish supervision over the clergy and the Church by the appointment of provincial commissaries (a traditional diocesan officer) as his deputies, to Virginia in 1689 and to Maryland in 1700. His first appointment as commissary for Virginia was James Blair, a protégé of Bishop Gilbert Burnet of Salisbury, a native Scot, and founder of the College of William and Mary in 1693. He occupied the post with a high degree of political acuity until his death in 1743. Compton then appointed his assistant at Fulham Palace, Thomas Bray, as commissary for Maryland. Bray travelled to the colony immediately and held a visitation of the clergy in 1700.[15] During the colonial era Compton and his successors appointed seventeen men to serve as commissaries, including one in New England, two each in New York and Pennsylvania, three each in Maryland and South Carolina, and six in Virginia.[16] Bishop Gibson appointed Alexander Garden, a native Scot, as his deputy in South Carolina in 1726, where he is remembered as the leader who brought judicial proceedings against the celebrated evangelist George Whitefield in 1741 without resolution.

A new era for the Anglican Church in mainland America began in 1701 with the founding in London of the SPG by the Revd Thomas Bray. The new Society was diligently led by Archbishop Thomas Tenison as president and Bishop Compton as vice-president during more than a decade; they were followed by William Wake and Edmund Gibson during the years until 1748. Now the Society became the centre for the administration, selection, appointment, maintenance, and supervision of men to serve as missionaries in North

---

[15] Bell, *Imperial Origins*, pp. 27, 28, 29.   [16] Bell, *Imperial Origins*, pp. 58–73, 211.

America and the focus of sustained objection, criticism, and attack by Dissenters. It aided and supported the establishment of congregations and the recruitment, appointment, maintenance, and supervision of men for posts in the New England, Middle, and Southern colonies until the beginning of the War for Independence in 1776. It was aided by several forces, including royal governors and provincial legislatures. Without its assistance, the increase in congregations and ministers would probably have been considerably more modest north of Maryland and south of Virginia. Arguably the Church could not have been established or survived in early America without the Society's extensive assistance and financial support.[17]

The revocation in 1684 of the 1629 charter of the Massachusetts Bay Colony brought dramatic political and administrative change to the province as a jurisdiction of the crown. Two years later a royal governor was appointed to administer the colony and represent the crown and the Board of Trade, and the first Anglican minister, Robert Radcliff, arrived in Boston to serve the first Anglican congregation in the province. Immediately, New England's established ministers, led by the Revd Increase Mather, legatees and keepers of the vision and faith of the founders of the colony, objected stridently to the Anglican presence; this contrasted sharply with the initial appearance of the Church in Charleston (1688), Philadelphia (1695), and New York (1697). Their objection was a reflection of the settlement's original and fundamental sense of its civil and ecclesiastical mission. This was a vision of order and faith that was shaped by the Dissenters' religious experiences in England that had forced their flight to North America. Across the decades the memory was recovered and remembered by such Puritan leaders as John Cotton, Richard Mather, and his son Increase and grandson Cotton Mather. Fear of royal government, a crown-appointed governor, bishops, and the real purpose of the missionaries of the SPG shadowed the Anglican Church in New England without relief until the Declaration of Independence in 1776 and the end of the War for Independence in 1783. It would restrain the reorganization and reconstitution of the Church for at least half a century in the new independent nation.

As early as 1701, the SPG took steps to enlist the support and assistance of governors in several provinces. Correspondence between colonial and London officials recounts their assistance over the years. Thirty governors were elected to membership in the Society and reported from time to time on the state of the Church in their jurisdictions. Several officials played key supportive roles on behalf of the Church in their colonies, including Joseph Dudley, William Shirley, Thomas Pownall, and Francis Bernard in Massachusetts; Benning Wentworth and his son John in New Hampshire; Lewis Morris and Robert

---

[17] Rowan Strong, *Anglicanism and the British Empire c.1700–1850* (Oxford, 2007), pp. 41–117; Bell, *Imperial Origins*, pp. 90–6; Daniel O'Connor and others, *Three Centuries of Mission: The United Society for the Propagation of the Gospel 1701–2000* (London, 2000).

Hunter in New Jersey; Robert Hunter in New York; Francis Nicholson, Alexander Spotswood, William Gooch, and Robert Dinwiddie in Virginia; Arthur Dobbs and William Tryon in North Carolina; and Francis Nicholson in South Carolina.[18] But the interest and assistance of the governors was no substitute for the presence and authority of a bishop, a prospect that remained a continuing fear for Congregational church leaders and which was transformed into a civil issue by John and Samuel Adams during the 1760s and 1770s.[19]

Local residents interested in forming a new congregation in their communities were required to request approval from the bishop of London. He usually endorsed the proposal and passed the matter on to the leaders of the Society for their consideration and assistance, which was unfailingly granted. Local congregations were responsible for the construction and maintenance of church buildings, parsonages, and glebes, an obligation that was regularly fulfilled for churches but often delayed for parsonages and glebes (if indeed these were provided at all). While the bishop of London controlled the ordination and assignment of men to American posts, the Society approved the appointments and paid their annual salaries. Wherever an Anglican congregation was formed, it represented a familiar bridge to England and its religious practices. Yet in every instance it was an American congregation in membership, commonly served by a native-born minister in New England and increasingly also in the other provinces.

A chain of accomplished Congregationalist leaders in subsequent generations restated for their auditors and readers the English Dissenters' experiences at the hands of Anglican partisans. The objections of Increase Mather and his son Cotton to the presence and purpose of the Anglican Church in Massachusetts, Connecticut, and New England were revisited by Noah Hobart, Jonathan Mayhew, and laymen John and Samuel Adams. This provided a recollection of the past of both England and New England that cast a permanent shadow over the Anglican experience in every town of the region in which congregations were established. In each community the story of the English Church varied, but it was the intense and persistent New England controversy as retold by subsequent historians that shaped the national profile of the Church during the colonial era. The availability of the printing press in Boston rather than the Chesapeake and Southern colonies did much to facilitate the ready publication of works by critics of Anglicanism. Absent from the printed record was any reference to sustained theological controversy, for instance regarding the doctrines of grace and election.[20]

[18] Bell, *Imperial Origins*, pp. 43–57, 210.

[19] Bell, *A War of Religion*, pp. 91–120; Strong, *Anglicanism in the British Empire*, pp. 88, 112–16.

[20] Isaiah Thomas, *The History of Printing in America, With a Biography of Printers and an Account of Newspapers* (Worcester, MA, 1810; ed. Marcus McCorison, New York, 1970).

CONGREGATIONS

Between 1701 and 1776, 492 Anglican congregations were founded, including 332 in the Chesapeake colonies, 66 in New England, 63 in the Middle colonies, and 31 in the Southern colonies. The circumstances of the Church in the religiously diverse Middle colonies differed from those in Connecticut, Massachusetts, New Hampshire, and Rhode Island. In New York, where the Church was one of several religious groups in 1775, there were only 36 English churches in a province that included 80 Dutch Reformed, 61 Presbyterian, and 35 Lutheran churches. A similar pattern was repeated in New Jersey, where 26 Anglican congregations were founded in a community that included 75 Presbyterian, 34 Dutch Reformed, and 27 Baptist churches. The diverse social origins of Pennsylvania's population were reflected in the number of religious groups active in the province: there were only 26 English churches, among 140 Lutheran, 136 German Reformed, 79 Presbyterian, and Mennonite churches. A similar situation existed in Delaware, where the 15 English churches were outnumbered by 32 Presbyterian ones.[21]

Even in the Chesapeake colonies, circumstances demonstrated a limited degree of religious diversity. In Virginia there were at least 249 Anglican congregations in a province that included 92 Baptist and 61 Presbyterian churches, while in Maryland there were 83 Anglican churches, with 32 Presbyterian, 20 Roman Catholic, and 19 German Reformed. The Chesapeake colonies included the largest number of Anglican ministers (749) in early America.[22]

In the Southern colonies, there were 31 Anglican congregations and 209 ministers.[23] North Carolina accounted for 24 English churches, 56 Baptist, and 35 Presbyterian. In South Carolina there were 25 churches with 141 ministers, 48 Presbyterian churches, and 37 Baptist churches. In thinly populated Georgia there were 5 churches each for the Anglicans, Presbyterians, and Baptists.[24]

Between 1686 and the close of the War for Independence in 1783, New England Anglicanism presented a contrast with the other regions of

[21] James B. Bell, 'The Colonial American Clergy of the Church of England Database', <http://www.JamesBBell.com>; Frederic Lewis Weis, *The Colonial Clergy and the Colonial Churches of New England* (Lancaster, MA, 1936), p. 15; Peter Benes, *Meetinghouses of Early New England* (Amherst, MA, 2012), pp. 281–324; Frederic Lewis Weis, *The Colonial Clergy of the Middle Colonies, 1628–1776* (Lancaster, MA, 1957); Frederick Lewis Weis, *The Colonial Clergy of Maryland, Delaware and Georgia* (Lancaster, MA, 1950).

[22] Bell, 'Colonial American Clergy Database'; Weis, *Colonial Clergy of Maryland, Delaware and Georgia*, pp. 94–9; Frederick Lewis Weis, *The Colonial Clergy of Virginia, North Carolina and South Carolina* (Boston, MA, 1955).

[23] Bell, *Imperial Origins*, p. 199.

[24] Bell, 'Colonial American Clergy Database'; Weis, *Colonial Clergy of Maryland, Delaware and Georgia*, p. 103; Weis, *Colonial Clergy of Virginia, North Carolina, and South Carolina*.

early America, having the lowest numbers of both congregations and ministers. The Church was vastly outnumbered, with 76 congregations, as against 720 Congregational ones (72 per cent of the total of 1,001 church buildings). Connecticut had 200 congregations, Massachusetts 334, the District of Maine 48, New Hampshire 101, and Rhode Island 15.[25] Ranking second in terms of numbers of church buildings were the Baptists, with 26 in Connecticut, 63 in Massachusetts, 5 in the District of Maine, 11 in New Hampshire, and 41 in Rhode Island, a total of 148 (15 per cent of the total).

By contrast, Anglicans had 40 primary and secondary church buildings in Connecticut, 22 in Massachusetts, 4 in the District of Maine, 3 in New Hampshire, and 7 in Rhode Island, a total of 76 churches (7.5 per cent of the total).[26] Of the congregations in Connecticut, 17 offered weekly services, as did 10 in Massachusetts, 2 each in the District of Maine and New Hampshire, and 3 in Rhode Island. The remainder were secondary congregations that held services fortnightly, monthly, or quarterly: there were 23 in Connecticut, 5 in Massachusetts, 2 in the District of Maine, and 1 each in New Hampshire and Rhode Island.

THE MINISTERS

Essential to the gradual advancement of the Church in every region of mainland America was the attraction of an increasing number of men to serve established and new congregations. Numerically outdistancing the thirteen provinces were the two Chesapeake colonies of Virginia and Maryland, with 749 ministers (215 in Maryland and 534 in Virginia), followed by the Middle colonies with 234 (92 in New York, 49 in New Jersey, 57 in Pennsylvania, and 36 in Delaware). The Southern colonies had 211 ministers (54 in North Carolina, 141 in South Carolina, and 16 in Georgia).

Arguably the Church of England could not have survived in the New England, Middle, and Southern colonies without the sustained financial support of the SPG. In 1706, after a bitter campaign, the South Carolina legislature established the Church in the province and each congregation and minister received stipends from the government. Only in Virginia and Maryland, where the Church was established by the legislatures and ministers were paid in tobacco at a rate set by legislation, was it independent of economic support from London. There were substantial variations in SPG support

---

[25] Weis, *Colonial Clergy and the Colonial Churches of New England*, p. 15.
[26] Weis, *Colonial Clergy and the Colonial Churches of New England*, p. 15.

between the four regions: this amounted to £68,909 for New England, £99,376 for the Middle colonies, £798 for the Chesapeake colonies, and £33,507 for the Southern colonies. Yet even an approximate figure for the substantial expense of extending the Church to New England and elsewhere in early America is elusive. Rarely can much detail be found regarding the expenses of each congregation for the acquisition of land and the construction and maintenance of church buildings and parsonages.

Between 1701 and 1783 the Society sponsored 309 men to serve in the mainland American provinces. In New England the distribution of the missionaries included 47 to Connecticut, 33 to Massachusetts, 4 to New Hampshire, and 11 to Rhode Island. The numbers for the Middle colonies included 58 for New York, 44 for New Jersey, and 47 for Pennsylvania and Delaware combined, while in the Southern colonies South Carolina accounted for 54 men, North Carolina 33, and Georgia 13. In Maryland, during the first decade of the eighteenth century, 5 itinerant men were aided by the Society.

Almost all the ministers in North America until about 1685 had been born in England; after that there began a steady and increasing stream of men from the other parts of the kingdom, including Scotland and Ireland. Among the 1,291 men who served the Church during the early American era, 425 were natives of England (33 per cent), 249 were native colonists (19 per cent), 176 were Scottish (14 per cent), and 89 Irish (7 per cent). There were 142 (11 per cent) whose places of birth are unknown but who were probably of English origin; if combined with the known Englishmen, this would give a total of 566 (44 per cent). In addition 51 (4 per cent) were natives of other nations, including France (17), Wales (15), Switzerland (9), Barbados (2), Holland (2), Spain (2), and one each from Curaçao, the Leeward Islands, Sweden, and the West Indies.

The highest proportion of native colonists serving as ministers was in New England. Connecticut had 41 native-born out of 52 ministers (79 per cent), in Massachusetts there were 27 out of 64 (42 per cent), and in New Hampshire 3 out of 5 (60 per cent). Rhode Island's 25 clergy included 10 native colonists (40 per cent). Englishmen represented the largest segment of non-American ministers, with 24 (37 per cent) in Massachusetts, 6 (24 per cent) in Rhode Island, and 8 (15 per cent) in Connecticut. Scots numbered 4 (6 per cent) in Massachusetts, 4 (16 per cent) in Rhode Island, and 1 (2 per cent) in Connecticut.

In the Middle colonies of New York, New Jersey, Pennsylvania, and Delaware, the proportion of native-born American clergy was somewhat below that in New England. In New York 37 (40 per cent) were native colonists, in New Jersey 19 (39 per cent), in Pennsylvania 13 (23 per cent), and in Delaware 9 (25 per cent). Of English-born ministers there were 22 (25 per cent) in New York, 13 (27 per cent) in New Jersey, 12 (21 per cent) in Pennsylvania, and 10 (28 per cent) in Delaware. Among New York's 92 clergymen 12 (13 per cent) were Scots and 6 Irish (7 per cent). The situation was similar in New Jersey, where the clerical ranks included 7 Scots (14 per cent) among the 49 colonial parsons and 3 (6 per cent) Irish. Pennsylvania was served by 9 native Scots (16 per cent) and 7 Irish (12 per cent). In Delaware 8 of the 36 clergy were natives of Scotland (22 per cent).

Until the early 1680s, Virginia ministers were born, educated, and ordained in England, but after the rejection of episcopal government by the Established Church of Scotland in 1690 an increased number of Scottish-born episcopal clergy migrated to posts in America, particularly to Virginia and Maryland. Among the 215 clergymen in Maryland associated with the Church during the colonial period, 40 (19 per cent) of the men were natives of the province, while in Virginia, the colony with the largest number of ministers (534), 78 (15 per cent) were native-born. The number of Englishmen in Maryland was 69 (32 per cent), and in Virginia 201 (38 per cent). Maryland included 27 men from Scotland (13 per cent) and 23 Irishmen (11 per cent), while in Virginia 92 (17 per cent) were of Scottish origins and 30 from Ireland (6 per cent). Several congregations in Virginia and Maryland complained over the years to bishops of London about the difficulty of understanding the speech of Scottish-born incumbents.

In North and South Carolina and Georgia, the national origins of the 211 ministers who served Anglican congregations before 1783 differed from the three northern geographical regions. In North Carolina 11 out of 54 ministers (20 per cent) were native colonists, in South Carolina 6 out of 141 (4 per cent), and in Georgia 4 out of 16 (25 per cent). English clergy were the largest segment, including 58 (41 per cent) in South Carolina, 11 (20 per cent) in North Carolina, and 5 (31 per cent) in Georgia. The next largest group was the 29 Irishmen: 18 (13 per cent) in South Carolina, 9 (17 per cent) in North Carolina, and 2 (13 per cent) in Georgia. Scots numbered 8 (15 per cent) in North Carolina, 13 (9 per cent) in South Carolina, and 1 (6 per cent) in Georgia. There were 23 ministers who were natives of other countries: 18 (13 per cent) in South Carolina, 3 (6 per cent) in North Carolina, and 2 (13 per cent) in Georgia. The national origins of 39 remain unknown: 25 (18 per cent) in South Carolina, 12 (22 per cent) in North Carolina, and 2 (13 per cent) in Georgia.

The social and educational profile of the parsons in the New England region contrasted with that of their colleagues in the Middle, Chesapeake, and Southern colonies. In the first instance, the men were overwhelmingly native-born and educated at the local colleges, Harvard or Yale. In Connecticut, only 2 men were educated at Scottish colleges, 10 at Oxford or Cambridge, 1 at Trinity College, Dublin, 9 at Harvard, 3 at Yale, and 16 at three other American colleges, while the college background of 3 ministers is unknown. The high number of Yale graduates entering the Anglican ministry is in large measure linked to the oversight, interest, and educational efforts of one of the

Yale 'apostates', Samuel Johnson, minister in nearby Stratford.[27] Among the group were 27 converts from Congregationalism and 1 from the Dutch Reformed Church; 16 of the Congregational converts had been ministers in that tradition and 1 was a former Presbyterian minister. In Massachusetts the clergymen followed a similar pattern: 4 were graduates of two of the Scottish colleges, 3 from Trinity College, Dublin, 21 from Oxford, 9 from Cambridge, 22 from Harvard, 7 from Yale, and 2 from two other American institutions, while the college experience of 6 men is unknown. The count in sparsely settled New Hampshire included 3 graduates from Trinity College, Dublin, 2 from Harvard, and 1 from Yale. In Rhode Island 5 ministers were graduates of three Scottish colleges, 5 from Oxford, 3 from Cambridge, 3 from Trinity College, Dublin, 6 from Harvard, 2 from Yale, and 4 from two other American institutions, with 4 men whose college affiliation is unknown.

In the Chesapeake colony of Virginia, 92 ministers were educated at one of the four Scottish colleges, 100 at Oxford and 75 at Cambridge, 21 at Trinity College, Dublin, 46 at the College of William and Mary, and 15 at one of the other early American colleges, with 204 whose college affiliation, if any, is unknown. In Maryland the ministerial ranks included 30 educated at a Scottish institution, 38 at Oxford, 23 at Cambridge, 18 at Trinity College, Dublin, and 23 at one of the American institutions, as well as 90 for whom no college details are available.

In the Southern colonies of North and South Carolina and Georgia the proportions were similar. Among the North Carolina men 9 were graduates of Scottish institutions, 6 of Oxford or Cambridge, 5 of Trinity College, Dublin, and 6 of American institutions; there were 31 whose educational background is unknown. South Carolina included 17 graduates of Scottish institutions, 56 of Oxford and Cambridge, 8 of American colleges, and 50 whose educational background is unknown. In Georgia only 1 minister was educated at a Scottish institution, 3 at Oxford, and 1 each at Harvard and Yale; the college experience of 9 is unknown.

The lack in the eighteenth-century American colonies of a resident bishop and a diocesan structure meant that clergy, whether of English, Scottish, Irish, or native colonist backgrounds, were prompted to meet regularly, whether provincially or regionally, to discuss matters of mutual interest. Between 1685 and 1749 the number of such conventions remained relatively constant, but for thirty years after 1750 it increased significantly after increased public questioning of the historical legitimacy of episcopacy and the voicing of suspicions that the Society was probably seeking to convert members of the established New England Congregational churches to the Church of England. A total of 157 conventions were held in early America, including provincial

---

[27] Bell, *Imperial Origins*, pp. 152–3.

sessions in South Carolina (40), Connecticut (24), New York (18), Pennsylvania and Virginia (14 each), and Maryland (4). The meetings were not by any means a Society-encouraged solution to the absence of the episcopal office but an American procedure that may have been based on the annual town meetings held in the colonies.[28] Creating a new diocese and a bishopric was not an administrative decision in the hands of the bishop of London or the archbishop of Canterbury but the responsibility of Parliament alone, and the government did not present such a request for consideration during the colonial era.

THE UNITED STATES: AN INDEPENDENT EPISCOPAL CHURCH, 1783–1829

Following the controversies regarding imperial administration during the run-up to the Declaration of Independence on 4 July 1776, and the end of the War for Independence in October 1783, the English Church became a victim of the new political circumstances, in company with the British military forces and customs officers. Abruptly, the early American Anglican Churches ceased after 176 years to be under the authority or supervision of the bishop of London. No longer were native-born candidates for the ministry eligible to be ordained by English bishops, and the salaries of the missionaries appointed by the SPG were terminated. In step with the emerging civil government of the new United States, the Church faced a process of transition from the era of British America to the innovative age of the early independent republic.[29] Throughout each of the thirteen states and nationally, Anglican churches faced the task of reorganizing and reconstituting themselves, a process that would play out over more than half a century and which was marked by distinctive historical, geographical, and economic characteristics. A revision of the Book of Common Prayer was required, as was the establishment of ecclesiastical canons for the independent American Church, which was burdened in New England and elsewhere by its characterization in the popular mind as the national Church of the enemy England. New political circumstances required that it must be reformed, while yet embracing the basic elements of the English Church. A movement in this direction during the 1780s was led by the 34-year-old minister of Christ Church, Philadelphia, William White, and others, primarily in Pennsylvania, Maryland, and New York. This culminated in the formation of the Protestant Episcopal Church in the

---

[28] Bell, *Imperial Origins*, pp. 110–14.
[29] Frederick V. Mills Sr, *Bishops by Ballot: An Ecclesiastical Revolution* (New York, 1978).

United States of America in 1789. The reconstitution and reorganization was neither speedy nor seamless, either nationally or in the individual states. Local congregations reassembled with new leadership and struggled to meet the inevitable and substantial financial burdens without the assistance of the London-based SPG. Dioceses needed to be organized and bishops elected and consecrated in each state to provide supervision, ordinations for ministerial candidates, and confirmation rites for members. The process was slow, complicated, and without an urgent sense of purpose, apart from in Connecticut, where the largest numbers of parsons and congregations were found. There the surviving band of ministers elected Samuel Seabury Jr as their bishop; he sailed to seek consecration from the hands of English prelates but without success. At the time, English law required bishops to give an oath of loyalty to the crown and Parliament, which Seabury could not do, and so he was encouraged to travel to Scotland and seek consecration from bishops of the Scottish Episcopal Church. Scottish prelates dutifully performed the ceremony on 12 November 1784, and he returned to Connecticut in June 1785 to fulfil his duties.[30]

Following Seabury's consecration, reservations were raised in the United States regarding the historic legitimacy of the Scottish episcopal office. After the consecration by British prelates of William White of Pennsylvania and Samuel Provoost of New York in 1787 and James Madison of Virginia in 1790, the four men consecrated Thomas John Clagget of Maryland in New York in 1792, and the American Church's uncertainty was stilled.

Elsewhere in New England, the Middle, Chesapeake, and Southern states, the recovery and reconstitution of the Church moved at a considerably more modest pace. Between 1784 and 1829 twelve dioceses were organized, beginning with Connecticut (1784) and New York and Pennsylvania (both in 1787). During the 1790s five additional dioceses were established: Rhode Island and Virginia (1790), Maryland (1792), South Carolina (1795), and Massachusetts (1797). With continuing diminished membership and straitened financial circumstances throughout the New England states with the exception of Connecticut, several Massachusetts congregations, instead of seeking to establish a diocese limited to the state, petitioned the General Convention in 1809 for the creation of an eastern diocese to serve the new states of Massachusetts, the District of Maine, Rhode Island, and Vermont; New Hampshire joined two years later. In 1811 Alexander Viets Griswold was elected and consecrated as the twelfth bishop of the Church in the United States and first prelate of the new diocese. Additional dioceses were subsequently created in New Jersey (1815), west of the Appalachian Mountains, in Ohio (1819), North Carolina (1823), Mississippi (1826), Vermont (1832),

[30] Bruce E. Steiner, *Samuel Seabury, 1729–1796: A Study in the High Church Tradition* (Athens, OH, 1971), pp. 222–4.

Delaware (1841), and Maine (1847). Between 1784 and 1829 twenty-two bishops were elected and consecrated to serve the new American dioceses, eleven of whom died before 1830.[31]

The first triennial meeting of the General Convention of the Protestant Episcopal Church in the United States of America, the Church's governing body, took place in New York City in 1791. The pages of the published *Journals* of the first and subsequent sessions provide a census of the names and numbers of clergymen and churches in each state or diocese.[32] There were 179 clergymen listed, although there was no report from Massachusetts or New Hampshire. Thirteen years later, in 1804, the *Journal* of the Convention indicated that the situation was little changed, noting that there were now 203 ministers on the national roster.[33] A decade later at the triennial meeting of the Church there was no representation from the states of New Hampshire, North Carolina, or Georgia, nor from any of the new states admitted to the Union since 1790 except Vermont (thus omitting Kentucky, Tennessee, Ohio, and Louisiana) or any of the established territories (Mississippi, Indiana, Michigan, Illinois, and Missouri). The number of clergymen on the national rolls had declined from 203 in 1804 to 186, although the Church in Virginia, with the largest number of clergy and churches during the colonial era, did not report on the number and status of its ministers and congregations.[34] It is estimated that perhaps as many as fifty ministers were serving the Church in Virginia, yet the statistics indicate that the Church's centre of gravity was shifting from the Chesapeake states to Connecticut, New York, and Pennsylvania.[35] Fifteen years later, at the General Convention in Philadelphia in August 1829, the *Journal* recorded a substantial increase in the number of ministers listed on the register to 488, with the largest number (128) residing in New York, followed by 65 in Pennsylvania, and 59 in Connecticut.[36]

Efforts to establish Church-related colleges by diocesan leaders gradually came to fruition in the early nineteenth century. Hobart and William Smith College in Geneva, New York, was founded in 1822, Trinity College in Hartford, Connecticut, the next year, and Kenyon College in Gambier, Ohio, in 1824. There was fervent debate within the Church for more than twenty years regarding the establishment of a seminary for the theological education of candidates for the ministry, some strongly supporting a national seminary and state leaders urging the founding of diocesan institutions. A measure of resolution of the dispute came with the founding of the General Theological

---

[31] *The Episcopal Church Annual, 2016* (New York, 2016).
[32] *Journals of General Conventions of the Protestant Episcopal Church in the United States, 1785–1835*, ed. William Stevens Perry, 2 vols. (Claremont, NH, 1874), I, pp. 175–9.
[33] *Journals of General Conventions*, ed. Perry, I, pp. 291, 305.
[34] *Journals of General Conventions*, ed. Perry, I, pp. 400–2, 441–6.
[35] Bell, *Imperial Origins*, p. 207.
[36] *Journals of General Conventions*, ed. Perry, II, pp. 248–75.

Seminary in New York City in 1817, a name chosen to reflect the intention of its founders to serve the whole Protestant Episcopal Church. Six years later the Virginia Theological Seminary was founded in Alexandria, Virginia.

BRITISH NORTH AMERICA

Elsewhere in North America, from the late seventeenth century the Anglican Church extended its reach to the easternmost edge of New France, the remote and modest fishing villages of Newfoundland. The distant venture was linked to continental European diplomatic, political, and military conflicts, controversies, and rivalries. English commercial settlers in the bays along the Atlantic coast were relentlessly exposed at least from 1668 to hostile controversy, conflict, and objection from French officials.[37] The vast territory of the region was controlled by the Company of New France in 1660, and three years later Louis XIV made it a royal province. It was settled by French-speaking colonists, under the jurisdiction of the French government and law and the Roman Catholic Church.

However, the government of Charles II asserted a historic interest in the territory of Newfoundland, claimed in 1583 by Sir Humphrey Gilbert. It became a valued centre for trade and fishing by English seamen during the seventeenth century and of substantial value to the crown. In 1668 the government reported that it produced £50,000 customs income yearly from fish exported to foreign countries, and yielded £500,000 for the government. England and France both asserted their control over the region and the French immediately took the situation seriously. The contested territory was exposed to strong and numerous French naval and military forces, the construction of forts, and the establishment of control of the three bays of Newfoundland, circumstances that quickly reduced substantially English income from the region.[38]

As early as 4 February 1669/70, on the recommendation of the Lords of Trade and Plantations, the king in Council approved that 'a chaplain shall be sent thither (to Newfoundland) on a convoy ship, and that the captains shall have power to regulate abuses there', a region without a resident governor or official in charge of civil affairs.[39] But the first traceable appointment of an Anglican minister at the edge of what is now eastern Canada did not occur until 1686, when John Jackson was assigned to the fishing settlement of

---

[37] See Peter M. Doll, *Revolution, Religion, and National Identity: Imperial Anglicanism in British North America, 1745–1795* (Madison, NJ, 2000).

[38] *Calendar of State Papers, Colonial Series, 1661–1668* (London, 1880), pp. 558–89.

[39] *Calendar of State Papers, Colonial Series, 1685–1688* (London, 1899), p. 635.

St John's, Newfoundland. With his appointment Bishop Compton was exercising his imperial ecclesiastical authority and jurisdiction at the same time that he appointed the first English clergyman to New England at Boston and gave attention to Church affairs in Virginia and Maryland. It remains unclear how Jackson was paid, but it may perhaps have been from Compton's episcopal purse, or William III's Secret Service account, or England's Treasury Office as in Virginia and Maryland.[40] Probably a native of Llanvrynach in the Welsh county of Brecon, and a graduate in 1680 of Jesus College, Oxford, in 1703 Jackson began to receive a 'benefaction of £30 per annum for three years' from the newly founded SPG to support his family of eight children, although he was not an appointed missionary of the Society.[41] Jackson served at the post for nineteen years before being recalled by Compton in 1705 following complaints of 'a violent temper and scandalous life'.[42] Shipwrecked on the return passage, he lost all his belongings and received further assistance from the SPG until Queen Anne granted him a living in England in 1709. Jackson was replaced by Jacob Rice, a 23-year-old graduate of Magdalen Hall, Oxford, recently ordained by Compton and appointed a missionary of the Society. Unfortunately, he was charged in a military court seven years later with an unscrupulous attempt to collect his clerical allowance in fish in 1712, which may have been more valuable.[43]

By the early eighteenth century the population of New France had reached 16,000, but from the 1720s the number of French emigrants began to dwindle, and the flow was replaced by a steadily increasing number of English and Scottish settlers to Newfoundland and Nova Scotia.

As happened further south, New France settlers engaged in numerous wars with Indians and others from the late seventeenth century, including the Beaver Wars and Anglo-French conflicts such as King William's War (1689–97) and Queen Anne's War (1702–13). During the latter, New England forces fought against the French and Indians in Nova Scotia, and the British captured Fort Royal in 1710. Three years later, under the terms of the Treaty of Utrecht, France ceded to Britain its claims to Newfoundland, the Acadia Colony of Nova Scotia, and the Hudson's Bay Company territories in Rupert's

---

[40] Bell, *Imperial Origins*, pp. 20–4.

[41] *Annual Report, Society for the Propagation of the Gospel in Foreign Parts* [hereafter: *SPG Annual Report*] (London, 1705), p. 31; Ernest Hawkins, *Historical Notices of the Missions of the Church of England in the North American Colonies previous to the Independence of the United States: Chiefly from the MS. Documents of the Society for the Propagation of the Gospel in Foreign Parts* (London, 1845), p. 347.

[42] Edward Carpenter, *The Protestant Bishop: Being the Life of Henry Compton, 1632–1713 Bishop of London* (London, 1956), p. 295.

[43] Hawkins, *Historical Notices*, p. 348; Clergy of the Church of England Database, <http://theclergydatabase.org.uk/>, accessed 16 Aug. 2016; Testimonial of military court held before Sir Nicholas Trevanion, 20 October 1712, Fulham Palace Papers, 1, fos. 3–4, Lambeth Palace Library, London; Jacob Rice to Bishop Compton, 6 Nov. 1712, Fulham Palace Papers, 1, fos. 5–6.

Land. France then sought to maintain its influence in the region by building the strong fortress of Louisbourg on Cape Breton Island. Conflicts recurred for the next thirty years, including Father Role's War (1722–5), King George's War (1744–8), Father le Loutre's War (1749–55), the Seven Pontiacs' War (1763–6), and finally the War for American Independence.

After 1710, mainland Nova Scotia was under the control of New England, but present-day New Brunswick and virtually all of present-day Maine remained contested territory between New England and New France. At its peak in 1712 the territory of New France was divided by France into colonies, each with its own administration, including Canada, Acadia, and Newfoundland.

By June 1727 London officials began to take steps to extend the Church to Newfoundland with the appointment of Jacob Rice to serve as chaplain to the garrison at Placentia.[44] The same year, Henry Jones, a Church of England minister but not an appointee of the SPG, began serving a congregation at Bonavista, a fishing centre in Newfoundland; he sought the Society's financial support because 'the people are poor and unable to maintain their minister', and received a £40 grant.[45] Seven years later the SPG engaged Robert Kilpatrick, recently ordained by Bishop Gibson of London, as a missionary at the migratory fishery at Trinity on Trinity Bay.[46] For almost a century thereafter, men were recruited and appointed to serve as missionaries, usually at a salary of £50 per annum, at Newfoundland posts that included Bay Balls, Bonavista, Carbonear, Conception Bay, Ferryland, Fortune Bay, Harbor Grace, Perlican, Placentia, Scylly Cove, St John's, St Mary's, Trepassey, and Trinity Bay.[47] By 1738 Jones and Kilpatrick were each receiving an annual stipend of £40 but three years later Jones noted that his colleague had died and left a widow and five children in need of the 'compassion of the Society'.[48]

English circumstances took a new turn in 1749 with the British defeat of French forces at Annapolis Royal, Nova Scotia. London imperial officials moved quickly to establish English rule. Edward Cornwallis, a British military officer, was charged immediately with establishing a new British settlement in the province to counter France's Louisbourg, and in 1754 he was appointed lieutenant-governor of the colony. The Church of England, a component of the unwritten constitution, was a primary element of the process of Anglicization of Nova Scotia and was quickly established by the legislature in the new colony.[49] Immediately the Board of Trade and Plantations in London issued Royal Instructions to the governor for the 'Protection and Encouragement of the Established Church', and ordered the 'Bishop of London's Ecclesiastical

[44] *Calendar of State Papers, Colonial Series, 1726–1727* (London, 1936), p. 308.
[45] *SPG Annual Report 1727*, p. 38.   [46] *SPG Annual Report 1735*, pp. 62–3.
[47] Hawkins, *Historical Notices*, pp. 348–52.
[48] *SPG Annual Report 1738*, p. 33; *SPG Annual Report 1741/2*, p. 45.
[49] Doll, *Revolution, Religion, and National Identity*, pp. 35–65.

Jurisdiction' and 'Religious Liberty' for Dissenting groups.[50] The Revd James Peden, deputy chaplain to the British troops, maintained a school supported by the SPG. The Commissioners of the Board of Trade ordered that 400 acres of provincial land be set aside for the construction of churches, and 200 acres for the maintenance of ministers. Immediately the Society appointed the Revds William Tutty and William Anywil to accompany the first settlers from England to the new colony. They were joined on a later voyage of colonists by Charles Frederick Moreau, a graduate of Clare Hall, Cambridge, and a former Roman Catholic priest. By 1754, Moreau was transferred to a post at Lunenburg; he was succeeded in 1767 by Paul Bryzelius, and in 1771 by Peter Delaroche, who noted in 1775 that his communicants included 120 German speakers and fifty French speakers.[51]

In 1750 the first Anglican Church in Nova Scotia was established at Halifax, a town of 4,000 persons excluding military troops, and the next year the Swiss-born Peter Christian Burger was ordained and appointed to minister there. He was succeeded by the Revd Thomas Wood, appointed by the SPG to serve congregations at Halifax and Annapolis Royal in 1751 and also to serve the French and Indian settlements. He was able to speak the Mickmack language, into which he translated the Book of Common Prayer.[52] In 1752 the provincial General Assembly enacted a statute for completing St Paul's church in Halifax, which was frequently used by all religious groups for services.

English civil administration was introduced with the appointment of Jonathan Belcher as chief justice of the Nova Scotia Supreme Court on 21 October 1754. He was the son of the influential and wealthy Massachusetts, New Hampshire, and New Jersey royal governor of the same name. The first legislative assembly in Halifax, under the governorship of Edward Cornwallis, met on 2 October 1758. Joseph Bennet became the SPG's first missionary at Horton, Cornwallis, Falmouth, and Newport, Nova Scotia, in 1763. John Eagelson, a Society appointee ordained by Bishop Thomas Terrick of London in 1768, began serving a community in the Cumberland District of about equal numbers of Presbyterians and Anglicans and their children, who were instructed in the Prayer Book catechism.[53] At the request of the governor of the Island of St John in the autumn of 1773, he visited Charlottetown, St Peter's, Stanhope, Traccady, and Malpeck or Prince Town.[54] In 1769 the first Foreign Auxiliary Committee of the SPG was established at Halifax, to advise London officials on locations for settling missionaries and founding missions.[55]

---

[50] Labaree (ed.), *Royal Instructions*, II, pp. 482–3, 489–90, 494.
[51] *SPG Annual Reports 1749–1771*; Hawkins, *Historical Notices*, pp. 356–60.
[52] Hawkins, *Historical Notices*, pp. 112–13.
[53] Hawkins, *Historical Notices*, pp. 112–13.   [54] *SPG Annual Reports 1768*.
[55] Hawkins, *Historical Notices*, p. 113.

During the years between 1713 and 1763 France's territorial claims in North America gradually diminished at the European peace conferences addressing continental disputes. At the Paris conference in 1763, France ceded to Great Britain nearly all of its North American possessions except two islands and the Louisiana Territory, and was removed as a threat to the thirteen American colonies. Great Britain now controlled the major portion of the Western hemisphere, including the thirteen American colonies, and faced the formidable task of administering its historically differing overseas territories. Included in Britain's extended territory in North America were approximately 80,000 primarily French-speaking peoples who were governed by different legal systems, had different systems of land ownership, and embraced widely different religious traditions and practices.

George III issued a Royal Proclamation on 7 October 1761 that organized Great Britain's new North American empire and moved to ameliorate relations with the native peoples on the matters of trade, settlement, and land purchases on the western frontier. The British government also protected most of the property, political, religious, and social culture of French-speaking residents. Canadians were guaranteed the right to practise the Catholic faith as acknowledged in the 1774 Quebec Act, and maintained French civil law in a form of land ownership known as the seigneurial system; but the proclamation also contained provisions which precluded civic participation by Roman Catholic Canadians. The Board of Trade in London issued Royal Instructions to the governor of Quebec that provided for the 'Protection and Encouragement of the Establish Church' and recognized the 'Bishop of London's Ecclesiastical Jurisdiction' in the region.[56]

Between 1749 and 1785 the effort to extend the Church of England in British North America was limited geographically to Newfoundland and Nova Scotia, with ministers recruited by the SPG. From 1749 to 1759 the Society allotted £2,910 for the salaries each year of two missionaries for Newfoundland and three in Nova Scotia. During the 1760s the number of men appointed to serve in the regions ranged from a low of four to a high of nine, accounting for expenditure of £4,070. The pattern continued during the following decade, with the Society making payment of £5,500 for the men's salaries while serving congregations. Yet the pattern of the previous thirty years continued between 1780 and 1785, with the number of clergymen, congregations, and expenses the SPG incurred amounting to £2,460. It was a transformational decade for Anglicanism in North America. As early as 1777 a trickle of refugee loyalist Anglican ministers, particularly from Massachusetts and Connecticut, supplemented by a few from New York and New Jersey, began migrating with their families to Nova Scotia, New Brunswick, and Cape Breton. The number

---

[56] Labaree (ed.), *Royal Instructions*, II, pp. 482–3, 489–90.

accelerated after the Treaty of Paris of 1783 that ended the war, and increased substantially in 1788 and 1789. Mather Byles of Boston and Portsmouth, New Hampshire, a great-grandson of Increase Mather, arrived in Halifax in 1777 and he was followed later by Joshua Wingate Weeks of Marblehead, Massachusetts, to Annapolis, and Jacob Bailey of Pownalborough, in the District of Maine, to Cornwallis, both in Nova Scotia. In 1783 John Stuart, missionary to the Mohawk Indians at Fort Hunter, and John Doty of Schenectady, both in New York, were settled at Kingston and Sorel, Canada, respectively. Two years later the provincial assembly of New Brunswick, formerly a part of Nova Scotia, made provision for four Anglican missions. These were served by fleeing American loyalist refugees: John Beardsley from New York at Maugerville; Samuel Cooke from New Jersey at St John's; and from Connecticut, James Scovil at Kingston, Samuel Andrews at St Andrews, and Richard Samuel Clarke at Gagetown.[57] In 1785 the number of Society-sponsored missionaries in Newfoundland, Nova Scotia, New Brunswick, and Canada had increased to 15 at an annual expense of £730, while four years later the ranks reached 27: 4 in Newfoundland, 12 in Nova Scotia, 6 in New Brunswick, 1 at Cape Breton, and 4 in Canada, at an annual charge of £1,340.

During the War for American Independence there was a limited degree of interest in the cause, but not active participation, on the part of colonists in British North America, even among the Acadians and New Englanders who had settled in Nova Scotia. A limited invasion of Canada by the Continental Army in 1775 in hope of capturing Quebec from the British was arrested. The defeat of the British army at Yorktown, Virginia, in October 1781 brought an end to the war.

In 1775 the SPG sponsored nine missionaries to British North America, three to Newfoundland and six to Nova Scotia. Thirteen years later the number increased to twenty-four, including three in Newfoundland, eleven in Nova Scotia, three in Canada, and one in Cape Breton, thanks to the arrival of seventeen ministers, mainly from Massachusetts and Connecticut. For more than a generation, this influx eased the need for London officials to recruit men in Great Britain. An inestimable loss for the New England Church became an opportunity for the strengthening and increase of the Church in British North America. The population of Halifax and Nova Scotia had increased, with 35,000 loyalist refugees and 5,000 free Negroes from the former mainland American colonies.

The devastating impact of political and military events on New England congregations and ministers provided a positive opportunity for expansion of the Church in Canada. New independent political institutions, the legislatures, ordered the churches closed in Massachusetts and Connecticut, and prompted

---

[57] Labaree (ed.), *Royal Instructions*, II, pp. 125–9.

many loyalist parsons to seek refuge in the Canadian Maritime Provinces. The course of the war, particularly in New England, reshaped the Church's standing and ministry in British North America. The SPG faced the task of financially maintaining and reassigning the corps of ministers formerly serving primarily Massachusetts and Connecticut congregations who streamed into the Maritime Provinces during the 1780s. Their arrival allowed the Church in Nova Scotia, New Brunswick, Cape Breton, Prince Edward Island, and Canada to dramatically increase the number of congregations.

A steady stream of the Society's missionaries and their families migrated to the region between 1776 and 1786 to fill vacant established missions and to serve new posts. Included among them were, from Connecticut, Samuel Andrews to St Andrews, New Brunswick; Richard Clarke to Gagetown, New Brunswick; John Sayre to Maugerville, Nova Scotia; James Scovil to Kingston, New Brunswick; and Roger Viets to Digby, Nova Scotia. From Massachusetts came Mather Byles Jr to St John, New Brunswick, and Joshua Wingate Weeks to Nova Scotia;[58] from the District of Maine, Jacob Bailey to Annapolis, Nova Scotia;[59] from New Hampshire, Ranna Cossit to Sydney, Cape Breton Island; from Rhode Island, George Bissett to St John's, Newfoundland; from New York, John Doty to Sorel, Quebec; Charles Inglis to Halifax, Nova Scotia; John Beardsley to St John, New Brunswick; and John Stuart to Kingston, Quebec. From New Jersey came Isaac Browne to Annapolis, Nova Scotia; Samuel Cooke to Fredericktown, New Brunswick; and George Panton to Yarmouth, Nova Scotia. These formed a coterie of experienced and committed men who provided years of service to Anglicanism in British North America. The refugees were each granted £50 by the provincial assembly to relieve their distressing financial circumstances.[60]

In 1777, John Doty, the Society's missionary at Schenectady, New York, and to the Mohawk Indians at Fort Hunter, was serving as chaplain to His Majesty's Royal Regiment of New York, near Montreal. He made two trips to England between 1781 and 1783 and reported on the current state of the English Church in British North America. He noted that the Roman Catholics were strong and French Protestants few; weekly prayer days were rarely observed by English congregations; saints' days were totally neglected; and the sacrament celebrated only three or four times a year at Montreal, and even less often at Quebec and Trois-Rivières. Doty offered a general estimate of the number of Protestant English families in Canada: 746, with 250 at Quebec, 60 at Montreal, and 40 at Niagara, with a total population of about 50–60,000 people.[61]

---

[58] James S. Lemon, *The Reverend Jacob Bailey, Maine Loyalist: For God, King, and for Self* (Amherst, MA, 2012), pp. 158–61, 163–5.

[59] Lemon, *Reverend Jacob Bailey*, pp. 148–77.

[60] Hawkins, *Historical Notices*, pp. 115–16, 371–4.

[61] Hawkins, *Historical Notices*, pp. 139–40.

When British forces and officials evacuated New York City in October 1783, they took many loyalist refugees to Nova Scotia, while others migrated to south-western Quebec. Many New Englanders fled to settlements on the shores of the St John River, a separate colony that gave rise to the creation of New Brunswick in 1784. Former New France, Quebec, was divided into two provinces by the Constitutional Act of 1791. The legislation continued the seigneurial system of land ownership in Lower Canada and established land reserves in Upper Canada to serve Anglican ministers, known as the Clergy Reserves. These were intended from time to time to be leased or sold to generate income for the benefit of 'Protestant clergy'.

Quebec, with its largely French-speaking population, was renamed Lower Canada, and included the region along the St Lawrence River and the Gaspé Peninsula. The territory of Upper Canada included a large portion of loyalist refugees, overwhelmingly from New England and New York, with a capital by 1796 at York, present-day Toronto. After 1790 most of the new settlers were American farmers searching for new lands; although generally favourable to republicanism, they were relatively non-political and stayed neutral in the second war for independence between the United States and Great Britain (1812–15).

Great Britain's loss of the thirteen original colonies prompted new questions about ecclesiastical and civil affairs and policies from Parliament and London imperial officials regarding its remaining provinces in the region. The controversial issues associated with governing the distant colonial Church and state during the 1760s and 1770s were familiar to ecclesiastical and government leaders in London during the 1780s and 1790s, and steps were taken to address circumstances in Canada.[62] In 1786 the politically well-connected Archbishop John Moore of Canterbury and Bishop Robert Lowth of London petitioned the crown for the appointment of a bishop for British North America. The next year George III approved the creation of the diocese of Nova Scotia, which included the entire remaining territory of the region, and the appointment of the former loyalist minister of Trinity Church in New York, the Irish-born Charles Inglis, as the first Church of England bishop. A year later he made his first diocesan visitation.[63]

In 1793 there were only six ministers in the Lower Province, and Jacob Mountain became the first bishop of Quebec, serving until 1825. He reported to the English government that the churches in Quebec and Nova Scotia were 'rather on the decline' because of lack of funds, unable to maintain themselves except at Montreal, Quebec, and Trois-Rivières. Ministers were dependent on

[62] Judith Fingard, *The Anglican Design in Loyalist Nova Scotia, 1783–1816* (London, 1972), pp. 13–19.

[63] Fingard, *Anglican Design*, pp. 19–38; Strong, *Anglicanism and the British Empire*, pp. 118–20.

the SPG and were not legally established or confirmed in their churches, and the building of churches in each province was slow. The Roman Catholics had a great advantage over the Protestants, as by an Act of Parliament they had their parishes and tithes.[64]

During the last decade of the eighteenth century the number of missionaries increased from a low of 27 in 1790 to a high of 51 in 1797, with 44 in 1799. Nova Scotia remained the province with the largest number of Anglican ministers, increasing from 12 men in 1790 to a high of 24 in 1798; numbers in New Brunswick rose from 6 in 1790 to 10 in 1799. The SPG's annual expenditure for missionaries in British North America gradually increased from £1,595 in 1790 to £2,335 in 1799, an increase of 68 per cent, exclusive of the unknown cost of the distribution of books and tracts to churches served by the Society's appointees.[65]

During the period between 1660 and 1829, two decades were particularly significant for the advancement of the English Church in British North America. The first was the 1780s, which saw the arrival of a band of loyalist refugee ministers from the now-independent New England states of Massachusetts and Connecticut. The second was the 1810s, marked by an increase in the number of missionaries appointed to the region, an increase in the number of congregations and communities served by the men, and the new and significant supplementing of the Society's vital financial role by the introduction and appropriation of funds for the maintenance of the Church by government and Parliament. Such financial arrangements were familiar in England but without precedent in North America.

During the first two years of the nineteenth century, the number of clergy-men and the level of financial support continued little changed from the last three years of the 1790s.[66] Between 1810 and 1819 the number of ministers in the region increased from 40 to 56, while annual expenditure rose from £2,190 to £11,210, a situation that reflected the substantial additional funds granted by Parliament for underwriting the national Church's expenses in the region.[67] It was a noteworthy turn of financial affairs for the SPG that had struggled for more than a century to generate the funds to carry the burden of extending the Church to North America. Led by a former government official, William Knox, London leaders undertook to bring the funding of the Church in British North America into line with imperial policy.[68] Nearly two decades passed before Parliament approved in 1812 the first annual money bill allocating funds for the maintenance of the Church in British North America. Nova Scotia, the centre and stronghold of the Church, received the first

[64] Hawkins, *Historical Notices*, pp. 143–4.
[65] Fingard, *Anglican Design*, pp. 39–48; *SPG Annual Reports 1776–1830*.
[66] *SPG Annual Reports 1797–1802*.   [67] *SPG Annual Reports 1810–1819*.
[68] Fingard, *Anglican Design*, 2–4.

allotment of parliamentary funds in 1813, followed by Newfoundland the next year, and New Brunswick in 1816. Without reservation, the civil and ecclesiastical leadership in London and British North America recognized that the Church was an element of the Anglicization process of imperial administration, in company with the corps of schoolmasters appointed and supported by the SPG who instructed students in every province for 130 years.

Between 1820 and 1829 numbers of ministers and congregations increased steadily, particularly in Nova Scotia, New Brunswick, and Upper and Lower Canada. In 1820 the SPG sponsored 75 men in the region, ending the decade with 133 men on its rolls. Numbers increased in Nova Scotia from 19 to 29, from 14 to 24 in New Brunswick, from 16 to 37 in Upper Canada, and from 17 to 29 in Lower Canada. Annual expenditure increased during the decade from £14,775 to £24,465.[69] Between 1815 and 1829 the SPG's annual expenditure on salaries of its missionaries in British America increased from £5,115 to £24,465, a rise of nearly 500 per cent. Over the period of eighty years the Anglican Church in British North America had been driven in large measure by the engine of imperial policy, the financial resources and oversight of the London-based Society, and more than a decade of Parliament's money bills. A strong foundation had been constructed for the expansion of the Church to British Columbia during the remainder of the nineteenth century.

CONCLUSION

The Church of England's presence in America in 1660 lacked any basis in a coherent policy established by English civil and ecclesiastical officials regarding the extension of the Church overseas. It was the legacy of the Virginia Company of London's efforts in 1619 which ended with its collapse five years later. For nearly half a century afterwards the Church was adrift without leadership or attention, until the efforts of Bishop Henry Compton and the Board of Trade and Plantations in the late 1670s and 1680s transformed the situation. The seventeenth century closed with the American Church strongest in Virginia, followed at a distance by Maryland, and only token representation along the Atlantic frontier in Boston, New York, Philadelphia, and Charleston. On this slim foundation a new era was launched after the founding of the SPG in 1701 and its steadily increasing recruitment and appointment of missionaries in all colonies except Virginia and Maryland until the close of the War for Independence in 1783.

---

[69] *SPG Annual Reports 1820–1829.*

Sustained efforts to extend the Church of England to British North America did not begin until the 1730s, twenty years after the Treaty of Utrecht and the acquisition of the Nova Scotia peninsula. The settlements of Newfoundland were the first benefactors of the SPG's appointment of ministers to posts after the mid-1730s. It was followed in 1750 with the appointment of a royal governor and Anglican minister at Halifax, Nova Scotia. A measured increase of British and Scottish settlers in the decades between the 1740s and 1770s was accompanied by a rising number of SPG appointees. Circumstances changed abruptly during the course of the American Revolutionary War, with the migration of thousands of loyalist refugees especially to Nova Scotia, New Brunswick, and Quebec. This population was served by numerous loyalist New England and New York missionaries of the SPG, seeking to continue their service, association, and salary. For the next three decades the SPG struggled to generate the contributions and income to maintain its establishment in North America.

Pursuing a different course from that taken in the early American colonies, Parliament established its first diocese and bishop in the Western hemisphere and appointed Charles Inglis as first bishop of Nova Scotia in 1787 at Halifax. A second diocese was created six years later at Quebec. Twenty-five years later, Parliament began granting substantial annual funds to maintain the salaries of the Society's appointees to serve the gradually increasing number of churches in each of the Canadian provinces.

SELECT BIBLIOGRAPHY

Annual Reports of the Society for the Propagation of the Gospel in Foreign Parts (London, 1704–1829).

Bell, James B., *Anglicans, Dissenters and Radical Change in Early New England, 1686–1786* (Basingstoke, 2017).

Bell, James B., *Empire, Religion and Revolution in Early Virginia, 1607–1786* (Basingstoke, 2013).

Bell, James B., *The Imperial Origins of the King's Church in Early America, 1607–1783* (Basingstoke, 2004).

Bell, James B., *War of Religion: Dissenters, Anglicans and the American Revolution* (Basingstoke, 2008).

Carey, Hilary M., *God's Empire: Religion and Colonialism in the British World, c.1801–1908* (Cambridge, 2011).

Carrington, Philip, *The Anglican Church in Canada* (Toronto, 1963).

Doll, Peter M., *Revolution, Religion, and National Identity: Imperial Anglicanism in British North America, 1745–1795* (Cranbury, NJ, 2000).

Fahey, Curtis, *In His Name: The Anglican Experience in Upper Canada, 1791–1854* (Ottawa, 1991).

Fingard, Judith, *The Anglican Design in Loyalist Nova Scotia, 1783–1816* (London, 1972).

Glasson, Travis, *Mastering Christianity: Missionary Anglicanism and Slavery in the Atlantic World* (New York, 2011).

Hawkins, Ernest, *Historical Notices of the Missions of the Church of England in the North American Colonies previous to the Independence of the United States: Chiefly from the MS. Documents of the Society for the Propagation of the Gospel in Foreign Parts* (London, 1845).

Mills Sr, Frederick V., *Bishops by Ballot: An Ecclesiastical Revolution* (New York, 1978).

O'Connor, Daniel and others, *Three Centuries of Mission: The United Society for the Propagation of the Gospel 1701–2000* (London, 2000).

Pascoe, C. F., *Two Hundred Years of the S.P.G.: An Historical Account of the Society for the Propagation of the Gospel in Foreign Parts, 1701–1900*, 2 vols. (London, 1901).

Strong, Rowan, *Anglicanism and the British Empire, c.1700–1850* (Oxford, 2007).

10

The Caribbean and West Indies

Natalie A. Zacek

In comparison not only with metropolitan Britain but with its North American colonies, the history of the Anglican Church in the West Indies—defined for the purposes of this chapter as Barbados, Jamaica, and the federated Leeward Islands colony, which consisted of the islands of Antigua, Montserrat, Nevis, and St Kitts (also known as St Christopher)—has not received significant scholarly attention, due not only to the paucity of surviving local records but also to a long-standing tendency for both contemporary observers and modern scholars to view these plantation-centred settlements as 'tropical hellhole[s] of dissipated whites'.[1] In a much quoted phrase, the writer Charles Leslie, who visited Jamaica in the 1730s, described that island's elite as 'lov[ing] a Pack of Cards better than the Bible'.[2] But while the Church struggled to establish itself in the West Indian colonies, it nonetheless played a crucial role in the secular, if not always in the confessional, identity of the islands' white inhabitants, emerging as an integral element of their self-image as 'Englishmen transplanted'.[3]

Throughout the period under study, metropolitan observers were on the whole highly critical of the state of Anglican observance in the West Indian colonies. The clergyman-philosopher George Berkeley spoke for many of his fellow churchmen when he wrote in 1725 that 'there is at this day, but little sense of religion, and a most notorious corruption of manners, in the English colonies settled on the continent of America, and the islands'. To Berkeley, this unhappy state of affairs could best be remedied by sending more and better qualified clergy 'to reform morals, and soften the behaviour of men', as in his view the Anglican churches throughout the colonies were 'a drain for the very

---

[1] Ron Chernow, *Alexander Hamilton* (New York, 2004), p. 8.

[2] Quoted in Michal J. Rozbicki, 'The Curse of Provincialism: Negative Perceptions of Colonial American Plantation Gentry', *Journal of Social History*, 63 (1997): 727–52 (pp. 732–3).

[3] Larry Dale Gragg, *Englishmen Transplanted: The English Colonization of Barbados, 1627–1660* (New York, 2003).

dregs and refuse' of British clergymen.[4] The physician Robert Poole, who was an adherent of George Whitefield, and who travelled throughout the West Indies in the late 1740s, complained repeatedly that the various churches at which he attended services were 'thinly visited and carelessly attended to', which he interpreted as a sign of the settlers' irreligious nature, as corroborated by the fact that 'many of those who call themselves Christians, [were] keeping open Shop, with their Goods publickly exposed to Sale' on Sunday, and that even those who attended services 'by their Behaviour, seem'd pretty great Strangers to the Duty of worshipping God with Decency and Reverence'.[5] The situation was apparently little improved in Jamaica in the 1820s, as the Revd Richard Bickell observed the 'too general profanation of the Sabbath' by white and black residents alike. Although Bickell praised the attempts, however fruitless, of Jamaican clergy to bring about the moral reformation of their communities, he complained that a dearth of 'regular and pious clergymen' in the colony had resulted in the ordination of some ministers 'that would not otherwise have been admitted into the church, and several of whom . . . have not been so attentive to their arduous duties as they should have been'.[6] Maria Nugent, the wife of the governor of Jamaica (1801–6), was similarly critical of the quality of that colony's clergy; she found Kingston's church 'pretty, and well fitted up', but 'the service was miserably performed, by a *Scotch* reader, and a *Welsh* preacher'. Lady Nugent was still less impressed by the religiosity, or lack thereof, displayed by members of the local elite; following a dinner-party conversation, she reported that 'some of the opinions of the gentlemen were shocking. No one professed to have the least religion, and some said it was all a farce.'[7]

But despite these criticisms, it would be inaccurate to conclude that the majority of colonists in the English West Indies were either hostile or indifferent to the practice of Anglican religion. The majority of the settlers prided themselves on their English heritage, and even those inhabitants who were apathetic in spiritual matters, or who begrudged payment of the taxes levied to construct and maintain churches and pay clergymen, viewed the Anglican Church as a principal source of English national identity, and saw at least tacit conformity with that Church as a line which definitively separated the true-born Englishman from a variety of feared or despised 'others'. These were, principally, the Spanish, England's original enemy in the settlement of the Americas; the French, their principal opponent from the mid-seventeenth

---

[4] George Berkeley, 'A Proposal for better supplying of Churches in our Foreign Plantations', in *The Works of George Berkeley*, ed. G. N. Wright, 2 vols. (London, 1843), II, p. 281.

[5] Robert Poole, *The Beneficent Bee: or, Traveller's Companion* (London, 1753), pp. 353, 330, 315.

[6] Richard Bickell, *The West Indies as they are* (London, 1825), pp. 95–6.

[7] Frank Cundall (ed.), *Lady Nugent's Journal* (Kingston, Jamaica, 1907), pp. 215, 99 (italics in original).

century until the end of the Napoleonic Wars; and the Irish in the metropole and the empire. They also included commercially useful but culturally alien groups such as the Jews; the Puritans, Quakers, and other Nonconformists, who symbolized the religious extremism of the Cromwellian era; Native Americans and enslaved or free persons of African descent. Even the least enthusiastic Anglican communicant was aware that his religion differentiated him from those whom he considered his enemies or inferiors, and that it afforded him a privileged legal and political status in colony and metropole alike, one which made him a full participant in the political, social, and economic life of his community. West Indian colonial governors might have been willing to overlook their constituents' indifference to spiritual matters, or to grant certain rights and privileges to wealthy settlers who were probably covert Catholics, as long as they outwardly conformed to Anglicanism. But as their appointments granted them authority over spiritual as well as administrative and military matters, they were also keen to prove to metropolitan authorities that 'God Almighty [was] devoutly and duly served throughout [their] Government'.[8]

Numerous challenges presented themselves to those who hoped to create a fully functioning Church of England within the West Indian colonies. The first order of business was the creation of parishes; while Barbados had been thus organized as early as 1629, with Jamaica following suit within a few years of its accession by England from Spain in 1655, progress was considerably slower in the Leeward Islands, sections of which continued to record their inhabitants by the use of the military unit of the division as late as 1681.[9] But the formation of parishes was the beginning, not the end, of the process of creating a religious infrastructure; once an island had come under the Church's aegis through the establishment of these units of religious authority, it was necessary that each parish be provided, by the combined efforts of colony and metropole, with churches and clergymen. But in the politically and environmentally volatile world of the seventeenth- and eighteenth-century West Indies, neither buildings nor ministers were easily acquired or maintained.

The French raids of 1666–7, in conjunction with the Anglo-Dutch conflict at that time, saw the destruction of three of St Kitts's churches and both of those which had been erected on Montserrat. The latter were rebuilt, but were destroyed again in an earthquake which struck the island on Christmas Day 1672. Leeward governor Charles Wheeler reported in 1671 that 'the islands have made liberal provisions for the maintenance of clergy, and are everywhere

---

[8] 'Instructions for our Trusty and Welbeloved Daniel Parke Esqr', 18 June 1705, Ann Arbor, University of Michigan, William L. Clements Library, Shelburne Papers.

[9] Robert Schomburgk, *The History of Barbados* (Cambridge, 2010), p. 92; Donald B. Cooper, *The Establishment of the Anglican Church in the Leeward Islands* (Stillwater, OK, 1966), p. 15.

erecting churches and chapels'.[10] Nonetheless, he expressed his disgust that the 'near 10,000 Christian Subjects' of the Leewards relied for their spiritual well-being upon 'but two in Holy Orders, both scandalous livers, and one a notable schismate'. When Wheeler's successor, Sir William Stapleton, made a report to the Board of Trade in 1673, he claimed that, although Nevis had 'some few Ministers', there were none anywhere else in the Leewards.[11] While Barbados had not suffered French attacks in the course of these hostilities, in the 1670s several parishes lacked incumbents, and those who were in post appear to have been unordained men recruited from amongst the island's laity.[12] At this time there were only four clergymen to serve Jamaica's fifteen parishes, and one of these was also the island's sole schoolmaster.[13]

Such complaints would be heard again and again over the next century. Governors bemoaned the lack of clergy and the perceived shortcomings of those available, and ministers were infuriated by the paucity of attenders and by the lack of churches or the smallness and dilapidation thereof. Meanwhile, islanders often resisted paying taxes for the support of the Church. This was not always the case; by the late seventeenth century, the islands boasted a number of impressive religious edifices. In Port Royal, Jamaica, the merchants of this booming port paid for the construction of an imposing church build-ing, which 'provided a physical space for business affairs and granted the merchants a degree of moral legitimacy' in a town notorious throughout the Atlantic world as a sink of iniquity.[14] In Bridgetown, Barbados's capital, St Michael's church, completed in 1665, was a substantial brick structure with tall, arched windows, a crenellated parapet, and two rows of interior columns.[15] The cartographer Richard Blome described one of Montserrat's churches, rebuilt after the depredations of warfare in the 1660s, as being 'very fair...of a delightful Structure...the Pulpit, Seats, and all the rest of the Carpenters and Joyners Work, being framed of the most precious and sweet-scented Wood'; while in St Kitts 'the English have erected five fair Churches, well furnished with Pulpits, and Seats of excellent Joyners work of

[10] Cooper, *Establishment*, pp. 20–1; British Library [BL], Egerton MS 2395, Papers Relating to the English Colonies in America and the West Indies, 1627–99, f. 528; petition of Wheeler to Charles II, 20 July 1671, in W. Noel Sainsbury (ed.), *Calendar of State Papers, Colonial Series, America and the West Indies, 1669–1674* (London, 1889), p. 243.

[11] Cooper, *Establishment*, p. 94.

[12] Larry Dale Gragg, *The Quaker Community on Barbados: Challenging the Hegemony of the Planter Class* (Columbia, MO, 2009), p. 77.

[13] Richard S. Dunn, *Sugar and Slaves: The Rise of the Planter Class in the English West Indies, 1624–1713* (Chapel Hill, NC, 1972), p. 157.

[14] Louis P. Nelson, 'Anglican Church Building and Local Context in Early Jamaica', in Kenneth A. Breisch and Alison K. Hoaglund (eds.), *Building Environments*, Perspectives in Vernacular Architecture 10 (Knoxville, TN, 2005), p. 66.

[15] Louis P. Nelson, *The Beauty of Holiness: Anglicanism and Architecture in Colonial South Carolina* (Chapel Hill, NC, 2009), p. 255.

precious Wood'. But this rapid development of the ecclesiastical landscape was undercut by the effects of ongoing warfare between the English settlers and their French neighbours. In 1712, the church of St Thomas Lowland, Nevis, was burned; that of St Anthony on Montserrat 'was much defaced by the Enemy, the few Books . . . Stolen and Lost and the ministers Robb'd of all they were masters of', to such a degree that David Bethun, the rector, begged the bishop of London in 1715 to send him some books, ornaments, bibles, and prayer books to replace those that had been lost or destroyed.[16]

Even in times of peace, West Indian colonists were often reluctant to devote tax revenues to the construction of new churches or the repair of existing ones. In 1720, for example, the Antiguans expressed a deep unwillingness to pay for the erection of a church in the parish of St Philip, as 'there was already a Church and a Chappel of Ease, both in very good repair', and 'it was unreasonable to build a new church for the convenience of eight or ten people, who were the only men that contended for building the same, when the majority of the inhabitants were against it'.[17] A few years later, when Antigua's new parish of St George was separated from that of St Peter's, the residents of the former elected not to construct a new church or chapel, but instead to use the small chapel at Fitch's Creek as their place of worship.[18]

It would be easy to interpret this unwillingness to devote public funds to the building, maintenance, and rebuilding of churches as an indication of the low value which West Indian colonists placed on religious observance. But as we have seen, between 1666 and 1713 the Leeward Islands were raided and ruined on numerous occasions by French attack, and all of the English colonies in the West Indies were constantly subject to hurricanes, earthquakes, and other natural disasters, in the course of which the built environment was repeatedly devastated. Vere parish church in Clarendon, Jamaica, for example, was damaged in the great earthquake of 1692, rebuilt, then devastated by hurricanes in 1712 and 1722.[19] To many settlers, it made little sense to devote large sums of money to the erection or repair of elaborate church buildings if they were likely to be destroyed within a few years; low wooden structures were far more likely to survive hurricanes and earthquakes than were taller ones built of stone. Unlike, for example, colonial Virginians, West Indian planters did not conceive of 'the house of God [as] the residence of the greatest gentleman in the neighbourhood'; as Robert Poole noted, they seemed no more or less

---

[16] Governor Walter Douglas to Mr Hoare, 5 Apr. 1714, Oxford, Rhodes House Library, SPGL C/WIN/ANT1L; Bethun to the bishop of London [1715], Lambeth Palace Library [LPL], Fulham Palace Papers, General Correspondence: Section B–WI, vol. XIX, Leeward 1, 1681–1749.

[17] *Journal of the Commissioners for Trade and Plantations, from January 1722–3 to December 1728* (London, 1928), p. 20.

[18] Vere Langford Oliver, *The History of the Island of Antigua*, 3 vols. (London, 1894), I, p. xcvi.

[19] Nelson, 'Anglican Church Building', p. 65.

keen to attend services in a church 'almost destroyed by Time and Negligence' than in one which boasted 'a very neat Altar-Piece' and 'ornamental Gilding and Painting'.[20] Moreover, individual residents frequently made generous gifts to their parish churches. In Nevis, St Thomas Lowland's parish church was the beneficiary in 1679 of the will of Sir Francis Morton, the president of the island's council and the colonel of its militia, who left twenty thousand pounds of sugar for the maintenance of the church and the purchase of communion plate for it. In 1703 Henry Carpenter of Nevis left the sum of £200 sterling to St Paul's parish, Charlestown, for the purchase of books on history and divinity 'to found a Library... for the encouragement of Piety and Learning'; and St John's church in Antigua had by the mid-eighteenth century acquired an impressive set of communion silver, as well as life-sized lead figures of Saints John the Baptist and John the Divine, apparently prizes seized from a French ship from Martinique at the beginning of the Seven Years War.[21] As early as 1645, Barbadian settlers were leaving funds to their parish churches for the purchase of 'some ornament' or 'other needful things', and guidebooks to Jamaica repeat the unfortunately unverifiable legend that the communion silver of St Peter's church, Kingston, was the gift of the notorious pirate-turned-governor Henry Morgan.[22] After the parish church of St Michael, Barbados (later the island's cathedral) was destroyed by a hurricane in 1780, the vestry raised £10,000 by public subscription to rebuild it.

The quantity and quality of available clergy remained a vexed issue within the West Indian colonies throughout the period under study. Charles II had commanded the bishop of London to supply ministers to the island colonies, and William III directed the bishop to apply to the Treasury for funds to cover the costs of these clergymen's passages across the Atlantic.[23] The governors of the various West Indian colonies were designated by the bishop as his ordinaries, an ordinary being 'a sort of lay bishop' responsible for appointing ministers to the islands' parishes, but a governor who was indifferent to religion or who was preoccupied with warfare, slave rebellion, mercantile crisis, or a poor sugar crop was unlikely to devote much effort to locating appropriate candidates, giving rise to situations such as that of late eighteenth-century Jamaica, in which there was one Anglican minister for every 1,500

---

[20] Dell Upton, *Holy Things and Profane: Anglican Parish Churches in Colonial Virginia* (New Haven, CT, 1986), p. 164; Poole, *Bee*, pp. 363, 30.

[21] William Smith, *A Natural History of Nevis* (Cambridge, 1745), pp. 213–14; Vere Langford Oliver, *The Monumental Inscriptions of the British West Indies* (Dorchester, 1927), 108; Vere Langford Oliver, *Caribbeana*, 6 vols. (London, 1909–19), IV, p. 289; 'A Layman', *Antigua: The Story of the Cathedral and Parish Church of St John, 1678–1932* (Guildford, 1933), pp. 28, 31.

[22] Gragg, *Englishmen Transplanted*, p. 73; Calvin Bowen, *Guide to Jamaica* (Kingston, Jamaica, 1958), p. 35.

[23] Gerald Fothergill, *A List of Emigrant Ministers to America, 1690–1811* (Baltimore, MD, 1965), p. 1.

white residents.[24] Moreover, few clergymen were keen to commit themselves to even a short term of service in the islands, as many of the reports submitted to the bishop by those who made the voyage described their experiences in highly negative terms. Not only were the individual churches frequently in an advanced state of dilapidation, but from a financial standpoint life in the islands could be very difficult. In 1705, the Revd Francis Le Jau, who had served for five years as Montserrat's only Anglican cleric, reported to the newly founded Society for the Propagation of the Gospel that 'everything there, particularly cloathing...[was] three times as dear as in England', that his parishioners had provided him with 'a house built with wild canes, thacht, but never finished', and that they had never made good on their promise to pay him an annual supplement of £60 sterling; he claimed that without the financial assistance provided by the famously pious Governor Christopher Codrington and a few other leading residents, 'he must have perished through want'.[25] In 1720 John Anderson, formerly a grammar school teacher in Lambeth, London, made similar complaints, claiming that the clergy of St Kitts 'have had no other settlement but voluntary contributions...which is the reason this place has had more ministers...than I can well remember to reckon up, the incumbent being required to shift for himself by going to some Colony as soon as any considerable arrears became due to him'. As the Reverend Henry Pope wrote from Nevis to the bishop of London, Edmund Gibson, in 1723: 'Your Lordship may plainly perceive there is little encouragement for clergymen to waste themselves in this scorching climate; for after many years we are but where we were, tied down to a poor stipend which will scarce find us meat, drink, and clothes.' He implored Gibson to find him a living in the metropole, 'resolving rather there to accept of the smallest thing in your Lordship's gift, than to live miserably here'.[26]

These difficulties notwithstanding, the quality of the West Indian clergy, in contrast to their quantity, was relatively high, although one English visitor to Jamaica in the late eighteenth century claimed that its clergymen were 'much better qualified to be retailers of salt-fish, or boatswains to privateers, than ministers of the Gospel'.[27] Le Jau had received a doctoral degree from Trinity College, Dublin, and had been made a canon of St Paul's Cathedral, a comfortable and prestigious post he chose to leave in favour of ministry in the West Indies and, later, in South Carolina.[28] The clergy of eighteenth-century

---

[24] Edward Brathwaite, *The Development of Creole Society in Jamaica, 1770–1820* (Oxford, 1971), p. 25.

[25] Quoted in C. F. Pascoe, *Two Hundred Years of the S.P.G.: An Historical Account of the Society for the Propagation of the Gospel in Foreign Parts, 1701–1900*, 2 vols. (London, 1901), I, p. 211.

[26] Quoted in Cooper, *Church*, pp. 10, 28.

[27] Quoted in Nelson, 'Anglican Church Building', p. 68.   [28] Cooper, *Church*, p. 20.

Montserrat included Rees Daly, Lewis Gaillard, and Richard Molineux, all of whom had matriculated at Oxford; in Nevis, William Smith and John Langley were Oxford graduates, and Thomas Powers had been a fellow of Trinity College, Cambridge. Kittitian clergy included Walter Thomas (MA Oxon), John Merac, who held a law degree from Cambridge, Thomas Paget, a fellow of King's College at the same university, and James Ramsay, a former naval surgeon who became a celebrated abolitionist via his widely read *Essay on the Treatment and Conversion of African Slaves in the West Indian Colonies* (1784).[29] Jamaican ministers included the Cambridge graduate Thomas Pierce Williams (active 1812–13) and David Duff from the University of Aberdeen (1793–1814), and in Barbados the Revd Benjamin Spry (1773–1806) was not only an Oxford graduate but also the brother of William Spry, the island's governor between 1767 and 1772.[30]

The criticisms posed by West Indian ministers regarding the progress of the Church within the islands should be interpreted with a degree of scepticism. On the one hand, those who regaled the bishop and the Society for the Propagation of the Gospel with triumphant accounts of their endeavours may have hoped to advance their metropolitan careers; on the other, those whose letters were replete with details of their poverty and of the settlers' irreligion may have done so in order to justify their lack of success, or to convince sympathetic readers to find them positions in England. Others may have suffered initial disappointment when faced with low attendance at services or popular ignorance of Anglican doctrine, but learned to adjust their expectations to their environment. Robert Robertson, who served as minister at St Paul's, Nevis, from 1707 to 1737, appeared to have accepted the prevailing opinion amongst the island's white population that '[they] thought they did pretty well in keeping the Face of Religion amongst themselves on the Lord's Day', although he was sad to note that, whereas he had at the time of his arrival attracted 150 or more attenders to his Sunday services, by 1724 that number had dropped to sixty or seventy, which he attributed not to a loss of communal piety but to 'the strange decay' of Nevis's white population in the face of warfare and natural disaster. He wrote wryly that 'most people here are fond enough of frequent preaching... they would have the Minister go to church, but will not do so themselves, and none are louder this way than some that never go to church', a plaint echoed around the same time by Charles Leslie, who reported that the churches of Jamaica were in a

---

[29] Oliver, *Monumental Inscriptions*; Margaret Deanne Rouse-Jones, 'St. Kitts, 1713–1763: A Study of the Development of a Plantation Colony', PhD thesis, Johns Hopkins University, 1977, p. 160.

[30] Clergy of the Church of England Database, <http://theclergydatabase.org.uk>, accessed 11 June 2014; Oliver, *Caribbeana*, III, p. 209.

'dismal' state and rarely open for services.[31] William Smith claimed that West Indian planters were not innately irreligious, but rather were frustrated by the fact that, instead of being allowed to choose their own clergymen, they were reliant upon those selected by the governor or the bishop, most of whom were not true 'West India Clergymen' but rather 'Great Persons Sons, Relations, and Dependants' from the metropole.[32] Even the generally censorious physician Poole, who so harshly criticized the unimpressive churches and small congregations he encountered in the islands, found some grounds for optimism regarding the settlers' commitment to the Church; at Parham, on Antigua's northern coast, 'the Congregation was pretty large, considering the Place, and we had a very excellent Discourse, by an old Gentleman'. Poole praised the women he saw at services in Montserrat, noting that, rather than using religious gatherings as a venue in which to display the latest fashions, a criticism frequently lodged in London and in the southern mainland colonies, 'they go in a decent Matron-like Manner, regarding Dress but little, after the Manner of true Housewives, whose Minds are occupied in something more noble'.[33] By contrast, Charles Leslie reported that in Jamaica church service was the venue for a fashion parade, in which the planters replaced their usual attire of head-kerchiefs, linen drawers, and vests with wigs and 'silk Coats, and Vests trimmed with Silver'.[34]

As Donald Cooper has noted, West Indian settlers throughout the period under study were 'not anti-religious as such', and they 'were willing to give lip service to the church so long as it did not oppose them'.[35] The Anglican Church of the region developed a 'latitudinarian philosophy' in the face of the limited availability of clergy and the general lack of religious fervour among its white residents. Yet it was also a Church which 'complemented a slave-owning society with its emphasis on hierarchy, authority, and obedience'.[36] Until the nineteenth century, while the Moravians, the Methodists, and especially the Baptists made many converts among the enslaved, it was almost exclusively the Church of the islands' white residents. On rare occasions a slave or a free person of colour, usually female and often of mixed race, might be in attendance. Poole saw a 'young Negro Woman receive the holy Sacrament' on Easter Sunday in Antigua, and the minister of St John's Fig-tree Church, in Nevis, baptized in the summer of 1763 Eve, an 'Adult Mulatto the property of Frances Brodbelt'. But from the beginnings of slavery in the English colonies the perceived clash between making a man a Christian and holding him as

---

[31] Robert Robertson, *A Letter to the Right Reverend the Lord Bishop of London, from an Inhabitant of His Majesty's Leeward-Caribbee Islands* (London, 1730); Oliver, *Caribbeana*, III, p. 322; Nelson, 'Anglican Church Building', p. 68.

[32] Smith, *Natural History*, p. 212.   [33] Poole, *Bee*, pp. 327, 361.

[34] Quoted in Nelson, 'Anglican Church Building', p. 72.   [35] Cooper, *Church*, p. 35.

[36] Andrew Jackson O'Shaughnessy, *An Empire Divided: The American Revolution and the British Caribbean* (Philadelphia, PA, 2000), p. 31.

chattel encouraged slave-owners to oppose aggressively the conversion of their slaves to Anglicanism. As early in the development of the slave system as the late 1640s, the English traveller Richard Ligon reported that Sambo, an African slave on Barbados, was 'kept out of the Church' because his owner feared that, 'being once a Christian, he could no more account him a slave'. As a result, nearly all such attempts by Church of England ministers were met with hostility. Le Jau, for one, claimed that masters refused to allow the conversion of their slaves because they would then be forced 'to look upon 'em as Christian brethren and use 'em with humanity'.[37] While the Moravians, who arrived in the Leewards in the 1750s, and the Methodists, whose theology was introduced to Antigua in 1760 by a prominent convert, the planter Nathaniel Gilbert, were both keen to include slaves and free people of colour in their services, most West Indian clergymen appear to have upheld the colour bar, often, like William Smith, sharing their parishioners' anxiety that 'a Slave... once Christened, conceits that he ought to be upon a level with his Master, in all other respects'. When James Ramsay adopted an abolitionist stance and offered religious instruction to St Kitts's slaves, his actions inflamed communal opinion to the point that local whites attacked him in print, refused to attend services at his church, and caused him to flee to England for his own safety.[38]

Despite facing discouragement and sometimes open hostility from the ranks of the planters, the Anglican Church did not entirely abandon the project of evangelizing the enslaved. Other than Ramsay, the most famous proponent of the religious instruction of slaves was the younger Christopher Codrington, an Oxford scholar, military commander, Barbadian planter, and Leeward Islands governor, who in 1710 left his two Barbadian estates and their hundreds of slaves to the Society for the Propagation of the Gospel. Codrington's intent was that the revenues generated by these vast sugar plantations would support the creation and maintenance of a college for the training of Anglican missionaries, at which were to be 'maintained a convenient number of professors and scholars who should be under the vows of poverty, chastity, and obedience, and be obliged to study and practise physick and chirurgery as well as Divinity, that by the apparent usefulness of the former to all men they might both endear themselves to the people and have the better opportunities of doing good to men's souls whilst taking care of their bodies'.[39]

---

[37] Oliver, *Caribbeana*, IV, p. 23; C. S. S. Higham, 'Early Days of the Church in the West Indies', *Church Quarterly Review*, 92 (1921), p. 127; Pascoe, *S.P.G.*, p. 211. See also C. S. S. Higham, 'The Negro Policy of Christopher Codrington', *Journal of Negro History*, 10 (1925): 150–3; Richard Ligon, *A true and exact History of the Island of Barbadoes*, ed. Karen Ordahl Kupperman (Indianapolis, IN, 2011), p. 101.

[38] O'Shaughnessy, *Empire*, p. 31.

[39] Quoted in W. T. Webb, 'Codrington College', *Mission Life*, 5 (1874): 207–8.

While the estate's slaves were to be the source of revenues which would support this project, Codrington's intention was that they would also serve as a model population of enslaved converts. But, as Travis Glasson has observed, the college's experience 'starkly reveals how the Society's program intersected with the bitter reality of slavery'; in 1745 the missionary Joseph Bewsher was forced to admit that fewer than twenty Codrington slaves 'could repeat their catechism', let alone be considered fully converted to Anglicanism. In a situation in which the plantation's white personnel 'wielded both the Bible and whip in the SPG's name', it is not surprising that the majority of the enslaved rejected Christianity, often in favour of obeah or other African-derived spiritual traditions which appalled the missionaries and their supporters.[40] On the Codrington plantation, as elsewhere in the West Indies, the slaves were suspicious of any minister or missionary 'who eat with manager, and drink with manager, and manager tell him what to say to us', and were all too aware of the power of what David Lambert has termed the 'clergy–planter nexus'.[41]

As described earlier, throughout the seventeenth and eighteenth centuries the Anglican Church struggled to find its footing in the West Indian colonies. It was frequently short of money, churches, clergymen, and (perhaps most importantly) public commitment, let alone enthusiasm. Yet Anglicanism in and of itself was a crucial source of identity at both the individual and the communal level in these colonies. To be an Anglican was to be part of an Atlantic community centred upon a Protestant vision of empire, one which in this period was in the process of commercially and militarily eclipsing its 'papist' rivals, Spain and France. The Church placed colonists and colonies within a 'Great Chain of Being' which linked them to God, the monarch, Parliament, and the English people, and endowed them with a set of rights and responsibilities which they believed, with some accuracy, to grant them a degree of political and spiritual liberty unique within early modern Europe and its overseas empires. Within the colonies, being a part of the Anglican Communion differentiated between white and black, master and slave, as well as between people who could claim the right to full participation within the political realm and those who could not. Churches, even if little used or dilapidated, 'played a specific role in the [West Indian] landscape... [they were] signifiers of white authority in a landscape that was more African than English in appearance', and they allowed white colonists to believe that they had succeeded in transforming tropical islands inhabited largely by enslaved

---

[40] Travis Glasson, *Mastering Christianity: Missionary Anglicanism and Slavery in the Atlantic World* (New York, 2012), pp. 143, 166, 163.

[41] Joseph Sturge and Thomas Harvey, *The West Indies in 1837* (London, 1968), p. 129; David Lambert, *White Creole Culture, Politics, and Identity during the Age of Abolition* (Cambridge, 2005), p. 19.

Africans into 'little Englands'.[42] Simultaneously, being an Anglican communicant, however minimal one's spiritual or financial commitment to the institution, allowed the islands' white male inhabitants full participation in the local militias and political establishments, opportunities denied throughout this period to the West Indies' significant populations of Jews, Quakers, and Catholics, and so defined the parameters of normative masculinity.[43] Thus, the history of the Anglican Church in Britain's West Indian colonies can be read as one of success as well as of struggle, and the Church's position in colonial West Indian society appears as simultaneously marginal and central.

SELECT BIBLIOGRAPHY

Cooper, Donald B., *The Establishment of the Anglican Church in the Leeward Islands* (Stillwater, OK, 1966).

Glasson, Travis, *Mastering Christianity: Missionary Anglicanism and Slavery in the Atlantic World* (New York, 2012).

Nelson, Louis P., 'Anglican Church Building and Local Context in Early Jamaica', in Kenneth A. Breisch and Alison K. Hoaglund (eds.), *Building Environments*, Perspectives in Vernacular Architecture 10 (Knoxville, TN, 2005), pp. 63–80.

Pascoe, C. F., *Two Hundred Years of the S.P.G.: An Historical Account of the Society for the Propagation of the Gospel in Foreign Parts, 1701–1900*, 2 vols. (London, 1901).

Zacek, Natalie A., *Settler Society in the Leeward Islands, 1670–1776* (Cambridge, 2010).

---

[42] Nelson, 'Anglican Church Building', p. 69.

[43] See Natalie A. Zacek, *Settler Society in the Leeward Islands, 1670–1776* (Cambridge, 2010), chs. 2–3.

11

India

Daniel O'Connor

Earlier manifestations of Christianity in India included one associated with the apostolate of St Thomas and bearing the spiritual stamp of the oriental Churches, while a second, Roman Catholic presence was pioneered by Vasco da Gama and the Portuguese from the late fifteenth century. Anglicanism first came to India through the agency of the East India Company. This 'Company of Merchants of London trading into the East Indies' was founded by authority of Queen Elizabeth I on 31 December 1600 and functioned until 1858, with a monopoly of Anglican religious involvement in the region for the first two hundred years. Further contributions to the Anglican presence, personnel sent by mission agencies, appeared from the second decade of the nineteenth century.

The company was controlled by a governor and court of directors who were staunchly Anglican, though their royalist inclinations were put aside during the period of the civil war and commonwealth, with constant deferential reference in the minutes at that time to Cromwell, and a number of Presbyterians appointed as chaplains.[1] The religiously radical governor during much of this short period, Maurice Thomson, was clearly at home under such a regime, but judiciously ensured at the Restoration a substantial gift of silver plate from the company to Charles II, soon followed by massive loans to the king. Thereafter, English Church affairs hardly registered with the company until late in the eighteenth century, and loyalty to the sovereign never wavered. Company rule in India gave way to that of Queen Victoria as empress in 1858.

Indian Anglicanism's '*magisterium*' thus rested essentially in the company, with the lay governor and court of directors assuming responsibility for the religious and moral character of its operations. Only very occasionally did the

---

[1] Daniel O'Connor, *The Chaplains of the East India Company, 1601–1858* (London and New York, 2012), pp. 7–8.

court turn to ecclesiastical authority, specifically to the archbishop of Canterbury and the bishop of London, for example to improve the recruitment of chaplains, though several of the archbishops took a lively interest in the company's affairs.

ANGLICAN FIRST-FRUITS, 1600–1700

During the seventeenth century the company was a purely mercantile project in which the merchants of a small and remote European nation ventured into a vast region of vigorous trade extending from the Persian city of Isfahan to the Japanese port of Hirado, with most company business at first located among the spice islands of the Indonesian archipelago. In 1682, the company's last foothold there was relinquished to Dutch rivals. Thereafter, its principal trade was on the south Asian mainland, initially at Surat and on the Coromandel coast.

The company during this period was a remarkably pious Anglican enterprise. The frequently daily meetings of its court in London were alive to a sense of divine presence, providence, and judgement in every aspect of operations. The governor regularly began court proceedings with prayers, including prayers of thanksgiving for the return both of a fleet and on investments. Frequently, to mark special occasions in the company's affairs, the court would repair to the local parish church (initially St Benet Gracechurch) for prayers and a sermon. Sermons, indeed, were a staple of the religion of the company at this time, while its chaplains were selected chiefly on the strength of a sermon preached before the court.

The court paid great attention to religious observance on the company's voyages and in the factories (trading posts) established in the East. Fresh instructions were invariably issued for each new venture. Regular worship was required, with certain times in every day set apart for public prayer. Fines for absence from worship were specified, and for misbehaviour, drunkenness, swearing, and so on. The merchant leader of each voyage and the president at each factory were responsible for these matters, assisted by a chaplain. Some 660 chaplains were appointed in the company's lifetime, 97 in the first century, serving then for an average of five years each.

In support of this observance, a bible bound with the Book of Common Prayer and a volume of sermons were regularly entrusted to a ship's purser. Eucharistic worship, related to the Church calendar, with fasting communion, was taken for granted, while psalm singing was a marked feature of this seventeenth-century Anglicanism, with every ship required to be provided with psalters and music. An episode in contemporary travel literature describes an encounter between the crew on a company voyage exchanging a performance of the psalms with a group of Muslims at Aceh, the crew explaining that they sang them daily.[2]

Sound learning was clearly a marked expectation of Anglicanism in India at this time, and the provision of theological literature for the chaplains and the more educated among the ships' and factories' personnel was a concern, with all the major factories including a library. Those of the early factories at places like Surat were particularly strong on contemporary puritan writers such as Baxter and Perkins. An intention to keep up to date was reflected in 1663 in the provision for Surat of the 1660 nine-volume Latin biblical commentary, *Critici Sacri*, while both Surat and 'the Coast' received a set of the recently published *Biblia Sacra Polyglotta* to assist in propagating the gospel among the local people. Acquaintance with the Fathers is widely evident in surviving sermons by the chaplains, though the lay president at Surat, George Oxenden, complained that, while their library had the epistles of Ignatius, it lacked those of Clement of Rome. By 1719, the catalogue of books in the library at Fort St George (Madras) included 23 books in Hebrew and Arabic, 75 in Greek, 357 in Latin, 698 English books, 48 French and Dutch, and 13 'translated into Tamil and into the Gentoo Languages'.[3]

Christian worship and conduct were impressive in some ships and factories. From Surat in 1672 the layman Streynsham Master, one of the company's finest mercantile minds, provided in a letter (probably to a member of the court) 'an account of the Manners of the ENGLISH Factors &c., their Way of Civil Converse and Pious Comportment'. It is a long and extremely interesting letter on religion practised 'as in Churches in England'.[4] Master ends his account of factory religion thus: 'with much discourse of Religion, Philosophy, the government of the Passions and affections, here is a most excellent governed Factory, indeed more like a College, Monastery, or a house under religious Orders than any other'. Master saw his concern for factory religion as a matter of emulating the ordered devotion of the Indian people, with Anglicanism finding its place within a hospitable Indian pluralism. At other factories, where the leadership was lax, drunkenness and disorder prevailed, usually to the dismay of the chaplain and the indignation of the court in London.

The company's worship remained largely private throughout the seventeenth century, conducted in an ordinary room set aside in the gated factory for that purpose, although Madras, under the progressive Streynsham Master, now governor, led the way with India's first Anglican church, St Mary's,

[2] R. Kerr, *General History and Collection of Voyages and Travels*, vol. 8, part ii (Edinburgh, 1824), bk 3, ch. 10, sect. 5.

[3] T. G. Percival Spear, *Nabobs: A Study of the Social Life of the English in Eighteenth-Century India* (Calcutta, 1991), pp. 186–8.

[4] Henry Yule (ed.), *The Diary of William Hedges, Esq (afterwards Sir William Hedges) during his Agency in Bengal; as well as on his Voyage out and Return Overland, 1681–1687*, Hakluyt Society, 74, 75, 78, 3 vols. (London, 1887–9), II, pp. cccv–cccvi.

consecrated in 1680. Contemporary with the classicism of Wren's London churches, St Mary's was modern in an English way, where an English community could worship as they were accustomed, and with a chaplain wearing an ample wig, all as in an English parish except that he walked abroad under his state roundel.[5] There were two distinctive features to the church. Designed and built, as most Anglican churches in India were, by military engineers, St Mary's had massive walls, a castellated parapet, and a roof reinforced to resist cannon balls, measures subsequently justified. Master further intended that the provision and accessibility of the church as a public building would attract Indian proselytes.

Many instructions underline the company's concern for the impression made on the people with whom they came into contact, and concern with mission was a recurring feature, first evident in a triumphant account of a baptism in 1616.[6] The need to understand other religions as a prerequisite for mission recurred throughout the company period, starting with Henry Lord's distinguished studies[7] and evident later in the work of William Jones, Warren Hastings, John Howell, Alexander Dow, Nathaniel Halhed, and Charles Wilkins.

The concern with mission surfaced strikingly from the 1660s, when a little-known evangelizing impulse rippled through the company in London and its associates at Oxford. This had been first signalled in a letter from the governor to Cambridge and Oxford in 1658 seeking prospective chaplains, 'having resolved to endeavour and advance the spreading of the gospel in India'.[8] Over the next three decades, the planning involved the Oxford scientist Robert Boyle, the orientalist Thomas Hyde, who proposed the foundation of a *Collegium de propaganda fide* to train chaplains at Oxford, and (leading the project) John Fell, bishop of Oxford. The court was enthusiastic, and large sums of money were earmarked. With Fell's poor health, however, and his death in 1686, the original scheme ran out of steam, but there were significant outcomes.

The first of these was led by Fell's close friend and student, Humphrey Prideaux, who in 1695 wrote to Archbishop Tenison with an accompanying paper, 'An Account of the English Settlements in the East Indies, together with some Proposals for the Propagation of Christianity in those Parts of the World'. Noting that there were already a million Indian people within the company's sphere of influence, and a further half a million of Portuguese

---

[5] The earliest reference to a 'parish' in India is 1708, when the Church in Bengal was described as an 'out-parish' of the diocese of London: Henry Barry Hyde, *Parochial Annals of Bengal, being a History of the Bengal Ecclesiastical Establishment of the Honourable East India Company in the 17th and 18th Centuries* (Calcutta, 1901), p. 56.

[6] O'Connor, *Chaplains*, pp. 41–2.   [7] O'Connor, *Chaplains*, pp. 68–9.

[8] Daniel O'Connor, 'Renewing the Missionary Work of East India Company Chaplains in the 17th Century', <http://divinity-adhoc.library.yale.edu/Yale-Edinburgh/Papers/OConnor2012.pdf>, p. 1.

origin, Prideaux urged the archbishop to address this missionary opportunity by seeking to influence the revision of the by-laws of the company's charter, due in 1698. That revision included a requirement that chaplains learn Portuguese and a vernacular language 'to instruct the native servants and slaves of the Company in the Protestant religion', and the provision of a church, school, and schoolmaster in each settlement.[9] Foundations were thus laid for an expansion of Anglican Christianity beyond the small groups of British seamen and merchants, hitherto the chaplains' only responsibility, and giving Anglicanism some possibility of a broader and more rooted presence.

A second outcome traceable to this Oxford missionary impulse was the formation by Thomas Bray of the two agencies, the Society for Promoting Christian Knowledge (SPCK) in 1699 and the Society for the Propagation of the Gospel in Foreign Parts (SPG) in 1701, which were to exert significant influences on the company's Anglicanism in the eighteenth century.

'PAROCHIAL ANNALS', c.1700–c.1780

By the end of the seventeenth century, textiles and tea had replaced spices as the company's principal commercial commodities (opium was to follow), with trade based largely on factories on the south Asian mainland, at the Mughal city of Surat, and in three small settlements which were to become Bombay, Madras, and Calcutta. Already, by 1700, these had begun their meteoric rise and would become three of Asia's greatest mega-cities. Madras, for example, on the Coromandel coast, had started in 1639 with the company's fortified factory built on a strip of land bought from a local landowner, the only immediate neighbours being a dozen houses of fisherfolk. The company establishment comprised eight merchants and twenty-four soldiers as guards, with a first chaplain in 1646. Within a year, three hundred families of weavers and dyers of the renowned Coromandel textiles had migrated from nearby towns into a settlement adjacent to the fort, with other trades, interpreters, merchants, and bankers soon to follow. By 1700, Madras was a city of approximately a quarter of a million inhabitants, with a spacious White Town and a thronging Black Town. Similar stories can be told of the rise of Bombay and Calcutta. The company establishment remained proportionately a very small element, and indeed each city continued to have an English population—including a growing number of private European traders and a garrison including 250 European soldiers—little more than that of a large

---

[9] John Shaw (ed.), *Charters relating to the East India Company from 1600 to 1761* (Madras, 1887), pp. 143–4.

village. The number of chaplains appointed remained fairly constant, with maybe a dozen in post at any given time until the later eighteenth century.

Church building followed the example of Madras, with St Anne's, Calcutta, named in respectful acknowledgement of England's reigning monarch and consecrated in 1709, and, in 1718, St Thomas's, Bombay, honouring the apostle of India. These churches became the focus for a more public church life as the English society of the presidency cities grew, and some Indians and Eurasians were attracted. The first chaplain at St Thomas's, Bombay, Richard Cobbe, submitted to the president a scheme including the provision of morning and evening prayers in church every day throughout the year, with a sermon every Sunday, and the sacrament on specified holy days. Catechizing was programmed, as was the observance of all holy days and Lent. At St Mary's, Madras, an organ was installed, while the impressive replacement for St Anne's in Calcutta, St John's, consecrated in 1787 and modelled on St Martin-in-the-Fields, soon acquired an organ with 1,400 pipes, a ring of six bells, and an orchestra loft. A military band with Eurasian musicians and a choir of boys from the charity school were soon features of each of the three presidency churches. Seating arrangements made company hierarchy visible—provision for the president was the priority, but in addition the Madras Council Minute Book in 1693 ordered that:

> The Churchwardens do herewith cause a handsome seat to be made in the Church for the Mayor, next below the Clerk's desk in the said aisle, with a place for a Mace... And that the Mayor's wife be placed next below him on the same side. And take care to seat those gentlewomen, that will be displaced... where best it may be to their content having due regard to their qualities.[10]

All this represented, with small exceptions, a ministry to the White Towns and the nabobs, the financially flourishing merchant community. Church-going being socially fashionable, an individual's church-going might require the accompaniment of at least seven servants.

It was not an easy ministry for a conscientious chaplain. William Anderson, in a sermon in Calcutta in 1707, compared those who were 'always either openly quarrelling... or secretly undermining one another' to 'the fiends in hell... everlastingly embroiled in feuds and discords'.[11] Reports of wealth and ostentation worried the court in London, as (in the 1750s) did reports of 'great licentiousness' prevailing in Bengal, but their calls for reform were met with ridicule. Underlying much of this was society's precarious hold on life in the face of extreme mortality rates. During the four months of hot weather at

---

[10] Frank Penny, *The Church in Madras: Being the History of the Ecclesiastical and Missionary Action of the East India Company in the Presidency of Madras in the Seventeenth and Eighteenth Centuries*, Vol. 1 (London, 1904), p. 114.

[11] Hyde, *Parochial Annals*, pp. 54–5.

Calcutta shortly after the consecration of St Anne's, 460 burials were recorded from a total English community of 1,200, three or four burials every day. A chaplain's fees from 'Superior Class' funerals were described as immense, though only about half lived to enjoy them.

In the later eighteenth century, the company began to develop from its role as trader to despotic narco-military state,[12] manipulating land ownership and seizing land revenues and the control of opium across the subcontinent, with a rapidly expanding army. The development of a public discourse about the British Empire constructed by SPG preachers and Church of England bishops in this period reflected something of this imperialism in India, noted by the Calcutta chaplain, William Johnson, in his proposal for the new St John's church submitted to governor-general Warren Hastings in March 1776.[13] The present chapel in the fort was too small, he wrote. Something better was required, now that the city housed the 'Government...of three extensive and populous provinces'. 'Temporal prudence' suggested 'paying a more than ordinary regard to the external rites and solemn ceremonies of religion in the sight of the nations of Bengal', for it was now no longer a matter merely of a merchant company, but 'the Government of the English nation, that in ... [God's] strength has been introduced and fixed over such extensive dominions of the Earth'.[14] The authorities liked this sort of thing, and Johnson was only one of several chaplains who began to provide the rhetoric for this imperial Anglicanism.

Three other developments served to shape aspects of eighteenth-century Indian Anglicanism. The first was that envisaged by Prideaux, with the co-option of some Indian and Luso-Indian employees of the company, the latter descendants of the earlier Portuguese Empire, not least in the area of Bombay. When Anglicanized, these were seen as potential allies. Books of Common Prayer in Portuguese were provided, and the SPCK added catechetical material in Portuguese to aid the process.

A further considerable expansion of Anglican numbers came as a result of militarization. The company and royal armies were hugely increased to deal with Portuguese, Dutch, and subsequently French rivals and to oppose the Mughal and other indigenous powers. What was virtually a corporate takeover of extensive regions of the subcontinent brought a considerable increase in chaplaincy appointments later in the eighteenth century, but also a new population, the children of British soldiers, officers, and other ranks, and

---

[12] The phrase 'narco-military' is D. A. Washbrook's: 'India, 1818–1860: The Two Faces of Colonialism', in A. Porter (ed.), *The Oxford History of the British Empire*, vol. III: *The Nineteenth Century* (Oxford, 1999), pp. 395–421 (p. 404). Washbrook points out that opium sales to China and south-east Asia were by the early nineteenth century 40 per cent of the total value of India's exports.

[13] See Rowan Strong, *Anglicanism and the British Empire, c.1700–1850* (Oxford, 2007), ch. 3.

[14] Hyde, *Parochial Annals*, pp. 164, 172.

Indian or Eurasian mothers, so many that in a few decades these 'country-born' outnumbered the British-born in the subcontinent. Hitherto, the church-wardens of the presidency churches, as overseers or fathers of the poor, had developed support for widows and orphans with a poor stock fund, and charity schools, including some modelled on that at Christ's Hospital, then in London. Subsequent developments were on a much greater scale. The story of these 'poor relations' is complicated by issues of race, class, and gender, and periodic shifts of policy.[15] Essentially, the company's attitude to these mixed-race people combined politico-economic calculation about the acquisition of servants for the company and potential allies with pastoral concern for the children of British fathers. Combining the political and the pastoral, the army preferred its soldiers to be married, and their children to be baptized as Christians and educated as Europeans. Chaplains were involved in a variety of ways, in one case gaining support from Lord Clive's Fund for native as well as British widows of European soldiers. The Scottish chaplain, Andrew Bell, in addition to his popular lectures on new scientific discoveries, made a significant contribution in developing a system of edu-cation at the Male Asylum, Madras, imaginatively promoted in a series of books and pamphlets, widely copied in India, and eventually championed by the National Society as the 'Madras system' in all its schools in Britain. While some of these 'poor relations' missed out on these new opportunities and ended up a 'half-pagan population fallen away from Christian rites in the slums' of the presidency cities, many more achieved something of a life, even a career, though always as the company's second-class citizens.[16] Not all, of course, became Anglicans, but large numbers did, with ordination for some in the nineteenth century.

A third development in this period saw seeds sown not merely of Angli-canism in India but, remarkably, of a robust Indian Christianity. Inspired by the formation of the SPCK and SPG, the Royal Danish Mission moved to recruit German Lutheran missionaries from Halle to work in south India, the missionaries Bartholomäus Ziegenbalg and Heinrich Plütschau being sent to Tranquebar in 1706. They were the first of some sixty-three Lutheran mission-aries in India over the coming century. They were welcomed by the company leadership and the chaplains in Madras, free passage was provided on company ships, and twenty-five of them were paid for by the company and 'managed' by the SPCK in what became known as the English Mission, working in the Black Towns, establishing schools for Tamil and Eurasian children, and using the

---

[15] C. J. Hawes, *Poor Relations: The Making of a Eurasian Community in British India, 1773–1833* (Richmond, 1996); and the fictional version, I. Allan Sealy, *The Trotter-Nama: A Chronicle, 1799–1984* (London, 1988).

[16] William Wilson Hunter, *The Thackerays in India and some Calcutta Graves* (London, 1897), p. 11.

Anglican Prayer Book and Catechism. Several company chaplains collaborated in their evangelism, Benjamin Schultze observing how William Leake, the chaplain at Fort St George 1721–8, delighted in the work of the conversion of the heathen, the archbishop of Canterbury, William Wake reciprocating in 1730 with a Latin letter to Schultze expressing his joy in the spread of the gospel. Later Lutherans such as Christian Friedrich Schwartz and effective later chaplains such as James Hough helped nurture the early generations of a flourishing Tamil Christianity, both Lutheran and Anglican.[17]

'THE ULTIMATE CIVILIZATION OF THE NATIVES', c.1780–1813

Increasingly violent militarization brought British victories in Mysore and over the Maratha Confederacy, and further disintegration of the Mughal Empire. The period also saw the company's formal role gradually diminishing, to be eventually succeeded by increasing imperial British rule, culminating in the Government of India Act of 1858. With the expansion of British interests throughout the subcontinent, but particularly westwards in the Bengal Presidency, chaplaincies reached Delhi in 1825 and Peshawar on the north-west frontier of the empire in 1849. The company appointed over 410 chaplains between 1780 and 1858, twice as many as in the previous two centuries. They stayed longer, an average of fifteen years, most being assigned to particular garrisons or to campaigns. Though the court of directors insisted in 1846 that their chaplains were not military servants, the militarization of their work and status was largely irresistible. Church of Scotland chaplains were also appointed from 1814, some nineteen to 1858, while Roman Catholic clergy were permitted to function as chaplains in the various garrisons.

Contemporary with these developments was the rising Evangelical movement, significant for Indian Anglicanism. A number of lay Christians in the company and in Parliament were in the forefront of the Evangelical cause, as were a number of new chaplains, together with supporters in Britain of a growing missionary movement. The principal focus of attention initially was the renewal of the company's charter in 1793, Evangelicals wanting to formalize the communication of Christianity to the native population. The company had always had a missionary concern, but Evangelicalism stressed, at its best, earnest evangelizing, at its worst something more moralizing and aggressive, in accord with the ruthless and violent imperialism of the times.

---

[17] O'Connor, *Chaplains*, pp. 91–4.

A key figure throughout the entire period was a company official, Charles Grant. A religious crisis around 1776, eight years after his arrival in India, led him to Evangelicalism. As Grant saw things, the Indian people lacked those qualities 'of integrity, truth and faithfulness' needed to participate in the emerging society. This moral judgement would sound throughout the coming century. Only Christianity would solve the problem, 'helping these poor people whose land we enjoy . . . to recover the almost lost life of nature, and to become acquainted with the truth and excellence of Revelation'.[18]

In 1786, an Evangelical chaplain newly arrived in Calcutta, David Brown, met Grant and encouraged him to share his ideas with the Cambridge clergyman Charles Simeon. Simeon's response was to use his influence among Evangelicals to recruit chaplains, while Grant's return in 1790 to an influential role for the next thirty-three years in the court of directors enabled him to collaborate with Simeon over many such appointments, among them that of the much admired and pious linguist Henry Martyn. Grant's effort to influence the revision of the 1793 company charter to include a 'Pious Clause' requiring company support for a programme of Christian teaching was effectively opposed by leading company figures, including Henry Dundas, President of the Board of Control, who persuaded Parliament that an official mandate for evangelism was unwise. It could even, in the light of events in France, nurture a politicized population with 'Jacobinical' ambitions, or a repeat of recent events in America. Significant Evangelical influence upon Anglicanism in India would have to wait until the next revision of the charter in 1813, when Claudius Buchanan, the first of Simeon's recruits and Grant's first appointee to the company chaplaincy, seized the initiative.

Buchanan was gifted, vigorously imperialistic, and vigorously Evangelical. In 1799 he became junior to Brown in the Calcutta chaplaincy. There, an early opportunity to display his views came at a service at St John's in 1800 to celebrate two recent victories, that of Wellesley over Tipu Sultan at Seringapatam and Nelson's over the French at the Battle of the Nile. As preacher, Buchanan spoke of 'Great Britain, like the Guardian Angel of the Christian world . . . the INSTRUMENT of God's choice', holding out the promise 'not only to establish the interests of our own country, but to accelerate the final triumph' of Christianity in India.[19] Wellesley liked the sermon and ordered its printing and distribution throughout India. While vice-provost of the new Fort William College, Buchanan exercised his skill as a publicist to influence the forthcoming revision of the charter, beginning in 1803 a programme of prize essays and prize poems, promoted throughout Britain's universities and

---

[18] Henry Morris, *The Life of Charles Grant: Sometime Member of Parliament for Inverness-shire, and Director of the East India Company* (London, 1904), pp. 19, 96–7.

[19] Claudius Buchanan, *A Sermon preached at the New Church of Calcutta, . . . on Thursday, February 6th, 1800* (Calcutta, 1800), pp. 20–1.

public schools, on themes touching upon Britain's imperial and Christian responsibilities in India. This proved an effective form of publicity, though provoking hostility towards mission among more cautious company personnel. Buchanan followed this up in 1805 with his *Memoir of the Expediency of an Ecclesiastical Establishment for British India, both as a Means of perpetuating the Christian Religion among our own Countrymen; and as a Foundation for the ultimate Civilization of the Natives*. The reference to 'civilization of the natives' was to echo throughout the nineteenth century, but was also Buchanan's calculated retort to the leading Scottish Enlightenment historian William Robertson's sympathetic account of the religion and culture of ancient India.[20] The *Memoir* was very specific, calling for a government-supported missionary establishment and 'men of episcopal dignity, an archbishop and metropolitan' in Bengal, and bishops for Bombay and Madras, thus enabling 'a remote commercial empire... [to] maintain its Christian purity, and its political strength amidst Pagan superstitions and voluptuous and unprincipled people'.[21] Wilberforce was enthused, lamenting Britain's neglect of its missionary obligations in India as a great national crime. Buchanan sent his *Memoir* to the archbishop of Canterbury, writing: '[w]e want something... to awaken to life this sluggish and inert race vegetating in ignorance and passive misery', an episcopal establishment 'for the abject subjects of this great eastern empire to look up to'.[22] Buchanan spent his last two years in India, from 1806 to 1808, visiting the south and writing lurid accounts of the 'Pagan superstitions' he witnessed there.

Returning to England as the debate leading up to charter revision intensified, Buchanan published his *Christian Researches in India* (1811), piling on the horrors of India's moral degeneracy to undoubted effect, nine editions appearing in two years. The more prudent Grant thought Buchanan's outspoken style counterproductive. Usefully, it prompted the directors to clarify their position: '[w]e are very far from being averse to the introduction of Christianity into India... but we have a fixed and settled opinion that nothing could be more unwise or impolitic... than... to introduce it by means which should irritate and alarm the religious prejudices of the Natives'.[23] At the same time, the SPCK acknowledged gratefully the company's century-long assistance to their missionary endeavours. A pamphlet battle with several senior members of the company followed. Between March and July 1813, during the charter's consideration in Parliament, some nine hundred petitions were

---

[20] Stewart J. Brown, 'William Robertson, Early Orientalism and the Historical Disquisition on India of 1791', *Scottish Historical Review*, 88 (2009): 289–312.

[21] C. Buchanan, *Memoir of the Expediency of an Ecclesiastical Establishment for British India* (London, 1805), pp. 9, 12.

[22] Hugh Pearson, *Memoirs of the Life and Writings of the Rev. Claudius Buchanan, D.D.* (Oxford, 1817), p. 374.

[23] Penny, *Church in Madras*, pp. 6–7.

initiated by Evangelical mission interests. In Parliament, Wilberforce, who had supported Buchanan during much of the previous debate, contrasted 'our Christian religion... sublime, pure and beneficent' with 'the Indian religious system... one grand abomination'.[24] Judiciously, nevertheless, he opposed Buchanan's government-sponsored missionary establishment. It was rejected. The new charter, approved in July, had three components important to Indian Anglicanism: support for education (including 'literature... encouragement of the learned natives... knowledge of the Sciences'), a regulated process to admit missionaries into India, and provision for the appointment of a bishop and three archdeacons.

Buchanan's health declining from 1811, he turned to his scholarly interest in oriental liturgies, and took a relatively subdued part in the final stage of the charter discussions. Nevertheless, we may take his distinctive and spirited career, with its rhetoric of contempt for the religious culture of India and its insistence upon moral difference, as a powerful marker for the bigotry and intolerance which characterized much of nineteenth-century Anglican mission in India, and for the stereotyping that favoured empire.

'A TRUE AND APOSTOLIC BRANCH OF THE CHURCH OF CHRIST', 1813–29

The 1813 charter's authorization of an ecclesiastical establishment with a bishop of Calcutta was of particular significance. Episcopal confirmation and ordination would help build up the Church, and Anglicans in India would now have a sense of belonging to something less remote than the diocese of London. Thomas Fanshaw Middleton arrived to remedy that deficiency in November 1814, supported by three archdeacons, one for each presidency. The company, alarmed by suggestions made in the charter renewal debate of Indian hostility, played down his arrival. Middleton commented: 'all this precaution was quite superfluous with respect to the natives, who are the most tolerant people in the world and wondered why we had no head of our Religion here'.[25]

The charter renewal campaign had been led by Evangelicals, so the choice of Middleton, a High Churchman, might appear surprising. However, consider-able influence in the Church of England still rested with the old High Church party led by the Hackney Phalanx. Middleton was a Phalanx insider, and his affectionate correspondence throughout his years in India with its leading

---

[24] *Hansard (series 1)*, vol. 26, col. 164 (22 June 1813).
[25] Thomas Fanshaw Middleton to William Van Mildert, 14 Feb. 1815, Durham University Library [DUL], Van Mildert Papers, VMP 1457/1.

members, the brothers Joshua and John Watson, Henry Norris, and William Van Mildert, provides important insights on his episcopate.

As a High Churchman, Middleton focused unwaveringly on building strong structures for Anglicanism in India. He was hindered by the ambiguous terms of his appointment in 'His Majesty's Letters Patent constituting the Episcopal See of Calcutta'. These caused him endless frustration. His long-term vision was of an Indian Church, built on the work of ordained Indians, hence his emphasis on founding an institution in which to train them: Bishop's College, Calcutta, his most treasured object. His immediate task, however, was to draw together the chaplains and missionaries, the English laity, and the growing numbers of Eurasian and Indian Christians, into an Anglican community recognized by the state as its established Church. As he explained in his first sermon in his cathedral, St John's church, on Christmas Day 1814, he came to India 'to set in order the things that...[were] wanting' by providing in episcopacy 'the bond of unity and the safeguard of truth'.[26] He sensed, however, many problems, with 'not a particle of Church feeling in the country'. People had no concept of a functioning Church, and he had to find his way 'through brushwood and jungle, where bishop never trod before'. An Anglican Church 'completely established' was many years emerging. The court of directors, attached to its powers of patronage, was little help, sending as chaplains 'whom they please[d]', and insisting that, bypassing the bishop, chaplaincy appointments remained with the governor-general and presidency governors, military chaplaincy appointments resting with the commander-in-chief.[27] These arrangements persisted, endlessly frustrating Middleton.

Establishment had, of course, significant implications for the chaplains themselves, as Middleton indicated when he first addressed those in Bengal in 1815. 'Hitherto a small body of detached individuals, acting without concert, and not subject to any local superintendence', they were 'thenceforward to become the members of a compacted body, and united under the regimen which prevailed in the earliest ages of the Gospel'. They would be 'no longer subject to all the inconveniences...implied by the name of military chaplains', but, bound by licence and an oath of canonical obedience, 'completely and exclusively, under ecclesiastical jurisdiction, at permanent stations, to which they would thenceforward be nominated by himself'. All this was indeed formally the case, but would only be fully realized after years of frustration for Middleton and his immediate successors. 'It is exceedingly galling to a clergyman', he wrote, 'to be told by a commanding officer, that there shall, or shall not, be service on such a day, and that such and such

---

[26] Charles Webb Le Bas, *The Life of the Right Reverend Thomas Fanshaw Middleton, D.D., late Lord Bishop of Calcutta*, 2 vols. (London, 1831), I, p. 228; unless otherwise stated, quotations in this section are from Le Bas.

[27] Middleton to Van Mildert, 14 Feb. 1815, DUL, VMP 1457/1.

portions of the Liturgy must be omitted'. These matters belonged to the bishop. The governors were another problem, only reluctantly surrendering their authority over the chaplains. Cornwallis, he wrote, was giving him 'a great deal of trouble and weakening...[his] authority over the Clergy', and he wrote of the 'despotism' of the governor of Madras.[28] The two presidency chaplains there, Edward Vaughan and Marmaduke Thompson, also resented the new situation, agreeing, 'though they agree[d] in hardly anything else', to exclude the archdeacon from the pulpit at St Mary's.[29] Intervention was necessary there and in Bombay, while in Calcutta the provocations of the senior chaplain, Henry Shepherd, compelled Middleton to assemble the clergy and deliver 'a very strong and not a very brief admonition'. Rigid and unimaginative military and bureaucratic mindsets and the grudging adjustment of chaplains to episcopal rule constantly slowed his work and clouded his visionary hopes. As his biographer notes, he had 'every foot of ground to contest'. His long letters to his Phalanx friends, lively, amusing, and full of intelligent fascination with all that was new to him, constantly alluded to these frustrations. The support of his wife was vital, as both amanuensis and constant companion. Friends attributed his death after eight years as bishop not least to continual obstructions encountered in his work.

Particular difficulties arose regarding the first Church of Scotland chaplain, James Bryce, who saw himself as the senior representative of a parallel establishment. Indeed, his first sermon, in January 1815, 'Preached at the Opening of the Church of Calcutta', declared it a superior establishment, Anglicanism being 'still grievously infected with the corruptions of the Church of Rome'. A particular irritant to Middleton lay in the matter of church buildings. Of the new St Andrew's at Madras, he wrote: '[Our] church at Madras is very handsome...but the Kirk is to eclipse it; the English has a stone floor, but the Scots are to have marble...our steeple is...the highest in India; but theirs is to be a few feet higher'.[30] It is unfortunate that such things came between two serious churchmen, for in fact Middleton's High Churchmanship and Bryce's Moderate missiology, with the stress both laid on education, should have made them natural allies. Fortunately relationships mellowed over time.

The competition over church buildings touched an important issue for Middleton. The directors had always insisted that new churches be as plain and simple as possible, and that all unnecessary expense be avoided. Though Middleton thought St John's, Calcutta, 'the handsomest modern Church... [he] ever saw', most of the rest were 'barn-like'. He suggested that 'if we would recommend our religion to the natives', good church buildings were vital. 'What must the worshipper in mosques and pagodas...in a country whose

[28] Middleton to Van Mildert, 28 Jan. 1816, DUL, VMP 1458/1.
[29] Middleton to Van Mildert, 17 Jan. 1818, DUL, VMP 1459/1.
[30] Middleton to Van Mildert, 3 May 1819, DUL, VMP 1460.

places of worship are the proudest monuments of native art... think of men who, possessing all the resources of the country, and pretending to a better faith, worship their Maker in buildings not distinguishable from barracks or godowns?' Throughout his episcopate he pressed for better standards. His Bishop's College was in 'pure, ancient, collegiate Gothic'. The new cathedral, St Paul's, only completed a quarter of a century after his death, would have pleased him in its Gothic Revival grandeur.

One weighty chaplaincy matter concerned the SPCK. Before his appointment, Middleton, with the other Phalanx members, had ardently supported the society. He came to India, then, aware of those Lutherans who had staffed the SPCK-supported English Mission over the previous eighty-five years. His two tours into south India enabled him to see this mission and its five serving missionaries. He was impressed with the successor to Schwartz at Tanjore, J. C. Kohlhoff, describing him to Joshua Watson as 'almost another Swartz... when I came away he pronounced over me a prayer for my future welfare... I could not but feel that the less was blessed of the greater'. Middleton's conversations with the Lutherans were an inspiration for the future Bishop's College. Kolhoff asked him to devise a means of educating the children of the missionaries in 'a sort of missionary college'. The advantages to the cause of Christianity were evident, 'especially as Mr. Kolhoff assured me that they might all... be regularly ordained by the bishop of Calcutta'. It would be a step towards transferring 'all the native Christians of the south, into the bosom of the Church'. Another step involved the two elderly Lutherans at Tranquebar, Caemmerer and Schreyvogel, who, in the prolonged absence of Danish support, offered to the SPCK, 'who have extended to us for a century so many valuable gifts and supplies, our humble services and the whole mission and its property'. Middleton saw an opportunity. 'It would be a creditable and popular thing for the... [SPCK] to consolidate the two missions', and thus bring all of Protestant native Christianity in south India 'into communion with the Church of England', episcopal ordination creating 'a genuine Asiatic branch of the Church of England'. The initial consolidation was effected in 1820, transferring eleven congregations and around two thousand Christians, with their catechists and chapels, to the care of the SPCK missionary, Kolhoff. The subsequent transfer of a large part of the SPCK Lutheran community, some twenty thousand Tamil Christians, to a specifically Anglican bosom, was completed under Middleton's successor, Reginald Heber. A wider union involving the Syrian Christians, already explored by two chaplains, Buchanan and Kerr, was also much on Middleton's mind following his tours of the south.

Mission issues were also important to Middleton. Perceptively he judged it a propitious moment. His episcopate coincided with the emergence of 'a revolution of knowledge and sensibilities... [among] tens of thousands of high-caste Bengali Hindus'. Middleton's encounters with Ram Mohun Roy convinced him that these 'higher classes... without whose concurrence all hope of extensive conversion must be groundless', were open to Christianity.[31] Fear of stirring hostility, expressed by opponents of the 1813 charter, was not the problem: 'ordinary discretion is all that is required . . . [and avoidance of] direct and open affront to the prevailing superstitions'. What was required was 'a preparation of the native mind to comprehend the importance and truth of the doctrines proposed to them: and this must be the effect of education'. The 'general diffusion of knowledge and the arts' through the medium of English could serve as 'preparatory to a feeling of interest about our religion'. Hence the twelve elementary schools he founded around Calcutta, managed by his chaplain, John Hawtayne. These 'schools of useful knowledge' would 'make the boys too wise for the Brahmins; after which, we trust that with God's blessing a purer and a more reasonable faith will find its way'. Even the Baptists could help by engaging in education, breaking the ground for the seed of the gospel which the Anglican Church would then sow. Related to this, in a scholarly discursus on early Church history, he showed how mission was always, within 'the order and system' of the Church, led by and under the authority of the bishop. This was a prerequisite for 'the expansion of the Catholic Church', for 'all antiquity . . . [showed] that the propagation of the Gospel was in close connection with order and discipline'. The social transformation of contemporary Bengal, consolidated by 'schools of useful knowledge', suggested a context in which 'civilization and religion . . . [might] be expected in the ordinary course of Providence to follow the successes of a Christian state'.

Meanwhile, Middleton emphasized the responsibility of the chaplains 'to maintain Christianity and Christian ordinances among Christians'. By constant pressure on the directors, numbers of chaplains in the Bengal Presidency doubled during his brief episcopate, but his two long tours underlined the general shortage and he contrasted the Anglican position with the 'sort of omnipresence' of the Roman Catholic Church. The difficulties faced by the chaplains were rehearsed in a sermon that Thomas Robinson preached before him in Bombay, speaking of the few chaplains 'in a remote part of the sacred vineyard', isolated from one another so that mutual support was impossible.[32] Addressing these problems, Middleton maintained what contact he could by his tours, confirmations, correspondence, and hospitality, and by providing, through the SPCK, libraries and teaching resources for the chaplains. He valued highly the pastoral and liturgical ministry of the chaplains, carried out, as he stressed, within 'order and system'. Especially important for them was his commitment to provide a context for their work, no longer merely as

---

[31] Nisith Ranjan Ray, 'Bishop Middleton (the first Lord Bishop of Calcutta) and Raja Rammohan Roy', *Bengal Past and Present*, 83 (1964): 83–9.

[32] Thomas Robinson, *The Peculiar Difficulties of the Clergy in India: A Sermon* (London, 1821).

chaplains to a company, but as priests in 'a true and apostolic branch of the Church of Christ'.

Middleton's accounts of his episcopal tours are pertinent here. For the overland part of his first tour, the governor-general provided him and Mrs Middleton and their personal staff with four to five hundred soldiers, servants, and attendants, the bishop's party travelling in palanquins approximately twelve miles between 4 a.m. and 8 a.m. daily for several months. An episcopal visitation in India, the bemused bishop commented, was 'no trifle...a complete Asiatic caravan...camels carry our baggage, and we dwell in tents... altogether patriarchal'. At sea off Bombay, Admiral Blackwood in courtesy lowered his topsail to Middleton's armed cruiser; '[h]ow strange [he remarked] is the life of a bishop in this country'. This sort of thing, and his concern about his own rate of pay and his place within the absurdly contrived orders of precedence have been interpreted as pomposity, but no one was less pompous in his letters to his friends, and it is clear that he was responding as an old-style High Churchman to 'the acquisition, by a Christian state, of the sovereignty of Hindostan'. He concluded from what he saw of Indian society that 'an ecclesiastical establishment, conspicuous by the number of its clergy, and invested with all the dignity and consideration which the Orientals invariably associate with the higher sacerdotal functions, so far from alarming them...by inducing them to inquire into the grounds and evidences of our faith, would lead them, gradually, to adopt it'.

Aside from this existing 'sovereignty', Middleton's hope lay in what his college might do 'to further the missionary designs' of a Church whose clergy would be 'bred and ordained on the spot'. Bishop's College opened in 1824, two years after his death. His prayers at the laying of the foundation stone in December 1820 emphasized 'a school of pastors and teachers, for the work of the ministry and the edifying of the body of Christ; increasing more and more, until this land of darkness be illumined in all its recesses with the light of the everlasting Gospel'. Two months later, the scholarly indologist, Phalanx associate, and SPG missionary W. H. Mill arrived to be principal, a role he fulfilled with distinction for eighteen years; his Sanskrit poem on Christ was a unique achievement, while his friendship with the Poona chaplain Thomas Robinson identified Robinson's Persian translation of the Old Testament as a project of the college. To Middleton, such indigenizing developments were as vital as the groundbreaking work of English education. To 'embrace and combine these objects' summed up his missionary vision, 'a Christian university, a centre of Christian learning which should be the heart and mind of the Church of India to be'.[33]

---

[33] T. G. Percival Spear, 'The Early Days of Bishop's College, Calcutta', *Bengal Past and Present*, 89 (1970): p. 187.

Scrutiny of the Letters Patent for a bishop of Calcutta, which we have only briefly touched upon here, makes clear how thoroughly inappropriate they were for the context, 'a travesty of episcopacy' lumbering bishop and diocese with ambiguous and anomalous elements from the ecclesiastical law of England.[34] It is a measure of Middleton's ability and vision that his episcopate, despite endless vexatious frustration, and within an unrelievedly imperialistic context, provided enough of an apostolic foundation for Indian Anglicanism ultimately to commend itself in the formation of united Churches in independent India.

The years after Middleton's death saw the next three bishops of Calcutta, including the charismatic Reginald Heber, come and die in that rapid succession which had so frequently been the way of things throughout the company period in India. Despite Middleton's impressive plans for Bishop's College, the learned and devoted leadership of Mill, and generous funding from the SPCK, SPG, and the Church Missionary Society, it was many years before the college came into its own. To end on a more positive note, however, two years before our period ended, Krishna Pillai was born, later to bring to expression in his beautiful Tamil poetry an authentically Indian Anglicanism.

*   *   *

The period reviewed here saw an Indian Anglicanism develop only slowly. Taking into account its dependence on the key role of the East India Company, however pious in its leadership and direction in the seventeenth century, and notwithstanding periodic efforts to advance a notion of mission, it could hardly have been otherwise. The small number of chaplains was there essentially to minister to the very small communities of expatriate personnel, their influence rarely reaching beyond the factory gates. Certainly, in the next century, the membership base broadened considerably, including in a relatively small way Indians and Luso-Indians associated with the company, in a much bigger way the mixed-race community engendered by the company and royal regiments, and in the south the Tamil and other indigenous congregations raised by the labours of the English Mission and its Lutheran associates, but the company, while calling for and intent upon enabling conversion in these three sectors, was never going to prioritize a more general Anglican expansion. As the century advanced, however, ideas of empire, interwoven to an extent with the aspirations of the emerging Evangelical movement, paved the way for the transition that an Anglican episcopate allowed for and which Thomas Middleton struggled to realize. He was wholly relaxed at the prospect of 'the acquisition by a Christian state of the sovereignty of Hindostan' as the context for the development of 'a genuine Asiatic branch of the Church of England', so that the foundations were laid for an Indian Anglicanism with its distinctive nineteenth-century combination of pastoral strength and imperial loyalty.

---

[34] Cecil John Grimes, *Towards an Indian Church: The Growth of the Church of India in Constitution and Life* (London, 1946), p. 63.

SELECT BIBLIOGRAPHY

Ashley-Brown, William, *On the Bombay Coast and Deccan: The Origin and History of the Bombay Diocese* (London, 1937).

Chatterton, Eyre, *A History of the Church of England in India, since the Early Days of the East India Company* (London, 1924).

East India Company, *Charters granted to the East-India Company from 1601...* (London, 1773).

Frykenberg, Robert Eric, *Christianity in India: From Beginnings to the Present* (Oxford, 2008).

Gibbs, Mildred E., *The Anglican Church in India, 1600–1970* (Delhi, 1972).

Gross, Andreas, Y. Vincent Kumaradoss, and Heike Liebau (eds.), *Halle and the Beginning of Protestant Christianity in India*, 3 vols. (Halle, 2006).

Hyde, Henry Barry, *Parochial Annals of Bengal, being a History of the Bengal Ecclesiastical Establishment of the Honourable East India Company in the 17th and 18th Centuries* (Calcutta, 1901).

Neill, Stephen, *A History of Christianity in India: The Beginnings to AD 1707* (Cambridge, 1984).

Neill, Stephen, *A History of Christianity in India: 1707–1858* (Cambridge, 1985).

O'Connor, Daniel, *The Chaplains of the East India Company, 1601–1858* (London and New York, 2012).

Paul, Rajaiah David, *Triumphs of His Grace: Lives of eight Indian Christian Laymen of the Early Days of Protestant Christianity in India, every one of whom was a Triumph of his Grace* (Madras, 1967).

Penny, Frank, *The Church in Madras: Being the History of the Ecclesiastical and Missionary Action of the East India Company in the Presidency of Madras in the Seventeenth and Eighteenth Centuries*, 3 vols. (London, 1904–22).

12

Africa

Elizabeth Elbourne

Africa was imagined by British Anglicans in the eighteenth century more than it was experienced, and African converts to Anglican Christianity, while important, were few. This is not to say, however, that Anglicanism and Africa did not have a significant mutual impact. The relationship was largely brokered by empire and by the slave trade: the stakes were accordingly high. This chapter focuses on those regions of the continent where Anglicanism had an impact or at least a presence in the eighteenth century: primarily coastal regions of West Africa, and to a more limited extent North Africa and southern Africa. In all these cases, the institutional presence of Anglicanism was linked to the slave trade or to colonization. I also discuss African–British educational and scientific networks in which Anglicans played a key role; debate over the appropriate British role in Africa and in the slave trade; and the foundation of Sierra Leone.

ANGLICANISM AND NORTH AFRICA

Christianity had deep roots on the African continent, as seen in the key role of North Africa in early Christianity, or the ongoing vibrancy of the Coptic and Ethiopian Churches. In Central and West Africa, the Portuguese attempted to establish slave-trading Christian kingdoms in the period in which they dominated the slave trade. Mvemba a Nzinga of the Kongo (King Afonso I) (c.1456–1542/3) is a prime example of an African leader who attempted, in conjunction with fellow elites, to Christianize his own kingdom, despite frustration over his inability to contain Portuguese slaving. There was a long history of Catholic missions, again tied to commerce and the slave trade (albeit often hampered by underfunding, the risky political implications of conversion for African leaders, and the frequent dabbling of missionaries themselves in the slave trade).[1] For the most part, however, Iberian and French Catholic missions faltered, and despite pockets of strength Christianity remained overshadowed by Islam and by indigenous religions in much of the continent.

Following abortive efforts to settle in Madagascar, England itself first held significant territory in Africa in 1664, when Charles II was granted the city of Tangier, in modern-day Morocco, by the Portuguese crown as part of the dowry of the Portuguese Infanta Catharine of Braganza. The English presence was short-lived. The sultan of Morocco forced the English to withdraw a mere twenty years later; they scrambled to blow up their own painstakingly built fortifications as they retreated.[2] The Anglican chaplain to the colony, Lancelot Addison (father of the better known Joseph) was the first Anglican clergyman to attempt to missionize in Africa. He sought, unsuccessfully, to convert those around him, whether Muslim or Jewish, to Christianity: it may be telling that in a later study of North African Jewish communities Addison claimed that the Jews were not 'forward to enter into Disputes' concerning the Scriptures, but when they were compelled to discuss Christianity were 'generally so fiery and cholerick, that they cannot refrain from an ill-bred railing'.[3] On his return to Britain, Addison wrote a history of the Berbers, as well as an account of North African Jewish communities and a biography of the Prophet Muḥammad, among other works.[4] While Addison's scholarship was informed by a deep conviction of the superiority of Christianity in general and of Anglicanism in particular, he nonetheless attempted, as William Bulman argues, to use historical scholarship to understand the region better and to convey information about it to an English-speaking audience. In this sense he contributed to an early modern explosion of Anglican writing about comparative religion and politics that Bulman considers to be a crucial part of what he terms the 'Anglican enlightenment'.[5]

Not all participants in the Anglican encounter with North Africa were elite. There was trade between Britain and North African states but also piracy. Many thousands of British people were captured by corsairs at sea and sent to Barbary coast states as slaves, albeit subject to ransom. A number wrote

---

[1] J. K. Thornton, 'Afro-Christian Syncretism in the Kingdom of Kongo', *Journal of African History*, 54 (2013): 53–77; Peter B. Clarke, *West Africa and Christianity: A Study of Religious Development from the 15th to the 20th Century* (London, 1986), pp. 7–28; Bengt Sundkler and Christopher Steed, *A History of the Church in Africa* (Cambridge, 2000), pp. 42–80.

[2] Linda Colley, *Captives: Britain, Empire and the World, 1600–1850* (New York, 2004 edn.).

[3] Lancelot Addison, *The Present State of the Jews* (London, 1675), p. 15.

[4] Lancelot Addison, *West Barbary, or, A short narrative of the revolutions of the kingdoms of Fez and Morocco with an account of the present customs, sacred, civil, and domestick* (Oxford, 1671); Addison, *Present State of the Jews*.

[5] William Bulman, *Anglican Enlightenment: Orientalism, Religion and Politics in England and its Empire, 1648–1715* (Cambridge, 2016), p. 10. On Anglican theories of difference and the English Enlightenment, see Travis Glasson, *Mastering Christianity: Missionary Anglicanism and Slavery in the Atlantic World* (Oxford, 2012), pp. 41–72.

popular memoirs about their experiences or were celebrated in ballads. Ordinary Anglicans may also have learned about North Africa from Church-sponsored ceremonies, in which redeemed captives were paraded through the streets and required to participate in public services of thanksgiving. Such ceremonies reflected the role of the Anglican Church (among others) in organizing collections for the redemption of captives, and they may well have helped shape a popular sense of the Church as protector and Islamic Africa as a place of danger, as well as economic opportunity.[6] The experience of slavery helped shape early modern British views of North Africa and of Islam, but largely through the experience of enslavement, rather than that of slave ownership. More generally, Anglican perceptions of North Africa were part of a much wider early modern European exploration of the Islamic world. North Africa was important in Anglican historical memory, given the importance of North African Christianity to the early Church. The Anglican Church had, however, little institutional presence in the region before the twentieth century.

ANGLICANISM IN WEST AFRICA: SLAVERY, EDUCATION, AND TRANSATLANTIC NETWORKS

The story of Anglicanism in West Africa in the eighteenth century was different. Here the British were (with occasional exceptions) slave traders rather than potential slaves. Although early English trade with West Africa dealt mainly in commodities other than slaves, the Company of Royal Adventurers Trading to Africa, founded in 1660 and eventually to become the Royal African Company (RAC), began to develop a significant English slave trade. It maintained a number of slave forts or 'factories' along the West African coast, including a headquarters at Cape Coast Castle in modern-day Ghana. In 1689, after the Glorious Revolution, the company lost its monopoly after a long struggle with independent traders and the slave trade was thrown open to competition from other merchant companies—ironically in the name of a particular vision of freedom, as William Pettigrew observes.[7] In 1752, the RAC was closed down and its slave forts given to the recently formed and government-sponsored Company of Merchants Trading to Africa. Despite being latecomers, the British dominated the transatlantic slave trade by the

---

[6] Colley, *Captives*.

[7] William Pettigrew, *Freedom's Debt: The Royal African Company and the Politics of the Atlantic Slave Trade, 1672-1752* (Chapel Hill, NC, 2013), esp. pp. 83–114; P. E. H. Hair and Robin Law, 'The English in Western Africa to 1700', in Nicholas Canny (ed.), *The Oxford History of the British Empire*, vol. I: *The Origins of Empire* (Oxford, 1998), pp. 241–63.

eighteenth century, and the West Indian plantations to which many enslaved victims were sold were crucial to the British imperial economy.[8]

The British did not try to create colonies in West Africa in the early modern period, despite their economic entanglements, but rather engaged with African intermediaries at coastal enclaves. Europeans did not have immunity to a number of diseases prevalent in sub-Saharan Africa and often feared to travel in the interior: much of the continent was *terra incognita* for Europeans. Furthermore, powerful West African kingdoms such as Dahomey, Ashanti, or Benin had trading relationships with Europeans but preferred to keep their trading partners largely confined to shipboard or to coastal enclaves.

The first Anglican missionary to West Africa was the Revd Thomas Thompson, who in 1751 volunteered to serve with the SPG as a missionary to Africa, following earlier service with the SPG in New Jersey. Thompson was based at the Cape Coast Castle slave fort, and was also employed as the chaplain of the government-sponsored Company of Merchants Trading to Africa (CMTA).[9] This appointment echoed a wider tradition of slave fort chaplains, pioneered by Catholic powers. On the Protestant side, chaplains included men such as Jacobus Capitein, a former slave who was educated and ordained in Holland and returned to work in a Dutch factory, and the Moravian Christian Jacob Protten, son of a Danish slave trader and a Ga woman, who proselytized and ran a school in a Danish slave fort, in conjunction with his wife Rebecca, a former slave from the West Indies.[10]

Among other things, chaplains were responsible for running schools for the children of people associated with the slave trade. These children often had white or mixed-descent fathers and African mothers, although the schools sometimes also included the children of wealthy families for whom literacy and arithmetic might facilitate employment. As this suggests, the slave trade gave rise to a community of potential intermediaries, and Christianity was often initially spread through such communities. A small but consistent number of Africans and so-called 'mixed-race' children were sent to Britain for schooling, mostly from slave-trading communities: in 1788, for example, some fifty such children from the Windward and Gold Coasts were attending schools in Liverpool.[11]

---

[8] David Richardson, 'Through a Looking Glass: Olaudah Equiano and African Experiences of the British Atlantic Slave Trade', in Philip Morgan and Sean Hawkins (eds.), *Black Experience and the Empire* (Oxford, 2006), pp. 59–61.

[9] Thomas Thompson, *An Account of Two Missionary Voyages: By the Appointment of the Society for the Propagation of the Gospel in Foreign Parts* (London, 1758); Vincent Carretta and Ty M. Reese (eds.), *The Life and Letters of Philip Quaque, the First African Anglican Missionary* (Athens, GA and London, 2010), pp. 7–8, 44 n. 2.

[10] David N. A. Kpobi, 'African Chaplains in Seventeenth-Century West Africa', in Ogbu U. Kalu (ed.), *African Christianity: An African Story* (Trenton, NJ, 2007), pp. 140–70. On Rebecca Protten, see Jon Sensbach, *Rebecca's Revival* (Cambridge, MA, 2005).

[11] Sundkler and Steed, *History of the Church in Africa*, p. 47.

In 1772, long after his return to England, Thompson published *The African Trade for Negro Slaves Shewn to be Consistent with Principles of Humanity and with the Laws of Revealed Religion*, a brief and, even by the standards of pro-slavery literature, singularly logically inconsistent pamphlet. The fact that Thompson argued both that it was hard to defend people being 'sold like bullocks at a fair' and that slavery was acceptable because sanctioned by the Bible and economically impossible to abolish perhaps reflects the extent to which even Anglican elites had begun to feel discomfiture with slavery at this juncture but also refused to disavow it.[12] On the contrary, slavery was increasingly economically important to the SPG over the course of the eighteenth century, with the development of its Codrington plantation in Barbados and the more general expansion of the British slave trade; indeed, Travis Glasson points out that over the course of the eighteenth century the SPG owned more people as slaves than worked for it as missionaries.[13] In the meantime, an Anglican slave ship captain named John Newton had an evangelical conversion after being saved from drowning off the coast of Africa (and penned 'Amazing Grace' about the experience); it was not until the 1780s, however, that Newton would become an open abolitionist.[14] When he did, he would become part of an important network of abolitionist Evangelical Anglicans, but it was ill health that ended his career in what he said at the time was accounted a 'genteel employment'.[15]

Thompson sought to train elite African men to work as ministers and missionaries in Africa, despite his public support for slavery. In 1754 the SPG sponsored three boys sent by Thompson to Britain, William Cudjo, Thomas Caboro, and Philip Quaque (also spelled Quaicoo), the latter the relative of a prominent Fante middle-man in the slave trade. Cabaro died and Cudjo had a breakdown and was confined to an asylum in Britain, but Quaque was ordained as an Anglican minister (in the Chapel Royal at St James's Palace) in 1765 and returned to the Cape coast in 1766. He thereby became the first African Anglican priest. In West Africa, Quaque worked as an SPG missionary and CMTA chaplain until his death in 1816, and oversaw a number of schools along the coast.[16] Quaque's first wife, an Englishwoman

---

[12] Thomas Thompson, *The African Trade for Negro Slaves Shewn to be Consistent with Principles of Humanity and with the Laws of Revealed Religion* (London, 1772).

[13] Glasson, *Mastering Christianity*, p. 6.

[14] [John Newton], *An Authentic Narrative of some Remarkable and Interesting Particulars in the Life of *****, communicated in a Series of Letters to the Reverend Mr Haweis (London, 1765); John Newton, *Thoughts upon the African Slave Trade* (London, 1788); Matthew Wyman-McCarthy, 'Rethinking Empire in India and the Atlantic: William Cowper, John Newton and the Imperial Origins of Evangelical Abolitionism', *Journal of Slavery and Abolition*, 35 (2014): 306–27.

[15] Newton, *Authentic Narrative*, p. 155.

[16] Travis Glasson, 'Missionaries, Methodists and a Ghost: Philip Quaque in London and Cape Coast, 1756–1816', *Journal of British Studies*, 48 (2009): 29–50; Kpobi, 'African Chaplains', pp. 160–3.

named Catherine Blunt, accompanied him to Africa but died within a year of arrival. He remarried first the servant who had accompanied his wife from England and then an African woman. His mission had mixed results. He was undercut both by Europeans who sometimes refused to respect a black priest and were scarcely models of piety, and by Africans, who saw him as declutured, particularly as he had lost his knowledge of the Fante language while in Britain. Quaque is nonetheless an important figure in the early history of education in Ghana.

Quaque spent his professional life working in a slave fort and for a slave-trading company, and his close kin were directly involved in the slave trade. Nonetheless, he entered into transatlantic correspondence with abolitionists and expressed increasing opposition to the slave trade through his life. Travis Glasson argues convincingly that Quaque should be seen as a 'transitional figure whose life experiences help chart the development of circum-Atlantic black Christianity', demonstrating the emerging linkages between black Christianity, Evangelicalism, and anti-slavery throughout the Atlantic world.[17]

These linkages were more famously evident in the life of leading abolitionist and fellow convert to Anglicanism Olaudah Equiano. An Igbo speaker, Equiano was almost certainly born in modern Nigeria[18] and captured as a child with his sister, from whom he later became separated. After an adventurous life as a sailor, which among other things saw him fight in the Seven Years War, purchase his freedom, and travel to the Arctic, Equiano became a leading abolitionist spokesperson in Britain. He wrote a widely circulated autobiography that became a key abolitionist text.[19] It is noteworthy, however, that Equiano also considered becoming an Anglican missionary to Africa as late as 1779, before the full-fledged emergence of an organized abolitionist movement in the 1780s.[20] Equiano was a member of the Sons of Africa, a group of Africans in Britain who opposed the slave trade. The group also included Christian convert and former slave Ottobah Cugoano whose *Thoughts and Sentiments on the Evils of Slavery* in 1787 denounced oppression and enslavement as unchristian and predicted slave uprisings.[21]

Despite the growing importance of these transatlantic black networks and the role of Christianity in the lives of particular individuals, Anglicanism

[17] Glasson, 'Missionaries, Methodists and a Ghost', p. 50.

[18] There is some controversy on these points, well summarized in Paul Lovejoy, 'Autobiography and Memory: Gustavus Vassa, alias Olaudah Equiano the African', *Slavery and Abolition*, 27 (2006): 317–47. I find Lovejoy's argument that Equiano was indeed born in West Africa to be convincing.

[19] Olaudah Equiano, *The Interesting Narrative of the Life of Olaudah Equiano* (London, 1789); Richardson, 'Through the Looking Glass'.

[20] As Christopher Brown points out: *Moral Capital: Foundations of British Abolitionism* (Chapel Hill, NC, 2007), p. 293.

[21] Ottobah Cugoano, *Thoughts and Sentiments on the Evil and Wicked Traffic of the Slavery and Commerce of the Human Species* (London, 1787); Brown, *Moral Capital*, pp. 296–7.

made limited headway in African communities themselves during the late eighteenth and early nineteenth centuries. Anglicanism was not widespread in the territory that is now Ghana, the homeland of Quaque and Cugoano, for example, until the mid-nineteenth century, when Britain imposed direct rule, and even then its growth was constrained by the popular perception that Anglicanism was the religion of government and colonial elites.[22]

BRITAIN, AFRICA, AND ABOLITIONISM: CHANGING ANGLICAN PERSPECTIVES

In the meantime, in Britain itself new forms of engagement with Africa gathered steam from the late eighteenth century onwards. On the one hand, there was increasing interest in African exploration and in the commercial potential of the continent; on the other hand, there was also increasing debate over the morality of slavery, paralleled by the emergence of a serious abolitionist movement. Anglicans played important roles in all these trends.

From 1758 to 1783, between the Seven Years War and the American Revolution, the British held the territory of Senegambia, briefly wresting it from the French. The colony was a failure but, as Christopher Brown argues, its very existence strengthened the hand of those in Britain who wanted to extract economic resources from Africa other than slaves, and who often supported the occupation of substantial swathes of territory, rather than a precarious foothold at slave factories. Brown traces arguments both for more substantive occupation of African territories and for reduction in dependence on slavery from late eighteenth-century debates forward to the foundation of Sierra Leone (and by implication on to the period of high imperialism).[23]

A second significant strand of public engagement with Africa, closely related to the drive to colonize, involved efforts to promote the exploration of the African interior and to create maps; it included the quest for the source of the River Niger.[24] In 1788, a small group of wealthy men, headed by Sir Joseph Banks, founded the Association for Promoting the Discovery of the Interior Parts of Africa (the 'African Association'). The group included

[22] Glasson, *Mastering Christianity*, p. 194; John S. Pobee, 'The Anglican Church in Ghana and the SPG', in Daniel O'Connor and others, *Three Centuries of Mission: The United Society for the Propagation of the Gospel, 1701–2000* (London, 2000), pp. 409–21.

[23] Brown, *Moral Capital*, pp. 275–8. See also Christopher L. Brown, 'From Slaves to Subjects: Envisaging an Empire without Slavery, 1772–1834', in Morgan and Hawkins (eds.), *Black Experience and the Empire*, pp. 111–40.

[24] David Lambert, *Mastering the Niger: James MacQueen's African Geography and the Struggle over Atlantic Slavery* (Chicago, IL, 2013).

both abolitionists and supporters of slavery.[25] Members contributed funds to sponsor expeditions to explore Africa. Banks, a naturalist, head of the Royal Society, and a member of the Anglican gentry, sat at the centre of multiple scientific networks that gathered information about the non-Western world. As such, he exemplified the role of gentlemen amateurs in Anglican-dominated information-gathering networks in late eighteenth- and early nineteenth-century Britain—although it is important to note that other networks, such as Quaker networks, also played important, and sometimes competing, roles in gathering imperial knowledge.[26] The African Association privately sponsored several expeditions to Africa including, most famously, the travels of Mungo Park.[27] In the early nineteenth century, the British government took over the sponsorship of exploration expeditions, reflecting the close relationship between public and private quests for imperial knowledge, in both cases involving key roles for members of Anglican elites. As David Lambert observes, Park's second expedition from 1805 (during which all British participants died) was 'government backed and militarized'.[28]

The greatest explosion of debate over Africa, however, developed over the issue of whether or not the slave trade in which Britain was so profoundly involved was immoral and ought to be halted. Reasons for the abolition first of the slave trade in 1807 and then of slavery itself in 1833 have been extensively debated. Should intellectual or economic arguments be prioritized? What role was played by Christianity, or the desire to make the empire more manageable and moral in the wake of the upheavals of the American Revolution, or by strategic objectives? Did capitalism help or hinder abolition? Whatever the relative balance of factors, elite Anglican abolitionists clearly played a key role in moving the abolitionist cause onto the political agenda after the trail had been blazed by Quaker and other Nonconformist activists, even as Anglicans also continued to be prominent among supporters of slavery. This domestic story is also part of a wider transnational story that includes the impact of slave revolts, and in particular the Haitian revolution.[29]

[25] Lambert, *Mastering the Niger*, p. 12.
[26] On Quaker networks, see Starr Douglas, 'The Making of Scientific Knowledge in an Age of Slavery: Henry Smeathman, Sierra Leone and Natural History', *Journal of Colonialism and Colonial History*, 9(3) (Winter 2008), online journal, <https://muse.jhu.edu/>, accessed 9 Oct. 2016.
[27] Mungo Park, *Travels in the Interior Districts of Africa: Performed under the Direction and Patronage of the African Association, in the Years 1795, 1796, and 1797* (London, 1799).
[28] Lambert, *Mastering the Niger*, p. 12.
[29] Some key works in a very large field include: Eric Williams, *Capitalism and Slavery* (Chapel Hill, NC, 1944); David Brion Davis, *The Problem of Slavery in the Age of Revolution* (Ithaca, NY, 1975); Roger Anstey, *The Atlantic Slave Trade and British Abolition, 1760–1810* (London, 1975); Brown, *Moral Capital*; Seymour Drescher, *Abolition: A History of Slavery and Antislavery* (Cambridge, 2009); Robin Blackburn, *The American Crucible: Slavery, Emancipation and Human Rights* (London, 2011).

The abolitionist cause became politically prominent in the late 1780s. The Society for Effecting the Abolition of the Slave Trade was founded in 1787 by a group of twelve men, nine of whom were Quakers and three of whom, Thomas Clarkson, Philip Sansom, and lawyer Granville Sharp, were Anglicans. In the Anglican camp, some important early political energy came, as Brown argues, from a circle centred on Barham Court in the village of Teston, home of philanthropist Elizabeth Bouverie. This tight-knit group included Lady Margaret Middleton and her husband Sir Charles Middleton, author and charity school advocate Hannah More, and abolitionist bishop Beilby Porteus. The local clergyman, James Ramsay, had worked as a surgeon on a ship commanded by Charles Middleton in the West Indies, and had then, changing careers, worked as a priest in St Kitts. He returned as an ardent abolitionist, and wrote an abolitionist book with support from the Teston circle, which had widespread influence and sparked a lively debate with the advocates of slavery.[30] In the meantime, Anglican Evangelical MP William Wilberforce led the parliamentary campaign at a time when non-Anglicans were not permitted to be Members of Parliament. The Anglicans who pioneered abolitionism in the late eighteenth century were largely Evangelicals in the contemporary Anglican sense of that term. They believed that God was using them to create change in the world. They also believed in the necessity of individual salvation. Elite Evangelicals such as William Wilberforce or Hannah More wanted to effect moral reformation both domestically and overseas. They cooperated cautiously with Dissenters (although this could not be too open a collaboration in the fevered atmosphere of the French Revolution era). Like Evangelicals outside the Anglican fold, they believed that the cause of virtue was a transnational movement, and they frequently supported missionary societies as well as domestic reform initiatives such as Sunday schools and penal reform movements. The attack on the slave trade was part of a wider effort to remake the world and to discipline unruly 'others'. Abolitionism became a widespread popular movement in Britain, notable among other things for the fervent participation of women.[31]

SIERRA LEONE

Abolitionist sentiment, economic desires to exploit African produce, black hopes to return to Africa, white desires to remove the black poor from Britain,

---

[30] James Ramsay, *An Essay on the Treatment and Conversion of African Slaves in the British Sugar Colonies* (London, 1784). On the Teston circle, James Ramsay, and early Anglican Evangelical abolitionists, see Brown, *Moral Capital*, pp. 333–89.

[31] Clare Midgley, *Women against Slavery: The British Campaigns, 1780–1870* (London and New York, 1992).

and the drive to evangelize the continent all came together in the foundation of what would eventually become the colony of Sierra Leone. In 1787, the London-based Committee for the Relief of the Black Poor sponsored a settlement in a small area of the modern-day country of that name, near to well-established slave-trade infrastructure including a fort. The aim was to resettle from Britain black loyalists and former slaves who had earned their liberty by fighting on the British side during the American Revolution. The idea of a commercial colony was initially promoted by Henry Smeathman, an entomologist who had lived in the region for four years, sponsored by the Royal Society and Joseph Banks on the one hand and by Quaker networks on the other, to gather information about African insects.[32] Smeathman's aims to make money were tempered by the conversionist enthusiasm of fellow sponsor Granville Sharp. Before the first voyage, Olaudah Equiano was briefly Commissary to Sierra Leone for the Committee for the Relief of the Black Poor but was dismissed after having criticized corruption among suppliers, claiming before the voyage departed that government was being cheated and 'my countrymen plundered and oppressed'.[33] Despite high hopes, the first settlement had failed disastrously by 1789 in the face of disease, a French attack, crop failure, and opposition and armed resistance from locals, led by the Temne leader the British called 'King Jimmy', who ultimately had the settlement burnt to the ground. In the wake of this initial failure, a small group of wealthy British Anglican reformers formed the Sierra Leone Company in 1791. They facilitated the large-scale emigration from 1792 onwards of many former American slaves who had resettled in Nova Scotia.[34] After a number of further vicissitudes, including settler rebellion, Sierra Leone became a crown colony in 1808.

Sierra Leone's Claphamite backers thought the colony would create a community of Christians who would in turn evangelize the continent. Many early settlers from North America brought, however, a different form of Christianity with them than Anglicanism. This was a Christianity forged in slavery and influenced by Evangelicalism and nonconformity, as well as by African American and African spiritual and intellectual traditions. New Light preachers such as the Particular Baptist leader David George were important figures in the early settlement, to the disquiet of men such as Governor Zachary Macaulay, who clashed with George and many others on both political

---

[32] Douglas, 'The Making of Scientific Knowledge'; Deirdre Coleman, *Romantic Colonization and British Anti-Slavery* (Cambridge, 2005), pp. 28–62.

[33] Equiano, *Interesting Narrative*, ch. 12.

[34] Brown, *Moral Capital*, pp. 259–330; Maya Jasanoff, *Liberty's Exiles: American Loyalists in the Revolutionary World* (New York, 2011); Simon Schama, *Rough Crossings: Britons, the Slaves and the American Revolution* (London, 2005); Cassandra Pybus, *Epic Journeys of Freedom: Runaway Slaves of the American Revolution and their Global Quest for Liberty* (Boston, MA, 2006).

and theological grounds.[35] In 1800, many settlers rebelled, although the rebellion was suppressed with the assistance of British troops and Jamaican 'maroons'.

When Macaulay returned to Britain in 1799, he brought with him twenty boys and four girls for education and (he hoped) Christianization: many of these were the children of Sierra Leonean African and Afro-European elites, and it was hoped that they would become agents of Christianity and 'civiliza-tion' on their return. This exemplified the Anglican search for African agents of Christianization. Tellingly, after initial confusion, Macaulay took the pro-ject firmly out of the hands of Scottish collaborators, including controversial Calvinist Evangelical Robert Haldane and the director of the largely Congre-gationalist London Missionary Society (LMS), John Campbell. Instead of sending the children to Edinburgh, Claphamites created an 'African Academy' in London to give the children a religiously and politically appropriate Anglican education. The academy closed in 1806, when the last of the children were sent back to Sierra Leone; in its final years, leading abolitionists such as Wilberforce and Macaulay himself sent their own sons to be educated there, where, as younger children in a monitorial system, they would have been taught by the older African boys. Sadly, however, the majority of the Africans seem to have died while in Britain, although details are unclear as not all can be identified. Nonetheless, a number returned to Sierra Leone and some occupied promin-ent roles, such as John Macaulay Wilson, who became house surgeon of the Liberated African Hospital in Freetown and eventually ruler of the Kafu Bulom people.[36]

The 'Liberated Africans' who were brought to the colony from captured slave ships after the abolition of the slave trade in the British Empire in 1807 doubtless seemed another promising target to be remoulded as an Anglican community. Although born in Africa they had been deracinated—often vio-lently wrenched from their families and communities—and spoke a diversity of languages. The largest group were Yoruba speakers, originally enslaved in a region roiled by warfare. Yoruba convert Samuel Ajayi Crowther wrote a trenchant autobiographical account in 1837 for the Church Missionary Society (CMS), describing the trauma of the loss of home, family, and lan-guage, before Sierra Leone offered some possibility for the remaking of self. He described being captured as a boy in a large-scale attack by slave raiders on

---

[35] Mark A. Noll, 'Evangelical Identity, Power and Culture in the "Great" Nineteenth Century', in Donald M. Lewis (ed.), *Christianity Reborn: The Global Expansion of Evangelicalism in the Twentieth Century* (Grand Rapids, MI and Cambridge, 2004), pp. 31–51 (pp. 37–8); Cassandra Pybus, '"One militant saint": The Much-Travelled Life of Mary Perth', *Journal of Colonialism and Colonial History*, 9(3) (Winter 2008), online journal, <https://muse.jhu.edu/>, accessed 9 Oct. 2016.

[36] Bruce L. Mouser, 'African Academy: Clapham 1799–1806', *History of Education*, 33 (2004): 87–103 (pp. 102–3 on Wilson); Pybus, '"One militant saint"'.

Osogun, then a town of some twelve thousand people: the town was torched, Crowther's family scattered among different slave traders, and he himself passed from one owner to another in a long, brutal movement towards the coast. He measured his passage from one dialect group to another until he could no longer understand the language. He was finally sold at the coast to a Portuguese trader. British warships intercepted the Portuguese vessel shortly after it put to sea. The British ships cruised on the sea for two and a half months (during which over a hundred men drowned when a brig was sunk during a storm), finally anchoring at Sierra Leone on 17 June 1822.

> From this period I have been under the care of the Church Missionary Society; and in about six months after my arrival at Sierra Leone, I was able to read the New Testament with some degree of freedom; and was made a Monitor [in school], for which I was rewarded with sevenpence-halfpenny per month. The Lord was pleased to open my heart to hearken to those things which were spoken by His servants; and being convinced that I was a sinner, and desired to obtain pardon through Jesus Christ, I was baptized on the 11th of December 1825, by the Rev. J. Raban.[37]

Over the course of an eventful life, Crowther became the first Anglican bishop of African descent and a major advocate of self-governing African Churches.

From the outset, Church and state worked closely together to try to convert former slaves. The CMS began a mission to Sierra Leone in 1804. The very high death rate of white missionaries throughout the early nineteenth century helped confirm the CMS in its commitment to evangelization by African agents. In 1816, more completely fusing Church and state, Governor McCarthy split the colony into sixteen parishes, created Christian villages, and appointed missionaries to be administrators of each parish.[38] In 1827 the CMS established the Fourah Bay Institution as a seminary to train teachers, catechists, and priests, eventually to educate many members of a West African Christian elite.[39] In 1850 a higher percentage of children in Sierra Leone attended school than in England.[40]

African American settlers, 'Liberated Africans', and Jamaican maroons formed the core of what would become the 'Krio' community in Sierra Leone. Many did in fact convert to Christianity, or maintain their existing

---

[37] Samuel Ajayi Crowther, 'Letter of Mr. Samuel Crowther to the Rev. William Jowett, in 1837, then secretary of the Church Missionary Society, detailing the circumstances connected with his being sold as a slave', in J. F. Ade Ajayi (ed.), *Journals of the Rev. James Frederick Schön and Mr Samuel Crowther* (2nd edn., London, 1970), pp. 371–85 (quotation at p. 384).

[38] Padraic Scanlan, 'The Colonial Rebirth of British Anti-Slavery: The Liberated African Villages of Sierra Leone, 1815–1823', *American Historical Review*, 121 (2016): 1085–113; Clarke, *West Africa and Christianity*, pp. 35–6.

[39] Daniel J. Paracka Jr, *The Athens of West Africa: A History of International Education at Fourah Bay, Freetown, Sierra Leone* (New York and London, 2003).

[40] Kevin Ward, *A History of Global Anglicanism* (Cambridge, 2006), p. 116.

Christian belief, and they formed the core of subsequent missionary efforts to West Africa, particularly to the former homelands of many in Nigeria. In particular, the evangelization of Yoruba homelands was enormously important, and would bear fruit by the turn of the century in the use of Christianity by many to forge a specifically 'Yoruba' identity.[41] Nonetheless, recent scholarship suggests that Islam was more important in the Krio community than the traditional view of the Krios as solidly Christian suggests, and was in part fostered through trade networks.[42] At the same time, Christians maintained or adopted many traditions indigenous to Africa, particularly Yoruba practices.[43]

In describing the improved state of Christianity in the 'recaptive' villages in the late 1830s, Crowther hinted at earlier community conflict:

> For often, when school was opened with about a hundred or more scholars, it was not often closed with many above fifty; for many of them, under pretence of going out, slipped away to their homes. Some there were who openly expressed their displeasure at school, by an artifice most ridiculous in its nature. These were the inhabitants of Wellington. Upon agreement, they soon assembled at the call of the bell; but before school was opened, they all, with one accord, simultaneously rushed out of the grass chapel, through the doors and windows, in the utmost confusion possible. To crown the whole, they shouted, in their country language, as soon as they got out, with an expression of their victory over the schoolmaster.[44]

As this suggests, CMS education plans were not always as readily accepted as more triumphalist accounts might imply, and there was doubtless more conflict than missionary sources allow.

ANGLICANISM IN SOUTHERN AFRICA

In temperate southern Africa, Europeans had not been discouraged from settlement by disease. The Dutch East India Company (VOC) established a refreshment station at the Cape of Good Hope in 1652 and governed it until

---

[41] J. D. Y. Peel, *Religious Encounter and the Making of the Yoruba* (Bloomington, IN, 2000).

[42] Gabril Raschid Cole, *The Krio of West Africa: Islam, Culture, Creolization, and Colonialism in the Nineteenth Century* (Athens, OH, 2013).

[43] C. Magbaily Fyle, 'The Yoruba Diaspora in Sierra Leone's Krio Society', in Toyin Falola and Matt D. Childs (eds.), *The Yoruba Diaspora in the Atlantic World* (Bloomington, IN, 2004), pp. 366–82.

[44] [Samuel Crowther], 'Narrative of Events in the Life of a Liberated Negro, Now a Church Missionary Catechist in Sierra Leone', *Missionary Register* (Oct. 1837): 433–40 (quotation at p. 439). This is an earlier version of the letter cited in note 37, published anonymously; the later version omits this discussion of schools.

1795. The British held the colony from 1795 to 1802 and again from 1806, with a brief interregnum under the Batavian Republic. British possession in international law was confirmed at the Treaty of Amiens in 1814, after which Britain initiated a programme of colonization. The colony had thus been under Dutch control, and influenced by Dutch Calvinism, for over 150 years before British rule.

Christianity had a long and complicated history in the Cape Colony, which only became more complicated as the colony expanded. Settlers used particular versions of Christianity to justify their presence and to define the boundaries of the 'white' community; for example, while people of Khoekhoe and San descent used Christianity to claim respect and equal status in a context of violent abuse and labour coercion.[45] Among missionary societies, the LMS, which began work in 1799, proved to be particularly important in early nineteenth-century Cape politics: it was both influential in Britain at some key moments and highly controversial. The LMS was putatively interdenominational and had some early Evangelical Anglican backing, but in practice was dominated by Congregationalists.

Although Anglicanism had very little vernacular presence, most early colonial officials were Anglicans (unless they were Presbyterians from Scotland), and Anglican military chaplains accompanied the British troops who were garrisoned at the Cape. In the early days of British colonialism at the Cape Colony, as the echoes of the French Revolution still reverberated, the Anglicanism of men such as Governor Charles Somerset pushed them to be instinctively distrustful of politically radical Nonconformists.[46] For example, Somerset tried to restrict the movements of missionaries beyond the frontiers of the colony in the 1810s. At the same time, the LMS was politically successful when it proved able to make alliances with powerful British Anglican officials in Britain, notably the abolitionist Sir Thomas Fowell Buxton, who was prepared to take up the cause of the Khoekhe and San at the Cape.

The early nineteenth century saw an explosion of missionary work in southern Africa, as the LMS established missions beyond the boundaries of the Cape Colony and a number of other missionary societies moved into the region in the aftermath of the Napoleonic Wars. In 1818 the LMS began an influential mission to Madagascar, for example. The CMS, however, did not launch a mission to southern Africa until the late 1830s. Even then the would-be Anglican mission rapidly fell apart in the welter of bloodshed between *voortrekkers* and the Zulu and personal quarrels, exacerbated by bitter quarrels over the death of the baby of a missionary couple whom Africans and other

---

[45] Elizabeth Elbourne, *Blood Ground: Colonialism, Missions and the Contest for Christianity in the Eastern Cape and Britain, 1799–1853* (Montreal and Kingston, ON, 2003).
[46] On Anglicans and imperial administration, see C. A. Bayly, *Imperial Meridian: The British Empire and the World, 1780–1830* (London and New York, 1989).

missionaries accused of killing through neglect.[47] Even if Anglican missionaries themselves did not play important roles and not many Africans converted to Anglican Christianity in this early period, Anglican officials tried to protect their own authority by limiting non-Anglican missions and Anglican parliamentarians at the imperial centre intervened in South African politics in the 1830s in response to LMS concerns. In other words, imperial Anglican politics mattered at the Cape, even in the absence of a significant Anglican institutional presence.

Despite a cluster of churches and chaplains, the Anglican Church did not develop a major footprint in southern Africa until 1848 when Robert Gray was appointed as the first bishop of Cape Town, and set out to organize an Anglican structure of province, diocese, and synod.[48] The Anglican Church and Anglican converts would subsequently play an important political and cultural role in southern Africa, but this story lies well beyond the purview of the current chapter.

AT THE TURN OF THE CENTURY

By the early nineteenth century, Anglicanism was poised to become a significant African religion. Under the direction of Henry Venn, honorary secretary from 1841 to 1873, the CMS would adopt a policy of supporting the 'euthanasia' of missions in favour of the creation of self-supporting local churches. This reflected, however, the existing reality of locally run missions in West Africa and in this sense was reactive as well as proactive. The history of bitter disputes over this policy in the colonial era, including its eventual rejection by many white missionaries (and the subsequent explosive growth of African Independent Churches) lies beyond the mandate of the current chapter. Subsequent history is worth highlighting, however, not least because it underscores the continuing interconnections between colonialism, Christianity, and politics that were so important to the history of Anglicanism in Africa in the long eighteenth century. It is also worth noting the paradox that Venn's policy actually reflected some earlier practices in the slave trade era.

Although Anglicanism did not have many adherents in eighteenth-century Africa, it was politically important, not least in struggles over the slave trade

[47] Adam Kuper, 'The Death of Piet Retief', *Social Anthropology*, 4 (1996): 133–43; Elizabeth Elbourne, 'Mother's Milk: Gender, Power and Anxiety on a South African Mission Station, 1839–1840', in Patricia Grimshaw and Andrew May (eds.), *Missionaries, Indigenous Peoples and Cultural Exchange* (Brighton, Portland, OR, and Toronto, ON, 2010), pp. 10–23.

[48] Ward, *Global Anglicanism*, p. 137; Peter Hinchliff, *The Anglican Church in South Africa: An Account of the History and Development of the Church of the Province of South Africa* (London, 1963).

and in the impetus to establish Sierra Leone, while a number of early African intellectuals were given a platform by Anglican networks. Both Africans and British Anglicans were to some extent imagining one another: Africa was highly diverse and in practice much of the continent was little known to the British in the eighteenth century, while Church politics and the precise denominational rules governing the Anglican Church were almost certainly less important to African interlocutors than to British Anglicans. Nonetheless, by the end of the period under consideration in this chapter, African Anglicanism was becoming an important reality.

SELECT BIBLIOGRAPHY

Brown, Christopher, *Moral Capital: Foundations of British Abolitionism* (Chapel Hill, NC, 2006).

Bulman, William J., *Anglican Enlightenment: Orientalism, Religion and Politics in England and its Empire, 1648–1715* (Cambridge, 2016).

Carretta, Vincent and Ty M. Reese, *The Life and Letters of Philip Quaque, the First African Anglican Missionary* (Athens, GA and London, 2010).

Equiano, Olaudah, *The Interesting Narrative of the Life of Olaudah Equiano, or Gustavus Vassa, the African* (London, 1789).

Everill, Bronwen, *Abolition and Empire in Sierra Leone and Liberia* (New York, 2013).

Glasson, Travis, *Mastering Christianity: Missionary Anglicanism and Slavery in the Atlantic World* (Oxford, 2012).

Hastings, Adrian, *The Church in Africa, 1450–1950* (Oxford, 1994).

Morgan, Philip D. and Sean Hawkins (eds.), *Black Experience and Empire* (Oxford, 2004).

Peel, J. D. Y., *Religious Encounter and the Making of the Yoruba* (Bloomington, IN, 2003).

Peterson, Derek R., *Abolitionism and Imperialism in Britain, Africa and the Atlantic* (Athens, OH, 2010).

Pettigrew, William, *Freedom's Debt: The Royal African Company and the Politics of the Atlantic Slave Trade, 1672–1752* (Chapel Hill, NC, 2013).

13

Australia and New Zealand

Joseph Hardwick

Scholars of Australian Anglicanism have commonly labelled the period between the arrival of the First Fleet in 1788 and the age of reform in the 1830s as a moment of Anglican 'ascendancy' or 'establishment'.[1] The small coterie of chaplains who made up the tiny Church establishment in New South Wales and Van Diemen's Land (modern Tasmania) are conventionally portrayed as the allies of the ruling military elite and agents of a brutal convict regime. The image of the parson-magistrate Samuel Marsden dolling out severe punishments to Irish political prisoners stands as a symbolic moment in early Australian Church history, one that supposedly captures the close ties between the 'flogging parson' and the autocratic colonial state.[2]

It is not hard to find other moments in Australian history when the colonial Church appears dressed in the guise of loyal accomplice of an authoritarian colonial state. Recent historiography has nevertheless tried to give a more positive account of the role played by the clergy and the Church of England in Australia's transition from a 'convict farm' to a settler society. The clergy who made up the early colonial chaplaincy did not necessarily see their primary role as building a hierarchical colonial society or upholding the interests of the colonial 'fiscal-military' state. Clergy were journalists, educators, intellectuals, farmers, community leaders, convict advocates, and progenitors of colonial families.[3] They were also missionaries: while Marsden worked with the Evangelical Church Missionary Society (CMS) to establish the first Anglican mission in New Zealand in 1814, other Australian clergy were involved in small-scale mission ventures among Australia's indigenous peoples. The early

---

[1] Brian Fletcher, 'The Anglican Ascendancy 1788–1835', in Bruce Kaye (ed.), *Anglicanism in Australia: A History* (Carlton, Victoria, 2002), pp. 7–30.

[2] *Manning Clark's History of Australia*, abridged by Michael Cathcart (London, 1995), pp. 27, 50.

[3] Michael Gladwin, *Anglican Clergy in Australia, 1788–1850: Building a British World* (London, 2015).

Australian Church of England cannot, therefore, be understood as a monolithic institution: convicts, emancipated felons, free settlers, colonial officials, military personnel, and clergy—we might also add indigenous communities to the list—all held different views on the functions that the Church of England should play in colonial settings. There was little agreement about how the Church should be structured, what its mission in colonial society should be, and what kind of relationship it should adopt towards the secular authorities. This chapter will show that labels such as 'ascendancy' and 'establishment' fail to capture the diversity of the Anglican presence in early Australia and New Zealand.

THE CHARACTER OF EARLY AUSTRALIAN AND NEW ZEALAND ANGLICANISM

The Church in New South Wales and Tasmania (the latter became a separate colony in 1825) was a privileged establishment whose primary responsibility was to provide spiritual ministrations to a European population of convicts, military personnel, and free settlers. The Church was 'established' in the sense that the clergy—they are more accurately termed state-appointed chaplains— were appointed by the crown and were subject to the authority of the military governors who ran the early convict regime. By the late 1810s the state was paying the salaries of Roman Catholic ministers, but for most of our period the Anglican clergy enjoyed a privileged status: Anglican ministers led national days of thanksgiving and they also enjoyed privileged access to the convict community. This Church 'establishment' was neither a large nor powerful institution. Clergy in New South Wales were particularly overworked. In 1836 there were only seventeen in a colony that stretched to the Lachlan River in the east and Port Macquarie (modern Newcastle) in the north. Anglicans set down firm institutional roots in Tasmania (it had thirteen clergy in 1836), but the Church had a more limited presence in the new colonies of Western Australia (founded 1829) and South Australia (1836).[4]

New Zealand's infant Church had a very different character. New Zealand had no large European population in the early nineteenth century, and it did not become a British colony until the infamous Treaty of Waitangi of 1840 organized the transfer of sovereignty from Māori communities to the crown. The Church that Samuel Marsden founded at Rangihoua Bay in the far north of New Zealand in 1814 was very much a missionary institution orientated

---

[4] John Barrett, *That Better Country: The Religious Aspect of Life in Eastern Australia* (Melbourne, 1966), pp. 16–17.

towards the Māori population; the small communities of transient Europeans who clustered around coastal whaling and flax stations were largely ignored. Yet elements of the traditional establishment model did make it to early colonial New Zealand: the early CMS missionaries were, for instance, designated as justices of the peace. Quite what this role entailed in a country that was not yet a British territory was not clear.

Despite these differences, the Australian and New Zealand Churches should both be treated as outposts of the Evangelical wing of the Church of England. High Churchmen viewed Australia's Church establishments as remote and insignificant institutions until at least the early 1830s. The Society for the Propagation of the Gospel (SPG)—the Church's main outreach association—only supported a handful of schoolteachers in New South Wales in the pre-1830 period, and it was not until an Anglican bishopric was established in New Zealand in 1841 that the Church hierarchy gave any sustained attention to that part of the world. The same colonial administrators who were strengthening the Church in what was left of Britain's North American empire showed little interest in doing the same in distant Australia.

In the early years of Australian settlement the imperial authorities were happy to let the Evangelical network known as the Clapham Sect find suitable clergy for New South Wales.[5] The first three appointments—Richard Johnson, Samuel Marsden, and John Crowther—were Yorkshire Evangelicals who had all been educated at Hull Grammar School and Magdalene College, Cambridge (Crowther never reached Australia, returning to England after his ship hit an iceberg). All three had come under the influence of the prominent Evangelicals Joseph Milner, the master at Hull, and Charles Simeon, a prominent Clapham figure. Underlying Yorkshire's Evangelical networks was the Elland Society, a voluntary organization that provided funds for aspiring clergy. Marsden was definitely connected to the society and it is probable Johnson was too.[6] The two clergy whom Marsden recruited in England in 1808—Robert Cartwright and William Cowper—were also drawn from the Evangelical Yorkshire ferment and both were the kind of 'plain pious men' of 'sincere piety & religious zeal' that Richard Johnson thought were needed in the rough-and-tumble world of colonial Australia.[7] Marsden also recruited two artisan missionary settlers for New Zealand, and in the following years these men would be joined by another lay missionary—Thomas Kendall, a Lincolnshire draper—and two ordained ministers, John Gare Butler (who arrived in 1819) and Henry Williams (arrived 1823), both of whom

---

[5] Fletcher, 'Anglican Ascendancy', p. 8.

[6] John Walsh and Stephen Taylor (eds.), *The Papers of the Elland Society, 1769–1828* (Woodbridge, 2016); Stuart Piggin, *Evangelical Christianity in Australia: Spirit, Word and World* (Oxford, 1996), p. 5.

[7] Richard Johnson to Bishop Howley of London, 16 Mar. 1815, Lambeth Palace Library [LPL], Howley Papers, vol. 7, f. 111.

had followed non-religious careers before coming under the influence of Evangelical Christianity.

The state's failure to support the Church in the Australia colonies adequately had the knock-on effect of forcing colonial administrators to appoint clergy who had arrived in Australia through unconventional and unofficial means. Henry Fulton, who served at Norfolk Island, was a Church of Ireland clergyman who had been transported after being implicated in the 1798 rebellion. John Youl served spells as a Congregational missionary in Tahiti and as a Nonconformist minister in New South Wales before being appointed to Port Dalrymple in northern Tasmania in 1817. Youl's appointment is important on two counts: on the one hand it shows how colonial administrators were forced to adopt a pragmatic approach to recruitment; on the other, it tells us something about the porous nature of the boundaries separating Anglicanism and Dissenting religion in early colonial Australia. As we shall see, a later generation of Anglican clerics would insist on more strictly defined denominational identities.

Clergy were not, of course, the only vectors through which Anglicanism was exported overseas. Lay settlers led Anglican services and read printed sermons to scratch congregations in remote European settlements.[8] Shipments of prayer books and bibles were sent to the Australian colonies by the Prayer Book and Homily Society and the Society for the Promotion of Christian Knowledge (SPCK). Senior Anglicans recognized that donations of this sort were the only way that prisoners in distant convict stations could be kept within the Anglican fold. Richard Johnson, the first chaplain, brought out hundreds of bibles and prayer books when he travelled with the First Fleet. But, like the clergy, religious literature did not always arrive through officially prescribed channels. In 1814, for instance, colonial officials accused the clergy and Evangelical mission societies of smuggling unauthorized versions of the Psalms into the colony.[9] The image of convict and non-Anglican clergy delivering services from non-official prayer books vividly illustrates the limitations of the British Empire's Napoleonic-era 'Anglican design'.

THE COLONIAL CLERGY

Recent scholarship has given a more rounded portrait of the Australian clergy than the stereotype of the 'flogging parson' would suggest. Colonial clergy

---

[8] Joanna Cruickshank, 'The Sermon in the British Colonies', in Keith Francis and William Gibson (eds.), *The Oxford Handbook of the British Sermon, 1689–1901* (Oxford, 2012), pp. 513–29.

[9] Governor Macquarie to Earl Bathurst, 7 Oct. 1814, *Historical Records of Australia, Series I, Governors' Despatches to and from England*, 26 vols. (Sydney, 1914–25), VIII, p. 337.

were not always the cringing lackeys of an authoritarian state; for the most part this was a group that was struggling to maintain its clerical authority and independence in an inhospitable environment. Meting out horrific punishments was only one way to impose authority; others chose more humane strategies.

Colonial officials assumed that the role of the colonial chaplain was to stand as a moral leader and impose a degree of 'Awe and religious Restraint' over the convict population.[10] Chaplains found it difficult to do this, not least because they were tasked with serving huge geographical areas—Robert Knopwood's 'parish' was the whole of Tasmania. Furthermore, like their counterparts elsewhere in the early nineteenth-century British world,[11] Australian chaplains found that their modest salaries (new chaplains got £250 a year, while Marsden as senior chaplain received £400) made it difficult to project the kind of social authority that was expected of a minister of the Church of England. Robert Cartwright had to take up farming to feed his family, and later clergy would complain when they were forced to go cap in hand to parishioners for financial aid. Some chaplains profited from grants of land and cattle from the crown (Marsden had amassed over 5,200 acres by 1827), but hand-outs of this kind only strengthened the clergy's dependence on the civil authorities.

Chaplains also found that the demands placed on them by the colonial state sat uneasily with their personal interests, religious ambitions, and sense of social justice. Certainly we can find moments when clergymen did perform the role of moral policeman. Evangelicalism of the moderate, early nineteenth-century Claphamite kind had both its emancipatory and disciplinary aspects, and clergy who ran successful farms wanted to stamp down on recalcitrant convict workers just as much as the secular authorities. Cartwright, for instance, claimed in 1814 that he had convinced Governor Lachlan Macquarie to force convicts to attend Anglican services.[12] Clerics coerced intelligence out of condemned prisoners and ordered degrading punishments, such as the shaving of convict women's heads.[13] Alison Vincent and Michael Gladwin have both tried to argue that the clergy were not always the unthinking agents of a repressive convict bureaucracy. The clergy's concern with salvation did indeed lead them to voice concerns about the conditions and treatment of the

[10] Macquarie to Lord Liverpool, 27 Oct. 1810, *Historical Records of Australia* I, VII, p. 346.

[11] Michael Gauvreau, 'The Dividends of Empire: Church Establishments and Contested British Identities in the Canadas and the Maritimes, 1780–1850', in Nancy Christie (ed.), *Transatlantic Subjects: Ideas, Institutions, and Social Experience in Post-Revolutionary British North America* (Montreal, 2008), pp. 199–250.

[12] See Cartwright's evidence to Commissioner Bigge in November 1819: John Ritchie (ed.), *The Evidence to the Bigge Reports: New South Wales under Governor Macquarie*, 2 vols. (Melbourne, 1971), I, p. 152.

[13] Macquarie to Earl Bathurst, 4 Dec. 1817, *Historical Records of Australia* I, IX, p. 509; Michael Gladwin, 'Flogging Parsons? Australian Anglican Clergymen, the Magistracy, and Convicts, 1788–1850', *Journal of Religious History*, 36 (2012): 386–403 (p. 399).

convict community. Ministers advocated the causes of individual convicts, appealed for reduced sentences, arranged convict marriages (sometimes without the consent of masters), and provided legal advice to illiterate convicts.[14] This more positive view of relations between convicts and clergy has been accompanied by a reassessment of convict religiosity: recent scholarship has used unlikely source material, such as tattoos, to find signs of popular religious devotion among the convict and emancipist community.[15] The number of former convicts who went on to serve as sextons and church patrons suggests that the Church held out benefits for those who were looking to enter 'respectable' civil society.

The Anglican clergy were one of a number of expatriate colonial groups who were trying to find a way of asserting their rights and privileges in what was still an authoritarian and militaristic empire.[16] One of Marsden's chief aims in the 1810s and early 1820s was to carve out an independent position for both the Anglican clergy and the Church itself. Marsden, like Richard Johnson before him, complained that the Church's close association with the military regime compromised the clergy's independence and authority: as Marsden put it in 1821, 'a naval or military government imagines the clergy are to obey all orders, however degrading to themselves, and unbecoming religion'.[17] Clergy were constantly searching for the independence that would allow them to propose reforms of the convict regime and put forward plans for Australia's commercial development. The most vocal did find ways to make their views heard in metropolitan Britain. Marsden, for instance, communicated his criticisms of Lachlan Macquarie's governorship through a network of London lobbyists; he also took the opportunity presented by the parliamentary inquiry that arrived in New South Wales in 1819 to voice his ideas on how the system of convict discipline could be made more efficient and effective.[18]

Clergy also tried to assert their independence by initiating an evangelizing programme that went beyond the narrow aims of the state's religious policy. Richard Johnson's Evangelical ambitions are reflected in the church he built in 1793 and the *Address* that he disseminated to New South Wales's inhabitants in 1792. While the T-shaped church, with its separate naves for the military, convicts, and free settlers, underlined that all were equal before God, the *Address* sought to encourage the 'unhappy convicts' and free settlers to read,

---

[14] Gladwin, 'Flogging Parsons?', pp. 394–8; Alison Vincent, 'Clergymen and Convicts Revisited', *Journal of Australian Colonial History*, 1 (1999): 95–114.

[15] For a contrary and older view, see Allan M. Grocott, *Convicts, Clergymen and Churches: Attitudes of Convicts and Ex-Convicts towards the Churches and Clergy in New South Wales from 1788 to 1851* (Sydney, 1980).

[16] C. A. Bayly, *Imperial Meridian: The British Empire and the World* (London, 1989).

[17] Marsden to Bishop Howley, 11 Mar. 1821, LPL, Howley Papers, vol. 1, f. 737.

[18] A. T. Yarwood, *Samuel Marsden: The Great Survivor* (Melbourne, 1977), pp. 153–4, 218–19.

pray privately, and attend communal worship.[19] When the expected Evangelical revival failed to materialize, chaplains focused their attention on communities who seemed ripe for instruction. One was the colonial youth. Marsden
helped to build female orphanages at Sydney in 1801 and Parramatta in 1814
because he felt the spiritual instruction of young women was the 'principal
means of checking the growing national sins'—primarily because it would
temper 'the vicious inclinations of young men'.[20] The education of Australia's
young people would remain under the control of the Anglican clergy until
Richard Bourke—an Anglo-Irish liberal—took the reins of government in
1831 and ushered in a new era of religious pluralism by providing money
for non-Anglican schools.[21]

MISSION IN AUSTRALIA AND NEW ZEALAND

The Evangelical project also extended to the indigenous inhabitants of Australia
and New Zealand. Even the staunchest apologist would have to admit that
Anglican clergy took a leading role in the destruction of indigenous communities and cultures. In 1830 the Revd William Bedford—who was then the
senior chaplain in Van Diemen's Land—blessed the infamous 'Black Line'
that tried to flush the last indigenous Tasmanians out of Van Diemen's
Land.[22] In New Zealand, Anglican missionaries were responsible for compiling a translation of the 1840 Waitangi Treaty that failed to communicate
European notions of sovereignty and possession to Māori communities. Even
humanitarian intentions had damaging legacies. Richard Johnson and later
Anglican missionaries would help to lay the foundations of Australia's
shameful history of child removal when they took Aboriginal children into
their homes for protection and Christian instruction. That these children
acted as translators and intermediaries for the colonial authorities usefully
illustrates the extent to which the clergy's Evangelical ambitions could coincide with the aims of the secular authorities.[23]

---

[19] Alan Atkinson, *The Europeans in Australia: A History*, vol. I: *The Beginning* (Melbourne,
1997), pp. 177–80.

[20] Marsden to John Stokes, 8 Oct. 1814, in George Mackaness (ed.), *Some Private Correspondence of the Rev. Samuel Marsden and Family, 1794–1824* (Sydney, 1942), letter no. 23.

[21] Fletcher, 'Anglican Ascendancy', pp. 17–19.

[22] John Harris, *One Blood. 200 Years of Aboriginal Encounter with Christianity: A Story of
Hope* (Sutherland, NSW, 1990), p. 95; Tom Lawson, *The Last Man: A British Genocide in
Tasmania* (London, 2014), esp. chs. 3–4.

[23] Meredith Lake, 'Salvation and Conciliation: First Missionary Encounters at Sydney Cove',
in Amanda Barry, Joanna Cruickshank, Andrew Brown-May, and Patricia Grimshaw (eds.),
Evangelists of Empire? Missionaries in Colonial History (Melbourne, 2008), pp. 87–102.

Clergy also consciously set out to destroy Aboriginal cultures. Most— Marsden was one exception—assumed that indigenous communities could attain the civilizational standards reached by whites. There was little to distinguish Anglican missions from those pursued by Presbyterians, other Nonconformists, and Catholics—all assumed that Aboriginal people could be weaned from their 'roving habits' and schooled in the arts of agriculture and manufacture if they were settled on permanent mission stations.[24] However, it was not until 1832 that the CMS sent two missionary husband-and-wife teams—one was Anglican, the other Lutheran—to open a station among the Wiradjuri people in the Wellington Valley in the far east of New South Wales. In 1836 the missionaries were reporting that between forty and sixty Aboriginal people were 'regularly addressed on the Subject of religion'.[25] The history of the mission lies outside our period, but we should note that it was not a long-term success. The mission could not isolate itself from settler society and the small number of indigenous people who were on site left permanently when it emerged that one of the missionaries—William Watson—had forcibly taken Aboriginal children from their parents.[26] The mission collapsed in 1843 and Watson established a new mission at nearby Apsley with his wife and 'family' of twenty-six 'adopted' Aboriginal children.[27]

Anglican missionaries had a limited impact on Australia's Aboriginal cultures and religions. Missions could only attract a tiny proportion of the indigenous population and missionaries found that their chief role was not to convert but to protect: missions quickly became refuges harbouring Aboriginal people fleeing from the encroachment of a frontier that brought disease, dispossession, and death.[28] Christian missionaries were spurred on when they found evidence that Aboriginal communities believed in a 'High God' or 'All-Father', but most became pessimistic about the possibility of conversion. This pessimism stemmed in part from the fact that missionaries had definite ideas about what conversion amounted to. Watson and his Wellington colleagues would only, for instance, baptize those who acknowledged their sin and who could display some outward sign that they had experienced conversion. Reading out loud passages from the Prayer Book

---

[24] Jean Woolmington, '"Writing on the Sand": The First Missions to Aborigines in Eastern Australia', in Tony Swain and Deborah Bird Rose (eds.), *Aboriginal Australians and Christian Missions: Ethnographic and Historical Studies* (Bedford Park, South Australia, 1988), pp. 77–92 (p. 79).

[25] 'Rev. Watson's Third Report (1836)', pp. 1–2, Transcripts of Letters, Journals, Diaries and Reports sent to the London Corresponding Committee of the Church Missionary Society, 1832–40, <http://www.newcastle.edu.au/school/hss/research/publications/the-wellington-valley-project/watson/>, accessed 3 Oct. 2013.

[26] Woolmington, '"Writing on the Sand"', p. 83.   [27] Harris, *One Blood*, p. 73.

[28] Hilary Carey, *Believing in Australia: A Cultural History of Religions* (St Leonards, NSW, 1996), pp. 58–63.

was not enough.[29] Twentieth-century historians have adopted similarly rigid definitions of Christian conversion: for Tony Swain, conversions were short-lived and superficial; for Jean Woolmington, pre-existing Aboriginal cosmologies made Christian conversion unlikely if not impossible.[30]

Conversion may have been rare and improbable when such rigid criteria were applied, but this does not mean that Aboriginal communities wholly rejected missionary teachings. Swain has found evidence that in the pre-1830 period Aboriginal cosmologies in New South Wales changed in a way that cosmologies elsewhere did not, and that these changes were directly linked to the expansion of the settler and missionary dominion.[31] For Swain, Aboriginal communities responded to destruction of their land by developing a new belief system that postulated that the spirits of the dead ascended to the sky (some on questioning called this 'heaven'), as opposed to a local and earth-bound site, as was the custom in 'traditional' beliefs. The settler invasion also led Aboriginal communities to adopt concepts of good and evil that were apparently alien to pre-colonial Aboriginal cosmologies. All this does not mean that indigenous communities were abandoning their religions for Christianity; a better explanation is that Aboriginal communities were appropriating aspects of Christian teachings in order to make sense of, and cope with, the death and dispossession that came with the European invasion.

Anglican missionaries felt that their chances of success were much greater in New Zealand as there the Māori seemed to possess recognizable religious systems built on a belief in gods (*atua*). Historians have credited Anglican missionaries with laying the foundations of a Māori Church, though again pioneer missionaries had to battle through an early survival period.[32] The three 'Godly mechanics' that the CMS sent out to Rangihoua between 1809 and 1813 were supposed to orchestrate a 'civilize first' policy that was predicated on demonstrating the superiority of European arts, manufactures, and agriculture to the Māori. This they failed to do. The mission was dependent on the support of Māori sponsors and the missionaries were soon arguing with one another. Two were dismissed in 1823 (one for adultery, the other drunkenness), though one of the malcontents—Thomas Kendall—had made a contribution to European–Māori communication when he published *A Grammar and Vocabulary of the Language of New Zealand* with the help of two high-status Māori and a Cambridge orientalist.

---

[29] Harris, *One Blood*, p. 69.

[30] Tony Swain, *A Place for Strangers: Towards a History of Australian Aboriginal Being* (Cambridge, 1993), p. 125; Woolmington, '"Writing on the Sand"'.

[31] Swain, *A Place for Strangers*, pp. 125–33.

[32] Allan Davidson, 'Culture and Ecclesiology: The Church Missionary Society and New Zealand', in Kevin Ward and Brian Stanley (eds.), *The Church Missionary Society and World Christianity, 1799–1999* (Grand Rapids, MI, 2000), pp. 198–227 (p. 207).

It was not until a strong-minded former naval officer, the clergyman Henry Williams, arrived to take over the mission in 1823 that Anglican outreach in New Zealand gained traction.[33] By the early 1840s Anglican missionaries were reporting that tens of thousands of Māoris had converted to Christianity. Even if we reject such claims as hyperbolic we still have to explain why Māori communities showed greater interest in Christianity from the late 1820s onwards. This interest was nothing new; what was different was that missionaries like Williams were catching up with demand by providing the Māori with the bibles and prayer books that would tell them about Christianity and Anglicanism. Changes in missionary strategy are, however, only part of the explanation. Jamie Belich has pointed out that the rising Māori interest in Christianity was connected to the changing landscape of Māori politics in the aftermath of the bloody inter-tribal 'Musket Wars' of the mid-1820s. In the ensuing period of peace Christianity replaced the European musket as a means by which rival communities accumulated prestige and power (*mana*). Churches and European priests were a marker of status and honour; they would also help Māoris acquire the literacy skills that would facilitate trade with Europeans.[34]

The limited nature of the European settlement in the pre-1840 period meant that Māoris could engage largely on their own terms with Western society. Māoris converted Christianity to their own uses. One of Williams's many worries was that the Māori understanding of baptism was not the same as his own. Examples of this Māori sampling of European religion can be clearly seen in the Māori prophetic movements that burst on to the scene from 1830 onwards. Williams noted that the founder of one of these movements, a seer (*matakite*) of the Nga Puhi people named Papahurihia, had resided 'awhile with us & obtained a superficial knowledge' but had 'gone forth two-fold more the child of the Devil'. Papahurihia used elements of Christian ritual (Williams noted in 1834 that his followers had 'services & baptism'),[35] but what he really got from his time among the Anglican missionaries at Rangihoua was knowledge of the Bible: one of his key teachings was that the Māori were a chosen people like the Israelites in the Old Testament, and he also seems to have invoked the serpent from the book of Genesis as a familiar-like figure. Missionaries may have had firm understandings on what conversion to Christianity amounted to, but no one could stop non-European communities from building their own syncretic forms of religion out of the various

---

[33] Davidson, 'Culture and Ecclesiology', p. 207.

[34] Jamie Belich, *Making Peoples: A History of New Zealanders—From Polynesian Settlement to the End of the Nineteenth Century* (Auckland, 1996), pp. 217–23.

[35] Allan K. Davidson and Peter J. Lineham, *Transplanted Christianity: Documents Illustrating Aspects of New Zealand Church History* (Palmerston North, 1987), p. 45.

Christian messages that were being handed to them by Catholic, Wesleyan, and Anglican missionaries.

A LAY CHURCH

Lay European settlers developed their own ideas on how an Anglican Church should operate in the colonies. The 1820s saw tensions develop between Anglican clergy who were trying to express their authority and clerical independence and an Anglican laity calling for a louder voice in Church administration.[36] We know that the 1820s saw the emergence of a popular reform movement that demanded representative political institutions, trial by jury, and the extension of religious toleration to non-Anglicans; what has received less attention is that the Church in the Australian colonies generated its own internal reform movement around the same time. In both New South Wales and Tasmania lay Anglicans demanded a democratic form of Church government that was based on elected churchwardens, rentable pews, and the public auditing of church accounts. Before then observers had commonly argued that Australia had neither a political public nor an Anglican laity. Marsden claimed that the government's control over the chaplaincy had alienated the free population and left the impression that religion was purely 'for children, the common soldier, & the convict in irons'.[37] But in the early 1810s there were signs that a lay community was beginning to stir: laypersons gained experience from funding and running Sydney's many charitable organizations, and private colonists helped fund school buildings, chapels, and burial grounds from 1812 onwards.[38]

While the lay community was starting to call for a louder say in how the Church was run, clergy were taking steps to exert the kind of ministerial control over Church property that they thought was the custom back in England. The two campaigns could clash. Thomas Hobbes Scott, New South Wales's first archdeacon, caused a stir when he evicted the banker, publisher, and reform advocate Edward Smith Hall from a pew in St James's church in Sydney in July 1828—an action that Scott claimed fell within his rights as the 'ordinary' of the church. The issue of the archdeacon's power to manage church pews quickly became bound up in a larger debate about what Hall's newspaper, the *Monitor*, called 'the capricious power' of the clergy and, by

[36] Joseph Hardwick, *An Anglican British World: The Church of England and the Expansion of the Settler Empire, c.1790–1860* (Manchester, 2014), ch. 2.

[37] Marsden to unnamed correspondent, undated, in Mackaness (ed.), *Some Private Correspondence*, letter no. 14.

[38] Brian Fletcher, 'Christianity and Free Society in New South Wales 1788–1840', *Journal of the Royal Australian Historical Society*, 86 (2000): 93–113; Yarwood, *Samuel Marsden*, p. 137.

extension, the authoritarian rule of the existing colonial administration.[39] Hall took the case to Sydney's Supreme Court but neither he nor anyone else was satisfied with the final ruling: Hall was found to have trespassed into the pew; Archdeacon Scott was told he could not claim the rights of an ordinary in England; and the judge ruled that there could be no churchwardens in New South Wales as colonial churches were in no way comparable to English parishes.[40] The designs of both the lay and clerical members of the Anglican community were therefore frustrated by the ambiguities surrounding the legal status of a Church struggling to free itself of its chaplaincy past.

ECCLESIASTICAL REFORM AND THE CHANGING SHAPE OF AUSTRALIAN ANGLICANISM

The vision of an inclusive and lay-orientated colonial Church was not shared by imperial administrators. Recent scholarship has shown how a new kind of centralizing agenda influenced the world of colonial governance in the 1820s and early 1830s. Appointments to colonial posts were increasingly made in London and officials at the Colonial Office discovered new ways of gathering information on empire.[41] Similar processes can be seen in the ecclesiastical sphere. In 1824 an 'Ecclesiastical Board' was set up to regulate the selection of colonial chaplains and find out more about the workings of colonial Church establishments. Colonial governors were now asked to send back statistical breakdowns of the denominational composition of colonial populations. An Anglican archdeacon—on a salary of £2,000 a year—was appointed in 1824, a Church and Schools Corporation oversaw a system of Anglican schooling, and in 1826 the clergy reserves (which were modelled on an earlier Canadian experiment) were established. Under the reserves system, one-seventh of all colonial land was set aside for the benefit of Anglican churches, schools, and clergy. These developments fed into a wider imperial religious policy that sought to build a Church that was independent of the military regime and rooted in a parochial landscape, just like the Church at home.[42] This revived 'Anglican design' of the post-1815 period was not necessarily part of a wider

---

[39] *The Monitor*, 5 July 1828.

[40] Governor Darling to Sir George Murray, 25 Aug. 1829, *Historical Records of Australia I*, XV, pp. 131–40.

[41] Zoë Laidlaw, *Colonial Connections: Patronage, the Information Revolution and Colonial Government* (Manchester, 2005).

[42] Hardwick, *An Anglican British World*, ch. 1; Meredith Lake, 'Provincialising God: Anglicanism, Place, and the Colonisation of the Australian Land', *Journal of Religious History*, 35 (2011): 72–90 (p. 77).

Tory revival. Thomas Hobbes Scott, the architect of New South Wales's revived establishment, was branded a High Tory by the Sydney press, but in fact Scott was more closely connected to the Whig opposition; indeed the letters that Scott sent to his patron—the Northumberland Whig MP W. H. Ord—tell us that his plans for a strong Church formed part of a broader programme of colonial commercial development that was some way distant from the unreformed empire of trade monopolies that Scott found himself working in.[43]

This attempt to strengthen the Church establishment has usually been written off as a failure. The clergy reserves, which were often land of poor quality, could never sustain the clergy and the system was wound up in 1829. But this new centralizing agenda did change Anglicanism in the Australian colonies in important ways. Evangelicals could no longer labour in isolation and an independent civilian Church began to emerge. The 'Anglican design' of the 1820s also led to the recruitment of a specialist colonial clergy. The later clergy were selected for their educational qualifications, professional competency, and possession of certain skills—such as familiarity with teaching—that were considered necessary in the colonies.[44] Brian Fletcher has pointed out that the arrival of these clergy led to a more diverse Anglican presence in Australia.[45] The 1820s cohort included men who had been born in England, Australia, and Ireland; men who were not Evangelicals; and men who came from relatively elevated social backgrounds.

The other important point about these later clergy—and one that is often overlooked—is that their arrival prompted new questions about what an Anglican was and what the essentials of Anglican belief were. This had rarely been an issue in the era of Evangelical dominance before 1815. Thomas Hobbes Scott raised doubts about the Anglican credentials of the Evangelical clergy when he told the Ecclesiastical Board in 1827 that the 'rising Church of this Colony should consist of members firmly attached to the Establishment'. For Scott, the Evangelical clergy looked more like Methodist preachers than ministers of the Established Church: he claimed the early chaplains ignored elements of the Prayer Book liturgy in their services; drew up catechisms 'of their own composition'; fraternized with non-Anglican ministers; and delivered sermons full of 'unconnected sentences' in a 'violent ranting manner'.[46]

---

[43] Thomas Hobbes Scott to W. H. Ord, 29 Apr. 1822, Ashington, Northumberland Archives, Blackett-Ord MSS, NRO 324/A/32.

[44] Joseph Hardwick, 'Anglican Church Expansion and the Recruitment of Colonial Clergy for New South Wales and the Cape Colony, 1790–1850', *Journal of Imperial and Commonwealth History*, 37 (2009): 361–81; Gladwin, *Anglican Clergymen*; Ian Breward, *A History of the Churches in Australasia* (Oxford, 2004), p. 16.

[45] Fletcher, 'Anglican Ascendancy', p. 21.

[46] Scott to Archdeacon Anthony Hamilton (secretary of the Ecclesiastical Board), 21 May 1827, Oxford, Rhodes House Library, C/AUS/SYD/4/2, f. 31; Scott to the secretary of the SPG, 3 Mar. 1827, Sydney, Mitchell Library, 'Extracts from the Records of SPG 1808–1833', As143/44.

This tension between an Anglicanism that emphasized liturgical and sacramental worship and one that focused on personal conversion, preaching, and salvation by faith would become more marked after Scott—a perennially unpopular figure—resigned in 1829. His replacement, the orthodox High Churchman William Grant Broughton, would help to connect Australia with the English High Church revival of the mid-1830s. This High Church influence would offer colonial church-goers another alternative definition of Anglicanism and Anglican identity. In this sense 1829 marked a definite break in the history of Anglicanism in the Australian colonies.

CONCLUSION

In early Australian colonies different kinds of colonist and different kinds of Anglican entered into a conversation about the role that the Church of England should play in a colonial society that was both convict and free, indigenous and European. The differing visions that military governors, Evangelical chaplains, free settlers, and emancipated convicts had for the Church sat uneasily with one another, but each group would find space in future decades to realize their aims. Missions remained problematic. Mounting tensions between communities of settlers and Māori in New Zealand placed Anglican missionaries in a difficult position, and later disputes over the sale of land raised questions about how a single Church could protect the interests of both Pākehā and Māori.[47] One project that was not carried into the future was the Anglican establishment. There was an establishment in the early Australian colonies, but the 'confessional state' had always rested on insecure foundations. Not only was establishment understaffed, it was also unpopular. Non-Anglicans opposed an ecclesiastical settlement that benefited only a minority of the population, and Anglican authority sat uneasily with the political culture of the colonies. New South Wales's Church and School Corporation was abolished in 1833, and the introduction of the 1836 Church Act—a piece of legislation that invited non-Anglicans to apply for state aid—ushered in a new era of religious pluralism and multiple establishments.

SELECT BIBLIOGRAPHY

Border, Ross, *Church and State in Australia, 1788–1872: A Constitutional Study of the Church of England in Australia* (London, 1962).
Breward, Ian, *A History of the Churches in Australasia* (Oxford, 2004).

---

[47] Davidson and Lineham, *Transplanted Christianity*, p. 118.

Davidson, Allan K., 'Culture and Ecclesiology: The Church Missionary Society and New Zealand', in Kevin Ward and Brian Stanley (eds.), *The Church Missionary Society and World Christianity, 1799–1999* (Grand Rapids, MI, 2000).

Davidson, Allan K. and Peter J. Lineham, *Transplanted Christianity: Documents Illustrating Aspects of New Zealand Church History* (Palmerston North, 1987).

Fletcher, Brian H., 'Christianity and Free Society in New South Wales 1788–1840', *Journal of the Royal Australian Historical Society*, 86 (2000): 93–113.

Gladwin, Michael, *Anglican Clergy in Australia, 1788–1850: Building a British World* (London, 2015).

Hardwick, Joseph, *An Anglican British World: The Church of England and the Expansion of the Settler Empire, c.1790–1860* (Manchester, 2014).

Harris, John, *One Blood. 200 Years of Aboriginal Encounter with Christianity: A Story of Hope* (Sutherland, NSW, 1990).

Judd, Stephen and Kenneth Cable, *Sydney Anglicans: A History of the Diocese* (Sydney, 1987).

Kaye, Bruce (ed.), *Anglicanism in Australia: A History* (Carlton, Victoria, 2002).

Strong, Rowan, *Anglicanism and the British Empire, c.1700–1850* (Oxford, 2007).

Part III

Anglican Identities

14

The Book of Common Prayer, Liturgy, and Worship

Bryan D. Spinks

In a sermon of 25 April 1797 the future bishop of Durham and its last prince bishop, William Van Mildert, could claim: 'Our Liturgy, indeed, in its present state, is a most valuable repository of Christian knowledge. It serves as a manual of faith and practice; nor can any person be thoroughly conversant in it, without finding his understanding enlightened, his thoughts spiritualized, and his heart improved.'[1] He asserted confidently: 'Upon the preservation, therefore, of our excellent Liturgy in its present improved state, must depend, in a great measure, the preservation of the Church of England.'[2]

Commenting on the Prayer Book through the 'long eighteenth century', William Jacob has observed:

> By 1700 the Prayer Book, as revised in 1662, was largely accepted in parishes as the common prayer of the Church ... [It] served as the primer for prayer, worship and doctrine for the great majority of the population, only about 6.7 per cent of whom, it was estimated, dissented from the Church of England ... The Prayer Book's Liturgies, and the ways in which they were conducted, functioned as a social mortar for holding together and reinforcing community and social networks and doctrines.[3]

However, as Jacob also acknowledged, this was a gradual process. Furthermore, although it became fashionable to speak of the 1662 Prayer Book as an 'incomparable' liturgy, its framers probably had little idea that their work

---

[1] William Van Mildert, *The Excellency of the Liturgy, and the Advantage of being Educated in the Doctrine and Principles of the Church of England* (London, 1797), p. 13.
[2] Van Mildert, *Excellency of the Liturgy*, p. 15.
[3] William Jacob, 'Common Prayer in the Eighteenth Century', in Stephen Platten and Christopher Woods (eds.), *Comfortable Words: Polity, Piety and the Book of Common Prayer* (London, 2012), pp. 83–97 (pp. 83–4).

would remain largely unchallenged until the mid-nineteenth century, and
without a legal alternative until the mid-twentieth century.

THE MAKING OF THE 1662 LITURGY

The Restoration of the monarchy brought with it a restoration of the national
Church comparable to its pre-civil war days. Even before the liturgical settlement, Samuel Pepys noted that on 5 August 1660 he attended St Margaret's,
Westminster, 'where for the first time I ever heard Common Prayer in that
Church'.[4] In the wake of the Declaration of Breda, which promised liberty to
tender consciences, Charles II undertook in the Worcester House Declaration
to appoint divines of the different persuasions to review the liturgy and make
recommendations for alterations. A royal warrant of 25 March 1661 established a commission to do just that, and the deliberations that followed were
held at the master's lodge of the Savoy. The Presbyterian party, which included
figures such as Edward Reynolds and Richard Baxter, was encouraged to
submit a lengthy list of their 'exceptions' to the 1604/1625 Prayer Book, and
Baxter authored an alternative liturgy of a Presbyterian hue.[5] However, the
conference ended without compromise or agreement, and the task of settling
the liturgical question passed to Convocation in November 1661. Proposals
for revision included the *Advices* of Bishop Wren, and the alterations drafted by
John Cosin—the so-called Durham Book. Revision was begun on 21 November
1661 and concluded in twenty-two days. Taking aim at the preface of the
Westminster *Directory* of 1644, the preface to the revised Prayer Book suggested
that it was a reasonable and moderate liturgy, representing

> the mean between the two extremes, of too much stiffness in refusing, and of too
> much easiness in admitting any variation from it . . . Our general aim therefore in
> this undertaking was, not to gratify this or that party in any their unreasonable
> demands; but to do that, which to our best understanding we conceived might
> most tend to the preservation of Peace and Unity in the Church; the procuring of
> Reverence and exciting of Piety and Devotion in the publick Worship of God; and
> the cutting off occasion from them that seek occasion of cavil, or quarrel against
> the Liturgy of the Church.[6]

---

[4] *The Diary of Samuel Pepys*, vol. I: *1660*, ed. Robert Latham and William Matthews (Berkeley,
CA, 1970), p. 215.

[5] Colin Buchanan, *The Savoy Conference Revisited*, Alcuin/GROW Joint Liturgical Study 54
(Cambridge, 2002); Glen Segger, *Richard Baxter's Reformed Liturgy: A Puritan Alternative to
the Prayer Book* (Farnham, 2014).

[6] Brian Cummings (ed.), *The Book of Common Prayer: The Texts of 1549, 1559, and 1662*
(Oxford, 2011), pp. 209–11.

Moderation was regarded as the virtue of the liturgy, though simply by retaining most of the text of 1604 it was the Presbyterian party that bore the brunt of the non-gratification. The 'Laudian' group was certainly unsuccessful in many of its aspirations to restore material and the sequence of the communion prayers of the 1549 Prayer Book, and William Sancroft was to record: 'My LL. ye BB. at Elie house Orderd all in ye old Method'. However, some of their demands were met, especially by means of rubrics, so as to suggest a higher doctrine of the sacraments. In the rite of baptism, provision was made for the explicit blessing of the water in the prayer which came immediately before the baptismal act: 'sanctifie this Water to the mysticall washing away of sin'. In the Lord's Supper, the rubrics directed the place for setting of bread and wine on the table, and indicated manual actions during the recitation of the words of institution. The rubrics also made provision for consecrating additional bread and wine, and distinguished between consecrated and non-consecrated elements. The prayer over the bread and wine was headed 'The Prayer of Consecration'. Although the 'Black rubric' of 1552—absent from 1559 and 1604—was now restored, it was altered. It no longer repudiated any 'reall and essential presence', but only a 'corporal' presence. Many divines did believe in a 'reall and essential presence', but not a corporal (physical) presence. The Ordinal was revised to make clear that bishops were a separate order, and that episcopal ordination was essential for the polity of the Church of England. New prayers were also added: the General Thanksgiving, which was expanded from the outline for thanksgiving over the communion elements in the Westminster *Directory*, and, inspired by the Westminster Assembly's *A Supply of Prayer for Ships* (1645), a form of prayers for those at sea. In response to a lax attitude to infant baptism by some ministers during the Interregnum, and to native conversion in the colonies, a new rite for baptism of those 'Of Riper Years' was also included. Two new prayers were added for use at Morning Prayer.

The new liturgy was to come into use no later than 24 August (St Bartholomew's Day) 1662. Delays in printing and procrastination by some parishes meant that it was not everywhere adopted by the appointed date. A copy only reached Dean Honeywood of Lincoln on 23 August. It was not read at Taunton until 25 August, and Ralph Josselin, the incumbent of Earls Colne in Essex—no doubt with the connivance of the churchwardens—did not introduce it until 30 May 1663.[7]

The pattern of Sunday services was that of the Elizabethan and Jacobean periods: in the morning, Morning Prayer, Litany, and ante-communion (called

---

[7] Bodleian Library [Bodl.], Tanner MS 48, f. 17, cited by I. M. Green, *The Re-establishment of the Church of England 1660-1663* (Oxford, 1978), p. 145; William Gibson, *Religion and the Enlightenment 1600-1800: Conflict and the Rise of Civic Humanism in Taunton* (Bern, 2007), p. 88; A. Macfarlane (ed.), *The Diary of Ralph Josselin 1616-1683* (Oxford, 1976), p. 498.

the 'second service'), with communion being celebrated in some places monthly, but in most parish churches quarterly, around the principal festivals. Evening
Prayer was usually followed by instruction in the catechism. The Interregnum
had interrupted the Prayer Book choral tradition, with cathedrals and other
choirs disbanded and organs destroyed. In 1661 Edward Lowe published *A
Short Direction for the Performance of Cathedrall Service*, which offered advice
for those who had forgotten or who had no knowledge of how cathedral services
were sung. An expanded edition, *A Review of some Short Directions for the
Performance of Cathedral Service*, was published in 1664. Whatever advices
were published to provide some uniform and orderly performance of the
services, at least according to the lawyer Dr Dennis Granville, ministers frequently used their own authority and discretion to abbreviate, omit, and
supplement the prescribed order of service: In January 1683 he wrote:

> I Confesse I am much offended and Disturbed, whensoever I hear any Minister
> Maime God's Publick Service, or add any New Matter of his own, or else Exalt his
> own Prudence, in Varying from the Forme or Order thereof, tho' hee should use no
> other Prayers, but what are Conteined in the Book … Wee have yet as many severall
> wayes of Worshipp, as wee have Ministers … One Cuts of[f] the Preparatory
> Exhortacion, Dearly Beloved Brethren etc., Another the Benedictus and Jubilate,
> and satisfyeth himself with a Psalme in Meeter in stead thereof, out of Sternald and
> Hopkins, which, all know, is no part of your Office, and a bad Translacion,
> considering the language of our Age (tho' probably it was very tolerable when it
> was first Composed) and never approved of in a Convocacion. A Third brings in
> part of the Visitacion Office, Comanded to bee said in the Sick Man's presence, into
> the Publick Congregacion … A Fourth Adds very Formally a Preface of his own to
> the Recitall of the Creed … A Fifth Jumbles both first and Second Service together,
> Cutting of[f] not only the Concluding Prayer of St. Chrysostome, and the Grace of
> our Lord Jesus Christ, but allso our Lord's Prayer, in the Front of the Comunion
> Office … A Sixth more presumptiously not only Cuts of[f] the Lord's Prayer alone,
> but both the Lord's Prayer and Nicene Creed allsoe. A Seventh, who avoids those
> Irregularityes, yet Presumes after Sermon to Cut of[f] the Prayer for the Church
> Militant, and the Final Benediction, The Peace of God, etc. hoping to satisfye his
> Congregacion, (but I am sure hee never Satisfied mee) with a Benediction of his
> own Choice, and Prayer of his own Composure.[8]

New churches that were built were designed to showcase the 1662 rite. That is
true of the new St Paul's Cathedral and other Wren churches, as well as those
of Hawksmoor. Reflecting on his work of the 1670s and 1680s, Wren wrote:

> in our reformed religion, it should seem vain to make a parish church larger, than
> that all who are present can both hear and see. The Romanists, indeed, may build
> larger churches, it is enough if they hear the murmur of the mass, and see the

---

[8]   Bodl., MS Rawlinson D 851, edited in J. Wickham Legg, *English Church Life from the Restoration
to the Tractarian Movement* (London, 1914), pp. 112–13.

elevation of the Host, but ours are to be fitted for auditories. I can hardly think it practicable to make a single room so capacious, with pews and galleries, as to hold above 2000 persons, and all to hear the service, and both to hear distinctly, and see the preacher. I endeavored to effect this, in building the parish church of St. James's Westminster, which, I presume, is the most capacious, with these qualifications, that hath yet been built; and yet at a solemn time, when the church was much crowded, I could not discern from a gallery that 2000 were present. In this church I mention, though very broad, and the middle nave arched up, yet as there are no walls of a second order, nor lanterns, nor buttresses, but the whole roof rests upon the pillars, as do also the galleries; I think it may be found beautiful and convenient, and as such, the cheapest of any form I could invent.[9]

THE CRISIS OF 1688/9

With the death of Charles II and the accession of his Roman Catholic brother, James II, renewed Protestant fears of popery resulted in some dialogue between more moderate Dissenters and the clergy of the Established Church. As part of a response to the Roman threat, a proposed revision of the 1662 liturgy was begun in 1688. Archbishop Sancroft appointed a committee which included Simon Patrick, John Sharp, John Moore, and Thomas Tenison. The results of their deliberations are found in a folio Prayer Book, MS 886 in Lambeth Palace Library. With the arrival of William of Orange and the Dutch invasion, a new situation was created, resulting in the non-juring crisis. A new commission began work on revision in October 1689, and its suggestions are found in another folio Prayer Book in Lambeth Palace Library, MS 2173, the so-called Liturgy of Comprehension. The commission consisted of thirty people: ten bishops or bishops-elect, seven deans, four academics, four canons, and five archdeacons. Amongst the proposals were the provision of the Beatitudes as an alternative to the Ten Commandments, and the use of the term 'sacrifice' of Christ's body and blood in the Prayer of Humble Access. As concessions to the Presbyterian-minded ministers, among other things, the surplice, the sign of the cross in baptism, the ring in marriage, kneeling for communion, and the phraseology of regeneration in the baptismal rite were all to be optional. Other alterations included the separation of Morning Prayer from the Litany and ante-communion, making them two separate Sunday services rather than one long service which was the practice. The final text was presented to Convocation on 4 December 1689. The proposals, however, were never formally discussed, and with the flight of James any need for

[9] Sir Christopher Wren, 'Letter of Recommendation to a Friend on the Commission for Building Fifty New Churches', reprinted in Pierre de la Ruffinière du Prey, *Hawksmoor's London Churches: Architecture and Theology* (Chicago, IL, 2000), Appendix 2, pp. 135–6.

comprehension evaporated. With the dissolution of Convocation on 13 February 1689/90, the 1662 book without change remained the lawful liturgy.

We are fortunate to have some account of worship in London, as recorded by a Scottish minister, Robert Kirk, in 1689. He carefully recorded descriptions with comments on the many services—established, Nonconformist, and Roman Catholic—that he attended while staying in the capital. Of the churches of the Church of England he noted:

> Every Church in London have not organs, but the most have—all the pulpits have a deep velvet cloth & cushion, Red, purple, checquerd & stript, or such other colours, with large fringes of the same colour intermixed with Gold, some are wholly gold or silver. They have their fonts within the entry of the Churches, & the minister or Reader (in orders) Christens the children after sermon, when the people are dismissed; These take the children in their own arms from the godmother, sprinkles water on their faces, signs the cross with their finger, then dryes the child's Face with its own linens, & gives it back to the Godmother which named it, the Father & a Gossip standing by, but the Godfather & Godmother engaging to train up the Child in the true Religion.[10]

According to Kirk, Covent Garden church had no organ, 'but psalms once sung when the minister is a coming. Women sing little. The men sing divers grave tunes, but all the tunes have only 2 notes for easiness to the commons, a higher & a lower.'[11] On 8 March 1690 he heard Henry Compton, bishop of London, preach on John 14:15, and afterwards, Compton 'going to the communion table at the east end of the Church, he prayed & laid his hands on the heads of about 300 young men & gentlewomen to confirm them; having been examined the week before', which apparently he did in different London churches throughout the season of Lent.[12] Kirk recorded that at Christmas all windows were beset with green laurel and holly berries. 'There is sermon in all the Churches before-noon; most of the people communicate that day, & then feast sumptuously for that & some days after.'[13] The seats in churches were also adorned with green branches.

NON-JURING LITURGICAL EXPERIMENTS AND NEWTONIAN BLUEPRINTS FOR REFORM

The Revolution of 1688/9 brought a crisis of conscience for some clergy of the Church of England. They had given their assent to King James II and his

---

[10] Robert Kirk, 'Sermons, Conferences...with a Description of London. Ann 1689', f. 157, University of Edinburgh, Department of Manuscripts, La.III.545.
[11] Kirk, 'Sermons, Conferences', f. 22.   [12] Kirk, 'Sermons, Conferences', fos. 85–6.
[13] Kirk, 'Sermons, Conferences', f. 123.

lawful descendants. As much as they disliked James, William and Mary were not his lawful descendants, since he had a son and heir to the throne, Prince Charles. A number of bishops, including Archbishop William Sancroft, felt unable to take a new oath of loyalty to William and Mary, and were therefore deprived of office. In 1693 the 'non-juring' bishops consecrated successors, and so began the non-juring secession, which in England would eventually become extinct. In Scotland, a condition for accepting William and Mary as lawful monarchs was freedom for the Church of Scotland to become Presbyterian in polity, and rid itself of bishops, and the Scottish bishops had in fact declined to take the oath to William and Mary. As a result of expulsions, a 'non-juring' Episcopal Church continued alongside the Presbyterian Church of Scotland. Once the last of the immediate Stuart line died without issue, the Scottish non-jurors felt able to take the oath, and thus continued as the Scottish Episcopal Church. Both the English and Scottish non-jurors eventually made liturgical changes to their inherited worship patterns. In England divisions over certain ceremonies led to splits between various non-juring leaders and their congregations.

The one cause that held the English non-jurors together was the principle of the binding nature of oaths. They considered themselves the continuing true Church of England, which meant strict allegiance to the 1662 rite. However, in 1716 a dispute arose over ceremonies, which has become known as the Usages controversy. Some of the non-jurors looked back to the 1549 Book of Common Prayer and wished to introduce a visual mixing of the chalice of wine with water, prayers for the faithful departed, an *epiclesis* of the Spirit upon the communion elements, and the prayer of oblation immediately after the prayer of consecration. The Non-Usagers were led by Bishop Nathaniel Spinckes, who argued that these ceremonies were *adiaphora* at best and should not be insisted on. However, Bishops Jeremy Collier and Thomas Brett were adamant that these four ceremonies were essential. The two parties broke communion, and embarked on a long internecine pamphlet war. The Usagers were attracted to the liturgy in the *Apostolic Constitutions*, VIII, and demanded not only a restoration of the four uses, but also a better liturgical expression of them than even the 1549 Book of Common Prayer. The Usagers appealed to the work on the eucharist by John Johnson of Cranbrook, and also to the writings of Edward Stephens and Johannes Grabe, both of whom had held opinions similar to the Usagers and had authored liturgies giving expression to such a theology. On 11 March 1718 the text of a eucharistic liturgy was issued and a lengthy explanation and defence for it set out by Thomas Brett, in *A Collection of Principall Liturgies, Used by the Christian Church in the Celebration of the Holy Eucharist: Particularly the Ancient*. An offertory prayer articulated the idea of the eucharist as a sacrifice, as taught by John Johnson—'this reasonable and unbloody sacrifice for our Sins and the Sins of the people'. The post-Sanctus of the eucharistic prayer was inspired by those of St James, St Basil, and the *Apostolic Constitutions*, VIII, and contained a distinct *epiclesis* of the Holy Spirit upon the elements. A compromise was reached between the two factions in 1732, in which the mixed chalice would be done privately, the words 'Militant here on earth' would not be omitted from that 1662 exhortation to prayer; that the words 'hear us etc' in the prayer of consecration were to be counted as an *epiclesis*, and the 1718 rite would be laid aside. In fact the result was three factions—one refusing any usages, one accepting the compromise, and a third continuing the usages. The leadership of the latter fell to Bishop Thomas Deacon of Manchester. He published his own liturgy in 1734, which made liberal use of *Apostolic Constitutions*, VIII. The liturgies of 1718 and 1734 are of considerable interest to liturgical scholars, but those who experienced these texts as their regular worship were an exceedingly small number.

Their Scottish Episcopalian counterparts in 1689 worshipped in exactly the same manner as their hitherto Presbyterian brethren. However, in 1709 a Church of England cleric, James Greenfield, opened a meeting-house opposite St Giles in Edinburgh and used the 1662 Book of Common Prayer. A complaint was made against him, and he was arrested and imprisoned, and the Court of Session confirmed the magistrates' sentence. However, by the provisions of the Act of Union of 1707, Greenfield appealed to the House of Lords in England, who found in his favour and awarded costs against the Edinburgh magistrates. By an Act of 1712, toleration was granted, and chapels for English expatriates in Scotland began to be established. It seems that the non-juring Episcopalians started to use the 1662 Book of Common Prayer, and their worship began to move away from the form shared with the Presbyterians. A Presbyterian minister, John Willison, asked of them in a pamphlet of 1712, 'Are you not likewise turned Schismatick from your own Episcopal Church of Scotland, by devising a new Form of Worship, never allowed by Her in former Times, nor practiced by such as are indulged in Churches to this Day?'[14] In the same year George Seton, fifth earl of Winton, reprinted the proposed Scottish rite of 1637; because of the expense, from 1722 only the communion office (the offertory onwards) with some omissions, such as exhortations, was printed and used by the Scottish Episcopalian party. They were thus able to distinguish themselves from the Church of England and the Church of Scotland. Their contact with the English non-jurors led to sharing liturgical dreams and experiments, so that in 1743 Bishop Thomas Rattray published a version of the liturgy of St James with an extended essay. In 1748 it was published in a form intended for actual use, under the title *An Office for the Sacrifice of the Holy Eucharist, being the Ancient Liturgy of the Church of Jerusalem, to which Proper Rubricks are added for Direction*. Stuart Hall has

---

[14] John Willison, *Queries to the Scots Innovators in Divine Service, and Particularly, to the Liturgical Party in the Shire of Angus* ([Edinburgh?], 1712), p. 3.

described the leather-bound manuscript he discovered in the safe of St John's church, Pittenweem, now deposited in St Andrews University Library.[15] It seems to be Rattray's compilation, and draws on the 1637 Book of Common Prayer and Rattray's own historical reconstruction of the Jerusalem liturgy; it was clearly intended for use. However, in 1764 the Scottish communion office became the normative communion liturgy for the Episcopal Church of Scotland, which ceased to be non-juring after the death of Charles Edward Stuart in 1788.[16]

The reforms made by the non-jurors came from outside the Established Church. Other calls for reform came from those who had no trouble remaining inside the national Church, and whose churchmanship was decidedly cutting-edge in terms of acceptance of Enlightenment knowledge and reasoning. Isaac Newton combined the new science with an interest in alchemy, and combined belief in a deity with private disbelief in the Christian Trinity. John Locke's views on the Trinity are less clear, but his refusal to accept dogma unless clearly stated in Scripture and his posthumously published paraphrases of the Pauline Epistles suggest a similar suspicion concerning the divinity of Christ.

Two of Newton's most able pupils, William Whiston and Samuel Clarke, both clergymen, made public their views on the Trinity, and both offered ideas for liturgical reform that this implied. Whiston succeeded Newton in the Lucasian Chair of Mathematics at Cambridge. By 1705 he had come to view Arianism as being the biblical doctrine from which Athanasius and the Church had deviated. He wrote to the two archbishops advising them of the Church's error. In 1708 he applied to the vice-chancellor of Cambridge for a licence to print his findings, but permission was refused. Undeterred, Whiston went ahead and published some of his ideas and conclusions in 1709, under the title *Sermons and Essays upon several Subjects*. In 1710 he was deprived of his chair for heresy, and in 1711 published his *Primitive Christianity Reviv'd*, in which he defended the *Apostolic Constitutions* as being an apostolic document. In 1713 he published *The Liturgy of the Church of England reduc'd nearer to the primitive Standard. Humbly propos'ed to Publick Consideration*. The preface argued that the Prayer Book had been too influenced by Calvin (here he was agreeing with High Churchmen such as Edward Stephens), and that it had departed from the primitive standards. In his proposals he sought to conform the Prayer Book to the norms of the *Apostolic Constitutions*. In Morning and Evening Prayer the doxology was changed to 'Glory be to the Father, through the Son, in the Holy Ghost'. This indeed had been a primitive

---

[15] St Andrews University Library, Deposited MS 84; see Stuart G. Hall, 'Patristics and Reform: Thomas Rattray and *The Ancient Liturgy of the Church of Jerusalem*', in R. N. Swanson (ed.), *Continuity and Change in Christian Worship*, Studies in Church History 35 (Woodbridge, 1999), pp. 240–60.

[16] On liturgical matters, see, in this volume, Chapter 8 by Alasdair Raffe.

and orthodox doxology prior to the full development of Trinitarian doctrine. Its revival implicitly challenged the equal status of the persons of the Trinity. Alterations in the Creed and the Gloria in Excelsis also indicated a lowering of Christological understanding. To be fair, his obsession with the apostolicity of the *Apostolic Constitutions* meant that he remodelled the 1662 prayer of consecration on the lines of 1549, he used the *Hagia Hagiois*, and he restored anointing in baptism.

His friend and fellow Newtonian prodigy was Samuel Clarke. His mastery in natural philosophy had already been displayed when he gave the Boyle Lectures, and in 1709 he was appointed rector of St James, Westminster, which was often a stepping-stone to a bishopric. However, further preferment ended with the publication of his *Scripture-Doctrine of the Trinity* in 1712. There he wrote:

> The reason why the Scripture, though it stiles the *Father* God, and also stiles the *Son* God, yet at the same time always declares there is but *One God*; is because in the *Monarchy* of the Universe, there is but *One Authority*, original in the *Father*, derivative in the *Son*: The *Power of the Son* being, not *Another* Power *opposite* to That of the *Father*, nor *Another* Power *co-ordinate* to That of the *Father*; but it self *The Power and Authority of the Father*, communicated *to*, manifested *in*, and exercised *by* the *Son*.[17]

If Clarke echoed Newton's conception of God, he seems to have echoed Locke's understanding of person. In the *Essay*, Locke wrote of 'a thinking intelligent Being, that has reason and reflection, and can consider itself as itself, the same thinking thing, in different times and places; which it does only by that Consciousness which is inseparable from thinking...consciousness always accompanies thinking...and 'tis that, that makes everyone to be, what he calls *self*'.[18] Newton had defined person as '*substantia intellectualis*', but applying strict logic, held that the three persons are three substances.[19] Throughout the *Scripture-Doctrine of the Trinity*, Clarke consistently defined person as 'intelligent agent': in God, three such persons would yield three Gods. Clarke set out what his contemporaries perceived to be a heterodox understanding of the Trinity in three parts. The third part set out how the 1662 Book of Common Prayer should be altered to bring it into harmony with Clarke's 'Scripture' doctrine of the Trinity. His further thoughts are recorded in an interleaved Prayer Book of 1724, where we find alterations such as 'Glory be to God, by Jesus Christ, through the heavenly assistance by the Holy Ghost'. Clarke inspired others, as is evidenced in John Jones's *Free and Candid*

---

[17] Clarke, *Scripture-Doctrine*, pp. 332–3.

[18] John Locke, *An Essay Concerning Human Understanding* 2.27.9, ed. Peter H. Nidditch (Oxford, 1975), p. 335.

[19] *Rationes*, No. 7, cited by Thomas C. Pfizenmaier, *The Trinitarian Theology of Dr Samuel Clarke (1675–1729): Context, Sources, and Controversy* (Leiden, 1997), p. 163.

Disquisitions relating to the Church of England (1749), William Hopkins's *The Liturgy of the Church of England in its Ordinary Service, Reduced nearer to the Standard of Scripture* (1763), and Theophilus Lindsey's *The Book of Common Prayer reformed to the Plan of the Late Dr Samuel Clarke* (1774). Lindsey himself seceded to form a Unitarian congregation, and it was in Unitarian liturgical compilations that the seeds of Clarke's ideas bore practical fruit.

The ideals of the non-jurors and the wish-list of the Newtonians certainly influenced the liturgical thinking of High Churchmen and 'liberals' respectively, but neither resulted in any great shift in worship in England. They were to bear some fruit in the aftermath of the crisis of the War for Independence in the American colonies. Independence posed an acute problem for members of the Church of England. With the consecration of Samuel Seabury for Connecticut by the non-juring Scottish bishops, and then provision for consecration of further bishops in England, the Protestant Episcopal Church of the United States of America came into being, and with it a new Prayer Book of 1789/90. The preface made it clear that it wanted to remain as close as possible to the liturgy of the Church of England, but in addition to the omission of prayers for the royal family, the book incorporated some of the more moderate and practical proposals of the Newtonians in terms of abbreviations such as the omission of the Athanasian Creed. However, in the communion office it incorporated the concept of offering and a strong petition for consecration of the elements (*anamnesis* and *epiclesis*) from the Scottish communion office, derived from the proposed 1637 Book of Common Prayer for Scotland. Although it shared some characteristics with Wesley's *Abridgement* for America, it was an official Anglican liturgy, though not that of 1662.

WORSHIP IN THE EIGHTEENTH CENTURY

Contemporary accounts of worship in eighteenth-century England are furnished by two visitors from Germany in the 1780s, Gebhard Friedrich Augustus Wendeborn and Carl Philip Moritz. Wendeborn wrote:

> Whoever has not been brought up in the English church, will not think himself much edified, when he attends in it for the first time divine service. The Common-Prayer book contains some very excellent prayers; but as they are read all the year round, and frequently without much devotion in a hasty manner, with a voice not always sufficiently loud and intelligible, it is no wonder, that the congregation should appear rather tired, and without many signs of fervent devotion. The alternate reading verses of the Psalms, by the clergyman and his congregation, the loud repeating of the Litany, the Creed, and other parts of the service by the latter, makes it rather resemble a Jewish synagogue. The frequent repetition of the reading of the prayers, and the psalms, is the cause, that many of

those who constantly attend the church, know both by heart; and therefore their thoughts seem to be much absent, when they recite this part of the service... the singing is generally not very harmonious; that recitation of some parts of the service, which, as I have observed before, is divided between the clergyman and the congregation, is done in a manner that betrays rather carelessness than attention; the perpetual motion of kneeling and rising again, that monotony which prevails, and that inanimated manner in which sermons are commonly delivered, have, in my opinion, nothing of solemnity in them, and can hardly promote edification and devotion.[20]

His views on the style of sermon delivery were echoed by his fellow country-man, the theologian, philosopher, and pastor Carl Philip Moritz, who referred to 'the monotonous tone the English always affect'. Moritz recorded the following after a visit to Nettlebed, Oxfordshire, in 1782:

I went out of the village for a short walk towards where I saw some men coming from another village to attend divine service in ours.

At last the parson [Revd John Reade] arrived on horseback. The boys took off their hats and bowed low to him. He had a somewhat elderly appearance, with his own hair dressed very much as if in natural curls.

The bell rang and I went into the church with the general public, my prayer-book under my arm. The clerk or verger showed me into a seat in front of the pulpit very politely.

The furnishing of the church was quite simple. Right above the altar were displayed the Ten Commandments in large letters on two tablets. And indeed there can be no better way of impressing the essential qualities of the faith on a waiting congregation than this.

Under the pulpit was a reading-desk where the preacher stood before the sermon and read out a very long liturgy to which the parish clerk responded each time, the congregation joining in softly. When, for example, the preacher said: 'God have mercy upon us,' the clerk and congregation answered: 'and forgive us our sins'. Or the preacher read a prayer and the whole congregation said 'Amen' to it... After the ritual had gone on for some time I noticed some shuffling in the choir [in the West Gallery]. The clerk was very busy and they all seemed to be getting ready for some special ceremony. I noticed also several musical instru-ments of various sorts as the preacher stopped his reading and the clerk announced from the choir: 'Let us praise God by singing the forty-seventh Psalm. "Awake, our hearts, awake with joy".'

How peaceful and heart-uplifting it was to hear vocal and instrumental music in this little country church, not made by hired musicians but joyfully offered by the happy dwellers in the place in praise of their God. This kind of music now began to alternate several times with the ritual prayers, and the tunes of the metrical

[20] Friedrich Augustus Wendeborn, *A View of England towards the Close of the Eighteenth Century*, 2 vols. (German edn., 1785–8; London, 1791), II, pp. 281–2.

psalms were so lively and joyful—and yet so wholly sincere—that I gave my heart unrestrainedly to devotion and was often touched to tears.

The preacher now stood up and gave a short address on the text: 'Not all who say "Lord! Lord!" shall enter into the Kingdom of Heaven.' He dealt with the subject in common terms and his presentation was sturdy. He spoke of the need to do God's will, but there was nothing out of the usual run in his matter. The sermon lasted less than half-an-hour.

Apart from all this the preacher was unsociable; he seemed haughty when he acknowledged the greetings of the country people, doing so with a superior nod.[21]

Georgian churches also give some indication of how the service was celebrated and adorned. St Peter's church, Gayhurst, Buckinghamshire (*c.*1728), is by an unknown architect. The interior retains its plain panelling, box pews, wrought-iron communion rail, fluted octagonal wooden font, and two-decker pulpit with large tester. The ceiling above the altar has three cherub heads surrounding the sun, with fronds, leaf whorls, and baskets of flowers. The reredos has the Ten Commandments in the centre, with the Creed on the left and the Lord's Prayer on the right. St Andrew's, Wheatfield, in Oxfordshire was rebuilt in the 1740s and combines classical and gothic styles. The interior furnishings are in the classical style, with box pews (some of which have hat pegs), an urn-shaped font, and two-decker pulpit with tester on the north side of the nave. The reredos text boards are like those of Gayhurst. The communion table is decorated with a cherub's head, grapes, and wheat. Neither of these two small churches provided a space for singers, but Avington in Hampshire (built 1768–71), has a west gallery which probably housed the singers, and Keding-ton, refurbished after the Restoration, had a west gallery added, and its three-decker pulpit presupposes a service presided over by parson and parish clerk.[22] These give us some idea of Georgian ideals.

The 1662 rites remained without official alteration, but there was a change in music styles during the period. From its Reformation beginnings, Church of England musical traditions fell roughly into two distinct types. The best known, because it still survives, was music of the cathedrals and collegiate churches, whose foundations provided for singers and musicians. Composers compiled music for the versicles and responses, the psalms, canticles, and verse anthems, as well as those elements that had been retained in the Prayer Book from the ordinary of the mass, such as the Gloria in Excelsis and the Sanctus. This music was out of the reach of most small parishes, whose repertoire was largely confined to the metrical psalms of either Sternhold and Hopkins (the Old Version, 1562) or Tate and Brady (the New Version,

---

[21] Carl Philip Moritz, *Journeys of a German in England in 1782*, trans. and ed. Reginald Nettel (New York, 1965), pp. 126–7.

[22] For more examples, see Mark Chatfield, *Churches the Victorians Forgot* (rev. edn., Ashbourne, 1989).

1696). The eighteenth century saw the rise of west gallery singers and bands, who, thanks to local composers, developed the west gallery style of parish music, often derogatorily called 'fuguing' by those of more refined musical taste. The Revd Dr John Burton remarked of the music at Shermanbury, Sussex, in 1752: 'in church they sing psalms, by preference, not set to the old and simple tunes, but as if in a tragic chorus, changing about with strophe and antistrophe and stanzas, with good measure, but yet there is something offensive to my ears, when they bellow to excess, and bleat out some goatish noise with all their might'.[23] And at Over Stowey in 1800, William Holland recorded: 'The Church was full this evening, some strangers with instruments of various kinds among the Singers. Poor Ben [the Clerk] could not make it out this day being in the background with these youngsters. He is old Sternhold and Hopkins for ever in the plain old stile and cannot well comprehend this grunting and tooting.'[24]

Revision of the actual liturgy was undertaken by John Wesley: in 1784 for the Methodist societies in America, and in 1786 a version for British Methodists. In a sense, with the ordination of elders and superintendents for America and the revised liturgy, the secession from the Established Church was now final. If this was true for the Arminian Methodists, it was also true for the English Calvinistic Methodists under the wing of Selina, Countess of Huntingdon. When, in order to save her chapel of Spa Fields, she seceded from the Church of England, she insisted that her chapels should still use the Book of Common Prayer—but with modifications, as evidenced in a manuscript she herself prepared outlining the changes.[25] However, the main contribution of both Arminian and Calvinistic Methodists, together with a number of those Evangelicals who remained within the Established Church, such as Martin Madan, Charles Simeon, and Thomas Haweis, was the collection and composition of hymns that were gradually introduced into public worship. Haweis cited a forgotten Elizabethan injunction: 'For the comforting of such as delight in music it may be permitted, that in the beginning or end of Common Prayer, either at morning or evening, there may be sung an hymn, or such like song, to the praise of almighty God, in the best melody and music, that may be conveniently devised, having respect that the sentence of the hymn may be understood and perceived.'[26]

Forgotten it certainly had been, and not until court cases in the nineteenth century was it finally established that it was perfectly legal to sing hymns in the

[23] W. H. Blaauw, 'Extracts from the "Iter Sussexiense" of Dr John Burton', *Sussex Archaeological Collections*, 8 (1856), p. 257.

[24] Jack Ayers (ed.), *Paupers and Pig Killers: The Diary of William Holland, a Somerset Parson 1799–1818* (Gloucester, 1984), p. 26.

[25] Cambridge, Westminster College, Cheshunt Foundation Archives, A4/5, 25.

[26] Thomas McCart, *The Matter and Manner of Praise: The Controversial Evolution of Hymnody in the Church of England, 1760–1820* (Lanham, MD, 1998).

Church of England. It is perhaps no accident that with the appearance of hymn books in the nineteenth century, metrical psalmody disappeared rapidly from Anglican worship.[27] However, the musical dam had already been burst in Evangelical congregations. Madan's *Collection of Psalms and Hymns* (1760) was drawn up for use at the Lock Hospital, London, where he was chaplain. In this sense it was for 'private use', or at least outside the setting of public worship. That was true also for many of the Wesley hymns, which were originally for societal use, not public worship, though Charles Wesley's eucharistic hymns were certainly intended for the public worship of the Church. The title of Simeon's collection of 1795 made quite clear his intention: *A Collection of Psalms and Hymns from various Authors, chiefly designed for the use of Publick Worship*. Haweis published his *Carmina Christo* in 1792, and in the preface wrote: 'I am persuaded also that no other method of communicating the knowledge of religious truths hath been attended with happier effects, or serves to leave deeper impression of them on the memory and conscience of the common people, than sacred songs. And for whom should we delight to labour but for these? "To the poor the Gospel is preached".'[28] The hymns were set out under headings, and the first part of the collection followed the liturgical calendar, commencing with hymns for the Nativity, including 'Hark! The bright seraphic quire', and 'By night whilst shepherds on the plain'. Hymns were provided for Easter, Ascension, Pentecost, and Trinity Sunday. An Easter hymn celebrated the cosmic dimension of the Resurrection, and a hymn for Trinity Sunday boldly attested Haweis's orthodoxy over against those of Clarke's persuasion. He also provided hymns for use at the communion service. The words and tunes brought a different tone to Anglican worship.

Contrary to the rather negative perception of the Hanoverian Church of England held by the Victorians, recent historiography has shown that it was vigorous and alive, and generally well supported.[29] Confirmations were popular and were occasions of importance.[30] It is evident that the Book of Common Prayer was valued by many sons and daughters of the Church and its virtues extolled over against what were regarded as the excesses of Romanism and Dissent. In his will (1727) John Hutchins, a London goldsmith, endowed an annual sermon on the excellence of the liturgy of the Church of England, to be preached each year on St Mark's Day. In the sermon for 1752, Samuel Shuckford noted the biblical nature of the Prayer Book, in its provision for confession of sin and recitation of the psalms. One of its 'excellencies' was 'that its Service is

[27] Susan Drain, *The Anglican Church in Nineteenth-Century Britain: Hymns Ancient and Modern (1860–1875)* (Lewiston, NY, 1989).

[28] Thomas Haweis, *Carmina Christo* (Bath, [1792?]), preface.

[29] E.g. William Gibson, *The Church of England 1688–1832: Unity and Accord* (London, 2001).

[30] Phillip Tovey, *Anglican Confirmation 1662–1820* (Farnham, 2014).

performed in short Prayers; and that these are so composed as to fill our Minds continually with a right Sense of almighty God, and of our blessed Saviour'.[31] Though it was not absolutely perfect, nevertheless 'its Worship is so framed, as to answer well all the Ends of a reasonable Service of God, truly to set forth his Honour and Glory, by leading his People, to believe and to do *as becometh the Gospel of Christ*.[32] In the sermon for 1760, Henry Stebbing argued that a public liturgy seemed essential for maintaining public devotion, and that there was no more need to change the Church of England liturgy than there was for changing the government. In conclusion, he stated:

> The liturgy of the Church of England is a treasure of Christian devotion, both publick and private. And those who are true christians and soberly devout have always esteemed and used it as such. As to those who, by making alterations in it, would lead the way to an entire abolition of it; and to others who, under the pretence of a more convenient liturgy, have a secret wish for the removal of what a Christian Church cannot part with, and an Established Church ought not; they are Both out of the question; because they are no friends to the Church of England, or not sound friends to Christianity.[33]

Many would agree with East Apthorp that the liturgy of the Church of England was 'so rational, so touching, so eloquent, so pious, devout and scriptural'.[34] Jeremy Gregory has noted that by constantly hearing the same services, the illiterate were able to gain an understanding of the Anglican rites, and many had learned the Prayer Book services by rote.[35] It was ingrained in what might be termed the English 'moderate' establishment religious psyche, and in the first three decades of the nineteenth century many like John Skinner, incumbent of Camerton, Somerset, referred to 'the excellent Liturgy of the Church of England'.[36] However, by the mid-nineteenth century its hegemony was under attack. Both Tractarians and Evangelicals would want enrichment, abbreviation, freedom to supplement, and the 'mean between the two Extremes of too much stiffness in refusing, and of too much easiness in admitting any variation from it' was on the way to being declared too narrow for the religious life of many in the Church of England.[37]

---

[31] Samuel Shuckford, *The Use of a Liturgy, and the Excellency of the Liturgy of the Church of England considered* (London, 1752), p. 18.

[32] Shuckford, *Use of a Liturgy*, p. 22.

[33] Henry Stebbing, *A Sermon preached at the Parish Church of St Mary-le-Bow, on St Mark's Day, 1760* (London, 1760), p. 19.

[34] East Apthorp, *The Excellence of the Liturgy of the Church of England: A Sermon at the Church of St Mary le Bow* (London, 1778), p. 21.

[35] Jeremy Gregory, '"For all sorts and conditions of men": The Social Life of the Book of Common Prayer during the Long Eighteenth Century: or, Bringing the History of Religion and Social History Together', *Social History*, 34 (2009): 29–54 (p. 50).

[36] John Skinner, *Journal of a Somerset Rector 1803–1834*, ed. Howard and Peter Coombs (Oxford, 1984), p. 269.

[37] See the *Report of the Royal Commission on Ecclesiastical Discipline* (London, 1906).

SELECT BIBLIOGRAPHY

Buchanan, Colin, *The Savoy Conference Revisited*, Alcuin/GROW Joint Liturgical Study 54 (Cambridge, 2002).

Fawcett, Timothy J., *The Liturgy of Comprehension 1689* (Southend-on-Sea, 1973).

Gregory, Jeremy, '"For all sorts and conditions of men": The Social Life of the Book of Common Prayer during the Long Eighteenth Century: or, Bringing the History of Religion and Social History Together', *Social History*, 34 (2009): 29–54.

Grisbrooke, W. Jardine, *Anglican Liturgies of the Seventeenth and Eighteenth Centuries* (London, 1958).

Jacob, William, 'Common Prayer in the Eighteenth Century', in Stephen Platten and Christopher Woods (eds.), *Comfortable Words: Polity, Piety and the Book of Common Prayer* (London, 2012), pp. 83–97.

Legg, J. Wickham, *English Church Life from the Restoration to the Tractarian Movement* (London, 1914).

McCart, Thomas, *The Matter and Manner of Praise: The Controversial Evolution of Hymnody in the Church of England, 1760–1820* (Lanham, MD, 1998).

Segger, Glen, *Richard Baxter's Reformed Liturgy: A Puritan Alternative to the Prayer Book* (Farnham, 2014).

Spinks, Bryan D., *Liturgy in the Age of Reason: Worship and Sacraments in England and Scotland 1662–c.1800* (Farnham, 2008).

Tovey, Phillip, *Anglican Confirmation 1662–1820* (Farnham, 2014).

15

Sermons

William Gibson

INTRODUCTION

The seventeenth and eighteenth centuries represent the golden age of the sermon in Britain.* It was the period in which sermons were the central feature of the Anglican liturgy and parish worship, and in which sermons exerted an extraordinary influence over the cultural life of the nation and dominated its print culture. The number and breadth of Anglican sermons, both printed and performed, is demonstrable evidence of the vitality and intellectual activity of the Church of England. Sermons were a primary medium for public discourse, including the fiercest political and religious controversies and polemics generated by Church and state. It was in preaching and sermons that the principal expression of the Evangelical movement was also seen.

Preaching enjoyed a remarkable presence in society: in addition to parish churches, sermons were delivered in Parliament, schools, universities, assizes, missions, and all manner of other locations and events. Even the architecture and arrangement of church buildings were dominated by the centrality of the pulpit, literally and figuratively. Sermons were also an important element in the ecclesiastical economy: for example, in just a few months in 1736 and 1737 George Whitefield raised £1,300 from collections at preaching.[1] Such was the demand for sermons that by the middle of the eighteenth century speculative builders were constructing chapels in London and elsewhere on the basis that the income from sales of tickets for sermons would defray the costs and return

* I am grateful to the Armstrong Browning Library at Baylor University, Waco, Texas, and the Lewis Walpole Library, Yale University, New Haven, Connecticut, for appointing me to visiting research fellowships in 2009 and 2011 respectively, to enable me to study collections of sermons and related manuscripts which contributed to the production of this chapter.

[1] Boyd Stanley Schlenther, 'Whitefield, George (1714–1770)', *ODNB*.

a good profit.[2] Reading sermons, like other forms of literature, moved from being an intensive to an extensive experience.

In 1662 most people heard sermons in their parish church, preached by their own parson, though there were increasing opportunities to sample other preachers' work. There was a number of classic sermons and collections of sermons, such as those by Tillotson, Sherlock, and Hoadly, that were widely reprinted and well known. While this remained the case, by 1829 there were far more opportunities to hear sermons and preachers: many churches had Wednesday and Sunday lectures (which had been suppressed under Laud), often delivered by clergy other than the incumbent. In addition, sermons for charity schools, the Society for Promoting Christian Knowledge (SPCK), and the Society for the Propagation of the Gospel (SPG) were complemented by missionary and Bible societies, as well as philanthropic societies, all of which offered public sermons. So the occasions on which a sermon might be heard grew significantly over the long eighteenth century.

QUANTITIES OF SERMONS

It is natural that scholars should have paid most attention to the published sermons, but it is important to recognize that printed sermons were an infinitesimally small percentage of the total of actual pulpit performances in Anglican churches of this period. An estimate is that there were a quarter of a billion sermon opportunities in the two centuries after 1688, but fewer than 100,000 individual printed sermons. The same is true for people's experience of sermons: a parishioner who attended a church where double duty was achieved (two services with a sermon at each) probably heard more than a hundred sermons a year, especially when weekday, occasional, and feast-day sermons are added. Most parishioners are likely to have read (or heard read) many fewer than this. A parson over his career might preach as many as 5,000 sermons, but it is unlikely that he used this number of published sermons as his sources. Consequently, published Anglican sermons were unrepresentative of the numbers of performances heard in the pulpits of the nation.[3] Published sermons were likely to have been delivered by the most educated, fashionable, influential, or senior clergy of the time. Accordingly, some of the assumptions

---

[2] John Trusler, 'Memoirs', Part 2 [1809], f. 17, Yale University, Lewis Walpole Library, MS 71; William Gibson, 'John Trusler and the Sermon Culture of the Late Eighteenth Century', *Journal of Ecclesiastical History*, 66 (2015): 302–19.

[3] William Gibson, 'The British Sermon 1689–1901: Quantities, Performance, and Culture', in Keith A. Francis and William Gibson (eds.), *The Oxford Handbook of the British Sermon 1689–1901* (Oxford, 2012), pp. 3–30; cf. John Gordon Spaulding, *Pulpit Publications, 1660–1782*, 6 vols. (New York, 1996).

derived from published sermons about popular preaching must be regarded as highly contingent. For example, it seems likely that there was a gradual change in styles of preaching towards the end of the seventeenth century, and that Archbishop John Tillotson inspired a move to a rational and ordered form of discourse.[4] Nevertheless this is a judgement derived principally from published sermons. That is not to say that such judgements should be dismissed, simply that they should be regarded with caution and tempered by evidence from the surviving manuscript sermons and from accounts of preaching in the parishes.[5] Published sermons can, however, provide evidence of the popular consumption of sermons, since it is clear that the sales of sermons dominated the printing industry in the first half of the eighteenth century. Publishing houses and non-commercial organizations like the SPCK were organized around meeting the large demand for printed sermons.[6] With the growth of provincial printers, booksellers' profits, at least initially, were often dependent on the publication and sale of sermons.[7]

PREACHING IN THE PARISH

It is sometimes difficult to appreciate the level of demand for preaching in parishes throughout the country. It was a demand that was not confined to Anglicans; in the late seventeenth and early eighteenth centuries it was common for Dissenters to attend Anglican churches to hear the sermon and leave afterwards. Sermons were clearly seen by some clergy as a major weapon in the armoury of the Church after the Toleration Act of 1689 effectively created a free market in Protestant worship. In Salisbury diocese Bishop Gilbert Burnet told his clergy that the strength of Anglican preaching was a reason why the Church was holding back the tide of Protestant Dissent.[8] In the

---

[4] James Downey, *The Eighteenth-Century Pulpit* (Oxford, 1969); O. C. Edwards Jr, *A History of Preaching* (Nashville, TN, 2004); Rolf P. Lessenich, *Elements of Pulpit Oratory in Eighteenth-Century England (1660–1800)* (Vienna, 1972).

[5] This trend has begun in Joris van Eijnatten (ed.), *Preaching, Sermon and Cultural Change in the Long Eighteenth Century* (Leiden, 2009); cf. Jeffrey S. Chamberlain, 'Parish Preaching in the Long Eighteenth Century', in Francis and Gibson (eds.), *The British Sermon 1689–1901*, pp. 47–62; Gibson, 'The British Sermon 1689–1901'.

[6] Terry Belanger, 'Booksellers' Trade Sales, 1718–1768', *The Library*, 5th series, 30 (1975): 281–302; Rosemary Dixon, 'The Publishing of John Tillotson's *Collected Works*, 1695–1757', *The Library*, 8th series, 2 (2007): 154–81; Michael F. Suarez and Michael L. Turner (eds.), *The Cambridge History of the Book in Britain*, vol. V: *1695–1830* (Cambridge, 2009).

[7] C. Y. Ferdinand, 'Newspapers and the Sale of Books in the Provinces', in Suarez and Turner (eds.), *Cambridge History of the Book*, V, pp. 434–47 (p. 434).

[8] Gilbert Burnet, *A Charge given at the Triennial Visitation of the Diocese of Salisbury in October 1704: To which is added a Sermon preach'd at Salisbury, and some other Places, in the said Visitation* (London, 1704), pp. 9–10.

competitive world of post-Toleration Act England, Anglican clergy came to realize that impressive sermons were an important means of fighting for the attendance of their parishioners.[9] As the principal objective of many church-goers was to hear the sermon, it was natural that disappointing preachers were censured and impressive preachers were in high demand. If there were occasional complaints about sermons, they were about the desire for more.[10] Novelty was important: despite being one of the best preachers in the country, Francis Dawes, incumbent of Solihull in the 1760s, found that his parishioners did not appreciate his sermons because, as one put it, 'we have heard him so often that we are tired of him'.[11] Sermon-gadding might have been initiated by seventeenth-century puritans but it remained common in this period as celebrated preachers, especially in the towns and cities, attracted large con-gregations from outside their parishes. John Trusler found that in 1759, when his sermon on the death of the Princess of Orange, daughter of George II, had attracted widespread attention, his church at Hertford was so full of people from his own and neighbouring parishes that he could hardly make his way to the pulpit.[12] The system of sermons and lectures on Wednesdays and Sunday afternoons, which was very strong in London and the major towns, often attracted attenders from other parishes.[13] In such an environment the quality of sermons was generally agreed to have improved—from Bishop Thomas Sprat in 1695 to John Trusler in 1809, opinions seemed strongly to support the view that sermons were not just good but improving.[14]

A paradoxical consequence of the rise of the sermon in Anglicanism was its elevation of the preacher in a Protestant Church that distanced itself from the sacerdotal claims of the Catholic priesthood. Seventeenth-century pur-itans had asserted the claim of *sola scriptura*, but the sermon intruded the parson into the relationship between God and humanity. While the sermon carried with it no sacerdotal function—and could be delivered by the laity—nevertheless it brought the priest to a prominence not enjoyed since the Reformation.

There was a strong tradition in the Church of England of clergy reading the published sermons of others. This was not the plagiarism it might appear to the twenty-first-century observer. Indeed, it was recommended practice for young clergy to read the sermons of other leading preachers—and thereby to give their congregations the best available fare—before they began to write

---

[9] Gibson, 'The British Sermon 1689–1901'.

[10] Donald Spaeth, *The Church in an Age of Danger: Parsons and Parishioners, 1660–1740* (Cambridge, 2000), p. 189.

[11] Trusler, 'Memoirs', fos. 191–2.

[12] John Trusler, *Memoirs of the Life of the Rev Dr Trusler, Part I* (Bath, 1806), pp. 113–16.

[13] James Paterson, *Pietas Londinensis, or the Present Ecclesiastical State of London* (London, 1714).

[14] Gibson, 'The British Sermon 1689–1901'.

their own sermons. Gilbert Burnet recommended this in one of the most enduring manuals for clergy training, *The Discourse of the Pastoral Care*, first published in 1692.[15] Reading the sermons of distinguished clergy was the apprenticeship of the pulpit and gave incumbents an effective model of how to preach. Otherwise the principal training, at least for graduate clergy, was listening to university sermons. For eighteenth-century clergy, quality usually won over novelty and originality; it mattered less who had written the sermon than whether it was a good one and whether it was appreciated by a congregation.

Manuscript sermons were sometimes shared between local clergy and between fathers and sons in clerical families and often bear the evidence of adaptation and amendment for specific audiences.[16] Volumes of manuscript sermons also indicate that clergy repeated popular sermons, and sometimes developed cycles of sermons. John Longe, vicar of Coddenham, Suffolk, from 1787 to 1832, is rare in leaving records of his sermon-writing. He composed his own sermons and adapted those of his father and blended them with extracts of the published sermons which he liked.[17] Similarly, John and Charles Wesley shared sermons which they had composed—and wrote them in a unique shorthand.[18] Many clergy laboured long and hard over their sermons, in some cases taking many hours to compose them. This was in part because sermons were regarded as a key aspect of pastoral care by both clergy and parishioners. Notwithstanding the use of preaching materials from a range of sources, as a whole, sermons represent the single most significant intellectual endeavour in Britain during the long eighteenth century. They absorbed and reflected the talents of the largest body of the educated population.

Sermons dominated worship and religious observance in part because of the infrequency of Holy Communion, which the canons of 1603 required to be held three times a year. Although there was in this period a significant rise in the frequency of communion, it was rarely celebrated weekly.[19] Moreover hymnody, though emergent in the eighteenth century, was not highly developed. With the settled liturgy of the Book of Common Prayer, which involved repetition of familiar prayers and devotions, the only regular feature of novelty and originality in worship was the sermon. Unsurprisingly, therefore, the sermon represented much of the focus of parishioners' attention and interest.

---

[15] Robert D. Cornwall (ed.), *Gilbert Burnet's Discourse of the Pastoral Care* (Lampeter, *c.*1997).

[16] Collections of manuscript sermons, c88, c104, c247, c250, c264, c410, c420, c550, Yale University, Beinecke Library.

[17] Michael Stone (ed.), *The Diary of John Longe, Vicar of Coddenham, 1764–1832* (Woodbridge, 2008), pp. 171–4.

[18] Richard P. Heitzenrater, 'John Wesley's Early Sermons', *Proceedings of the Wesley Historical Society*, 37 (1970): 110–28 (p. 113).

[19] F. C. Mather, 'Georgian Churchmanship Reconsidered: Some Variations in Anglican Public Worship 1714–1830', *Journal of Ecclesiastical History*, 36 (1985): 255–83.

PREACHING AND POLITICS

The interest in sermons lay not simply in their pastoral and devotional content. Sermons in this period were also a medium through which some of the most important political and public discourses were conducted. In the immediate aftermath of the Toleration Act, sermons reflected the tension between the Church of England and Protestant Dissent. The case for and against the separation of Dissent was hotly contested and debated: from the farewell sermons of the clergy ejected in 1662 following the Act of Uniformity, to the attempts to recover Dissenters to the Church in the various *Dissenters Cases*—first published in the 1670s, but frequently republished in collections well into the eighteenth century. The legitimacy, or otherwise, of schism and the Dissenters' use of occasional conformity to show their charity to Anglicanism as well as to qualify for office under the Test Act were often discussed in controversial sermons. These themes featured especially prominently in sermons when there were moves to outlaw occasional conformity in the first two decades of the eighteenth century.[20]

Sermons also defined the relationship of Anglicanism to Catholicism in the 1670s and during the reign of James II. James's fury at the anti-Catholic sermons preached in London churches resulted in the suspension of Bishop Henry Compton from his diocese; such Anglican anti-Catholic sermons were a constant thorn in his side and were important weapons in the Church's response to his rule.[21] Anti-Catholic sermons throughout the eighteenth century were a significant element in the mixed economy of the pulpit, and were particularly widespread during wars with Catholic nations and periods of Jacobite danger.[22] After the Revolution of 1688, sermons often focused on the enduring national anxiety about the legitimacy of expelling an anointed king. If the execution of one king had been a sin in 1649 perhaps the expulsion of a second was equally sinful in 1688. For more than two decades a principal occupation of many published sermons was the issue of whether the nation had offended God in 1688–9 and whether it had acted legitimately, at least in divine terms. Consequently a number of the sermons on such events as the deaths of Mary II, of Archbishop John Tillotson, and of William III, and on the great storm of 1703 sought to discern, and invite, providential sanction on Britain for 1688.

---

[20] David J. Appleby, *Black Bartholomew's Day: Preaching, Polemic and Restoration Nonconformity* (Manchester, 2007); William Gibson, 'Dissenters, Anglicans and the Glorious Revolution: The Collection of Cases', *Seventeenth Century*, 22 (2007): 168–84.

[21] William Gibson, *James II and the Trial of the Seven Bishops* (Basingstoke, 2009), pp. 48–58, 73–96.

[22] Colin Haydon, *Anti-Catholicism in Eighteenth-Century England c.1714–80* (Manchester, 1994); Pasi Ihalainen, *The Discourse on Political Pluralism in Early Eighteenth-Century England* (Helsinki, 1999); Tony Claydon, *Europe and the Making of England, 1660–1760* (Cambridge, 2007).

This national anxiety was a result of the settlement of the throne, but also the settlement of religion and the Toleration Act of 1689. The Act seemed to make the Dissenters' schism permanent and therefore, to many clergy, it threatened the Anglican monopoly and the salvation of Anglicans and Dissenters alike. It was this concern that motivated Henry Sacheverell's sermon of 1709. The sermon was one of the most significant pulpit performances of the century, leading to Sacheverell's impeachment in March 1710. The sermon and trial were responsible for unrest and riots in London and across the country, and an important ingredient in the Tory victory in the 1710 election. The sales of the Sacheverell sermon, estimated in its first edition alone to have been 40,000, must have achieved almost complete saturation of the literate public and it was probably heard by many of the illiterate, as clergy read the sermon, and answers to it, from their pulpits.[23]

The Sacheverell sermon represented a challenge to the Glorious Revolution and the Hanoverian succession, and revealed the strength of popular opinion in defence of the Church of England. Ultimately Sacheverell's High Church Tory agenda failed in the wake of the Whig revival of 1714. The Hanoverian settlement produced its own politico-theological controversy in the form of Benjamin Hoadly's Bangorian sermon in 1716. Hoadly's assertion—that Christ left no visible authority on earth to shackle human consciences—struck at the basis of the Church's claim to enforce theological doctrines. It also challenged the state's use of the Test Act to establish an Anglican monopoly on public offices and to deny Dissenters a role in the public life of the country. The sermon, an elite Whig performance before the king, electrified the country, just as Sacheverell's had. It produced hundreds of responses in print, many of which were sermons themselves, preached to endorse or denounce Hoadly's views.[24]

From Sacheverell and Hoadly onwards, the pulpit remained the foremost public forum for controversy in the eighteenth century. The detection of heterodoxy was largely undertaken by careful reading of the sermons of the clergy, and defences of orthodox Anglicanism were also undertaken in the pulpit. The principal theological arguments of the eighteenth century, including opposition to Deism and natural religion, the arguments for and against miracles, and for and against clerical subscription, were fought out in

---

[23] Geoffrey Holmes, *The Trial of Doctor Sacheverell* (London, 1973); Mark Knights, *The Devil in Disguise: Deception, Delusion, and Fanaticism in the Early English Enlightenment* (Oxford, 2011); Mark Knights (ed.), *Faction Displayed: Reconsidering the Impeachment of Dr Henry Sacheverell*, a special issue of *Parliamentary History*, 31 (2012).

[24] William Gibson, *Enlightenment Prelate: Benjamin Hoadly, 1676–1761* (Cambridge, 2004), ch. 5; see also Guglielmo Sanna, *Religione e vita pubblica nell'Inghilterra del '700. Le avventure di Benjamin Hoadly* (Milan, 2012); [Thomas Herne], *A Continuation of the Account of all the considerable Pamphlets that have been published on Either Side in the present Controversy, between the Bishop of Bangor and others, to the end of the Year, MDCCXIX* (London, 1720).

sermons.[25] Even in the second half of the eighteenth century individual sermons had the power to raise political temperatures. Thomas Nowell's 30 January sermon before the House of Commons in 1772 advanced High Toryism; the sermon provoked such a reaction by defending Charles I from any responsibility for the English Civil War that a motion in the Commons to abolish the anniversary 'martyrdom' service was only narrowly defeated.

The pulpit was also an important means for the state to defend itself from political and military danger. In 1715 and 1745 the government used the pulpit as a vital weapon in defence of the Hanoverian succession against the Jacobite risings; and the sermons which defended the state were a significant means to mobilize the population.[26] Sermons thus became an instrument in the process of eighteenth-century nation-building, sanctioning and endorsing a social and political structure which was under attack from outside by forces which were constitutionally and religiously antagonistic.

SERMONS AND NATIONHOOD

Sermons were also the principal means of nation-building through public commemorations. Major martial events, such as victories on land and at sea, were celebrated with services of thanksgiving and the publication of sermons, often praising generals and admirals such as Marlborough and Nelson. There were days of fasting and prayer for victory during wars which were also attended by a sermon. When, during the American War of Independence, defeat seemed likely, Bishop Yorke of St David's urged in a fast-day sermon in 1778 that 'vigour, prudence and temper are necessary to recover our former harmony'.[27] Constitutional events, including the Union of England and Scotland in 1707 and that of Britain and Ireland in 1801, were celebrated with sermons.[28] Most of these sought to advance a British exceptionalism as a

[25] Robert G. Ingram, '"The Weight of Historical Evidence": Conyers Middleton and the Eighteenth-Century Miracles Debate', in Robert D. Cornwall and William Gibson (eds.), *Religion, Politics and Dissent, 1660–1832: Essays in Honour of James E. Bradley* (Aldershot, 2010), pp. 85–109.

[26] James J. Caudle, 'The Defence of Georgian Britain: The Anti-Jacobite Sermon 1715–1746', in Francis and Gibson (eds.), *The British Sermon 1689–1901*, pp. 245–60.

[27] James Yorke, *A Sermon preached in the Cathedral Church of Lincoln, on Friday, February 27, 1778* (Lincoln, 1778), p. 13; G. M. Ditchfield, 'Sermons in the Age of the American and French Revolutions', in Francis and Gibson (eds.), *The British Sermon 1689–1901*, pp. 275–88.

[28] Pasi Ihalainen, 'The Sermon, Court, and Parliament, 1689–1789', and Warren Johnston, 'Preaching, National Salvation, Victories, and Thanksgivings: 1689–1800', in Francis and Gibson (eds.), *The British Sermon 1689–1901*, pp. 229–44, 261–74; Tony Claydon, 'The Sermon Culture of the Glorious Revolution: Williamite Preaching and Jacobite Anti-Preaching, 1685–1702', in Peter McCullough, Hugh Adlington, and Emma Rhatigan (eds.), *The Oxford Handbook of the Early Modern Sermon* (Oxford, 2011), pp. 480–94.

new Israel. In parishes far distant from the centre of government, sermons also marked the history and culture of the nation by providing a cycle of preaching on a series of annual commemorative days. Church bells were rung and sermons preached on, among others, 30 January, the anniversary of the execution of Charles I; 29 May, the anniversary of the Restoration of Charles II; 5 November, the joint anniversary of the discovery of the Gunpowder Plot in 1605 and of the landing of William of Orange in 1688; and 17 November, the anniversary of the accession of Queen Elizabeth I. In this way sermons were a means for the history of England, and the culture of Protestantism, to be inculcated into congregations; such celebrations formed part of the religious calendar alongside Christmas, Easter, Whitsun, and Michaelmas.

The lives of monarchs and men and women great and small were remembered and honoured in funeral sermons, in which there was a healthy trade in printed versions. There were sometimes significant disparities between the numbers of funeral or commemorative sermons on the deaths of individuals. Queen Mary II easily outstripped her husband William III and sister Queen Anne in the number of funeral sermons published on her death. The death of Princess Charlotte in 1819, which robbed George IV and the country of an heir, was marked by scores of published mourning sermons.[29] In other aspects of national life, sermons were also associated with moral behaviour and criminal justice through preaching before the Societies for the Reformation of Manners and at assizes, which usually indicated the divine sanction of both the law and the state.[30] In workhouses and charity schools, sermons were part of the divine sanction of the orders of society. In this way the sermon was an important joist in the buttressing of the state and society by the Church. It was the major religious and political public address system, utilized for the ends of both institutions.

SERMONS AND THE CHURCH

Sermons were used as an important managerial instrument within the Church. In visitation sermons, bishops and archdeacons laid down the professional expectations and demands which they wished to make on the clergy. The published visitation sermons of both bishops and archdeacons formed the largest single corpus of information and advice on the training and continuing

[29] Penny Pritchard, 'The Protestant Funeral Sermon in England, 1688–1800', in Francis and Gibson (eds.), *The British Sermon 1689–1901*, pp. 322–37; Paul S. Fritz, 'The Trade in Death: The Royal Funerals in England, 1685–1830', *Eighteenth-Century Studies*, 15 (1982): 291–316.

[30] Hugh Adlington, 'Restoration, Religion, and Law: Assize Sermons 1660–1685', in McCullough et al. (eds.), *The Early Modern Sermon*, pp. 423–41.

professional development of clergy in the discharge of their duties. In the case of Archdeacon Thomas Sharp of Northumberland, such sermons were collected together into an anthology of guidance and counsel for the clergy, and remained in print for many years.[31] Daniel Whitby's suite of visitation sermons as archdeacon of Middlesex was frequently reprinted as the best orthodox defence of the eucharist.[32] Equally, sermons preached at the consecration of bishops were often used as an agenda for an episcopate. They provide a window onto the principal preoccupations of the episcopate in this period.[33]

Sermons were important as moments of instruction and direction by a parson to a congregation. Preaching provided an opportunity for clergy to censure the behaviour of parishioners. Some contemporaries clearly felt that clergy were too disapproving in the pulpit.[34] Parsons sometimes made strong statements about a congregation's morality, sexual behaviour, and 'filthy and smutty discourses'. But after the Toleration Act it was clear that preaching could not be too censorious lest it discourage parishioners from attending, nor could preachers threaten the wrath of God for the same reason. Consequently many clergy often preferred to speak in more general terms about obedience to God and religious teaching.[35]

The form of sermons in the eighteenth century varied considerably, but they were longer than those of the Victorian era. On average, sermons probably lasted between thirty minutes and an hour, though there are numerous examples of much longer performances. The assumption, mentioned earlier, that this period saw a distinct shift from elaborate poetic sermons to rational Tillotsonian preaching was also associated with a clearly announced division of the sermon into text, the parts of the arguments a preacher would consider, and an application to the immediate needs of the congregation. These regular features of both published and manuscript sermons are often assumed to have occluded the emotional content of sermons. But even Benjamin Hoadly, who preached a cycle of sermons while rector of St Peter Poor and was known for his latitudinarian rationalism, could preach sermons

[31] William Gibson, '"This itching ear'd age": Visitation Sermons and Charges in the Eighteenth Century', in Francis and Gibson (eds.), *The British Sermon 1689–1901*, pp. 289–304.

[32] Daniel Whitby, *A Review of the Doctrine of the Eucharist* (London, 1737).

[33] Colin Haydon, 'Consecration Sermons', in Francis and Gibson (eds.), *The British Sermon 1689–1901*, pp. 305–21; William Gibson, 'Brother of the More Famous Benjamin: The Theology of John Hoadly', *Anglican and Episcopal History*, 75 (2006): 401–22.

[34] David Vaisey (ed.), *The Diary of Thomas Turner 1754–1765* (Oxford, 1984), pp. 125–6; Jeffrey S. Chamberlain, '"A regular and well-affected" Diocese: Chichester in the Eighteenth Century', in Jeremy Gregory and Jeffrey S. Chamberlain (eds.), *The National Church in Local Perspective: The Church of England and the Regions, 1660–1800* (Woodbridge, 2003), pp. 73–98 (pp. 85–7).

[35] Jeffrey S. Chamberlain, 'Parish Preaching in the Long Eighteenth Century', in Francis and Gibson (eds.), *The British Sermon 1689–1901*, pp. 47–62.

infused with emotion. One example was Hoadly's sermon on the crucifixion, in which he praised the decision of 'the thief on the cross' to grasp his one opportunity for salvation.[36]

PERFORMANCE IN THE PULPIT

Performance was an important aspect of preaching and sermon culture. Those who witnessed Sacheverell's performance in 1709 were undoubtedly affected by the sight of it. Witnesses wrote about his goggling eyes, inflamed cheeks, and saliva-flecked lips as he bellowed his words from the pulpit in St Paul's.[37] The effect of such a performance was to intensify the experience of his vehemence by the congregation. The same is true of George Whitefield, who is said to have driven fifteen people mad by his histrionic preaching in London in 1736.[38] Whitefield's impact was achieved partly by the novelty of his direct engagement with the congregation. Despite his condemnation of the stage, Whitefield's sermons were highly theatrical: by frequent repetition he knew many sermons by heart and therefore rarely stumbled in his speech. He often used props, donning a judicial black cap when condemning the unrepentant sinner to damnation, and when he spoke of the tears of St Peter he sometimes wiped his eyes with the sleeves of his gown. Even those who were not interested in the subject of the sermon found themselves spellbound by the performance.[39] Whitefield's frequent dissolution into tears in the pulpit was such a regular feature of his preaching that John Wesley became suspicious of its authenticity. William Hogarth's print *Credulity, Superstition, and Fanaticism* (1761) satirized the frenzied preaching and responses of the Evangelical movement. Ecstasy, grief, and horror were the sensations of the congregation in Hogarth's print, as they were in some of the congregations of the most dramatic and unrestrained Evangelical preachers. Other preachers, like David Simpson of Macclesfield, delivered sermons in which they debated issues with themselves, putting opposing ideas into speeches and answering them in the voice of the preacher. How these sounded when delivered is doubtful; in the printed versions, Simpson indicated quotation marks when he presented opposing ideas and comments.[40]

---

[36] Benjamin Hoadly, *Several Discourses concerning the Terms of Acceptance with God* (London, 1719), p. 240.

[37] Holmes, *Trial of Sacheverell*, p. 63.   [38] Edwards, *History of Preaching*, p. 432.

[39] Schlenther, 'Whitefield'.

[40] David Simpson, *Sermons on useful and important Subjects* (Macclesfield, 1774).

EVANGELICAL PREACHING

The Sacheverell sermon shows that extempore preaching did not hold a monopoly on melodrama, but emotion from the pulpit became associated with the extempore preaching of eighteenth-century Evangelicals. Evangelical clergy sought spiritual renewal, which was not an experience entirely responsive to reason and reflection; conversion relied more heavily on emotion and feeling. For this reason, Evangelical preachers adopted new behaviour in the pulpit. They addressed themselves directly to their congregation, asking questions and demanding introspection. Moreover, as some Evangelical clergy were denied parishes, and therefore churches in which they could perform all the usual liturgical functions of a minister, they turned to preaching outside churches. Whitefield's caustic condemnation of his fellow Anglican clergy was so offensive that he could rarely find a parson willing to invite or allow him to preach. In 1740, Whitefield's followers forced the rector of St Margaret's, Westminster, to admit him to the pulpit by obstructing the incumbent's choice of preacher from entering the pulpit.[41] Following the example of Howell Harris in Wales, Whitefield and then Wesley adopted field preaching as a means to evangelize. Consequently extempore preaching, rather than reading a written or published sermon, was most suited to the purpose and circumstances of Evangelicals. These circumstances of Anglican Evangelical preaching should not obscure the fact that it often adopted new rhetorical forms. One of the features of many Evangelical sermons was their 'rhetorical direction' towards personal interaction with God and an emphasis on the personal that has been called 'the communality of "us", or the introversion of "me"'.[42]

Methodism, and the Anglican Evangelical movement generally, provided the most significant examples of celebrity preaching in this period. There were, of course, preachers who built up a reputation for excellence who were not Evangelicals: Thomas Secker's church at St James's, Piccadilly, was said to be always full when he was due to preach. Even a priest who was unpopular with his own parishioners, like Parson Skinner of Camerton, could attract a good congregation when he preached.[43] But it was the Evangelical clergy who attracted huge audiences and developed powerful reputations for their sermons. Such reputations were often made by word of mouth. There were some guides to which were the best preachers, such as *Pulpit Elocution, or Characters and Principles of the most popular Preachers of each Denomination in the Metropolis and its Environs* (1782), which offered Londoners pen-portraits of

[41] Schlenther, 'Whitefield'.
[42] Bob Tennant, 'The Sermons of the Eighteenth-Century Evangelicals', in Francis and Gibson (eds.), *The British Sermon 1689–1901*, pp. 114–35.
[43] Downey, *Eighteenth-Century Pulpit*, p. 90; John Skinner, *The Journal of a Somerset Rector 1803–1834*, ed. Howard Coombs and Arthur N. Bax (Oxford, 1984), p. 167.

each of the preachers and suggestions of which to go and hear. In the rest of country there were no such directories, yet people there also sought out impressive preachers. In Wales, the preaching of Daniel Rowlands and Griffith Jones attracted enormous crowds. Rowlands in particular had the reputation of emptying local churches when he agreed to preach in a particular locality, as people flocked to hear him.[44]

PREACHING AND ANGLICAN GLOBALIZATION

Sermons were an important means by which Anglicanism spread across the world as Britain gained territorial possessions in a succession of wars in this period. The SPG was founded in 1701 with the mission to supply clergy for British colonies, and to convert the indigenous peoples in North America and in the Caribbean. The sermons preached for the Society in London, and by its missionaries in the plantations and colonies, began the process of constructing an overseas identity for Anglicanism. The London preachers were the elite clergy, often bishops, and their sermons were published annually for the public to buy and read. They chose biblical texts which resonated with the SPG's mission, often those relating to Jewish expansion and to Christ's injunctions to evangelize. Naturally they tended to show some antagonism to Britain's foes in the colonial field, especially the French and Spanish. But their central message was the providential Anglican mission to Christianize and Protestantize the populations in British colonies. It was a providential mission because Britain was presented as a new Israel, expanding outwards with a heavenly sanction and a divine duty. These preachers placed great emphasis on the moral behaviour to be demanded of native peoples. The loss of the North American colonies was a blow to the SPG, though Beilby Porteus did his best in 1783 to argue that the Society needed to refocus its work on the black slaves of the Caribbean, who might be transformed into smallholders enjoying all the benefits of Anglicanism, including marriage.[45] Above all, SPG sermons emphasized that, though distant from home and despite having no parish or diocesan structure, colonists remained Anglican and possessed all the duties and benefits of the Church of England.[46]

The character of Anglicanism which developed in the colonies carried with it an emphasis on the sermon. In the Caribbean and North America, and later

[44] A. Skevington Wood, *The Inextinguishable Blaze* (London, 1960), p. 46.

[45] Beilby Porteus, *A Sermon preached before the Incorporated Society for the Propagation of the Gospel in Foreign Parts . . . on Friday, February 21, 1783* (London, 1783).

[46] Rowan Strong, 'Eighteenth-Century Mission Sermons', in Francis and Gibson (eds.), *The British Sermon 1689–1901*, pp. 497–512.

colonies in the East and Africa, missionaries were initially without church buildings and had limited access to episcopal ministry. In consequence, sermons were a principal form of religious instruction, observance, and devotion. In colonial North America, the puritan Cotton Mather referred to the sermon as the 'net of salvation', it being the main means to capture and hold believers; the same was true for Anglicans.[47] Consequently the sermon, especially in North America, became the centrepiece of religious life, with weekday sermons complementing Sunday worship. As in England, sermons in North America both reflected and formed attitudes and cultural identity.[48] With the building of the King's Chapel in Boston in 1689, sermons gradually began to shed their puritan character and became part of a liturgical suite of worship with prayers, eucharist, and Bible reading.

The SPG, like the SPCK, developed a large publishing network to supply thousands of printed sermons to the colonies. Sermons were also responsible for the growth of publishing in North America as they had been in Britain. Between 1738 and 1741 George Whitefield's publications made up more than half of the output of all publishers in the American colonies; and Benjamin Franklin built a substantial business from his association with Whitefield.[49] This print culture created a transatlantic religious community as, increasingly, Whitefield's sermons preached and printed in America were imported to Britain and vice versa.

Missionaries in North America and the Caribbean were able to use sermons to build congregations because the centres of population were developing alongside the Churches. In India this was not the case. The East India Company employed chaplains to serve the Anglican colonists in the factories of Madras and Calcutta but it was only late in the eighteenth century that missionaries, not employed by the company, were sent to evangelize the people of India. Consequently sermons in Britain's colonies in the East often appeared first in printed form, as it was much easier and cheaper to send published sermons than to train and send missionaries. Joanna Cruickshank has dated the arrival of the sermon in Australia to 3 February 1788, when the chaplain of the First Fleet, Richard Johnson, preached at Sydney Cove to convicts, sailors, and soldiers. Johnson brought with him books published by the SPCK, including a hundred copies of Stephen White's sermon on stealing, first published in 1747. Four years later Johnson was also to preach the first published sermon in Australia (though it had previously been printed in Britain). Anglican sermons dominated the growing print culture of Australia up to the middle of the nineteenth century,

[47] E.g. Ronald A. Bosco, 'Lectures at the Pillory: The Early American Execution Sermon', *American Quarterly*, 30 (1978): 156–76 (p. 158).

[48] E.g. Perry Miller, *The New England Mind: The Seventeenth-Century* (Cambridge, MA, 1939); Perry Miller, *The New England Mind: From Colony to Province* (Cambridge, MA, 1953).

[49] Schlenther, 'Whitefield'.

and the majority of these were the sort of occasional and commemorative sermons which were also found in Britain, for visitations, ordinations, consecrations, funerals, and national events.[50] As in Britain, the printed sermon represented only a tiny fraction of preaching; from 1795 the preachers of the London Missionary Society adopted itinerant preaching in the colonies as their principal activity. Another similarity with Britain was the preoccupation of many sermons with behaviour: Sabbath-breaking, swearing, drunkenness, theft, and immorality were favourite subjects for preaching and for the printed sermon.

SERMONS AND CAMPAIGNS

Anglican sermons were also central to the growth of humanitarianism and philanthropy in Britain. Many humanitarian organizations adopted the sermon as a means of raising funds. In 1782 it was said that when Colin Milne at St Sepulchre's, Snow Hill, was asked to preach to raise funds 'a handsome collection was made and the subscription (for the Humane Soc) was enlarged' and that 'people, when they go elsewhere to be entertained must pay'.[51] The campaign against the slave trade employed sermons as a means of raising both funds and public interest in their cause. It drew together Evangelicals and Tories such as William Agutter, who preached against slavery in Oxford in 1788, arguing that Christianity had superseded the Old Testament sanction of slavery.[52] Sermons were the principal means by which most people encountered the anti-slavery campaign and they were heard in some of the most fashionable churches and chapels of the country, and delivered by some of the leading preachers.[53] In 1788, Bishop Porteus, a long-standing supporter of the movement, and a critic of the Anglican use of slaves on the Codrington estate in Barbados, preached a highly influential sermon which added to the growing national debate.[54] The demand for abolition was taken up in pulpits throughout the country and here too they became a method of public broadcast, this time in a cause that won widespread support as a result. Besides

[50] Joanna Cruickshank, 'The Sermon in the British Colonies', in Francis and Gibson (eds.), *The British Sermon 1689–1901*, pp. 513–29.

[51] *Pulpit Elocution* (1782), pp. 13, 16.

[52] William Agutter, *The Abolition of the Slave-Trade considered in a Religious Point of View: A Sermon preached before the Corporation of the City of Oxford at St Martin's Church, on Sunday, February 3, 1788* (London, 1788).

[53] Philip Peckard, *Justice and Mercy recommended, particularly with reference to the Slave Trade: A Sermon preached before the University of Cambridge* (Cambridge, 1788).

[54] Bob Tennant, 'Sentiment, Politics, and Empire: A Study of Beilby Porteus's Antislavery Sermon', in Brycchan Carey, Markman Ellis, and Sara Salih (eds.), *Discourses of Slavery and Abolition: Britain and its Colonies, 1760–1838* (Basingstoke, 2004), pp. 158–74.

printed tracts, it is difficult to find a means by which the anti-slavery movement was spread which was as effective as the sermon.

SERMONS, CHURCHES, AND PULPITS

Preaching was so significant that it determined the architecture and arrangement of Anglican churches and strongly influenced their rebuilding and renovation. The auditory church, which dominated church architecture from 1660 to 1820, was essentially an expression of the central place of sermons in the Anglican liturgy. Single-chamber churches gave equal, and often greater, attention to the pulpit than to the altar. Wren's St James's, Piccadilly, of 1684 was the model for such churches in London and was emulated by many others, including Gibbs's St Martin-in-the-Fields, built in 1726. Such architects made careful calculations of acoustics from the pulpits of their churches, and architects regarded the pulpit as a central feature of the architecture of the buildings they designed.[55] Parson James Woodforde even moved his pulpit in 1775 so that it had greater prominence. The placing of the pulpit was a central concern in the arrangement of churches; at St Peter's, Leeds, in 1714 it was moved twice during the renovation.[56] Acoustics were important to enable preachers' voices to reach the whole congregation. In March 1790 the pulpit at All Saints, Newcastle, was resited in front of the communion rails because of the 'auditory difficulties' of the building's circular design—although Jane Harvey complained in Newcastle four years later that the shape of the church still led to the 'drowning of the voice of the preacher ... rendering it impossible for those seated at a distance to hear distinctly'.[57] The same problem was resolved in the chapel of the Foundling Hospital in London in 1780 by repositioning the pulpit so that the 'Congregation would hear much better'. In 1799 a committee of MPs led by William Wilberforce sought a solution for the acoustic problems of St Margaret's, Westminster, where the large space of the nave 'considerably weakens [the] voice of [the] preacher' and the frequent removal of the pulpit for the annual music festival had damaged it. In historic churches where nothing could be done about the acoustics, novel solutions were sometimes found. In St Mary le Strand in 1728, the noise from the street was so great that the preacher used a 'speaking trumpet' to magnify his voice to the congregation. In 1791 the architect C. R. Cockerell was instructed to renovate St Mary's,

---

[55] Terry Friedman, *The Eighteenth-Century Church in Britain* (London, 2011), p. 99.

[56] W. M. Jacob, *The Clerical Profession in the Long Eighteenth Century, 1680–1840* (Oxford, 2007), p. 257; Jonathan Oates (ed.), *The Memoranda Book of John Lucas 1712–1750*, Thoresby Society, 2nd series, 16 (London, 2006), p. 41.

[57] [Jane Harvey], *A Sentimental Tour through Newcastle; By a Young Lady* (Newcastle, 1794), p. 13.

Banbury, in such a way as to enable the pulpit to be central to the church and also to design a suitably imposing tester for it.[58]

The ability to see the preacher was also important. At Beverley Minster the problem of restoring the church and making the pulpit a central feature was resolved by constructing it with wheels so that it could be moved to the centre of the minster for sermons.[59] In November 1789, when St Paul's, Covent Garden, was renovated, the *Public Advertiser* claimed that the new pulpit 'deserves as much attention as...[any] other part of [the] repair'.[60] In the renovation of St Nicholas's, High Street, Bristol, in 1798 the effect was 'well calculated for [the] audience all to see [and] hear [the] preacher'.[61] In St Paul's, Liverpool, in 1774 it was noted that the church contained a remarkable pulpit with a movable staircase 'unseen by [the] congregation, by which [the] preacher gradually ascends to public view'.[62]

Sermons were often the means by which clergy appealed to their congregations to fund new church buildings.[63] Such a sermon in Leeds in January 1722 produced subscriptions of £35 from the Newcastle Corporation, £200 from Christopher Watkinson of Hamburg, £50 from Sir Thomas Wentworth, and £50 from the earl of Burlington.[64] Equally a subscription in May 1788 for extending St Chad's Cathedral in Lichfield was raised because the nave could not accommodate the size of the congregation during sermons.[65] In August 1712, when Nathaniel Crewe, bishop of Durham, consecrated a new church in Stockton, his chaplain, Mr Smith, preached of the 'commendable zeal for building churches which distinguished the reign of Queen Anne'.[66] Because the opening of a new church was attended by a sermon it was often referred to as its 'preaching in'. By the end of the century the architect George Steuart was so frequently asked to install new pulpits in churches that he had a number of standard designs from which builders could choose.

SERMONS AND CULTURE

Anglican sermons were a reflection of, and an influence upon, the wider culture of Britain. They featured in works of fiction, both poetry and the

[58] Friedman, *Eighteenth-Century Church in Britain*, CD-Rom, 'Documents', pp. 302, 589, 734, 760, 18, 21.

[59] Friedman, 'Documents', p. 38.   [60] *Public Advertiser*, 3 Nov. 1789, p. 4.

[61] [George Heath], *The New Bristol Guide* (Bristol, 1799), p. 118.

[62] Friedman, 'Documents', p. 276.   [63] Friedman, 'Documents', pp. 245–6.

[64] Accounts from the rebuilding of Holy Trinity, Leeds, f. 37, Leeds, West Yorkshire Archive Service, Accounts 35.

[65] Friedman, 'Documents', p. 258.

[66] John Brewster, *The Parochial History and Antiquities of Stockton upon Tees* (Stockton, 1796), pp. 121–2.

emerging form of the novel. In Henry Fielding's *Joseph Andrews*, he compared the popularity of sermons to that of plays. Fielding was a layman who
wrote sermons, and was not beyond mocking them, but his gentle scorn for
some sermons was derived in part from their popularity. Sermons also
featured strongly in Samuel Richardson's novels. The popular sermons
preached at the Three Choirs Festival in Hereford, Worcester, and Gloucester
from the 1720s also reached a London audience in printed form and demonstrated the extensive connections between music and preaching. This was
not unique: the Corporation of the Sons of the Clergy organized music
festivals with sermons and local clergy took up this model in organizing
events in Norfolk (1684), Bristol (1692), Chester (1697), Suffolk (1704), York
(1722), and Durham (1726).[67] St Cecilia's Day services were also often attended with sermons which marked the association between music and religion.

Sermons spawned a wide material culture also. There were preaching
gloves, preaching cloths, cushions, hourglasses, and candle-holders in pulpits.
'Sermon paper' (a standard size of paper named because of its popularity for
use in printed sermons), parish and circulating libraries (which were initially
dependent on sermons for their stock), commemorative medals of sermons
(such as Sacheverell's, Whitefield's, and Wesley's), and china models of
popular preachers such as Wesley and Whitefield were all ways in which the
sermon reached beyond the experience of hearing in church into the homes
and the economy of Britain.

In the twenty-first century sermons and preaching have, in the colloquial,
acquired a negative connotation, but it is important to recall that this was not
always so. For many, perhaps most, people in the long eighteenth century, to
be preached to and to hear a sermon was often inspiring and stimulating.
Preaching brought moral instruction, religious devotion, and often new ideas
and controversies to the public. In remote places, rural parishes, and overseas
they connected congregations with the rest of the Church. The printed sermon,
whether singly or in collections, dominated the best-sellers in the period.
Consequently they were the principal means for Anglicanism to broadcast its
religious, political, moral, educational, and controversial goals both to England
and to its growing empire.

---

[67] Andrew Pink, 'Order and Uniformity, Decorum, and Taste: Sermons Preached at the
Anniversary Meeting of the Three Choirs, 1720–1800', in Francis and Gibson (eds.), *The British
Sermon 1689–1901*, pp. 215–27; Nicholas Cox, *Bridging the Gap: A History of the Corporation of
the Sons of the Clergy over 300 Years, 1655–1978* (Oxford, 1978), pp. 36–9.

SELECT BIBLIOGRAPHY

Appleby, David J., *Black Bartholomew's Day: Preaching, Polemic and Restoration Nonconformity* (Manchester, 2007).

Downey, James, *The Eighteenth-Century Pulpit* (Oxford, 1969).

Eijnatten, Joris van (ed.), *Preaching, Sermon and Cultural Change in the Long Eighteenth Century* (Leiden, 2009).

Ellison, Robert H. (ed.), *A New History of the Sermon: The Nineteenth Century* (Leiden, 2010).

Francis, Keith A. and William Gibson (eds.), *The Oxford Handbook of the British Sermon 1689–1901* (Oxford, 2012).

Friedman, Terry, *The Eighteenth-Century Church in Britain* (London, 2011).

Gibson, William, *Enlightenment Prelate: Benjamin Hoadly, 1676–1761* (Cambridge, 2004).

Gibson, William, *James II and the Trial of the Seven Bishops* (Basingstoke, 2009).

Gibson, William, 'John Trusler and the Sermon Culture of the Late Eighteenth Century', *Journal of Ecclesiastical History*, 66 (2015): 302–19.

Haydon, Colin, *Anti-Catholicism in Eighteenth-Century England c.1714–80* (Manchester, 1994).

Ingram, Robert G., '"The Weight of Historical Evidence": Conyers Middleton and the Eighteenth-Century Miracles Debate', in Robert D. Cornwall and William Gibson (eds.), *Religion, Politics and Dissent, 1660–1832: Essays in Honour of James E. Bradley* (Aldershot, 2010), pp. 85–109.

Jacob, W. M., *The Clerical Profession in the Long Eighteenth Century, 1680–1840* (Oxford, 2007).

Lessenich, Rolf P., *Elements of Pulpit Oratory in Eighteenth-Century England (1660–1800)* (Vienna, 1972).

McCullough, Peter, Hugh Adlington, and Emma Rhatigan (eds.), *The Oxford Handbook of the Early Modern Sermon* (Oxford, 2011).

Stone, Michael (ed.), *The Diary of John Longe, Vicar of Coddenham, 1764–1832* (Woodbridge, 2008).

16

Church, Parties, and Politics

J. C. D. Clark

Church parties and their conflicts were an embarrassment for the pre-Tractarian Church of England. In 1822 Richard Whately, fellow of Oriel, saw party divisions as threatening enough to devote his Bampton Lectures to 'the evils which arise from the perversions and the inordinate violence of party-feeling'. 'The baneful effects of party-spirit, and its train of accompanying evil passions, are too common (unhappily) and well-known especially in the Christian Church, to need being much insisted on. In fact, ecclesiastical history consists mainly of a detail of them.' He named few names. In footnotes, he censured only Wesley, Priestley, and unnamed theologians 'who have written on the Calvinistic questions'. In his text, Whately specified no recent parties within the Church except, and that only once, theological ones ('Calvinist, Arminian, Hutchinsonian') or those that relied on the appropriation of words in common use ('such terms as, "Serious," "Evangelical," "Religious," or, "Orthodox"').

For tactical reasons, Whately's advice was 'to avoid as much as possible the *names* of parties', even though 'many of them have been so established by long usage'. 'This plan, if steadily pursued, will have a tendency to bring many of them, gradually, into comparative disuse.' Consequently, although he wrote of 'the two opposite parties', he also asserted: 'With respect to the parties actually existing in our Church, an attempt to characterize them distinctly, and to describe fully the respective faults which are most prevalent in each, would not only be invidious, and perhaps mischievous, but would in fact be in some degree foreign to the purpose of these lectures.' Whately congratulated himself on 'steering a middle course between opposite extremes'. But his purpose was irenic chiefly because of his belief that 'practically speaking, all truth is relative' in a present in which 'there are no supernatural gifts'.[1]

---

[1] Richard Whately, *The Use and Abuse of Party-Feeling in Matters of Religion considered* (Oxford, 1822), pp. 30, 46–7, 50–1, 119, 122, 258–9, 262, 269–70.

Others were similarly influenced by their own theologies, and similarly tried to avoid labels. In a work published in 1798 a High Churchman, Charles Daubeny, used no party names even while arguing that the Church was 'a spiritual society under the regular establishment of its Divine Founder', separation from which was schism; mentioning Latitudinarianism only once, as a 'way of thinking and acting', not a party; and citing in defence of episcopacy William Law's second reply to Benjamin Hoadly of 1717 (in his second edition of 1804, however, Daubeny defended himself from 'the titles of bigot and high-churchman', since the second should mean only 'a decided and principled attachment to the Apostolic government of the Church').[2] An Evangelical conceded that 'The Ministers of the National Church may be divided into the Secular, the Latitudinarian, the Orthodox, and the Evangelical', but he diagnosed them in terms of 'energetic spirituality' and termed each a 'class' rather than a 'party'. For him, 'Evangelical' was a label 'applied ... in common parlance' to the friends of 'vital Christianity'; he almost never used 'High Church', and even ignored its reassertion in Bishop Horsley's *Charge* of 1790, which he cited.[3] It was an outsider, the Unitarian Thomas Belsham, who openly asserted that 'The ESTABLISHED CHURCH is at this time divided into two great parties': 'the High Church party', who 'adhere to the Church upon the ground of *political expedience*', and 'those who are commonly called Evangelical', plus a group within the Church who thought for themselves and were 'watchful for an opportunity' of reforming its theology.[4]

From the 1790s to the 1810s there was much common ground between High Church and Evangelical, and although conflicts were growing by 1822, battle lines were not then drawn. Yet just this eventually happened: Orthodox, Evangelical, and Oriel Noetic began to pull apart, a trend that Tractarianism accentuated but did not originate.[5] The moment of definition came in 1853 when the *Edinburgh Review* published a lengthy untitled account of three recent books, under the running head 'Church Parties'.[6] Of these parties the anonymous reviewer posited three: the 'High'; the 'Broad', a term devised by himself; and the 'Low', or Evangelical. The 'High' and 'Low' were further

---

[2] Charles Daubeny, *A Guide to the Church, in several Discourses* (London, 1798), pp. vii, 2, 16, 27, 423, 457 (2nd edn., 2 vols. [London, 1804], I, pp. xliii–xliv).

[3] John White Middleton, *An Ecclesiastical Memoir of the First Four Decades of the Reign of George the Third* (London, 1822), pp. 20, 32.

[4] Thomas Belsham, *The Present State of Religious Parties in England represented and improved* (London, 1818), pp. 9, 11–13.

[5] Peter B. Nockles, 'Church Parties in the Pre-Tractarian Church of England 1750–1833: The "Orthodox"—Some Problems of Definition and Identity', in John Walsh, Colin Haydon, and Stephen Taylor (eds.), *The Church of England c.1689–c.1833: From Toleration to Tractarianism* (Cambridge, 1993), pp. 334–59 (pp. 347, 351–5).

[6] W. J. Conybeare, 'Church Parties', ed. Arthur Burns, in Stephen Taylor (ed.), *From Cranmer to Davidson: A Church of England Miscellany* (Woodbridge, 1999), pp. 213–385, reprinting the essay from *Edinburgh Review*, 98(200) (Oct. 1853): 273–342.

subdivided ('exaggerated', 'stagnant', 'normal') in ways that disparaged most of their alleged adherents. 'High Church' and 'Low Church' were categories of long standing; the reviewer was original in claiming the existence of a separate, intermediate, and moderate 'Broad Church' position which could correct the other two. Now the Evangelicals and High Churchmen were to be demoted and parodied, and a liberal tradition elevated, or invented, as a solution to the problem that the other two allegedly posed.[7]

The essay caused a sensation, and was several times reprinted in the 1850s as a separate work. After its author was revealed as the Revd William John Conybeare (1815–57), he included a revised version in his *Essays Ecclesiastical and Social* (1855); the piece became an influential academic analysis, beyond its initial journalistic purpose. Conybeare was a former fellow of the then liberally inclined Trinity College, Cambridge, a man of (in his own terms) Broad Church sympathies, currently vicar of the well-endowed living of Axminster, Devon, but dying slowly of tuberculosis. His object may have been to overstate the reification of Church parties in the 1850s in order to condemn the idea of such division per se, but to reunite them on a Broad Church basis.[8]

By virtue of his early death, Conybeare was unable to witness life imitate art: the Church of England came increasingly to act out his polemical analysis, and to resolve itself in its self-understanding into three parties, in mutual rivalry for the spoils of the establishment. Anglican historians, too, often came in the nineteenth century to echo this three-party model, adopting it as an interpretative framework and projecting it back onto the long eighteenth century in order to blame the alleged 'spiritual lethargy' of that period on another party than the historian's. Academic debate was mainly between optimists and pessimists in their assessment of the Church's pastoral effectiveness; its tripartite party composition was generally taken as given.[9]

This investigation concerns the decades before Conybeare's survey. He had begun his review:

> The three writers whose works are named above may be taken as representatives of the three great parties which divide the Church of England. These parties have always existed, under different phases, and with more or less of life. But they have been brought into sharper contrast, and have learned better to understand themselves and one another, during the controversies which have agitated the last twenty years. They are commonly called the Low Church, the High Church, and the Broad Church parties... It would be an interesting task to trace these parties historically, from the Reformation downwards; to show how far they may

[7] Nockles, 'Church Parties', pp. 347–8.

[8] Burns, in Conybeare, 'Church Parties', ed. Burns, p. 233.

[9] John Walsh and Stephen Taylor, 'Introduction', to Walsh et al. (eds.), *The Church of England*, pp. 1–64 (pp. 1–4).

be regarded as continuous branches, how far as modern revivals, how far as new modifications of ancient schools of opinion. But this would require researches far too extensive for our limits.[10]

Such historical reconstruction was a task less urgent to the combatants of the 1850s than the prosecution of their current antagonisms. It was, indeed, never properly undertaken.

Historians in the late twentieth century became cautious of accepting a variety of Victorian claims to long intellectual antecedents. The historians' emphasis was instead on the differences of late seventeenth- and eighteenth-century practice, doctrine, and sensibility from what came later. This caution was entirely proper. But it established a dominant assumption: the eighteenth-century Church of England, in the work of historians from Norman Sykes (1897–1961) onwards, was generally depicted as consensual, unified, and moderate, pursuing its pastoral task with more or less efficiency (according to the historian), but without the profound divisions suffered by its Victorian descendant. It is appropriate to reconsider this genealogy, and to ask how far Conybeare had grounds for seeing the alignments of 1853 as having been long anticipated.

Any attempt to trace long antecedents for the groups or 'parties' of 1853 raises problems of definition: in one approach, their existence depended on the possibility of the objective classification of Church members, yet this eluded Conybeare for his own day and is even more difficult for earlier centuries.[11] In another approach, the historian's task is only to record what contemporaries said about the matter: parties had no objective existence, but were influential insofar as people thought them real. Party language from the seventeenth century onwards was polemical, designed to achieve certain ends, not an anticipation of the sociology of religion: yet, as such, it could be powerful.

HIGH CHURCH

Conybeare's partisanship was evident in his account of the origins of the High Church party. They were 'The "Church and King men," who flourished thirty, fifty, or seventy years ago'; they 'were a political, and not a religious party. They sometimes talked of Orthodoxy, at Visitation Dinners or University Elections; but they meant by Orthodoxy not any theological creed, but love of tithes and hatred of Methodists.' Conybeare distinguished them from the 'true High Church theology' which 'represents the dominant school of the

---

[10] Conybeare, 'Church Parties', ed. Burns, p. 259.
[11] Burns, in Conybeare, 'Church Parties', ed. Burns, pp. 229–31.

Caroline epoch … This party died out at the beginning of the last century, after its exaggerated phase (with which we have recently been again familiarised) had developed itself in the Non-jurors.' Conybeare sought to disparage the High Churchmen of his time by dissociating them from churchmen of the seventeenth century, who held 'that system of belief which was maintained by Bull and Pearson'. According to Conybeare, in his own day 'the watchwords of the School are *"Judgment by works," "Baptismal Regeneration," "Church Authority,"* and *"Apostolical Succession"'*. But he claimed that High Church tenets concerning the apostolic succession and Church authority were, by the 1850s, 'not the basis of their system, but only secondary and ornamental details'. Only among the Tractarians was this different: 'a fabric may be built upon them [those tenets] at which the Anglican stands aghast'; Tractarians were 'those bold essayists who revived, twenty years ago, the theology of Laud'.[12]

To Conybeare, between the Caroline divines and the French Revolution lay a chasm. The Tractarians' arguments meant that 'Christianity becomes a system of magical forms and incantations, tending to the exaltation of the sacerdotal office'; but such magical forms had faded away in the torpor of the mid-Hanoverian period.[13] Recent scholarship casts doubt on this polemical scenario.[14] Many churchmen responded to Interregnum sectarianism by emphasizing the essentially episcopalian nature of church polity, the catholicity of the Church of England, the real presence, the authority of the priest to remit sins, the insufficiency of the Scriptures without an authoritative guide, and prayers for the dead: during the Restoration these might attract, if only occasionally, the disparaging label '*High-Church-Man*'.[15] Previously, 'High' and 'Low' churches referred literally to the elevation of buildings, a locution that for obvious reasons survived in Scotland.[16] The metaphorical use of these terms to refer to ecclesiology was widely propagated only after the conflicts produced by the Revolution of 1688 and the impetus it gave to the further reification of Whig and Tory identities in politics.[17]

[12] Conybeare, 'Church Parties', ed. Burns, pp. 300–2, 305, 313.

[13] Conybeare, 'Church Parties', ed. Burns, p. 314.

[14] Richard Sharp, 'New Perspectives on the High Church Tradition: Historical Background 1730–1780', in Geoffrey Rowell (ed.), *Tradition Renewed: The Oxford Movement Conference Papers* (London, 1986), pp. 4–23; F. C. Mather, *High Church Prophet: Bishop Samuel Horsley (1733–1806) and the Caroline Tradition in the Later Georgian Church* (Oxford, 1992), pp. 1–23; Peter B. Nockles, *The Oxford Movement in Context: Anglican High Churchmanship 1760–1857* (Cambridge, 1994), pp. 1–32, 44–57, 104–9, 146–56.

[15] *The Reformed Papist, or High-Church-Man: Characterized in Reflections on his Principles and Designs* (London, 1681), pp. 2–4.

[16] E.g. Henry Hibbert, *Waters of Marah: Drawn forth in two Funerall Sermons, October 1653* (London, 1654), sig. A3ʳ.

[17] George Every, *The High Church Party 1688–1718* (London, 1956), pp. xiii, 1–2.

By the 1690s, these identities were well established; each side was eager to characterize the other. In 1702, the High Churchman Henry Sacheverell pointed to the moderate puritan Richard Baxter (1615–91) as 'the *God-Father, and Original of these Party-Names*' in 'his Answer to that Great Pillar and Light of our Church, the Venerable Mr. *Hooker*', High Church being 'the greatest Brand of Reproach'. It contrasted with 'the Fashionable and Endearing Name of *Low-Church-Man*'.[18] Sacheverell outlined the beliefs of a Whig author: the Whig would insinuate that his High Church opponent

> was *High* for the *Divine Right* of *Episcopacy*, *High* for the *Uninterrupted Succession* [to the throne], *High* for the *Liturgies* against *Extemporary Prayers*, *High* for the Primitive Doctrine and Discipline of the *Antient Church*: And, perhaps he would add, that he much lamented the Destruction of the *Episcopal Church* in *Scotland*, and should be for Addressing Her Majesty to restore it; that he believes *Separation* from the *Church of England* to be a Damning Schism, and...the Dissenters, to be in a very *dangerous* State, notwithstanding the *Toleration*. And Ten to One he [the Whig] would whisper, that he [his opponent] is an Enemy to all *Accommodations*, to *Comprehension* and *Trimming Moderation*; That he is so *High*, as to Observe the *Traditional* Customs, as well as the *Written* Laws of the Church; that he always *Bow'd* very low towards the *Altar*, and at the Name of Jesus. And to Sum up his Character, perhaps he would not omit his Hatred to *Conquest* [as a theory of the Revolution] and *Translations* [of bishops, to prevent which the High Church MP Sir John Packington had introduced a Bill].

But these, contended Sacheverell, were merely the positions of the Church itself. 'If therefore they will make any *Distinction*, let it be of *Church-Men* and *Atheists, High-Church*, and *No-Church*'.[19]

In Anne's reign the party labels were still new enough to elicit elaborate exercises in definition, one author similarly disputing 'the Distinction of *High-Church* and *Low-Church*' since the first, on examination, was merely synonymous with a zealous churchman, 'truly and sincerely for the Church of *England*', 'strict in the Observance of its Rules and Orders' and having 'Concern for its Safety', but the latter, who 'enjoy her Dignities and Preferments, and maintain a sort of outward Conformity, but at the same time have no inward liking to her Constitution', were indeed '*no* Church-Men'.[20] Sacheverell had no hesitation in using party names; but another author condemned 'that foolish and pernicious Distinction of *High* and *Low* Church, which you and I could not understand the Meaning of', and lamented that

---

[18] [Henry Sacheverell], *The Character of a Low-Church-man: Drawn in Answer to the True Character of a Church-Man: Shewing the false Pretences to that Name* ([?London], 1702), pp. 7, 27.

[19] [Sacheverell], *Character of a Low-Church-man*, pp. 26–8.

[20] Anon., *The Distinction of High-Church and Low-Church, distinctly considered and fairly stated: With some Reflections upon the popular Plea of Moderation* (London, 1705), pp. 7, 22–4, 28–30, 34–5.

friends had been forced into different camps 'for so the contending parties will have it', only to propose, as terms of unity, an obviously High Church ecclesiology.[21]

High Churchmen of the Restoration sought to reinstate an ideal of uniformity of practice and homogeneity of religious worship in the Established Church. This attempt has sometimes been held to have been terminated by the Toleration Act of 1689, but clergy continued to fight the battle; the Occasional Conformity Act of 1711 and the Schism Act of 1714 were achievements of this phase, and although both were repealed in 1719, no one could know if or when the political tide might reverse itself. In subsequent decades, excluded from the highest office, a Tory and High Church tradition survived on the basis of private patronage and the networks still fed by Oxford University.

By the 1720s, the idea of a High Church identity was so clearly established that a freethinker could combat it by linking it with a political identity, denigrating 'the High-Church *Jacobite* Clergy of *England*'. This link was appropriate, he claimed, since any argument for 'a sole, divine, apostolick, and independent Power in the Bishops to govern the Church' had to end in '*Popery*'. The author, probably the anti-clerical polemicist Thomas Gordon, analysed the High Church into component parts. The first part he named after 'Dr. Bungey', John Dunton's satirical nickname for Henry Sacheverell:

> Dr. *Bungey*'s High-Church stands distinguish'd from the *True Church of England*; by their *Arminian* Doctrines, contrary to our old Orthodox *Calvinistical* Articles; by their Enmity to the Act of Toleration, and to the Principles on which it is grounded; by their claiming an Independent Power in Priests to make Laws, and govern the Church; which is contrary to the laws of *England*, that place the Power of making Church-Laws in other Hands, and particularly contrary to the Oath of Supremacy, which makes his Majesty Supreme Head of the Church; by teaching the Doctrines of Hereditary Right and Passive Obedience, contrary to the Judgment and Practice of the Legislature at and since the Revolution, and to the *Determination* of the House of Lords, on the Impeachment of Dr. SACHEVEREL, and their *Condemnation* of the *Oxford Decree*;[22] and by a Spirit of Faction against the present Establishment in State, and against his Majesty's Measures; by rebellion and Perjury, by Uncharitableness to all Foreign, and more especially to Domestick Protestants; and by an implacable Fury and Malice towards all Dissenters among us, besides *Jews* and *Papists*.

---

[21] Anon., *A Letter to a Friend concerning the new Distinction of High and Low Church* (London, 1704), pp. 2–7.

[22] *The Judgment and Decree of the University of Oxford past in their Convocation July 21. 1683, against certain pernicious Books and damnable Doctrines destructive to the Sacred Persons of Princes, their State and Government, and of all humane Society* (Oxford, 1683).

Even this Church was divided in two:

> Some of his High-Church are Swearers to the Government, and say the Church Prayers for His Majesty King GEORGE and his Family, continuing at the same Time disaffected to him, and Enemies to his Legal Title. Others of the Doctor's High-Church are *Non-swearers*; and, tho' they come to the Church, disown joining with the *Swearers* in the Prayers for the King and his Family; whose Practice the profound Mr. DODWELL has defended in a Book.

There was also the non-juror 'Mr. [Charles] LESLEY's High-Church'.

> At the *Revolution* several Bishops, who were deprived by Act of Parliament, for not taking the Oaths to the Government, made an open Separation from the Church of *England*; and pretended, that they and their Adherents were the Church, charging those who fill'd their Sees with being Usurpers, and setting up Altar against Altar; and also charging them and their Adherents, together with all the other Bishops, Clergy and Laity, who join'd in the same Communion with the usurping Bishops, with *Schism*. Hereby also they distinguish themselves in Principles from the Church of *England*; which, being a legal Establishment, asserts to the Legislature, which has a Right to preserve their Peace, a Right to deprive Bishops for Crimes against Law. They do not indeed so much distinguish themselves in Principles from Dr. *Bungey's* Church, as they do from the true Church of *England*: For the Doctor's Church equally contends with Mr. *Lesley's* Church against the Parliament's Right to deprive Bishops, and calls it Usurpation on the Rights of the Church; but is for Submission to such usurp'd Exercise of Power; and contends, Schism to be on the Side of those, who separate on a Principle of defending the Rights of the Church, against an Usurpation of those Rights.

There was a contrast with another component, to which was assigned the name of another non-juror, 'Dr. [Thomas] *Brett's* High-Church':

> Soon after King GEORGE'S Accession to the Crown, the Bishops of the last mention'd High-Church did all, except one, assemble in a Synod, where they resolv'd upon making *Four Alterations* in the Common-Prayer Book, *viz*. I. *To mix Water with the Wine in the Sacrament*. 2. *A Prayer for the Dead*. 3. *A Prayer for the Descent of the Holy Ghost upon the Bread and Wine in the Sacrament*. 4. *An Oblatory Prayer; which goes upon the Ground, that the Eucharist is a proper Sacrifice*. All which Dr. *Brett* is not only an Advocate for, as an Author, but (perhaps) as *Titular* Archbishop of *Canterbury*, exercised his Authority in enjoining. This has split the last High-Church into two Churches.[23]

This was the Usages controversy, which deeply divided the non-jurors. Although from a hostile perspective, *The Independent Whig* acutely observed the problems of the High Church party.

---

[23] [John Trenchard and Thomas Gordon], *The Independent Whig* (3rd edn., London, 1726), no. 12 (6 Apr. 1720), p. 123; no. 16 (4 May 1720), pp. 152, 154; no. 50 (24 Dec. 1720), pp. 447–51. I owe this reference to Richard Sharp.

Those problems did not prevent the survival of High Church positions within the Whig episcopate, in men like Archbishop John Potter $(c.1674-1747)^{24}$ and Bishop Edmund Gibson (1669–1748). Yet if the High Church party survived as a politically aware group, it could only be weakened by the Whig stranglehold on senior appointments and by the eclipse after the 1740s of the Jacobite option. Historians have discerned the entry into office after *c*.1740 of a new generation of clergy, whose minds had not been shaped by older polarities. In each diocese, contrasting styles of churchmanship were increasingly expressed in personal rather than party terms.[25] Yet 'High Church' survived in liturgical practice and in theology more clearly than in political conflict.[26]

As public debate subsided after the Bangorian controversy, the term 'Low Church' tended to fall out of use first; 'High Church' survived longer, as a term of abuse. By the 1760s it too had faded, sharing in the general decline of party political discourse. In 1768 William Knox explicitly linked the two languages: 'Whilst party distinctions of Whig and Tory, High Church and Low Church, Court and Country subsisted, the nation was divided, and each side held an opinion for which they would have hazarded every thing, for both acted from principle... But the abolition of party names seems to have destroyed all public principles among the people.'[27]

Yet from the 1750s, a surviving High Church tradition was given a theological rallying point by the followers of John Hutchinson (1674–1737); from the 1760s, George III's programmatic openness to former Tory politicians extended to churchmen also;[28] and from 1776, worldly loyalties placed High Churchmen on one side of a newly emerging political divide. A reverence for patristic tradition was made once again relevant by the attacks on it of Unitarians like Joseph Priestley. The political legacy of the early eighteenth century continued to deter use of the label 'High Church', but it finally came back into currency. As in the early eighteenth century, so in the later, a binary view of political conflict acted to promote a binary view of the alternatives within the Church of England, however divines might sense that the two categories did not map exactly onto each other.[29] In the age of the French Revolution, when political options were increasingly polarized, a prominent Unitarian could claim: 'The clergy of the Church of England may be divided into two classes, the HIGH and the LOW Church', stigmatizing the first, looking

[24] John Potter, *A Discourse of Church-Government* (London, 1707).

[25] Jeremy Gregory and Jeffrey S. Chamberlain (eds.), *The National Church in Local Perspective: The Church of England and the Regions, 1660–1800* (Woodbridge, 2003).

[26] Sharp, 'New Perspectives'.

[27] [William Knox], *The present State of the Nation: Particularly with respect to its Trade, Finances, &c. &c.* (London, 1768), p. 32.

[28] Walsh and Taylor, 'Introduction', p. 54.

[29] Walsh and Taylor, 'Introduction', pp. 34–5.

back to the early eighteenth century to claim that party's continuity, and contending that 'passive obedience and non-resistance are still the avowed principles of the Church'. Samuel Heywood asserted that Bishop Horsley's only claim to any special authority, the apostolic succession, had been, as Bishop Warburton 'admitted...lost in the English church at the revolution' of 1688. Among other historic sources, Heywood cited Bishop Gilbert Burnet, Lord Somers, Dr Sacheverell, *The Independent Whig*, and the role of Dissenters in the disturbances of 1715 and 1745: his analysis was historically preoccupied.[30]

Sacramental and liturgical practice, ecclesiology, and debates on Trinitarianism and Calvinism still divided the mid-eighteenth-century Church and created a large group, far beyond the Hutchinsonians, conscious of subscribing to a distinct theological position. If the name 'High Church' fell into disuse, inconvenient for its former political associations, it was generally replaced by a more diverse yet more ecumenically united identity, 'Orthodox'.[31] But 'High' and 'Low Church' were still easily intelligible terms, and could be revived, as they were by Charles James Fox in the Commons debate on the unsuccessful attempt to repeal the Test and Corporation Acts in 1790.[32]

This old debate now occurred in a dramatically new context. The circumstances of the French Revolution (both political and theological) posed new challenges, and the term 'High Church' was deliberately reasserted by Bishop Samuel Horsley in 1790. He claimed a theological meaning for it, and dissociated himself from its early eighteenth-century political baggage:

> a High-Church-Man, in the true sense of the word, is one that is a bigot to the secular rights of the Priesthood. One, who claims for the Hierarchy, upon pretence of a right inherent in the sacred office, all those Powers, Honours and Emoluments, which they enjoy under an establishment; which are held indeed by no other tenure, than at the will of the Prince, or by the law of the Land.

The older position he termed 'a folly, long since eradicated'. His clergy should not therefore be 'scared from your duty by the idle terror of a Nick-Name', but accept 'the spiritual authority of the priesthood': 'we must be content to be High-Churchmen according to this usage of the word, or we cannot at all be Churchmen'. As antidotes to the prevalent equation of religion and morality he recommended the works of Clement and Ignatius, 'either in the Original or in Bishop WAKE's translation', Hooker's *Ecclesiastical Polity*, the works of 'the

---

[30] [Samuel Heywood], *High Church Politics: Being a seasonable Appeal to the Friends of the British Constitution, against the Practices and Principles of High Churchmen; as exemplified in the late Opposition to the Repeal of the Test Laws, and in the Riots at Birmingham* (London, 1792), pp. 1–6, 9–10.

[31] Nockles, 'Church Parties', pp. 338–43.

[32] *The Debate in the House of Commons, on the Repeal of the Corporation and Test Acts, March 2d, 1790* (London, 1790), p. 55.

celebrated CHARLES LESLIE', and William Jones of Nayland's *An Essay on the Church* (1787).[33] This commanded much assent; but by 1822 an Evangelical assessed Horsley against Evangelical standards:

> High-churchmen were gratified by the dignified manner in which he maintained all questions of ecclesiastical privilege; by his zeal for episcopacy; by his powerful defence of orthodoxy, and keen opposition of heresy; by his remarkable attention to pontifical exterior, and by his demand of obsequious submission from the commonalty and laity to their temporal and spiritual governors.[34]

So the French Revolution polarized religious life as it did politics. After the Birmingham riots of 1791, the Unitarian Dissenter Joseph Priestley blamed Edmund Burke's *Reflections on the Revolution in France* (1790), 'which has contributed more than any other to excite a spirit of party; the clergy almost universally approving of it, and the low church party and Dissenters as generally condemning it'.[35] A moderate Whig thought it unnecessary to explain his reference to 'The author of *the Reflections* and the high church party'.[36] Another commentator condemned the anti-Jacobin reaction of which events at Birmingham were a part: 'The exploded *High Church and King* doctrines were now revived in full vigour.'[37] Such reactions tended to ignore High Church ecclesiology. By 1818, a Unitarian argued that only a few High Churchmen 'still contend for the divine right of episcopacy'; most defended it on 'the far more tenable ground of *political expedience*'.[38]

   One historian has estimated that half the bishops fell into the High Church party by 1800:[39] it was the group that Conybeare was later to subdivide as 'High and Dry'. Yet '[a]longside this school, and sharing many of its concerns, existed a doctrinally "Catholic" strain of High Churchmanship, represented on the bench by Horne and Horsley, more openly committed to the principle of apostolicity and engaged in a fervently sacramental piety'.[40] High Church-manship, then, still had a political dimension: from Conybeare's perspective, the events of 1833 had begun a civil war within an increasingly powerful High Church position between those who emphasized its ecclesiology and those who prioritized its political theology.

---

[33] *The Charge of Samuel [Horsley], Lord Bishop of St. David's, to the Clergy of his Diocese, delivered at his Primary Visitation, in the Year 1790* (Gloucester, 1790), pp. 33–6, 38.

[34] Middleton, *Ecclesiastical Memoir*, p. 328.

[35] Joseph Priestley, *An Appeal to the Public, on the Subject of the Riots in Birmingham* (Birmingham, 1791), p. 23.

[36] Sir Brooke Boothby, *Observations on the Appeal from the New to the Old Whigs, and on Paine's Rights of Man* (London, 1792), p. 23.

[37] [Thomas Bigge], *Considerations on the State of Parties, and the Means of effecting a Reconciliation between them* (London, [1793]), pp. 17, 33.

[38] Belsham, *Religious Parties*, p. 9.   [39] Mather, *High Church Prophet*, pp. 17, 210–12.

[40] Walsh and Taylor, 'Introduction', p. 35.

Inconsistently, Conybeare also presented 'the Anglican [High Church] party' as being of recent formation. They had not been responsible for 'such great measures of public morality as are due to the school of Wilberforce and Buxton. But this is no reproach to them; for they did not exist as a distinct party till those national reforms were accomplished.' It was indeed a revival; 'its creed is the same which nourished the piety of the best Churchman and the best Churchwoman of the seventeenth century'.[41] But this was a failure of historical understanding on Conybeare's part. He was not wholly wrong: the High Church tendency did take on greater coherence in the early decades of the nineteenth century, with expression in identities like that of the Hackney Phalanx, journals like *The British Critic* (1793), *The Orthodox Churchman's Magazine* (1801), and *The Christian Remembrancer* (1818), and in the clearly denominational National Society for the Education of the Poor (1811), and the Church Building Society (1817).[42] But its continuity was greater than Conybeare knew. Consequently, he reproved the Tractarians more than he understood them.

LOW CHURCH

Conybeare argued that the Low Church or Evangelical party 'originated in the revival of religious life, which marked the close of the last and the beginning of the present century,—the reaction against a long period of frozen lifelessness. The thermometer of the Church of England sank to its lowest point in the first thirty years of the reign of George III.' The Thirty-Nine Articles were regarded as merely token: 'by most they were neither believed nor disbelieved'. Conybeare argued that even the SPCK had fallen into 'languor and decrepitude' after the mid-eighteenth century.[43] Yet recent scholarship suggests that the failings of which Conybeare complained (jobbery, corruption, worldliness) were found in the Church in all ages, while episodes like the Bangorian controversy of 1717–19 and the Subscription controversy of 1772–4 engaged combatants who showed a high degree of principled commitment.

Conybeare's scenario here too showed a failure of historical understanding. The term 'Low Church' was at least as old as the 1690s, partly led by political divisions that followed the Revolution. Divisions persisted: William III sought to promote reliable clergy, and this accentuated the sense of a binary opposition, which was similarly reinforced after the Hanoverian accession in 1714.

---

[41] Conybeare, 'Church Parties', ed. Burns, pp. 306, 312.
[42] Walsh and Taylor, 'Introduction', p. 51.
[43] Conybeare, 'Church Parties', ed. Burns, pp. 259, 261, 267 n.

The long reigns of George I and George II gave ample scope for appointing Whig bishops and deans, who in turn operated a patronage network in the same cause; it 'produced, by 1740, an overwhelmingly Whiggish archidiaconate', and increasing numbers of parochial incumbents.[44] This was a victory for a self-aware Low Church rather than for 'frozen lifelessness': even Hoadly defended the ecclesiology of the Church in which his career flourished after 1714.

To Low Churchmen also, party divisions in the Church were both theological and political. In 1702 the High Churchman Henry Sacheverell offered a polemical account of the position of his archetypal Low Church opponent:

> *He believes very little or no* Revelation, *and had rather lay his* Faith *upon the substantial Evidences of his own Reason, than the precarious Authority of Divine Testimony. So that if he does* suppose *the being of a* God, *as for the Nature of* Jesus Christ, *he is not concern'd about his* Divinity, *whether his Union is* Hypostatical *or Accidental, being an utter Enemy to* hard Terms in Religion. *And therefore the* scholastick Jargon *of the* Trinity *will ill suit with one of so* polite a Genius, *so that he had rather be a* Deist, Socinian *or* Nestorian, *than Affront to his own Understanding with believing what is* Incomprehensible, *or be so rude, as to obtrude on others what he cannot* himself Explain. *He thinks the* Articles of the Church, *too* Stiff, Formal, and Strait-lac'd a Rule *to confine his* Faith in, *and Complements 'em out of their Rigour and Severity. He sets loose to all Opinions, can embrace those of every Sect, and is too good Natur'd to Prosecute any one for* Heresy or Schism. *He looks upon the Censuring* Atheism, Infidelity *or* False Doctrin, *as a Dogmatical Usurpation, as an Intrusion or breaking in upon that* Human Liberty *which he sets up as the* Measure *and* Extent *of his Belief. He makes the most he can of this* World, *being not over* Confident *of any other.*

In addition, the Low Churchman permitted 'occasional Communion, the most pernicious and Destructive Principle that ever the *Church of England* suffer'd under', and contended that 'Obedience' was due only to 'a *Legal Government*', of which legality 'the People are to be the *Judges*'. If so, 'there can be no such Thing as *Rebellion* in the World'. The Low Churchman adopted no 'Exalted Pretences' to 'Church-government'.

> *He looks upon the* Homilies *as* tolerably good, for the *Time* they were Compiled in; *but, that They contain some Doctrins, not so* suitable *to this Age. Being a Man of a* Condescending *and* Peaceable Temper, *He is for* making the Articles *and* Liturgy *to* comply with *Tender Consciences; and so very* Charitable, *as to let his* Dissenting Brethren *even into the Enjoyment of the* Church-Revenues. *He will not maintain the* Divine Right *of* Episcopacy, *for fear of Offending the* Reform'd Churches Abroad; *and to please his dear Friends, the* Fanaticks *at home, will, in case of Necessity, allow even a* Lay-Brother *to Ordain a* Presbyter. *He thinks the*

---

[44] Walsh and Taylor, 'Introduction', p. 31.

Ecclesiastical Canons *an* Encroachment *upon the* Civil Power, *and that* Christ's Kingdom *is not to be Establish'd by Force and Usurpation.*[45]

This was the hostile picture.

But Low Churchmen had a positive case to present. One agreed that High and Low Church was 'a silly and groundless Distinction', but only because *'the two Parties differ in little or nothing that is of any concern to the Church'.*[46] Low Churchmen too regarded themselves merely as true church-men; it was their opponents who deserved a party label, High Church, by going beyond the Church's position.[47] On 12 November 1712 the Whig bishop of Salisbury, Gilbert Burnet (1643–1715), finished a new preface to the third edition of his 'favourite Book', looking back on his ministerial career but with extreme anxiety: 'I see imminent Ruin hanging over this Church, and by consequence over the whole Reformation.' The new preface was mainly concerned with 'the unhappy Consequences that follow formed Parties', since 'Politics and Party eat out among us not only Study and Learning, but that which is the only Thing that is more valuable, a true Sense of Religion'. What had the Whig bishops done, Burnet asked, 'to occasion such tragical Out-cries; and to ingage so many of the Bodies of the Clergy into Jealousies of their Bishops, and into Combinations against them, as if they were betraying the Church and its Liberties?' Could the bishops have been to blame? 'What Reason have we given to the World by our manner of Living, to think we had our Posts only for the Advantages we reap by them, and that we do it even against our Consciences, and are only waiting an Opportunity to betray them?' In his day, 'we are unhappily broken among our selves, and under the Names of *High* and *Low* Church, there is a new Scene opened for Jealousy and Animosity'.

Burnet accepted that 'I my self am ranked among the *Low* Church-men', and offered an account, if idealized, of their position:

> They are cordially and conscientiously zealous for the Church, as Established by Law: But yet they think no human Constitution is so perfect, but that it may be made better, and that the Church would be both more secure and more unex-ceptionable, if the administration of the Discipline were put into other Hands, and in a better Method. They lay the Foundation of all that they believe in the Christian Religion in the Scriptures: These and these only are the Measures and Standard of their Faith. No great Names nor Shews of Authority over-awe them: They search the Scriptures, there they seek and find their Faith.

---

[45] [Sacheverell], *Character of a Low-Church-man*, pp. 9–10, 18–19.

[46] Anon., *The Low-Church-Men vindicated from the unjust Imputation of being No-Church-Men* (London, 1705), p. 4.

[47] [Richard West], *The true Character of a Church-Man, shewing the false Pretences to that Name* ([?London, ?1702]), pp. 4–5.

The idea of *adiaphora* underpinned their ecclesiology:

> They think that in Matters declared to be indifferent, no Harm could follow on it, if some Regard were had to the Scruples of those who divide from us, in order to the fortifying the Whole by Uniting us among our selves: But till that can be done, they think a kind Deportment towards Dissenters softens their Prejudices, and disposes them to hearken to the Reasons which they offer to them, with all the force they can, but without the asperity of Words, or a contemptuous Behaviour; in which they have succeeded so well, that they see no cause to change their Conduct.

But Burnet was explicit in his politicized anti-popery.

> [Low Churchmen] do indeed make a great difference between Dissenters and Papists: They consider the one as a handful of People true to the Protestant Religion, and to our national Interests, not capable of doing us much Mischief, and who are, as far as appears to them, contented with their Toleration, and are only desirous to secure and maintain it. They have another and a very different Opinion of Popery: They consider that Church, not only with relation to the many Opinions and Practices held by them; such as Transubstantiation, Purgatory, and the worshipping Saints and Images, and a great many more; they are persuaded that these are false and ill grounded, but they could easily bear with them, as they do with other Errors: But they consider Popery as a Conspiracy against the Liberty and Peace of Mankind, on design to engross the Wealth of the World into their own hands; and to destroy all that stand in their way, sticking at no Practice, how false, base, or cruel soever, that can advance this. This is the true ground of their Zeal against Popery, and indeed against every thing that has a Tendency that way.

This was a key part of the Low Church commitment to Erastianism:

> The pretending to an Independency of the Church on the State, is not only in their Opinion a plain attack made on the Supremacy, vested by Law in the Crown, and casting a Disgrace on our Reformers, and on every Step made in the Reformation, which are openly owned by the chief Promoters of this new Conceit: But it is a direct Opposition to the famed Place, so much stretched by the same Persons to serve other purposes, in the *13th* of the Romans, *Let every Soul be subject to the higher Powers*; in which all Subjects are equally comprehended. The Laws of GOD are certainly of a superiour Obligation to any human Authority; but where these Laws are silent, certainly all Subjects of what sort soever, are bound to obey the Laws of the Land where they live.

Erastianism went with anti-sacerdotalism. 'The raising the Power and Authority of sacred Functions beyond what is founded on clear Warrants in Scripture, is, they think, the readiest way to give the World such a Jealousy of them, and such an Aversion to them, as may make them lose the Authority that they ought to have, while they pretend to that they have not.'

And this, in turn, created for Low Churchmen common ground with all other Protestants:

> They dare not Unchurch all the Bodies of the Protestants beyond [the] Sea; nor deny to our Dissenters at home, the federal Rights common to all Christians, or leave them to uncovenanted Mercy. They do not annul their Baptisms, or think that they ought to be baptized again in a more regular manner, before they can be accounted Christians. They know of no Power in a Priest to pardon Sin, other than the declaring the Gospel-Pardon, upon the Conditions on which it is offered. They know of no Sacrifice in the Eucharist, other than the Commemorating that on the Cross, with the Oblation of the Prayers, Praises, and Almsgiving, prescribed in the Office. They are far from condemning private Judgment in Matters of Religion: This strikes at the Root of the whole Reformation, which could never have been compassed, if private Men have not a Right to judg for themselves; on the contrary, they think every Man is bound to judg for himself, which indeed he ought to do, in the Fear of God, and with all Humility and Caution. They look on all these Notions as Steps towards Popery; tho they do not conclude, that all those who have made them, designed that by so doing.

These theological positions had been indelibly reified in recent politics.

> This is a short Account of the *Low* Church-men's Notions, with relation to Matters of Religion among us. As to our temporal Concerns, they think that all Obedience and Submission that is settled by our Laws, to the Persons of our Princes, ought to be paid them for Conscience sake: But if a misguided Prince [James II] shall take on him to dissolve our Constitution, and to subject the Laws to his Pleasure, they think that if God offers a Remedy, it is to be received with all Thankfulness. For these reasons they rejoiced in the Revolution [of 1688], and continue Faithful and True to the Settlement then made, and to the subsequent Settlements. They think there is a full Power in the Legislature to settle the Crown, and to secure the Nations: And so they have taken the Oaths [of allegiance and abjuration] enjoined with a good Conscience, and with fixed Resolutions of Adhering firmly to them, without any other views but such as the Laws and the Oaths pursuant to them do direct. They know of no unalterable or indefeasible Right, but what is founded on the Law.

Clearly, politics and religion were inextricably interwoven for Burnet and his contemporaries. Burnet held up the continuing threat of a Stuart claimant: 'his Religion is still the same cruel and bloody Conspiracy against Protestants that it was'. Yet he claimed an irenic spirit, 'my Design being to do all I can to heal our Breaches'. 'I have thus freely opened all that I know of the Principles of those called the *Low* Church-men among us. I will not pretend to tell what are the Principles of those called *High* Church-men; I know them too little to pretend to tell what their Maxims and Views are.' But this was obviously untrue: Burnet's Low Churchmanship was a mirror image of what he imagined High Churchmanship to be. As to the High Churchmen's politics, 'the Impiety of Mens taking Oaths [of allegiance and abjuration] against their Consciences, and, in hope to compensate for that, their acting contrary to them, is of so monstrous a nature, that our Language does not afford Words black enough to set out its Deformity'.[48]

Burnet had said too much, and his irenic professions were confronted by the realities of his party commitment. A freethinker, John Asgill, seized on this text and satirized Burnet for his 'Appearance of Honesty', his appetite for the spoils of the establishment at which popish clergy too might aim, his contempt for the poverty of the non-juring clergy, his unyielding hostility to the blameless son of James II. Asgill acknowledged also a theological divide: the two parties were differently educated. He imagined a scene at which Burnet rejected a High Church candidate for ordination:

> Methinks I see Your L......p lolling in an Easy Chair, when a young *Prig* from one of the Universities disturbs Your Repose, and demands *Ordination* at Your Hands.—Well, What's your Name? My L..d, my Name is——. Whence come you? From *Oxford*, My L..d. What College there? *Christ Church*, My L..d. What Books have you read? *Hammond, Barrow, Pearson, Beveridge, Bull, Wells, Mills,* &c. My L..d. What think you of *Le Clerc, Whitby, Burkett, Henry, Whiston,* the *Exposition* of the Thirty Nine Articles, or the *Racovian* Catechism? My L..d, I was never directed by my Tutor to read any of them.—I thought so; but come then, supposing I were a *Jew*, how would you go about to convert me to *Christianity*?— And thus Your L......p goes on, if it so happens that he answers all Your Objections on that Head, to make Yourself a *Turk*, a *Pagan*, &c. and if he does not give you Satisfaction upon the Whole, as 'tis Ten Thousand to one if he can, he is sent away like an ignorant Coxcomb, to seek for *Orders*, where he can get them. But if a Convert from the *Presbyterians, Independents, Anabaptists, Quakers*, or even a Gifted *Clothier*, or the like, addresses You upon the same Account, Your L......p turns Your blind Side; he has You there, and passes Muster, not unlike the *Faggots* at t'other end of the Town.

One controversial text was by the bishop himself: Gilbert Burnet's *An Exposition of the Thirty-Nine Articles of the Church of England* (London, 1699), while the Racovian catechism of 1605 had been based on the work of Socinus.

Asgill implied that Burnet was actuated by the very party zeal he disclaimed; the freethinker suggested that the work of '*C[o]ll[i]ns*, and *T[o]l[a]nd*, and

---

[48] Gilbert Burnet, *A Discourse of the Pastoral Care* (4th edn., London, 1713), unpaginated, pp. [v–vi, ix–xiv, xvii], italic and roman reversed. Burnet's characterization, emphasizing theological distinctions, was echoed by Anon., *The Principles of the Low-Church-Men fairly represented and defended* (London, 1714). For a Low Church account prioritizing politics, see [John Fransham], *The Criterion: or, a Touchstone, By which to judge of the Principles of High and Low-Church* (London, 1710); for a freethinker's account, [John Toland], *The Jacobitism, Perjury, and Popery of High-Church Priests* (London, 1710); for a High Church account of the Low Church, prioritizing their claimed right of private judgement, Anon., *Honesty the best Policy: or the Mischiefs of Faction shewed in the Character of an High, and a Low-Church Clergy-Man* (London, 1711).

T[i]nd[a]ll, and the rest of our Legion' would be 'very little advanc'd, were it not for the seasonable Assistance of two or three of Your L......p's Bench, and such as *Cl[a]rke, H[oa]dly, Wh[i]st[o]n*, and some others of their Brethren'; Asgill ironically wished Burnet 'a good and speedy *Translation*' to a richer bishopric.[49]

Some men had tactical reasons to keep up the old language stigmatizing High Churchmen. Others had tactical reasons to play it down. In the 1730s, an opposition to Sir Robert Walpole's ministry was constructed, seeking to unite extreme Whig and Tory-Jacobite elements. Its leading journal had to urge: 'Forget, therefore, Gentlemen, the foolish and knavish Distinction of *High-Church* and *Low-Church*, of *Whig* and *Tory*; Sounds, which continue in your Mouths, when the *Meaning* of them is gone, and are now only used to set you together by the Ears, that Rogues may pick your Pockets.' Magna Carta itself had been won when '[t]hose of the *high Church* and Those of the *low Church* united in one common Cause'.[50] 'That turbulent and noisy Cry of *High-Church* and *Low-Church*, *Whig* and *Tory*, laugh'd at and contemn'd by all thinking Men, has too too long spirited up and fermented our Party Divisions.'[51] Dissenters, meanwhile, had every reason for reviling 'the High-Church party, who, generally speaking, were enemies to the Revolution it self'; Dissenters recalled the end of Anne's reign, '*when High-Church and Jacobitism triumphed in the prospects of Persecution and the Pretender*'.[52]

The survival of the Hanoverian monarchy slowly changed the landscape. By the 1780s, a visiting German Lutheran minister observed:

> The English Episcopal church was formerly divided into the *high* and the *low* church. Those who were for extending the authority and the power of bishops, so as to render them and the church almost independent of the state, went under the former denomination; those, on the contrary, who were for extending the power of the king in ecclesiastical matters, and over the bishops, came under the denomination of the low church. The former might be compared to the tories in the state, and the latter to the whigs. I believe, however, that at present the distinction of these church-parties is extremely faint, since in modern times the convocation, or as it may be called the church parliament, is immediately prorogued as soon as it meets, and is as it were almost abolished. The sentiments of the low churchmen prevail, and very few, it may be supposed, maintain at present those principles which formerly distinguished high-churchmen in the stricter or more eminent sense.[53]

---

[49] *Mr. Asg..l's congratulatory Letter to the L..d B....p of S...m, upon the excellent modern Preface just publish'd by his L......p* (London, 1713), pp. 7–8, 10–11, 23.

[50] *The Craftsman*, 14 vols. (London, 1731–7), II, p. 104; VII, p. 53.

[51] Anon., *The Loyal: or, Revolutional Tory* (London, 1733), p. 7.

[52] [Samuel Chandler], *The Dispute better adjusted, about the proper Time of applying for a Repeal of the Corporation and Test Acts, by shewing that some Time is proper* (London, 1732), pp. 12–13.

[53] Friedrich Augustus Wendeborn, *A View of England towards the Close of the Eighteenth Century*, 2 vols. (German edn., 1785–8; London, 1791), II, pp. 278–9.

But the world was already changing after a mid-century lull. John Brewster looked back to the reign of George II: 'Ecclesiastical controversies lessened in number and in virulence. The characteristic terms of *High Church* and *Low Church* became imperceptibly changed into *Court* and *Country-party*, even though '*Whig* and *Tory* were still considered as political distinctions'. Nevertheless, '[t]he two parties alluded to, may be traced through a succession of many years, varying indeed with the times, but still holding a decided, if not a respectful, distance from each other'; they were 'ready to be re-united, when similar times, or men of similar dispositions, might be inclined to call them into action'. This indeed occurred in the reign of George III when 'the fear of popery became again the *watchword* of party': Archdeacon Blackburne's *The Confessional* of 1766 caused a sensation, led to the Subscription controversy, and generated 'parties' on 'both sides'.[54]

High and Low Church partly converged during the eighteenth century. Conybeare argued that on the issue of 'judgment by works', for example, there was 'no real difference between the moderate [High Church] Anglican and the moderate Evangelical'.[55] Evangelicals began to be perceived as a party from about the 1770s, an Evangelicalism defined by pastoral zeal more than by reviving Calvinism. Yet Evangelicals were not Low Churchmen. It was because late eighteenth-century Evangelicals gave little attention to ecclesiology (unlike their Low Church forebears) that they provoked other churchmen to a lesser degree to frame an antithesis. Other things did it for them in the age of the French Revolution.

Conybeare argued that the sweeping Evangelical victory of the late eighteenth century revealed victorious combatants arranged in 'three separate armies . . . From this period the Evangelical party began to assume the form which it still retains.' He recognized a problem with this analysis, conceding that the Evangelicals (Joseph Milner, Henry Martyn, William Wilberforce) had originally 'comprehended many different shades of theological opinion', including Methodists, but claimed that they became united by their shared tenets: the necessity of conversion, justification by faith, and the sole authority of Scripture.[56] This was evidently so: the Evangelicals by 1800 had developed a strong sense of distinctiveness, defined over against the body of the Church. Evangelical clergy generated 'the rudiments of a national framework' in the shape of local clubs that corresponded on a national basis and cooperated with national societies like the Church Missionary Society. This sense was soon promoted by journals like *The Christian Observer* (1802) and *The Record* (1828), the latter especially ridiculed by Conybeare.[57]

---

[54] John Brewster, *A Secular Essay: Containing a retrospective View of Events connected with the Ecclesiastical History of England, during the Eighteenth Century* (London, 1802), pp. 89–90, 245, 247–8.

[55] Conybeare, 'Church Parties', ed. Burns, p. 302.

[56] Conybeare, 'Church Parties', ed. Burns, pp. 261–2.

[57] Walsh and Taylor, 'Introduction', pp. 49–50.

Without ecclesiology, by c.1800–29 the use of the term 'Low Church' had almost disappeared in England: the landscape had changed too much since Burnet's day. Only from the mid-1830s did Tractarians attach the old label 'Low Church' to Evangelicals, who evidently accepted it.[58] Nor was the Evangelical versus High Church divide of c.1780–1829 as reified as the Low Church versus High Church divide of c.1690–1740. In the later period, the Church was far more united in political matters: only two bishops, John Hinchliffe of Peterborough and Hoadly's protégé Jonathan Shipley of St Asaph, had been openly against the ministry's American policy in the 1770s;[59] there was still less dissension during the French Revolution;[60] and in a key division on 8 October 1831, the bishops voted 21 to 2 against the Reform Bill. Their opposition failed, and after 1832 the Church moved into a transformed landscape.

LATITUDINARIANS AND BROAD CHURCH

Against the High and Low Church parties, which Conybeare in places depicted as recent formations, he argued, 'another party of a different character has always existed in the Church of England. It is called by different names; Moderate, Catholic, or Broad Church, by its friends; Latitudinarian or Indifferent by its enemies. Its distinctive character is the desire of comprehension. Its watchwords are Charity and Toleration.' It has escaped attention that while Conybeare de-emphasized the unity and continuity of High and Low Church, he did the opposite for his idea of a Broad Church party. Indeed he idealized it. He added an historical thesis: 'It will appear, from what we have said, that the Broad Church are, to the middle of the nineteenth century, what the Low Church were to its beginning—the originators of ecclesiastical reform, and the pioneers of moral progress.' The difference was that the Low Church or Evangelicals had been 'united closely to one another' and 'acted as a compact body', while the Broad Church 'have so little organisation or mutual concert of any kind, that they can scarcely be called a party at all'. Only a revival of Convocation 'would force the Broad party into an organised alliance'.[61]

How much continuity was there in this third and last party? 'Latitudinarianism' was a term known from the 1660s, preceding Low and High Church.

---

[58] Nockles, *Oxford Movement in Context*, p. 32.
[59] G. M. Ditchfield, 'Ecclesiastical Policy under Lord North', in Walsh et al. (eds.), *The Church of England*, pp. 228–46.
[60] Mather, *High Church Prophet*, pp. 223–4.
[61] Conybeare, 'Church Parties', ed. Burns, pp. 340–7.

Some used it to disparage churchmen who had collaborated during the Interregnum but subsequently professed their adherence to episcopacy and Arminianism. One author defended Latitudinarians' (post-1662) theological orthodoxy in order to vindicate their interest in natural science.[62] Richard Baxter thought Latitudinarianism held 'that Mr. *Edward Stillingfleet's Irenicon* hath well proved, That no Form of Church Government is of Divine Institution. And therefore when the Magistrate commandeth any, he is to be obeyed.'[63] Latitudinarianism could (but did not have to) reinforce 'comprehension', that response to separated Dissent after *c.*1662 that sought its reincorporation into Anglicanism by broadening the terms of Church membership. But this option receded with the political events of 1688 and 1714: Anglicans and Dissenters increasingly agreed on the regrettable but irreversible separation of Protestant nonconformity. Consequently, Latitudinarians never evolved to form a party. Even for a satirist in 1699, the Latitudinarian was a character type, not a party member.[64]

Instead Sacheverell in 1702 depicted Latitudinarianism as a policy commitment of the Low Church party, 'that noble Design of *Archbishop Tillotson,* in the beginning of the *Last Revolution,* to have fetch'd in all Dissenters upon the same Bottom with that of the Church of *England;* and by Altering, Circumscribing and Abolishing its *Rubrick, Liturgy and Canons,* to have Established the *Low Church Party* upon their Own Universal and Comprehensive Principles'. For Sacheverell, a phrase like 'this Vile *Latitudinarian Party*' was synonymous with the Low Churchmen. Indeed, Low Churchmen were not Christians, since 'a Man that is of no Religion, can never pretend to that Name ... They Stile themselves, in *Indefinite* Terms, *Protestants at Large,* that is, of all Religions, besides the *Popish,* which they will not allow to be such; and so by an *Universal Latitude, Comprehension* and *Indifference* to every Sect and Party, they run into the common Herd.'[65]

Conybeare did not live to see his 'Broad Church' reified by the revival in 1852 of Convocation after its *de facto* suspension in 1717. Indeed he had difficulty in listing characteristic Broad Churchmen, apart from the admired but unique Thomas Arnold (1795–1842) and F. D. Maurice (1805–72). This difficulty is easily explained: 'Latitudinarianism' had almost disappeared from eighteenth-century discourse. In his preface of 1712, Burnet had not employed the terms 'Latitudinarian' and 'Latitudinarianism'; he was, in his

---

[62] S. P. [?Simon Patrick], *A brief Account of the new Sect of Latitude-Men* (London, 1662).

[63] *Reliquiae Baxterianae: or, Mr Richard Baxter's Narrative of the most memorable Passages of his Life and Times,* ed. Matthew Sylvester (London, 1696), Book I, Part II, p. 388; Edward Stillingfleet, *Irenicum: A Weapon-Salve for the Churches Wounds* (London, 1660).

[64] [Thomas] Brown, *A Collection of Miscellany Poems, Letters, &c. To which is added, a Character of a Latitudinarian* (London, 1699).

[65] [Sacheverell], *Character of a Low-Church-man,* pp. 8, 12, 16, 25, 28.

self-perception, a Low Churchman.[66] In the 1720s, *The Independent Whig* made no use of 'Latitudinarianism', and presented the divide as one between Low and High Church. The terms 'Latitudinarian' and 'Latitudinarianism' were rarely used in the eighteenth century, and then chiefly by Catholics to disparage Anglican ecclesiology. William Darrell wrote '[t]o shew the Unreasonableness of Atheism and Latitudinarianism'; Edward Hawarden warned: 'must he not be a *Latitudinarian* with a witness, whoever perswades himself, that *Men*, or *Nations*, may be Members of the *Catholick Church*, tho' they deny all the *Sacraments*'; Richard Challoner bracketed '*Atheism, Deism, Latitudinarianism*, and barefaced Impiety'; Sebastian Redford argued that the Protestant reformers had 'opened a gap to Latitudinarianism and Deism, and established a state of Anarchy'.[67] Eighteenth-century Anglican condemnations of Latitudinarianism were rare.[68] But Darrell's, Hawarden's and Challoner's were uncommon asides, from a Church lastingly unreconciled to schism.

Theology as well as politics remained at issue. William King, in 1709, observed that on the doctrines of foreknowledge and predestination 'the difference is so great, that on account thereof, there yet remain form'd and separate Parties, that mutually refuse to communicate with one another'. His ambition, anticipating Whately, was so to explain the differences as to abolish 'those Animosities, that yet remain between the contending Parties'.[69] Yet theological controversies over Deism, Calvinism, and Trinitarianism did not exactly correspond with the alignments that comprehension had created into the 1660s: despite King, there was no unified Latitudinarian theology.

John Jones's key text of 1749 ignored 'Latitudinarian' and 'Latitudinarianism'; Francis Blackburne's of 1766 used 'Latitudinarian' just once, and in reference to Charles I's reign.[70] By 1785, Richard Watson argued that the 'great lesson' to be drawn from ecclesiastical history was 'Moderation', by distinguishing between 'the word of God' and 'the additions which men have made to it'. In 'many questions in Divinity' the only outcome was 'irksome

---

[66] Burnet, *Pastoral Care.*

[67] [William Darrell], *A Gentleman instructed in the true Principles of Religion, with a full Confutation of Atheism and Latitudinarianism: The Second Part. Written for the Instruction of a Young Nobleman* ([?London], 1707), p. 113; [Edward Hawarden], *The true Church of Christ, shewed by concurrent Testimonies of Scripture, and Primitive Tradition* (London, 1715), p. 70; [Richard Challoner], *The Grounds of the Catholick Doctrine, contained in the Profession of Faith, publish'd by Pope Pius the Fourth, by way of Question and Answer* (5th edn., [?London], 1736), p. 59; [Sebastian Redford], *An important Enquiry; or, the Nature of a Church Reformation fully considered* (London, 1751), p. 54.

[68] E.g. John Wesley, *Catholic Spirit: A Sermon on 2 Kings X. 15* (London, 1789), p. 16.

[69] William King, *Divine Predestination and Fore-knowledg, consistent with the Freedom of Man's Will: A Sermon* (London, 1709), p. 4.

[70] [John Jones], *Free and candid Disquisitions relating to the Church of England* (London, 1749); [Francis Blackburne], *The Confessional* (London, 1766), p. 185.

uncertainty'. Some might charge him with being 'an encourager of sceptical and Latitudinarian principles', but 'I have no regard for Latitudinarian principles, nor for any principles but the principles of Truth'. He looked forward to an era of 'liberal toleration'.[71] Watson's 'Latitudinarian principles' had more to do with epistemology than with ecclesiology.

A lack of focus on possible historical antecedents of the Broad Church party has derived also from the scarcity until recently of historical attention to the two great controversies that illuminate the nature of theological challenges to Trinitarian Anglicanism: the Bangorian controversy of 1717–21[72] and the Subscription controversy of 1772–4, the latter according to John Disney a protest against 'the galling yoke of Spiritual Tyranny' and an appeal to 'the simple and universal Principle of Protestantism'.[73] Disney did not analyse the ecclesiastical opponents of the petition in party terms, although he knew the category 'Latitudinarian'.[74] Participants in neither of these controversies appealed to a Latitudinarian position, or to any synonym for one. In these two controversies there were heterodox Anglicans, but they were perceived as a concealed theological problem rather than as a Church party. They lacked a label, a social base, symbols, and a support network. Their aim was no longer the 'comprehension' of Dissenters (often, inconveniently, Trinitarian Calvinists) but freedom for themselves to pursue careers within the Church while not holding its (for them) problematic doctrines. The Feathers Tavern Petition of 1770, signed by some two hundred clergy, did not create a sense of party identity in the following decades: its rejection by the House of Commons provoked only nine clerical secessions from the Church into a newly organized Unitarian movement.

In the 1780s Wendeborn wrote for his German readers that 'the appellation Low-churchman' had sometimes been wrongly applied 'to those who contended, that the difference between the Episcopal and other Protestant churches, was of no great moment, for which reason some strict high-churchmen did not hesitate to reckon them among the *Latitudinarians*'. Few if any English clergy, he reassured German Protestants, now maintained that 'old exploded doctrine' of the High Churchmen.[75] This lack of definition was true also in the early nineteenth century. An Anglican Evangelical in 1822, looking back on the late

---

[71] Richard Watson (ed.), *A Collection of Theological Tracts*, 6 vols. (Cambridge, 1785), I, pp. xiii–xvi, xviii.

[72] Philanagnostes Criticus [Thomas Herne], *An Account of all the considerable Pamphlets that have been published on Either Side in the present Controversy, between the Bishop of Bangor, and others, to the end of the Year MDCCXVIII: With occasional Observations on them* (London, 1719); Andrew Starkie, *The Church of England and the Bangorian Controversy, 1716–1721* (Woodbridge, 2007).

[73] [John Disney], *A short View of the Controversies occasioned by The Confessional, and the Petition to Parliament for Relief in the Matter of Subscription to the Liturgy and Thirty-Nine Articles of the Church of England* (2nd edn., London, 1775), pp. vii, xx.

[74] John Disney, *Memoirs of the Life and Writings of John Jortin, D.D.* (London, 1792), p. 279.

[75] Wendeborn, *View of England*, II, p. 279.

eighteenth century, wrote that the Latitudinarians like Edmund Law 'merged, indeed, the character of divines in that of philosophers'. He did not see them as a party.[76] The Oxford Noetics, men like Richard Whately, drew such group identity as they enjoyed from their membership of a single college, Oriel, rather than from being the heirs to a great tradition.

Even the Broad Church, Conybeare argued, had shared in the grand decline of the eighteenth century: 'The natural indolence of men causes them to pass from the toleration of unimportant differences to the belief that all differences are unimportant. Thus, in the last century, the comprehensive Christianity of Tillotson and Burnet degenerated into the worldliness of the Sadducean Hoadly.' Conybeare added a footnote: 'Hoadly defends (in his "Reasonableness of Conformity") the practice of signing the Articles without believing them.'[77] Other historians, too, assumed that the mid- and late Georgian Church had been 'dominated by a tepid yet all-pervasive "Latitudinarianism"'.[78] This picture has been modified by new scholarship on eighteenth-century High Churchmanship and Evangelicalism rather than by academic attention to anything that might be called Latitudinarianism; indeed the coherence of any such position through the eighteenth century is in doubt.

The term 'Latitudinarianism' has reality only as an organizing category for present-day historians, signifying in their pages 'enlightened moderation' held by 'liberals' who professed 'religious liberalism', not an actual phenomenon of the years c.1700–1829. But enlightened moderation is too imprecise a term to be historically revealing, and 'liberal' was not a substantive noun until the 1810s, at which time it meant one who mounted a far from moderate attack on the old culture of Church and state. The use of 'Latitudinarianism' for this period may indeed only be part of the familiar retrojection into the eighteenth century of ideas that were formulated later, like radicalism, social class, and 'the Enlightenment'.

CONCLUSION

High and Low Church, then, were familiar ideas throughout the eighteenth century; Conybeare underestimated their survival. A greater difficulty arises with his category of 'Broad Church' and its possible antecedents. Even in 1853, contemporary reactions often claimed that a 'Broad Church' position had been

[76] Middleton, *Ecclesiastical Memoir*, p. 27.

[77] Conybeare, 'Church Parties', ed. Burns, p. 348; Benjamin Hoadly, *The Reasonableness of Conformity to the Church of England* (2 parts, London, 1703), Part I, pp. 29–135, esp. 36–7, 41–2, 105–6.

[78] Walsh and Taylor, 'Introduction', p. 32.

wrongly characterized, or that it did not exist.[79] Conybeare therefore modified his characterization of it in his 1855 edition, in ways that undermined the claims of the Broad Church to be a mean that held the solution to the extremes.[80] Yet this analytical qualification counted for little after the heated controversies over liberal theology, notably *Essays and Reviews* (1860), that divided opinion from the 1860s. The assumption therefore strengthened that the Broad Church party was as reified as the other two. If this was not the case before 1853, however, it casts doubt on any tripartite party analysis of the period 1662–1829. If Conybeare's disparagement of mid-Hanoverian torpor is revised, persisting contemporary perceptions of two Church parties, High and Low, are more evident; not in exactly their forms of 1853, but in the forms of the 1690s that continued to evolve, not only into the forms of the 1850s but beyond.

SELECT BIBLIOGRAPHY

Conybeare, W. J., 'Church Parties', ed. Arthur Burns, in Stephen Taylor (ed.), *From Cranmer to Davidson: A Church of England Miscellany* (Woodbridge, 1999), pp. 213–385.

Every, George, *The High Church Party 1688–1718* (London, 1956).

Hunt, John, *Religious Thought in England from the Reformation to the End of the Last Century*, 3 vols. (London, 1870–3).

Hylson-Smith, Kenneth, *Evangelicals in the Church of England 1734–1984* (Edinburgh, 1988).

Marshall, John, 'The Ecclesiology of the Latitude-Men 1660–1689: Stillingfleet, Tillotson and "Hobbism"', *Journal of Ecclesiastical History*, 36 (1985): 407–27.

Mather, F. C., *High Church Prophet: Bishop Samuel Horsley (1733–1806) and the Caroline Tradition in the Later Georgian Church* (Oxford, 1992).

Nockles, Peter B., *The Oxford Movement in Context: Anglican High Churchmanship 1760–1857* (Cambridge, 1994).

Sharp, Richard, 'New Perspectives on the High Church Tradition: Historical Background 1730–1780', in Geoffrey Rowell (ed.), *Tradition Renewed: The Oxford Movement Conference Papers* (London, 1986), pp. 4–23.

Spellman, W. M., *The Latitudinarians and the Church of England, 1660–1700* (Athens, GA, 1993).

Spurr, John, '"Latitudinarianism" and the Restoration Church', *Historical Journal*, 31 (1988): 61–82.

Starkie, Andrew, *The Church of England and the Bangorian Controversy, 1716–1721* (Woodbridge, 2007).

Walsh, John, Colin Haydon, and Stephen Taylor (eds.), *The Church of England c.1689–c.1833: From Toleration to Tractarianism* (Cambridge, 1993).

[79] Burns, in Conybeare, 'Church Parties', ed. Burns, p. 241.
[80] Burns, in Conybeare, 'Church Parties', ed. Burns, pp. 242–5.

17

The Church of England and
the Churches of Europe

Tony Claydon

THE MUDDLED INHERITANCE OF ANGLICANISM

As all the volumes in this series make clear, the Anglican Church was not just shaped, but was plagued, by its Tudor birth. For centuries after Henry VIII's break with Rome, and the Elizabethan Settlement, opponents accused this communion of being founded on a king's lust, or being merely a parliamentary religion. The Church also had a mixed parentage that divided its adherents. The medieval heritage of episcopacy, liturgy, and cathedral worship encouraged sensibilities very different from the concentration on preaching, the iconoclasm, and the anti-clericalism gleaned from the Reformation. Polarizing loyalties to these two birthrights led to the rupture of the early Stuart era, the ejection of Dissent in 1662, and the long struggle between 'High' and 'Low' factions that has lasted from the Glorious Revolution to the twenty-first century. This Tudor inheritance also complicated and compromised the Anglican Church's relationship with the other communions of Europe. The effects lasted through the long eighteenth century.

At one level, of course, the establishments of Henry and Elizabeth had severed all connection with the wider *ecclesia*. Henry had broken with European Catholicism, claiming that England was a sovereign and self-sufficient empire.[1] Elizabeth had imposed an Erastian settlement that recognized no authority above national legislation to shape the Church.[2] Both monarchs had fashioned styles of ecclesiastical governance, doctrine, and worship that had no close counterparts elsewhere, especially in their uniquely eclectic combination of traditional and evangelical religion. Yet while the Church of England might

---

[1] Most famously in 24 Hen. VIII. c. 12, the Act in Restraint of Annates (1553).

[2] See Norman Jones, *The Birth of the Elizabethan Age: England in the 1560s* (Oxford, 1993).

appear isolated, strong forces wove it back into larger European wholes. Its Protestantism, though idiosyncratic, was real. A doctrine rejecting purgatory, transubstantiation, and papal authority placed the Church firmly within the Reformation. As historians of the sixteenth century have shown, this encouraged loyalty to an international community of Protestants—though continental divisions, especially between Lutherans and Calvinists, posed the puzzle of which groups in particular the English should endorse.[3] At the same time, the Church's claim for continuity with its medieval predecessor maintained ties with other (usually Rome-led) heirs of that European body. England's bishops, like Roman Catholic bishops abroad, claimed apostolic succession from Christ, and through the same channels. The daily cycle of worship was held to be a purified version of ancient rites that were also preserved—albeit in corrupted form, thought English clerics—by the Roman communion.

Of course, these different international loyalties were contradictory. Though initially contained by ecclesiological fudge, the alternative conceptions of the English Church's European position soon pulled apart. Anthony Milton has shown how central this international confusion was to the ecclesiastical disputes of James I's and Charles I's reigns. The battle between Laudian and puritan can be retold as a struggle between catholic and reformed visions: and both of these were conceptions of England's place in the struggle between European Christianities.[4] The civil war and its aftermath transformed much for the Church: but the events of the mid-seventeenth century recast, rather than removed, the competition of European identities. For the whole period from 1662 to 1829, clerics and their lay parishioners negotiated competing visions of where they sat within European Christendom.[5]

And placing the Anglican Church in the diverse spectrum of European belief would always be a live issue in the 170 years after Charles II's restoration, since events on the continent could still be understood as wars of religion. In the earlier decades of this period, the expansion and intolerance of Louis XIV threatened the Reformation in the west of Europe, whilst the defeat of Sweden at the hands of Orthodox Russia in the Great Northern War weakened another Protestant power, and began to pose the question of England's relations with Eastern Christianity. Foreign policy after the Treaty of Utrecht in 1713 was more confessionally confused (Britain was in alliance with France for a couple of decades after the treaty) and the existential threat to continental

---

[3] See Patrick Collinson, *The Birthpangs of Protestant England* (Basingstoke, 1988), ch. 1; Peter Lake and Maria Dowling (eds.), *Protestantism and the National Church in Sixteenth-Century England* (London, 1987).

[4] Anthony Milton, *Catholic and Reformed: Roman and Protestant Churches in English Protestant Thought, 1600–1640* (Cambridge, 1994).

[5] Tony Claydon, *Europe and the Making of England, 1660–1760* (Cambridge, 2007), pp. 284–353.

Protestantism might have appeared less urgent.[6] Yet in the Seven Years War (1756–63), diplomatic realignments counterposed the leading Catholic powers, France and Austria, against the Protestant forces of Britain and Prussia. And after the 1789 Revolution in France, the future of Christianity as a whole looked insecure. Revolutionary and Napoleonic forces burst across Europe, frequently opposing clerical power and even Christian beliefs. This forced English churchmen to consider whether they should retain any narrowly confessional allegiances if there were an existential danger to their faith as a whole. Given the close engagement with continental affairs that marked eighteenth-century English politics and culture, Anglicans would have been constantly called to define themselves with relation to the Christians of Europe, even if their muddled Tudor inheritance had not already made this central to their concerns.[7]

CATHOLIC AND REFORMED: THE CHURCH OF ENGLAND'S EUROPEAN IDENTITIES IN THE LATER STUART AGE

The most noticeable feature of Anglicanism in the first decades after 1662 was the increasing assertion of its catholic, perhaps even Rome-leaning, identity. This shift was entirely understandable, given the experience of the 1640s and 1650s. In the civil war years, and under the republic, the Church had been proscribed by politicians hostile to what they saw as the remnants of popery in its doctrine, ceremony, and government. This naturally caused those who kept the faith to value what was being attacked (the 'catholic' heritage of episcopacy and liturgy), and to be highly suspicious of the comparisons with unequivocal foreign Protestantism that seemed to have driven their foes. Consequently, when the Church's supporters triumphed after 1660, they pressed a vision of the establishment that was at some distance from its 'Reformation' identity.[8]

Much of this shift was rhetorical. In the Restoration era, more Anglican apologetic centred on the transmission of sanctity through the episcopal and Europe-wide Catholic Church of the Middle Ages than had been the case earlier, or at least before the Laudian advances of the 1630s. More of it also

---

[6] Though see arguments for the continuing purchase of Protestant solidarity through the early eighteenth century: Andrew Thompson, *Britain, Hanover and the Protestant Interest, 1688–1756* (Woodbridge, 2006); Claydon, *Europe*, pp. 192–219.

[7] Claydon, *Europe*; Stephen Conway, *Britain, Ireland, and Continental Europe in the Eighteenth Century: Similarities, Connections, Identities* (Oxford, 2011).

[8] Jeffrey R. Collins, 'The Restoration Bishops and the Royal Supremacy', *Church History*, 68 (1999): 549–80; Jacqueline Rose, *Godly Kingship in Restoration England: The Politics of the Royal Supremacy, 1660–1688* (Cambridge, 2011).

hinted that the Roman communion might be a true—if corrupted—Church; and more of it distanced the English establishment from foreign reformed Christians.[9] The change was particularly profound in ecclesiastical history. Peter Heylyn, a leading polemicist as well as Laud's former chaplain, used a series of historical works to retell the Tudor Reformation as a wholly English renewal of the medieval structures; any influence that had come from Protestants abroad had been disruptive and unwelcome. Heylyn denounced the pre-civil war puritan movement as an alien invasion; and charted the journey of its false principles from Geneva, through France, and the Netherlands, to infect a dangerous faction of Englishmen.[10]

The Romeward drift of Anglican identity also had practical effects in ministry. Before the civil war, and even under Laud, foreign Protestant ministers who came to England could take up posts in the local Church, even if they had not received episcopal ordination. Their clerical status was held to have been legitimate, since it conformed to the conditions in each person's homeland, and had occurred within Churches the English establishment saw as sister communions. Under the Act of Uniformity (1662), however, this ceased. Incoming clergy had to be reordained by an English bishop. This was a pretty explicit statement that Anglicans no longer thought foreign Protestant Churches had valid ministry.[11]

This severing of connections with the continental Reformation created profound tension. It played a central, though often underplayed, role in the Dissenting schism of 1662. Many ministers found they could not take a place in the Caroline Church because they could not accept episcopal ordination. This was partly because being reordained denigrated the former ministry exercised without a bishop's endorsement; but often—and prominently in a case such as that of John Humfrey, which was argued out in a vigorous pamphlet exchange—because people could not accept the implied slight to non-episcopal Protestants abroad.[12] If there could be no real ministers without bishops—some worried—were all the Reformed clerics of France, Switzerland, and the Netherlands unqualified? If bishops had to have unimpeachable succession from the medieval *ecclesia*, then the Protestants of Germany and Scandinavia might be Churchless too, since episcopacy in these regions had

---

[9] John Spurr, *The Restoration Church of England, 1646–1689* (New Haven, CT, 1991), pp. 107–32.

[10] Peter Heylyn, *Ecclesia restaurata: or, the History of the Reformation of the Church of England* (London, 1661); Peter Heylyn, *Cyprianus anglicus: or, the History of the Life and Death of... William... Archbishop of Canterbury* (London, 1668); Peter Heylyn, *Aerius redivivus: or, the History of the Presbyterians* (London, 1670).

[11] 14 Car. II c. 4: An Act for the Uniformity of Public Prayers (1662).

[12] John Humfrey, *The Question of Re-ordination* (London, 1661); [Zachary Crofton], *A Serious View of the Presbyters Re-ordination by Bishops* (London, 1661); R. I., *A peaceable Enquiry into that novel Controversie about Reordination* (London, 1661); John Humfrey, *A Second Discourse about Re-ordination* (London, 1662).

been refounded after a break. Pondering these questions, many Nonconformists concluded that the establishment had left the international Reformation, and this became one of their standard taunts. Richard Baxter, for example, skewered Anglican opponents. One of his most powerful techniques was to point out that if the non-episcopal Huguenots in France were not the true Church there (as English intolerance of non-episcopalian groups seemed to imply), then the only alternative was the superstitious, persecuting, and worldly Catholicism of the French hierarchy.[13]

The Romeward drift of the Church also unsettled those who remained within. One can debate when 'High' and 'Low' Church positions emerged (it is true that many people later described as Low Churchmen, and so thought to be more generous to Dissent, saw no justification for Nonconformist behaviour in Charles II's reign), but some clergy were disturbed by the unchurching of foreign reformed communions in the Restoration era, and this eventually pushed them towards a 'Low Church' position.[14] This sort of cleric came to see English Nonconformists as suffering some of the same wrongs at the hands of the establishment as the alienated Protestants on the continent. A key moment in the shift was the exclusion crisis of 1679–83. Faced both with reversals for the Protestant cause in Europe, such as Louis XIV's occupation of Strasbourg in 1681, and the domestic prospect of a Catholic successor to Charles II in the form of his brother, James, duke of York, some churchmen reasserted the Reformation identity of their communion. As part of this, they argued that differences between Protestants, both at home and abroad, might have to be accommodated if the cause as a whole was to survive.

Accordingly, Gilbert Burnet published his massive *History of the Reformation* in two volumes in 1679 and 1681.[15] At an important level this was a rebuttal of Heylyn. It retold the continental influences on the Tudor Church as positive encouragements to reform, and used this to argue for forbearance in disputes between Protestants. Around the same time, churchmen such as Daniel Whitby and Samuel Bolde pointed to truces between opposed brands of Protestantism in parts of Europe. For these writers, such arrangements offered a model for a desperately needed local settlement with Dissent.[16] Effectively, a group of clerics was reconceiving the Church as part of a

---

[13] E.g. [Richard Baxter], *An Answer to Mr Dodwell and Dr Sherlocke* (London, 1682).

[14] John Spurr, 'The Church of England, Comprehension, and the Toleration Act of 1689', *English Historical Review*, 104 (1989): 927–46, questions an early emergence of a 'Low Church' party.

[15] Gilbert Burnet, *The History of the Reformation of the Church of England: The First Part* (London, [1679]); Gilbert Burnet, *The History of the Reformation of the Church of England: The Second Part* (London, [1681]).

[16] Samuel Bolde, *A Sermon against Persecution, preached March 26. 1680* (London, 1682); Samuel Bolde, *A Plea for Moderation towards Dissenters* (London, 1682); [Daniel Whitby], *The Protestant Reconciler* (London, 1683).

complex and flexible European Protestantism. In their version of the international Reformation, different heirs of Luther and Calvin could overlap in one geographical area, and find ways of living in reasonable harmony. This simultaneously argued for an accommodation with Nonconformists in England and eased the problem of which foreign folk to endorse as true spiritual brethren.

This reaction set up a tension that would govern the internal Church disputes of the late Stuart age. It is possible to describe most of these arguments in terms of rival appeals—either to the brotherhood of episcopal Churches that attracted High Churchmen, or to the flexible international Protestantism that was at the core of the Low Church creed. For instance, the disputes over toleration and comprehension in 1689 centred on whether the Church of England was part of the European Reformation, and whether that movement might allow different sorts of Protestants in one place if it were. As Low Church proponents of a broad settlement with Dissent set their establishment within a broad and flexible international Protestantism, their High Church opponents objected.[17] Later, arguments over occasional conformity made reference to the need (or not) to accommodate foreign Protestants visiting England. Some clerics actually praised the practice of occasional conformity, both because it allowed foreigners access to English communion services if their own denomination had no local branch, and because it permitted members of other Protestant Churches to show solidarity with the English establishment.[18] Still later, Henry Sacheverell was accused of unchurching foreign Protestants as his extreme High Church views led to his state trial in 1710; whilst many of the opponents of Benjamin Hoadly in the Bangorian controversy (1717–21) stressed that the Church had to have the sort of institutional autonomy that episcopal succession—of the kind exemplified by Roman Catholicism in Europe—best provided.[19] Given the constant bickering between clerics that marked this era, it appeared that the Church's basic confusion over its European identity was bringing it to an insoluble crisis.

Yet, despite all this, the Church held together after 1662. There was the non-juring schism of 1689: but this was about the binding powers of oaths and the political legitimacy of William III, issues that were largely unrelated to the

---

[17] See Claydon, *Europe*, pp. 319–26.

[18] Claydon, *Europe*, pp. 333–5: Andrew Starkie, *The Church of England and the Bangorian Controversy, 1716–1721* (Woodbridge, 2007).

[19] Anon., *A True Answer to Dr Sacheverell's Sermon before the Lord Mayor* (1710); John Toland, *Mr Toland's Reflections on Dr Sacheverell's Sermon preach'd at St Paul's: Nov. 5, 1709* (London, 1710); Thomas Brett, *The Independency of the Church upon the State* (London, 1717); Thomas Brett, *The Divine Right of Episcopacy: And the Necessity of an Episcopal Commission for preaching God's Word, and for the valid Ministration of the Christian Sacraments, proved from the Holy Scriptures, and the Doctrine and Practice of the Primitive Church* (London, 1718); Anon., *A Letter to the Reverend Dr Bradford* (London, 1718).

tensions we have been describing. Although scholars have charted a particular vision of the Church emerging in those who could not come to terms with the post-revolutionary regime, before William invaded there seems to have been little ecclesiologically in common between those who would become non-jurors.[20] On the wider issues around the Church's European identity, clerics bickered, but never quite divorced. In large part, this was because the factions defined by rival continental visions were in fact quite blurred. The fissure between Catholic and Protestant allegiance was deep, but it often ran through individual clergymen, rather than marking a clear boundary between rival groups. Many Anglicans appeared to value both a sense of universal episcopacy and a sense of brotherhood with reformed Christians, and were reluctant to abandon either completely. The result was much hybrid rhetoric, blunting of argument, and appeals to principles from the other side of a dispute.

Particularly remarkable here was the use of Reformation loyalties by what we might call 'High' Churchmen, even as they castigated Dissenters for their 'Protestant' rejection of the establishment. This happened repeatedly. At the Restoration, potential Nonconformists were told that foreign Protestants had the highest respect for the Church of England, so leaving the establishment would be an insult to reformed Churches abroad.[21] One bizarre tract by Jean Durel (himself an exiled Frenchman), used quotes from Luther, Bucer, Calvin, Melanchthon, and other heroes of sixteenth-century European Protestantism to construct a sort of fantasy council in favour of the restored Church.[22] Later, those arguing for modifications in the Church's liturgy to attract Dissenters in 1689 were told that such changes would horrify the continental godly. Protestants abroad had always looked to England as the stable and most excellent core of their movement, so if its establishment were changed on an expedient whim, the whole European movement would be demoralized.[23] Again, in the

---

[20] J. C. Findon, 'The Nonjurors and the Church of England, 1689–1716', DPhil thesis, University of Oxford, 1979; for the emerging churchmanship among non-jurors, see Mark Goldie, 'The Nonjurors, Episcopacy, and the Origins of the Convocation Controversy', in Eveline Cruickshanks (ed.), *Ideology and Conspiracy: Aspects of Jacobitism, 1689–1759* (Edinburgh, 1982), pp. 15–35; Jacqueline Rose, 'By Law Established: The Church of England and the Royal Supremacy', in Grant Tapsell (ed.), *The Later Stuart Church, 1660–1714* (Manchester, 2012), pp. 21–45, esp. pp. 31–3.

[21] *Reliquiae Baxterianae: or, Mr Richard Baxter's Narrative of the most memorable Passages of his Life and Times*, ed. Matthew Sylvester (London, 1696), book 1, part 2, pp. 242–7; John Gauden, *Considerations touching the Liturgy of the Church of England* (London, 1661); [Thomas Morton], *Confessions and Proofes of Protestant Divines of Reformed Churches, that Episcopacy is in respect of the Office according to the Word of God, and in respect of the Use the best* ([London], 1662).

[22] Jean Durel, *A View of the Government and Public Worship of God in the Reformed Churches beyond the Seas* (London, 1662).

[23] E.g. [Thomas Long], *The Letter for Toleration decipher'd, and the Absurdity and Impiety of an Absolute Toleration demonstrated* (London, 1689); M. M., *A Letter from the Member of Parliament, in answer to the Letter of the Divine, concerning the Bill for uniting Protestants*

late 1690s, when Francis Atterbury argued for a convocation to discipline nonconformity, he suggested that Dutch and French Protestants were demanding action in England to stamp out emerging heresies.[24] Finally, when High Churchmen attacked Hoadly's vision of an other-worldly Church, free of coercive doctrine, they asked what this said about a European Protestantism that had received state support and made binding confessional statements.[25] On the other side, 'Low' clerics made similar appeals across the ideological divide. They retained a clear sense of belonging to a European episcopal Church, and could speak or act on this at particular moments. So men such as Gilbert Burnet celebrated any sign of hostility to the pope, or attacks upon superstition, within continental Roman Catholicism. They clearly hoped the evils of that deluded Church would be ended by an internal reform that might leave its bishops and liturgical heritage intact. This was probably more likely than, and ultimately preferable to, its overthrow by local Protestant rivals.[26]

So, dual identity within individual clerics prevented internal Church warfare going too far. Each side felt the pull of the other's European loyalties, preventing any utter rupture of principles. One sign of this was a marked reluctance to take arguments to their logical conclusion. For example, several writers in the Restoration period argued vigorously against those who rejected episcopacy, but then said they were too ignorant of conditions on the continent to judge disputes there, and did not want their words used to attack Protestants suffering under Catholic hierarchies.[27] Similarly, when many Low Churchmen saw Hoadly's extreme version of their suspicion of a Catholic institutional Church, they recoiled. Not only did they join their High Church colleagues in complaining that his insistence on a purely other-worldly community of the faithful would forbid secular support for reformed Churches, but they objected that it invalidated the imposed credal statements that were the common heritage of all Christians, and that underpinned Roman Catholic as much as most mainstream Protestant communions.[28]

[London, 1689]; [John Willes], *The Judgement of the Foreign Reformed Churches concerning the Rites and Offices of the Church of England* (London, 1690).

[24] [Francis Atterbury], *A Letter to a Convocation-Man concerning the Rights, Powers, and Priviledges of that Body* (London, 1697), pp. 3–6.

[25] Andrew Snape, *A Letter to the Bishop of Bangor* (London, 1717); Thomas Dawson, *Suspiria sacra* (London, [1718]); William Law, *A Reply to the Bishop of Bangor's Answer to the Representation of the Committee of Convocation* (London, 1719).

[26] E.g. Gilbert Burnet, *Some Letters, containing an Account of what seemed most remarkable, in Switzerland, Italy, &c.* (Rotterdam, 1687), esp. p. 175; Norman Sykes, *William Wake, Archbishop of Canterbury, 1657–1737*, 2 vols. (Cambridge, 1957), ch. 4.

[27] E.g. Robert Conold, *The Notion of Schism stated according to the Antients, and considered with reference to the Nonconformists* (2nd edn., London, 1677), p. 104; Henry Dodwell, *Separation of Churches from Episcopal Government, as practised by the present Non-conformists, proved schismatical* (London, 1679), Preface, p. iv; [William Sherlock], *A Discourse about Church-Unity* (London, 1681), p. 607.

[28] Claydon, *Europe*, pp. 349–51.

THE CHURCH'S EUROPEAN ECLECTICISM IN
THE LONG EIGHTEENTH CENTURY

As it turned out, the Bangorian controversy ended a period of Anglican history that had been marked by the effects of the Romeward drift of the mid-seventeenth century. In the decades after 1720, disputes sparked by this drift continued, but there were fewer set-piece battles, and, as a number of scholars have shown, eighteenth-century Anglicanism was characterized by broad collaboration on a number of pastoral and apologetic projects.[29] Yet the rejection of extremes was really a continuation of the long-standing muddle in Church thinking. The English establishment still saw itself both as part of a European Reformation, and as part of a universal episcopal Church, and— valuing both identities—it never made serious efforts to think its way out of the contradiction. This set up the pattern for the whole of the 'long' eighteenth century in areas well beyond abstract ecclesiological theory. Through the entire era, churchmen of all stripes reached out to a highly eclectic collection of Christians abroad, in a series of practical, organizational, and rhetorical approaches.

The Reformation allegiance of the establishment remained strong through-out. One of the clearest signs of this was the Church's willingness to present contemporary events on the continent as the latest stages in Protestantism's global struggle for survival, and to offer concrete help to non-Roman Christians who suffered in the struggle. This was often steered from an official level. All through this period, the Church led national participation in the fast and thanksgiving days that were called regularly to win God's blessings on Britain's military efforts in Europe, and it frequently composed prayers, or generated sermons, that saw the wars as crusades for the continental 'Protestant interest' against the cruelties of popery. This had been particularly true in the struggles against the persecuting Louis XIV. Fast liturgies under William III and Anne had included supplications for all the reformed Churches, and preachers had repeatedly presented those monarchs' wars as struggles for the very survival of the European Reformation.[30] Yet, if it had been Louis's aggression and intolerance that had caused the establishment to consider international Protestantism in its response to England's wars, this focus lasted beyond the Sun King's death. In 1746, Thomas Rutherford, preaching to the House of Commons, could call for mobilization against France in the

---

[29] E.g. Jeremy Gregory, 'The Eighteenth-Century Reformation: The Pastoral Task of the Anglican Clergy after 1689', in John Walsh, Colin Haydon, and Stephen Taylor (eds.), *The Church of England c.1689–c.1833: From Toleration to Tractarianism* (Cambridge, 1993), pp. 67–85; also the comments in John Walsh and Stephen Taylor's 'Introduction' to the same volume, pp. 51–2.

[30] Tony Claydon, *William III and the Godly Revolution* (Cambridge, 1996), ch. 4; Claydon, *Europe*, pp. 168–72.

War of Austrian Succession, telling MPs they had a duty to be 'the glory and strength of the reformation', and to 'take the lead in the Protestant cause'.[31] This has been called 'the highest point of international Protestantism within the genre of eighteenth-century state sermons'.[32] Although overtly Protestant rhetoric appears to have been less prominent during the Seven Years War, a preacher such as Isaac Smithson could still speak of an enemy whose religion led it to massacre and extirpate those it labelled 'heretics', and here he concurred with the Supreme Governor of the Church, George II, whose messages to Parliament at the start of the conflict had condemned 'oppression to the Protestant Interest'.[33]

Aid to distressed Protestants abroad could be similarly official. Repeatedly through the eighteenth century, monarchs and archbishops gave orders for clerics to lead fundraising for foreign reformed Christians in their parishes. A series of 'church briefs', or warrants for ministers to collect money, were issued: examples included ones to gather funds for the Protestant refugees from Orange in southern France in 1703, for the Protestants of Copenhagen in 1729, and for the Protestant colonists of Moldova in 1764.[34] Similarly a Royal Bounty was established in 1696 to aid those French Huguenot refugees who had settled in England. Paid out of the civil list, this continued to support ministry and charitable causes within the Huguenot community until the end of the eighteenth century.[35]

Yet whilst official action was important, concern for the sufferings of the Reformation abroad was also a feature of voluntary and lay initiative within the Church. It thus formed part of the broadening of religious activism beyond the clerical hierarchy that has been seen as a key development in decades after 1662.[36] Particularly in the early eighteenth century, voluntary action clustered around the Society for the Promotion of Christian Knowledge (SPCK). This was a largely Anglican body, which drew support from both 'High' and 'Low' wings of the Church, and concentrated on providing religious literature to the congregations of England. Yet despite this domestic focus, the society also had a network of correspondents across Europe. This network acted as a clearing-house for information about the fate of foreign Protestants, and the news it conveyed frequently prompted charitable activity in Anglican parishes. For decades after its 1699 foundation, the society was involved in fundraising for a

[31] Thomas Rutherford, *A Sermon preach'd before the honourable House of Commons...* *January 30, 1746* (London, 1746), pp. 15–16.

[32] Pasi Inhalainen, *Protestant Nations Redefined* (Leiden, 2005), p. 258.

[33] Isaac Smithson, *A Sermon, occasioned by the Declaration of War against France* (London, 1756), p. 5; *Journals of the House of Lords*, 29/4 (1756–60), pp. 197–8.

[34] Wyndham Anstis Bewes, *Church Briefs; or, Royal Warrants for Collections for Charitable Objects* (London, 1896).

[35] Raymond Smith (ed.), *Records of the Royal Bounty and Connected Funds* (London, 1974).

[36] Mark Goldie, 'Voluntary Anglicans', *Historical Journal*, 46 (2003): 977–90.

number of groups suffering Catholic persecution, in a whole swathe of Europe from the Alps to the Russian border.[37] Some have detected a waning of interest in the fate of foreign Protestants as the eighteenth century wore on, but even late in our period it could be revived. In the 1820s, the SPCK was key to a renewal of Anglican interest in, and succour of, the Waldensians. These folk were a minority, and frequently persecuted, sect of non-Roman Christians who had inhabited the Alpine valleys since the late Middle Ages, and had been the object of continuing fascination and financial support from England since the seventeenth century.[38]

As well as illustrating the broad Anglican concern with the fate of the European Reformation, the SPCK exemplified other ways in which the Church was imbricated in a continental Protestant community. The society's continental contacts were a subset of a wider group of European correspondents, who kept in close touch with Anglicans throughout our period, relaying news, doctrinal opinion, and the results of scholarly research, in a Protestant republic of letters. These people also recommended, sent, and translated books for one another. This promoted a common stock of spiritual classics that meant that English religious writers were held in high regard on the continent, and that the leading manifestos of the central European Evangelical Revival became well known among Anglicans.[39] Such communication was facilitated and enhanced by frequent personal travel. This was in both directions across the English Channel, and could be for the purposes of education, career advancement, or—highly significantly—to escape local persecution.

In this general exchange, it is perhaps important to remember the royal court as a crucial point of entry for foreign Protestant personnel and ideas. Between 1689 and 1760 all the monarchs except Mary and Anne (and so all the Supreme Governors of the Church) had been baptized into a European Protestant communion other than the Church of England, and they maintained intimate contacts with their native confession. Even the two reigning queens had close foreign Protestant associations. Mary had spent well over a decade in the Netherlands and shared her role as ecclesiastical governor with

---

[37] Sugiko Nishikawa, 'The SPCK in Defence of Protestant Minorities in Early Eighteenth-Century Europe', *Journal of Ecclesiastical History*, 56 (2005): 730–48.

[38] Nishikawa, 'SPCK'; William Stephen Gilly, *Narrative of an Excursion to the Mountains of Piemont* (London, 1824). There had been church briefs for the Waldensians in1689 and 1698: Bewes, *Church Briefs*, pp. 222–32; and note William Wake, *The Case of the exiled Vaudois, and French Protestants, stated* (London, 1699); Nicholas Brady, *A Sermon preach'd at the Parish-Church of Richmond . . . for a Publick Humiliation and Collection for the Vaudois* (London, 1699). Archbishop Secker had lobbied for funds for the Waldensians in 1768: *The Autobiography of Thomas Secker, Archbishop of Canterbury*, ed. John S. Macauley and R. W. Greaves (Lawrence, KS, 1988), p. 68.

[39] W. R. Ward, *The Protestant Evangelical Awakening* (Cambridge, 1992), esp. pp. 1–11; W. R. Ward, 'The Eighteenth-Century Church: A European View', in Walsh et al. (eds.), *The Church of England*, pp. 285–98.

her Dutch Calvinist husband. Anne's consort, Prince George of Denmark, had come from that Lutheran kingdom, and usually worshipped in the Lutheran chapel at St James. George introduced at least one highly significant influence when he appointed the German Pietist Anton Wilhelm Böhm as his chaplain in 1705. Böhm became a leading light in the SPCK, translating German spiritual writings for English parishioners and importing ideas from the German city of Halle, where he had attended university.[40]

The result of these frequent and multi-layered contacts was that many Anglicans, and at all levels, had close personal knowledge of foreign reformed Christians. We can take random examples to show the chronological and thematic range. We might consider the parishioners of All Saints, Oxford, in the 1660s, and later the congregation at the Savoy in London, who were ministered to by the Palatinate-born and Calvinist-trained Anthony Horneck (1641–97). This influential cleric, central to the later seventeenth-century rise in ministerial standards in the capital that has been called the 'small awakening', had come to Oxford for his education and been inducted to the Anglican Church, but had then returned to Germany to serve as chaplain to the elector in Heidelberg between his two English postings.[41] We could consider Gilbert Burnet. Already a scholar of European reputation, who wrote regularly to many continental men of letters, Burnet was forced into exile in 1685 when his political enemy, James II, came to the throne. He then spent the next three years visiting Geneva, witnessing the persecution of Huguenots in France, and living in The Hague, before returning to England as part of William III's 1688 expedition and being rewarded for his services to the new king by the bishopric of Salisbury.[42] We could also talk of John Wesley, the founder of Methodism, but himself a lifelong Anglican. His spiritual development was greatly influenced in the 1730s by contact with the refugee Salzburgers he met in Georgia and the Moravian community of London.[43] Again, Thomas Secker spent much of his time as archbishop of Canterbury (1758–68) dealing with lobbyists from distressed Protestant communities abroad. Though worried that too many official calls for charity would strain English patience (Secker talked of 'monthly' church briefs raining down), he did what he could, providing personal gifts, and encouraging wider donations where he felt it appropriate.[44]

Of course, this sort of close contact facilitated transfer of religious ideas. Again to cite a random list, we could consider the apocalypticism of many

---

[40] Daniel L. Brunner, 'Boehm, Anthony William (1671–1722)', *ODNB*.

[41] W. R. Ward, 'Horneck, Anthony (1641–1697)', *ODNB*.

[42] Martin Greig, 'Burnet, Gilbert (1643–1715)', *ODNB*.

[43] Henry D. Rack, *Reasonable Enthusiast: John Wesley and the Rise of Methodism* (Peterborough, 1999), pp. 107–37, 202–7.

[44] Robert G. Ingram, *Religion, Reform and Modernity in the Eighteenth Century: Thomas Secker and the Church of England* (Woodbridge, 2007), pp. 266–80.

French Huguenots. Reacting to persecution, important voices of this community interpreted their suffering as a sign of the end of times, and this almost certainly influenced the more millennial readings of the 1688 Revolution within the English establishment.[45] We could mention the central European influences on Methodism (which remained an Anglican movement until the last years of the eighteenth century, and inspired many who stayed in the Church after this); and we could cite the impact of German Pietist ideas on the Church's approach to 'social' issues. The Anglican charity school movement, and those who interested themselves in workhouses, orphanages, and prisons frequently took their inspiration from the pioneering institutions of Halle in Saxony.[46] Strands of Anglican opinion sceptical about Church orthodoxy also looked abroad. Throughout the eighteenth century, those who rejected the official position on the Trinity, or at least questioned the establishment's dogmatism on the point, looked to parts of the European Reformation marked by more flexible thinking. In particular, anti-Trinitarians cited the protest movement in Switzerland led by Jean Frederik Osterwald.[47]

What should be clear from this list of contacts and influences is the very wide variety of European Protestants with whom Anglicans found sympathy. Their foreign brethren ranged from strict Calvinists such as the Huguenots to Lutherans such as Daniel Jablonski, the leader of the Church in Brandenburg with whom the English tried to agree a merger of communions in the 1720s.[48] Partly this was the result of that 'Low' Church understanding of the Reformation as a diverse movement that had to live with different strands. Yet it also marked the continuing confusion about the English Church's position in European Christianity. For just as the earlier Protestant heritage of the Church survived into the high eighteenth century, so did the interest in foreign episcopal Churches. This certainly encouraged talk of union with Lutherans who had preserved the bishop's office, at least in some form: but it also, of course, promoted links with Catholicism.

---

[45] The writings of the exile Pierre Jurieu were particularly influential; see also Lionel Laborie, 'Millenarian Portraits of Louis XIV', in Tony Claydon and Charles-Édouard Levillain (eds.), *Louis XIV Outside In: Images of the Sun King beyond France, 1661–1715* (Aldershot, 2015), pp. 209–28.

[46] M. G. Jones, *The Charity School Movement* (Cambridge, 1938); Daniel L. Brunner, *Halle Pietists in England: Anthony William Boehm and the Society for Promoting Christian Knowledge* (Göttingen, 1993); Tim Hitchcock, 'Paupers and Preachers: The SPCK and the Parochial Workhouse Movement', in Lee Davison, Tim Hitchcock, Tim Keirn, and Robert B. Shoemaker (eds.), *Stilling the Grumbling Hive: The Response to Social and Economic Problems in England, 1689–1750* (Stroud, 1992), pp. 99–120.

[47] Brian Young, 'A History of Variations: The Identity of the Eighteenth-Century Church of England', in Tony Claydon and Ian McBride (eds.), *Protestantism and National Identity: Britain and Ireland, c.1650–c.1850* (Cambridge, 1998), pp. 105–28, esp. pp. 119–20.

[48] Sykes, *Wake*, II, pp. 60–80.

As an example we might take that network of correspondents we cited linking Anglican with Protestants across the continent. This Reformation alignment was very real, but at the same time it was hard to disentangle from a wider web of contacts and friendship that crossed the great confessional divide. As Anne Goldgar has shown, the European republic of letters was often, indeed often strove to be, non-confessional. Its Anglican members did not reject sources of news, scientific insight, or humanist scholarship just because they were Roman Catholic. In fact, to bring religious dispute into discussions was seen as an impolite breach of the rules of the community, or of the expectation that at the least people of different faiths should listen and learn from each other's witness.[49] A related form of toleration, and one that had even wider cultural impact was the willingness of Anglican aristocrats to let their heirs meet European Catholics on the Grand Tour. If part of the point of sending sons to the continent was to learn from the excesses of popery, it was also to appreciate the finest Catholic libraries, art, and architecture. As part of the education, one should be introduced to the learned Catholic keepers of such cultural treasures; these men were seen as sources of wisdom, whose willingness to engage with Protestant visitors might be interpreted as a sign of a coming Catholic reformation.[50]

Catholic erudition was seen as a possible sign of Romanist enlightenment and reform across Europe. Yet it was the Church in France for which the English held out most hope. The French clerical establishment was thought to be closer to reform than others for a number of reasons. First, France's role as the cultural leader of Europe opened her Church to the most advanced ideas from across the continent; and, second, France's geographical position—neighbouring Britain, the Netherlands, Germany, and Switzerland—gave her close contact with Protestant societies. As English travel literature explained, Catholics near to the confessional frontier had absorbed positive influences from the Reformation. Third, and most importantly, the French Church had shown a spirit of national independence over centuries. This characteristic has been labelled 'Gallicanism', and was thought to have rendered France relatively free of papal dogma. If the French Church took this a little further, and declared itself free to correct its own Romish errors, English clerics hoped it could follow the path they had taken in the sixteenth century.[51] If it did, it would finally create a sister Church for them on the continent. France would have a national establishment, reformed and free of the papacy, but retaining episcopacy and the other uncorrupted inheritances from the medieval *ecclesia*.

---

[49] Anne Goldgar, *Impolite Learning: Conduct and Community in the Republic of Letters, 1680–1750* (New Haven, CT, 1995), ch. 4.

[50] Jeremy Black, *France and the Grand Tour* (Basingstoke, 2003); Jeremy Black, *Italy and the Grand Tour* (New Haven, CT, 2003).

[51] See, for example, John Northleigh, *Topographical Descriptions* (London, 1702), p. 164; Joseph Addison, *Remarks on Several Parts of Italy* (London, 1705), pp. 197–8.

For some, this might even create a model for a 'new reformation': something that could unite the continent's Protestants and Catholics.[52]

The result of these hopes was a constant interest in French ecclesiastical politics. Anglican commentators looked with eager anticipation for each new breach between France and Rome, or went further to assert that the Gallicans already mirrored the purity and independence of the English Church. In 1706, for example, Joseph Bingham wrote a volume quoting Gallican clerics and using arguments for their own position to defend the nature of the English establishment.[53] Throughout the century, Anglicans noted the civility and tolerance of many French clerics, and notions of Anglo-French sisterhood reached their high-water mark in 1717. Then Archbishop William Wake attempted a broad reconciliation between the French and English Churches, to result in some sort of intercommunion between the two institutions. Misunderstanding of what the two sides were willing to concede scuppered this initiative: but the fact that it was tried at all tells us much about many Anglicans' understanding of their place within a community of European episcopal Churches. This was particularly true as much of Wake's effort centred on convincing the French that Anglicans retained an unbroken succession of bishops from the primitive Church, and thus that they enjoyed an institutional and spiritual continuity with the Gallican hierarchy.[54]

The story was similar with Anglican interest in Eastern Orthodoxy. Most English people knew very little about the true beliefs of the Churches of Greece, the Balkans, and Russia: but at a very superficial glance, these seemed almost as good candidates for brethren abroad as the Gallicans. The Orthodox were led by bishops. They had escaped the tutelage of the papacy. In fact, they had been independent so long that they had avoided the corruptions of Roman Christianity. In Anglican eyes popery had come to its rank culmination in the high Middle Ages, well after the schism between Latin and Greek Christianities. Building on these assumptions, churchmen repeatedly reached out to the East. In the 1670s, Bishop Henry Compton of London encouraged the building of a Greek church in Soho (this explains the name of Greek Street in that part of the city). Between 1699 and 1705 there was a Greek college in Oxford, albeit short-lived, and modern scholars have detected a continuing Orthodox influence on Anglican liturgies and architecture, based on the premise that Eastern Christians retained pure practices from the ancient, patristic Church.[55]

This long-standing interest in a community of episcopal Churches set much of the context for the Anglican reaction to the French Revolution. At a

---

[52] E.g. Leonard Adams (ed.), *William Wake's Gallican Correspondence and Related Documents, 1716–1731*, 7 vols. (New York, 1988–93), I, p. 98.

[53] Joseph Bingham, *The French Churches Apology for the Church of England* (London, 1706).

[54] Stephen Taylor, 'Wake, William (1657–1737)', *ODNB*.

[55] Peter M. Doll (ed.), *Anglicanism and Orthodoxy 300 Years after the 'Greek College' in Oxford* (Oxford, 2006).

superficial glance, the rapid political changes in France from the late 1780s might have appealed to English churchmen. The freedom granted to reformed Christians, the dissolution of monasteries, and the attacks on mighty Catholic prelates might have spoken to the Protestant parts of their heritage, as they did to sections of the radical Dissenting community.[56] Soon and overwhelmingly, however, English churchmen recoiled from what was happening over the Channel. They protested at the despoliation of the French Catholic Church, and reacted with horror to the militant Deism or even atheism that the authorities (at least for a brief period in 1793–4) promoted as an alternative.[57] Most practically, they welcomed French Catholic clergy. By 1800, more than five thousand priests had come over from France. Although the Emigrant Relief Committee set up to help the exiles was established by the government, leading churchmen sat on the body, and much of the fundraising was led by local clergy.[58] The Church also, of course, played its accustomed part cheer-leading wars, but this time against the new atheist danger. Its sermons and liturgies for the military fasts and thanksgivings of the 1790s were often clarion calls against the French clergy's godless enemies. Preachers and prayers spoke of the 'idolatry of a monstrous form' that had arisen in France, or of foes who were 'avowed blasphemers'.[59]

Of course, much of this reaction was a visceral defence of Christianity—of whatever form—against extreme forces that seemed even more destructive than popery. In a curious way that illustrates the continuing hybridity of Anglican identity, French Catholics may also have benefited from a strand of the Church's Reformation heritage. Dating back to the sixteenth century, and to John Foxe in particular, this saw persecution as the defining mark of Babylon, and tended to treat anyone who had suffered it as a probable member of Christ's true communion.[60] Much too might be political. The Catholics' conservative rejection of revolutionary radicalism might seem a useful ally for an establishment trying to secure its privileges, powers, and property from any English revolution. Yet the argument for collaboration with European Catholicism had been at least half-made before the 1790s' turmoil in France. There were sympathies with French clergymen facing the Revolution, because

[56] Clarke Garrett, 'Joseph Priestley, the Millennium, and the French Revolution', *Journal of the History of Ideas*, 34 (1973): 51–66.

[57] E.g. Robert Nares, *Man's Best Right* (London, 1793); Henry Poole, *A Sermon preached in . . . Lewes . . . 28th of February, 1794* (Lewes, 1794).

[58] Dominic Aidan Bellenger, 'Fearless Resting Place: The Exiled French Clergy in Great Britain, 1789–1815', in Kirsty Carpenter and Philip Mansel (eds.), *The French Émigrés in Europe and the Struggle against Revolution, 1789–1814* (Basingstoke, 1999), pp. 214–29.

[59] Charles Manners-Sutton, *A Sermon preached before the Lords Spiritual and Temporal . . . on Friday, February 28, 1794* (London, 1794), p. 10; *A Form of Prayer, to be used in all Churches and Chapels, upon Friday the 28th day of February, 1794* ([London?], 1794), p. 7.

[60] Claydon, *Europe*, pp. 165–8.

they were already thought to be fellow ministers in another heir of the pre-Reformation Church.

EUROPEAN IDENTITIES AND THE END OF
THE EIGHTEENTH-CENTURY CHURCH

This volume in the history of Anglicanism begins with the 1662 settlement and ends with Catholic and Dissenting emancipation. Considering the Church's relations with the Christians of Europe during this period suggests there may be an interesting story that links these bookending events. The year 1662 marked the definitive rescue of an understanding of the establishment's place in continental Christianity that had been in deep trouble twenty years before. Laudian over-reach had brought the episcopal vision of the Church's heritage into deep disrepute by 1640; but the next two decades rehabilitated this identity as it stiffened the Church's resistance to its enemies. This ensured that the Restoration ecclesiastical settlement would institutionalize a 'catholic' conception of England's place in Christendom, and that this would continue to complement the deep sense of participation in the European Reformation. As we have seen, this meant that Anglicans of the long eighteenth century had sympathies with a very wide range of foreign Christians. They were alive to the practices and ideas of many other Churches, and so could never really conclude that their own communion was the sole source of inspiration, godliness, or even orthodoxy.

Ultimately, this opened the establishment to the claims of other kinds of Christian in England itself. Reflection on the diversity of Christian brethren abroad undermined arguments for rigid monopoly among the English themselves. From as early as the 1680s, some churchmen began to argue for accommodation with local Protestant Dissent. The 'Low' party saw the danger to the international Reformation, and began to suspect that forbearance in internal Protestant disputes was essential for survival. In part, the 1689 Toleration Act was the price the whole Church paid for its concern for foreign Protestants. William III demanded an accommodation with nonconformity as part of his European strategy against the persecuting Louis XIV, and very few churchmen baulked.[61] From that point, there were always those willing to work with Dissenters, and, despite setbacks for the cause in the high eighteenth century, this undoubtedly eased the path to final emancipation in 1828. At the other end of our period, the horrifying fate of European Catholicism during the French Revolution softened Anglican attitudes to its British and

---

[61] For William's role in 1689, see Jonathan I. Israel, 'William III and Toleration', in Ole P. Grell, Jonathan Israel, and Nicholas Tyacke (eds.), *From Persecution to Toleration: The Glorious Revolution and Religion in England* (Oxford, 1991), pp. 129–71.

Irish adherents. As Stephen Conway and others have pointed out, sympathy for French clergy seems to have accelerated moves away from penalizing Rome's domestic adherents in the 1790s, and to have built a momentum that led towards 1829.[62]

If this is right, then the Anglican Church of the long eighteenth century was both characterized and overthrown by its confused European identity. Finding brethren across the ecclesiastical spectrum on the continent certainly provided churchmen with rich sources of apologetic, and allowed a very diverse communion to stick together. Yet it also questioned why Anglicans should enjoy privileges over those of their fellow countrymen who shared beliefs with Churches abroad. Ultimately, the establishment could not claim to be the local representative of universal true Christianity, and so legitimately to suppress other opinions, because it could never say exactly what that universal true Christianity was.

SELECT BIBLIOGRAPHY

Bellenger, Dominic Aidan, 'Fearless Resting Place: The Exiled French Clergy in Great Britain, 1789–1815', in Kirsty Carpenter and Philip Mansel (eds.), *The French Émigrés in Europe and the Struggle against Revolution, 1789–1814* (Basingstoke, 1999), pp. 214–29.

Claydon, Tony, *Europe and the Making of England, 1660–1760* (Cambridge, 2007).

Conway, Stephen, *Britain, Ireland, and Continental Europe in the Eighteenth Century: Similarities, Connections, Identities* (Oxford, 2011).

Goldgar, Anne, *Impolite Learning: Conduct and Community in the Republic of Letters, 1680–1750* (New Haven, CT, 1995).

Inhalainen, Pasi, *Protestant Nations Redefined* (Leiden, 2005).

Nishikawa, Sugiko, 'The SPCK in Defence of Protestant Minorities in Early Eighteenth-Century Europe', *Journal of Ecclesiastical History*, 56 (2005): 730–48.

Spurr, John, *The Restoration Church of England, 1646–1689* (New Haven, CT, 1991).

Sykes, Norman, *William Wake, Archbishop of Canterbury, 1657–1737*, 2 vols. (Cambridge, 1957).

Thompson, Andrew, *Britain, Hanover and the Protestant Interest, 1688–1756* (Woodbridge, 2006).

Walsh, John, Colin Haydon, and Stephen Taylor (eds.), *The Church of England c.1689–c.1833: From Toleration to Tractarianism* (Cambridge, 1993).

Ward, W. R., *The Protestant Evangelical Awakening* (Cambridge, 1992).

Young, Brian, 'A History of Variations: The Identity of the Eighteenth-Century Church of England', in Tony Claydon and Ian McBride (eds.), *Protestantism and National Identity: Britain and Ireland, c.1650–c.1850* (Cambridge, 1998), pp. 105–30.

---

[62] Conway, *Britain, Ireland and Continental Europe*, pp. 180–8.

18

Church Building and Architecture

Louis P. Nelson

One might expect a sanctity of style
August and manly in a holy pile,
And think an architect extremely odd
To build a playhouse for the church of God;
Yet half our churches, such the mode that reigns,
Are Roman theatres, or Grecian fanes;
Where broad arch'd windows to the eye convey
The keen diffusion of too strong a day;
Where, in the luxury of wanton pride,
Corinthian columns languish side by side,
Closed by an altar exquisitely fine,
Loose and lascivious as a Cyprian shrine.[1]

In 1754, English poet James Cawthorn engaged a question that would frame debates over church construction a century later: 'What was the best architectural style for a church to express "true" religion?' For Cawthorn, classical columns and temple pediments signalled the lasciviousness of ancient Athens or Rome. By contrast, the pointed arches and stained glass windows of Gothic or medieval forms more readily communicated the faithfulness, even sanctity, of a church in England. By the mid-nineteenth century, of course, the question had been settled; A. W. N. Pugin and the Ecclesiologists had won the debate and English churches of that period generally were presumed to be Gothic.[2] And their victory has been long-lived, buoyed in recent decades by the persistent associations of form and faith and the lasting historical perception of the eighteenth century—especially the eighteenth-century Church of England—as

---

[1] James Cawthorn, 'Of Taste: An Essay spoken at the Anniversary Visitation of Tunbridge School, 1754', in *The Poems of Hill, Cawthorn, and Bruce* (Chiswick, 1822), pp. 170–1.
[2] See Giles Worsley, 'The Origins of the Gothic Revival: A Reappraisal', *Transactions of the Royal Historical Society*, 6th series, 3 (1995): 105–50.

feeble at best and corrupt at worst.[3] Yet recently historians have undertaken a vigorous revision of this thesis, demonstrating the continuing vitality of Anglican faith.[4] This chapter follows that argument by demonstrating that the long eighteenth century was a period of significant church building and that the architecture of the Church of England in this era played a critical role in religious vitality and theological formation.

While certainly not to the expansive scale of Victorian church construction, the century and a half from 1662 to 1829 was an era of significant building. Taking centre stage in this story, of course, are the extraordinary efforts by Christopher Wren, his many assistants, and hundreds of artisans involved in the building of St Paul's Cathedral and more than fifty parish churches in the decades following the Great Fire of London in 1666.[5] Begun in 1676 and declared complete in 1711, St Paul's is rightly celebrated as the major architectural achievement of its era. Lost in its shadow, however, Wren's fifty parish churches were a major contribution in themselves. They were the first broad programme of experimentation in Anglican church form. Furthermore, the restoration of the episcopate in 1660 opened the door to an intensive wave of church inspection and repair across England after twenty years of neglect. If the diocese of York is any indication, more than half of England's churches required—and received—some repair in the latter decades of the seventeenth century.[6] And, despite Victorian aspersions of neglect, the regular maintenance of churches was continued in practice through the eighteenth century as well.[7] If both rural and urban parishes persisted in the upkeep of their churches—and given that the vast majority were medieval in origin, that was a constant issue—the rapid urbanization of eighteenth-century England was a major catalyst for new church construction. In 1710, Parliament appointed a building commission to undertake the construction of fifty new churches in London and Westminster's expanding suburbs. While this programme resulted in only eleven finished churches, it triggered a vibrant conversation among architects and churchmen about the

---

[3] Arthur Burns, *The Diocesan Revival in the Church of England, 1800–1870* (Oxford, 1999); Peter Virgin, *The Church in an Age of Negligence: Ecclesiological Structure and Problems of Church Reform, 1700–1840* (Cambridge, 1989).

[4] John Walsh, Colin Haydon, and Stephen Taylor (eds.), *The Church of England c.1689–c.1833: From Toleration to Tractarianism* (Cambridge, 1993); Jeremy Gregory, *Restoration, Reformation and Reform: The Archbishops of Canterbury and their Diocese* (Oxford, 2000); Jeremy Gregory and Jeffrey S. Chamberlain (eds.), *The National Church in Local Perspective: The Church of England and the Regions, 1660–1800* (Woodbridge, 2003); Terry Friedman, *The Eighteenth-Century Church in Britain* (New Haven, CT, 2011).

[5] For St Paul's Cathedral, see Kerry Downes, *Christopher Wren: The Design of St. Paul's Cathedral* (London, 1988); for the City churches, see Paul Jeffrey, *The City Churches of Sir Christopher Wren* (London, 1996).

[6] J. S. Purvis, *The Condition of Yorkshire Church Fabrics* (York, 1958), pp. 15–20.

[7] W. M. Jacob, 'Clergy and Society in Norfolk, 1707–1806', PhD thesis, Exeter University, 1982, esp. pp. 276–7.

proper form of an Anglican church, one that would generate scores of architectural drawings, sixteen wooden models, and have an impact across England and her empire.[8] Beyond London, the rapid expansion of many cities and towns during this period required the subdivision of urban parishes and the construction of a substantial number of new urban churches in cities like Birmingham and Bristol.[9] Over the course of the eighteenth century, Parliament passed 114 separate Acts concerned with the construction or reconstruction of parish churches, the majority of which were in cities and towns outside of London.[10] But an equal number of new Anglican churches were constructed in lands beyond British shores. Anglicans built new churches in places ranging from New England to the Caribbean to India, although the greatest concentrations were in Virginia, North and South Carolina, and Jamaica.[11] From the heart of London, to towns across Britain and her empire, Anglicans expended great time and energy on the repair and construction of new parish churches between 1662 and 1829.

The churches built across these locales varied quite widely in plan and appearance. Yet, as Nigel Yates has made clear, the majority of Anglican churches defaulted to a conservative tradition that espoused the division of the church interior into two chambers, a nave for ordinary service and a chancel for the celebration of the eucharistic sacrament (Fig. 18.1).[12] At least one-third, but more likely something closer to one-half, of all churches newly erected across England in this era took this form, achieved through a narrow, deep chancel projecting from a wider nave, or the installation of a chancel screen, creating two chambers of one longitudinal footprint, or both. This segregation into distinct chambers gave primacy to two of the three liturgical centres of the church; the preaching pulpit dominated the nave, while the communion table sat either centrally within the chancel or against the east wall. The third liturgical centre, the font, generally retained its ancient position near the main or west door of the church.

The Anglican sermon, generally well ordered and dispassionate, was delivered from a pulpit that clearly signified the authority of the preacher to

[8] Howard M. Colvin, 'Fifty New Churches', *Architectural Review*, 107 (1950): 189–96; M. H. Port (ed.), *The Commissions for Building Fifty New Churches: Minute Books, 1711–27. A Calendar*, London Record Society 23 (Woodbridge, 1986).

[9] W. M. Jacob, *Lay People and Religion in the Early Eighteenth Century* (Cambridge, 2002), pp. 201–3; Peter Borsay, *The English Urban Renaissance* (Oxford, 1991), pp. 110–11.

[10] Basil F. L. Clarke, *The Building of the Eighteenth-Century Church* (London, 1963), Appendix II.

[11] Dell Upton, *Holy Things and Profane: Anglican Churches in Colonial Virginia* (New York, 1986); Louis P. Nelson, *The Beauty of Holiness: Anglicanism & Architecture in Colonial South Carolina* (Chapel Hill, NC, 2008); Louis P. Nelson, 'Anglican Church Building and Local Context in Early Jamaica', in Kenneth A. Breisch and Alison K. Hoagland (eds.), *Building Environments, Perspectives in Vernacular Architecture* 10 (Knoxville, TN, 2005), pp. 63–79.

[12] Nigel Yates, *Buildings, Faith and Worship: The Liturgical Arrangement of Anglican Churches, 1600–1900* (Oxford, 2000 edn.), ch. 4.

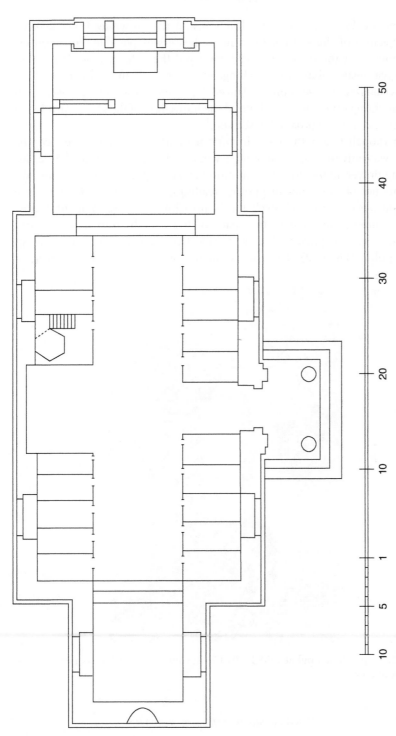

Fig. 18.1. James Gibbs, Plan for St Mary's, Patshull, Staffordshire (1740s). Image courtesy Joint Record Office, The Friary, Lichfield.

interpret the Word of God. Its elevation and the crowning tester assisted the projection of the sermon to as many hearers as possible. Furthermore, the canopy over the preacher's head conveyed the authority of his position in the great responsibility of preaching, and the beauty and refinement of the pulpit visualized the sermon's balanced logic and structure. A dove, often found alighting on the top, symbolized the indwelling of the Holy Spirit in the minister and in the words of his sermon.[13]

Even though it was the most important event of the weekly service, the sermon was only one aspect of Sunday worship. Depending on the 'Order for Morning Prayer' in the Book of Common Prayer, Anglican services followed a fairly predictable sequence of prayers, readings, recitations, and song. Since the pulpit was reserved exclusively for the preaching of the sermon, this liturgy required another location in the space of the church from which to lead reading, song, and prayers. This generated the distinctive form of a triple-decker pulpit (Fig. 18.2). The entirety of the service of Morning Prayer, or

Fig. 18.2. Triple-decker pulpit, mid-1730s, Christ Church, Lancaster County, Virginia. Photo by author.

---

[13] Nelson, *Beauty of Holiness*, pp. 190–4.

Matins, which was often one component of a three-part liturgical programme, was conducted from the reading desk. Seated in the upper reading desk, the minister was generally responsible for directing the service and leading the confession, prayers, and creed, and reading the Scriptures. From the lower desk, the parish clerk initiated hymns and psalms. And the sermon alone was delivered from the pulpit.

If the pulpit dominated the nave, the communion table dominated the chancel. Celebration of the Lord's Supper, also called the Holy Communion and the eucharist, was a spiritual practice central to the life of the faithful Anglican. The directives found in the Book of Common Prayer regarding the setting for Holy Communion were fairly simple. 'The Table at the Communion-time, having a fair white Linen Cloth upon it, shall stand in the body of the Church, or in the Chancel . . . And the Priest shall stand at the North Side of the Table . . . the people kneeling.'[14] The service began in a manner very similar to Morning Prayer with a series of prayers, preparations, and Scripture readings, followed by a sermon. After the sermon, the priest was to 'place upon the table so much Bread and Wine as he shall think sufficient', and those intending to partake in the communion were to be 'conveniently placed for the receiving of the Holy Sacrament'. The essential elements for the celebration of the communion, then, were a space for the communicants to gather, a communion table, and vessels to contain the elements. As Yates has demonstrated, the majority of eighteenth-century Anglicans who partook of communion did so in a church that provided a structurally distinct chancel.[15] Together with a triple-decker pulpit and a longitudinal nave, the structurally distinct chancel was a typical feature of Anglican church building throughout this period. Even so, alternatives emerged.

The Great Fire of London in 1666 set the stage for the first broad experimentation with Anglican church planning. Christopher Wren has been widely recognized as the popularizer of the Anglican model of an 'auditory church'. Writing near the end of his career, Wren drafted a letter that expounded at length on his experience in London parish church design. In addition to commentaries on materials, building in an urban setting, and the inappropriateness of urban cemeteries, he also argued that church plans should respond to the practical constraints of audibility, an extension of his scientific interest in sound.[16] To that end, Wren argued that churches should not be more than 60 feet wide and 90 feet long in order that everyone inside might be able to hear the preacher since 'a moderate Voice may be heard 50 feet distant before

---

[14] *The Book of Common Prayer* (London, 1760).

[15] Yates, *Buildings, Faith and Worship*, pp. 66–76; Friedman, *Eighteenth-Century Church*, p. 97.

[16] Lydia Soo, *Wren's 'Tracts' on Architecture and other Writings* (Cambridge, 1998), pp. 107–11, 'Letter on Building Churches'; see also Penelope Gouk, 'The Role of Acoustics and Music Theory in the Scientific Work of Robert Hooke', *Annals of Science*, 37 (1980): 573–605.

the Preacher, 30 feet on each side, and 20 behind the Pulpit . . . without losing the Voice at the last Word of the Sentence'. He further argued that given differences in emphasis, 'a *French* Man is heard further than an *English* Preacher', reinforcing for his readers the fact that his recommendations resulted from experimentation.[17] When providing an exemplar in his letter, Wren offered St James, Piccadilly (1676–84), a compact rectangular auditory.

To assign the introduction of the Anglican auditory church entirely to Wren, however, is to misunderstand the historical development of architectural typologies. As Peter Guillery has demonstrated, London had a number of pre-Fire examples of 'auditory' churches and meeting-houses, most especially the Broadway chapel in Westminster.[18] Furthermore, the development of auditory planning for new Anglican churches occurred beyond London before and during Wren's city church building programme.[19] Similar meeting-houses could be found across the continent as well, from France to the Netherlands.[20] So while occasional examples of direct inspiration can be found—St Mary's in Dublin (1697) appears to emulate Wren's St Clement Danes—the significance of Wren's auditory churches lies most securely in his experimentation and articulation of auditory principles for the London church-building efforts of the early eighteenth century. One of the earliest and most important examples of an auditory city church in the American colonies was St Philip's in Charleston, built in the 1720s (Fig. 18.3).

The rise of the auditory church in the seventeenth century foregrounded the importance of hearing the words of the sermon. This focus shifted the attention in the space of the church from the spatial segregation of the chancel to the strategic positioning of the pulpit. Increasingly over the course of the eighteenth century, the pulpit moved to the location in the church where hearing the sermon from all quarters in the church was most easily facilitated.[21] The rising importance of vocal clarity also meant that pulpits were surmounted with a canopy or tester, a flat surface positioned over the preacher's head to deflect sound down towards the pews.

[17] The whole letter is reprinted in Soo, *Wren's 'Tracts'*, pp. 112–18.

[18] Peter Guillery, 'Suburban Models, or Calvinism and Continuity in London's Seventeenth-Century Church Architecture', *Architectural History*, 48 (2005): 69–106; Peter Guillery, 'The Broadway Chapel, Westminster: A Forgotten Exemplar', *London Topographical Record*, 26 (1990): 107–14.

[19] For examples, see Yates, *Buildings, Faith and Worship*, ch. 5.

[20] Keith L. Sprunger, 'Puritan Church Architecture and Worship in a Dutch Context', *Church History*, 66 (1997): 36–53; Keith L. Sprunger, *Dutch Puritanism: A History of English and Scottish Churches of the Netherlands in the Sixteenth and Seventeenth Centuries* (Leiden, 1982); Bernard Reymond, *L'Architecture religieuse des Protestants* (Geneva, 1996). For a broader picture, see James White, *Protestant Worship and Church Architecture* (Oxford, 1964), ch. 4, 'Reformation Experiments'.

[21] Yates, *Buildings, Faith and Worship*, pp. 86–7; Friedman, *Eighteenth-Century Church*, pp. 97–9.

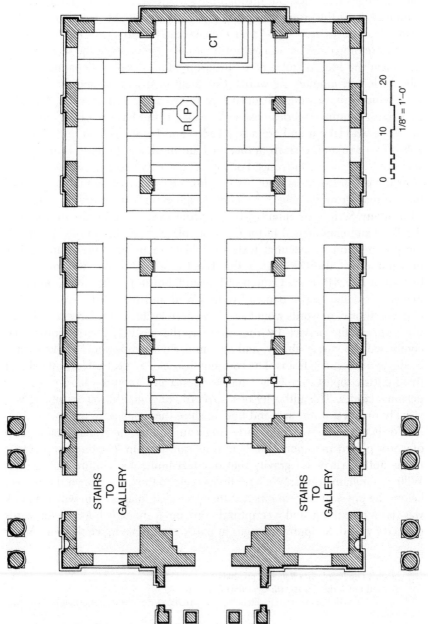

Fig. 18.3. St Philip's Church, Charleston, South Carolina, 1720s (burned 1835). Reconstruction drawing by author.

But in addition to hearing the sermon, early Anglicans were also familiar with seeing the Scriptures. Ornamentation of the church interior was an ancient English practice, but through the seventeenth century that ornament commonly took the form of Scripture. In most surviving English examples, the written Scriptures are located near the chancel, the pulpit, or the font, in an effort to reinforce the biblical authority of the sacraments or the sermon. The walls near the altar in Stokesay in Shropshire, for example, are painted with a tabernacle surrounding the words 'Come eat of my bread and drink of the wine which I have mingled forsake ye food... [the rest is lost]'. An early eighteenth-century American example reads (from Matthew 11): 'Come unto me all ye who labour and are heavy Laden and I will give you rest. Take my yoke upon you and learn from me; for I am meek and lowly in heart and ye shall find rest unto your souls. For my yoke is easy and my burden is light.' Near the pulpit the walls read: 'As new born Babes desire ye milk of ye word that ye may grow thereby.'[22] In 1710, Keighley in Yorkshire was beautified with 'many Scripture sentences (besides the Creed, the Lord's Prayer, and the Ten Commandments) fit for that holy place'.[23] Yet the most explicit was the presentation of essential texts on tablets in or near the chancel. The presentation of the Decalogue—the Ten Commandments—was prescribed by Canon LXXXII of the Church of England, but in practice the Commandments were often accompanied by the Creed and the Lord's Prayer.[24] The divine authority of words would also have been visible in the large folio books used during the service by the minister, the smaller, quarto books that comprised the parish library, and the similarly sized personal books owned by the wealthiest Anglicans. The common usage of a 'great Bible' implied that these parish copies were larger and more visually imposing than private or personal copies. The authority of the Word contained in the Scriptures was visually manifest in the size and fine finish of these bibles.[25]

Words were so powerful in early Anglicanism that the visual consumption of words played an important role in Anglican worship. The implied presence of the author carried a gravity that our text-inundated culture has lost. As William Graham argues: 'We have little access to the sense of awe and respect before the physical copy of *any* text that prevailed in ages... in which a book was (is) a rare thing, and a scriptural book often the *only* book.'[26] As words penned by God, Scripture passages in part or the Bible in whole took on the

---

[22] Jacobs, *Lay People and Religion*, pp. 208–9.

[23] Quoted in Clarke, *Eighteenth-Century Church*, p. 170.

[24] G. W. O. Addleshaw and F. Etchells, *The Architectural Setting of Anglican Worship* (London, 1956), p. 158.

[25] Paul Gutjahr, *An American Bible: A History of the Good Book in the United States* (Stanford, CA, 2002).

[26] William Graham, *Beyond the Written Word: Oral Aspects of Scripture in the History of Religion* (Cambridge, 1993), pp. 119–25.

sensuous presence of divine 'aura'. Describing sacred images, David Morgan defines aura as 'a presence or power that impresses upon the viewer the authenticity, veracity, or authority of whomever or whatever the image depicts'.[27] In an early modern Protestant context, sacred words would have had similar 'aura', especially for the illiterate majority who could certainly see and hear but not read. Leigh Schmidt argues that '[w]ords became printed objects more than breathed speech, things to be seen rather than voices to be heard'.[28] In a culture that still read out loud, written words were 'a repository of the vocal words of an author'.[29] Reinhard Wittman describes the most pervasive form of reading in the eighteenth century as 'naïve, non-reflexive and undisciplined, and for the most part performed aloud. It constituted the sole form of reading among the rural population and a large section of the urban lower classes too.'[30] When seeing holy writ, the early modern viewer would not have given it silent intellectual consideration as we might, but would have seen and heard the voice of God.[31]

The rising importance of hearing the sermon and seeing the Scriptures was paralleled by an increasing emphasis on church music. The most common form of music in the seventeenth-century Anglican liturgy was the practice of lining out the psalms.[32] In this mode of church music the parish clerk read or sung a line of the psalm and the congregation followed, singing the same line to one of a handful of popular tunes.[33] In the larger city churches, the voice of the parish clerk was particularly important for this reason. The clerk or minister selected the tune from what by the seventeenth century had become a fairly small handful of a dozen or so options with names like NORWICH, ST DAVIDS, SOUTHWEL [sic], and YORK.[34] These tunes had a simple, declamatory character with repetitive rhythms and one note per syllable, a musical structure

[27] David Morgan, *Protestants and Pictures: Religion, Visual Culture and the Age of American Mass Production* (Oxford, 1999), p. 6.

[28] Leigh Eric Schmidt, *Hearing Things: Religion, Illusion, and the American Enlightenment* (Cambridge, MA, 2002), p. 16.

[29] Graham, *Beyond the Written Word*, p. 39.

[30] Reinhard Wittman, 'Was there a Reading Revolution at the End of the Eighteenth Century?', in Guglielmo Cavallo and Roger Chartier (eds.), *A History of Reading in the West* (Amherst, MA, 1999), pp. 284–312 (p. 290). See also William Dyrness, *Reformed Theology and Visual Culture: The Protestant Imagination from Calvin to Edwards* (Cambridge, 2003), p. x.

[31] Graham, *Beyond the Written Word*, pp. 9–44.

[32] For examples, see Robert Stevenson, *Protestant Church Music in America: A Short Survey of Men and Movements from 1564 to the Present* (New York, 1966), pp. 13–21, 'New England Puritanism, 1620–1720'.

[33] Stephen Marini, *Sacred Song in America: Religion, Music, and Public Culture* (Champaign, IL, 2010), p. 75.

[34] Stevenson, *Protestant Church Music in America* (New York, 1970 edn.), pp. 18–19. A complete discussion of English church music from this period appears in Ruth M. Wilson, *Anglican Chant and Chanting in England, Scotland, and America, 1660 to 1820* (Oxford, 1996). See also Nicholas Temperley, 'The Old Way of Singing: Its Origins and Development', *Journal of the American Musicological Society*, 34 (1981): 511–44.

that clarified each word and emphasized the text over the music. Lining out the psalms to popular tunes did not require any books and meant that the entire congregation could participate. Although the practice led to embellishments and departures, it generally ensured that the congregation was singing together as a body.[35] In the opening decades of the eighteenth century, however, the dependence on familiar tunes for lining out the psalms was slowly replaced by singing both psalms and anthems from printed musical compositions.[36] The new repertoire of music was usually organized in three or four parts and printed together with the words, producing much more sophisticated, aesthetically rich, musical arrangements.

The adoption of more complex musical performance was accelerated significantly through the publication of new parish music collections. Foremost among these was John Chetham's *A Book of Psalmody* (1718), through which he hoped 'to better improve this excellent & useful part of our Service, to keep up an uniformity in our Parish-Churches, and bring them as much as may be to imitate their Mother Churches the Cathedrals'.[37] Over the course of the eighteenth century, this increasingly sophisticated musical performance was accompanied by an organ. While organs introduced the possibility of fundraising concerts, they were also an aid to piety. As early as 1708, one writer from Leeds argued that organs aided in 'promoting the Glory and Worship of the Almighty and Raising the Devotions of Pious Christians by Harmoniously praising his Holy Name with Psalms & Hymns'.[38] Whereas organs were a rarity in the seventeenth century throughout the Anglican world, they were becoming increasingly common by the middle of the eighteenth century.[39]

This emphasis first on the audibility of the sermon and then on the importance of beautiful performance of music changed Anglican church architecture. Eighteenth-century builders recognized that architecture facilitated or deadened sound quality and they designed their buildings accordingly. The relationship between architecture and the soundscape of the Christian liturgy had an ancient history. The complex spaces of the medieval church established a sequence of reverberations that created a fullness of sound reinforcing the mystery and awe central to pre-Reformation theology. Conversely, the simplicity of Protestant spaces created a clarity of voice critical to a religion of the Word. The complexity of singing in parts, the introduction of organs, and the increasing attention paid to the beauty of music imposed new demands on

---

[35] Stevenson, *Protestant Church Music* (1970 edn.), p. 22.

[36] Wilson, *Anglican Chant*, pp. 163–91, 'Chants and Chanting in Parish Churches, *c.*1710–1820'; cf. Stevenson, *Protestant Church Music* (1970 edn.), pp. 21–31, 'Regular Singing, 1720–1775'.

[37] John Chetham, *A Book of Psalmody* (London, 1718), Preface, quoted in Wilson, *Anglican Chant*, p. 164.

[38] Quoted in Friedman, *Eighteenth-Century Church*, p. 80.

[39] Temperley, *Music*, p. 7; Yates, *Buildings, Faith and Worship*, pp. 64–5.

the eighteenth-century church interior. The practice of designing spaces that best facilitated musical performance surfaces in the English context as early as the late seventeenth century, when Thomas Mace published the design for an octagonal music room in *Musick's Monument* (1676). Attention to the shape of the room was important, Mace informed his readers, because 'a *Good Room* will make [Instruments] seem *Better* and a *Bad Room, Worse*'. Mace argued that a room best suited musical performance when it had an '*Arch'd Seiling . . . Plain, and Very Smooth*' with an open interior and walls free from ornamental work, so that '*Sound* has Its *Free, and Un-interrupted Passage*'.[40] Such practical recommendations were realized in the music rooms of early eighteenth-century London.[41] One of these, Hickford's Great Room, near Piccadilly, was the most fashionable place for music in London by the mid-eighteenth century. It was no accident that its ceiling was a tray ceiling with coved sides, much like the larger parish churches of London in the same decades.[42] Mid-eighteenth-century church builders recognized that a compact rectangular footprint with an uninterrupted interior—an auditory—diminished musical reverberation far more successfully than longitudinal churches.

Changes in communion practice over the course of the century also transformed the church interior. In the earlier decades of the eighteenth century most if not all the communicants gathered in a chamber chancel for the communion service. Chancels of the later eighteenth century, however, either intruded into the nave of the church or were housed in shallow apses (Fig. 18.4). This shift in material form corresponds to changing liturgical practice.[43] By the middle of the century, the entire congregation began to remain in the church to observe the communion service, and communicants remained in their pews with the rest of the congregation through the prayers and exhortations, approaching the chancel only to partake of the elements. The practice of surrounding the table—so essential to creating the community in earlier celebrations of the sacrament—had been abandoned as communicants now knelt before the altar table. Under these new liturgical conditions, vocal projection from the chancel to communicants in their pews became a practical challenge. The shallow, curved chancel of later eighteenth-century churches functioned as a sound shell, projecting the voice of the minister speaking in the chancel to the entire congregation. Underneath a coved ceiling, the organ at the west end and the curved chancel at the east became

[40] Thomas Mace, *Musick's Monument* (London, 1676), pp. 238–40.
[41] Michael Forsyth, *Buildings for Music: The Architect, the Musician, and the Listener from the Seventeenth Century to the Present Day* (Cambridge, MA, 1985), pp. 21–43.
[42] Forsyth, *Buildings for Music*, p. 28.
[43] Addleshaw and Etchells, *Architectural Setting*, p. 56.

Fig. 18.4. St Catherine's Church, Dublin, Ireland, 1760s. Photo by author.

facing acoustic centres in an eighteenth-century space far better equipped to clarify and amplify the sacred sounds of the liturgy.

In addition to serving as a sound shell, the tall, shallow chancel also became a dramatic frame for the visual consumption of the communion by the entire congregation. By the end of the eighteenth century, pews began to orient towards the chancel, offering direct lines of sight to the communion table for a larger proportion of the congregation. In the same decades the gathered three-decker pulpit dissolved into two separate fixtures—a pulpit and a reading desk—positioned either side of the nave.[44] By the 1820s, this division was commonplace, fully orienting the interior along the east–west axis. Finally, the communion table was often elevated on a dais of three steps raised above the floor of the nave.[45] In the same decades clusters of box pews with ringing benches—which resulted in hearers facing all directions—were replaced with ranks of pews, turning all eyes towards the east end of the church.[46] This late eighteenth-century material change foregrounded the importance of seeing. As written by early nineteenth-century Church Building Commissioners, '[d]ouble or square pews were consequently forbidden, and pews were to be of a uniform low height, so that all may see'.[47] By the early nineteenth century,

---

[44] Yates, *Buildings, Faith and Worship*, p. 116.
[45] Yates, *Buildings, Faith and Worship*, p. 120.
[46] Yates, *Buildings, Faith and Worship*, pp. 116–20; Nelson, *Beauty of Holiness*.
[47] Yates, *Buildings, Faith and Worship*, p. 119.

the space of the Anglican church interior accommodated an increasing demand for clarity of sight in addition to the earlier drive towards clarity of hearing.

A brief survey of those churches erected by Anglicans in the American colonies offers a telling perspective on various dimensions of late seventeenth- and eighteenth-century church-building practices. Dell Upton's careful analysis of Anglican parish churches in Virginia makes clear that seventeenth-century churches were generally longitudinal with a conceptual division between the nave and the chancel, as in similar examples in contemporary England. When these parishes felt the need for larger buildings, they often expanded through the construction of an addition perpendicular to the main building, resulting in a T-plan. But some early eighteenth-century parishes, faced with the prospect of building a new church, erected instead a cruciform planned church. Upton understands these buildings as accommodating the new demands on audibility in large church buildings. The planning of early Virginia's Anglican parish churches mirrored quite closely those of their counterparts in parishes across the motherland; in all cases they functioned very clearly to buttress the local elite.[48]

There are, however, two interesting patterns that set colonial church construction apart from that in the motherland. The first is Carl Lounsbury's observation that the establishment date of a colony appears to have played a role in the planning of Anglican church design. Agreeing with Upton, Lounsbury argues that the generally longitudinal parish churches in Virginia do parallel their counterparts in England through the seventeenth and well into the eighteenth century. Yet in Maryland, the much younger colony just to the north, parish churches correlate more strongly to the more compact auditory planning of the fashionable urban churches built in London in the very late seventeenth and early eighteenth century. Without the inscription of the older tradition in the landscape, Lounsbury argues, the younger colony more freely adopted the newer formula.[49] The second observation is that the cruciform plan appears far more commonly in the colonies than it does as new construction in Britain.[50] If newly built cruciform churches were rare in Britain, they were a strong minority in Virginia and in South Carolina, and the majority in Jamaica and Bermuda (Fig. 18.5). Eighteenth-century cruciform churches are also common in rural parishes in Ireland.[51] It seems likely that

---

[48] Upton, *Holy Things and Profane*, esp. ch. 5, 'Churches'.

[49] Carl Lounsbury, 'Anglican Church Design in the Chesapeake: English Inheritances and Regional Interpretations', in Alison K. Hoagland and Kenneth A. Breisch (eds.), *Constructing Image, Identity, and Place*, Perspectives in Vernacular Architecture 9 (Knoxville, TN, 2003), pp. 22–38.

[50] On the general absence of newly built cruciform plans in England and Wales, see Yates, *Buildings, Faith and Worship*, pp. 100–1.

[51] Consider St Finnian's, Kinnitty, and St Catherine's, Tullamore, both in County Offaly; and St Paul's, Newtown Forbes; Killoe church; and Clonbroney parish church, all in County Longford.

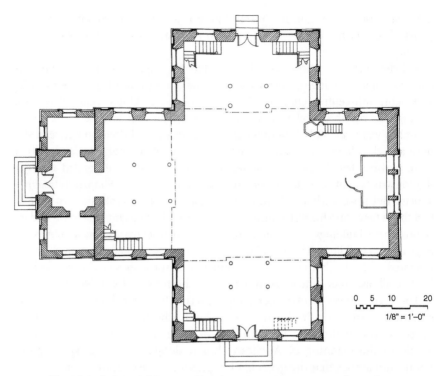

Fig. 18.5. St James, Montego Bay, Jamaica, 1760s. Drawing by author.

the cruciform shape of the church was intended to be symbolic. St Paul's
parish church in South Carolina was described as bearing 'the form of a cross';
St Andrew's parish church, also in South Carolina, was described as enlarged
'in the form of a cross'.[52] In their desire to distinguish or set apart their newly
constructed churches, in a newly colonized landscape Anglicans revealed a
theological parallel between the baptism of a child and the consecration of a
church. Both were ritual acts of inscription that extended a claim about the
spiritual indwelling of God, one in a person, the other in a building. Making
the sign of the cross on the forehead of a child consecrated him or her for
service in the Church. Similarly, the use of a cross in the form of the church
might have been seen as consecrating the land upon which it stands and
protecting it 'against sin, the world, and the devil'. Even so, the shape was
never entirely theological. As I have argued elsewhere, the cruciform plan
in Jamaica might have been a comforting and familiar cultural marker of
Englishness in a dangerous and racially African landscape.[53] Anglicans in

[52] Cited in Nelson, *Beauty of Holiness*, p. 152.
[53] Nelson, 'Anglican Church Building'.

colonial contexts built churches that responded both to their memories of homelands and the realities of their new circumstances.

If architectural planning was the central consideration for the vast majority of Anglican church builders in this period, the implications of historical inspiration dominated the imagination of some very few. The most profound contributions in this arena were certainly offered by Nicholas Hawksmoor, the leading architect in the effort to build fifty new churches in London and Westminster after the 1711 establishment of a commission for that purpose.[54] Architectural historian Pierre de la Ruffinière du Prey has examined in detail Hawksmoor's unbuilt design for a 'Basilica after the primitive Christians', an extraordinary design produced in concert with the wave of debates over Anglican church design triggered by the work of the commission.[55] As du Prey makes clear, Hawksmoor's basilica is a carefully studied and learned design informed by the most recent scholarship on the forms of the earliest Christian churches, especially *Origines Ecclesiasticae: or, the Antiquities of the Christian Church*, published in 1711 by the Revd Richard Bingham. Based on a deep study of ancient forms, Hawksmoor invested in his London churches clear references to the ancient past and an intentional emulation of his imagined early Christian archetype. Yet if Hawksmoor was the most articulate and prolific architect in this vein, there are certainly other examples that suggest an interest in connecting contemporary Anglican church design to the ancient world. The architect Batty Langley, whose pattern books included numerous designs for Anglican liturgical fittings, often wrote under the pseudonym Hiram, the presumed architect of Solomon's Temple.[56] St Philip's church in Charleston, South Carolina, might reflect an interest in early reconstructions of the Temple of Solomon.[57] The architect John Wood Sr worked to restore the cathedral in Llandaff, Wales, in order to return it to what he believed to be its early Christian origins.[58] The 1739 design for a Protestant cathedral in Waterford, Ireland, includes a centralized bapisterium of early Christian inspiration.[59] And in the early nineteenth century, Lewis Way, a leading proponent of the conversion of Jews, built a church at Stansted in West Sussex replete with Old Testament symbolism.[60]

---

[54] For an introduction to this project, see Port (ed.), *Commissions for Fifty New Churches*. On Hawksmoor, see Kerry Downes, *Hawksmoor* (London, 1970); Vaughn Hart, *Nicholas Hawksmoor: Rebuilding Ancient Wonders* (New Haven, CT, 2002).

[55] Pierre de la Ruffinière du Prey, 'Hawksmoor's "Basilica after the Primitive Christians": Architecture and Theology', *Journal of the Society of Architectural Historians*, 48 (1989): 38–52; argument expanded in Pierre de la Ruffinière du Prey, *Hawksmoor's London Churches: Architecture and Theology* (Chicago, IL, 2000).

[56] Friedman, *Eighteenth-Century Church*, p. 519.

[57] Nelson, *Beauty of Holiness*, ch. 1, 'The City Churches'.

[58] Friedman, *Eighteenth-Century Church*, p. 384.

[59] Friedman, *Eighteenth-Century Church*, p. 387.

[60] Yates, *Buildings, Faith and Worship*, p. 113.

But if the study and emulation of specific ancient or biblical buildings was not widespread, the general emulation of antique temples was commonplace. In his monumental study of the eighteenth-century church in Britain, Terry Friedman has argued convincingly that by the early eighteenth century architects intentionally designed churches in the form of an antique temple. Designs ranged from the fully peripheral temple with freestanding columns entirely surrounding the body of the church, to the more common practice of designing the primary façade of a church with a portico or temple front.[61] The most famous Anglican church design of this era—James Gibbs's St Martin-in-the-Fields—is squarely in this tradition. With the church body encased in classical pilasters fronted by a protruding Corinthian portico and surmounted by an elegant steeple design, St Martin's was widely recognized as a monumental design achievement. Furthermore, the church appeared prominently in the architect's *A Book of Architecture*, published soon after the completion of the building. Through this publication, Gibbs's design became the inspiration for urban churches from Dublin, Ireland, to Charleston, South Carolina, to Kolkata, India, creating a shared visual urban form across the expanding British Empire. Based on an extensive examination of this practice in the English context, Friedman has suggested that this intensive pursuit of antique models for contemporary Protestant churches was distinctively Anglican; no similar scholarly endeavour animated continental architecture—Protestant or Catholic—and in this way the antique temple-cum-church shaped not just Britain but the British Empire as well.[62]

By way of conclusion, it is worth attending to the importance of sensibility and emotion in both Anglican worship and architecture. In the later eighteenth century, Penuel Bowen, a Congregationalist visitor to Charleston, South Carolina, described for a Boston friend Charleston's two Anglican churches:

> They accord to my material sensations, being efforts and effects of great cost and ingenuity. They appear without and within quite superb and grand, tho neither gothic and heavy [*sic*] The Furniture is rich and good and the organs large and full. One of them especially is finely played and the assemblies of people large and splendid and well behaved too.

Bowen observed his own response to the rich aesthetics of the church and the impact of these aesthetics on 'the assemblies', a term denoting audience rather than congregation. As he continued, however, he expressed the conflict between the effect these churches had on him and his own Calvinist theology, which rejected the agency given to church aesthetics by Anglicans. 'I will own to you Sir these things have and always had an agreeable effect on the sensitive, nay the feeling part of Devotion in me. You will lampoon the idea if you please

---

[61] Friedman, *Eighteenth-Century Church*, ch. 21.
[62] Friedman, *Eighteenth-Century Church*, pp. 383–92, 402.

and beat it out of me if you can please ... I am too much a materialist.'[63] The 'feeling part of Devotion' that had tempted Bowen was a critical aspect of Anglican worship through the course of the eighteenth century. Whether classical or Gothic, architecture engaged the regularity of the liturgy, music sung in parts, with or without an organ, and visual representations of God's voice to integrate the senses into the formation of the religious self.

If early eighteenth-century Anglican theologians and church architects explored the potential of ancient building forms for newly built churches, their later counterparts began to express deep concern for the antiquity of the buildings already in the landscape. As Terry Friedman has clearly demonstrated, eighteenth-century Anglicans began an expansive campaign to make studied and sensitive repairs to their own ancient churches.[64] Publications on the fabrics of ancient cathedrals appeared through the century and buildings were preserved as testaments to earlier generations of the faithful. In his 1720s history of Canterbury cathedral, John Dart declared: 'the venerable Grandeur ... [struck] a distant Awe upon the Beholder'.[65] As a result, an increasing awareness of the antiquity of the churches in the British landscape generated a degree of awe that served to reinforce the romantic power of these places. For some eighteenth-century Anglicans, the power of the medieval meant that Gothic was best suited to modern church architecture. Examples of new work in the Gothic taste become increasingly popular over the course of the eighteenth century. As reported in a 1760s *New History of London*, Gothic architecture was preferred for church buildings '[b]ecause it was thought to be better suited to the purposes of devotion, striking the imagination with a religious dignity, and holy awe, so as to dispose the mind to the worship of the deity'.[66] By the end of the century, these sensations would be described as sublime. By the early nineteenth century, churches newly built in the Gothic style were fairly commonplace. These stylistic changes coordinated with the newly important eastward orientation from within the body of the nave— facilitating visibility—that all the senses might be enlisted to the purposes of devotion. And in each of these changes—architectural style and internal orientation especially—the late eighteenth- and early nineteenth-century church set the stage for the architectural and liturgical revolution of the Oxford Movement, which would introduce profound transformations in

[63] 'Letter from Penuel Bowen in Chas to Gen Lincoln, July 9, 1786', Bowen Cooke Papers, South Carolina Historical Society, Charleston.

[64] Friedman, *Eighteenth-Century Church*, chs. 12–16; see also Rosemary Sweet, '"A Neat Structure with Pillars": Changing Perceptions of the Temple Church in the Long Eighteenth Century', in Robin Griffith-Jones and David Park (eds.), *The Temple Church in London: History, Architecture, Art* (Woodbridge, 2010), pp. 175–94.

[65] Friedman, *Eighteenth-Century Church*, p. 232.

[66] Quoted in Friedman, *Eighteenth-Century Church*, p. 185.

Anglican architecture through the middle decades of the nineteenth century and launch the next major season of Anglican church design.[67]

SELECT BIBLIOGRAPHY

Addleshaw, G. W. O. and F. Etchells, *The Architectural Setting of Anglican Worship* (London, 1956).

Bremner, Alex, *Imperial Gothic: Religious Architecture and High Anglican Culture in the British Empire, 1840–1870* (New Haven, CT, 2013).

Clarke, Basil F. L., *The Building of the Eighteenth-Century Church* (London, 1963).

Colvin, Howard M., 'Fifty New Churches', *Architectural Review*, 107 (1950): 189–96.

Du Prey, Pierre de la Ruffinière, *Hawksmoor's London Churches: Architecture and Theology* (Chicago, IL, 2000).

Friedman, Terry, *The Eighteenth-Century Church in Britain* (New Haven, CT, 2011).

Gregory, Jeremy and Jeffrey S. Chamberlain (eds.), *The National Church in Local Perspective: The Church of England and the Regions, 1660–1800* (Woodbridge, 2003).

Guillery, Peter, 'Suburban Models, or Calvinism and Continuity in London's Seventeenth-Century Church Architecture', *Architectural History*, 48 (2005): 69–106.

Jeffrey, Paul, *The City Churches of Sir Christopher Wren* (London, 1996).

Nelson, Louis P., *The Beauty of Holiness: Anglicanism & Architecture in Colonial South Carolina* (Chapel Hill, NC, 2008).

Upton, Dell, *Holy Things and Profane: Anglican Churches in Colonial Virginia* (New York, 1986).

Yates, Nigel, *Buildings, Faith and Worship: The Liturgical Arrangement of Anglican Churches, 1600–1900* (Oxford, 2000 edn.).

---

[67] Alex Bremner, *Imperial Gothic: Religious Architecture and High Anglican Culture in the British Empire, 1840–1870* (New Haven, CT, 2013); Phoebe Stanton, *The Gothic Revival and American Church Architecture: An Episode in Taste, 1840–1856* (Baltimore, MD, 1968); Megan Aldrich, *The Gothic Revival* (New York, 1994).

19

Anglicanism and Music

Nicholas Temperley

THE MUSIC OF WORSHIP (1): ENGLISH CATHEDRALS AND CHORAL FOUNDATIONS

In music as in other forms, the prevailing sentiment guiding the Church of England has been the maintenance of tradition, especially in the face of movements towards Catholicism, Protestant Dissent, or rationalism. The grand, immemorial custom of daily choral services symbolized permanence and stability, as it still does for many people today, and offered reassurance in times of religious change. In terms of musical history, the choral foundations have preserved a unique body of music with an almost continuous performing record from long before the Reformation.

The Georgian period was not the most distinguished in the long history of English cathedral music. Waning financial and moral support for the institutions led to a decline in standards of performance and in the creative energy that was needed to maintain its vitality. Indeed Edmund Fellowes, a leading historian of cathedral music, considered that 'after the very lean period, extending over a hundred years, a great revival took place in the early years of Victoria'.[1] Before that lean period, however, there was a time of high achievement, when the overall conservatism was tempered by an exciting strain of innovation and creativity centred on the Chapel Royal.

Veneration of tradition was especially strong when the Established Church was reinstated in 1660, because of the fierce desire to counteract and obliterate the recent interruption. Just as Gothic churches and black-letter type enjoyed a brief revival, so also was there a vigorous effort to recover the ancient forms of church music. Unlike buildings and bibles, music ultimately depends on regular performance for survival, and a generation was growing

---

[1] Edmund H. Fellowes, *English Cathedral Music from Edward VI to Edward VII* (London, 1941), p. 203.

up that had never heard the music of the cathedral service or the sound of trained choirs and organs. Energetic action was needed to bring them back to life.

The 1662 Act of Uniformity, overruling puritan objections, fully restored the stately language and ritual of earlier times. Like its predecessors, the revised Prayer Book had few direct references to music, but it did contain a new rubric after the collects in Morning and Evening Prayer: 'In quires and places where they sing, here followeth the anthem.' This often quoted rubric did not represent an actual innovation. Anthems had been sung after the third collect ever since the royal Injunctions of 1559 authorized 'in the beginnyng, or thend of common prayers, eyther at mornyng or evenynge, . . . an hymne, or suche lyke songe, to the prayse of almyghte God, in the best sort of melodye and musicke that maye be convenientlye devysed'.[2] It was the addition of closing prayers in 1662 that made it necessary to reauthorize the custom by means of a rubric. 'Quires and places where they sing' were those foundations that had endowments to support choral music: the Chapel Royal; the royal peculiars of Westminster Abbey and St George's Chapel, Windsor; twenty-two English cathedrals; four collegiate parish churches; six colleges at Oxford and Cambridge; and the colleges of Winchester and Eton. In most of these places, urgent steps were taken to restore the choral service.[3] One of the greatest difficulties was to find and educate an adequate body of choirboys. They had to be trained from scratch, and to learn the entire musical repertoire. Captain Henry Cooke (*c.*1616–72), Master of the children at the Chapel Royal, had been authorized to conscript boys with good voices from anywhere in England and bring them to Whitehall, which certainly added to the difficulties at some provincial foundations.

Publications of a kind never previously thought necessary were now issued to describe and explain fully the music of choral worship, forestalling any attempts to take advantage of the Prayer Book's vagueness in musical matters. Edward Lowe, one of the organists of the Chapel Royal, published *A Short Direction for the Performance of Cathedrall Service* (1661), to inform 'Persons as are Ignorant of it, And shall be call'd to officiate in Cathedrall, or Collegiate Churches'. A second edition (*A Review of Some Short Directions*, 1664) incorporated the changes found in the 1662 Prayer Book. This was complemented by James Clifford's *The Divine Services and Anthems usually Sung in His Majesties Chappell, and in all Cathedral and Collegiate Choirs in England and Ireland* (1663), which included the words of 172 anthems; in a second edition (1664) the number was increased to 406.

---

[2] *Injunctions geven by the Quenes Majestie* (London, 1559), article 49.
[3] See Ian Spink, *Restoration Cathedral Music 1660–1714*, Oxford Studies in British Church Music (Oxford, 1995), part 3.

These publications served to re-establish the music of Elizabethan times. Services[4] by Thomas Tallis and William Byrd were recommended, and most of the anthems in Clifford's wordbook were from that period or the early seventeenth century; very few were from Charles I's time. They included some magnificent music in a well-developed polyphonic style, but by the 1660s they were conservative to the point of archaism.

At the Chapel Royal, however, there was a strong modernizing force. The king, whose musical tastes had been formed during his long exile at the court of Louis XIV, did not hide his impatience with the older styles.[5] A consort of viols was introduced, which both accompanied the voices and played a 'symphony' between the verses of the anthem—'and very fine it is', as Pepys wrote in his diary on 14 September 1662. By 1670 there were fifteen instruments of the violin family, and from 1673 until the end of the reign a total of twenty instrumentalists were involved, obviously on the model of Louis's '24 violons du roi'. Their annual cost of £400 is an indication of the level of Charles's interest in the music of the chapel.[6]

With the new accompaniments came a new style, partly influenced by French and Italian models, but with a strong native element as well. Charles liked to tap his foot to a lively rhythm. Triple time, dance-like dotted rhythms, passages of vocal display, and sprightly closing alleluias became the fashion, and there was increasing use of the solo voice. The verse anthem, in which a group of soloists alternate with the full choir, had been developed in late Elizabethan times, but it was now taken to a point where the full choir was often relegated to an insignificant closing section. A further departure was the development of the solo anthem, where a single singer carried the lion's share of the music, which he could ornament at will. Some remarkable soloists were available in the chapel choir, above all John Gostling (1644–1733), a bass of extraordinary range and power, or later the star countertenor Richard Elford (d. 1714). Soloists were encouraged to show off their voices in a manner that some described as theatrical.

What is often called the 'Restoration style', as developed in these stimulating conditions, combined continental fashions with a vivid new manner of setting English words and a daring extension of accepted harmonic conventions. The result was a second golden age of English cathedral music. Matthew Locke (c.1621–77), the leading English composer at the time of the Restoration, was

---

[4] A 'service', as a musical composition, was a choral setting of at least the morning and evening canticles (usually Te Deum, Jubilate, Magnificat, and Nunc Dimittis) and three texts from the ante-communion service: the Responses to the Commandments (sometimes misnamed the Kyrie), Creed, and Sanctus. Some included the alternative canticles. All the movements were in the same key.

[5] Fellowes, *English Cathedral Music*, p. 133.

[6] Spink, *Restoration Cathedral Music*, p. 102; Peter Holman, *Four and Twenty Fiddlers: The Violin at the English Court 1540–1690* (Oxford, 1995 edn.), esp. p. 398.

a Roman Catholic who was appointed organist of the Queen's Chapel, but he also wrote English anthems for the Chapel Royal. Described by Spink as 'a genius—though of a peculiar and almost perverse kind',[7] he, more than any other composer, was the chief source of the singular flavour of much music of the period, with its harsh dissonances, its bold melodic and rhythmic surprises, and its intensity of word setting. A group of Cooke's students, led by Pelham Humfrey (1647–74), John Blow (1649–1708), and William Turner (1651–1740), eagerly developed the new style. 'This, his Majesty greatly encourag'd, by indulging their youthful fancys...In a few years more, several others, Educated in the Chappell, produc'd their Compositions in this style, for otherwise, it was in vain to hope to please his Majesty.'[8] Finally, Henry Purcell (1659–95), still today regarded by many as England's greatest composer, brought these brilliant developments to their summit.

Not everyone shared Charles's tastes, and the Chapel Royal composers also produced more conservative work, probably for use when the king was not in attendance. The provincial cathedrals, with few exceptions, kept to a conservative repertoire and style. Neither James II nor William III took much interest in the Chapel Royal. The choir was reduced in size, and in 1689 the string orchestra was disbanded. Spink sees a decisive change in Purcell's church music after the death of Charles II: 'The anthems he wrote for the chapel up to 1685, for all their extravagance, have an intimacy, warmth, and even good humour that is lacking in those he wrote for James or William. There is something haughty and less human about them.'[9] Anne was the last monarch who took a personal interest in the services, and there was a brief revival of standards at the chapel to go with her High Church predilections. The anthems of William Croft (1678–1727) and John Weldon (1676–1736) suggest that active royal patronage was once again encouraging innovation and self-confidence.

The arrival of the Hanoverian kings initiated more than a century of slowly declining standards of performance in choral foundations. They and their German entourage attended the Lutheran chapel at the Court of St James, founded by Prince George of Denmark in 1702. Naturally George I and II, as Lutherans, paid little attention to the Chapel Royal, while cathedral choirs were also losing support, for reasons already outlined. The sorry state of things in the late eighteenth century was recorded by Lord Torrington, a connoisseur of cathedral music who toured the country and reported on what he heard.[10]

---

[7] Spink, *Restoration Cathedral Music*, p. 111.

[8] Thomas Tudway, introduction to 'A Collection of the Most Celebrated Services and Anthems both Ancient and Modern used in the Church of England beginning at the Restoration of K. Charles II', vol. 2 (1716?), British Library, Harleian MS 7338; quoted in Spink, *Restoration Cathedral Music*, pp. 115, 437.

[9] Spink, *Restoration Cathedral Music*, p. 166.

[10] John Byng, 5th Viscount Torrington, *The Torrington Diaries (1781–94)*, ed. C. Bruyn Andrews, 4 vols. (London, 1934–8); Nicholas Temperley, 'Music in Church', in H. Diack

Deans and chapters diverted funds intended to support the choral services, and absenteeism of both clergy and choir members, not to mention frequent drunkenness among the latter, made it impossible to maintain proper musical standards. These disgraceful conditions prevailed in many cathedrals well into the Victorian period.[11] Increasingly, the organ took on the duty (once fulfilled by cornetts and sackbuts) of covering up gaps in the choral texture. Theodore Aylward, organist of St George's Chapel, Windsor, from 1788 to 1801, one day received a message from the choir that they were unable to sing the anthem he had selected, 'because Mr. —— had a cold'. He returned the answer that 'they could do as they liked about singing it, but he intended to play it'.[12] Attendance at cathedral services also sank to its lowest historical levels. Torrington thought he might 'live to see when none will be present at a cathedral service, but a reader, a verger, and 2 singing boys, who will gallop it over in a few minutes'.[13]

In spite of these lapses, continuity was maintained to a surprising degree. The wordbooks of the Chapel Royal and several cathedrals show that all earlier periods continued to be represented in the music of the daily services, while the output of new music was quite impressive. Some encouragement was provided by annual charity meetings centred on the cathedrals (to be discussed later). In the composition of anthems and services, the period after 1700 saw a growing Italian influence. Anthems were now subdivided into recitatives and arias or duets, adopting the forms of Italian opera as well as its developing conventions of tonality; the role of the chorus was gradually reduced. Styles of performance moved in the same direction, with a growing use of ornamentation, cadenzas, and other devices serving to display the solo voice.[14] Nevertheless, 'full' anthems (for the whole choir) were never entirely abandoned. In general the English anthem retained its distinctive character in the work of many soundly trained composers and a few exceptionally gifted ones such as Maurice Greene (1696–1755) and William Boyce (1711–79). Services were necessarily more stereotyped than anthems. The long texts of most of the canticles, which could not legally be abridged, placed limits on the possibility of any form of expansive music, whether soloistic or contrapuntal; and they had been set to music so many times that true originality was difficult to achieve.

An important feature that developed in this period was the Anglican chant, derived ultimately from Gregorian chant but now taking on the form of a miniature piece of classical music, consisting of ten or twenty chords, to which

---

Johnstone and Roger Fiske (eds.), *Music in Britain: The Eighteenth Century*, Blackwell History of Music in Britain 4 (Oxford, 1990), p. 364.

[11] See Nicholas Temperley, 'Cathedral Music', in Nicholas Temperley (ed.), *Music in Britain: The Romantic Age 1800–1914*, Blackwell History of Music in Britain (Oxford, 1990), V, pp. 172–3.

[12] George Job Elvey, *Life & Reminiscences*, ed. Lady Elvey (London, 1894), p. 37.

[13] Torrington, *Diaries*, I, p. 55.   [14] Temperley, 'Music in Church', pp. 363–4.

the daily psalms were sung. There was considerable variation in the way the syllables were distributed among the notes. In 1834 a study was published recording different modes of chanting that had evolved in the cathedrals of Lincoln, York, Canterbury, and Bangor.[15]

The Church of England was the only religious body that allowed organs in its worship, and so became the chief patron of the voluntary, another form that flourished in Georgian times. Voluntaries, as their name implies, had traditionally been improvised; but as more and more parish churches acquired organs, it began to be worthwhile for publishers to print sets by leading organists. The first, by Thomas Roseingrave (1690/1–1766), organist of St George, Hanover Square, was published in 1725. English organs at this time lacked pedals, and possessed only a modest range of stops compared with those of North Germany and the Netherlands, but a distinctive type of voluntary in several movements was developed, making use of solo stops imitating orchestral instruments. There were two outstanding composers of voluntaries: John Stanley (1712–86) and Samuel Wesley (1766–1837).

THE MUSIC OF WORSHIP (2): ENGLISH PARISH CHURCHES

Unlike choral foundations, most parish churches had no endowments for their music. At the time of the Restoration and for many decades after, very few had organs,[16] let alone choirs. The Prayer Book services were therefore spoken throughout. The only music was congregational, and consisted of metrical psalms and a few hymns, gathered in *The Whole Book of Psalms, Collected into English Meter, by Thomas Sternhold, John Hopkins, and others*, which was first published in complete form in 1562 and went into hundreds of editions over the next three centuries.[17] It was widely believed that 'Sternhold and Hopkins', also known as the 'Old Version', contained the only psalms and hymns that could legally be sung in Anglican worship, and it was not until 1820 that this theory was successfully challenged in the Consistory Court of York.[18]

---

[15] Jonathan Gray, *Twenty-Four Chants: To which are prefixed, Remarks on Chanting* (London and York, 1834); Ruth M. Wilson, *Anglican Chant and Chanting in England, Scotland, and America, 1660 to 1820* (Oxford, 1996).

[16] See Nicholas Temperley, 'Organs in English Parish Churches, 1660–1830', in Nicholas Temperley, *Studies in English Church Music, 1550–1900* (Farnham, 2009), pp. 175–92.

[17] See Beth Quitslund and Nicholas Temperley (eds.), *The Whole Book of Psalms: A Critical Edition of the Texts and Tunes*, Renaissance English Text Society Publications, 36 (Tucson, AZ, forthcoming).

[18] Thomas K. McCart, *The Matter and Manner of Praise: The Controversial Evolution of Hymnody in the Church of England 1760–1820*, Drew Studies in Liturgy 8 (Lanham, MD and London, 1998), pp. 93–103.

Earlier attempts to dislodge the collection, including those made by Parliament in the 1640s, were largely unsuccessful. In 1696 *A New Version of the Psalms* by Nahum Tate and Nicholas Brady was published by authority of the king in council, but it was another century before it overtook the Old Version in popularity.[19]

Psalms were generally sung before and after the sermon. The priest would retire to the vestry to change from a surplice to a Geneva gown (before sermon) or back into a surplice (after sermon). Meanwhile the parish clerk, usually an uneducated man with little or no musical training, would 'line out' the psalm by reading the first line or pair of lines in a loud voice, for the benefit of those who could not read or had no book, and then lead the seated congregation in the singing of that line, choosing one of a dozen well-known tunes, and setting the pitch at whatever level he thought convenient. In this fashion some six to ten stanzas would usually be sung. By the later seventeenth century the singing had reached an almost unbelievably slow tempo, perhaps two to three seconds per note, and it could take as long as an hour to get through the singing of a long psalm, as Pepys recorded at St Olave, Hart Street, in his diary for 6 January 1661.

This kind of singing was truly the music of the people. With few exceptions the gentry, and even the clergy, openly dissociated themselves from the proceedings, while both literary and musical critics, as well as the church hierarchy, were ever more scornful of the psalm paraphrases and tunes, and of the way they were sung, often called the 'Old Way of Singing' and characterized by dragging, scooping, and the addition of subsidiary notes between the proper notes of the tune.[20]

Efforts to reform the Old Way began almost immediately after the Restoration. The most efficient tool of reform was an organ, and organs were gradually acquired by the more affluent parishes in London and many provincial cities, usually from an individual donor or by subscription. Meanwhile some High Church clergy were forming religious societies to regulate the lives of the young men of their parishes.[21] They practised the psalms and their tunes at their meetings, and were encouraged to spread themselves around the church to lead the congregation in song.

These reforms gave birth to two distinct traditions, which can be roughly categorized as urban and rural.[22] In town parishes that could afford an organ

[19] Nicholas Temperley, *The Music of the English Parish Church*, 2 vols. (Cambridge, 1979), I, p. 122.

[20] Nicholas Temperley, 'The Old Way of Singing: Its Origins and Development', in Temperley, *Studies*, pp. 69–102.

[21] Garnet V. Portus, *Caritas Anglicana, or an historical Inquiry into those Religious and Philanthropical Societies that flourished in England between the Years 1676 and 1740* (London, 1912).

[22] Temperley, *Parish Church*, I, chs. 5, 6.

and a charity school, the clerk and congregation were essentially displaced by a treble-dominated choir, supported by young men if there was a religious society. The most successful tune-book catering for this development was John Playford's *The Whole Book of Psalms... Composed in Three Parts* (20 edns., 1677–1757). Each psalm and hymn from the Old Version was provided with a tune set out in a way that allowed for performance by either boys or men, with an optional second voice part and a bass for either vocal or instrumental use. As time went on, the tenors and basses gradually dropped out of urban choirs, leaving the children to sing alone with the organ, unless they were joined by a few brave voices from the congregation.

From time to time efforts were made to restore hearty communal singing. With the publication of Henry Playford's *Divine Companion* (1701) and *A Supplement to the New Version of Psalms* (6th edn., 1708) began a new tradition of commissioning leading composers to create new tunes, such as Croft's ST ANNE's and HANOVER, both of which have remained among the most esteemed hymn tunes until the present time. At its best the union of an organ with 'the voices of a well-instructed congregation' could form 'one of the grandest scenes of unaffected piety that human nature can afford'.[23]

The rural model started with the same premise: a rehearsed choir to lead the congregation in singing metrical psalms. But without an organ or a qualified schoolmaster to teach the children, it was the adult male volunteers, mostly farmers and artisans and their families, who came to dominate the singing. It was soon found expedient to assemble them in a special gallery or pew. A new breed of country singing teachers arose, who earned a living by visiting many parishes in a neighbourhood to instruct the voluntary choirs. The most successful ones published and sold their own collections, encouraging the choirs to perform more and more elaborate music. Ornate tunes were developed, varied by solos and duets, and eventually 'fuguing' tunes, in which the different voices sang overlapping texts. Many country choirs aspired to anthems, and even, in some northern parishes, chanted the canticles and responses. Naturally these developments discouraged congregations from taking part, and this was a cause of strong objection from both parishioners and church authorities. Edmund Gibson, bishop of London, issued a stern warning to his clergy in 1724:

> But when I recommend the bringing your people, whether old or young, to a decent and orderly way of singing, I do by no means recommend to you or them the inviting or encouraging those idle instructors, who of late years have gone about the several counties to teach tunes uncommon and out of the way (which very often are as ridiculous as they are new: and the consequence of which is, that

---

[23] John Brown, *A Dissertation on... Poetry and Music* (London, 1763), p. 213; see also Temperley, *Parish Church*, I, pp. 141–51.

the greatest part of the congregation being unaccustomed to them, are silenced, and do not join in this exercise at all), but my meaning is that you should endeavour to bring your whole congregation, men and women, old and young, or at least as many as you can, to sing five or six of the best known tunes in a decent, regular, and uniform manner, so as to be able to bear their part in them in the public service of the church.[24]

But this was a difficult goal to attain without professional direction. The amateur choirs persisted, often without resistance from the local parson, and soon became an immovable part of parish life. To maintain pitch and rhythmic order, a bass viol, cello, or bassoon was often employed, and after 1750 a band of several instruments could be heard in many churches. A distinct style of country psalmody flourished well into the Victorian era, only loosely based on established principles of harmony, musical form, and choral performance.[25] (It has recently been treated with more respect on its own terms, and revived with success by the West Gallery Music Association, whose journal, *West Gallery*, carries many articles reporting on the history of country psalmody in individual parishes and regions.) Out of this tradition came a number of fine psalm tunes that still have a permanent place in modern hymnals, including John Chetham's BURFORD (1718), Francis Timbrell's BEDFORD (c.1725), William Knapp's WAREHAM (1738), and Aaron Williams's ROCKINGHAM (1778) (the personal names and dates refer to first printings; there is little certainty as to authorship). The more elaborate compositions, along with the country choirs themselves, would succumb to various reform movements, and to the nearly universal introduction of organs and harmoniums during the nineteenth century.

'Gallery' music, as this kind of psalmody has been labelled in recent times, was criticized by John Wesley, who attacked 'complex tunes which it is impossible to sing with devotion' and 'the repeating the same words so often (but especially while another repeats different words—the horrid abuse which runs through the modern church music) as it shocks common sense, so it necessarily brings in dead formality and has no more of religion in it than a Lancashire hornpipe'.[26] Wesley, though he had little opportunity to initiate musical reforms within the Church, conducted a lifelong effort to improve and inspire the singing at Methodist meetings. Metrical psalms were replaced by hymns, above all those of his brother Charles, which combined immediate personal appeal with Arminian principles of rebirth in Christ. New types of

[24] *Directions given by Edmund Lord Bishop of London to the Clergy of the Diocese, in ... 1724* (London, 1724).

[25] Nicholas Temperley and Sally Drage (eds.), *Eighteenth-Century Psalmody*, Musica Britannica 85 (London, 2007).

[26] At the Bristol Conference, 1768; cited by J. T. Lightwood, *Methodist Music of the Eighteenth Century* (London, 1927), pp. 35–6. A Lancashire hornpipe was a type of folk dance.

tune were introduced, based on the most fashionable secular music (and in some cases parodies of actual secular songs). New modes of singing were enforced, with all standing up and taking part, in strict time, '*lustily* and with a good Courage', and above all '*spiritually*'.[27] Though Wesley's ideas were long resisted by most Anglican authorities, they were highly successful in attracting supporters. In the opinion of William Vincent, later dean of Westminster, 'for one who has been drawn from the Established Church by preaching, ten have been induced by music'.[28]

There was clearly a need for improvement, but there was no consensus on what forms it should take. Beilby Porteus, the reform-minded bishop of London from 1787 to 1809, rebuked his clergy for neglecting psalmody and charged them to improve it, primarily by recruiting children from the newly opened Sunday schools. He was by no means in favour of parish choirs' imitating cathedral music with chanting or anthems, and urged a return to the old simple psalm tunes, sung by all.[29] Evangelicals also aimed to restore the people's part in the song of praise, but many, like Wesley, wanted to draw on the riches of secular music. Some believed that the whole service should be performed congregationally, a truly revolutionary notion. Vincent reported in 1790 that he had heard the doxology successfully chanted at one church.[30] Next came the canticles and responses, which were sufficiently familiar for a reasonable degree of uniformity to be achieved without rehearsal. Ultimately, in 1831, the first fully pointed psalter was published.[31] At York in particular, a sustained effort had been made to introduce congregational chanting in several churches under the inspiration of an evangelistic High Church layman, Jonathan Gray.[32]

Because of the still prevalent resistance in the Church to the singing of hymns of human composition, pioneering efforts in that direction were often made in licensed proprietary chapels not subject to episcopal supervision.[33] These included London hospital chapels (to be considered later). A desire for more tasteful and artistic church music was felt by many who were not in sympathy with the Evangelical movement, and it could only be attained by

---

[27] Isabel Rivers and David L. Wykes (eds.), *Dissenting Praise* (Oxford, 2011), pp. 211–12.

[28] William Vincent, *Considerations on Parochial Music* (2nd edn., London, 1790), p. 15.

[29] Beilby Porteus, *A Charge delivered to the Clergy of the Diocese of London … in the Year MDCCXC* (London, 1790), pp. 16–21.

[30] Vincent, *Considerations*, p. 10.

[31] J. E. Dibb, *Key to Chanting. The Psalter … and Portions of the Morning and Evening Services of the Church, appointed to be sung or chanted, with a peculiar Arrangement to facilitate the Practice* (London, 1831).

[32] Nicholas Temperley, *Jonathan Gray and Church Music in York*, St Anthony's Hall Publications 51 (York, 1977), repr. in Temperley, *Studies*, pp. 287–318.

[33] Nicholas Temperley, assisted by Charles G. Manns and Joseph Herl, *The Hymn Tune Index: A Census of English-Language Hymn Tunes in Printed Sources from 1535 to 1820*, 4 vols. (Oxford, 1998), I, p. 13.

trained choirs with organ accompaniment. Dr Charles Burney, a leading figure in the musical and literary worlds, considered that 'the greatest blessing to lovers of music in a parish-church, is to have an organ that is sufficiently powerful to render the voices of the clerk and of those who join in his *out-cry*, inaudible'.[34] Several influential psalmody collections appeared in the 1790s, with new and elegant tunes, often adapted from secular music or commissioned from leading composers, and providing for harmony and organ accompaniment.[35] The ultimate stage in this development was reached by William Gardiner, a Leicester stocking manufacturer, who published *Sacred Melodies, from Haydn, Mozart and Beethoven, adapted to the best English Poets, and appropriated to the Use of the British Church*.[36] Though the trend towards professional standards and styles was generally beyond the reach of country choirs and bands, it was spread more widely after 1800 by the increasing use of barrel organs, whereby correctly harmonized tunes were made available to any parish clerk who could turn a handle.[37] After the legal decision of 1820 there began the vast production of hymns that, within a few decades, would reduce the metrical psalms to a marginal position in the Church.

THE MUSIC OF WORSHIP (3): THE WIDER ANGLICAN COMMUNION

In Wales and Ireland the Church had inherited the medieval cathedrals, where it conducted English-language choral services; but in most cases the endowments were not sufficient to maintain daily services at an acceptable standard. In Wales, only St David's maintained a reasonably continuous choral tradition. At Dublin, the two cathedrals sometimes offered dual positions to lay clerks and organists, which allowed them to induce experienced English cathedral musicians to settle in Dublin, and a high standard of performance resulted.[38] Parish church music in both countries was largely congregational, with only a few wealthy churches able to afford organs. A selection of metrical

---

[34] Charles Burney, *A General History of Music*, 4 vols. (London, 1776–89), III, pp. 60, 64.

[35] Edward Miller, *The Psalms of David for the Use of Parish Churches* (London, [1790]); Samuel Arnold and John Wall Callcott, *The Psalms of David for the Use of Parish Churches* (London, 1791); William D. Tattersall, *Improved Psalmody, Vol. I* (London, 1794): Temperley, *Parish Church*, I, pp. 215–16, 228–9.

[36] 2 vols. (London, 1812, 1815).

[37] Noel Boston and L. G. Langwill, *Church and Chamber Barrel-Organs* (Edinburgh, 1967); Temperley, *Parish Church*, I, pp. 234–9.

[38] W. H. Grindle, *Irish Cathedral Music* (Belfast, 1989).

psalms with monophonic tunes was printed for St Michan's, Dublin, in 1752.[39] A more comprehensive collection was David Weyman's *Melodia Sacra... adapted to the Version of Nicholas Brady and Nahum Tate, as used in the United Churches of England and Ireland* (Dublin, [c.1816]).

In Scotland, renewed efforts by the Stuart kings to impose episcopal government and liturgy were at last abandoned with the Presbyterian settlement of 1691. After 1712 'qualified chapels' that accepted the English Prayer Book (with its prayer for Queen Anne, or later King George) were allowed to offer public worship, while others, especially in Aberdeenshire, quietly preserved the Scottish form of the liturgy. Chanting, services, and anthems were performed in several episcopal chapels.[40]

In North America the Church of England was established in the southern colonies. The Society for the Propagation of the Gospel (SPG) made some headway in the north as well. Thomas Bray, in his visitation to Maryland as representative of the bishop of London in 1700, introduced the *New Version* and instructed the few available clergy in the singing of metrical psalms. In 1713 the vestry of the Queen's chapel, Boston, voted 'the psalms of Tate and Brady to be sung in the Church';[41] an organ was presented to the chapel by Thomas Brattle in the following year, the first to be used in a church in English-speaking North America. John Wesley, during his incumbency in Savannah, Georgia (1735–7), encouraged the singing of both metrical psalms and hymns.

By the later eighteenth century the principal North American cities such as Boston, Charleston, Halifax, New York, and Philadelphia had prosperous Anglican churches with music provided by organ and charity children along the lines of English town churches. Francis Hopkinson composed anthems for Anglican use as early as 1761. Daniel Bayley, parish clerk of St Paul's church, Newburyport, Massachusetts, reprinted and extended a number of English country psalmody collections of psalm tunes and anthems from 1764 onwards. However, the vestry of St Paul's, Halifax, Nova Scotia, in 1770 banned both anthems and voluntaries, allowing the organist in future only 'to play the Psalm Tunes in a plain Familiar Manner without unnecessary graces'.[42] After independence the Protestant Episcopal Church's Book of Common Prayer

[39] The second edition (1771) was entitled *A Collection of Select Psalms for the Use of Parish Churches in general, but particularly intended for that of New St Michan's, Dublin*: cf. Barra Boydell, 'St Michan's Church, Dublin: The Installation of the Organ in 1725 and the Duties of the Organist', *Dublin Historical Record*, 46 (1993): 101–20.

[40] Wilson, *Anglican Chant*, pp. 192–216.

[41] Henry W. Foote, *Annals of King's Chapel*, 2 vols. (Boston, 1882), I, p. 204.

[42] Timothy McGee, 'Music in Halifax, 1749–1799', *Dalhousie Review*, 49 (1969): 377–87; Nicholas Temperley, 'Worship Music in English-Speaking North America, 1608–1820', in Timothy McGee (ed.), *Taking a Stand: Essays in Honour of John Beckwith* (Toronto, 1995), pp. 166–84.

(1786) departed from its English model in providing an official supplement of metrical psalms with eighteen tunes, and also two chants. These were revised from time to time in authorized hymnals, something the mother Church has never had. Prose psalms were chanted in Episcopal churches at least as early as 1783, when Andrew Law included them in his *Rudiments of Music,* which Richard Crawford has associated with Law's efforts to establish himself as choirmaster of St Peter's church, Philadelphia.[43] A full range of tunes, chants, and anthems for parish churches was incorporated in many published Episcopal tune-books, most comprehensively in the collections of John Cole of Baltimore.[44]

Anglican missionaries in many parts of the world found that singing was the great magnet for attracting indigenous people to the colonists' churches. This was the case in Virginia from the earliest times. In 1772 a Connecticut clergyman actually declined to distribute fifty copies of Tate and Brady's Psalms provided by the SPG for Iroquois Indians 'lest these people, who are more fond of psalm singing than of any other part of Divine Worship ... might be induced to neglect providing themselves with prayer Books'.[45] Elsewhere expatriate Anglicans sought to maintain for themselves musical traditions as close as possible to those of the mother country. Examples are an edition of Tate and Brady published at Amsterdam, with 123 monophonic tunes, 93 of them new, approved by the Dutch authorities for the use of the Gereformeerde Orthodoxe Engelsche Gemeente; and a book of tunes and anthems, harmonized in three parts, compiled by William Day, singing master at St Mary's church, Fort St George, India.[46]

ANGLICAN MUSICAL CULTURE: CHARITIES AND CEREMONIAL MUSIC

One of the earliest recorded uses of Anglican music to encourage charitable donations was the annual psalm of thanksgiving sung on Easter Monday by the children of Christ's Hospital for their benefactors, going back at least to 1610. New hymns and tunes were often composed and printed for the

---

[43] Richard A. Crawford, *Andrew Law: American Psalmodist* (Evanston, IL, 1968), p. 37.

[44] Temperley, *Hymn Tune Index,* I, pp. 12–13. See also Arthur H. Messiter, *A History of the Choir and Music of Trinity Church, New York* (New York, 1906); George W. Williams, *Jacob Eckhard's Choirmaster's Book of 1820* (Columbia, SC, 1971).

[45] Kenneth Walter Cameron (ed.), *The Church of England in Pre-Revolutionary Connecticut* (Hartford, CT, 1976), p. 276.

[46] *A New Version of the Psalms...Set to Music by J. Z. Triemer* (Amsterdam, 1753; 2nd augmented edn., 1765); William Day, *Sacred Harmony* (Madras, 1818).

occasion.[47] The custom was later imitated by the charity schools that led the singing in urban parish churches. An annual charity sermon was preached in many churches, when the choir would often sing a specially composed hymn, sometimes by a distinguished composer.[48] Other public charities were served by music. As early as 1664, it became customary to sing Psalm 133, or its metrical equivalent, at charitable meetings around the country. James Clifford added the following note to the words of Albertus Bryne's anthem on this text ('Behold, how good and joyful a thing it is, brethren, to dwell together in unity'): 'This is to be sung at the charitable Meeting of each County, &c.' He added the same note to Adrien Batten's anthem on William Whittingham's paraphrase of the same text from the Old Version, 'O how happy a thing it is'.[49] It is not entirely certain that 'charitable' here carries its principal modern meaning of giving to the poor; the choice of psalm suggests that it may only mean friendship.

On 22 November 1683, there was a new departure at an unknown location in London: a celebration of the birthday of St Cecilia, patron saint of music. From 1684 to 1700 the feast took place in Stationers' Hall. At first it was entirely secular. Each year a new ode was written and composed by leading court poets and composers. Purcell's three contributions, above all his 'Hail, bright Cecilia' of 1692, have become deservedly famous. Beginning in 1693 the event was accompanied by a church service, normally at St Bride's, Fleet Street, which featured a sermon in defence of religious music; elaborate settings of the Te Deum and Jubilate with instrumental accompaniments (again, Purcell's is the most renowned example); and sometimes a special anthem, such as William Turner's 'The king shall rejoice'. For the first time in Anglican sacred music, trumpets were heard.[50]

These services, and especially the sermons justifying the use of instrumental music in worship, were a clear assertion of Anglican values against Calvinist restrictions, and more specifically (as Whyte suggests) a reaction to William III's banning of instruments from the Chapel Royal services in 1689. Six of the eight sermons are extant in printed form; the first, by Thomas Battell,

---

[47] Susi Jeans, 'The Easter Psalms of Christ's Hospital', *Proceedings of the Royal Musical Association*, 88 (1961–2): 45–60; Temperley, *Hymn Tune Index*, I, pp. 109–10; John Nightingale, 'Catalogue of Compositions of Charles Wesley the Younger', in N. Temperley and S. Banfield (eds.), *Music and the Wesleys* (Urbana, IL, 2010), pp. 236–7.

[48] Nicholas Temperley, 'Croft and the Charity Hymn', *Musical Times*, 119 (1978): 539–41, repr. with Croft's hymn, 'To thee, O Lord of hosts', in Temperley, *Studies*, pp. 207–20.

[49] James Clifford, *The Divine Services and Anthems usually sung in His Majesties Chapel* (London, 1664 edn.), pp. 45, 56.

[50] This and the next paragraph are based on an unpublished paper by Bryan White, '"What the end of musick is": The Profane and the Sacred on St Cecilia's Day', delivered at a symposium on Restoration Cathedral Music, at Western Illinois University, Macomb, Illinois, on 19 March 2013. I am grateful to Dr White for allowing me to quote from this paper. He is preparing a book on *Music for St Cecilia's Day from Purcell to Handel*.

sub-dean of the Chapel Royal, set the tone for the others, taking Psalm 100:1–2 as its text.[51]

Though the annual celebrations did not last beyond 1700, St Cecilia's Day remained a likely occasion for the glorification of music in the first half of the eighteenth century. The London example was followed in other cities, for instance at Salisbury, Winchester, Gloucester, and Dublin.[52] Odes in praise of music were regularly performed at Oxford, in some cases as academic exercises for a degree.[53] Among the masterpieces of the genre were Maurice Greene's setting of Pope's 'Ode for St Cecilia's Day', 'Descend ye nine, descend and sing' (performed at Cambridge, 1730);[54] Handel's *Alexander's Feast* (1736), based on Dryden's second ode, originally set by Jeremiah Clarke in 1697, with additions by Newburgh Hamilton; and Handel's *Ode for St Cecilia's Day*, from Dryden's first ode, 'From Harmony, from heavenly Harmony', which had been set by G. B. Draghi for the 1687 celebration.

Another charity under Anglican auspices was the Sons of the Clergy, which held an annual service in May for the relief of distress among clerical families, starting during the Commonwealth (in 1655) and still observed today. It was first held in old St Paul's Cathedral, and after 1697 in the rebuilt St Paul's, with orchestral accompaniment by prominent professional musicians, followed by a banquet at the Merchant Taylors' Hall.[55] Purcell's Te Deum and Jubilate were regularly performed until displaced by Handel's 'Utrecht' and 'Dettingen' settings of the same canticles.

All these events can now be seen as leading towards the grand tradition of choral festivals that became the crowning events of English musical life in the later eighteenth and nineteenth centuries. At first these were developed chiefly in the provinces. The earliest was the Three Choirs Festival, in which Gloucester, Hereford, and Worcester pooled their choral resources and took turns to provide the venue.[56] It may have started as early as 1713, with little more than the three cathedral choirs taking part. Similar meetings, often triennial, were established at many other cities including Salisbury (from 1748), Winchester (1766), Birmingham (1768), Norwich (1772), Manchester

---

[51] Ralph Battell, *The Lawfulness and Expediency of Church-Musick asserted* (London, 1693), p. 1.

[52] E.g. Thomas Naish, *A Sermon preach'd at the Cathedral Church of Sarum, Novemb. 22. 1700. Before a Society of Lovers of Musick* (London, 1701).

[53] Rosamond McGuinness and H. Diack Johnstone, 'Concert Life in England, I', in Johnstone and Fiske (eds.), *The Eighteenth Century*, pp. 89–91.

[54] In H. Diack Johnstone (ed.), *Maurice Greene: Ode on St Cecilia's Day and Anthem: Hearken unto me*, Musica Britannica 58 (London, 1991).

[55] Nicholas Cox, *Bridging the Gap: A History of the Corporation of the Sons of the Clergy over 300 Years, 1655–1978* (Oxford, 1978).

[56] Watkins Shaw, *The Three Choirs Festival* (London, 1954).

(1777), Nottingham (1782), and York (1791).[57] The choirs of Yorkshire, Lancashire, and Derbyshire, both Anglican and Dissenting, were often in demand in other parts of the country. The solo singers and instrumentalists were generally brought in from London and the whole ensemble directed by the cathedral organist. Smaller versions existed in many other towns, and they had spread to North America by 1780.[58] Provincial festivals were often timed to coincide with assizes, race meetings, or other local events. The central feature was always an Anglican service in the cathedral or principal church, often augmented by instruments and extended by additional anthems. (Nearly 120 orchestral anthems were composed between 1700 and 1775, some for choral festivals, others for royal occasions, installations, and degree presentations.[59]) There was nearly always a sermon, once again extolling the virtues of vocal and instrumental music in the service of religion, and a collection of money for the poor. In the evenings balls and secular concerts were held, and at least one oratorio; for some time there was opposition to performing oratorios in church.

The English oratorio, in the words of Howard Smither, 'is Handel's creation, his remarkable synthesis of elements found in the English masque and anthem, the French classical drama, the Italian *opera seria* and *oratorio volgare*, and the German Protestant oratorio'.[60] With a few exceptions it was a three-act drama with a libretto in verse based on a biblical story, using a 'French' overture and recitatives, airs, and ensembles similar to those of Italian opera, combined with choruses influenced by English cathedral and ceremonial music. It was performed in a theatre or concert hall. In 1732 Bernard Gates, master of the children of the Chapel Royal, presented a private, staged performance of Handel's *Esther* at the Crown and Anchor tavern in London, sung by the choristers. Handel wanted to repeat this publicly at the King's Theatre, the home of Italian opera, but was prevented from doing so by Bishop Gibson, who was also dean of the Chapel Royal, on the grounds that the opera house was an immoral place. He therefore compromised by performing it in the theatre without staging, and this became the norm. Oratorio concerts at Covent Garden and Drury Lane theatres became a fixture of the Lent season for nearly a hundred years. In two of his works, *Messiah* and *Israel in Egypt*, Handel moved a step further from opera towards church music, by using a

---

[57] Brian Pritchard and Douglas J. Reid, 'Some Festival Programmes of the Eighteenth and Nineteenth Centuries: 4. Birmingham, Derby, Newcastle upon Tyne and York', *Royal Musical Association Research Chronicle*, 4 (1970): 1–33.

[58] Nicholas Temperley, *Bound for America: Three British Composers* (Urbana, IL, 2003), pp. 24–7.

[59] Monte Edgel Atkinson, 'The Orchestral Anthem in England, 1700–1775', DMA thesis, University of Illinois at Urbana-Champaign, 1991.

[60] Howard Smither, 'Oratorio', §8, in *The New Grove Dictionary of Music* (London, 2001), p. 515.

prose text entirely compiled from the Bible in the King James Version, and dispensing with named characters. Beginning in 1750 he performed *Messiah* each year in the Foundling Hospital chapel. This was the first step on its path to Westminster Abbey.

Despite their operatic and secular connections, Handel's oratorios were received by their audiences as 'unprecedented, unequalled expressions of the religious sublime'.[61] They appealed predominantly to the middle classes, for whom Italian opera was a closed book, but who were very familiar with the Bible stories, and who identified strongly with the Israelites in their national-ism and sense of being a chosen people. In addition, as Ruth Smith has shown, the oratorios were an aggressive assertion of traditional Christian values against Deism, which had made much headway in the 1720s. They showed 'that God could aid man with miracles; that he had thus aided the Israelites; . . . and that Jesus fulfilled the Old Testament prophecies of the Messiah'.[62] Since the Dissenting sects and most Methodists strongly disapproved of dramatizing Scripture, it was the Church of England that was primarily identified with the enormous success of Handel's works. The pomp and splendour of the ora-torios, as well as the profound insights into individual character in those that carried a dramatic story (such as *Saul, Samson, Judas Maccabaeus, Solomon, Theodora,* and *Jephtha*), made them a national treasure rarely equalled in English history. But *Messiah*, though initially disapproved, would eventually outstrip all the others in popularity, even acquiring the definite article (not part of its original title) in common speech.

Handel also provided sacred music for many national events: Te Deum settings for the Treaty of Utrecht (1713) and the victory of Dettingen (1743); four anthems for the coronation of King George II and Queen Caroline (1727), the most famous being 'Zadok the priest'; 'The ways of Zion do mourn', an anthem for the queen's funeral (1737); and anthems for two royal weddings and the Peace of Aix-la-Chapelle (1749).[63]

His exalted status was recognized in five gigantic commemorations in Westminster Abbey between 1784 and 1791, commissioned and attended by George III and employing unprecedented numbers of singers and players.[64] Handel had attained an almost godlike position as the unchallengeable master of sacred music. No work by a native composer established a permanent place

---

[61] Ruth Smith, *Handel's Oratorios and Eighteenth-Century Thought* (Cambridge, 1995), p. 168.

[62] Ruth Smith, 'Intellectual Contexts of Handel's Oratorios', in Christopher Hogwood and Richard Luckett (eds.), *Music in Eighteenth-Century England: Essays in Memory of Charles Cudworth* (Cambridge, 1983), pp. 115–34 (p. 126).

[63] Donald Burrows, *Handel and the English Chapel Royal*, Oxford Studies in British Church Music (Oxford, 2005).

[64] Charles Burney, *An Account of the Musical Performances in Westminster Abbey and the Pantheon . . . in Commemoration of Handel* (London, 1785).

in the British oratorio repertory for the next century: only Haydn's *Creation*, Spohr's *Last Judgment*, and Mendelssohn's *Elijah* succeeded in doing so, but still far behind Handel. Beginning in the 1790s, some cathedral choirs began to sing extracts from the oratorios as anthems. Many had already been adapted as psalm or hymn tunes, first by the Methodists and then, more hesitantly, by Anglican compilers. A flood of hymn tunes based on Handel's works, both sacred and secular, now appeared in countless British and American publications. For instance, 217 printings of tunes based on 'I know that my redeemer liveth' appeared between 1790 and 1820.[65]

There were other important links between music and charity. The eighteenth century saw a notable rise in institutions dedicated to specific classes of disadvantaged people. With the Enlightenment had come a declining faith in divine intervention to relieve suffering, and a correspondingly greater emphasis on human endeavour. Some of the new charities, like the Foundling Hospital (founded in 1737) and the Asylum for Female Orphans (1758), dealt directly with the increasing number of births outside marriage among the poor. Others, such as the Lock Hospital (1746) and the Magdalen Hospital (1758), attempted to relieve the problems of venereal disease and prostitution respectively. All four institutions had chapels in which Anglican worship was practised, though they were free from direct diocesan control, which allowed them to move boldly in new directions, especially in the use of non-scriptural hymns. And all generated printed anthologies of music that were widely used domestically and in church and chapel.[66]

The Lock Hospital was perhaps the most influential of these institutions in moving church music in the direction of secular art music. From 1763 there was an annual fundraising performance at the Lock Hospital of an oratorio, *Ruth*, by Felice Giardini (at first aided by Charles Avison, but from 1768 with Giardini's music alone),[67] clearly following the precedent of *Messiah* at the Foundling Hospital. Martin Madan (1726–90), benefactor, chaplain, and chief hymn-writer and composer at the Lock, drew on the most fashionable secular styles of the day in compiling its music collection, even calling on Italian opera composers such as Giardini. The music achieved an elegance that was far removed from the typical psalmody of the time. In this Madan was following

---

[65] Nicholas Temperley, 'Adaptations', in Annette Landgraf and David Vickers (eds.), *The Cambridge Handel Encyclopedia* (Cambridge, 2009), p. 6, based on details in Temperley, *Hymn Tune Index*, I, pp. 39–40.

[66] Nicholas Temperley, 'The Hymn Books of the Foundling and Magdalen Hospital Chapels', in David Hunter (ed.), *Music Publishing & Collecting: Essays in Honor of Donald W. Krummel* (Urbana, IL, 1994), pp. 1–37; Nicholas Temperley, 'The Lock Hospital Chapel and its Music', *Journal of the Royal Musical Association*, 118 (1993): 44–72, reprinted in Temperley, *Studies*, pp. 258–86. The various editions of all four institutions' tune-books are set out in Temperley, *Hymn Tune Index*, I, pp. 108–15.

[67] Simon McVeigh, 'Music and the Lock Hospital in the 18th Century', *Musical Times*, 129 (1988): 239–40.

the principles of the Wesleys: Charles Wesley had called on composers of church music to 'Plunder the carnal lover, Strip him of every moving strain, Every melting measure, Music in virtue's cause retain, Rescue the holy pleasure'. John Wesley was quite intolerant of the kind of rough, plebeian music that was beginning to be used in revival meetings.[68] Madan, also, was clearly appealing to upper-class tastes rather than to the uncultivated masses.

In the late Georgian era there arose another, countervailing trend: the romanticization of ancient psalmody. Musical antiquarianism had gained an early start in England with such institutions as the Academy of Ancient Music (1726), the Madrigal Society (1741), and the Concert of Ancient Music (1770).[69] It now began to focus on the Elizabethan and Jacobean psalm tunes that were still the main resource of urban parochial music. William Crotch, professor of music at Oxford, was convinced that the music of the sixteenth and seventeenth centuries was superior to that of his own time: 'Few productions of the present day', he asserted, 'will ever become fit for divine service at all'.[70] He reprinted thirty-two early psalm tunes in *Tallis's Litany... [and] a Collection of Old Psalm Tunes... for the Use of the University Church, Oxford* (Oxford, 1803). The charity children of the City of London had gathered once a year since 1704 to sing en masse in one church, initially as a fundraising event; it now began to take on an aspect of the sublime, and profoundly impressed many visitors, including Haydn. In 1801 the ceremony was moved from Christ Church, Newgate Street, to St Paul's Cathedral. A fashion developed for performing ordinary hymns or metrical psalms as concert items, with full orchestral accompaniment.[71] At the York Festival of 1823, hymns or psalms were sung in the minster on three occasions by the entire cast of soloists (led by Angelica Catalani), chorus, and orchestra, one of them with a trumpet solo. A commentator said that this 'produced the greatest impression during the whole of this extended festival... The sound of the trumpet, proceeding from nearly the top of the orchestra, appeared as if it descended from the tower above: and the thrill of awe, not unmingled even with terror... was such as we shall not attempt to describe.'[72]

This movement recalls the veneration for the music of the past that we noted at the time of the Restoration, but with somewhat different motives and

---

[68] Temperley and Banfield (eds.), *Music and the Wesleys*, pp. 18–25.

[69] William Weber, *The Rise of Musical Classics in Eighteenth-Century England: A Study in Canon, Ritual, and Ideology* (Oxford, 1992).

[70] William Crotch, *The Substance of Several Courses of Lectures on Music* [delivered at Oxford between 1800 and 1805] (London, 1831).

[71] Temperley, *Parish Church*, I, pp. 244–9.

[72] J. Crosse, *An Account of the Grand Musical Festival, held in September, 1823, in the Cathedral Church of York* (York, 1825), pp. 339–40. For a longer quotation, see Temperley, *Parish Church*, I, pp. 245–6.

emphasis. Soon the Oxford Movement would delve still further back in time to revive Gregorian chant, office hymns, and other music of the Sarum use.

SELECT BIBLIOGRAPHY

Burrows, Donald, *Handel and the English Chapel Royal*, Oxford Studies in British Church Music (Oxford, 2005).

Fellowes, Edmund H., *English Cathedral Music from Edward VI to Edward VII* (London, 1941).

McCart, Thomas K., *The Matter and Manner of Praise: The Controversial Evolution of Hymnody in the Church of England 1760–1820*, Drew Studies in Liturgy 8 (Lanham, MD and London, 1998).

Smith, Ruth, *Handel's Oratorios and Eighteenth-Century Thought* (Cambridge, 1995).

Spink, Ian, *Restoration Cathedral Music 1660–1714*, Oxford Studies in British Church Music (Oxford, 1995).

Temperley, Nicholas, 'Music in Church', in H. Diack Johnstone and Roger Fiske (eds.), *Music in Britain: The Eighteenth Century*, Blackwell History of Music in Britain 4 (Oxford, 1990).

Temperley, Nicholas, *The Music of the English Parish Church*, 2 vols. (Cambridge, 1979).

Temperley, Nicholas, *Studies in English Church Music, 1550–1900* (Farnham, 2009).

Temperley, Nicholas, assisted by Charles G. Manns and Joseph Herl, *The Hymn Tune Index: A Census of English-Language Hymn Tunes in Printed Sources from 1535 to 1820*, 4 vols. (Oxford, 1998).

Wilson, Ruth M., *Anglican Chant and Chanting in England, Scotland, and America, 1660 to 1820* (Oxford, 1996).

20

Anglicanism and Art

Clare Haynes

A history of the relationship of the visual arts and the Church of England since the Reformation has yet to be written, but were it to be, the story it would tell would be of a slow and tentative rapprochement, which has in the twenty-first century reached a quite unprecedented degree of intimacy and trust. The Church has not only embraced Orthodox traditions of icon writing, examples of which can be seen in many parish churches and cathedrals, it has also commissioned major works by leading contemporary artists, some of which have been experimental, problematic, daring.[1] By contrast, the role of Anglicanism in the arts outside the Church, beyond these commissions, is perhaps at its lowest point since the Reformation. In the eighteenth century, this situation was very nearly reversed: Anglicanism was a significant influence on the visual arts outside of the Church, while the roles for art inside the church were restricted, bound by concern over idolatry and popery. There was, however, a great deal more art in church than has hitherto been recognized, which was used to ornament the church and edify the congregation.

Eighteenth-century Anglicanism's presence and influence can be traced across the whole compass of the visual arts.[2] For example, if we begin with portraiture, some of the most interesting and characterful portraits of the period were made of bishops and priests.[3] They are much more varied in their means and effects than might be supposed, but a few contrasted examples must suffice to demonstrate the point: an unusual, rather anxious-looking, portrait of Archbishop John Tillotson (c.1691–4), by a follower of Kneller, is distinctive, as is the sheer energy of Hogarth's otherwise formal depiction of

---

[1] See Rowan Williams, *The Dwelling of the Light: Praying with Icons of Christ* (Norwich, 2003) and the journal *Art and Christianity*.

[2] Jeremy Gregory, 'Anglicanism and the Arts: Religion, Culture and Politics in the Eighteenth Century', in Jeremy Black and Jeremy Gregory (eds.), *Culture, Politics and Society in Britain 1660–1800* (Manchester, 1991), pp. 82–109.

[3] John Ingamells, *The English Episcopal Portrait 1559–1835* (London, 1981).

Fig. 20.1. Thomas Gainsborough, *The Rev. John Chafy Playing the Violincello in a Landscape*, *c*.1750–2. © Tate, London 2016.

Bishop Benjamin Hoadly in his Garter robes (1741).[4] Thomas Gainsborough's joyful portrait of his friend the Revd John Chafy (*c*.1750–2) playing the cello in front of a temple of Apollo (Fig. 20.1) contrasts with Joshua Reynolds's elegantly direct portrait of Archbishop Thomas Secker (1758). Similarly, John Hoppner's movingly sober portrayal of Bishop Beilby Porteus (1807) in weekday dress offers us a quite different vision of episcopal character from that provided by Sir Martin Archer Shee's extravagant depiction of Archbishop William Howley (1828). In each of the examples we see these men as the leaders they were, in local and national, as well as cultural, terms. We see too the subtle play of tradition and originality, as artists attempted, in what were frequently official portraits, to represent the public man, the manager, and the politician, as well as the individual of faith.[5]

While the originals had a restricted audience, many of these portraits were engraved. There was, in fact, an enormous market for clerical portrait prints,

---

[4] William Gibson, 'The Significance of the Iconography of Bishop Benjamin Hoadly (1676–1761)', *British Art Journal*, 7 (2006): 1–10.

[5] Jeremy Gregory, '*Homo Religiosus*: Masculinity and Religion in the Long Eighteenth Century', in Tim Hitchcock and Michele Cohen (eds.), *English Masculinities 1660–1800* (London and New York, 1999), pp. 85–110.

not just as frontispieces for books but also as single sheets. Some sold in huge numbers, spawning copies, such as the many prints made of the seven bishops who refused to read James II's Declaration of Indulgence in 1688, or Sacheverell's portrait, which circulated in great numbers in a variety of forms not just immediately after his infamous sermon in 1709 but for decades.[6] In the windows of the shops where they were sold, portraits of Anglican clergymen were often displayed alongside those of preachers of other denominations and thus the competition that existed for souls, which was the reality of the Established Church's situation under the Act of Toleration, was made visible (see, for example, J. R. Smith's *Spectators at a Print-Shop in St. Paul's Churchyard*, 1774).

As one would expect, in the period that has been called the golden age of satire, individual clerics, particularly the lord bishops, were subject to the satirist's attentions. In an anonymous mezzotint of the 1730s entitled *Blessed be the Lord for I am Rich*, Thomas Sherlock was shown in his study handing his mitre to the Devil, while in Gillray's *The Minister Endeavouring to eke out Dr. Pr+ty+++n's Bishoprick* (1787) (Fig. 20.2) William Pitt places the dome of St Paul's over the spire of Lincoln cathedral, referring to the 36-year-old George Pretyman's appointment as dean of St Paul's in the same month as he was appointed bishop of Lincoln. It is an elegant treatment of the common themes of pluralism and political cronyism. Satire in this period was as often direct and vicious as it was witty and playful. Prints also dealt very frequently with social types and the clergy were, like other professionals, the butt of satire. Thin curates, sometimes riding even thinner horses on their Sunday duties, were represented as often as overweight bishops, whose bellies spoke of their enormous incomes and their lack of fundamental Christian virtues. These types were neatly contrasted in *A Worldly Bishop and a Godly Curate* (1810), in which a massive bishop is importuned outside his palace by an emaciated and bent-figured curate, with his pocket full of sermons. The amorous clergyman caught in a variety of compromising situations continued another anti-clerical tradition, and print buyers had a choice of prints of monks, usually read as anti-Catholic propaganda, or slightly less lewd but essentially similar images of Anglican priests. In *Wolves in Sheeps Cloathing*, published in 1777, for example, three clergymen are at table, each accompanied by a scantily dressed young lady. Preaching was satirized in prints such as Gillray's *Pulpit Eloquence* (1795), where a red-faced cleric begins reading his sermon with the deathly phrase 'I shall divide my Discourse into seven heads, namely . . .'. Those who administered justice as clerical magistrates were increasingly targeted, especially after Peterloo, in prints such as George Cruikshank's

---

[6] Sacheverell's portrait was, for example, reproduced on ceramics such as the Delftware dish (*c*.1710) in the Fitzwilliam Museum: Michael Archer, *Delftware in the Collection of the Fitzwilliam Museum* (London, 2012), p. 88.

Fig. 20.2. James Gillray, *The Minister Endeavouring to Eke out Dr Pr*ty***n's Bishoprick*, 1787. © The Trustees of the British Museum.

Preachee & Floggy, too! (1819). Regrettably, the degree to which these prints are evidence of widespread anti-clericalism and whether it was of a new kind that would result in the reforms of the nineteenth century has yet to be investigated.

A quite different form of art was used to illustrate bibles of course. As they had been since the Reformation, bibles were often illustrated, but in this period the engravings were increasingly sourced at home rather than being imported from the Low Countries, as had been the case. Some of these editions, those printed by Baskett from 1717 and Baskerville in 1769, for example, provided opportunities for painters to design religious art in an unaccustomedly grand manner.[7] This reached its apogee in Thomas Macklin's Bible, which was published in serial form from 1791–1800 and featured the work of many Royal Academicians, including Phillip de Loutherbourg, Angelica Kauffmann, and Sir Joshua Reynolds. The works they produced for this and rival projects include some of the great art of the period, although they have received little

---

[7] C. H. Collins Baker, 'Sir James Thornhill as Bible Illustrator', *Huntington Library Quarterly*, 10 (1946–7): 323–7.

attention.[8] The first American illustrated Bible was produced by the patriot publisher Isaiah Thomas in Worcester, Massachusetts, in 1791, at the start of a decade that was a high point of Bible illustration. Prints were also sold to be bound into prayer books, and catechisms and commentaries began to be illustrated as well. Among the more genteel offerings, cheap and wholesome (if by the highest standards of the day crudely achieved) depictions of biblical subjects were available, such as those produced by the firm of Bowles and Carver in the 1790s. Often drawn after canonical paintings, these prints meant that some works of high European culture, such as Raphael's *Transfiguration*, circulated very widely as religious art. Such images seem never to have been of much concern with respect to idolatry, their size and usual position in texts apparently thought unlikely to entice the gaze, but it is not insignificant that they were always captioned with the appropriate biblical reference, however recognizable the subject. The text seems to have served both as warrant for the image and guarantor of an appropriate response.

A quite different way in which we might consider the presence of Anglicanism in eighteenth-century visual culture is in the depiction of churches in topographical and landscape art. While the practice of incorporating churches as eye-catchers in elite landscapes is well known, the depiction of churches in landscape paintings and other topographical art has not been studied.[9] Churches dominate many depictions of village and towns, not just because of their relative height and size but also because of the artist's choice of viewpoint. Furthermore, engravings of church exteriors and, to a much lesser extent, interiors were often the most illustrated elements of antiquarian and topographical accounts.[10] These engravings speak of a close identification of church and community but it remains unclear how widely shared these views were and in what ways they might be related to the identifications expressed in, for example, beating the bounds or attendance at church.[11]

Whilst churches had been emptied of any images that had been associated with idolatry and popery, Roman Catholic art in the form of canonical works

[8] T. S. R. Boase, 'Macklin and Bowyer', *Journal of the Warburg and Courtauld Institutes*, 26 (1963): 148–77. Naomi Billingsley has recently begun work on the Macklin Bible: <https://www. academia.edu/28615344/The_Formation_and_Reception_of_the_Macklin_Bible>.

[9] One exception is John Constable: Paul D. Schweizer, 'John Constable and the Anglican Church Establishment', *Artibus et Historiae*, 5 (1982): 125–39; Michael Rosenthal, *Constable: The Painter and his Landscape* (London, 1983), esp. p. 146.

[10] Compare, for example, William Maitland, *The History and Survey of London from its Foundation to the Present Time*, 2 vols. (London, 1756; first publ. 1739), and James Peller Malcolm, *Londinium Redivivum; or, an Antient History and Modern Description of London*, 4 vols. (London, 1802–7).

[11] For the sacred potential of rogation in this period, see Alexandra Walsham, *The Reformation of the Landscape: Religion, Identity, and Memory in Early Modern Britain and Ireland* (Oxford, 2011), esp. pp. 257, 267; David Fletcher, 'The Parish Boundary: A Social Phenomenon in Hanoverian England', *Rural History*, 14 (2003): 177–96.

exerted an increasing influence on Protestant culture, as the art market developed in the eighteenth century. Paintings of the Italian and French schools were valued as examples of painterly achievement and as demonstrations of the taste of their owners. The problem of their often 'idolatrous' content was resolved in ways that involved the tacit rejection of a cornerstone of art's moral capital, that great art always expressed universal truths. British art theorists developed new ideas of reception to deal with this issue, modifying the body of art theory that had been imported from the academies of Catholic France and Italy. Among these, Jonathan Richardson's writings stand out as promoting Anglicanism as, in fact, the only secure basis for connoisseurship.[12] There remained the more intractable problem of domestic artistic production. It was a commonplace of art historical understanding that if art was not used to serve religion, publicly, in church, it was not fulfilling its most important moral function, and that, furthermore, artists would never reach the heights of excellence that had been achieved by, for example, Raphael and Michelangelo without being given such work to do.[13] Whilst painters did produce significant numbers of religious paintings for print sellers, as well as small-scale works for domestic settings, the question remained alive for the whole of the period—could art be allowed to serve its highest calling in the Church without raising the twinned spectres of idolatry and popery?

The answers that were given to this question in the period were contradictory. For some the answer would remain 'no', for others, it was a cautious 'yes'. Art did re-emerge in the Church in the eighteenth century but not as the result of a concerted campaign or as the working out of a settled theological position but piecemeal, as individual communities arrived at the conclusion that the visual arts could be useful and appropriate means of expressing reformed Christianity. Whilst very little by way of a theology of art was written in the period and religious art had very little positive theoretical support, it is clear that a system of decorum operated to police Anglican art. Faculties were not required for the installation of a painting in a church per se, although parishes might mention them as part of a larger project of rebuilding, if it was to be paid for by them. The precise status of altarpieces as property is rarely made explicit in parochial records. Instead a number of largely tacit rules about material, place, rank, and biblical interpretation dictated the ways in which art was used in the service of the Church and its people, each based on one fundamental idea: the avoidance of idolatry. The inseparable association with popery operated as an additional stigma, and making the distinction obvious between the reformed Church and

---

[12] Clare Haynes, '"To put the soul in motion": Connoisseurship as a Religious Discourse in the Writings of Jonathan Richardson', *Religion in the Age of Enlightenment*, 5 (2015): 1–24; Clare Haynes, 'In the Shadow of the Idol: Religion in British Art Theory', *Art History*, 35 (2012): 62–85.

[13] Iain Pears, *The Discovery of Painting: The Growth of Interest in the Arts in England 1680–1768* (London, 1988), pp. 43–50.

what was perceived as popery was probably the main determining factor of the appearance of church interiors in the period.[14] Nevertheless, over the course of the century, confidence grew and there was significant expansion in the use of art in church, in terms of the numbers of paintings that were installed and the range of their subject matter: over 1,000 works of art have been identified.[15]

There was a rigid distinction between sculpture and painting and their uses because three-dimensional art was considered much more dangerously seductive than 'flat' art. Thomas Tenison put it most succinctly in *Of Idolatry*: 'There is not so great danger in the Images of things without life, especially if they be flat Pictures, not Protuberant Statues, nor Pictures which the Artist hath expressed with roundness. The worse and the more flat the work is, the less danger there is of its abuse.'[16] Thus freestanding sculpture was very rare indeed, and with very few exceptions sculpted stone was used in church only for funerary monuments and fonts. The funerary monument was a richly discursive document, which combined word and image to speak of piety, personal achievement, and character, as well as civic pride, local history, and national events. Among the very many eighteenth-century monuments that survive are some of the great works of eighteenth-century sculpture. While most sculptors deployed a restrained, often formulaic pattern of ornament, others, including Roubilliac, Rysbrack, Flaxman, and Westmacott, late in the century, made works of originality and splendid achievement: richly allusive, complexly imagined, and displaying great virtuosity.[17] While sculptors such as these had a national, even international clientele, local stonemasons developed distinctive patterns of ornament too. Out in the churchyard, gravestones and graveyard monuments also became more elaborate over the period, calling on a wider range of eschatological themes.[18] North American scholarship, much in advance of work on English and Welsh gravestones, demonstrates that they can reveal rich insights into religious and social attitudes to life, as well as death.[19]

While sculpted memorials for individuals were unproblematic inside church, as they had generally been since the Reformation, stone at the communion table was very rare.[20] In 1705–6 Queen Anne gave to Westminster Abbey the marble

---

[14] Nigel Aston, *Art and Religion in Eighteenth-Century Europe* (London, 2009).

[15] This section of the chapter is based on research for a forthcoming book entitled provisionally *In the Idol's Shadow: Art in the Church of England 1660–1839*.

[16] Thomas Tenison, *Of Idolatry* (London, 1678), p. 271.

[17] David Bindman and Malcolm Baker, *Roubiliac and the Eighteenth-Century Monument* (London, 1995); M. I. Webb, *Michael Rysbrack: Sculptor* (London, 1954); David G. Irwin, *John Flaxman 1755–1826* (London, 1979); Marie Busco, *Sir Richard Westmacott: Sculptor* (Cambridge, 1994).

[18] Frederick Burgess, *English Churchyard Memorials* (Cambridge, 2004 edn.).

[19] See, for example, *Markers* and the *AGS Quarterly*, both published by the American Association of Gravestone Studies.

[20] Nigel Llewellyn, *Funeral Monuments in Post-Reformation England* (Cambridge, 2000); Peter Sherlock, *Monuments and Memory in Early Modern England* (Aldershot, 2008).

altarpiece that Christopher Wren had designed for James II's Catholic chapel at Whitehall, which had lain in store at Hampton Court for some years. A number of elements thought too popish were removed, including some statues, but the rest was installed in the abbey. It was taken down in the early 1820s in a bid to restore a more unified Gothic appearance to the interior. Parts of it can now be seen in the parish church of Burnham-on-Sea in Somerset.[21] Plaster made to resemble sculpted stone was deployed at the communion table in a handful of examples, in the form of a frieze, akin to a monochrome painting. In the mid-1750s, the sculptor William Collins produced two such panels for the semi-private spaces of Magdalene College chapel, Cambridge, and the Beauchamp chapel in St Mary's, Warwick; a step further was taken in the small, coloured *Supper at Emmaus* after Titian, carved, in fact, in limewood by Sefferin Alken, which was installed in the House of Commons church of St Margaret, Westminster, in 1758–9. It survives *in situ* but as part of an elaborate Kempe reredos of the early twentieth century.[22] The rarity of these things, as well as their flatness, demonstrates well the sensitivities that existed in relation to material and form, as well as position.

Away from the eastern focus of most churches, fonts could be, in contrast, rather elaborately carved objects. The most famous example of the period is certainly Grinling Gibbons's Adam and Eve font (1686) for St James, Piccadilly. Its image circulated as a print and it was copied for at least one provincial church (All Saints, Moulton, Lincolnshire). Early fonts might include elements of biblical narrative, such as the late seventeenth-century one at St Margaret Lothbury, City of London, where in four panels Noah's Ark, the Baptism of Christ, Adam and Eve, and the Baptism of the Eunuch were carved. Over the century, fonts tended to get smaller and plainer, and as such quite distinctively modern when compared with medieval examples. The use of new materials, such as Wedgwood's Black Basalt, would have also contributed to this effect of modernity (one, from 1778, can be seen at St Mary's, Essendon, Hertford-shire).[23] Often using neo-classical forms, traditional symbolism signifying eternal life was incorporated, as they were often made in an octagonal or circular form. A small, exquisite example, with its tripod stand, designed by Robert Adam, survives at St Mary's, Ruabon, which was given to the church by the great patron Sir Watkin Williams-Wynn in 1772.[24] The pre-Reformation tradition of incorporating especially exuberant decoration into font covers was continued. A finial, or the pulley for the cover, might be made in the shape of

---

[21] Jocelyn Perkins, *Westminster Abbey: Its Worship and Ornaments*, 3 vols., Alcuin Club Collections, 33, 34, 38 (London, 1938–52), I, pp. 65–80.

[22] Terry Friedman, *The Georgian Parish Church: 'Monuments to Posterity'* (Reading, 2004), pp. 90–101.

[23] Nikolaus Pevsner and Bridget Cherry, *Hertfordshire* (London, 2002 edn.), p. 141.

[24] T. W. Pritchard, *Ruabon Parish Church, Denbighshire* (Much Wenlock, 1998), pp. 16–17.

Fig. 20.3. Anon., *Font Cover Pulley*, St Mary the Virgin, Charlton Marshall, Dorset, *c*.1713. © Author.

the dove, representing the Holy Spirit, or be ornamented with cherubs, as was made for St Mary, Charlton Marshall, Dorset (*c*.1715) (Fig. 20.3). Small statues of the evangelists or the Christian virtues could also be used to ornament the font, as in Canterbury Cathedral (made in 1639 and reinstalled in 1663) and the Coade Stone font installed in the new church of All Saints, Newcastle upon Tyne (*c*.1786).[25]

Throughout the period, carving was also used to ornament pulpits. A rich language of symbolism, much of it traditional, was used to embellish and add meaning to these objects, a language that speaks of attitudes to sacred space, to the importance and expectations of preaching in the period, and to the rewards of faith. While at the beginning of the period pulpits might bear small narrative panels of carving like fonts, these disappeared as styles in furniture, domestic and ecclesiastical, changed. However, a range of symbols, including the dove of the Holy Spirit, compass roses, palm trees, and cherubs continued to frame preaching and the reading of liturgy. Large numbers of

[25] T. Sopwith, *A Historical and Descriptive Account of All Saints' Church, in Newcastle upon Tyne* (Newcastle upon Tyne, 1826), p. 99.

Georgian pulpits do survive, although they have often been cut down. Particularly fine examples are to be found, for example, at St Swithun's, Worcester, St Botolph Aldersgate, City of London, and St Margaret's, King's Lynn (now the minster).

Painting was used much more extensively in the Georgian church than has been thought. Away from the chancel, for example, paintings depicting Time and Death were to be found at the west end of some churches, while paintings of King David as psalmist seem to have been quite commonly placed on the front of the singing gallery in churches, such as that given by Elihu Yale to his home parish of St Giles, Wrexham (*c.*1710). In some churches, symbols of the tribes of Israel or representations of the apostles ornamented the nave, such as those which remain at St Mary's, Thirsk, and St Mary's, West Walton.[26] The chancel was, however, the space in which painting was most frequently to be found. The word 'altarpiece' was used during the period to indicate any kind of object attached to the east wall behind the communion table. It did not indicate a figurative painting but a form, of which the most common was that of boards painted with the texts of the Ten Commandments, often accompanied by the Lord's Prayer and the Creed. Canon LXXXII required that the Commandments be displayed where they might best be seen and while they were often placed at the east end, in some churches, where the chancel was screened or the arch was very low, they were placed above the chancel arch, so that they were visible by the congregation in the nave.[27] While these boards have been seen as evidence of the triumph of the word over the image at this most sensitive of spaces, even the plainest sets of the texts usually included some visual representation, often cherubs, painted or carved. Easier to miss is that the Commandments were often painted in arched shapes, which was the traditional way in which the stone tablets that God inscribed and Moses brought down from Mount Sinai had been depicted. In some examples, this was made more obvious with painted effects indicating stone or three dimensions.

Surrounding the texts, painted (often carved and gilded) woodwork, perhaps supplemented by plasterwork, could endow the east end with a rich, sparkling appearance (Fig. 20.4). A diverse array of symbolism was employed on altarpieces, often typological suggesting the fulfilment of the promises of the old covenant in the new. Dorset is particularly rich in surviving stucco schemes, at, for example, St Nicholas, Abbotsbury (1751), and St Wolfrida, Horton (*c.*1755).[28] The texts themselves were usually painted in two colours, often gold on a coloured ground, usually black but sometimes blue or red. Designed akin to architecture, just as title pages to books often were, the idea

---

[26] Clare Tilbury, 'The Heraldry of the Twelve Tribes of Israel: An English Reformation Subject for Church Decoration', *Journal of Ecclesiastical History*, 63 (2012): 274–305.

[27] Gerald Bray (ed.), *The Anglican Canons 1529–1947*, Church of England Record Society 6 (Woodbridge, 1998), p. 377.

[28] John Newman and Nikolaus Pevsner, *Dorset* (London, 2002), pp. 72, 235.

Fig. 20.4. J. Le Keux after F. Mackenzie, *St Mildred's Church, Bread Street, London,* 1838. © Author.

that the east wall was imagined as akin to a portal was suggested by a host of ornament recalling the Tabernacle: curtains were often painted above the altarpiece, together with pairs of cherubim flanking a glory.

A glory was probably the most commonly used motif of all; from the Restoration on, it was frequently depicted on the altarpiece or the ceiling above. Sometimes containing the *Tetragrammaton*, glories made up of golden light-filled clouds, and sometimes rays of light, suggested God's presence and the culmination of the Christian journey. At St Giles Cripplegate, City of London, the glory was described in 1708 as 'very spacious . . . gilt with Gold, whose Rays dart thro the Clouds at a great distance'.[29] St Paul's chapel, New York, still has a more modest but equally elaborate glory altarpiece, dating from 1787.[30] This popular image can be seen to be associated with the pre-Reformation tradition of ornamenting ceilings as heavenly skies painted blue with clouds, which

[29] Edward Hatton, *A New View of London*, 2 vols. (London, 1708), I, p. 249.
[30] Michael Paul Driskel, 'By the Light of Providence: The Glory Altarpiece at St. Paul's Chapel, New York City', *Art Bulletin*, 89 (2007): 715–37.

survived well into the period. Chancel ceilings, or that part of the ceiling over the communion table in churches without a separate chancel, were very frequently ornamented distinctively to set them apart. Even in churches where the pulpit was placed centrally, the decoration of the chancel and its window made the east end present to the congregation. The Holy Spirit, in the form of a dove, was very often displayed there too, as at St Deiniol's, Worthenbury (*c.*1739).

At the beginning of the period, before the 1710s, the only panel paintings to form part of an altarpiece were the figures of Moses and Aaron, usually depicted full length either side of the Ten Commandments. These figures, based loosely on Bible title pages, were very common indeed (Fig. 20.5). While it would be easy to

Fig. 20.5. ? Joshua Kirby, *Moses and Aaron*, panels from an altarpiece, St Bartholomew, Orford, Suffolk, *c.*1745. © Author.

infer a church-party interpretation of these paintings, their significance to contemporaries was in fact much richer than this. Moses and Aaron were commonly referred to as types of Christ, and the history of the Israelites was frequently called on in sermons, fast and thanksgiving liturgies, as well as religious literature more generally, as exemplary for the British people.[31] This message was reinforced in most churches by the display of the royal arms.[32] Thus these figures resonated both with the texts and the liturgy, as well as with the congregation gathered in the nave. With or without a glory between them, they also suggested, very strongly, God's presence in the church. The popularity of Moses and Aaron as accompaniments to the texts was surely because of this rich allusiveness. Furthermore, they could be considered safe both because they were surrounded by text and because, by being paired, they divided the attention. Paintings of a single figure were only ever displayed at the east end in pairs until late in the eighteenth century, and were restricted to Moses and Aaron or Peter and Paul. So safe were Moses and Aaron considered that half a dozen or so pairs of small, freestanding sculptures of them have been identified. However, their status was potentially uncertain: those made for St Catherine's in Jamaica, which were damaged when the church was hit by a hurricane in 1722, were not replaced because, it was said, they were considered disruptive to worship.[33] By far the most common subjects for art in church until the 1760s, paintings of Moses and Aaron were to be found in churches all over England and Wales, as well as in Anglican churches across the growing empire.[34] Gradually, however, as narrative subjects were adopted, Moses and Aaron seem rarely to have been chosen in the second half of the eighteenth century as the possibilities for art expanded.

In turning to consider narrative painting and the possibilities for it, attention must first be given to place. In private chapels, in country houses, or in Oxford and Cambridge colleges, and other institutions, decorative schemes were often much more visually elaborate than those of any parish church or cathedral. In private spaces, patrons could, perhaps, have more confidence in the congregation's ability to look appropriately in their close-knit, hierarchical communities. In the less regulated congregations of parish churches and cathedrals, a more conservative approach to the ornament of the east end

[31] Tony Claydon and Ian McBride, 'The Trials of the Chosen People: Recent Interpretations of Protestantism and National Identity in Britain and Ireland', in Tony Claydon and Ian McBride (eds.), *Protestantism and National Identity: Britain and Ireland, c.1650–c.1850* (Cambridge, 1998), pp. 1–29.

[32] H. M. Cautley, *Royal Arms and Commandments in our Churches* (Ipswich, 1974).

[33] Nicholas M. Beasley, *Christian Ritual and the Creation of British Slave Societies, 1650–1780* (Athens, GA, 2009), pp. 103–4.

[34] E.g. Christ Church, Barbados, and in America: Dell Upton, *Holy Things and Profane: Anglican Parish Churches in Colonial Virginia* (New Haven, CT, 1997 edn.), p. 120.

was taken and in such circumstances it is not surprising that plainness maintained its attractions for some, as it still does.[35] Thus, famously, at St Paul's Cathedral in the 1770s, against a backdrop of increasing anti-Catholicism, a sextet of leading artists, including Sir Joshua Reynolds and Benjamin West, had their offer of six paintings refused because the bishop of London, Richard Terrick, was concerned it might be perceived as the 'introduction of Popery'.[36] By contrast, in country houses and other private spaces, chapels had long been filled with elaborate continentally inspired, or produced, ornament.[37] This distinction is perhaps most poignantly to be experienced at what is now the parish church of Great Witley, in Worcestershire. The church, once the chapel of Witley Court, incorporated the interior built for the duke of Chandos at Cannons, Middlesex.[38] A glorious confection of white and gold stucco work, papier mâché, paintings and painted glass, the church demonstrates both what was possible for the Anglican interior in the period but crucially too, in its uniqueness, the restraint that was everywhere else deployed.

Concern over the judgement of the congregation was not the only criterion that divided such interiors from the rest. Money had something to do with it too, for paintings, coloured glass, and elaborate stucco were very expensive and most parishes could not afford them. However, it is clear that in cities, where funds and skills were available, civic pride and competition between parishes encouraged the use of more elaborate decorative schemes.[39] Elsewhere, the presence of a patron with an interest in art might be a determining factor. Few parishes paid for the paintings that hung in their chancels; they were most usually given by a member of a local elite family, whose parish was in their gift, sometimes by a local artist, or occasionally they could be the work of the incumbent or a member of his family. For example, the windows of the choir of Norwich Cathedral were ornamented in the 1770s and 1780s by a number of transparencies painted by the wife of the dean, Joyce Lloyd.[40]

---

[35] Margaret Aston, *England's Iconoclasts: Laws Against Images* (Oxford, 1988), pp. 94–5, 119–21; Tara Hamling, *Decorating the Godly Household: Religious Art in Post-Reformation England* (London, 2011).

[36] Gregory, 'Anglicanism and the Arts', p. 9; Thomas Newton, *The Works of the Right Reverend Thomas Newton*, 6 vols. (2nd edn., London, 1787), I, p. 142.

[37] Annabel Ricketts, *The English Country House Chapel: Building a Protestant Tradition* (Reading, 2007).

[38] Susan Jenkins, *Portrait of a Patron: The Patronage and Collecting of James Brydges, 1st Duke of Chandos (1674–1744)* (Aldershot, 2007).

[39] Jonathan Barry, 'Cultural Patronage and the Anglican Crisis: Bristol c.1689–1775', in John Walsh, Colin Haydon, and Stephen Taylor (eds.), *The Church of England c.1689–c.1833: From Toleration to Tractarianism* (Oxford, 1993), pp. 191–208.

[40] R. G. Wilson, 'The Cathedral in the Georgian Period, 1720–1840', in Ian Atherton, Eric Fernie, Christopher Harper-Bill, and Hassell Smith (eds.), *Norwich Cathedral: Church, City, and Diocese, 1096–1996* (London, 1996), pp. 576–614 (p. 599).

Familiarity with art gained outside of church, which might be thought an encouragement to its use, could also engender caution. This can be discerned in a sermon that the Revd Andrew Burnaby delivered in 1766 in front of Sir Horace Mann and two other elite travellers and collectors, George Cowper, 3rd Earl Cowper, and John Child, 2nd Earl Tylney, in Leghorn, where he was chaplain to the British factory. Dealing with the 'moral advantages to be derived from travelling in Italy', Burnaby discussed the question of 'conversing with the fine arts'. Having established the ways in which the arts could engender moral improvement by stimulating sensibility, Burnaby went on to warn that they were as capable, if 'undirected and unrestrained', of generating a 'stronger propensity to vice'. Thus, 'it seems to have been for this reason that some of the wisest of the ancients were doubtful, whether it might not be more advisable to forego the advantages to be derived from them, than run the risk of their not being properly and usefully directed and applied'.[41] It was this same anxiety over the influence of the arts in society that continued to prevent art from being deployed in church more extensively. So, for example, this may well be the reason why Williams-Wynn was prepared to commission a font from Robert Adam for his parish church, discussed earlier, and a portrait of his son as the infant St John the Baptist from his friend Sir Joshua Reynolds but not an altarpiece.[42]

Nevertheless, there were many who quite clearly believed that in their parish the danger was past, that the Reformation had been effective; and where there were resources to allow it, paintings began again to play a part in church. The first subject that found favour after Moses and Aaron was the Last Supper. This proved a popular addition to the communion table. One of the few that survive *in situ* is William Kent's painting commissioned for St George's, Hanover Square, London, in 1725, although it is presented in a reordered setting. Johann Zoffany's *Last Supper* (1787), which has recently undergone a major restoration, can still be seen at St John's, Calcutta. Scenes from Christ's nativity began to supplement the subjects thought suitable, such as *The Three Wise Men* commissioned by General Wade for Bath Abbey in 1726.[43] Significantly, these subjects were ones that contained many figures. As William Hole put it in the most substantial Anglican defence of church art:

as Ornament, and Instruction are all we contend for, I should prefer large historical Paintings to single Figures; and this the more willingly, because Adoration has at no time, nor in any place, been paid to them. Indeed it is scarcely

---

[41] Andrew Burnaby, *Six Occasional Sermons* (London, 1777), pp. 120–1. The role of clerical connoisseurs and artists in the eighteenth-century British art scene has yet to be explored.

[42] An early nineteenth-century copy of this portrait (*c.*1778) survives at Hanbury Hall, Worcestershire.

[43] Susan Sloman, 'General Wade's Altarpiece for Bath Abbey: A Reconstruction', *Burlington Magazine*, 133 (1991): 507–10.

possible to conceive, when a Number of Objects are before the Eye in one Picture, that a particular one be selected for this Purpose.[44]

This concern over the eye was supplemented by a rigorous, if informal, policing of a painter's interpretation of the biblical text. A telling example of this is an encounter that Benjamin West had when presenting his designs to George III for the Chapel of Revealed Religion that was planned for Windsor, which if it had come to fruition would have been the most ambitious scheme of Anglican art of the long eighteenth century. Even though the plans had already met with the approval of a committee of clergymen appointed by the king, he also invited a number of bishops to examine West's designs. The king apparently declared, after West had laid out his plans to them, 'you see how well he understands these things, for whilst you bishops have been spending your time amongst heathen fables, he has been studying his bible!'[45]

It is not surprising that until the late 1760s choices over iconography were quite conservative, but gradually the repertoire did widen and the resurrection and ascension began to be depicted, attracting some of the ablest artists of the period, including William Hogarth (Fig. 20.6), Benjamin West, Joshua Reynolds, and John Constable. Work needs to be done to develop a contextual, specifically Anglican, interpretation of art that was used in the Church of England. It is clear, for example, that while both William Hogarth and Joseph Backler modelled their depictions of *Christ's Ascension* (at St Mary Redcliffe, Bristol, and St Thomas, Dudley) on Raphael's famous *Transfiguration*, they also presented the reformed eschatological speculations of the parochial incumbents for whom they were working.[46] From the 1780s, almost certainly under the influence of the new Evangelicalism, subjects began to be chosen that presented the viewer with a much more direct and concentrated opportunity to gaze on Christ and to engage with his suffering, in paintings of the Agony in the Garden, for example, such as that by Francis Eginton for St Asaph Cathedral, now at St Tecla's, Llandegla, Denbighshire (c.1800). The crucifixion was only very rarely depicted and, incidentally, crosses seem never to have been placed on or above the communion table of a parochial or cathedral church. However, it was at this point, late in the eighteenth century, that the meditative potential of art was re-embraced, although very few paintings were admitted that depicted Christ alone (see for example, John Jackson's *Agony in the Garden*, St Cedd's, Lastingham, Yorkshire, 1824).

[44] [William Hole], *The Ornaments of Churches Considered* (Oxford, 1761), p. 31.

[45] Jerry D. Meyer, 'Benjamin West's Chapel of Revealed Religion: A Study in Eighteenth-Century Protestant Art', *Art Bulletin*, 57 (1975): 247–65 (p. 248).

[46] Thomas Broughton (1704–74) and Dr Luke Booker (1762–1835). For these works see Haynes, *In the Idol's Shadow* (forthcoming).

Fig. 20.6. William Hogarth, *The Ascension*, central panel of the altarpiece of St Mary Redcliffe, 1756. © Bristol Culture.

Well into the 1840s, art at the communion table adhered to the academic traditions of French and Italian painting, which still dominated taste in Britain. Even as Gothic forms were reintroduced in furnishings and ornament, paintings remained classical in style. This began to change first in stained or (more usually) painted glass. There are two connected reasons for this. First, a great deal more medieval glass survived and was visible than did medieval painting, which, where it had not been removed, was almost always whitewashed over. Glass painters, who often had to make repairs, knew the idiom and it remained a common, sometimes celebrated, feature of the eighteenth-century church interior. Second, stained glass had never been seen as potentially as dangerous as paintings or sculpture.[47] Attraction to a Miltonic 'dim religious light' in church was not the monopoly of one Church party or another. Subjects which may have been considered a little indecorous for paintings above the communion table were possible in painted or stained glass, although they were subject to the same rule of close adherence to the biblical text that controlled all eighteenth-century Anglican art.

Many altarpieces and east windows were based directly or indirectly on the works of the European canon, on paintings by Raphael, Michelangelo, Rubens, and others, such as the window by William Collins after Raphael's *Christ's Charge to St Peter* (1828) in the chapel of the East India Company in Calcutta. From the 1750s, in addition, paintings that had been collected abroad, often by Grand Tourists, began to be given to parish churches. While it is now bereft of the glorious-sounding altarpiece designed for it that included 'very elegant emblematical figures in plaister of Paris on a dove colourd and blue ground', one of the few of these paintings still *in situ* is that of *The Lamentation of Christ* given in 1780 to St Mary's, Bridgwater, by the local MP, the Hon. Anne [sic] Poulett (Fig. 20.7). Many paintings of a similar provenance but often much smaller than this, are still to be found in odd corners of parish churches and cathedrals. Such gifts are useful reminders of the patronage relations that were such an important aspect of eighteenth-century parochial life.[48] By the end of the period, pre-Reformation continental stained glass was also being imported in large amounts, such as the Herkenrode glass installed in Lichfield Cathedral in 1801–3.[49] Just at the end of the period, foreign woodwork began to be imported too, as Gothicism came to dominate ecclesiastical taste.[50]

The introduction of continental paintings to Anglican churches was a development that contemporary artists would have looked on with some chagrin. Throughout the century, artists had given paintings to their home parishes in an act that surely combined generous impulses as well as the hope that it might encourage others to want something similar for their own churches. The most successful religious painter of the period was certainly Benjamin West, whose hugely ambitious and influential works graced the communion tables and windows of a number of churches and cathedrals, including Hereford, Winchester, and Rochester.[51] However, despite his royal

---

[47] Sarah Baylis, 'Glass Painting in Britain c.1760–1840: A Revolution in Taste', PhD thesis, Cambridge University, 1989, pp. 20–57.

[48] Mark McDermott and Sue Berry (eds.), *Edmund Rack's Survey of Somerset* (Taunton, 2011), pp. 231–2.

[49] Baylis, 'Glass Painting in Britain', pp. 234–51.

[50] Simon Bradley, 'The Gothic Revival and the Church of England 1790–1840', PhD thesis, Courtauld Institute, 1996; Charles Tracy, *Continental Church Furniture in England: A Traffic in Piety* (Woodbridge, 2001).

[51] Helmut von Erffa and Allen Staley, *The Pictures of Benjamin West* (New Haven, CT and London, 1986), pp. 286–399.

Fig. 20.7. Anon., *The Lamentation*, St Mary, Bridgwater, Somerset. © Author.

patronage, West did not achieve all he had hoped, as complete acceptance of art's place in the Church of England remained elusive.[52] Nevertheless, by the end of the period it can be said that paintings were a relatively common part of

---

[52] See, for example, Benjamin Robert Haydon, *New Churches considered with respect to the Opportunities they afford the Encouragement of Painting* (London, 1818). Treated in a broader context, see Thomas Ardill, 'Between God and Mammon: Religious Painting as Public Spectacle in Britain *c.*1800–50', PhD thesis, Courtauld Institute, 2015.

church ornament. By then, however, another change in taste was underway, which was already sidelining the altar painting in favour of Gothic Revival stained glass.[53] This was merely the beginning. Under the influence of the Cambridge Camden Society, founded in 1839, a campaign was undertaken that aimed to restore churches to what was considered an authentic religious language of the Middle Ages.[54] This resulted in what can be described as widespread iconoclasm. Within the space of forty years, vast numbers of Georgian church interiors, paintings, and fittings were lost. Even though it had been so carefully policed, the classicism that had been the highest expression of decorous Christian art for their forefathers became regarded by the Camdenites and their followers as pagan. In fact, without the accounts, albeit often incomplete and partial, of early nineteenth-century antiquarians we would now have little idea of the riches of the Georgian church interior. Through their records and the surviving works, it is nevertheless possible to glimpse aspects of the eighteenth-century Church that could otherwise be overlooked.

The eighteenth-century parish church was a space of diverse visual practices, of civic pride, and of the continuing working out of Anglicanism's reformed identity. Not only was art used to ornament the church fittingly, within the bounds that have been identified, setting the building apart for the worship of God, it directed the attention of the congregation, articulated theological ideas, and expressed collective expectations of worship, as well as the hopes that were the foundation of their Christian faith. While Anglicanism was hugely influential in the visual arts more widely in the long eighteenth century, it is nevertheless the case that its own use of art remained cautious, as it did throughout the nineteenth century. One only has to read, for example, of the opposition that greeted Walter Hussey's commission of a statue of the *Madonna and Child* by Henry Moore for St Matthew's, Northampton, in 1943, or George Bell's decision in the Goring judgement in 1954, to realize just how recently the rapprochement between art and the Church began to gather momentum.[55]

---

[53] Baylis, 'Glass Painting in Britain', pp. 187–233.

[54] Christopher Webster and John Elliott (eds.), 'A Church as It Should Be': The Cambridge Camden Society and its Influence (Stamford, 2000).

[55] Peter Webster, 'The "Revival" in the Visual Arts in the Church of England, c.1935–c.1956', in Jeremy Gregory and Kate Cooper (eds.), Revival and Resurgence in Christian History, Studies in Church History 44 (Woodbridge, 2008), pp. 297–306.

SELECT BIBLIOGRAPHY

Addleshaw, G. W. O. and F. Etchells, *The Architectural Setting of Anglican Worship* (London, 1948).

Barry, Jonathan, 'Cultural Patronage and the Anglican Crisis: Bristol *c.*1689–1775', in John Walsh, Colin Haydon, and Stephen Taylor (eds.), *The Church of England c.1689–c.1833: From Toleration to Tractarianism* (Oxford, 1993), pp. 191–208.

Black, Jeremy and Jeremy Gregory (eds.), *Culture and Society in Britain, 1660–1800* (Manchester, 1997).

Croft-Murray, Edward, *Decorative Painting in England, 1537–1837*, 2 vols. (London, 1962–70).

Friedman, Terry, *The Eighteenth-Century Church in Britain* (New Haven, CT and London, 2011).

Haynes, Clare, *Pictures and Popery: Art and Religion in England 1660–1760* (Aldershot, 2006).

Yates, Nigel, *Buildings, Faith and Worship: The Liturgical Arrangement of Anglican Churches 1600–1900* (Oxford, 2000).

21

Theology in the Church of England

B. W. Young

Recent studies of the Church of England during the long eighteenth century have seen scholarship advancing well beyond the predominantly negative appraisals made in long-influential work by Victorian students of the period.[1] Liberation from the interpretatively compromised cocoon of a Victorian catastrophist vision of the late Stuart and Hanoverian Church has long been a desideratum, and for most aspects of eighteenth-century Church history this has been, and continues to be, achieved.[2] Curiously, this is much less true of the intellectual history of the Church than of its more firmly institutional or pastoral aspects; despite or because of a huge explosion in scholarly activity surrounding the Enlightenment—from the 'early Enlightenment' of the second half of the seventeenth century to the 'High Enlightenment' of the first sixty to seventy years of the eighteenth century—intellectual historians of the Church (never a large party) have only just begun to free themselves from a long Victorian interpretative shadow. There are perfectly understandable and intellectually respectable reasons for this. On one hand, Enlightenment studies still tend to a secular bias, in which experience of Enlightenment is held to constitute an epochal liberation of the European intellect from the tutelage of centuries of 'superstition' (although increasingly students of the phenomenon are alert to its congruence with Christian commitment across Europe and North America).[3] On the other, students of eighteenth-century theology and religious philosophy usually owe much of their initial exposure to this still

---

[1] See John Walsh and Stephen Taylor, 'The Church and Anglicanism in the "Long" Eighteenth Century', in John Walsh, Colin Haydon, and Stephen Taylor (eds.), *The Church of England c.1689–c.1833: From Toleration to Tractarianism* (Cambridge, 1993), pp. 1–64.

[2] B. W. Young, 'Religious History and the Eighteenth-Century Historian', *Historical Journal*, 43 (2000): 849–68.

[3] See John Robertson, *A Very Short Introduction to the Enlightenment* (Oxford, 2015). On the 'liberation' interpretation, see Anthony Pagden, *The Enlightenment and Why It Still Matters* (Oxford, 2013).

neglected field of study to two pioneering and enormously influential studies that coincidentally inaugurated the serious study of intellectual history in England.[4] Both of these works also constituted a revolt from within the Church of England against both High Church and Evangelical traditions that were themselves antagonistic to much eighteenth-century religious thought and experience.

In 1860, Mark Pattison (1813–84), who would become the rector of Lincoln College, Oxford, the following year, contributed an essay to the Broad Church collection, *Essays and Reviews*, on 'Tendencies in Religious Thought, 1688–1750'. It was the most historically minded of the seven essays that a group of advanced churchmen had quietly if combatively assembled, and it was by no means the most controversial of those writings.[5] In 1876, Leslie Stephen, a former fellow and chaplain of Trinity Hall, Cambridge, before resigning his priesthood and supporting himself as a man of letters, published his *History of English Thought in the Eighteenth Century*. Stephen's celebrated study owed a good deal to Pattison's essay, and just as it effectively marked Stephen's rejection of his Evangelical inheritance, so Pattison's essay evidenced his distancing from his long repudiated allegiance to the Tractarian party of John Henry Newman, in whose Littlemore retreat the young Pattison had been an acolyte.[6] In order to demonstrate just how influential these appraisals (and particularly that of Pattison) have been, and also to record how modern students of the subject are finally beginning to move beyond them, this chapter will concentrate initially on the contours of an intellectual history of the Church of England as detailed by Pattison. Since Pattison only takes his readers to 1750, the remainder of the chapter will similarly follow the scholarly terrain regarding the Church of England up to around 1800, as this had been initiated in Stephen's pioneering and deservedly influential study. In so doing, it is well to bear in mind Pattison's concentrated and effective definition of theology as primarily constituting 'the contemplative, speculative habit, by means of which the mind places itself already in another world than this; a habit begun here to be raised to perfect vision hereafter. 2ndly, and in an inferior degree, it is ethical and regulative of our conduct as men, in those

---

[4] B. W. Young, 'Knock-Kneed Giants: Victorian Representations of Eighteenth-Century Thought', in Jane Garnett and Colin Matthew (eds.), *Revival and Religion since 1700: Essays for John Walsh* (London, 1993), pp. 79–93.

[5] Ieuan Ellis, *Seven against Christ: A Study of 'Essays and Reviews'* (Leiden, 1980); Josef L. Altholz, *Anatomy of a Controversy: The Debate over 'Essays and Reviews'* (Aldershot, 1994).

[6] On Pattison, see A. D. Nuttall, *Dead from the Waist Down: Scholars and Scholarship in Literature and the Popular Imagination* (New Haven, CT and London, 2003), pp. 72–122; H. S. Jones, *Intellect and Character in Victorian England: Mark Pattison and the Invention of the Don* (Cambridge, 2007). On Stephen, see J. W. Bicknell, 'Leslie Stephen's *English Thought in the Eighteenth Century*: A Tract for the Times', *Victorian Studies*, 6 (1962): 103–20; B. W. Young, *The Victorian Eighteenth Century: An Intellectual History* (Oxford, 2007), pp. 103–47.

relations which are temporary and transitory.'[7] Only thus considered can one begin to make sense of the central, perhaps damning, claim he makes in his essay, namely, that during the eighteenth century '[t]heology had almost died out'.[8] But had it? As will become clear, Pattison had considerably overplayed his hand: theology did not almost die in the eighteenth century, it simply accommodated itself to the thinking of its times, just as Church teaching always does, and Pattison was simply too close to the era he denigrated to realize this.

THEOLOGY IN AN AGE OF REASON

What is most telling in Pattison's essay is that he knowingly takes his chronology from political history, beginning with the era of the Glorious Revolution and closing with the Newcastle years of the Whig ascendancy. The succeeding era between 1750 and 1830, at which he occasionally glances in his essay, was characteristically christened by him 'the Georgian period'. As he implies, few churchmen took pride in either era in their religious history, and, before the concept of 'Enlightenment' gained momentum in the mid-twentieth century, no allied intellectual tendency helped either Pattison or more orthodox churchmen to imagine anything other than a purely political periodization of this epoch. It also allowed Pattison to begin his provocatively secularizing reading with an initial interpretative advantage, presuming rather than justifying such a claim. And he did so very cleverly by echoing his younger self, considering the eighteenth-century Church from the perspective of a High Churchman, who, he declared, closed his *Catenae Patrum* 'with Waterland or Brett, and leaps at once to 1833, when the *Tracts for the Times* commenced—as Charles II dated his reign from his father's death'.[9] Pattison's own more mature and decidedly more 'liberal', if not agnostic voice, nonetheless maintained a ground bass throughout the essay, but he ably kept up more than a suggestion of disinterestedness in his account. A number of registers are recognizably at work at various points in the essay, all subtly conveying to the reader that Pattison felt the defence of their faith by eighteenth-century theologians was in every way intellectually unsatisfactory. And 'defence' is the operative term, since Pattison emphasized the assault on Christian belief that had begun in the wake of Hobbes and was continued by later publicists as being at the centre of Anglican theology and apologetic activity in the first half

---

[7] Mark Pattison, 'Tendencies of Religious Thought in England, 1688–1750', in Vincent Shea and William Whitla (eds.), *Essays and Reviews: The 1860 Text and its Reading* (Charlottesville, NC and London, 2000), pp. 386–430 (quotation at p. 393).

[8] Pattison, 'Tendencies', p. 392.   [9] Pattison, 'Tendencies', pp. 387–8.

of the eighteenth century; for Pattison this was not an heroic age of faith, but rather a defensive era in which common appeals to 'reason' and its attendant 'proofs' were used by churchmen to 'demonstrate' the truths of Christian revelation against their cultured detractors, but all too often on the terms proposed by those very detractors.

How accurate, and how strategically aligned, is Pattison's interpretation? In addressing that question, one can learn a lot about the Church of England from the era of James II to that of George II, a period described by Norman Sykes, just a century later, as that between Archbishops Sheldon and Secker. (It took a twentieth-century churchman and Church historian to substitute a clerical for a political periodization in quietly challenging, and slightly extending, Pattison's sense of intellectual chronology, although, with some exceptions, Sykes's treatment of the Church's intellectual history is not so different, if altogether more charitably constructed, than that offered by Pattison.)[10] Pattison was first and foremost a scholar, and it is with the scholarly divines that he was most concerned. Modern scholars have taken a long time to catch up with him, let alone go beyond him, but recent work by specialists in the developing field of the history of scholarship has finally begun to challenge his general picture of the period.[11] To mount an intellectual challenge, however, demands familiarity with the claims made by Pattison.

At root, theology had died out, according to Pattison, because 'the supremacy of reason' had replaced it as a means of understanding religion: the freethinkers and Deists, the opponents of Christianity, had claimed to base their case on pure reason; in defending their position, churchmen had likewise appealed to reason when attempting to refute freethinkers, so that, as Pattison phrased it, the title of John Locke's *Reasonableness of Christianity* summarized an era of religious thought which, adverting to the periodization favoured by the late seventeenth-century patristic scholar William Cave, Pattison denominated the '*Seculum rationalisticum*', the age of reason (or rather, perhaps, the age of rationality or rationalism).[12] 'Dogmatic theology had ceased to exist' as reason substituted for faith, and 'abstract speculation was brought down from inaccessible heights and compelled to be intelligible'.[13] In such an atmosphere, he insisted, the distinction between Calvinists and Arminians had become meaningless. Philosophical theology had also sought to defend itself according to the criteria of rationalism, and this was how he interpreted the work of Bishops Butler and Berkeley. Himself a distinguished historian of classical philology, it is perhaps not surprising that the theologian Pattison

---

[10] Norman Sykes, *From Sheldon to Secker: Aspects of English Church History 1660–1768* (Cambridge, 1959), pp. 140–87.

[11] Most recently by Dmitri Levitin, *Ancient Wisdom in the Age of the New Science: Histories of Philosophy in England, c.1640–1720* (Cambridge, 2015).

[12] Pattison, 'Tendencies', pp. 389–90. [13] Pattison, 'Tendencies', pp. 390, 404–5.

most praised, and then with distinct reservations, was Richard Bentley (1662–1742), better remembered now as a student of classical literature than as an advocate for Christianity.[14]

It is indisputable that 'reason' was the dominant category of eighteenth-century theology, but it would be wrong to suggest, as Pattison does, that this implies a conscious distancing from 'mystery'. Robert South (1634–1717), who successfully and regularly preached at the epicentre of Anglican life, in London at Westminster Abbey, and in Oxford at Christ Church and the University Church of St Mary's, frequently emphasized to his learned auditors that mystery was an essential and inevitable component in revealed religion. Authority and mystery, for South, were as one in divinity; the accents of Augustine can readily be discerned in South's language whenever he discoursed on the divine nature:

> We may as well shut a Mountain within a Mole-Hill, or take up the Ocean in a Conch Shell, as read the stupendous Sacred Intricacies of the Divine Subsistence, by the short and feeble Notions of a Created Apprehension.

> A Christian, in these Matters, has nothing to do but to believe, and since I cannot scientifically comprehend this *Mystery*, I shall worship it with the Religion of *Submission* and Wonder, and casting down my Reason before it, receive it with the Devotions of Silence, and the noble Distances of Revelation.[15]

South was by no means alone in insisting that 'mystery' was necessarily present in a faith that might well otherwise have considered itself reasonable; without mystery, South and others insisted, religion, whether revealed or even if purely natural, would not have required faith of its adherents. Mystery was a constant in religion, and as such promoted in much Anglican theology. Nowhere was this more apparent than in discussion of the doctrine of the Trinity, about which there was considerable debate in the 1690s, some of it as a result of the thinking of John Locke and like-minded lay theologians, as well as by more or less explicit Socinians.[16] South, for example, pummelled away at another divine, William Sherlock (1639/40–1707), on the nature of the Trinity throughout the mid-1690s, emphasizing that it was a mysterious doctrine and that too close an examination and detailing of it resulted in such heresies as

---

[14] Pattison, 'Tendencies', pp. 403–11, 417–19. Cf. the subtitle of Kristine Louise Haugen, *Richard Bentley: Poetry and Enlightenment* (Cambridge, MA, 2011).

[15] Robert South, *Twelve Sermons*, 6 vols. (London, 1694–1717), II, pp. 302, 306.

[16] John Marshall, *John Locke: Resistance, Religion, and Responsibility* (Cambridge, 1994); John Marshall, *John Locke, Toleration and Early Enlightenment Culture: Religious Intolerance and Arguments for Religious Toleration in Early Modern and 'Early Enlightenment' Europe* (Cambridge, 2006); Sarah Mortimer, *Reason and Religion in the English Revolution: The Challenge of Socinianism* (Cambridge, 2010). Scholars tend either to flesh out or repudiate the argument of Hugh Trevor-Roper, 'The Religious Origins of the Enlightenment', in Hugh Trevor-Roper, *Religion, the Reformation and Social Change: The Crisis of the Seventeenth Century* (London, 1967), pp. 179–218.

Sabellianism, that is, stressing the difference within the Triune God to the extent that it effectively creates three distinct Gods, all of whom it worships. Oxford University joined in the debate, disputing the ends and purposes of the Cambridge-educated Sherlock's theological explorations, which it condemned; indeed, the atmosphere grew so nasty that central government stepped in, and William III himself declared it inadmissible for the clergy publicly to squabble over Trinitarian dogma.[17] This did not stop such controversies continuing well into the eighteenth century, with various divines, from Isaac Newton's theological lieutenant Samuel Clarke, to slightly later Cambridge-bred divines such as Bishops Hare and Rundle, being identified by their opponents as Arians. Arians, such as Newton and William Whiston, his clerical successor in the Lucasian Chair of Mathematics at Cambridge, believed that Christ was the favoured first creation of God, and accordingly that he was a creature, albeit one more directly connected to God the Father than any of his other creations.[18] Trinitarian debate entailed much discussion of the teachings of the Church Fathers as well as abstract philosophical speculation. It is not quite accurate, then, to say with Pattison that 'dogmatic theology' was not to be found in the first half of the eighteenth century; in fact there was rather a lot of it, as its modern historians can attest, although there is a tendency among them to read it more as an aspect of ecclesiology than as theology. And ecclesiology is a component of theology; theology subsumes ecclesiology.

Among the mysteries that South discussed, often obliquely, was the nature of salvation. Here again one has to challenge Pattison's assertion that the distinction between Calvinists and Arminians had become unimportant between the 1680s and 1750s. South's soteriology was one that emphasized grace over works, and in this he was at one with his colleague at Christ Church, William Jane, the Regius Professor of Divinity; from Jane's lectures to those preparing for the priesthood, as well as in reading ordained for such men by their clerical college tutors, something akin to Calvin's teachings could occasionally be discerned. But is this the same as calling it Calvinist teaching? In a recent study, Stephen Hampton plainly thinks so, but it might be rather better to say that they were not followers of Calvin so much as of Augustine; they saw themselves more as Reformed Catholics than as Reformed Protestants.[19] Certainly, whilst John Edwards (1637–1716) of St John's College, Cambridge,

---

[17] Robert South, *Animadversions on Dr. Sherlock's Book* (London, 1693); Robert South, *Tritheism Charged upon Dr. Sherlock's New Notion of the Trinity* (London, 1695); William Sherlock, *Vindication of the Doctrine of the Holy and Ever Blessed Trinity* (London, 1695); William Sherlock, *A Modest Examination of the Authority and Reasons of the late Decree* (London, 1696).

[18] See John Gascoigne, *Cambridge in the Age of Enlightenment: Science, Religion and Politics from the Restoration to the French Revolution* (Cambridge, 1989).

[19] Stephen Hampton, *Anti-Arminians: The Anglican Reformed Tradition from Charles II to George I* (Oxford, 2008).

might have identified himself as a follower of Calvin, other similarly inclined divines would be more apt to call themselves orthodox Augustinians on the matter.[20] This was especially true of those, such as South, who found themselves on the 'catholic' wing of the Church, and hence close to the revived Augustinianism of the Jansenist party in the Roman Catholic Church—and the lay masterpiece of that party, Pascal's *Lettres Provinciales*, had been translated at Christ Church in 1657 by Henry Hammond—rather than more explicitly Protestant Calvinists within the Church of England. South rarely preached on the subject of freedom of the will or the nature of the relationship between sin and grace without being aware that it was mired in controversy, and, unusually, in controversy he would rather avoid. Preaching at Christ Church in 1685, he observed of the originating text of such vexations, Romans 7, that it had been 'the Unhappy Source of so much Controversie about these Matters'. It was plain that he would rather have avoided contributing to such controversy, as he immediately stated the problem: 'it is *Practice* that divides the World into Vertuous and Vitious; but otherwise, as to the Theory and Speculation of *Vertue* and *Vice, Honest,* and *Dishonest,* the Generality of Mankind are much the same'. A good inclination habituated people to virtue, whilst an 'ill-disposed will, by the Super-induction of ill Habits, quickly deface[s] it'. Disposition became all, as he concluded with a typical antithesis between classical and Christian conceptions of religion: 'For, as in the Heathen Worship of God, *a Sacrifice, without a Heart,* was accounted *Ominous,* so in the Christian Worship of him, *an heart without a Sacrifice* is worthless and impertinent.'[21] South tended to emphasize the necessary difficulties of the Augustinian theory of redemption by contrasting it with the apparently straightforward, but actually confused, thinking of heathen religion about the rewards of virtue and the losses incurred by vice. Preaching on Romans 1:20—'For the invisible things of him from the creation are clearly seen, being understood by the things that are made, *even* eternal power and Godhead; so that they are without excuse'—South insisted that the gospel theory of satisfaction was at once more demanding and more rewarding than any other theory. All classical theories were as nothing on the matter, and Stoicism, a popular resort for moralists of the time, was very much included in this rebuttal. South drew a sharp analysis of the human will and its relationship with virtue; its actual operational intricacies, however, were subsidiary matters that he did not choose to elucidate to any great degree.[22] Aware that this was a model of the will that created anxieties amongst Christians, South attempted to mitigate them by observing that there were, occasionally, changes in the

---

[20] See John Edwards, *A Brief Vindication of the Fundamental Articles of the Christian Church* (London, 1697).
[21] South, *Twelve Sermons,* I, pp. 494–5, 521.   [22] South, *Twelve Sermons,* II, pp. 321–70.

human spirit overseen by the Spirit of God; he never questioned the efficacy of an undoubtedly perplexing doctrine:

> But still (I say) for all the *Rarity* and *Fewness* of such Examples, God will have all the world know (maugre all our flourishing Socinians and Pelagians) that under the Gospel Oeconomy there is such a thing, such a *Gratia Vorticordia*, as we have been speaking of... And indeed if we do but grant the *general Corruption of Human Nature thro' Original Sin*, it is infinitely sottish, as well as impious, to assert the contrary.[23]

For South, this was a matter of scriptural authority, and, to a lesser degree, of patristic and Scholastic study; it was not teaching he had explicitly, or even implicitly, imbibed from Calvin. And for South this had a political, as well as a religious dimension; memories of the republican Presbyterianism of the civil war period at Oxford were too strong for him, as can be heard echoed in his dismissal of Calvin's politics, denoting the great Protestant teacher as the 'Grand Mufti of Geneva'.[24] For South and other orthodox divines, it was the Church Fathers rather than the leaders of the Reformation whose teaching they affirmed when expounding their own theological positions, whether in the pulpit or from the professorial lectern. Theology was at least as much a practical matter as it was a prescribed subject of study in late Stuart and early Hanoverian Anglican divinity.

Study of the Church Fathers was integral to much Anglican theology in the late seventeenth and early eighteenth century, as the recent work of Jean-Louis Quantin has magisterially demonstrated.[25] Pattison was, therefore, quite wrong to scant such commitment in his description of the theology of the age. As Quantin has shown, the authority of the Fathers united different groups within the Church, although towards the end of the seventeenth century and the beginning of the eighteenth century it was increasingly the property of High Churchmen and non-jurors. And the man to whose work tribute was paid again and again was George Bull (1634–1710), who was to become the bishop of St David's, and above all the presentation in his *Defensio Fidei Nicaenae* (1685) of the orthodox Nicene Creed as the bulwark of the faith, for which he was awarded a doctorate in divinity at Oxford; to dispute such authority was, for Bull's many orthodox followers, to identify oneself as a heretic. When William Whiston questioned the Nicene authority of Athanasius, preferring the theology of Arius, which he read as the accepted teaching of the primitive ante-Nicene Church, he knowingly entered on a period of dissension from the Church of which he was a priest; his exile from Cambridge was punctuated by serial altercations with more orthodox divines, and there

---

[23] South, *Twelve Sermons*, VI, pp. 330–1.   [24] South, *Twelve Sermons*, IV, pp. 54, 207.
[25] Jean-Louis Quantin, *The Church of England and Christian Antiquity: The Construction of a Confessional Identity in the Seventeenth Century* (Oxford, 2009).

can be little doubt that he became almost an enthusiast for his variety of Christian rationalism.[26]

It is with such outstanding scholars as Bull that Quantin's study is mostly concerned, and his texts were central to university study well into the first third of the eighteenth century. The supremacy of Bull in such courses is of primary importance in understanding the training of clergy, but there were intermediaries between such deeply learned apologetic and the everyday study of the Fathers as this occurred in cathedral closes, college libraries, and the better-equipped parish studies of divines. And at the core of such practical reflection was the work of William Cave (1637–1713), a Cambridge-educated London divine, whose expositions of the Fathers as a living resource of orthodox theology were to secure him doctorates in divinity from Oxford and Cambridge and a canonry at Windsor. Cave's were timely interventions, written with immediate as well as generally educative purpose. His writings were, therefore, rather more than theological apologetic against Rome (and Dissent), although they could be exactly that on occasion, as in his short *Discourse concerning the Unity of the Catholick Church maintained in the Church of England*, published in 1684, at the height of the Tory Reaction. It was designed expressly to silence the question asked by such Roman Catholic grandees as Bossuet—whose work was seen as prominent in the elite circles in which conversions to Rome were taking place—namely, where the Church of England was before the Reformation, to which Cave responded:

> We answer, just where it is: Thereby no new Church was set up; no new Articles of Faith brought in; no new order of Priesthood to minister in holy things: all which would have required new Miracles, and a new immediate Authority from heaven so attested: only the old ones were purged from impurities in Doctrine, Writings, and Practice, which, in passing through so many degenerate Ages, they had contracted and that no ordinary Power might suffice to do.[27]

So far, so familiar; but what Cave also noticed was that if Rome was not to triumph again in England, and if the purified doctrines of a Reformed Catholic Church were to prevail, then behaviour had to reflect this providential gift: hence his exhortation at the close of his pamphlet: 'That our lives may be answerable to our Profession, and our pious, virtuous, peaceable, and charitable

---

[26] See Scott Mandelbrote, 'Newton and Eighteenth-Century Christianity', in I. Bernard Cohen and George E. Smith (eds.), *The Cambridge Companion to Newton* (Cambridge, 2002), pp. 409–30; Scott Mandelbrote, 'Eighteenth-Century Reactions to Newton's Anti-Trinitarianism', in J. E. Force and S. Hutton (eds.), *Newton and Newtonianism* (Dordrecht, 2004), pp. 93–111; James E. Force, *William Whiston: Honest Newtonian* (Cambridge, 1985); Maurice Wiles, *Archetypal Heresy: Arianism through the Centuries* (Oxford, 1996).

[27] William Cave, *A Discourse concerning the Unity of the Catholick Church maintained in the Church of England* (London, 1684), pp. 26–7.

Conversation may be in some proportion as defensible, and remarkable as the Principles we proceed upon, or the benefits we lay claim to.'[28]

There was an urgency to Cave's scholarship in the troubled 1680s, but there had also been a sense in which his earlier scholarship, particularly as evinced in his celebrated *Primitive Christianity* (1673), had been a direct intervention in the piety of his own times. And in this respect, Cave and South, both London divines, and hence direct observers of much that they attacked, were at one.

The dedication to Nathaniel Crewe, bishop of Oxford, affixed to *Primitive Christianity* revealed the fearful circumstances in which Cave wrote, and the purpose with which he did so: 'I beheld Religion generally laid waste, and Christianity ready to draw its last breath, stifled and oppressed with the vices and Impieties of a Debauched and Profligate Age: to contribute towards the Recovery whereof, and the reducing things (if possible) to the Ancient Standard, is the Design of the Book that is here offered to you.'[29] Four years later—in *Apostolici*, a study of the apostolic and immediately post-apostolic martyrs, and of the Church Fathers of the first three centuries—things had hardly changed, as Cave offered an even more emphatic jeremiad in his dedication, once more to Crewe, by then translated to Durham:

> For we are fallen into the worst of Times, wherein men have been taught, by bad Principles, and worse Practices, to despise the Holy Order, and to level it with the meanest of the People. And this is not only by profest *Enemies (for we then could have borne it)* but by pretended friends, who seem to have a high zeal for Religion, and themselves. By which means the hands of evil men have been strengthened, and the designs of those sufficiently gratified, who 'tis like would rejoice at the ruine of us both.

Cave was worried by the sort of 'Political Christianity' which so troubled South, and especially by the actions of anti-clerical grandees and other courtly scoffers. And beneath this, Cave detected the covert politics of atheism:

> I confess that the Persons and Credit of the Regular Clergy should by some Men be treated with Contempt and Scorn, is the less to be wondered at, when Religion itself is not secure from the rude and base Railleries of some, and the serious Attempts of others, who gravely design to banish the awe of Religion, and the impressions of whatever is Divine and Sacred, out of the minds of men.[30]

---

[28] Cave, *Discourse*, p. 56.

[29] William Cave, 'Epistle Dedicatory', in *Primitive Christianity, or, the Religion of the Ancient Christians in the First Ages of the Gospel* (London, 1673), sigs. A6ᵛ–A7ʳ.

[30] William Cave, 'Epistle Dedicatory', in *Apostolici: Or, the History of the Lives, Acts, Death, and Martyrdoms of those who were Contemporary with, or immediately Succeeded the Apostles, As also the most Eminent of the Primitive Fathers for the first Three Hundred Years* (London, 1677), sigs. A2ᵛ–A3ʳ.

By the time he turned to his 'Epistle to the Reader', things had become
yet more apocalyptic, as Cave contrasted the purity of the primitive ages of
the Church with the decadence of his own times; for all its intellectual
progress, his was, he adduced, an age of sorry decline by contrast with
those happier ages:

> For however Later Ages might have improved in knowledge, Experience daily
> making Additions to Arts and Sciences, yet former Times were most eminent for
> the practice and vertues of a holy Life. The Divine Laws, while newly published,
> had a stronger influence upon the minds of Men, and the Spirit of Religion was
> more active and vigorous till Man by degrees began to be debauched into that
> impiety and prophaneness, that in these last Times has over-run the World.[31]

Divinity, for Cave, was a means of correcting a fallen world, and the primitive
Church of the Fathers provided the ultimate court of appeal in correcting
Christian declension. And in this, he was not alone.

When, for example, some twenty years after Cave's patristic works had
made their way into learned clerical libraries, William Reeves (1667–1726)
concluded his preface, 'Concerning the Right Use of the Fathers', to his
translations of texts by Justin Martyr, Tertullian, and Minucius Felix, it was
with an eye both to enforce orthodoxy and to counter the freethinking critics
of Christianity, against whom he preached whenever opportunity allowed.
Reeves, a product of Eton and King's College, Cambridge, where he was briefly
a fellow, was close to the pious layman Robert Nelson, to whom his study was
dedicated, and he ended his quietly distinguished career as vicar of St Mary's,
Reading. In what he decried as 'this Age of Licentiousness', Reeves wished
through his writings to

> infuse an Ambitious Warmth in the Younger Clergy of entring upon the Study of
> Divinity, with the Scriptures in Conjunction with the Fathers, and to form their
> Notions, and Fashion their Minds by the Doctrine and Example of Christ and His
> Apostles and the Noble Army of Martyrs, and not to take up, and quench their
> Thirst with the Corrupted Stream of Modern Systems.[32]

The 'Corrupted Stream of Modern Systems', it is not hard to infer, was that
associated with what the High Church divine dismissed as 'the Cavils of the
Sons of Latitude'.[33] Similarly, adverting to John Locke's claim that a minimal
commitment to accepting that Jesus was the Messiah was enough to constitute
a believing Christian, Reeves set up the primitive Church against modern
philosophers, declaring that he hoped that 'the Martyrs were as much concerned for Truth as the Lockists'.[34] Polemic, as ever, was never far away in

---

[31] Cave, 'To the Reader', in *Apostolici*, sig. B1ᵛ.
[32] William Reeves, *The Apologies of Justin Martyr, Tertullian, and Minutius [sic] Felix*, 2 vols.
(London, 1716), I, p. lxxix.
[33] Reeves, *Apologies*, I, p. 12.   [34] Reeves, *Apologies*, I, p. xiii.

such everyday recommendations of something so basic to Anglican theology as study of the Church Fathers.

Building on the work of 'our Excellent Dr. Cave', Reeves saw in patristics the antidote to the modernism of latitudinarianism, insisting that: 'In the Study of Divinity not to begin with the Fathers, is not only an absurd Contempt of the best Men, and the soundest Christians, but it is in effect to begin at the wrong End, and to study backwards.'[35] In order to ensure that such a bedrock was available, Reeves encouraged lay patrons to provide libraries for parochial clergy; presumably his own work, which denounced the Huguenot Jean Le Clerc as well as the Cambridge divine Daniel Whitby for their critical treatment of the Fathers, was to be an essential part of such a library. There his volumes would sit alongside the more expensive, more pronouncedly learned work of Dr Cave; after all, what Reeves had provided were lively, animated, and deeply considered English translations of major patristic texts. The Fathers needed to be presented in the vernacular precisely to enable their ready availability to, and consequently influence on, clergymen in their parish work and, more deeply, in their thinking as preachers of the Word in what he routinely lambasted as 'this degenerate Age'.[36] Bull, and conceivably Cave, they would have read at the university; Reeves's work was conceived for the consideration of the parochial clergy.

Orthodox theology was central to Church teaching for Reeves: doctrine and pastoral concern were but two sides of the same coin. His sometimes rebarbative orthodoxy could be heard in his sermons as much as in his work on the Fathers of the Church, as when preaching on the faith requisite in a Christian, he emphasized the centrality of the Trinity to Christian doctrine and practice. The enemy was easily identified, as he opined that: 'We live in an Age that loves to distinguish itself by a notable Contempt of *Creeds* and *Creed-makers*; when every wretch that can *scratch Paper*, is scribbling against the tremendous Mystery of the ever-blessed Trinity, and in the very Face of the Law pulling down the establish'd Litany and Articles of our Church.' In withstanding such challenges, the modern Church should look to the likes of Bishop Bull, 'our great Gamaliel', in defending the Trinity, and the claims Reeves made in his work on the Fathers translated immediately and effectively into the pious observation (and wish) that a learned clergy were

Men, equal to the glorious Task they have undertaken, and marvellous well appointed with Scripture, Antiquity, Language and Logick, to drive our Enemies from their strongest Holds, and to ferret the Foxes out of all Wiles of little Sophistry and disingenuous Dealing. And indeed to strip them of Ambiguity, is to spoil the Cheat and convict the Jugglers.[37]

---

[35] Reeves, *Apologies*, I, pp. 1, 10.   [36] Reeves, *Apologies*, I, pp. 165–7, 12.
[37] William Reeves, *Fourteen Sermons preach'd on several Occasions* (London, 1729), pp. 114, 142–3.

The proper promotion of orthodoxy in theology led desirably, for Reeves and like-minded clergy, to orthodoxy in civil society. His was a consciously anti-Lockean stance, and one he shared with a great many clergy. If Locke's *Reasonableness of Christianity* provided the keynote of eighteenth-century Anglican theology, as Pattison insisted it did, Locke's own voice, however, was not universally respected, either by many of his contemporaries or by their immediate theological heirs. There was opposition to merely reasonable Christianity throughout the eighteenth century; and it was an opposition by no means confined to the Evangelical Revival, of which both Pattison and Stephen were deeply suspicious.

Such furious disapprobation of Lockean credal minimalism as that expressed by Reeves can be found again and again in theological writing of the period; and Pattison was therefore entirely right when he emphasized that, with rare exceptions, 'the theology of the Hanoverian period is of the most violently partisan character'.[38] Nowhere was it more partisan than when its proponents were insisting that they were above party; faction afflicted theology as well as political parties, but it cannot be reduced to being a mere reflection of purely political partisanship. And religious partisanship was in its turn regretted in particular by laymen, both religious and irreligious. John Locke, ritually rebuked by Reeves, returned such suspicion, observing regretfully, in private notes on the queen of the sciences, that:

> There is indeed one Science (as they are now distinguished) incomparably above all the rest where it is not by corruption narrowed into a trade or faction for meane or ille ends and secular interests, I mean Theologie, which conteining the knowledge of god and his creatures, our duty to him and our fellow creatures and a view of our present and future state is the comprehension of all other knowledge directed to its true end i.e. the honour and veneration of the Creator and the happynesse of mankinde. This is that noble study which is every mans duty and every one that can be called a rational creature is capable of.

So exalted a sense of its study and importance made Locke's fear of faction within theology all the sadder to him: 'This is that Science which would truly enlarge mens minds were it studied or permitted to be studied every where with that freedom, love of truth and charity which it teaches, and were not made contrary to its nature the occasion of strife faction, malignity and narrow impositions.'[39]

Locke, South's contemporary at Westminster School and Christ Church, Oxford, was deeply suspicious of the sort of clerical partisanship that South the often polemical divine relished, and there is something of a paradox in

---

[38] Pattison, 'Tendencies', p. 415.
[39] John Locke, 'Theologie', in Victor Nuovo (ed.), *John Locke: Writings on Religion* (Oxford, 2002), p. 3.

South's subsequently encouraging Locke to quash his fellow divine Edward Stillingfleet, when Locke was engaged in an extended philosophical dispute with the learned bishop of Worcester, who had begun his career with an important study in antiquarian and scriptural apologetic, his *Origenes sacrae*, which appeared in print alongside the Restoration of the Church of England, in 1662.[40]

Locke's critique of clerical factionalism stopped short of the familiar anti-clerical charge of 'priestcraft', an accusation that the freethinker Anthony Collins (1676–1729), one of the most consistent critics of the Established Church, frequently made in his writings against the clergy and theology. In *A Discourse on Free-Thinking* (1713), Collins opined, not without considerable evidence, that: 'The Priests do not study Divinity so call'd, but only how to maintain a certain System of Divinity.'[41] Earlier in his rebarbative treatise, Collins had observed, regarding the Calvinist John Edwards of Jesus College, Oxford, writing fervently against Whiston's alleged heterodoxy: 'according to this profound Divine, the Priests are never to have any regard for Truth, but where it happens to agree with the Oaths they have once taken, and the Subscriptions and Declarations they have once made'. Such a position, Collins provocatively deduced, would have kept Roman Catholics as Roman Catholics, and Muslims as Muslims.[42] Collins, who was ten years behind William Reeves at Eton and King's, turned Reeves's orthodox charges against him and like-minded clergy. Lay suspicions of theology were not easily allayed by its clerical opponents.

But as the example of Locke importantly attests, lay writers also played an important role in eighteenth-century Anglican apologetic. To consider but two later products of Locke's Oxford college, the cousins Gilbert West and George Lyttleton both initially rejected their religion when leaving Christ Church, only to recover it later in their lives. And they recovered it in the most public of forms, both writing considerable and influential defences of central aspects of the Christian faith. West was to be awarded a doctorate of laws at Oxford in 1748 for his *Observations on the Resurrection*, published the previous year, and which drew on historical reasoning in making its case. Also in 1747, Lyttelton produced his *Observations on the Conversion of St Paul*, described by another of their contemporaries at Oxford, Samuel Johnson—an equally effective lay theologian, and a regular supplier of sermons to rich if uninspired clergy—as 'a treatise to which infidelity has never been able to fabricate a specious answer'.[43] Lay Christians who had enjoyed an education

---

[40] Esmond de Beer (ed.), *The Correspondence of John Locke*, 8 vols. (Oxford, 1976–89), VI, pp. 63, 196–7, 753–4; VIII, pp. 356–8.

[41] Anthony Collins, *A Discourse on Free-Thinking* (London, 1713), pp. 109–10.

[42] Collins, *Discourse*, p. 84.

[43] Samuel Johnson, 'Lyttelton', in Roger Lonsdale (ed.), *The Lives of the English Poets*, 4 vols. (Oxford, 2006), IV, p. 186.

alongside the more learned of the clergy were able to draw on similar scholarly training when making common cause against sceptics and unbelievers. Nor were all lay theologians as orthodox as West and Lyttelton; in *The Light of Nature Pursued* (1768), Abraham Tucker expounded a distinctive metaphysics, occasionally through the disembodied spirit of John Locke: however, unsystematic and eccentric though the work was, William Paley adverted to its influence on his thinking in his *Moral and Political Philosophy* (1785). Lay divinity spoke to professional theologians throughout the eighteenth century.

It was, however, more usually the clergy who offered the most thorough replies to unbelievers, and nowhere so powerfully, as even Pattison acknowledged, as when Richard Bentley took on Anthony Collins in his *Remarks upon a late Discourse on Freethinking* (1713). By then, Bentley had established himself as the leading classical philologist of his age—and he also emended Scripture, controversially confirming Erasmus's suspicion that the one overt reference to the Trinity in the New Testament, at 1 John 5:7, was actually an interpolation.[44] The royal road to preferment, ending in Bentley's becoming Master of Trinity College, Cambridge, had been made possible when as a young London preacher he had initiated the Boyle Lectures on the evidences of the Christian religion in 1692. As is well known, in these celebrated lectures, in which he appealed to the work of Isaac Newton and other fellows of the Royal Society, Bentley laid the foundations of natural theology, adducing from the evidence of design that there was a designer, and that the Christian God was that designer. But the lectures went beyond this world; Bentley hypothesized a plurality of worlds in which providential ends were also at work, and whose denizens were destined for eternity as assuredly as were Bentley's human readers, and he took the opportunity to lambast Thomas Hobbes, axiomatic in Anglican apologetic between the Restoration and the early 1700s.[45] Bentley established a style of apologetic that remained in place until it reached its apogee in the work of William Paley and the Bridgewater Treatises of the 1830s. But the Boyle Lectures were devoted to the necessity of revelation, and Bentley's lectures were permeated by scriptural illustration, and his successor lecturers continued to appeal to Scripture. And here it is noticeable that, in his essay, Pattison made next to no appeal to the sustained exploration of the Bible and ancillary texts made in the first half of the eighteenth century. He mentioned John Rogers's Boyle Lectures, which centred on the necessity of revelation, but he did not choose to expound

---

[44] Haugen, *Richard Bentley*, pp. 194–205.

[45] Richard Bentley, *The Folly and Unreasonableness of Atheism* (London, 1693); Haugen, *Richard Bentley*, pp. 101–5. On disapprobation of Hobbes by Restoration divines, see Samuel P. Mintz, *The Hunting of Leviathan: Seventeenth-Century Reactions to the Materialism and Moral Philosophy of Thomas Hobbes* (Cambridge, 1962); Jon Parkin, *Taming the Leviathan: The Reception of the Politics and Religious Ideas of Thomas Hobbes in England, 1640–1700* (Cambridge, 2006).

them, perfectly respectable though they undoubtedly are.[46] (Rogers, a former fellow of Corpus Christi College, Oxford, and the son of a clergyman, illustrates how much the learning of the Church was dependent on will and circumstance; his biographer noted how his addiction to country sports as a young man had had occasionally to give way to his studies in divinity before his academic success could be guaranteed. Here, in one instance, the familiar Victorian cliché regarding a worldly Church supposedly vitiated by an equally worldly clergy is mitigated by the learned example of a divine who rode to hounds to the end of his days.)[47]

Pattison made up for ignoring scriptural studies in his 1860 essay by mentioning them at length in an essay of 1863 devoted to the English divine, William Warburton (1698–1779), whose specious classical learning provoked his ire almost as much as what Pattison saw as his equally tendentious theology. In the course of his excoriation of Warburton, Pattison discussed the lectures on Hebrew poetry given by Robert Lowth in the 1750s, which were to have a profound influence on the German biblical scholarship that subsequently undermined Pattison's own scriptural beliefs.[48] Lowth, consequently, he praised, and as Robert G. Ingram, amongst others, has shown in his study of Archbishop Thomas Secker's promotion of Hebrew scholarship in mid-eighteenth-century Oxford, serious study of the Bible continued to be made throughout the period.[49] Here also was the origin of a proof of scriptural veracity that increasingly appealed over the second half of the eighteenth century: prophecy. Up to 1750, similar apologetic value had regularly been accorded to the appeal to the miraculous, but in 1749 the decidedly heterodox Cambridge divine, Conyers Middleton (a sometime opponent of the ageing Bentley's dictatorial reign as Master of Trinity College), put paid to that by publishing his learned tract, *A Free Inquiry into the Miraculous Powers, which are supposed to have subsisted in the Christian Church, from the Earliest Ages through several successive Centuries.* This provoked a furore in which clergy argued *pro* and *contra* (and largely *contra*) Middleton, who had had the good sense to die before the controversy had reached its height. Even David Hume regretted that his own assault on the miraculous, the tenth section of his *Enquiries*, which appeared in the same year as Middleton's enquiry, had fallen out of notice, overwhelmed by a merely theological rather than a purely philosophical debate: proponents of a secular rather than a clerical Enlightenment in

---

[46] John Rogers, *The Necessity of Divine Revelation, and the Truth of the Christian Revelation, asserted in Eight Sermons* (London, 1727); Pattison, 'Tendencies', p. 395.

[47] John Burton, 'Life', prefixed to John Rogers, *Nineteen Sermons Preached on Several Occasions* (London, 1735), p. xvii.

[48] 'Life of Bishop Warburton', in Henry Nettleship (ed.), *Essays by the late Mark Pattison, sometime Rector of Lincoln College, Oxford*, 2 vols. (Oxford, 1889), II, pp. 119–76.

[49] Robert G. Ingram, *Religion, Reform and Modernity in the Eighteenth Century: Thomas Secker and the Church of England* (Woodbridge, 2007), pp. 86–100.

England necessarily face problems with this fact.[50] Much of Middleton's energy went against the authority of the Fathers, whom he portrayed as credulous peddlers of increasingly absurd miracles, and from this point their authority underwent a rapid decline in English divinity. And Middleton was not alone in gradually transforming the Fathers from witnesses of eternal truths into instances of more or less interesting moments in the evolution of Church history before the Reformation ushered in a new age of credibility, a narrative propounded with great care and scholarly panache by John Jortin (1698–1770), whose lack of any very obvious orthodoxy had kept back preferment until he was made archdeacon of London towards the end of his life. Jortin's *Remarks on Ecclesiastical History* (1751–73) were quarried by Gibbon, but so also was the more orthodox history offered by Joseph Bingham (1668–1723) in the ten volumes of his *Origenes ecclesiasticae, or Antiquities of the Christian Church* (1708–22).[51]

And Jortin, in common with any number of Anglican divines, had had his encounters with the irascible Warburton, whose *Divine Legation of Moses Demonstrated* (1738–41)—a work that rapidly gained him a European reputation—had taken on every conceivable heterodoxy, although its own value as orthodox apologetic was quickly to prove decidedly equivocal. Basing his claim on 'the principles of a religious deist', Warburton rested his argument that where all ancient societies had prudently based their laws on an efficacious, if entirely fictional, belief in an afterlife of rewards and punishments, the ancient Jews had not, and this because God interposed directly in the Jewish polity, although Moses had indeed had direct knowledge of the true logic of eternity. Warburton had been close to Middleton, but scenting trouble by such an association, distanced himself from controversy by publishing, in 1751, a tract, *Julian*, which attempted to verify a very late miracle, namely the 'fiery eruption' that obliged Julian the Apostate to abandon his blasphemous attempt to rebuild the temple at Jerusalem. For all the disseveration of Warburton's contemporaries, and the venting of later fury by Pattison and Leslie Stephen, his ambitious attempt at creating a scholarly case for the truth of Christian revelation has begun to be revalued by modern scholars, a revaluation initiated by J. G. A. Pocock, who sees in the *Divine Legation*,

---

[50] Hugh Trevor-Roper, 'From Deism to History: Conyers Middleton', in John Robertson (ed.), *History and Enlightenment* (New Haven, CT, 2010), pp. 71–119; Robert G. Ingram, 'The Weight of Historical Evidence: Conyers Middleton and the Eighteenth-Century Miracles Debate', in Robert D. Cornwall and William Gibson (eds.), *Religion, Politics, and Dissent 1660–1832: Essays in Honour of James E. Bradley* (Farnham, 2010), pp. 85–109; Brian Young, 'Conyers Middleton: The Historical Consequences of Heterodoxy', in Sarah Mortimer and John Robertson (eds.), *The Intellectual Consequences of Religious Heterodoxy 1600–1750* (Leiden, 2012), pp. 235–65.

[51] B. W. Young, 'John Jortin, Ecclesiastical History, and the Christian Republic of Letters', *Historical Journal*, 55 (2012): 961–81; B. W. Young, '"Scepticism in Excess": Gibbon and Eighteenth-Century Christianity', *Historical Journal*, 41 (1998): 179–99.

along with Gibbon's *History of the Decline and Fall of the Roman Empire*, one of the two masterpieces produced by England's clerical Enlightenment.[52] After publishing *Julian*, which was poorly received, Warburton retreated from the appeal to miracles, turning his attention instead to the apologetic currency of prophecy, something that had been earlier promoted by Thomas Sherlock (1677–1761), in his *The Use and Intent of Prophecy* (1725). Such was Warburton's conviction of the returns to be made on prophecy that he invested in 1768 in a series of Warburtonian Lectures to be delivered at Lincoln's Inn, which continued into the twentieth century as an opportunity for learned young divines to be introduced to the London preaching circuit. Warburton's was a decidedly mixed legacy; even as Pattison and Stephen lambasted his reputation, his faith in the apologetic value of biblical prophecy remained a central feature of fashionable London preaching.

The readmission of Warburton into the scholarly mainstream has been welcome, but it does demonstrate a strange bias in scholarship that began with Pattison and which recent revisionism has not dispelled. By emphasizing the role in Anglican apologetic of what might be called late Christian humanism, as represented by the likes of Cave, Warburton, and Jortin, scholars have tended to discount the specifically philosophical contribution made by Bishops Berkeley and Butler. Pattison was unusual in being as critical of both men, and particularly by probing the contribution of Joseph Butler, as both men enjoyed a singularly high reputation in nineteenth-century England, Berkeley as a proponent of Idealism long before German metaphysics had begun to suffuse British philosophical theology in the opening decades of the nineteenth century, and Butler not only as a philosopher but also as a moralist, who appealed as strongly to the residually Christian Matthew Arnold as much as he did to the resolutely orthodox William Gladstone, who edited Butler's works.[53] Historians of philosophy have begun the rehabilitation of Berkeley and Butler; it is time for historians of religion to absorb their work into a deeper appreciation of England's peculiarly Christian experience of Enlightenment.

George Berkeley and Joseph Butler produced, respectively, in *Alciphron* and *The Analogy of Religion*, classics of Christian philosophical apologetic, the

---

[52] J. G. A. Pocock, *Barbarism and Religion*, 6 vols. (Cambridge, 1999–2015), I: *The Enlightenments of Edward Gibbon, 1737–1764*; B. W. Young, *Religion and Enlightenment in Eighteenth-Century Britain: Theological Debate from Locke to Burke* (Oxford, 1997), pp. 167–212; David Sorkin, *The Religious Enlightenment: Protestants, Jews, and Catholics from London to Vienna* (Princeton, NJ, 2008), pp. 25–65; John Robertson, *The Case for the Enlightenment: Scotland and Naples 1680–1760* (Cambridge, 2005), pp. 280–8.

[53] Jane Garnett, 'Bishop Butler and the *Zeitgeist*: Butler and the Development of Christian Moral Philosophy in Victorian Britain', in Christopher Cunliffe (ed.), *Joseph Butler's Moral and Religious Thought: Tercentenary Essays* (Oxford, 1992), pp. 63–96; Boyd Hilton, *The Age of Atonement: The Influence of Evangelicalism on Social and Economic Thought 1785–1865* (Oxford, 1988), pp. 340–61; David Bebbington, *The Mind of Gladstone: Religion, Homer, and Politics* (Oxford, 2004), pp. 116–18, 247–53, 310–11.

authority of which was immediately acknowledged and which continued well into the nineteenth century. Until the closing decades of the nineteenth century, Butler and Berkeley had a higher reputation in Britain than had Hume; it was the likes of Leslie Stephen who made this change possible. But in doing so, Pattison and Stephen and others were not guilty, in making their assessments of eighteenth-century culture, of what John Robertson has characterized as 'premature secularisation'.[54] Indeed, when Pattison shiftily noted that High Churchmen closed their list of fathers either with Daniel Waterland or Daniel Brett, he knew exactly what he was doing. At first sight, the two names ought to be interchangeable, but they are not. Both were orthodox theologians, but what exactly constituted 'orthodoxy' is brought to the surface in making this claim, as Brett challenged Waterland's self-ascription as an orthodox divine over a central issue in theology. Waterland, the Master of Magdalene College, Cambridge, in the 1730s, successfully promoted the study of properly orthodox theology in a celebrated guide to reading prepared for his own under-graduates but rapidly adopted across his university. He also challenged, in his capacity as archdeacon of Middlesex, Mandeville's apology for selfishness, as Waterland saw it, his notorious *Fable of the Bees* (1714), and Matthew Tindal's *Christianity as Old as the Creation* (1730), which Waterland answered in terms which did not impress the heterodox Conyers Middleton, who answered him in his turn.[55] Thomas Brett, a late non-juror, preached orthodox sermons of an intensity which provoked the ire of heterodox churchmen and freethinkers alike. And Brett, a studious defender of the eucharist as a 'representative Sacrifice', took rather a different line on eucharistic doctrine than did Waterland, who saw the rite in a rather more distinctive light.[56]

In an age of faith that also prided itself on reason, the doctrine of the eucharist proved surprisingly divisive: Brett, Hoadly, and Waterland were most evidently in agreement in their rejection of transubstantiation, but in many other respects they were in profound disagreement regarding the literally elemental nature of Holy Communion. In his 1713 sermon, *The Christian Altar and Sacrifice*, Brett affirmed the distinctions between Roman Catholic and Anglican teaching, but he also condemned Dissenting ministers for making 'a profane Mockery of that Divine *Ordinance*'. Whilst he repudiated the Catholic refusal to give the cup to the laity as a 'sacrilege', he also derided those Protestants who, 'contrary to the Doctrine of the Holy Scriptures, and of the pure Catholick Church in the first Ages of Christianity', insisted that the eucharist was a purely commemorative rite. In the eucharist,

---

[54] Robertson, *Case for the Enlightenment*.

[55] Daniel Waterland, *Advice to a Young Student* (Cambridge, 1730); Daniel Waterland, *Scripture Vindicated* (London, 1730–2); Daniel Waterland, *Christianity Vindicated against Infidelity* (London, 1732); Conyers Middleton, *A Letter to Dr. Waterland containing some Remarks on his Vindication of Scripture* (London, 1731).

[56] Pattison, 'Tendencies', p. 387.

moral and pastoral theology united indissolubly with doctrinal orthodoxy: Brett emphasized the duty of taking communion regularly, enjoining his hearers and readers thereby '[t]o receive the Pardon of our Sins, Reconciliation with God, the Encrease of strengthening Grace, and become so firmly united to Christ, that nothing may ever be able to dissolve the Union'.[57] Brett's sermon was relatively uncontroversial; what followed, in 1720, was decidedly controversial. *A Discourse Concerning the Necessity of discerning the Lord's Body in the Holy Communion* was prefaced by a sustained critique of Roman Catholic, Lutheran, and Calvinist teaching, with a particular rebuke to the last named, who had '*substantiated in the Place of Truth an idle Fancy of their own*'. Brett was also afraid that yet more heterodox teachings were at large, as the doctrine of the Trinity continued to be undermined by Arian and Socinian theologians, leaving him to conclude, with what quickly proved to be foresight, that 'there is Reason to fear that this Socinian Notion of the Holy Eucharist has been too much spread amongst us'. In order to avoid *all* heretical teaching on the doctrine, Brett wanted the Church of England to revert to the original Prayer Book authorized by Edward VI, in which it was taught by authority that the Holy Ghost changes the bread and the wine into the body and blood of Christ, teaching undermined by the subsequent presence of Bucer and Peter Martyr in England, who had been sent over expressly 'to spoil our Reformation' by rendering it Calvinist. As with many of his Anglican contemporaries, for Brett patristic authority was principally a matter of practical rather than of speculative theology, and not least in regard to the eucharist, since: 'It is best to stick to the Doctrine of the truly Primitive, Catholick and Apostolick Church in this as in all other Matters; for in so doing, we shall find, that we adhere most steadfastly to the Divine Oracles.'[58]

Scripture was the basis of Brett's tract, which was built on 1 Corinthians 11:29 and the insistence that the eucharistic bread is Christ's body; the testimony of a number of Fathers was subsequently adduced to affirm this, as were ancient liturgies and the teaching of the Greek and other Orthodox Churches. But what Brett taught was very particular, namely that although there was no change in *substance* in the elements at consecration, there was a transformation '*Energetically* in full Power and Effect'. For this teaching he appealed to all that mattered theologically, to 'Scripture, Antiquity, Universality, and Consent'. He argued against Roman Catholic superstition, but was more wary of Protestant error, exhorting his readers that

> out of an imaginary, vain fear of Transubstantiation, let us not run into another Extreme, and believe that there is nothing in this Communion but a bare

[57] Thomas Brett, *The Christian Altar and Sacrifice* (London, 1713), pp. 20–3, 30–1, 34, 36, 39–40.

[58] Thomas Brett, *A Discourse concerning the Necessity of discerning the Lord's Body in the Holy Communion* (London, 1720), pp. iii–v, x, xii–xv, xxiv.

Remembrance of Christ's *Death*; that there is no Body or Blood of Christ in the Eucharist, only an empty Ceremony, a bare Sign, or an untrue Figure of a Thing absent, this is certainly directly contrary to the Doctrine of the Scriptures, of the Primitive Fathers, and of the Church of England.[59]

Hoadly's *Plain Account of the Nature and End of the Sacrament of the Lord's Supper*, which appeared anonymously in 1735, was all that Brett had explicitly repudiated fifteen years before; the distance between non-juring and more or less Socinian theology is nowhere more readily apparent. The one had repudiated Lutheran theology as a Lutheran dynasty secured the British throne; the other had over-compensated in making an accommodation with it.

In the preface to this lengthy tract, Hoadly stated that it had had its origins in sermons he had preached in a London living where he found that his parishioners were 'often in danger of great Errors or great Superstition'. He had in his sights unbelievers and infidelity, but Catholic teaching was no less clearly and directly in his line of vision. The only authorities he wished to attest throughout the text were passages from the New Testament, read by him as affirming Christ's words that the eucharist was a remembrance and a memorial; the rite was, for the heterodox bishop, supremely 'That Rational and Christian *Devotion*'. What he described and defended was exactly what Brett had denounced at the beginning of the previous decade: the bread and wine were the outward signs of a memorial, a pledge for the believer to behave morally as Christ had enjoined, a remembrance of the benefits that God has promised to those who follow these precepts, both in this world and in that which is to come; Holy Communion, in Hoadly's ultra-Protestant understanding, was to encourage believers in 'our perseverance in the practice of Every Instance of Virtue and Holiness required of Christians'.[60] It was, effectively, the eucharist moralized.

Hoadly's tract was a theological outlier in the thought and practice of the eighteenth-century Church; when Waterland explained the doctrine of the eucharist to the clergy of his archdeaconry of Middlesex in a charge in April 1738, he nowhere even alluded to it; he did, however, criticize Brett's theology in an appendix. As was usually the case with Waterland's reasoning, his was a historically weighted account of critical theology, and he traced disputes about eucharistic doctrine back to the mid-seventeenth century, before disputing their revival in the early eighteenth century. And again, when discussing the theology of the Church of England, he made his invariably pacific overtures when conversing in print with his fellow clergy, noting of this particular dispute that 'a great Part of it arose from some *Confusion* of Ideas, or Ambiguity of Terms'; in this instance, what was at variance was the notion of what constituted sacrifice. What he sought to do, by following agreed rules,

[59] Brett, *Discourse*, pp. 28–9, 33.

[60] [Benjamin Hoadly], *A Plain Account of the Nature and End of the Sacrament of the Lord's Supper* (London, 1735), pp. iii, viii, 5–7, 23–4, 71, 122, 191–2.

was to 'satisfy reasonable Men on Both sides'. The great error identified by Waterland was that originated by the theologian who had most influenced Brett's work on the eucharist, the obscure John Johnson (1662–1725), the author of a vast and eccentric treatise on the eucharist, *The Unbloody Sacrifice, and altar, unvail'd and supported*, published in 1714. In accord with eucharistic doctrine generally, Johnson had seen the communion as replacing the sacrifices of animals under the Mosaic law with that made by Christ himself as the Lamb of God; unlike the great majority of theologians, however, excepting the Cambridge Platonist Joseph Mede among a handful of others, Johnson had insisted that Christ's sacrifice was, in common with that of the Mosaic law, *material* in nature. According to Johnson, the sacrifices made of animals under the Mosaic law were replaced by the material elements of bread and wine at the eucharist. Brett affirmed Johnson's understanding, insisting that the bread and wine constituted a material sacrifice at the eucharist. Waterland considered this an invention sponsored by Johnson, 'a zealous *Materialist* if ever there was one'; and argued that, to save the bother of proving his assertion, Johnson was 'pleased to aver, that it was *given for granted*'. Johnson (and Brett) built the '*Superstructure*' of a doctrinal system around this entirely invented foundation of a material sacrifice; theirs, according to Waterland, was a basic error, as the Mosaic law had fully given way to Christ's sacrifice: 'They cannot do so much now, because their *legal* Oeconomy is out of Doors, and all Things are become *new*. In a word, our *Expiations* now are either *spiritual,* or *none*: And therefore such of course must our *Sacrifices* also be, either *spiritual,* or *none at all*.'[61]

The Middlesex charge grew out of Waterland's major statement on the nature of Holy Communion, *A Review of the Doctrine of the Eucharist, as laid down in Scripture and Antiquity*, authoritatively published at the University Press in Cambridge in 1738. A silent rebuke of Hoadly's work occurs early in this considerable and influential treatise, where Waterland reverses the impact of the contrast his clerical superior had earlier drawn in teaching on the eucharist: 'as there may be two Extremes, *viz*. of *Superstition* on one Hand, and of *Profaneness* on the other, it appears to be much safer and better to lean on the former Extreme, than to incline to the latter'. Basing his arguments securely on Scripture, the Fathers, and antiquity, an implicit rebuke of Hoadly's treatise was made in language that Brett had used before him: 'the Socinian Way is, to exclude God, as it were, out of the *Sacraments*, and to allow Him no part in them, but to reduce it all to a bare *Human Performance*, or *Positive Duty*: But we have not so learned Christ.'[62] Chapter XII of the *Review*

---

[61] Daniel Waterland, *The Christian Sacrifice Explained, in a Charge delivered in part to the Middlesex Clergy* (London, 1738), pp. 4, 43–4, 47.

[62] Daniel Waterland, *A Review of the Doctrine of the Eucharist, as laid down in Scripture and Antiquity* (Cambridge, 1737), pp. 11, 18.

challenged the view championed by Johnson and Brett, characterizing it as being a dispute 'more about *Names*, than Things'. Waterland made a careful calibration of patristic teaching as a counter to their eucharistic materialism. The gospel dispensation had abolished the material sacrifice of the Mosaic law; consequently, the sacrificial had given way to the predominantly commemorative view of eucharistic theology: Johnson and Brett had been quietly but effectively marginalized by Waterland, whose clarification of teaching on the matter was to become the last word on the subject within the Church of England for a century.[63]

Had Waterland not subsequently produced his charge to the Middlesex clergy, relations with Brett would have remained distant but respectful. Brett had initially replied to Waterland's *Review*, working on the assumption that theirs was indeed but a difference of terms, of '*logomachy*'. He traded texts and readings with Waterland, in time-honoured style, and submitted respectfully that the eucharist was indeed a material sacrifice, and that Waterland had only been over-scrupulous in insisting that 'burnt offerings' alone could meaningfully constitute a material sacrifice. Such was the extent of their disagreement; and Brett was determined to minimize their dispute, fearing that proponents of the Socinian teaching of the *Plain Account* could benefit by alleging Dissent among the orthodox on the nature of the eucharist. Hence Brett deliberately echoed his critic as he declared: 'I thought it necessary to make these Remarks, to shew that there is not such a great Difference between the learned Doctor and us as may at first Sight appear to be, and that it is rather a *seeming* than a *real* difference.'[64] But for Waterland, as his charge subsequently demonstrated, Brett's defence of antiquity resulted paradoxically in a theological novelty, and orthodoxy had therefore been dealt a blow that had to be returned; rapprochement was thereby rendered impossible, and a very real and fundamental difference between the two men was revealed in their conceptions of orthodox eucharistic doctrine. Brett, who had replied to Hoadly in 1736, now added to his earlier response to Waterland, regretting what he saw as betokening worse than a retreat on his former ally's part: Waterland was now in the company of Hoadly, and had indeed outpaced him. According to Brett, 'the learned and truly good and worthy Dr. Waterland' had been overcome by 'Party-Zeal', effectively writing against his own *Review*: 'and after he has learnedly and judiciously spoken so highly of the Eucharistick Elements, to run into the contrary Extreme, so that even the Author of the *Plain Account* can say nothing more degrading of or degrading to them'.[65] Orthodoxy had thereby

[63] Waterland, *Review*, pp. 466–535.

[64] Thomas Brett, *Some Remarks on Dr Waterland's Review of the Doctrine of the Eucharist* (London, 1738), pp. 213–14.

[65] Thomas Brett, *A True Scripture Account of the Nature and Benefits of the Eucharist* (London, 1736); Thomas Brett, *A Supplement to the Remarks on Dr Waterland's Review of the Doctrine of the Eucharist* (London, 1738), p. 26.

come to grief over one of the most basic elements of Church teaching; Hoadly had surreptitiously and unfairly won a theological victory.

Pattison slyly adverted to his readers that High Church theology was broken-backed, and that, like as not, it always had been. Perhaps, in justice, Brett should have the last word here: 'But what will not Men do to serve a Cause and a Party they have espoused? They know Popery is justly terrible to all good Protestants, and therefore hope if they do but loudly cry but *Popery, Popery,* that is sufficient to confute any Doctrine they dislike.'[66] Substitute 'Tractarian' for 'Popery' and that is an accurate assessment of Pattison's Broad Church 'disinterest' in detailing the tendencies of religious thought he discerned in the theology of the first half of the eighteenth century.

It was relatively easy for Pattison to suborn theology to rationalism in the eighteenth century as what he frequently avoided in his essay was a direct confrontation with theology. And even now, when students of Church history are familiar with the niceties of the Bangorian controversy provoked by Hoadly's apparently compromising vision of the nature of the Church, they are much less familiar with his no less heterodox understanding of the eucharist as evinced in his *Plain Account.*[67] This tract was at least as controversial as Hoadly's now infinitely better known sermon, *The Nature of the Kingdom, or Church, of Christ,* preached before George I, to consequent notoriety, in 1717, and it was immediately answered by Waterland—the scourge of Cambridge heterodoxy—in *The Nature, Obligation, and Efficacy of the Christian Sacraments Considered* (1730). Such tracts as those produced by Hoadly, as well as by Brett and Waterland, might have induced a studied indifference in Pattison, but they are of the essence of Anglican theology in the mid-eighteenth century. It is well, when reading Pattison, to bear in mind words spoken by Norman Sykes at Oxford in his Ford Lectures in 1958, just shy of a hundred years after the appearance of his essay, in which he reminded his auditors that 'the age of reason . . . in its own way and in a limited degree, was also a not inconsiderable age of faith'.[68]

Sykes's response to Pattison's scanting of the eighteenth century as an age of faith draws attention to the fact that, to use a distinction adverted to by Samuel Horsley in an archidiaconal charge delivered to the clergy of St Albans in 1783, Pattison privileged the speculative over the practical in his discussion of theology.[69] It was a distinction that academic theologians made rather more frequently than did parochial clergy; and it is one that made little sense to one

---

[66] Brett, *Christian Altar and Sacrifice,* p. ix; see further, Henry Broxap, *The Later Nonjurors* (Cambridge, 1928).

[67] See Andrew Starkie, *The Church of England and the Bangorian Controversy, 1716-1721* (Woodbridge, 2007).

[68] Sykes, *From Sheldon to Secker,* p. 185.

[69] Samuel Horsley, *A Charge delivered to the Clergy of St Albans, at a Visitation holden May 22nd, 1783* (London, 1783), p. 1. He reverted to the distinction when addressing his diocesan

of the most distinctive theologians of the first half of the eighteenth century, and who made only the most fleeting of appearances in Pattison's essay. William Law (1686–1761) is alluded to by Pattison as being one of those men 'at war with society, like the Nonjuring clergy, or a few isolated individuals of superior piety'; but even among his fellow non-jurors, Law was exceptional, as the premier historian of the non-juring clergy, Henry Broxap, acknowledged as long ago as 1924.[70] Why this was so is gestured at in the preface to the American edition of *Essays and Reviews*, in which F. H. Hedge referred to 'the mystic piety of Law'.[71] As Broxap stated it, 'William Law considered as a Non-Juror, stands apart. He cannot be classed as belonging to any particular section, and his mysticism which coloured the whole of his later life was foreign to the genius of the movement.'[72] The most sympathetic study of Law was made by a clergyman who had studied at Lincoln College during the period when Pattison had absented himself from Oxford for a lengthy period of study in Germany; J. H. Overton accepted Pattison's judgement that '"reasonableness" was the very keynote of the theology of the period', and that Law had paid homage to reason accordingly. But Abbey's was generally a much more positive view of eighteenth-century divinity than was that of the rector of his old college; he identified Law as 'one of the ablest of theological writers in a period remarkably fertile in theological literature', and in this judgement the studious parochial clergyman was closer to the truth of the matter than was the much more celebrated scholar.[73]

If the first half of Law's vigorous writing career was devoted to controversial divinity, largely, but not exclusively, devoted to his fellow clergy, the second half, when he had absorbed the mysticism of the seventeenth-century Silesian Jacob Boehme, saw him writing controversial theology for lay as much as for clerical readers; and he remains best known for two classics of practical spirituality addressed specifically to a pious lay readership, *A Practical Treatise upon Christian Perfection* (1726) and *A Serious Call to a Devout and Holy Life: Adapted to the State and Conditions of All Orders of Christians* (1728), the latter of which was especially admired by as disparate a duo as Samuel Johnson and Edward Gibbon. Both tracts were considerable literary achievements, their exhortations powerfully imagined through dextrous pen-portraits of those who had failed to achieve and those who thoroughly exemplified the life of the devout Christian. (It has been claimed that some of these pen-portraits

clergy as bishop of St David's: *The Charge of Samuel, Lord Bishop of St David's, to the Clergy of his Diocese, delivered at his Primary Visitation in the Year 1790* (London, 1790), p. 3.

[70] Pattison, 'Tendencies', p. 425; Broxap, *Later Nonjurors*, pp. 63, 101, 103, 154, 159–60, 162, 164, 167, 198.

[71] *Essays and Reviews*, p. 629.   [72] Broxap, *Later Nonjurors*, p. 217.

[73] J. H. Overton, *William Law, Nonjuror and Mystic: A Sketch of his Life, Character and Opinions* (London, 1881), pp. 43, 128, 1.

were based on members of Gibbon's family, Law having been employed to act as a tutor to the historian's father when his non-juring sentiments had obliged the theologian to resign from his fellowship of Emmanuel College, Cambridge.)[74] Law's engagements with erring fellow clergy and two Deist controversialists, however, are at least as important as his devotional treatises, and likewise as significant in literary as well as in strictly theological terms: Law was one of the great prose-writers of the eighteenth century.

Overton's estimation of Law's controversial writings remains fundamentally sound: as he put it in regard to Law's answers to Bishop Hoadly on the nature of the Church of Christ, their appearance 'raised him at once to the very highest rank of writers in controversial divinity'. His response to Mandeville, published in 1723, is undoubtedly 'the most caustic of his writings'. And it remains true that Law's tract on *The Unlawfulness of Stage Entertainments* 'is decidedly the weakest of his writings, and most of his admirers will regret that he ever published it'. Overton judged Law's reply to Matthew Tindal to be 'a good specimen of that adroitness which he always showed as a controversialist'. He was more equivocal about his *Answer to Dr Trapp*, but was much more appreciative of how, 'with marvellous keenness and vigour', Law had attacked the main propositions informing Warburton's *Divine Legation*.[75] Law's three letters to the bishop of Bangor are forensic and lapidary by turn; in the first he demonstrated how Hoadly's stricture that sincerity in religious conviction was the primary indication of Christian commitment would have opened up the Church to fellowship with such heretical outliers of republican Dissent as Muggletonians, Quakers, Ranters, Fifth-Monarchy Men, and Socinians, but not to non-jurors! In the second letter, Law argued that Hoadly's conciliatory tones had given hope to infidels and heretics, and pain to true lovers of the Church; it was hard, Law asserted, to distinguish Hoadly's beliefs, particularly his repudiation of what the bishop decried as 'hypocrisy' in religion, from the criticism levelled against the Church by Jews, Muslims, and Deists, not least as his 'Novel Doctrine' concerning the Trinity was far removed from orthodoxy; Hoadly's conception of the Church had strayed some way from the experience, and hence the authority, of primitive Christianity.[76] In his final response to Hoadly, Law repeated his earlier claims whilst occasionally, and daringly for an 'emotional Jacobite', drawing political parallels with the bishop's heretical ecclesiology; central to his exposition of the shortcomings of Hoadly's sermon on the nature of Christ's kingdom is his insistence that '[y]our Lordship here advances a mere human Speculation founded upon no other Authority, than

---

[74] See B. W. Young, 'William Law and the Christian Economy of Salvation', *English Historical Review*, 109 (1994): 308–22.

[75] Overton, *William Law*, pp. 19, 32, 37, 122, 293–307, 323–33.

[76] William Law, *The Bishop of Bangor's Late Sermon, and his Letter to Dr. Snape in Defence of it, answer'd* (London, 1718), pp. 3–6, 10, 15–16; William Law, *A Second Letter to the Bishop of Bangor* (London, 1719), pp. 14, 35, 62, 67, 73, 103, 106.

the uncertain signification of the Words, *King* and *Kingdom*'. Hoadly had promoted human authority against both the law and the gospel, leaving Law to conclude of the bishop's innovative teaching that 'a few more such *Defences* of Christianity and the Reformation, as you have given would compleat their Ruin, as far as *human Writings* can compleat it'. Regrettably, Hoadly had set up his 'new Religion ... out of pure Tenderness to the Laity'.[77]

Next to the presumptuous authority of the perniciously heretical Hoadly, the outspoken freethinker Mandeville was even more openly exposed to Law's pious ironies; his arguments were dismissed as being worse than those of any heathen, and as totally lacking in scriptural warrant. As the founder of a charity school himself, Law was outraged by Mandeville's criticism of such foundations, leading him to denounce his opponent's satire in the strongest of terms, placing Mandeville in the lewd company of those he had himself demeaned: 'Thus is your prostitute Pen wantonly employed, to put out as far as you can, the Light of Reason and Religion, and deliver up mankind to Sensuality and Vileness.'[78] As Law would go on to argue against Trapp's critique of being 'righteous over-much', he declared that this was simply impossible for humanity; they ought always to pursue righteousness, which was its own practical end.[79]

Reason was insufficient in defending religion, be it natural or revealed; this was the refrain of *The Case of Reason*, his response to Matthew Tindal's *Christianity as Old as the Creation*. But Law's mystically tinged reply was not destined to be influential; for as Overton observed (following Pattison's central claim):

> When it is remembered that the title of Locke's famous treatise—the 'Reason-ableness of Christianity'—gave the keynote to the dominant theology of Law's day, one can hardly be surprised that this vigorous crusade against reason should have been received by the friends of the Christian cause with indifference, if not with actual hostility.[80]

Overton was right to measure Law's distance from conventional theology; Law's comparatively late assault (it did not appear until 1757), on the *Divine Legation* as a treatise that veered dangerously in the direction of the infidelity it ostensibly opposed, was potently argued, but once again it was a theological tract that remained largely ignored.[81] Law had attacked one highly placed

---

[77] William Law, *A Reply to the Bishop of Bangor's Answer to the Representation of the Committee of Convocation* (London, 1719), pp. 39, 43, 227, 149.

[78] William Law, *Remarks upon a Late Book, Entituled, The Fable of the Bees* (London, 1724), p. 95.

[79] William Law, *Answer to Dr. Trapp* (London, 1740).

[80] Overton, *William Law*, p. 128.

[81] William Law, *A Short but Sufficient Confutation of the Reverend Dr. Warburton's Defence (as he calls it) of Christianity, in his Divine Legation of Moses* (London, 1757).

cleric too many; his retreat in the closing decades of his life into Behmenist mysticism (that had originally influenced those very Commonwealth sects he otherwise strenuously denounced), removed him altogether from the rational and historical theology of his contemporaries, inspiring only a pained rebuke by John Wesley, *A Letter to the Reverend Mr. Law: occasioned by some of his late writings*, which appeared in 1756.[82] The ascendancy of reasonable Christianity was to prove stronger during the eighteenth century than would any tendencies to the mysticism evoked by Law as providing *The Way to Divine Knowledge*, the title of his first fully-fledged Behmenist tract, published in 1752. As will become clear, by the mid-eighteenth century, two Cambridge-bred theologians, William and Edmund Law, had only a surname in common; their conception of the nature and purpose of theology was as dissimilar as could possibly be imagined as having subsisted, let alone flourished, in the Church of England.

THEOLOGY AND ENLIGHTENMENT

Mark Pattison had wanted to emphasize a *caesura* in Anglican scholarship around 1750, arguing that from the final quarter of the eighteenth century it was to be German scholarship that would truly revolutionize theological study, particularly in the field of scriptural studies, and thereby divorcing the parochialism that he associated with reactionary Tractarianism from an advanced European scholarly mainstream in which intellectual liberalism infused thoughtful piety. Leslie Stephen, who was also inspired by a pioneering work of German scholarship, was similarly concerned to demonstrate, as a proponent of agnosticism, how freethinking challenges to Christianity, from Hobbes to Hume and Paine, had been briefly smothered by the emotionalism of the eighteenth-century Evangelical Revival, and therefore saw it as the task of his generation to liberate people from an Evangelical legacy in which the (personally) distasteful doctrine of the atonement had proved a stumbling block to any belief in Christianity. For Stephen and his allies, the new concentration on the Incarnation was no solution to the problems thrown up by atonement theology; theirs was an all or nothing attitude, in which all compromises were to be jettisoned in favour of confronting a genuine loss of faith. And Stephen frequently berated eighteenth-century divinity as constituting compromise, as not being quite honest, and often as being intellectually disreputable. The true incarnation of all such highly dubious tendencies in Stephen's mind was

---

[82] Young, *Religion and Enlightenment*, pp. 122–36.

Warburton, with which 'knock-kneed giant' of Anglican theology he was mildly obsessed.

But there were theologians whom Stephen admired, and the language which he used to describe them—above all that of 'manliness'—denotes some degree of fellow feeling, as Stephen was himself an exponent of agnostic manliness and of what he identified as clarity and precision in thinking. In the proto-Unitarian circle presided over in mid-eighteenth-century Cambridge by Edmund Law (1703–87), Master of Peterhouse and bishop of Carlisle, Stephen discerned intellectual honesty and forthright clarity of diction which he associated with the North Country origins of many of its members.[83] Law had himself been a protégé of Waterland, but his progressive theology, nowhere better expressed than in his *Considerations on the State of the World, with regard to the Theory of Religion* (1745), had freed him to explore theology well beyond the orthodox barriers to which Waterland had moored his own divinity. With the publication of this pioneering tract in which theology is seen as progressing precisely as it is accommodated to the philosophy of an age of empiricism inaugurated by Locke, a specifically eighteenth-century brand of theology can be recognized.[84]

Law's theology meets both criteria of Pattison's definition of theology: it is concerned with a world beyond this—that of God and the spiritual realm—and also with how morality in the world has to be directed towards that realm, as that is where the rewards of heaven will be felt. Law and his followers discountenanced the likelihood of a hell with eternal punishment; their notion of a progressive God effected a separation of their eschatology from that of the Church Fathers, particularly the ritually despised Tertullian, and in this they built on the historico-theological dynamic initiated by Conyers Middleton and John Jortin. Eschatology in this instance reverted to divisions within the early history of the Reformation, in which the idea of mortalism, the sleep of the soul, was resurrected against the more orthodox eschatology championed most resolutely by Calvin. History and theology, from the Church Fathers to the Reformation and beyond, were—and are—necessarily and deeply intertwined.[85]

Where Law embraced progress as a means of accommodating theology, or what he called the 'theory of religion', to the advances of Enlightenment thought, his ally in seeking to overturn subscription to the Thirty-Nine Articles as necessary for study at the ancient universities and in clergy accepting preferment, Francis Blackburne (1705–87), looked to the history of theology, particularly Reformed theology, when making a weighty substantive case for

---

[83] Leslie Stephen, *History of English Thought in the Eighteenth Century*, 2 vols. (London, 1876), II, pp. 343–61.

[84] See Owen Chadwick, *From Bossuet to Newman* (Cambridge, 1957).

[85] See B. W. Young, '"The Soul-Sleeping System": Politics and Heresy in Eighteenth-Century England', *Journal of Ecclesiastical History*, 45 (1994): 64–81.

reform in *The Confessional* (1767). And where Stephen had insisted that Law's party at Cambridge was 'Socinian in all but name', Blackburne vehemently denied that he was a Socinian, and declared himself doctrinally 'a Calvinist of the most liberal sort'. Blackburne saw a continuity in the reform programme he and Law had initiated with the theological experiments of the seventeenth century; politically he and others of the circle were close to the 'Commonwealthman' ethos that permeated radical circles in the eighteenth century: and hence it was that he defended the memory and personal reputation of John Milton from the criticisms of Johnson in his *Lives of the English Poets*; a layman, in this instance, was more clerically minded than an advanced clerical historian and polemicist. Theological progressives looked backwards for inspiration and forwards for the fulfilment of their goals. The doctrine of the Trinity broke off the older generation from its immediate successors: Law and Blackburne remained in the Church, Theophilus Lindsey, John Disney, and John Jebb joined with such leaders of rational Dissent as Joseph Priestley in founding a new denomination, Unitarianism.[86]

Two of the leading figures from the younger generation formed in the Law circle also remained loyal to the Church of England, although both Richard Watson (1737–1816) and William Paley (1743–1805) were treated with suspicion by many of their clerical contemporaries. Richard Watson has been unfairly marginalized in much discussion of later eighteenth-century thought; many students of the period have remarked on his apparently random appointment to the chair in Chemistry at Cambridge long before he actually knew anything about the subject, although it ought to be remembered that he became a not insignificant chemist, and published in the field, if never reaching anything remotely akin to the eminence in the field of his contemporary, Joseph Priestley, an ordained Presbyterian minister who became one of the founders of Unitarianism. In recent years, Dissent has become the focus of rather more scholarly energy than has the history of the Established Church in the last half of the eighteenth century, and Priestley's reputation has benefited accordingly, whilst Watson's, never high, has plummeted.[87] This is unjust; Priestley's work is notably uneven, as one might expect of a man who wrote widely, perhaps too widely, on everything from the natural sciences to politics, from decidedly polemical ecclesiastical history to millenarian speculation: Watson wrote almost as widely, but much more circumspectly and, arguably, with a greater sense of immediate purpose. From the chair of chemistry, Watson was promoted to the Regius Chair in Divinity, again after having published little in the field, although as a clerical fellow of Trinity College, Cambridge, it can be confidently assumed that he had enjoyed a good classical

---

[86] Young, *Religion and Enlightenment*, pp. 45–80.

[87] Isabel Rivers and David L. Wykes (eds.), *Joseph Priestley: Scientist, Philosopher, and Theologian* (Oxford, 2008).

and theological education.[88] Whatever the actual details of such an education, Watson prided himself as a good Protestant on his devotion to Scripture and equally on his distance from the sort of ecclesiological and patristic scholarship that had prevailed in the Cambridge of Waterland (and Brett). Unlike many of his predecessors in the chair, Watson did at least take the trouble to lecture, and the image of his holding up a bible and declaring to his auditors 'In sacrum codicem' ('In this sacred text') tells one all one needs to know about his style of theological reflection. For Watson, as for Chillingworth, the Bible, and the Bible alone, was the religion of Protestants, and he justified it with a suitably scriptural adjuration: 'Here is the fountain of truth, why do you follow the streams derived from it by the sophistry, or polluted by the passions of man?'[89] What Watson said as an advanced liberal, many an Evangelical could have echoed: it should be no surprise that his Oxford-educated Cambridge ally, Peter Peckard, the Master of Magdalene College, successfully presided over a college that became increasingly attractive to Evangelicals.[90]

It was not, however, specifically at Cambridge that the fruits of Watson's theological labours were to be gathered in; rather, it was as a public divine, engaging with what he perceived to be dangerous assaults on the faith, that he eventually gave of his scholarly best, and it was scholarship that served a pressing purpose. In its own way, it was akin to the work of such earlier Cambridge divines as Bentley, although the enemies Watson confronted were a good deal more challenging than had been the 'Hobbists' against whom the erstwhile master of his Cambridge college had charged. When Edward Gibbon chose to conclude the first volume of his *History of the Decline and Fall of the Roman Empire* with two chapters that seemed to question the veridical foundations of the Christian Church, strongly implying that its progress was owed to natural rather than to supernatural means, and engaging in an exercise in comparative atrocity that suggested that rumours of a hecatomb of mass Christian martyrdom had been much exaggerated, he had knowingly provoked the ire of the clerical tribe. The squadron of divines who answered Gibbon did not greatly impress him, although their efforts have begun to be properly appreciated in revisionist scholarship, and their activities seem to have been encouraged by Thomas Secker, the then archbishop of Canterbury and a former bishop of Oxford, from which university the majority of these divines were recruited.[91] But there was one independent clerical respondent, and that was Richard Watson. In his *Apology for Christianity* (1776), Watson

[88] Denys Arthur Winstanley, *Unreformed Cambridge: A Study of certain Aspects of the University in the Eighteenth Century* (Cambridge, 1935), pp. 51–2, 56, 102–8, 144–5.

[89] Richard Watson (ed.), *Anecdotes of the Life of Richard Watson*, 2 vols. (London, 1818), I, pp. 62–4.

[90] Margaret Forbes, *Beattie and his Friends* (London, 1904), p. 247.

[91] David Womersley, *Gibbon and 'The Watchmen of the Holy City': The Historian and his Reputation, 1776–1815* (Oxford, 2002).

had not questioned Gibbon's scholarship in the way that Davis of Balliol, Chelsum of Christ Church, and Randolph of Corpus Christi had compromisingly, if bravely, done, but he did rather question the degree of emphasis that Gibbon placed on the natural, secondary causes of the growth of Christianity. Watson accepted their validity, but he did not wish to abandon the notion that the coming into the world of Christianity in an unpromising climate, which it then overcame, was itself a proof of its supernatural authority, an argument not unlike one promoted by two clerical historians, first in the 1730s by John Jortin and then in 1755 by the Presbyterian friend of Hume, William Robertson.[92] Well into the 1770s and 1780s, history was treated as a handmaid to revelation, and Watson's pithy statement of this did not discommode Gibbon. Indeed, one wonders if what Gibbon had had to say about Watson in his *Vindication* did not henceforth make him a marked man among more consciously orthodox divines, even if the amicability he stresses sometimes sounds a trifle equivocal:

> Dr Watson's mode of thinking bears a liberal and philosophic cast; his thoughts are expressed with spirit, and that spirit is always tempered by politeness and moderation. Such is the man whom I should be happy to call my friend, and whom I should not blush to call my antagonist . . . if in some instances he seems to have misapprehended my sentiments, I may hesitate whether I should impute the fault to my own want of clearness or his want of attention, but I can never entertain a suspicion that Dr Watson should descend to employ the disingenuous arts of vulgar controversy.[93]

In short, Watson had written and behaved like a gentleman, unlike Priestley (whom Gibbon despised and whose perhaps seditious writings he recommended to the attention of the public magistrate).[94] It is striking that in praising Watson, a Cambridge divine, and in castigating the Oxford clerical party who wrote against him, the Oxford-educated Gibbon, who grew to distrust what he perceived to be the limited self-serving clericalism of his own university, identified something akin to what Stephen would find in Watson and his allies: honesty and rationality, albeit of a constrained and intellectually constraining kind.

When preferred to the bishopric of Llandaff, to which insignificant see his alleged lack of 'orthodoxy' would confine him to the end of his days, Watson

[92] John Jortin, *Four Sermons on the Truth of the Christian Religion* (London, 1730), pp. 24–62; John Jortin, 'The Fitness of the Time when Christ came into the World', in *Discourses concerning the Truth of the Christian Religion* (2nd edn., London, 1747), pp. 158–75; William Robertson, *The Situation of the World at the Time of Christ's Appearance, and its Connexion with the Success of his Religion considered* (Edinburgh, 1755).

[93] *A Vindication*, in Patricia Craddock (ed.), *The English Essays of Edward Gibbon* (Oxford, 1972), pp. 282–3.

[94] Edward Gibbon, *The History of the Decline and Fall of the Roman Empire*, ed. David Womersley, 3 vols. (Harmondsworth, 1994), III, p. 439, n. 42.

identified an altogether more insidious foe; and this time his opponent was very much *not* a gentleman. In the altogether more charged political atmosphere of the revolutionary 1790s, the appearance in 1794 of Thomas Paine's *The Age of Reason*, an anti-clerical digest promoting a form of artisanal Deism, was a potentially more dangerous challenge than the sceptical ironies offered by Gibbon. Watson seized his opportunity and denounced Paine, effectively in the opinion of many of his readers, in his only popular work, *An Apology for the Bible* (1796), an exercise in scriptural exegesis that effected at the close of the eighteenth century what the work of such Boyle lecturers as John Rogers had done in the 1720s. Modern enthusiasts for the revolutionaries of the 1790s ritually denounce the likes of Watson as compromising, self-serving liberals who aided and abetted the younger Pitt's supposed 'reign of terror'.[95] This is a considerable overstatement; Watson, in common with his younger Cambridge contemporary Paley, had not compromised his own political principles so much as recognized in what Paine and his allies offered altogether too radical a political vision at a moment when England was at war with revolutionary France. And the last thing that divines such as Watson and Paley wanted to see was the importing of what they thought of as revolutionary atheism, but what was in fact a revival, in much more radical Anglo-French registers, of the Deism of a century before. There is, therefore, continuity, on both sides, of Anglican apologetic in the face of freethinking onslaughts, a recurrence in the 1780s and 1790s of debates that had begun in the 1680s and 1690s.

Watson had good reason to be wary of association with radical politics; his nephew by marriage was Fletcher Christian, the gentlemanly leader of the mutiny on the *Bounty*.[96] Paley had no such compromising associations, but, despite his able defence of the status quo in the 1790s and 1800s, his clerical career was to stall as firmly as had that of Watson. But whereas Watson at least made it to the episcopal bench, Paley was to enjoy no preferment beyond the archdeaconry of Carlisle. And yet his was perhaps the most effective clerical voice of his period. Unfortunately for Paley, George III had bridled at the prospect of promoting him to a bishopric, noting that he was not 'orthodox'. An Established Church did not always do justice to the intellectual ability of its more gifted clergy; dull, contented, unoriginal men littered the higher reaches of the Church in the closing decades of the eighteenth century, probably as a greater proportion of deans and bishops than had been true in the first half of the eighteenth century. Conformism in the state compromised intellectual originality in the Church, particularly when, as with Watson and Paley, such originality looked to its less imaginative critics like heterodoxy. And Paley was dogged by a

---

[95] E.g. Mark Philp, *Reforming Ideas in Britain: Politics and Language in the Shadow of the French Revolution, 1798–1815* (Cambridge, 2013).

[96] Greg Dening, *Mr Bligh's Bad Language: Passion, Power and Theatre on the Bounty* (Cambridge, 1992).

reputation for heterodoxy from the acts he took for his degree at Cambridge, in which he had defended the thesis that the punishment of the damned would be for a limited period and not for eternity, onwards. In the middle decades of the eighteenth century such daring brought its rewards, and Paley became a fellow of Christ's College, Cambridge, and would later turn down the mastership of Jesus College, Cambridge; but where the university could be open-minded enough to seek to promote a protégé of the Law circle, the national Church would prove altogether less accommodating as the eighteenth century progressed purely in chronological, and not necessarily in intellectual, terms.[97]

Unsurprisingly, then, a compromising degree of 'worldliness' has long clung to the reputation of Paley's theology. For later critics, he had accommodated the world too much in making theology a modern subject. This was especially so in his discussion of the 'dismal science' of political economy; and where Paley was here following such immediate clerical predecessors as Josiah Tucker, who had endured Warburton as his bishop when acting as dean of Bristol, he was also making it possible for such younger contemporaries as the Cambridge-educated Thomas Robert Malthus to see in population theory an aspect of a complex theodicy that fed directly into what Boyd Hilton has christened the 'Age of Atonement', an era in which natural theology had mutated into a less optimistic assessment than that initiated by Bentley and continued by Paley.[98] It was against this atmosphere that Leslie Stephen and his generation reacted. In many ways, this is a specifically Cambridge story with national resonances and consequences, as 'rational' Christianity ossified into conservative Evangelicalism. It is a world in which the Evangelical brothers Joseph and Isaac Milner revived a Calvinist theology, incarnated in their *History of the True Church of Christ*.[99]

Nor was Evangelicalism the only way in which the theology of the eighteenth-century Church reacted against what was widely perceived to be the arid rationalism of too many prominent divines. In Hutchinsonianism, a

---

[97] M. L. Clarke, *Paley: Evidences for the Man* (London, 1974); D. L. Le Mahieu, *The Mind of William Paley: A Philosopher and his Age* (Lincoln, NE, 1976).

[98] Hilton, *Age of Atonement*; J. G. A. Pocock, 'Josiah Tucker on Locke, Burke, and Price: A Study in the Varieties of Eighteenth-Century Conservatism', in J. G. A. Pocock, *Virtue, Commerce, and History: Essays on Political Thought and History, chiefly in the Eighteenth Century* (Cambridge, 1985), pp. 157–91; A. M. C. Waterman, *Revolution, Economics and Religion: Christian Political Economy, 1798–1833* (Cambridge, 1991); Robert J. Mayhew, *Malthus: The Life and Legacies of an Untimely Prophet* (Cambridge, MA, 2014); B. W. Young, 'Christianity, Commerce and the Canon: Josiah Tucker and Richard Woodward on Political Economy', *History of European Ideas*, 22 (1996): 385–400; B. W. Young, 'Christianity, Secularization and Political Economy', in David J. Jeremy (ed.), *Religion, Business and Wealth in Modern Britain* (London, 1998), pp. 35–54; B. W. Young, 'Malthus among the Theologians', in Brian Dolan (ed.), *Malthus, Medicine and Mortality: 'Malthusianism' after 1798* (Amsterdam, 2000), pp. 93–114.

[99] J. D. Walsh, 'Joseph Milner's Evangelical Church History', *Journal of Ecclesiastical History*, 10 (1959): 174–87.

peculiar form of fundamentalism made its way among a self-perpetuating circle of Oxford (and Edinburgh) divines, reaching its apologetic height in the 1790s. It was the only theological party in the eighteenth-century Church to take its leadership from a layman, and this is the sole respect in which it is in any way remotely akin to the seventeenth-century sects in which biblically inflected mysticism had originally flourished; indeed, it ritually denounced all such sects, repudiating William Law's Behmenist reveries in the process. John Hutchinson (1674–1737) was a naturalist and a theologian, but his study of nature was not that of such natural theologians as Richard Bentley, the friend and ally at Trinity College, Cambridge, of Isaac Newton. Newton and his theological lieutenants were the enemy in the eyes of Hutchinson, who discovered in a particular way of interpreting the language of the Hebrew Bible what Hutchinson pointedly called, in his own version of a systematic theology, *Moses's Principia*, the first volume of which revisionist study appeared in 1724. Restoring the missing vowel points to the Masoretic text, Hutchinson read the creation account of Genesis as providing a true natural theology, the antithesis of Newton's natural philosophy, which he considered to be rigidly mechanical and hence dangerously removed from direct divine interposition as this had been recorded throughout the Bible. Newtonian natural science and theology (revealed, with the posthumous publications of Newton's biblical researches, to be Arian in Christology), was considered a high road to infidelity by Hutchinson; in its stead, Hutchinson appealed directly to his own reading of the Hebrew Scriptures, adducing in support the writings of many of the Church Fathers: in this way, he allied the Mosaic narrative with primitive Christianity in a unique appeal to origins.[100]

'Hutchinsonianism' began to be systematized into a distinctive variety of divinity by Julius Bate, for whom Hutchinson had secured a Sussex living. Bate, an opponent of Warburton's directly contrary reading of the Old Testament, published Hutchinson's posthumous literary remains, and through allies at Oxford established a base for its promotion among High Church divines. It was essentially a fringe movement granted prestige by its directly institutional affiliations; George Horne (1730–92), President of Magdalen College, Oxford and bishop of Norwich, and who opposed every conceivable 'heretic' from Arians and Socinians to Edward Gibbon in his many writings, was the most prominent convert to the movement.[101] Horne's theology was further promoted by his biographer, William Jones, who declared of his theology: 'When a student hath once persuaded himself that he sees truth in the principles of Mr. Hutchinson, a great revolution succeeds in his ideas of the natural world

---

[100] John Hutchinson, *Moses's Principia* (London, 1724). Scott Mandelbrote's *ODNB* entry on Hutchinson is exemplary.

[101] See Nigel Aston, 'Horne and Heterodoxy: The Defence of Anglican Beliefs in the Late Enlightenment', *English Historical Review*, 108 (1991): 895–919.

and its economy.'[102] This conservative revolution in Anglican theology was ideally suited to apologetic in the 1790s, when the orthodox clergy were at war with such Unitarian defenders of 'atheistic' France as Joseph Priestley; it was in this charged atmosphere that Jones published his apologetic arsenal for the clergy (and the pious laity), *The Scholar Armed against the Errors of the Times*, which appeared in 1795, alongside his biography of his mentor, Horne.[103] At least one Hutchinsonian, William Romaine, was also an Evangelical, and the movement was thus at one both with the revived High Churchmanship of such opponents of Unitarianism as Samuel Horsley, bishop of Rochester (and a former secretary of the predominantly Newtonian Royal Society), and with Evangelical biblicism.[104]

As the eighteenth century gradually became recognizably the nineteenth century, the Evangelical Revival which had been such a marked feature of the 1730s and 1740s, and also of the 1760s and 1780s, began to affect the way people thought about eighteenth-century theology, and a predominantly negative series of judgements resulted. In his studies of the growth of the Oxford Movement, Peter Nockles has invaluably drawn attention to the High Church origins of the Tractarian moment (linking it occasionally with Hutchinsonian divines), but it is well to remember that, as the late Frank M. Turner reminded us, John Henry Newman had had an Evangelical phase, and that this can have played no small part in his own rejection of eighteenth-century theology.[105] The integument of nineteenth-century views of the eighteenth century has continued to influence views of later students of Anglican intellectual history.

Accordingly, as readers of Pattison and Stephen, as well as modern revisionist historians of the era in English Church history with which they engaged, it is well for us to reflect on what Pattison had reflexively had to say early in his essay: 'Both the church and the world of to-day are what they are as the result of the whole of their antecedents.'[106] In order to reach a reasonable understanding of eighteenth-century theology, we have to be sensitive to what nineteenth-century writers, their immediate successors, had to say. We cannot afford to be dismissive either of eighteenth-century theologians or yet of their successor generations if we are to be serious students of eighteenth-century theology.[107]

---

[102] William Jones, *Memoirs of the Life, Studies, and Writings of the Right Reverend George Horne, D.D., Late Lord Bishop of Norwich* (London, 1795).

[103] Young, *Religion and Enlightenment*, pp. 136–51.

[104] On which revival, see the invaluable study by F. C. Mather, *High Church Prophet: Bishop Samuel Horsley (1733–1806) and the Caroline Tradition in the Later Georgian Church* (Oxford, 1992).

[105] Peter B. Nockles, *The Oxford Movement in Context: Anglican High Churchmanship, 1760–1857* (Cambridge, 1994); Frank M. Turner, *John Henry Newman: The Challenge to Evangelical Religion* (New Haven, CT, 2002).

[106] Pattison, 'Tendencies', p. 388.

[107] I am indebted to Noël Sugimura, Sophie Smith, John Robertson, and Mishtooni Bose for their critical readings of this chapter.

SELECT BIBLIOGRAPHY

Bennett, G. V. and J. D. Walsh (eds.), *Essays in Modern English Church History, in Memory of Norman Sykes* (London, 1966).

Bulman, William J., *Anglican Enlightenment: Orientalism, Religion and Politics in England and its Empire, 1648–1715* (Cambridge, 2015).

Bulman, William J. and Robert G. Ingram (eds.), *God in the Enlightenment* (Oxford, 2015).

Champion, J. A. I., *The Pillars of Priestcraft Shaken: The Church of England and its Enemies, 1660–1730* (Cambridge, 1992).

Evans, A. W., *Warburton and the Warburtonians: A Study in some Eighteenth-Century Controversies* (London, 1932).

Patterson, Annabel, *Early Modern Liberalism* (Cambridge, 1997).

Pocock, J. G. A., *Barbarism and Religion*, 6 vols. (Cambridge, 1999–2015).

Reedy, Gerard, *The Bible and Reason: Anglicans and Scripture in Late Seventeenth-Century England* (Philadelphia, PA, 1985).

Reedy, Gerard, *Robert South, 1634–1716: An Introduction to his Life and Sermons* (Cambridge, 1992).

Rivers, Isabel, *Reason, Grace, and Sentiment: A Study of the Language of Religion and Ethics in England, 1660–1780*, 2 vols. (Cambridge, 1991–2000).

Sheehan, Jonathan, *The Enlightenment Bible: Translation, Scholarship, Culture* (Princeton, NJ, 2005).

Sirota, Brent S., *The Christian Monitors: The Church of England in an Age of Benevolence, 1680–1730* (New Haven, CT, 2014).

Spurr, John, *The Restoration Church of England, 1646–1689* (New Haven, CT, 1991).

Sykes, Norman, *Edmund Gibson, Bishop of London, 1669–1748: A Study in Politics and Religion in the Eighteenth Century* (London, 1926).

Sykes, Norman, *William Wake, Archbishop of Canterbury, 1657–1737*, 2 vols. (Cambridge, 1957).

Willey, Basil, *The Eighteenth-Century Background: Studies on the Idea of Nature in the Thought of the Period* (London, 1940).

Young, Brian, 'Theological Books from *The Naked Gospel* to *Nemesis of Faith*', in Isabel Rivers (ed.), *Books and their Readers in Eighteenth-Century England: New Essays* (London, 2001), pp. 79–104.

22

Anglican Religious Societies, Organizations, and Missions

David Manning

Over the course of its 'long eighteenth century', the Church of England learned to embrace those within its communion who formed voluntary associations to perform acts of public virtue. This was a brave move. Despite bouts of internal resistance, divisive fears about conventicles were replaced by a willingness to entertain extra-liturgical, mutually formative relations between clergy and laity. As a result, Church propaganda blossomed. There was, however, no overarching programme, official or otherwise, for utilizing voluntary, corporate activism to promote Church interests.

Just as recourse to a 'long eighteenth century' can give a false sense of historical coherence, grouping together the earliest societies to work under the rubric of the Church of England can also be misleading. Historians have, inadvertently, conspired to present three general phases of development. Only the first, covering the period between the 1660s and the 1740s, has benefited from sustained historiographical interest. Here the debate about the emergence of religious societies has been driven by discussions about either the psyche of the post-1689 Church or the prototypes of Methodist societies.[1] That said, Brent Sirota's *The Christian Monitors* (2014) has offered an audacious synthesis which envelops post-revolutionary fervour for pious association in a multi-faceted 'Anglican revival' which heralded the beginning of

---

[1] E.g. Garnet V. Portus, *Caritas Anglicana: or, an Historical Inquiry into those Religious and Philanthropical Societies that flourished in England between the Years 1678 and 1740* (London, 1912); Henry D. Rack, 'Religious Societies and the Origins of Methodism', *Journal of Ecclesiastical History*, 38 (1987): 582–95; John Spurr, 'The Church, the Societies and the Moral Revolution of 1688', and Craig Rose, 'The Origins and Ideals of the SPCK 1699–1716', in John Walsh, Colin Haydon, and Stephen Taylor (eds.), *The Church of England c.1689–c.1833: From Toleration to Tractarianism* (Cambridge, 1993), pp. 127–42, 172–90 respectively.

'modern civil society in Britain'.[2] Studies which acknowledge either the Church's response to early Methodism, or its most testing times in America, tacitly give expression to a second phase that ran from the 1740s to the 1790s.[3] During this period, Church Evangelicals used associational activism to their own advantage whilst Church missionaries tried to shore up loyalism in the colonies. Discussion about whether Evangelicalism was a force of social control or benevolent humanitarianism helped to frame a third phase in the history of religious societies from the 1790s to the 1830s.[4] However, in recent years, such a contention has been superseded by studies of Christian mission which, following the work of Rowan Strong, amongst others, has challenged this chronological focus by showing how missionary societies were amongst the most powerful engines of the British Empire from the early eighteenth century onwards. Notwithstanding this intervention, it may be said that scholars have hitherto tended to plunder the history of religious societies to make good on broader, but rather tired, arguments about the identity and status of the Church of England as an institution in one of three stereotypical phases of its 'long eighteenth century'.

There are other questionable interpretative paradigms too. The voluntary nature of these societies is noteworthy, but this does not necessarily mean that volunteerism constitutes a straightforward criterion of historical analysis. There was nothing inherently new about the phenomenon of voluntary religious association. Moreover, as Mark Goldie has highlighted, religious adherence in England had increasingly been a matter of choice from the early seventeenth century onwards: and this has surely put paid to the anti-ecclesiastical dimension of progressive voluntary association in Jürgen Habermas's theory of 'the public sphere'.

The associational quality of English religious societies was significant, but the relevant historiography is fragmented and underdeveloped. Frederick Bullock's classic *Voluntary Religious Societies 1520–1799* (1963) identified a continuous movement for non-separatist, religious association from the early Reformation in Germany to the English Evangelical missionary societies of the late eighteenth century.[5] Whilst Bullock's text remains an invaluable source of information on many well-known and lesser-known societies, its ahistorical,

---

[2] Brent S. Sirota, *The Christian Monitors: The Church of England and the Age of Benevolence, 1680–1730* (New Haven, CT, 2014), p. 260.

[3] E.g. John Walsh, 'Religious Societies: Methodist and Evangelical 1738–1800', in W. J. Sheils and Diana Wood (eds.), *Voluntary Religion*, Studies in Church History 23 (Oxford, 1986), pp. 279–302; Kenneth Elliot, *Anglican Church Policy, Eighteenth-Century Conflict, and the American Episcopate* (New York, 2011).

[4] E.g. Ford K. Brown, *Fathers of the Victorians: The Age of Wilberforce* (Cambridge, 1961), pp. 317–60; David Bebbington, *Evangelicalism in Modern Britain: A History from the 1730s to the 1980s* (London, 1989), pp. 69–72.

[5] F. W. B. Bullock, *Voluntary Religious Societies 1520–1799* (St Leonards-on-Sea, 1963).

decontextualized use of the Halle Pietist apologetic of *ecclesiolae in ecclesia* as a guiding principle of enquiry now lacks credibility. Eamon Duffy has since elucidated how a fascination with the supposed patterns of 'primitive Christianity' gave credence to inter- and intra-parochial religious association in late seventeenth-century England. For good or ill, the 'English conventicle' was part of the Elizabethan and Jacobean Church experience and, as John Spurr has pointed out, therefore a touchstone for later generations of communicants participating in acts of practical, collective piety. More generally, Peter Clark's sense of Britain's eighteenth-century 'associational world' certainly owed a debt to earlier forms of religious sociability. That said, the forces of urbanization also stimulated what has been teasingly construed by Jonathan Barry as 'bourgeois collectivism'. The Church was surely not immune to the 'urban renaissance' described by Peter Borsay. Historians may have finally discredited long-lived sociological theories about how the supposedly modernizing force of 'rationalization' informed a transition from medieval *Gemeinschaft* ('Community') to early modern *Gesellschaft* ('Society'), but they have yet to integrate historicized theological precepts of community into their understanding of early modern association. An uncritical focus on philanthropy is another potential distraction. Benevolence was rarely an end in itself, but rather a means of piety; and this was not only relativized through ideological filters but represented some sense of continuity with earlier times. Bob Tennant has also exposed the naïvety of using 'mission' and 'missionary' as uniform analytical categories.

Finally, recourse to 'Anglicanism' continues to be a point of controversy. Once deemed an unhelpful anachronism, the concept has been refashioned as a viable historiographical construct to help designate particular representations of Church 'orthodoxy'.[6] Finding meaningful labels for patterns of religious thought and practice is no easy task; but the charge of reductive essentialism plagues those of 'Anglican' and 'Anglicanism' perhaps more than most. Terminology aside, a singular focus on the Church of England should not negate a critical appreciation of the extent to which its identity was contextualized by evolving interconfessional dialectics.

Nearly twenty years ago, Martin Ingram cautioned against using simple notions of 'continuity' and 'change' to investigate the cultural shifts of enduring, protean phenomena.[7] The time has come to heed this warning more seriously. With a heightened sensitivity to the way in which historical contingencies became significant through long-term and short-term contexts, this

---

[6] Ian Green, 'Anglicanism in Stuart and Hanoverian England', in Sheridan Gilley and W. J. Sheils (eds.), *A History of Religion in Britain: Practice and Belief from Pre-Roman Times to the Present* (Oxford, 1994), pp. 168–87.

[7] Martin Ingram, 'Reformation of Manners in Early Modern England', in Paul Griffiths, Adam Fox, and Steve Hindle (eds.), *The Experience of Authority in Early Modern England* (Basingstoke, 1996), pp. 47–88 (p. 68).

chapter will provide a new chronological survey of those religious societies that worked for their interpretation of Church interests between 1662 and 1829.

If the Restoration Church of England's 'vision of the consecrated life of the laity was not new', then the practical undertaking of creating voluntary associations to realize such a cause was not new either.[8] From the early Reformation, biblical accounts of *koinonia* emphasized a participatory quality to communion that complicated notions of *sola fide*. In despairing of the religious credentials of evangelists, Martin Luther had appealed to 'Christians in earnest' to 'assemble by themselves in some house to pray, to read, to baptize and to receive the sacrament and practise other Christian works'.[9] In a more idealistic effort to get closer to the 'primitive Church', Martin Bucer had championed an experiment in inter-parochial *Christlichen Gemeinschaften* ('Christian Communities') at Strasbourg in 1547. When it came to turning heightened devotion into a force for public instruction and mission, Ignatius of Loyola's *Societas Iesu* was a powerful prototype. In Elizabethan England, the act of prophesying reflected an emerging 'godly' impulse for brotherhood and mutual edification; and, despite the suppression of the practice after 1576, household seminaries remained a valuable source of spiritual nourishment for some puritans well into the seventeenth century. Wherever people met, those of like mind had an opportunity to form cliques of various kinds. Academic colleges could offer an ideal of communal education, even if the reality was rather more mundane. The precocious Nicholas Ferrar (1593–1637) made friendship, learning, and Arminian piety the defining features of an esteemed community at Little Gidding (*fl.*1626–57), which was both innovative and yet also reminiscent of a medieval fraternity. In more rarefied intellectual circles, Johann Valenti Andreä's esoteric, mystical design for a *Societas Christiana* was a noted influence upon Samuel Hartlib (*c.*1600–62), an Anglo-Prussian polymath and educational reformer who underwrote an international network of scientific correspondence with a utopian vision of Christian community and whose endeavours count amongst the antecedents of the Royal Society (1660). Elsewhere, a distinctly 'primitivist' approach to divine inspiration was fostered by George Fox's Religious Society of Friends.

Reformation also brought about a crisis of organized sociability in England. As the medieval social diffusion of church-based religiosity gradually retracted, the relinquished space was opened up to forces of ideological negotiation and competition. Outside the formal act of public worship, participatory activities with a religious dimension not only required a greater degree of active, as

---

[8] John Spurr, *The Restoration Church of England, 1646–1689* (New Haven, CT, 1991), p. 371.

[9] Martin Luther, 'Preface to The German Mass and Divine Order of Service, January 1526', in B. J. Kidd (ed. and trans.), *Documents Illustrative of the Continental Reformation* (Oxford, 1911), p. 196.

opposed to passive, lay involvement but increasingly gave expression to new forms of religio-political identity. Movements for a 'reformation of manners' put a distinctive, sometimes divisive, moral gloss on aspects of pleasure, leisure, and sociability. Prophesying found its antithesis in the boozy airing of religious opinions at home or in the tavern; and the inter-parochial phenomenon of sermon-gadding rubbed against an entrenchment of local traditions such as bell-ringing and feasting. By the mid-1650s, counties and cities rivalled parishes as arenas of religious sociability: ministers came together to form ad hoc 'non-denominational' associations in at least seventeen counties, whilst a counterblast to Cromwellian austerity was sounded by county feasts in London. Amongst those who harboured a return to episcopacy, a sense of fraternal solidarity was keenly felt by those 'sons of the clergy' who attended the sermon of George Hall (bap. 1613, d. 1668) at St Paul's Cathedral on 8 November 1655 and contributed to a collection for sequestered clergy and their families, before retiring to dinner at Merchant Taylors' Hall. Suffice to say, post-1662 religious societies were part of an extending, multifarious phenomenon of practical, communal piety.

In the final quarter of the seventeenth century, various ambitious individuals founded societies that went on to redefine the scope and application of Protestant virtue for local and national interests. Societies within the communion of the Established Church led the way, acting both independently and as part of a wider Protestant collective. As an indication of the contextual complexity of the cause, many opening credits have been given to a naturalized German who championed an ascetically inflected sacramental piety as a preacher to a cosmopolitan (but down and out) congregation at St Mary-le-Savoy, and an Essex lad with puritan credentials from Emmanuel College, Cambridge, who walked the line between conformity and nonconformity as a curate at the effervescent parish of St Giles Cripplegate. From about 1678, the same year the Sons of the Clergy was incorporated by Charles II as a charitable society to look after the needs of clerical widows and their families, the respective endeavours of Anthony Horneck (1641–97) and William Smythies (bap. 1635?, d. 1715) secured their reputations among the most noted leaders of a growing number of parochial societies in London whose members sought to reaffirm their piety within the Church of England. Sharing in a long-lived protean movement to define religiosity with respect to the ideals of 'primitive Christianity', these groups engendered a disciplined approach to shared religious learning, frequent communion, ascetic living, and charitable works. Apostolic archetypes mixed with lingering memories of earlier experiments in voluntary association to form a backdrop to the more immediate need to save souls on the streets of London. The relationship between the spoken word, printed text, and pious deeds was also significant. Since the late sixteenth century, influential clergymen on both sides of the Calvinist–Arminian divide had advanced the cause of practical divinity from the pulpit and the press.

Following the providential warning of the Great Fire of 1666, Richard Alles-tree's *The Causes of the Decay of Christian Piety* (1667) reminded Londoners that the time to act was upon them. However, the way in which direct contact with charismatic preachers who led by example mixed with the appeal of constructing an edifying, primitive brotherhood with a sense of purpose was surely crucial. That said, despite few clergymen being able to replicate Hor-neck's combination of popularity and ascetic integrity the capital boasted at least fifteen similar societies 'belonging to the Church of England' by 1694.[10] In the afterglow of revolution, piety by association had become fashionable.

A few years earlier, one pious agitator by the name of Edward Stephens (d. 1706) had laid claim to starting societies in Tower Hamlets and the Strand in 1690 which, in being moved to action against vice, had organized them-selves into a more disciplined and effective movement for moral reform.[11] Working at the ragged, porous edge of orthodoxy, Stephens's campaign was initially born out of a short-tempered sense of moral disillusionment with the Williamite regime; this did not, however, detract the likes of Bishop Stilling-fleet from not only offering sympathy but also acting as an intermediary in gaining royal support. In 1691 Queen Mary intervened by encouraging the justices of Middlesex to be more diligent in enforcing the current laws against vice. This kind of lobbying was both part of a well-established, polymorphous phenomenon for a 'reformation of manners' and a particular reflection of 1690s angst. Local self-interest to rid the streets of prostitutes, drunkards, and Sabbath-breakers was often part and parcel of more abstract concerns about practical sins. Beyond what modern commentators call 'moral panic' there was a deep theological conviction that evil deeds were an expression of evil thoughts, and vice versa. Post-revolutionary spiritual paranoia surrounding the state of urban morality was given a nervous tweak by God's providential judgement upon Port Royal, Jamaica, in 1692 and an agonizing wrench by the untimely death of Queen Mary in 1694. With the gradual demise of the ecclesiastical courts and a perception amongst would-be activists that more could be done to enforce the criminal laws against vice and enact new legislation, these emerging Societies for the Reformation of Manners (SRMs) became a force for public morality by attempting to suppress public immor-ality. Much more than a pressure group, these societies worked as a para-legal franchise with the informal but active approval of London's ecclesiastical and civil authorities to lend a hand in matters of law enforcement. With approximately twenty separate groups in the London area by 1697, the SRMs established a network of informers who were armed with pre-prepared

---

[10] A list, and particulars, of fifteen religious societies in London and Westminster in 1694, Bodleian Library [Bodl.], Rawlinson MSS D 1312.

[11] Andrew Craig, 'The Movement for the Reformation of Manners, 1688–1715', PhD thesis, University of Edinburgh, 1980.

warrants that merely required a dutiful scribe to note down the name of an offender and the location of the alleged indiscretion before turning the paperwork over to a local constable. Between 1704 and 1716, 11,717 prosecutions were brought by the SRMs in and around London; all but 298 were for Sunday trading offences.[12] The SRMs had a meaningful socio-legal presence, even if much narrower in scope than their own rhetoric might suggest.

By the early eighteenth century, the SRMs had dozens of franchises in towns all over England, as well as outposts in Wales, Scotland, Ireland, America, and the Caribbean.[13] Their candle at Bristol burned bright and fast. Fifty-five men of public standing who were willing and able to meet a 10*s* annual subscription charge gathered at the home of the Bristol merchant Sir John Duddlestone (d. *c.*1716) to found the SRMs at Bristol in 1700. Initial momentum was created by members of the Society of Merchants and the Corporation of the Poor, who sought to extend their influence in the realm of law enforcement and moral reform. Yet poor attendance at meetings and an ideological shift towards preventing sin through education meant that the Society ceased business just five years later. The status of the Bristol SRMs as a religious society representing Church interests is a complex matter. The SRMs was not designed to promote interconfessional relations, but it did count several Nonconformists and Dissenters amongst its more prominent members. Having said that, at its inception the SRMs' *raison d'être* was grounded in a commitment to the Church-state, pressing constables and magistrates to act upon the royal proclamations against profaneness issued in the early 1690s. Furthermore, according to the later reflections of one of its clerical members, Arthur Bedford (bap. 1688, d. 1715), 'above three parts of the Society were members of the Church of England'. As an ardent supporter of uniformity, Bedford had no truck with Dissent; but he was nevertheless frustrated by those 'zealous for the Church, but cold in the Case of Immorality' who had sought to undermine the Society at Bristol.[14] It is not clear who, exactly, Bedford had in mind here; but, judging from reports elsewhere, the intervention of the SRMs was seen by some more senior clergy as troublesome meddling in the affairs of Church and state. The Bristol case perhaps exemplified the character of these bodies as a rather vague ideological franchise, created by (and at the mercy of)

---

[12] Record of prosecutions brought by the SRMs according to warrants issued by justices of the peace in and around London, 1704–16, Bodl. Rawlinson MSS D 1396–1404.

[13] Portus, *Caritas Anglicana*, pp. 125–7; Joel Bernard, 'Original Themes of Voluntary Moralism: The Anglo-American Reformation of Manners', in Karen Halttunen and Lewis Perry (eds.), *Moral Problems in American Life: New Perspectives on Cultural History* (Ithaca, NY, 1998), pp. 15–40.

[14] Arthur Bedford to J. T., Bristol, 23 Dec. 1710, Bristol Record Office, Temple Letter Book, P/Tem. Ka. 4, fos. 100–3, cited in Jonathan Barry (ed. and intro.), 'The Society for the Reformation of Manners 1700–5', in Jonathan Barry and Kenneth Morgan (eds.), *Reformation and Revival in Eighteenth-Century Bristol*, Bristol Record Society Publications 45 (Bristol, 1994), p. 55.

local agents and yet inspired by a translocal corporate identity emanating from the Church of England in London. The annual sermons preached to the SRMs at St Mary-le-Bow between 1696 and 1739 certainly made it appear as if they had some sense of a unified purpose. Whatever the successes or failures of individual societies, the SRMs also drew strength from their talisman Josiah Woodward (1657–1712), former minister to the East India Company, Oxonian Doctor of Divinity, and minister at Poplar, then in Middlesex. As the self-appointed chief propagandist of London's parochial religious societies and the SRMs, Woodward kept the flame for moral reform burning by publishing regular accounts of the SRMs' concerns, activities, and ambitions, as well as penning a series of moralizing pamphlets.[15] The aura of the SRMs' message was possibly more influential than their interventions as para-legal law enforcement organizations, especially outside London.

In 1695 Archbishop Tenison had set about renewing the Church's obligation to the rigour and discipline of catechesis, as set out in the fifty-ninth canon. In hindsight, this undertaking might be seen as particularly significant. In abstract terms, it gave fresh impetus to a sense of clerically led piety that was anchored in the authority of prescribed textual knowledge and yet open to practical lay application. This tapped into both a widespread conviction of the formative relationship between divine knowledge and pious behaviour and a growing swell of interest in how education in general might be put to better use to guard against future sins of thought, word, and deed. Furthermore, it tacitly worked to claw back ground lost to lay Nonconformists, such as Lord Wharton (1613–96), who had stolen a march on the Established Church by distributing bibles and catechisms to poor children. In a more tangible way, Tenison's intervention proved to be the stimulus which caused Thomas Bray (bap. 1658, d. 1730), rector of Sheldon in Warwickshire, to devise and then publish a lecture for other clergymen on effective catechesis. This caught the attention of Bishop Compton, just as he was trying to find suitable clergy to lead a new Church of England initiative in Maryland following the demise of the colony's Catholic proprietary governorship.[16] Bray was talented, ambitious, but poor. The promise of a mandate to orchestrate the Church's ambitious agenda in Maryland, combined with an annual salary of £400, was an offer Bray did not refuse. In preparation for his new duties, he gained a Doctorate in Divinity from Oxford in double-quick time, then moved to London; but jurisdictional wrangling delayed his departure to America. In the meantime, he busied himself planning how best to facilitate the Church's

---

[15] E.g. Josiah Woodward, *An Account of the Rise and Progress of the Religious Societies in the City of London, &c. And of the Endeavours for Reformation of Manners* (London, 1698); Josiah Woodward, *A Kind Caution to Prophane Swearers* (London, 1701).

[16] Geoffrey Yeo, 'A Case without Parallel: The Bishops of London and the Anglican Church Overseas, 1660–1748', *Journal of Ecclesiastical History*, 44 (1993): 450–75.

cause at home and abroad. Realizing that many clerics not only lacked sufficient funds but also the appropriate knowledge to promote the Church effectively, Bray set about arranging a subscription scheme to fund new parochial libraries and designing a list of edifying reading matter for well-intentioned but inadequate clergy.

In the mid-1690s, colonial ambition, interconfessional rivalry, and fears about both immoral behaviour and heterodox thought mixed to give a little frisson to age-old debates about the quality of the clergy. There was probably also a tinge of perverse jealousy amongst more outward-looking clerics such as Bray that the Church of England had nothing comparable to the Church of Rome's *Congregatio de Propaganda Fide* (1622). After gaining support from Bishop Compton, Bray and four laymen founded the Society for Promoting Christian Knowledge (SPCK) in March 1699.[17] According to the business of the first meeting of the SPCK, the initial aims of the Society were threefold: to redeem misguided Quakers; to promote catechetical schools; and to provide financial and practical assistance to missionaries and clergy in the plantations. These ambitions carried Bray's work forward and were part of an integrated ideological intervention in an emerging knowledge economy.

By March 1701, Bray had been to Maryland and returned. Inspired by his exploits, Zaccheus Isham (1652–1705) was moved to organize a committee in the Lower House of Convocation to look into ways of promoting the Church in the plantations yet further. Bray used this momentum to petition the king for a charter to form a Society for the Propagation of the Gospel in Foreign Parts (SPG) to put the colonial operation of the SPCK on a more formal footing.[18] Bray's wish was granted. This time there was much keener interest from the episcopate: the inaugural meeting of the SPG was held in June 1701 at Lambeth Palace. A rich combination of bishops, clergy, and laity (some of whom also had roles with the SPCK, the SRMs, and other charitable organizations) aimed first and foremost to serve better the clergy in the plantations, so that they might hold settlers to the Established Church. The challenge was immense. Set against the constitutional reconfiguration of the colonies after the Revolution of 1688–9, the SPG wanted to create (belatedly) scores of viable parish churches from scratch for thousands of disparate souls from the Caribbean to Newfoundland. The conversion of natives and slaves was a secondary, but no less weighty, ambition.

---

[17] W. O. B. Allen and Edmund McClure, *Two Hundred Years: The History of the Society for Promoting Christian Knowledge, 1698–1898* (London, 1898).

[18] *A Collection of Papers, printed by Order of the Society for the Propagation of the Gospel in Foreign Parts* (London, 1715); C. F. Pascoe, *Two Hundred Years of the S.P.G.: An Historical Account of the Society for the Propagation of the Gospel in Foreign Parts, 1701–1900* (London, 1901); Daniel O'Connor and others, *Three Centuries of Mission: The United Society for the Propagation of the Gospel 1701–2000* (London and New York, 2000), pp. 5–44.

The experience of one early 'missionary' to Carolina gives an insight into the conflict between these two aims and, indeed, between the metropolitan ideals of the SPG and the realities of colonial life.[19] Aided by an annual stipend of £50 from the SPG and a one-off payment of £20 from a newly formed clerical charity known as the Queen's Bounty, Samuel Thomas (d. 1706) was initially tasked in the summer of 1702 with easing relations with the 'wild Indians', with a view to their conversion; and to this end the SPG provided an extra £10 for buying clothes for the natives.[20] Upon his arrival, however, Thomas was pressed into service as a minister to settlers and a teacher to 'poor Negroes' at Goose Creek.[21] Edward Marston (*fl.*1702–12), the non-juring rector of St Philip's, Charlestown, was incensed by what he viewed as the usurpation of hard-working clergy by upstarts from the SPG and charged Thomas with neglecting his primary duty vis-à-vis the natives. Whilst the tetchy relations between Marston and Thomas were symptomatic of wider religio-political battles for authority in Carolina, Thomas was forced back to London to explain himself to the SPG leadership; he was subsequently exonerated, but died before making it back to Goose Creek. The seal of the SPG presented a noble society responding to a colonial call to '*transiens adjuva nos*' ('come over and help us'): the reality severely tested such idealistic propaganda. Nevertheless, the Society's annual sermons, preached at St Mary-le-Bow and subsequently published in print and distributed in their thousands, showed that the SPG's determination went undiminished.

Episcopacy had its pet 'project', even if the SPG proved to be something of a slow burner. Partly as a result, the SPCK was left to act 'as something of a free radical within the body of the eighteenth-century Church of England'.[22] Building upon the inter-parochial clerical networks which had been growing since the 1650s, the SPCK leadership encouraged provincial clergy to read and distribute all edifying books and papers sent to them; to meet each other frequently so that they might, by their collective will, become more effective in propagating Christianity and more zealous in performing their clerical duties; and to assist in the setting up of schools for poor children to instruct them in the principles of the 'true' religion. After just a few years of operation, diligent, if rather self-absorbed, corresponding members of the SPCK were reporting that clergy on the Isle of Man had been galvanized to action to raise funds for schools, farmers, and distressed sea passengers; how the Society's books and

---

[19] 'Letters of Rev. Samuel Thomas, 1702–1706', *South Carolina Historical and Genealogical Magazine*, 4 (1903): 221–30, 278–85; 'Documents concerning Rev. Samuel Thomas, 1702–1707', *South Carolina Historical and Genealogical Magazine*, 5 (1904): 21–55.

[20] Geoffrey Best, *Temporal Pillars: Queen Anne's Bounty, the Ecclesiastical Commissionaires and the Church of England* (Cambridge, 1964), esp. pp. 1–295, 515–39.

[21] Shawn Comminey, 'The Society for the Propagation of the Gospel in Foreign Parts and Black Education in South Carolina', *Journal of Negro History*, 84 (1999): 360–9.

[22] Sirota, *Christian Monitors*, p. 110.

papers had been distributed in Wigan; how catechetical lectures had been established in Newcastle; how Reigate in Surrey had benefited from a religious library but lamentably had no charity school; and how, apparently, there were no papists or Quakers in the town of Newcastle-under-Lyme. The SPCK had galvanized local activism and created, at least in theory, a national collective.

At the helm of the SPCK a relatively small group of committed souls, drawn from the most willing of the Society's all-male subscribing membership, set to work. In the early years, a gathering of just three constituted a quorate meeting of the SPCK. Bray's leadership was a tour de force and Sir John Philipps (*c*.1666–1737) brought political clout. Robert Nelson (1656–1715) radiated High Church solemnity, even if the first generation of the Society should be seen as basically non-partisan when it came to Church politics. The first secretary, John Chamberlayne (1669–1723), was a skilful linguist and advanced the Society's relations with friendly allies in Europe before becoming a Fellow of the Royal Society in 1702 and then shifting his more pious interests to the SPG. Joseph Downing (1676–1734) served as the SPCK's main printer from its inception to 1734. Henry Newman (1670–1743) wrote over 6,000 letters for the SPCK in the first five years of his tenure as secretary to the Society, a post he held from 1708 to 1743. Formerly a librarian at Harvard College and lay corresponding member for Newfoundland, Newman not only personified the transatlantic scope of the SPCK, but showed how apostates from Congregationalism could be drawn to the Church of England. The SPCK leadership kept a frenetic schedule of weekly meetings until 1722, moving to a monthly timetable thereafter. Early gatherings were typically convened at various private residences. The succour of mother Church was, however, never too far away; during the year of 1703 the Society met regularly at rooms in Sion College and by the 1720s the favoured venue was St Paul's chapter house. From 1728 the Society established a firm base in Bartlett's Buildings, Holborn. More convivial work was conducted regularly at either St Dunstan's or Nando's coffee house, both on Fleet Street. There was also an annual dinner for subscribing members which was initially held at St Dunstan's Quest House. Here the SPCK's business was, like its core members, social, bustling, and metropolitan.

Indeed, as a useful aside, the Church of England had rediscovered its role as master of ceremonies for many other associations. In defining a convivial interface between carnal and spiritual worlds, the stigma of 'priestcraft' was seemingly of little consequence to 'clubbable' clergy like those who met at John Lewis's clerical club at Melksham, Wiltshire, in the late 1710s and early 1720s. County feasts were also typically preceded by a church service which channelled mutually gratifying sentiments of Christian love and solidarity.[23]

---

[23] Newton E. Key, 'The Political Culture and Political Rhetoric of County Feasts and Feast Sermons, 1654–1714', *Journal of British Studies*, 33 (1994): 223–56.

At their annual sermon of 1713, the Gloucestershire Society of Bristol (established in 1657) were entreated by the vicar 'let us of the *Establish'd Church* be *United*'.[24] Founded in 1714, the Society of Ancient Britons brought together many of London's most distinguished Welshmen to affirm their cultural identity whilst displaying a proud allegiance to the Hanoverian regime. Annual celebrations took place on St David's Day, when the Church of England liturgy played host to a sermon delivered in Welsh at St Paul's, Covent Garden; dinner followed at Haberdashers' Hall, with the first health of the evening being drunk to 'King *GEORGE* and the Church of *England*, as by Law Established'.[25] Whilst the Society for Ancient Britons was superseded by the Honourable Society of Cymmrodorion (1751), it lived on into the nineteenth century as a supporter of its own charity school in London and as a medium by which Church of England clergymen contributed to a resurgent Welsh culture in Wales itself.[26] Running through this renaissance in Church sociability, the SPCK was able to weave its magic.

The SPCK became a master of the printed medium.[27] Bray's vision for a more knowledgeable, vital Church was, in no small measure, born out of a burning anti-Quakerism. Only by a learned solidarity could the clergy hope to vanquish the demon of 'enthusiasm' and its capacity to turn Church communicants into terrible apostates. A pledge made at the second meeting of the SPCK to print and disperse select texts, by the excommunicated Quaker schismatic turned virulent anti-Quaker George Keith (1638?–1716), soon snowballed into a dedicated programme to publish and disseminate edifying works to clergymen near and far in an effort to help promote and defend a notion of orthodoxy crafted by the SPCK leadership.

By early 1700 the Society had arranged to supply its clerical corresponding members with packets of books and papers designed to help them advance the cause of the SPCK. In the first instance these packets included stirring works on London's parochial societies and the SRMs, as well as Bray's foundational proposals for the SPCK. Within months this short roster was extended to take account of moral works by Bray, Woodward, and Allestree, amongst others, as well as Gilbert Burnet's *Exposition of the Thirty-Nine Articles of the Church of England* (1699). Within the next few years the SPCK would expand its remit

---

[24] Henry Abbot, *Unity, Friendship and Charity, recommended in a Sermon preach'd before the Gloucestershire Society, August 27, 1713* (Bristol, 1713), p. 19.

[25] Thomas Jones, *The Rise and Progress of the Most Honourable and Loyal Society of Ancient Britons* (London, 1717), p. 18.

[26] Sarah Prescott, '"What Foes more dang'rous than too strong Allies?": Anglo-Welsh Relations in Eighteenth-Century London', *Huntington Library Quarterly*, 69 (2006): 535–54.

[27] Scott Mandelbrote, 'The Publishing and Distribution of Religious Books by Voluntary Associations: From the Society for Promoting Christian Knowledge to the British and Foreign Bible Society', in Michael F. Suarez and Michael L. Turner (eds.), *The Cambridge History of the Book in Britain*, vol. V: *1695–1830* (Cambridge, 2009), pp. 613–30.

considerably. Complementing the charitable work of London's parochial societies and the campaigns of the SRMs, the SPCK ordered thousands of Woodward's moral pamphlets to be printed and then arranged for them to be distributed amongst seamen under the command of Admiral Benbow (d. 1702); it serviced several of London's prisons with bibles and other suitable religious literature; and it made a forceful intervention on the side of Jeremy Collier's protest against the immorality of the theatre by publishing anti-stage texts and distributing them in their thousands all over London.[28] The SPCK began commissioning the translation and publication of edifying foreign works as well as making select English texts available in other languages, starting with Jean Frédéric Ostervald's *The Grounds & Principles of the Christian Religion* (1704), translated from French into English by the SPCK's secretary Humfrey Wanley (1672–1726), and a plan to translate Josiah Woodward's *Earnest Persuasive to the Serious Observance of the Lord's Day* (1700) into Welsh—although it is not clear whether this was ever made a reality. The Halle Pietist and chaplain to Prince George of Denmark, Anton Wilhelm Böhm (1673–1722), brought reports of a Halle Pietist mission at the Danish settlement of Tranquebar (now Tharangambadi) in India to the attention of the SPCK by translating them into English and publishing them as *Propagation of the Gospel in the East* (1709). Whilst the SPG was mandated to British colonies only, the SPCK had greater liberty to court allies in Europe and further the cause of Protestantism in foreign lands. Böhm's privileged position helped ensure that his Lutheranism was no barrier to becoming a member of the SPCK, an act which was perhaps also symbolic of both the Society's inherent anti-Catholicism and its interest in international Protestantism— and as an indication of the complexity of this phenomenon, it should be noted that a parallel Society in Scotland for Propagating Christian Knowledge (founded in 1709) promoted Scottish Presbyterianism in both the Highlands and British colonial America.[29] Utilizing Josiah Woodward's connections with the East India Company, the SPCK sent a printer and a press to Halle missionaries at Tranquebar in 1711. Only the machine made it; nevertheless, this proved to be the beginning of a mutually agreeable endeavour which would see the SPCK become a key sponsor of Protestant missionaries in India for the rest of the eighteenth century. Whilst in many ways impressive, this operational expansion was engineered by the industry of a dedicated few.

---

[28] SPCK Minute Book 1, 1699–1706, fos. 272–80, 362, Cambridge University Library, SPCK MS A1/1; *The Postman*, 20/22 Jan. 1704.

[29] Nathan Philip Gray, '"A Publick Benefit to the Nation": The Charitable and Religious Origins of the SSPCK, 1690–1715', PhD thesis, University of Glasgow, 2011; Eamon Duffy, '*Correspondence Fraternelle*: The SPCK, the SPG, and the Churches of Switzerland in the War of the Spanish Succession', in Derek Baker (ed.), *Reform and Reformation: England and the Continent c.1500–c.1750*, Studies in Church History, Subsidia 2 (Oxford, 1979), pp. 251–80.

Initially, the SPCK attempted to supply their texts to diverse recipients free of charge. This proved unsustainable. From about 1705, it started to charge for its publishing services, although it still aimed to subsidize the cost of book production as best it could. As a result it was able to supply an ever-increasing number and range of carefully vetted religious books for parochial libraries, subscribing and corresponding members, clergy, missionaries, and charity schools; and here there was often close collaboration with the SPG and the SRMs. By 1712 there was a catalogue of over forty books recommended for purchase by or for the masters of charity schools: a quarto bible cost 18s, John Rawlet's *Christian Monitor* (1686) 3d, and Henry Hammond's *Practical Catechism* (1646) 5s; amongst these rather predictable works, there were more exotic translated offerings from Thomas à Kempis (c.1379–1471), Hugo Grotius (1583–1645), and August Hermann Francke (1663–1727).[30] The SPCK's *Account* for 1746 included an enlarged, consolidated book catalogue with over 180 titles for all of the SPCK's main activities. Small 'quires' were divided into lists of bibles, testaments and psalters, common prayers with psalms, and other religious books. Larger stitched books were listed under the following headings: '*On the* Holy Scriptures', '*Publick and Private* Devotion', '*On the* Catechism', '*The* Holy Communion', 'Christian Doctrine *and* Practice', '*Concerning* Particular Duties', 'Common Vices', 'Charity-Schools, Work-Houses, *and* Hospitals', and '*Against* Popery'.

This list formed the basis of a steadily evolving catalogue which was still very much in use in 1797; by that time, works by Kempis, Grotius, Francke, and Hammond had all seemingly been dropped, but Rawlet's classic remained available for purchase and a new section in the catalogue listed two texts against 'enthusiasm'. It is difficult to ascertain which items were bought from these catalogues, let alone in what quantities; however, available records for the circulation of the SPCK's publications account for 177,506 items (8,881 of which were bibles) in 1807, rising to 1,309,582 items (30,030 of which were bibles) in 1827.[31]

The SPCK's focus on schooling was a distinctly national enterprise. Given the success of the Blue Coat model, there was nothing novel about championing charity schools. More daring thoughts concerned the academic and spiritual education of wealthy young women.[32] Clement Barksdale (1609–87) had brought the campaign of Anna Maria van Schurman (1607–78) within the confines of the Church of England in his 1675 proposal for a 'College of Maids, or a Virgin-Society'. High-minded musings on the subject were also advanced by Mary Astell (1666–1731) in *A Serious Proposal to the Ladies* (1694). It was,

---

[30] *An Account of Charity-Schools in Great Britain and Ireland* (London, 1712), pp. 70–1.

[31] McClure, *Two Hundred Years*, p. 198.

[32] Bridget Hill, 'A Refuge from Men: The Idea of a Protestant Nunnery', *Past & Present*, 117 (1987): 107–30.

however, Edward Stephens, pioneer of the SRMs, who apparently founded a Religious Society for Single Women in London for the benefit of 'the Church and Nation' around 1695.[33] Here any sense of progressive pedagogy was tied up with ancient sacred ideals of female celibacy. More generally, the likes of Richard Bulkeley (1660–1710), member of the Royal Society, early protagonist of the SRMs, and a corresponding member of the SPCK for Ireland from November 1699, had also touted the idea of creating schools for more overtly pious ends in the early 1690s. It should be made clear, however, that the SPCK did not go about directly founding or governing charity schools; rather, it provided parishes with a powerful rationale for supporting education and thereafter made itself indispensable to fledgling institutions by supporting them with teaching resources, money, and publicity. The '*Chief Design*' of these schools was the '*Education of Poor Children in the Knowledge and Practice of the Christian Religion*, as profess'd and taught in the Church of England'.[34] In this regard there was a commitment to both sexes: boys were to be taught the three 'R's', whilst girls would be taught to read, write, knit, and sew; daily religious discipline, including prayers and reciting the catechism, was taken for granted. From the summer of 1702 a charge for promoting schools was levied upon all new subscribing members to the SPCK. Two years later the SPCK inaugurated a sponsored anniversary sermon at St Sepulchre's church for the trustees, staff, and children of charity schools in and around London: from 1782 the service was held at St Paul's Cathedral, where it was later represented in the 'Holy Thursday' poems in William Blake's *Songs of Innocence and Experience* (1789–94). This annual sermon also appears to have been held in lieu of a similar event explicitly for the SPCK. The society helped turn a mainly London-based charity school movement into a national phenomenon. By 1724, it could lay claim to helping to found 1,577 schools across Great Britain and Ireland, rising to 2,015 in 1746, before dipping to 1,853 by 1797.[35] Throughout the eighteenth century, the SPCK was, indirectly, the largest and most powerful educator of children in the country.

The second and third generations of the SPCK experienced mixed fortunes. On the one hand, it had reasons to be confident. In 1746 it boasted over 180 subscribing members, as well as two female contributors. At this time the actual figure for individual subscriptions was discretionary, but the SPCK's

---

[33] Edward Stephens, *The More Excellent Way; or, a Proposal of a Complete Work of Charity* (London, 1696), p. 1.

[34] *An Account of the Methods whereby the Charity-Schools have been erected and Managed* (London, 1705?), p. 3; Craig Rose, 'Politics, Religion, and Charity in Augustan London c.1680–c.1720', PhD thesis, University of Cambridge, 1989.

[35] Thomas Wilson, *The True Christian Method of Educating the Children both of the Poor and Rich* (London, 1724), p. 57; *The Account of the Society for Promoting Christian Knowledge* (London, 1746), p. 34; *An Account of the Society for Promoting Christian Knowledge* (London, 1797), p. 101.

finances seemed relatively resilient, aided by sizeable bequests like the legacy of £4,000 left by one Elizabeth Palmer back in 1728. By 1797, subscribing members paying a minimum annual fee of one guinea numbered well over a thousand, and the number of female annual contributors had eclipsed the 1746 count for male subscribers. On the other hand, the SPCK struggled for quality and unity amongst its leadership. As for the former, its long-serving fourth secretary, Thomas Broughton (1712–77), was a case in point. Broughton was a Methodist drop-out who found his way to the SPCK via a curacy at the Tower of London and a lectureship at All Hallows, Lombard Street, and then served as the Society's secretary from 1743 until his death. Before falling out with the Methodists, Broughton had learned the ways of practical collective piety as a member of John Wesley's 'Holy Club' at Oxford (active 1729–*c.*1738). Whilst this experience may have helped the SPCK refresh its core principles, Broughton hardly set the world alight. George Gaskin (1751–1829), Oxonian Doctor of Divinity and husband to Broughton's daughter, took over the secretarial reins between 1785 and 1823, by which time the SPCK was a rather different animal to the one created by Bray. The intra-Church non-partisanship that had served the Society well through the Bray years came under considerable strain. Traditional stalwarts of the Church-state were forced to contend with a series of powerful Evangelical, interdenominational rivals such as the Society for Promoting Religious Knowledge among the Poor (1750), the Sunday School Society (1785), the London Missionary Society (1795), the Religious Tract Society (1799), the British and Foreign Bible Society (1804), and the British and Foreign Schools Society (1808/14).[36]

In the shadow of the SPCK's operations in the second half of the eighteenth century, a range of new societies returned to the issue of clerical education in an effort to secure a particular vision of Church of England uniformity. After a brief spell as a fellow of Queen's College, Cambridge, and curate at St Matthew's, Friday Street, London, Henry Venn (1725–97) became curate at Clapham in 1754. Here the wealthy merchant and lay Church Evangelical John Thornton (1720–90) was in the process of turning Clapham into something of an Evangelical hotspot: an endeavour which would reach maturity a generation later with the 'Clapham Sect' (*fl.*1792–1815).[37] Inspired by his new environment, Venn became a formidable preacher and even used a period of

---

[36] Isabel Rivers, 'The First Evangelical Tract Society', *Historical Journal*, 50 (2007): 1–22; Thomas Laqueur, *Religion and Respectability: Sunday Schools and Working-Class Culture 1780–1850* (New Haven, CT, 1976), pp. 1–62; Anna Johnston, *Missionary Writing and Empire, 1800–1860* (Cambridge, 2003); Aileen Fyfe, 'The Religious Tract Society', in James Murphy (ed.), *The Oxford History of the Irish Book*, vol. IV: *The Irish Book in English, 1800–1891* (Oxford, 2011), pp. 357–63; Stephen Batalden, Kathleen Cann, and John Dean (eds.), *Sowing the Word: The Cultural Impact of the British and Foreign Bible Society, 1804–2004* (Sheffield, 2004).

[37] John Wolffe, 'Clapham Sect (act. 1792–1815)', *ODNB*.

ill-health to reinterpret and revise Richard Allestree's classic work *The Whole Duty of Man* (1658) to reflect a more Evangelical form of spirituality: Venn's *The Complete Duty of Man* was eventually published in 1763. In the meantime, Evangelical patronage brought Venn to the vicarage at Huddersfield in 1759. Venn's curate, George Burnett (*c.*1734–93), was also new to Yorkshire. An Aberdonian by birth, Burnett had first come to England to serve as assistant to his godfather George Conon (1698–1775), a graduate of Marischal College, Aberdeen, working as headmaster of Truro Grammar School in Cornwall. Conon was apparently a guiding spirit in the Evangelical conversion of Samuel Walker (bap. 1713, d. 1761), curate at St Mary's, Truro. By 1754 Walker had co-opted like-minded parishioners to form a religious society along similar lines to the Horneck model—whilst individual societies came and went, there were still at least fourteen parochial societies of this type in and around London at this time.[38] A year later he had started a clerical society not unlike those so eagerly encouraged by the early SPCK. Truro's Evangelicalism turned the young Burnett. After studying at Christ Church College, Oxford, he entered the ministry; and although Burnett's exact path to Huddersfield is somewhat unclear, the route was surely of an Evangelical design. In 1762 Burnett took on a curacy at Elland cum Stainland and Fixby. Venn and Burnett became firm friends. Whilst exploring their own relationship to Methodism, the two co-founded a religious society in 1767 that would go on to be known as the Elland Society.[39] For the first decade of its existence, the Society functioned to offer mutual learning and support to local Evangelical clergymen in a manner not unlike Walker's clerical society; this pattern was repeated when Venn left for Yelling, Huntingdonshire, in 1771 and founded a new clerical society there in 1783, and when Henry Venn's son John (1759–1813) established a similar type gathering at Little Dunham, Norfolk, in the early 1790s.

By 1777 the Elland Society had, under Burnett's leadership, diversified by raising funds to educate poor but able boys who were capable of entering the ministry and supporting the Evangelical cause within the Church of England. With prominent Evangelical connections across the country, the Elland Society did not lack wealthy backers. Its education fund grew from £88 10*s* in 1777–8 to £1,225 19*s* 6*d* in 1796–7; thereafter it averaged between £300 and £400 annually due to competition from other similar educational funds.

---

[38] William Dodd, *Unity recommended, in a Sermon on Ephesians, Chap. iv. Ver. 3. Preached before the Religious Societies in and about London* (London, 1759), p. 24.

[39] John Walsh, 'The Magdalene Evangelicals', *Church Quarterly Review*, 159 (1958): 499–511; A. T. Yarwood, 'The Making of a Colonial Chaplain: Samuel Marsden and the Elland Society, 1765–93', *Historical Studies*, 16 (1975): 362–80; Barbara Melaas-Swanson, 'The Life and Thought of the Very Reverend Dr Isaac Milner and his Contribution to the Evangelical Revival in England', PhD thesis, University of Durham, 1993, pp. 64–120; John Walsh and Stephen Taylor (eds.), *The Papers of the Elland Society, 1769–1828* (Woodbridge, 2017).

Clerical education societies were all the rage. Another clergyman with Truro connections, Thomas Tregenna Biddulph (1763–1838), started a society at Bristol in 1795. Thomas Jones (1752–1845), a peripatetic Evangelical curate who had successfully lobbied the SPCK to publish 10,000 copies of the Welsh Bible in 1799, founded a society at Greaton, Northamptonshire, in 1812. And the noted Church Evangelical, Charles Simeon (1759–1836), who had been influenced by both Henry and John Venn, founded the London Clerical Education Society in 1816. For all these, and several others, the Elland Society led the way partly because it was able to utilize a set of Yorkshire Evangelical contacts to strike up a most fruitful relationship with Magdalene College, Cambridge. From 1778, a steady stream of carefully vetted Elland pensioners matriculated at the College; by 1796–7 there were at least twelve in residence. Each student consented to a life of pious study that was monitored so as to produce Church Evangelicals immune to the 'enthusiastic' ways of Methodism.[40] The Elland Society exemplified a paradox at the heart of Church Evangelicalism: on the one hand it contributed to and benefited from both the Methodist movement and the wider interdenominational force of Evangelicalism; on the other, it disavowed these very formative links in an effort to control, secure, and legitimate its own doctrinal and ecclesiological identity solely within the uniformity and conformity of the Church of England.

The threat of Dissent was also a deep preoccupation of the curate at Nayland, William Jones (1726–1800). No humble clerical assistant, Jones not only had degrees from Oxford and Cambridge and a fellowship at the Royal Society for good measure, but was also a devotee of John Hutchinson's take on a 'conservative' spirituality which served as a bulwark against voguish 'rational' reconfigurations of natural theology. The Hutchinsonians (*fl.*1724–90) may have been a rather loose band of reactionaries, but their polemic was striking.[41] In 1751, George Watson's rousing sermon at St Mary's before the University of Oxford put the Hutchinsonians on a war footing against the supposed drift to 'deistical' apostasy by aiming to 'recover what is *diminished* of the Dignity of the *Church* of *England*', especially with regards to the education of 'the *rising Generation*'.[42] This message was picked up by Jones in his twilight years when, in 1792, he co-founded the short-lived Society for the Reformation of Principles with William Stevens (1732–1807), a lay Hutchinsonian, treasurer of the Queen's Bounty, auditor of the SPG, and benefactor to the Sons of the Clergy.

Offering financial assistance to clerical families went hand-in-hand with a desire to support clerical education. After over a century of rather piecemeal

---

[40] Walsh, 'Magdalene Evangelicals', pp. 501, 503.

[41] Nigel Aston, 'Hutchinsonians (act. *c.*1724–*c.*1770)', *ODNB*.

[42] George Watson, *A Seasonable Admonition to the Church of England: A Sermon preached before the University of Oxford, at St Mary's, on the twenty ninth of May, 1751* (Oxford, 1755).

development, the Sons of the Clergy finally gained some momentum under the presidential tenure of Archbishop Secker between 1758 and 1768, but this may also be seen in the light of shifting views in 'conservative' clerical thought. Secker's own bequest of £500 to the organization was dwarfed by the innovative and generous will of John Stock of Hampstead who, in 1780, left the Sons of the Clergy £300 plus a further £3,500 of consolidated annuities held in trust by the Painters-Stainers' Company, with arrangements for an annual drawdown of £100. And Stevens reportedly spent 'half of his income' on this charitable organization alone. By virtue of such sums it was in a position to enhance its provision to the children and widows of deceased clergy as well as helping impoverished clergy themselves.[43]

In the early 1790s, the Society for the Reformation of Principles returned to first principles by aiming to inculcate a renewed sense of the fundamentals of 'orthodox' Christianity amongst aspiring young men at university, and particularly those with clerical ambitions, in order to safeguard the future of the Church-state. Set against the outbreak of the French revolutionary wars, the Society feared an unholy alliance between irreligious sectaries, republicans, and infidels. At root such anxiety was hardly new. Echoing the perennial call for unity which was enshrined in the fifty-third canon, Jones declared that the 'members of a Society for the *Reformation of Principles* have no private ends to serve; they are of no *sect*, but *the sect of the Nazarenes*; nor of any *party*, but of the church of England'.[44] Despite potential affinity with Methodism through its Hutchinsonian heritage, the Society emerged out of a profound theological distrust of both 'rationalism' and 'enthusiasm'. This conviction helped to firm up a pre-Tractarian, anti-Evangelical strand of High Churchmanship which would expand and mature through the Society's unofficial journal, the *British Critic* (established 1793), the dining 'Club of Nobody's Friends' (1800) founded in honour of the publication output of William Stevens, and the seminal work of the 'Hackney Phalanx' (*fl.*1800–30)—a group headed by Joshua Watson (1771–1855), a wealthy merchant friend of Stevens and resident of Hackney.[45]

As they tried to protect their sense of the intellectual bloodline of clerical 'orthodoxy', select anti-Evangelical High Churchmen widened their ideological programme with gusto. The likes of Stevens and Watson poured considerable

---

[43] Nicholas Cox, *Bridging the Gap: A History of the Corporation of the Sons of the Clergy over 300 Years, 1655–1978* (Oxford, 1978), pp. 74–107.

[44] [William Jones] (ed.), *The Scholar armed against the Errors of Time; or, a Collection of Tracts*, 2 vols. (London, 1800), I, sig. A2.

[45] Peter B. Nockles, 'Church Parties in the Pre-Tractarian Church of England 1750–1833: The "Orthodox"—Some Problems of Definition and Identity', in Walsh et al. (eds.), *The Church of England*, pp. 334–59; Mark Smith, 'Hackney Phalanx (act. 1800–1830)', *ODNB*; E. A. Varley, *The Last of the Prince Bishops: William Van Mildert and the High Church Movement of the Early Nineteenth Century* (Cambridge, 1992), pp. 63–88.

time, energy, and money into the work of the SPCK, the SPG, and the Sons of the Clergy. All three institutions benefited from an upsurge in the kind of support such rich, business-minded lay High Churchmen were able to supply, but much to the detriment of a rapprochement with second-generation Evangelicals. However, in the tumultuous period of the late eighteenth and early nineteenth centuries, Church Evangelicals were in no mood to compromise. Interdenominational Evangelical societies were thriving, with not insignificant assistance from members of the Church of England, and the leadership of the SPCK and the SPG were viewed as obstinately out of touch with the influential thinking emanating from Clapham.

Frustrated by the lack of reform from within established societies, Church Evangelicals struck out on their own. Disestablishment in the United States had arguably helped to end the kind of conflicted sense of Church mission demonstrated by the case of Samuel Thomas in Carolina. Rather than shoring up an overly ambitious centralized scheme for parochial expansion in the colonies, missionaries could focus attention on caring for the 'heathen', with a view to conversion. Such a cause was naturally appealing to Evangelicals and sparked fresh interest in Africa and the Indian subcontinent, which technically fell outside the remit of the SPG. With strong links to Clapham patrons, the Evangelical interdenominational Eclectic Society (1783) had already proved a breeding ground for missionary thought when John Venn, now rector of Clapham, led a splinter group into founding the Church Missionary Society (CMS, 1799).[46] In a climate of anti-Dissent paranoia, the CMS made a conscious attempt to be unequivocal in its loyalty to the Church-state, notwithstanding a lack of support from the episcopate; but this led to the same paradox as that experienced by the Elland Society. Moreover, an inability to attract suitable recruits resulted in the CMS falling upon the same strategy as the SPCK to affect mission overseas: it had to make do with supporting German Lutherans. Working through their anniversary sermon, which was convened between 1801 and 1819 and followed by a general meeting and then dinner, as well as exchanges in print, in script, and in person, change proved to be over a decade in the making. Providential, patriotic responses to the Napoleonic Wars combined with a continued perverse jealousy of Catholic mission brought about renewed points of solidarity between the CMS and its interdenominational rivals, which eventually translated into gains for the former. Following the 'Vellore Massacre' (1806), the CMS was also able to make the most of an emerging discourse which called for the 'civilization' of non-Christians in India. And between 1808 and 1811, the Scottish Presbyterian

---

[46] Elizabeth Elbourne, 'The Foundation of the Church Missionary Society: The Anglican Missionary Impulse', in Walsh et al. (eds.), *The Church of England*, pp. 247–64; Bob Tennant, *Corporate Holiness: Pulpit Preaching and the Church of England Missionary Societies, 1760–1870* (Oxford, 2013), pp. 92–196.

turned Church of England protégé of Charles Simeon and one-time chaplain to the East India Company, Claudius Buchanan (1766–1815), almost single-handedly made the CMS fit for purpose by promoting the idea of a global Church 'in which dioceses . . . and their clergies were comprised primarily of indigenous peoples'.[47]

Whilst not forsaking the SPCK and the SPG, High Churchmen also looked to form new societies to serve better their own distinct vision of Christianity in Britain. Following the demise of the SRMs in the 1730s, episodic action against immorality had increasingly become the preserve of Evangelicals. Reflecting the original design of the SRMs, William Wilberforce's Society for the Enforcement of His Majesty's [i.e. George III] Proclamation against Vice and Immorality (1787) proved to be something of a primer for the more potent Society for the Suppression of Vice (1802); but then the latter, which constituted a relatively small group of just twenty-nine London men of the middling sort at inception, was something of a rearguard action of 'patriotic wartime conservativism'.[48] Indeed, a religious test was imposed to ensure Dissenters could not join the Society, although this was repealed in the late 1830s; and whilst it would go on to act as 'an auxiliary to government' during Richard Carlile's trial for blasphemy (1819), interest in the Society was seemingly sustained between the 1810s and the 1830s only through fear of socio-political unrest.[49] Somewhat predictably, one of the most prominent early members of the Society for the Suppression of Vice, the anti-Jacobin writer John Bowles (1751–1819), was also a member of the 'Hackney Phalanx'. Galvanized by the work of the pioneering educationalist Andrew Bell (1753–1832), another Scot turned Church of England clergyman, who viewed '"unsectarian religious teaching" as a contradiction in terms', a 'Hackney Phalanx' committee of John Bowles, Joshua Watson, and his clerical brother-in-law Henry Handley Norris (1771–1850), started planning what would become the National Society for the Education of the Poor in the Principles of the Established Church (1811). This society immediately gained the political and financial backing of the Church-state—the archbishop of Canterbury served as president and Lord Liverpool acted as one of the vice-presidents—and it even drew begrudging support from some Church Evangelicals. By 1833 the Society controlled some 690 schools across the country.[50] But the 'Hackney Phalanx' did not stop with education reform. For Watson and company, 'the want for church-room, especially for the lower classes, in all the populous parishes' of the kingdom, was the defining principle of their

---

[47] Tennant, *Corporate Holiness*, p. 127.

[48] M. J. D. Roberts, 'The Society for the Suppression of Vice and Its Early Critics, 1802–1812', *Historical Journal*, 26 (1983): 159–76.

[49] M. J. D. Roberts, 'Making Victorian Morals? The Society for the Suppression of Vice and its Critics, 1802–1886', *Historical Studies*, 21 (1984): 157–73 (p. 157).

[50] Varley, *Last of the Prince Bishops*, pp. 71–2, 75.

Society for Promoting the Building and Enlargement of Churches and Chapels (1818; renamed the Incorporated Church Building Society, ICBS, in 1828).[51] With backing similar in scale and scope to that of the National Society, the ICBS grew rapidly into the foremost association for organizing and funding the expansion of churches and parishes in Victorian Britain.

Taken together, the religious societies that were allied to the Church of England over the course of its 'long eighteenth century' typically had something of a split personality. On the one hand, they were very much part of a burgeoning, and distinctly British, 'associational world'. In this respect, they were surely little different from many other clubs and societies that, despite all their energy and enterprise, struggled to supersede the kind of traditional forms of association which reflected communal approaches to gaining sustenance and edification: after all, pubs remained pubs and churches remained churches.[52] On the other hand, these religious societies offered novel, atypical forms of association insofar as they constituted an extension, or perhaps an evolution, of more established models of parochial and ecclesiastical interpersonal relations. Their sense of purpose was as intense as it was profound, leading to both internal strife and towering achievement. Indeed, through their particular take on charity, education, moral activism, mission, and sociability, these societies became a crucial organ of Church propaganda.

SELECT BIBLIOGRAPHY

Andrews, Robert M., *Lay Activism and the High Church Movement of the Late Eighteenth Century: The Life and Thought of William Stevens, 1732–1807* (Leiden, 2015).

Barnhart, William C., 'Anglican Volunteerism, Ecclesiastical Politics, and the Bath Church Missionary Association Controversy, 1817–18', *Anglican and Episcopal History*, 77 (2008): 1–21.

Bullock, F. W. B., *Voluntary Religious Societies 1520–1799* (St Leonards-on-Sea, 1963).

Clark, Peter, *British Clubs and Societies 1580–1800: The Origins of an Associational World* (Oxford, 2000).

Collinson, Patrick, 'Night Schools, Conventicles and Churches: Continuities and Discontinuities in Early Protestant Ecclesiology', in Peter Marshall and Alec Ryrie (eds.), *The Beginnings of English Protestantism* (Cambridge, 2002), pp. 209–35.

Hammond, Geordan, 'The Revival of Practical Christianity: The Society for Promoting Christian Knowledge, Samuel Wesley, and the Clerical Society Movement', in Kate

---

[51] *Christian Observer*, 17 (1818): 198–9.

[52] Peter Clark, *British Clubs and Societies 1580–1800: The Origins of an Associational World* (Oxford, 2000), pp. 430–91.

Cooper and Jeremy Gregory (eds.), *Revival and Resurgence in Christian History*, Studies in Church History 44 (Woodbridge, 2008), pp. 116–27.

Ingram, Martin, 'Reformation of Manners in Early Modern England', in Paul Griffiths, Adam Fox, and Steve Hindle (eds.), *The Experience of Authority in Early Modern England* (Basingstoke, 1996), pp. 47–88.

Isaacs, Tina, 'The Anglican Hierarchy and the Reformation of Manners, 1688–1738', *Journal of Ecclesiastical History*, 33 (1982): 391–411.

Key, Newton E., 'The Political Culture and Political Rhetoric of County Feasts and Feast Sermons, 1654–1714', *Journal of British Studies*, 33 (1994): 223–56.

Lloyd, Sarah, 'Pleasing Spectacles and Elegant Dinners: Conviviality, Benevolence, and Charity Anniversaries in Eighteenth-Century London', *Journal of British Studies*, 41 (2002): 23–57.

Shell, Alison, 'Intimate Worship: John Austin's *Devotions in the Ancient Ways of Offices*', in Jessica Martin and Alec Ryrie (eds.), *Private and Domestic Devotion in Early Modern Britain* (Farnham, 2012), pp. 259–80.

Sirota, Brent S., *The Christian Monitors: The Church of England and the Age of Benevolence, 1680–1730* (New Haven, CT, 2014).

Strong, Rowan, *Anglicanism and the British Empire, c.1700–1850* (Oxford, 2007).

Tennant, Bob, *Corporate Holiness: Pulpit Preaching and the Church of England Missionary Societies, 1760–1870* (Oxford, 2013).

Walsh, John, 'The Magdalene Evangelicals', *Church Quarterly Review*, 159 (1958): 499–511.

Walsh, John, Colin Haydon, and Stephen Taylor (eds.), *The Church of England c.1689–c.1833: From Toleration to Tractarianism* (Cambridge, 1993).

Walsh, John and Stephen Taylor (eds.), *The Papers of the Elland Society, 1769–1828* (Woodbridge, 2017).

23

Anglican Evangelicalism

Gareth Atkins

Anglican Evangelicals have always been captivated by their early history. In few places is this more obvious than at Ridley Hall, Cambridge, founded in 1879 to produce educated ordinands and missionaries to combat what its founders considered to be evils that were peculiar to its age: rationalism, 'Romanism', and theological liberalism.[1] It was the product of a movement whose identity was fostered in print and in bricks and mortar through a range of educational and philanthropic institutions, and which raised hundreds of thousands of pounds a year through well-managed societies. Yet although—and perhaps because—the scale and sophistication of the movement would have been unimaginable a hundred years before, Evangelicals remained enthralled by an earlier, more rough and ready age. In few places was this more deeply felt than in Cambridge, where Charles Simeon, curate of Holy Trinity from 1782 and vicar there from 1783 until his death in 1836, was still venerated, his sway over generations of undergraduates, according to the historian Macaulay, being 'far greater than that of any Primate'.[2] Ridley Hall was a sort of reliquary, preserving Simeon's study sofa, his gown, his pocket-knife, and his correspondence.[3] The first principal of Ridley Hall, H. C. G. Moule, wrote a much-reprinted biography with the great man's bible open before him.[4]

Such hero-worship was pronounced, but it was not unusual. 'The history of the Evangelical Revival', one commentator has claimed, 'is essentially a history of personalities.'[5] Most of them were drawn from the rough century between

---

[1] James C. Whisenant, *A Fragile Unity: Anti-Ritualism and the Division of Anglican Evangelicalism in the Nineteenth Century* (Carlisle, 2003).

[2] T. B. Macaulay to his sister, 1844, in G. O. Trevelyan, *The Life and Letters of Lord Macaulay* (London, 1908 edn.), p. 50 n.

[3] F. W. B. Bullock, *The History of Ridley Hall, Cambridge*, 2 vols. (Cambridge, 1941), I, pp. 221, 264.

[4] H. C. G. Moule, *Charles Simeon* (London, 1892), pp. 16–17.

[5] Charles Smyth, *Simeon & Church Order: A Study of the Origins of the Evangelical Revival in Cambridge in the Eighteenth Century* (Cambridge, 1940), p. 6.

the conversion of Wesley in 1738 and the death of Wilberforce in 1833. From the cradle to the grave, pious readers feasted on biographies of William Wilberforce, Hannah More, and Henry Martyn. They repeated their words, too. Central to Simeon's aura had been his Friday evening conversation parties, where he dispensed tea and aphoristic advice with a light touch. Published accounts of them jostled on Evangelical bookshelves with William Cowper's *Table Talk* (1782), Thomas Adam's *Private Thoughts on Religion* (1786), John Newton's *Letters and Conversational Remarks* (1808), and Josiah Pratt's *Eclectic Notes* (1856), all packed with homely *bons mots* crystallizing the wisdom of the Evangelical fathers.[6] Pious households continued to follow the devotional patterns laid out in classics such as the Independent minister Philip Doddridge's *Rise and Progress of Religion within the Soul* (1745) and Henry Venn's *Complete Duty of Man* (1763). In the late nineteenth century, the philanthropic landscape was still dominated by the Church Missionary and Religious Tract Societies (both founded in 1799), the British and Foreign Bible Society (1804), and the London Society for Promoting Christianity among the Jews (1809). Their centenary celebrations showered the religious public with sermons and jubilee volumes rejoicing in the growth of late Hanoverian seedlings into mighty Victorian and Edwardian oaks.[7]

This emphasis on continuity was suggestive but misleading. For, as will become clear, this well-defined party bore little resemblance to the fluid milieu of the first, formative generations of the movement. Early Evangelicalism was based not so much on institutions as individuals, and even though, as Ford K. Brown famously quipped, Wilberforce and his 'Clapham Sect' coadjutors adopted 'ten thousand compassions and charities', the expansive voluntarism that would lead Sir James Stephen to apostrophize an 'age of societies', where every ill could be remedied by a public meeting, only flowered fully in the 1810s and 1820s.[8] Victorian myth-making was also misleading in other ways. While the informal networks that comprised the movement in its early years certainly laid foundations for later institutions, they also allowed for, and indeed generated, very diverse opinions on sacraments, hymnody, homiletics, and a host of other issues. Most significant among them was the issue of churchmanship. As early as the 1750s there was a developing consensus among 'gospel clergymen', as they called themselves, about the need to remain 'regular', i.e. to minister only within one's own parish, to obey one's bishop,

[6] Abner William Brown, *Recollections of the Conversation Parties of Charles Simeon* (London, 1863).

[7] Eugene Stock, *A History of the Church Missionary Society*, 4 vols. (London, 1899–1916); William Canton, *A History of the British and Foreign Bible Society*, 5 vols. (London, 1904–10); W. T. Gidney, *The History of the London Society for Promoting Christianity amongst the Jews* (London, 1908).

[8] Ford K. Brown, *Fathers of the Victorians: The Age of Wilberforce* (Cambridge, 1961), p. 317; [Sir James Stephen], 'The Clapham Sect', *Edinburgh Review*, 80 (1844): 306.

and to use only authorized forms of service and prayers. Yet boundaries also remained blurred: as late as the 1810s there remained 'semi-regulars' prepared to itinerate, to pray extempore, and to swap pulpits with Methodists and other Dissenters. Within the Church, partisan divisions developed only gradually, and not always along predictable lines. Evangelical regulars yielded nothing to High Churchmen in their love for the formularies, and indeed, as Mark Smith argues, differed doctrinally from some strands of pre-Tractarian High Churchmanship only on the details of justification by faith.[9] True, they might support pan-Evangelical endeavours that were not episcopally led or populated solely by churchmen, and within their parishes establish classes that divided believing sheep from formalist goats. Even then, though, they often did so only reluctantly.[10]

In terms of theology, too, Hanoverian Evangelicalism was worlds away from the rigorism associated with its later nineteenth-century counterpart. From the earliest stirrings of revival there had always been a sense that credal niceties mattered little in comparison with heart-religion—'the one thing needful'—but the bitterness of the mid-century Calvinistic controversies combined with enlightened empiricism to imbue Evangelicals with a profound distaste for wrangling about how salvation took place. 'I do not know any opinions separate from their practical uses that are worth contending for', sniffed the Hull clergyman-schoolmaster Joseph Milner.[11] The result was a deliberately undogmatic 'moderate Calvinism' or 'Bible Christianity', in which grace was to be offered to all, and whose emphasis on divine sovereignty was tempered with an awareness of human agency. 'If a man be not born again, it signifies little, whether he be called Calvinist or Arminian, whether he belong to Church or Kirk, Relief, Circus, or Tabernacle', Newton told a correspondent.[12] Preachers scrutinized their congregations less for correct beliefs than for the works that were evidence of genuine faith. While collections of systematic theology gathered dust, volumes of *Practical Sermons* poured from the presses, packed with moral guidance. By the 1780s and 1790s this shift, coupled with the spread of 'vital religion' or 'seriousness', as it was also known, among business-minded laymen, was fuelling an increasingly urgent activism. There was a growing sense that philanthropic ends justified the use of practical means, embodied in the big-hearted but hard-headed ecumenism of the

[9] Henry Ryder, 'A Charge Delivered to the Clergy of the Diocese of Gloucester in the Year 1816', ed. Mark Smith, in Mark Smith and Stephen Taylor (eds.), *Evangelicalism in the Church of England c.1790–c.1890* (Woodbridge, 2004), pp. 76–80.

[10] Grayson Carter, *Anglican Evangelicals: Protestant Secessions from the Via Media, c.1800–1850* (Oxford, 2001), pp. 31–57.

[11] Isaac Milner (ed.), *The works of the late Rev. Joseph Milner*, 8 vols. (London, 1810), VI, p. 174.

[12] John Campbell, *Letters and Conversational Remarks by the late Rev. John Newton* (New York, 1811 edn.), p. 149.

societies founded around 1800. 'I should be glad to get a Mahometan to receive and disperse our bibles', averred the London minister and Bible Society activist Rowland Hill. 'He might get good and would do good.'[13]

This chapter, then, traces the beginnings of an enduring movement, but it also outlines a distinct phase in its existence: one characterized by diversity of opinion and practice and concerned primarily with pragmatic accommodation to the realities of late Hanoverian politics and public life. It proceeds in three sections. The first considers the emergence of Evangelicalism as a distinct grouping within the Church of England, with its own sense of identity; the second, its ramification in clerical associations and among groups of prosperous laypeople; the third, its infiltration of metropolitan officialdom and provincial society. Although it would be possible to say much more about Evangelical thought, theology, and devotional practice, what follows focuses on the networks that spread Evangelical influence, and on the issues generated by the movement's expansion. Above all, what did it mean to be both Anglican and Evangelical? Or, to put it another way, how were the demands of churchmanship to be balanced against those of 'true' Christianity? This was undoubtedly a formative period in the development of Anglican Evangelicalism, but it also bequeathed tensions that would continue to trouble the movement well into the twentieth century.

'A ROPE OF SAND'? THE 1730s TO THE 1780s

In a magisterial essay first published in 1966, John Walsh set out the variegated influences acting on early Evangelicals, ranging from inherited High Church spirituality to puritan theology to Pietist emotionalism, and mediated through the late seventeenth- and early eighteenth-century Anglican-led Societies for the Reformation of Manners, through the Moravian *Unitas Fratrum*, and through other, more Calvinist diasporas: Scots Presbyterians such as George Conon, schoolmaster of Truro and mentor to Samuel Walker, and William Darney, the North Country pedlar-preacher; Huguenot descendants, too, such as Walter Sellon, James Rouquet, and the Perronets, not to mention William Romaine and, most famously, John Fletcher of Madeley, Shropshire, alias Jean Guillaume de la Flechère of Nyon, Switzerland.[14] While John Wesley's Aldersgate Street experience of 24 May 1738 at 'about a quarter to nine' has always provided a tempting starting point for tidy-minded historians, Charles

---

[13] Edwin Sidney, *The Life of the Rev. Rowland Hill* (London, 1834), p. 372.

[14] J. D. Walsh, 'Origins of the Evangelical Revival', in G. V. Bennett and J. D. Walsh (eds.), *Essays in Modern English Church History in Memory of Norman Sykes* (London, 1966), pp. 132–62.

Abbey and John Overton in the late nineteenth century and Elie Halévy in the early twentieth were mistaken in seeing Anglican Evangelicalism simply as an offshoot of 'the great Methodist revival'.[15] Walsh wisely echoed Gladstone's insistence that revival had no single source, being 'the result of the confluence of many tributaries' that surfaced in Wales, Scotland, New England, and elsewhere well before 1738.[16]

Scholarship since 1966 has delineated the often complicated courses that those tributaries took. Much of it emphasizes longer-term narratives. W. R. Ward has teased out how central European mysticism and millennialism were spread by North Atlantic travellers, traders, and refugees, especially after the revocation of the Edict of Nantes in 1685.[17] Scholars have also debated the extent to which the early Evangelicals appropriated the theological legacy of the puritans, both in Britain and in America.[18] Henry Rack, meanwhile, has shown how the 'Holy Club' of the Wesleys was one of several Oxonian bodies modelled on the religious societies pioneered by mainstream post-Reformation churchmen like Anthony Horneck (1641–97) and Josiah Woodward (1657–1712).[19] Evangelistic techniques once assumed to be Methodist innovations have been placed within much older traditions. Already between 1714 and 1718 Griffith Jones, rector of Llanddowror in Carmarthenshire, was being pilloried for 'invading' neighbouring parishes and preaching outdoors to huge congregations; while the outbursts of feeling that attended Scottish 'communion seasons' as early as the mid-seventeenth century have been put forward as potential precursors to later revivalism.[20] Recent work has also widened the parameters of discussion. David Bebbington has shown how Evangelicalism drew upon and redefined strands of Enlightenment thought,[21] an idea taken up by Phyllis Mack and Sarah Apetrei, whose close-textured explorations of the inner lives of Methodist and Quaker women reveal the careful balance between emotion and empiricism—the 'managed heart'—that

---

[15] Walsh, 'Origins', pp. 135–7.

[16] W. E. Gladstone, 'The Evangelical Movement, its Parentage, Progress, and Issue', in W. E. Gladstone, *Gleanings of Past Years*, 7 vols. (London, 1879), VII, p. 205.

[17] W. R. Ward, *Early Evangelicalism: A Global Intellectual History, 1670–1789* (Cambridge, 2006).

[18] Michael A. G. Haykin and Kenneth J. Stewart (eds.), *The Advent of Evangelicalism: Exploring Historical Continuities* (Nottingham, 2008); Andrew Cambers and Michelle Wolfe, 'Reading, Family Religion, and Evangelical Identity in Late Stuart England', *Historical Journal*, 47 (2004): 875–96.

[19] Henry D. Rack, *Reasonable Enthusiast: John Wesley and the Rise of Methodism* (London, 1989), p. 87.

[20] G. H. Jenkins, *Literature, Religion and Society in Wales, 1660–1730* (Cardiff, 1978), pp. 34–8, 305–9; Leigh Eric Schmidt, *Holy Fairs: Scottish Communions and American Revivals in the Early Modern Period* (Princeton, NJ, 1989).

[21] D. W. Bebbington, *Evangelicalism in Modern Britain: A History from the 1730s to the 1980s* (London, 1989), pp. 50–74.

lay at the centre of Evangelical ideas of the self.[22] Geordan Hammond
has unpicked the fabric of patristic interest—Anglican, non-juror, Lutheran,
Moravian—that lay behind the emphasis of Wesley and others on 'primitive
Christianity'.[23]

While our understanding is much richer, then, than it once was, it has
become more difficult to generalize about the genesis of Evangelicalism. What
is clear, however, is that the chaotic energy it imparted to existing religious
allegiances rendered them provisional and even meaningless. Hitherto, the
equilibrium ensured by the 1689 Toleration Act had guaranteed relative
denominational stability, the boundaries between establishment and Dissent
being jealously policed from both sides of the fence. Now, itinerant preachers
and white-hot revivalism swept through church and chapel alike, prompting
individual secessions, spinning off independent congregations, and spawning
new denominational bodies. Many found it an exciting time of ecumenical
cross-pollination. Take James Hervey (1714–58), for instance, rector of Weston
Favell in Northamptonshire, whose post-conversion career nicely exemplifies
this temper. 'Though I am steady in my Attachment to the established church,
I would have a Right-hand of Fellowship, and a Heart of Love, ever ready, ever
open, for all the upright evangelical Dissenters', he assured one correspondent
in 1748.[24] He admired Isaac Watts's hymns and used them in his services. His
friends and correspondents were an eclectic set of Methodists and Evangelicals,
including Wesley, Whitefield, the Countess of Huntingdon, Lady Frances
Shirley, and Nonconformists such as Philip Doddridge at nearby Northampton, with whom he was especially close.[25] Hervey's intellectual influences
were similarly broad: he was widely read in physico-theology and both
classical and modern poetry, and sought in his writings to combine puritan
meditation with Shaftesburian sublimity in order 'to bait the Gospel-Hook,
agreeably to the prevailing taste'.[26] Through *Meditations and Contemp-
lations* (1746–7) and *Theron and Aspasio* (1755), Hervey reached an urbane
readership, though not without revolting those who could not stomach
his Calvinism.[27] Although similarly cultivated, John Berridge of Everton
in Bedfordshire relished an earthier ministry, preaching in barns and
poaching converts in parishes as far as the outskirts of Cambridge.[28] Such
behaviour frequently attracted episcopal displeasure. Bishop Lavington of

[22] Phyllis Mack, *Heart Religion in the British Enlightenment: Gender and Emotion in Early
Methodism* (Cambridge, 2008); Sarah Apetrei, *Women, Feminism and Religion in Early Enlightenment England* (Cambridge, 2010).

[23] Geordan Hammond, *John Wesley in America: Restoring Primitive Christianity* (Oxford,
2014).

[24] James Hervey, *A Collection of the Letters of James Hervey*, 2 vols. (London, 1760), I, p. 264.

[25] Isabel Rivers, 'Hervey, James (1714–1758)', *ODNB*.

[26] Hervey, *Letters*, II, p. 101.   [27] *Meditations* reached twenty-six editions by 1800.

[28] Smyth, *Simeon & Church Order*, pp. 149–200.

Exeter's vitriolic *The Enthusiasm of Methodists and Papists Compar'd* (1749–51) was prompted in large part by irregularity in his diocese, including, perhaps, the 'circumforaneous vociferations' of George Thomson of St Gennys.[29]

Others were more cautious about crossing denominational and parochial divides. By 1764, when John Wesley wrote to all the 'serious' clergy he knew of in the Church of England, he could name thirty-four. His letter proposed union of action based on three shared 'fundamental truths': original sin, justification by faith, and the inward and outward holiness that resulted.[30] From some forty to fifty recipients, however, he was dismayed to receive only three replies, all lukewarm. Further invitations went unheeded. 'I can do no more,' he informed the Methodist Conference in 1769. 'They are a rope of sand, and such they will continue.'[31] He should not have been surprised. In part the objection was theological: leaning towards the qualified predestinarianism of the Thirty-Nine Articles, many such clergy were suspicious of the Wesley brothers' Arminianism and their stress on the possibility of perfection. More problematic, though, was the issue of regularity. Since the Commonwealth period anti-sectarian feeling had become bred in the Anglican bone, and while there were certainly those prepared to cooperate with Wesley, they were wary of his authoritarianism and warier still of his studied ambivalence about whether his connexion belonged in the Church. His proposal that the uniting parties could remain 'quite regular, or quite irregular, or partly regular and partly irregular' as they chose was, therefore, not at all reassuring.[32] Of course, we should be cautious about distinguishing too neatly between churchmen and Methodists. John and Mary Fletcher's saintly 'Church Methodism' at Madeley demonstrates how new, flexible practices could complement regular, parish-based work,[33] while the received caricature of Charles Wesley as John's sidekick has been replaced by rounded portrayals of a clerically-minded fifth columnist in the Methodist citadel who reined in his brother's separatist impulsiveness.[34] Still, lines were being more clearly drawn, especially where general concerns became specific complaints, such as when Henry Venn arrived in Huddersfield in 1759 and found a parish riddled with Methodist

[29] G. C. B. Davies, *The Early Cornish Evangelicals, 1735–60* (London, 1951), p. 25.

[30] Richard Watson, *The Life of John Wesley* (London, 1835 edn.), pp. 213–14.

[31] Joseph Benson (ed.), *The Works of the Rev. John Wesley*, 17 vols. (London, 1809–13), VI, pp. 382–3.

[32] Edwin Sidney, *The Life and Ministry of the Rev. Samuel Walker* (London, 1838 edn.), p. 236.

[33] David R. Wilson, 'Church and Chapel: Methodism as Church Extension', in Geordan Hammond and Peter S. Forsaith (eds.), *Religion, Gender, and Industry: Exploring Church and Methodism in a Local Setting* (Cambridge, 2011), pp. 53–76.

[34] Gareth Lloyd, *Charles Wesley and the Struggle for Methodist Identity* (Oxford, 2007).

preachers and societies. After two years of competition a compromise was reached, but this did little to dispel worries about Wesley's cavalier attitude.[35]

Although the Countess of Huntingdon's connexion and the Whitefieldite Calvinistic Methodists were theologically closer to the predestinarianism of most of the gospel clergy, relations with them eventually ran aground on similar reservations. In the 1760s and 1770s floundering clerics like William Romaine, Martin Madan, and Thomas Haweis were only too happy to accept the countess's scarf of office as her chaplains, while many more took occasional advantage of the ambiguous status of her chapels to preach to some of the largest congregations in London.[36] In the early 1780s, however, legal proceedings forced her to register her chapels under the Toleration Act. Prominent Anglican revivalists from Wales, such as David Jones of Llangan, David Griffiths of Llwyngwair, and Thomas Charles of Bala continued to occupy the Spa Fields pulpit regularly even after the connexion conducted its own ordinations in 1783, but others withdrew from what was now a *de jure* Dissenting sect. The enraged countess denounced her onetime charges as 'plausible leaders for Satan only', 'half hearted interested creatures' that 'would eat, drink and be merry' in plump establishment livings.[37] Her ire was understandable; yet so too was their caution. The connexion they now abandoned had endured a long and sometimes troubled informal existence in the interstices between Church and Dissent; but even though the countess's chapels used the Book of Common Prayer, and even if she, unlike Wesley, consistently rejected the idea that women ought to preach, they took their Anglican vows (and the prospect of prosecution) seriously enough to distance themselves from their former patroness. The countess, of course, was well aware of what was at stake: in 1772, for example, her own former preacher, the recently ordained Cradock Glascott, had scrupulously refused to speak in the laundry-cum-chapel of her house at Ashby-de-la-Zouch on the basis that this would constitute irregularity.[38] Nor could she have failed to notice that students of her college at Trevecca struggled to secure ordination, especially against the backdrop of High Church reaction that set in during the American wars.[39] 'The Countess of Huntingdon's people', observed one contemporary in 1777, 'are especially obnoxious to the bishops in general.'[40]

[35] Ryan Danker, 'Constrained to Deviate: John Wesley and the Evangelical Anglicans', DTheol thesis, Boston University School of Theology, 2012, pp. 164–7.

[36] Alan Harding, *The Countess of Huntingdon's Connexion: A Sect in Action in Eighteenth-Century England* (Oxford, 2003), pp. 296–357.

[37] Lady Huntingdon to Mr Evans, 10 June 1782, in John R. Tyson and Boyd Stanley Schlenther (eds.), *In the Midst of Early Methodism: Lady Huntingdon and her Correspondence* (Lanham, MD, 2006), p. 152.

[38] Harding, *Countess of Huntingdon's Connexion*, p. 316.

[39] Harding, *Countess of Huntingdon's Connexion*, pp. 173–233, 375.

[40] Thomas W. Aveling, *Memorials of the Clayton Family* (London, 1867), p. 33.

Especially galling to her, perhaps, was the existence of a nexus of 'serious' ministers, many of whom who had hitherto flirted with irregularity but were now determined to work within Anglican limits. Among the most influential was Venn, since 1771 retired to Yelling, in Huntingdonshire, where he acted as mentor to a number of young Cambridge-educated Evangelicals, Simeon among them.[41] Another was Romaine, who, after a succession of lectureships, preacherships, and curacies in the City of London, as well as irregular preaching expeditions further afield, had been elected rector of St Andrew-by-the-Wardrobe with St Ann Blackfriars in 1764, which post he retained until his death.[42] Romaine was the only beneficed Evangelical in the capital until 1780, when he was joined by the former slave trader John Newton, appointed to St Mary Woolnoth.[43] All three had revelled in the freedom of earlier decades; all had undertaken extra-parochial preaching and visiting; and all had benefited from the patronage of lay patrons who were relaxed about cross-denominational endeavour. Now they came down firmly on the side of regularity. One who had never taken the countess's shilling was Thomas Adam, incumbent of Wintringham in Lincolnshire since 1724. Like his friend and correspondent Walker, Adam was a staunch churchman who clashed with Wesley repeatedly. Although no barnstorming preacher, he shaped the nascent movement in crucial ways. One was in becoming a guru to pious laypeople, notably the earl of Dartmouth and the merchant-philanthropist John Thornton, both of whom visited in order to seek his advice. The other was in his writings. In the nineteenth century Adam's posthumously published *Private Thoughts* were likened to Pascal's *Pensées*, being lauded by Samuel Taylor Coleridge, Thomas Chalmers, and even John Stuart Mill.[44] During Adam's lifetime, however, he was known for his *Practical Lectures on the Church Catechism* (1753), which were hugely influential in reassuring his brethren of the fundamentally Evangelical nature of Anglican forms, and thus of the need for them to remain loyal to the Established Church.

'TRUE CHURCHMEN': THE 1780s TO THE 1800s

The protégés of such men were increasingly disinclined to ride roughshod over the disciplines of the national Church. In part this was because they had

---

[41] John Venn, *The Life and a Selection from the Letters of the Late Rev. Henry Venn* (London, 1834), esp. pp. vi–xv, 49–51.

[42] William Bromley Cadogan, *The Life of the Rev. William Romaine* (London, 1796).

[43] D. Bruce Hindmarsh, *John Newton and the English Evangelical Tradition: Between the Conversions of Wesley and Wilberforce* (Oxford, 1996).

[44] A. B. Grosart, rev. D. Bruce Hindmarsh, 'Adam, Thomas (1701–1784)', *ODNB*.

too much to lose. In a letter of 1795, the aged Newton eloquently summarized their gains. 'The gospel is preached in many parts,' he reflected.

> We have it plentifully in London; and many of our great towns, which were once sitting in darkness, have now the true light... And every year the gospel is planted in new places—ministers are still raising up—the work is still spreading. I am not sure that in the year 1740, there was a single parochial minister, who was publicly known as a gospel preacher, in the whole kingdom: now we have, I know not how many, but I think not fewer than four hundred.[45]

Burgeoning numbers fostered a sense of *esprit de corps*. Where communications between them had once been intermittent, by the end of the century gospel ministers were notorious for meeting to exchange prayers, pastoral tips, news, and gossip. Walker's clerical club, established at Truro in the 1750s for 'zealous Anglicans', was a key early exemplar, as was the Elland Society in Yorkshire (1767), and in the ensuing decades similar societies mushroomed, at Hotham and York in the north; at Bristol; at Creaton, Rauceby, Leicester, and Aldwinkle in the Midlands; at Little Dunham in Norfolk; in London, where the Eclectic Society first met in the Castle and Falcon Inn on Aldersgate Street in 1783; and in Ossory, whose episcopally sanctioned association became a seedbed for Evangelicalism in the Church of Ireland.[46] Instead of taking the world as their parish, their members regarded their parishes as their main and increasingly their sole sphere, and they valorized those who did likewise. They swapped anecdotes about pioneers like the fearsome William Grimshaw of Haworth, whose pre-sermon forays, riding-crop in hand, sent hardened absentees scurrying to church; or about Walker, of whom it was said that 'you might fire a cannon down every street of Truro in church time, without a chance of killing a single human being'.[47]

While revivalist trailblazers had benefited from the protection of a handful of aristocratic patrons, they had often been antagonistic towards respectability. Berridge had once rejoiced that a fellow clergyman had 'driven the Squire and his family from the church, which is a mighty good symptom'.[48] By the end of the century a more savvy generation was learning instead to woo the rich and influential. 'To do *now* as Berridge did *then* would do much harm', Simeon would later warn his undergraduate hearers.[49] Historians have rightly emphasized the importance of the revived Reformation of Manners movement of the

---

[45] Campbell, *Letters and Conversational Remarks*, p. 76.

[46] John D. Walsh, 'The Yorkshire Evangelicals in the Eighteenth Century: With Especial Reference to Methodism', PhD thesis, University of Cambridge, 1956, pp. 262–4; Alan Acheson, *A History of the Church of Ireland 1691–1996* (Blackrock and Dublin, 1997), pp. 131–4.

[47] Sidney, *Samuel Walker*, p. 17.

[48] Richard Whittingham, *The Works of the Rev. John Berridge* (London, 1838), p. 413.

[49] Brown, *Conversation Parties of Simeon*, p. 200.

1780s and 1790s in this shift.[50] Particularly important was the development of a broad-based coalition around the need to improve public morals in the aftermath of defeat in America. While bishops curious to attend the Countess of Huntingdon's chapel in Bath had once skulked behind curtains in the so-called 'Nicodemus Corner', endeavours like the Proclamation Society (1787) brought Evangelicals together with figures like Bishops Porteus of London and Barrington of Salisbury and Durham, who shared their urgency but not all of their convictions.[51] These allies came in useful in the reactionary 1790s, when episcopal charges resounded with denunciations of 'Methodistical' enthusiasm, and when even Hannah More's Mendip Sunday Schools could be accused of teaching crypto-Jacobinism.[52] While the Proclamation Society and its successor, the Society for the Suppression of Vice (1802), are usually remembered (and disparaged) for their efforts to combat popular immorality, Evangelical writers also warned elite readers that the moral health of society hinged on their behaviour, an idea set out most influentially in William Wilberforce's *Practical View of the Prevailing Religious System of Professed Christians in the Higher and Middle Classes of this Country Contrasted with Real Christianity* (1797).[53] Such arguments were at once sincere and tactical, highlighting a growing awareness that social and political suasion mattered as much as revivalist fervour. John Thornton's son Henry was especially alive to this. A London banker, MP for Southwark, and bachelor housemate of Wilberforce, Thornton junior was deeply critical of his father's support for non-Anglican divines: 'he therefore rendered the Bishops his enemies'. 'While he was doing much good to thousands and perhaps tens of thousands of the common people to whom he both sent preachers and distributed books innumerable', he added, 'he made little progress with the rich.'[54] Henry, by contrast, was acutely aware that appearances mattered, justifying the expenditure of £300 on a new coach by pointing out to his wife-to-be that 'to gain an influence over the minds of our equals ... cannot be done if we are not equally free from austerity and

---

[50] Joanna Innes, 'Politics and Morals: The Reformation of Manners Movement in Later Eighteenth-Century England', in Eckhardt Hellmuth (ed.), *The Transformation of Political Culture: England and Germany in the Late Eighteenth Century* (Oxford, 1990), pp. 57–118; M. J. D. Roberts, *Making English Morals: Voluntary Association and Moral Reform in England, 1787–1886* (Cambridge, 2004), pp. 17–95.

[51] [Aaron C. H. Seymour], *The Life and Times of Selina, Countess of Huntingdon*, 2 vols. (London, 1839), I, p. 477 n.

[52] Anne Stott, *Hannah More: The First Victorian* (Oxford, 2003), esp. pp. 232–57.

[53] John Wolffe, 'William Wilberforce's *Practical View* (1797) and its Reception', in Kate Cooper and Jeremy Gregory (eds.), *Revival and Resurgence in Christian History*, Studies in Church History 44 (Woodbridge, 2008), pp. 175–84.

[54] Henry Thornton, 'Recollections', f. 4, Cambridge University Library, Thornton MSS, Add. 7674/1/N. For his father's activities, see Isabel Rivers, 'The First Evangelical Tract Society', *Historical Journal*, 50 (2007): 1–22.

ostentation'.[55] 'By becoming a little more respectable,' he later put it more pithily, 'we become much more dangerous.'[56]

That process was facilitated by the multiplication of fashionable congregations, often around charismatic ministers. At the Lock Hospital chapel, near Hyde Park Corner, Martin Madan's electrifying preaching and his promotion of oratorios and hymn-singing had from the 1750s attracted growing numbers of well-heeled hearers, an upward trend that continued under his successors, Edward de Coetlogon and the celebrated Bible commentator Thomas Scott.[57] In the 1780s and 1790s worshippers there included Lord Dartmouth, Sir Charles Middleton, Wilberforce, Henry Thornton, and Edward Eliot—all MPs—and the agriculturalist and civil servant Arthur Young. 'We shall soon have gout numbered among the privileges of the gospel!' joked one member.[58] While London Evangelicalism has received considerable attention from historians, cultured congregations further afield are worthy of closer examination. At St Alkmund's, Shrewsbury, the former Irish Methodist Richard de Courcy ministered to a congregation who in 1795 expensively rebuilt the church on a grand scale in the modish Gothic style, complete with chandeliers, gilding, the latest cast-iron lancet tracery, and a unique east window depicting an allegorical figure of 'Evangelical Faith' kneeling on the cross, her arms extended towards a floating celestial crown: this alone cost no less than £110.[59] In Dublin, Bethesda Chapel became the centre of an influential philanthropic circle that spanned the professions, business, and Trinity College, including the founder of the Royal Irish Academy, Dr Robert Perceval, the Guinness brewing family, and the La Touche banking dynasty.[60] When Daniel Wilson, future bishop of Calcutta, visited Ireland on a CMS fundraising tour in 1814 he was pleasantly surprised by the reception he received among the Anglo-Irish aristocracy, noting the numerous 'clergymen of the first families and connections' who supported the CMS, the Hibernian Bible Society (1806), and the Sunday School Society for Ireland (1809).[61] Members of these and other prominent congregations gradually reshaped perceptions of the movement. As the *Christian Observer* noted in 1810, it was difficult to dismiss Evangelicals

---

[55] Marianne Thornton senior to Mrs Sykes, Feb. 1796, 'Family Letterbook', fos. 57–8, Thornton MSS, Add. 7674/1/N.

[56] Henry Thornton to Hannah More, 26 Jan. 1811, 'Family Letterbook', f. 286.

[57] Nicholas Temperley, 'The Lock Hospital Chapel and its Music', *Journal of the Royal Musical Association*, 118 (1993): 44–72.

[58] John Scott, *The Life of the Rev. Thomas Scott* (London, 1822 edn.), p. 243.

[59] Terry Friedman, *The Eighteenth-Century Church in Britain* (New Haven, CT and London, 2011), pp. 268–70. For De Courcy, see [Seymour], *Selina, Countess of Huntingdon*, I, pp. 381–5; Thomas Philips and others, *History and Antiquities of Shrewsbury*, 2 vols. in 1 (Shrewsbury, 1837 edn.), I, pp. 232–6.

[60] Acheson, *Church of Ireland*, pp. 98–100.

[61] Charles Hole, *The Early History of the Church Missionary Society for Africa and the East to the End of A.D. 1814* (London, 1896), p. 510.

as philistines when so many were now patrons of poetry, scholarship, and the visual arts.[62] Notwithstanding groundbreaking work by Antje Steinhöfel, this milieu awaits its historian: the sculptor John Bacon, the painter Francis Rigaud, and the pastellist John Russell were all known to be 'serious', and their catalogues read like a roll-call of the pious networks that now criss-crossed the country.[63]

The changing social composition of the movement opened up new career options for aspiring ministers. The expulsion of six Oxford 'Methodists' from St Edmund Hall in 1768 taught Evangelical strategists that educational open-ings mattered, and from the 1770s the Elland Society funnelled its 'pensioners' through northern grammar schools to Magdalene College, Cambridge, where the fellows were known to be favourable, and later to Queens' College, where another Yorkshire Evangelical, the natural philosopher Isaac Milner, became president in 1788.[64] The Bristol Clerical Education Society was founded in 1795 by the redoubtable Thomas Tregenna Biddulph and sponsored many of its recruits to attend St Edmund Hall.[65] As Sara Slinn has shown, these educational conveyor-belts were complemented and to some extent fed by 'domestic clerical seminaries': clergymen prepared to take in resident students in order to prepare them for ordination.[66] By founding formal societies, however, Evangelicals guarded both flanks, on the one hand demonstrating to churchmen that 'seriousness' and sound learning were compatible, and on the other advancing young men who might otherwise be drawn towards Dissent, with its academy system. 'I wish to know what state are the funds of your West Riding Charity for catching the colts running wild on Halifax Moor, cutting their manes and tails, and sending them to college', Wilberforce asked the Leeds surgeon William Hey. 'I would most cheerfully give something towards an institution I so highly approve.'[67] This symbiosis between lay sponsorship and clerical advancement was even more important once gradu-ates were ordained. The best among them attracted the attention both of patrons and of the influential clergymen who occupied nodal points in the emerging geography of Evangelical Anglicanism, men like Thomas Robinson of Leicester, Edward Burn of Birmingham, Thomas Dikes of Hull, Simeon at Cambridge, and Biddulph at Bristol. While their predecessors had been

---

[62] See Doreen M. Rosman, *Evangelicals and Culture* (London, 1984).

[63] Antje Steinhöfel, 'John Russell and the Impact of Evangelicalism and Natural Theology on Artistic Practice', PhD thesis, University of Leicester, 2005.

[64] John D. Walsh, 'The Magdalene Evangelicals', *Church Quarterly Review*, 159 (1958): 499–511.

[65] J. S. Reynolds, *The Evangelicals at Oxford, 1735–1871* (Abingdon, 1975 edn.).

[66] Sara Slinn, 'Sons of the Prophets: Domestic Clerical Seminaries in Late Georgian England', in John Doran, Charlotte Methuen, and Alexandra Walsham (eds.), *Religion and the Household*, Studies in Church History 50 (Woodbridge, 2014), pp. 318–30.

[67] Wilberforce to Hey, Dec. 1789, in Robert Isaac Wilberforce and Samuel Wilberforce, *The Life of William Wilberforce*, 5 vols. (London, 1838), I, p. 252.

content to take the crumbs from under the establishment table in the shape of poorer livings, unwanted curacies, and afternoon lectureships, well-qualified clerical neophytes could now afford to adopt a more calculating attitude. 'The land is full of Evangelical ministers from one end to the other,' marvelled the Carlisle clergyman John Fawcett in 1800, with pardonable exaggeration, 'so that it is now the fashionable Divinity.'[68]

Numerical success was paralleled by assertiveness about the movement's pedigree. Joseph Milner ranged across the entire Christian epoch in his *History of the Church of Christ* (1794–1809) retouching figures like Augustine, Jerome, and Gregory the Great to resemble late eighteenth-century 'vital believers'.[69] Gospel ministers also elaborated their Anglican lineage with growing sophistication and tactical awareness. Although in private many read the works of puritan writers, especially John Owen and Richard Baxter, in public they tended to name-check more straightforwardly Anglican authorities, regarding the label 'Calvinist' with suspicion and preferring instead to underline their place in an indigenous tradition of biblical churchmanship. Although some scholars have recently questioned the idea that the revival of the 1730s marked a new theological departure, most Evangelical historiographers undoubtedly thought in terms of discontinuity.[70] The Elizabethan and Jacobean reformed consensus, they believed, had been wrecked by reaction and counter-reaction under Laud and Cromwell, paving the way for the 'Great Ejection' of 1662 that placed so many of the pious outside the establishment pale, and the suppression of 'Calvinism' within the Church and its decay into Socinianism among Dissenters. When the streams of true religion re-emerged, they smugly pointed out, it was within the establishment. The idea that they and they alone preserved the reformers' inheritance became a fixation among the regular majority.[71] Its classic statement was the influential *True Churchmen Ascertained* (1801), in which the York clergyman John Overton quoted extensively (but selectively) from the Book of Common Prayer, Articles, and Homilies in order to confound High Church naysayers: '*We*...are the TRUE CHURCHMEN...they are *Schismatics*.'[72] That said, their affection for the formularies went far beyond pragmatism or partisanship. In describing vividly its author's life-changing encounter with dusty texts to which he had once

---

[68] John Fawcett to Thomas Scott, 24 May 1800, Birmingham University Library, CMS Papers, Home Correspondence, G/AC 3/1, no. 21.

[69] John D. Walsh, 'Joseph Milner's Evangelical Church History', *Journal of Ecclesiastical History*, 10 (1959): 174–87.

[70] See Haykin and Stewart (eds.), *Advent of Evangelicalism*.

[71] Gareth Atkins, '"True Churchmen"? Anglican Evangelicals and History, *c.*1770–1850', *Theology*, 115 (2012): 339–49.

[72] John Overton, *The True Churchmen Ascertained: Or, an Apology for those of the Regular Clergy of the Establishment, who are sometimes called Evangelical Ministers*...(York, 1801), p. 397.

carelessly assented, Thomas Scott's famous *Force of Truth* (1779) stood for the experiences of many others. By the turn of the century almost all gospel ministers could have echoed the sentiments of Richardson of York:

> My faith is exactly that of the Church of England; as far as I know, her doctrines are mine. Her forms of worship are preferred by me before any devotional service I ever heard, or saw. I have been shaken in mind by controversial writers of different sects and sorts; I have been tossed about by various winds of doctrines; I have thought deeply on every point that seemed to me to accompany salvation; and I have determined to live and die in the bosom of the Established Church.[73]

SPHERES OF INFLUENCE: THE 1800s TO THE 1830s

The first quarter of the new century was the heyday of Anglican Evangelicalism, if not numerically then in terms of its social and political clout. Where Methodism had taken advantage of weaknesses in establishment provision, Evangelicalism now exploited its strengths. Central to this was the coterie which formed around Henry Thornton and Wilberforce following the former's purchase of Battersea Rise in 1792, the group known at the time as the 'Saints' and to posterity as the 'Clapham Sect'. The latter label was coined in a famous *Edinburgh Review* article of 1844.[74] The author, Sir James Stephen, was a second-generation Claphamite, and his picture was, he admitted, 'whimsical' and highly impressionistic, not least since those he described did not all live there at the same time.[75] It was also partial, eulogizing the East India Company director, Charles Grant; the former governor-general of India, Lord Teignmouth; the rector of Clapham, John Venn; the businessman Zachary Macaulay; and his father, the lawyer James Stephen; but excluding others, including the angular anti-slavery campaigner Thomas Clarkson, whose radicalism did not sit easily with Claphamite conservatism, and the Evangelical prime minister, Spencer Perceval, who lived nearby but belonged to a different circle. Stephen's selectivity was understandable. The Saints had been integral to events the Victorians regarded as epoch-making. In the late 1780s they had helped to found the 'Province of Freedom', later Sierra Leone, for freed slaves; in Parliament they pushed for the abolition of the slave trade in 1807 and the passage in 1813 of the 'Pious Clause' allowing proselytization in British India; in 1802 they founded the *Christian Observer*, which exercised significant influence on genteel and influential readers. Nevertheless, by reducing the

---

[73] John Pearson, *Life of William Hey* (London, 1822), pp. 151–2.
[74] [Stephen], 'Clapham Sect'.
[75] Sir James Stephen to Joseph Sturge, 4 Oct. 1844, London, British Library, Add. MS 43845, f. 25.

movement to the activities of a few families, Stephen obscured the reasons for its success. By the reforming 1830s and 1840s, when Stephen and other filial biographers were writing, patronage had become a dirty word, but a generation earlier it had been the key that unlocked the professions, politics, and public life.

While many modern writers continue to be dazzled by the movement's celebrities, their rhetoric, and their personal charisma, contemporary critics were only too aware of the real basis of Evangelical strength.

> The party which [they have] formed in the Legislature, and the artful neutrality with which they give respectability to their small numbers,—the talents of some of this party, and the unimpeached excellence of their characters, all make it probable that fanaticism will increase, rather than diminish. The Methodists [i.e. Evangelicals] have made an alarming inroad into the Church, and they are attacking the Army and Navy. The principality of Wales, and the East India Company, they have already acquired. All mines and subterraneous places belong to them; they creep into hospitals and small schools, and so work their way upwards.[76]

It is worth emphasizing that the substance, if not the sentiment, would have been acknowledged with glee by those at whom it was aimed: the Saints, after all, were men and women of their time, and their methods reflected this.

Their influence was especially marked in the late Hanoverian business world. 'We are all City people and connected with merchants, and nothing but merchants on every side', Henry Thornton remarked, referring to a cousinhood which conjoined Hull business families, Russia merchants, and international bankers such as the Smiths of Nottingham and London.[77] Other family houses, including the Barclays, Drummonds, Hoares, Mannings, and Neales, were similarly 'serious' in complexion.[78] Sir Thomas Baring, heir to the mighty Barings Bank—the 'sixth great power in Europe'—was a friend and ally of the Saints. Thornton's own firm was based at Bartholomew Lane, in the shadow of the Bank of England, where his brother Samuel was director and later governor. While critics alleged that Threadneedle Street was an Evangelical fiefdom, their phobias were even more pronounced concerning the East India Company, whose headquarters was nearby, in Leadenhall Street. For the Whig churchman and essayist Sidney Smith, its neo-classical facade masked a teeming hive of pious place-finders. 'Methodism at home is no unprofitable

---

[76] [Sydney Smith], 'Ingram *On Methodism*', *Edinburgh Review*, 11 (1808), p. 361.

[77] 'Recollections of Marianne Thornton', MS, [1857], cited in Henry Thornton, *An Enquiry into the Nature and Effects of the Paper Credit of Great Britain*, ed. F. A. von Hayek (London, 1939), p. 12.

[78] Ian S. Rennie, 'Evangelicalism and English Public Life, 1823–1850', PhD thesis, University of Toronto, 1962, p. 11; Hector Bolitho and Derek Peel, *The Drummonds of Charing Cross* (London, 1967), pp. 137–44.

game to play', he sneered. 'In the East it will soon be the infallible road to promotion.'[79] There was truth in this. The Evangelical stockholders helped to ensure that in the 1800s and 1810s Charles Grant, Edward Parry, and Thornton's brother Robert played a significant part in East India Company affairs, for instance in the appointment of chaplains to Indian posts.[80] Spreading outwards from Somerset House and Whitehall, a nexus of like-minded civil servants, including figures like Sir Charles Middleton (later Lord Barham) in the navy, and Sir James Stephen at the Colonial Office, carried weight in officialdom.[81] Social contact, attendance at the same churches, and intermarriage served to reinforce and augment these networks. Hence Evangelicals might favour medical practitioners like John Pearson of Golden Square or his pupil William Blair of Bloomsbury; they published with Leonard Benton Seeley of Fleet Street or John Hatchard of Piccadilly, whose bookshop was a haunt for the pious; and if they went to law they did so through men like the solicitor William Cardale.

Such developments gave gospel ministers greater cachet. During service times the streets outside St John's, Bedford Row, near Gray's Inn, Welbeck Chapel, in the West End, and Wheler Chapel, Spitalfields were lined with gleaming carriages. The rising stars who preached there still sought to save souls, but talked openly about securing 'spheres of influence' through which to reach larger numbers and more respectable hearers. 'The importance of such a congregation is obvious at a glance; and the minister himself was quite sensible of it', observed Daniel Wilson's biographer.[82] In most cases this involved securing the right to present to a living. Evangelical strategists had long been aware of the 'problem of continuity': the risk that one of their own might be replaced by an unregenerate 'idol shepherd' who would undo his good work. There had always been localized attempts to remedy this, but by the 1810s and 1820s Evangelicals were notorious for their propensity for snapping up fashionable pulpits on a systematic basis. Under Simeon the trust bequeathed by John Thornton to preserve livings for suitably ardent ministers expanded rapidly, controlling ten in 1814 and thirty by 1836, including most of the churches in Bath.[83] The foundations thus laid transformed a city once described by John Wesley as 'Satan's headquarters' into a godly stronghold, a pattern repeated in Cheltenham, Buxton, Tunbridge Wells, and other nineteenth-century watering

[79] [Sydney Smith], 'Indian Missions', *Edinburgh Review*, 12 (1808), p. 173.

[80] Penelope Carson, *The East India Company and Religion, 1698–1858* (Woodbridge, 2012), pp. 52–150.

[81] Paul Knaplund, *James Stephen and the British Colonial System, 1813–1847* (Madison, WI, 1953); Gareth Atkins, 'Religion, Politics, and Patronage in the Late Hanoverian Navy, c.1780–c.1820', *Historical Research*, 88 (2015): 272–90.

[82] Josiah Bateman, *The Life of the Right Rev. Daniel Wilson*, 2 vols. (London, 1860), I, p. 178.

[83] Wesley D. Balda, 'Spheres of Influence: Simeon's Trust and its Implications for Evangelical Patronage', PhD thesis, University of Cambridge, 1981, pp. 130–1.

places. In nearby Bristol, Evangelical sympathizers among the merchantocracy and the local aristocracy controlled the disposal of corporation livings, making Biddulph 'virtually Bishop of Bristol'.[84] In the capital, and in provincial centres like Newcastle upon Tyne, Manchester, and Liverpool, immense sums were poured into strategic purchases and the building of proprietary chapels, which conferred patronage rights on the trustees who put up the funds. All this was conducive to striking growth. By Gladstone's reckoning, Evangelicals made up around one in twenty (i.e. about 600) of the established clergy by the death of George III in 1820, rising to some one in eight (about 1,500) ten years later.[85] Grassroots expansion was matched at higher levels. In 1815 Henry Ryder became the first Evangelical bishop when he was appointed to Gloucester. A cultured moderate who owed his elevation to the political influence of his brother, the earl of Harrowby, and who sought to play down partisan controversy, Ryder nonetheless stuffed canonries and arch-deaconries with zealous protégés, not to mention ordaining would-be CMS missionaries who had been turned away elsewhere.[86] He was joined on the episcopal bench in 1826 by Charles Richard Sumner at Llandaff and in 1828 by John Bird Sumner at Chester, while Power Le Poer Trench, archbishop of Tuam, became in the 1820s the acknowledged leader of the Evangelical cause in Ireland.[87]

Still more thrilling was the surging popularity of philanthropy in the euphoric decade after the 1807 Abolition Act. The raptures that greeted the measure were a far cry from 1795, 1797, or 1804, when food shortages, financial turmoil, and the threat of French invasion had attracted portentous warnings about national sins, blackest of them all being the slave trade.[88] Evangelicals had long championed the idea that to be pious was also to be patriotic. Now, with the tide turning in Europe, they credited moral reforma-tion at home with the success of British arms abroad, a message calculated to attract presidents and patrons from well beyond the bounds of those who would have identified as Evangelical.[89] 'The Christian world ... is improved beyond the fondest dreams of the visionary', breathed Zachary Macaulay in 1811. 'Behold our kings, and our princes, and the nobles of the land,

[84] L. P. Fox, 'The Work of the Reverend Thomas Tregenna Biddulph', PhD thesis, University of Cambridge, 1953, pp. 45–6, 307–8; Henry Budd, *A Memoir of the Rev. Henry Budd* (London, 1855), p. 267.

[85] Gladstone, 'Evangelical Movement', p. 210.

[86] Ryder, 'Charge', ed. Smith, pp. 53–62.

[87] G. H. Sumner, *Life of Charles Richard Sumner* (London, 1876), pp. 130–2, 150–2; Joseph D'Arcy Sirr, *A Memoir of the Honorable and Most Reverend Power Le Poer Trench* (Dublin, 1845), p. 46.

[88] John Coffey, '"Tremble, Britannia!" Fear, Providence, and the Abolition of the Slave Trade, 1756–1807', *English Historical Review*, 127 (2012): 844–81.

[89] Gareth Atkins, 'Christian Heroes, Providence, and Patriotism in Wartime Britain, 1793–1815', *Historical Journal*, 58 (2015): 393–414.

brightening their honours by patronising this divine work!'[90] The leaders of
the newly formed Bible, tract, and missionary societies also developed innovative forms of organization—local 'auxiliary societies'—turning metropolitan
associations into national and eventually international bodies, with branches
across not just the United Kingdom but across the global British world.
This was a financial masterstroke. The effects were most striking in the
Bible Society, whose income increased from some £6,000 in 1808–9 to a
staggering £65,748 in 1812–13, but other societies, too, experienced expo-
nential growth.[91] Simultaneously, year after year of packed meeting halls and
lengthening subscription lists stoked mounting post-millennial excitement.
Had the divine blueprint for a new epoch been revealed? In the aftermath of
Napoleon's defeat the answer seemed to be 'yes': 'No ten years, with the
exception of the apostolic age, have done more...towards the promotion of
true religion', gushed Macaulay in the *Christian Observer*.[92] Missionary publications were packed with diagrams, maps, facts, and figures demonstrating
that the conversion of the world required only the application of sufficient
means, all designed to convince readers to part with their money.

Amid the triumphalism, however, cracks in pan-denominational unity can
be glimpsed. For the hard-nosed lay businessmen who provided Evangelical
societies with much of their funding and financial expertise, gospel ends
justified pragmatic means.[93] 'The line of business is, with few exceptions, as
direct at the Bible Committee as it is at Lloyd's,' argued one member, 'and
there is as little reason to expect the peculiar tenets of Calvin and Socinus to
enter into a debate for dispersing an edition of the Scriptures, as there would
be if the same men met to underwrite a policy of insurance.'[94] Clergymen
accustomed to justifying their place in the Church were often more lukewarm
about cross-denominational activity. Hence the formation in 1799 of the CMS,
so called to distinguish it from the non-denominational (London) Missionary
and Baptist Missionary Societies, which many Anglicans initially supported,
and in 1812 of the Prayer-Book and Homily Society; hence, too, the Anglican
takeover in 1815 of the London Society for Promoting Christianity among the
Jews. In the Bible Society, balance was preserved by appointing three secretaries, one Anglican, one Nonconformist, and one for the 'Foreign Protestant
Churches', all under the deliberately uncontroversial rubric of distributing the

[90] 'Preface', *Christian Observer*, 10 (1811), unpaginated.

[91] Roger H. Martin, *Evangelicals United: Ecumenical Stirrings in Pre-Victorian Britain,
1795–1830* (London, 1983), pp. 80–98.

[92] 'Review of Owen's History of the Bible Society', *Christian Observer*, 15 (1816): 730.

[93] Leslie Howsam, *Cheap Bibles: Nineteenth-Century Publishing and the British and Foreign
Bible Society* (Cambridge, 1991).

[94] 'A Sub-Urban Clergyman' [John Owen], *A Letter to a Country Clergyman* (London, 1805),
p. 50.

Scriptures only, 'without note or comment'.[95] Naturally, none of this placated High Church polemicists like Charles Daubeny or Henry Handley Norris, who condemned the 'promiscuous' association of churchmen with Dissenters as diverting funds away from the existing Church missionary and Bible organizations, the SPG and SPCK. As Mark Smith has argued, such tensions bespeak divisions over how to tackle the challenges of industrialization and urbanization. One solution was to rejuvenate existing parochial and diocesan structures.[96] The other was to adopt a more voluntarist way of working, combining lay and clerical leadership, and adapting to new imperatives as they arose: 'nothing less than... a new model of Anglicanism', whose adherents remained sedulously loyal to the Church, but whose autonomous operations represented a *de facto* challenge to existing norms.[97] Of course, not everyone who favoured the latter course was a paid-up Evangelical. Plenty of non-Evangelicals supported the new societies, including Bishops Porteus, Barrington, and Burgess of St David's, while Ryder was the most prominent among the many mainstream Evangelicals who gave to the Bible Society and the SPCK alike. Voluntarism would become central to the economy of Victorian religion. In the 1810s and 1820s, however, as party divides began to widen, Evangelicals and their allies looked like they were deliberately flouting episcopal authority, which in a sense they were. Hence the otherwise disproportionate protest of Archdeacon Josiah Thomas of Bath against the formation of a CMS auxiliary in 1817: 'A Church of England Missionary Society, under the MANAGEMENT (that is the word) of A CORRESPONDING COMMITTEE!!!'[98]

By the 1820s success was also beginning to raise unsettling questions among Evangelicals themselves about their place in the Church and in the establishment more broadly. While there had always been periodic expressions of uneasiness about aspects of Anglican services, above all the baptismal and burial rubrics, which seemed to imply the salvation even of unrepentant sinners, these had usually remained restricted to the letters pages of pious periodicals.[99] Now, in the face of missionary setbacks, splits within the Bible Society over the status of the Apocrypha, 'infidel liberalism', and calls for Catholic Emancipation, ebullient young hardliners expressed mounting disquiet at a Church that seemed ever more obviously to jumble the elect together with the unregenerate. Not for them the carefully weighted subtleties of

[95] Canton, *Bible Society*, I, pp. 15–17.

[96] Arthur Burns, *The Diocesan Revival in the Church of England, c.1800–1870* (Oxford, 1999).

[97] Mark A. Smith, 'Henry Ryder and the Bath CMS: Evangelical and High Church Controversy in the Later Hanoverian Church', *Journal of Ecclesiastical History*, 62 (2011): 726–43 (p. 742).

[98] Josiah Thomas, *An Address to a Meeting holden in the Town Hall, in the City of Bath...* (Bath, 1818 edn.), p. 12.

[99] See W. J. C. Ervine, 'Doctrine and Diplomacy: Some Aspects of the Thought of the Anglican Evangelical Clergy, 1797 to 1837', PhD thesis, University of Cambridge, 1979.

moderate Calvinism: magnetic figures like Henry Bellenden Bulteel at Oxford and the Church of Ireland clergyman John Nelson Darby set forth a more full-blooded predestinarianism that eventually impelled them into secession.[100] They took with them personal followings and built new chapels to house them, often funded by strong-minded aristocratic supporters, as in the early days of the revival. The most prominent seceder was the London-based Church of Scotland minister Edward Irving, who decried Evangelical complicity with the establishment, blasting a movement that had become 'perverted by usefulness' and by chasing eminent patrons and donors instead of declaring the whole counsel of God. While cultured Evangelicals winced at Irving's frothing rhetoric, it hit a nerve, articulating doubts about a modus operandi that seemed to prioritize social and moral renovation over inward spirituality; doubts that many privately shared. It was symbolically apt that the circulation of the moderate, reformist *Christian Observer* was outstripped by the more uncompromising, anti-reformist *Record*, founded in 1828, which could soon boast that it was the 'parsons' paper'.[101] Evangelicals also found themselves outmanoeuvred on the other flank: by the late 1820s young Oxonians who sought a ginger group were more likely to head towards High Churchmanship, flocking to hear Keble and later Newman rather than aligning themselves with a movement whose radical appeal now appeared jaded.[102]

Thus even before the crisis of the Protestant state, the authority of the older generation was crumbling, and with it the unity and pragmatism that had characterized the preceding decades. If the constitutional upheavals of 1828–32 were undoubtedly as unsettling to Evangelicals as they were to other Anglicans, they were all the more traumatic because they served to widen the rifts in an already fractured movement. Was reform to be welcomed as a necessary preservative of public order, or denounced as inimical to the religious and political truths embodied in the Protestant settlement? Ought they to be pragmatic, and bow to the inevitable, or rail against the unholy alliance of papal antichrist and no-Church nonconformity? Should they engage with the world or withdraw from it? That such tensions did not induce mass secessions can be ascribed in part to the institutional strengths built up over the preceding decades. Patronage networks provided security of tenure, and the means for further expansion. Philanthropic organizations allowed continuing pastoral and practical innovation. Most importantly, perhaps, the vast majority of Evangelical clergy cleaved to the Church not just for pragmatic reasons but through affection and conviction in equal measure, holding that for all its faults, its doctrines were sound, and that national establishments

---

[100] Carter, *Anglican Evangelicals*, pp. 152–311.
[101] Rennie, 'Evangelicalism and English Public Life', pp. 78–81.
[102] David Newsome, *The Parting of Friends* (London, 1966).

were ordained by God.[103] At the same time, Anglican Evangelicals struggled to recapture the excitement of the decades either side of 1800, when the new piety had coursed through the veins of institutions and individuals alike. This nostalgia was already present in the 1820s, and was heightened by the passing of Wilberforce and More in 1833, of Simeon in 1836, and Macaulay in 1838. Nevertheless, even by 1829 that outward-looking movement was well on the way to becoming a party, one that was arguably geared more to defending its ancestors' gains than to expanding upon them.

SELECT BIBLIOGRAPHY

Atkins, Gareth, 'Wilberforce and his Milieux: The Worlds of Anglican Evangelicalism, c.1780–1830', PhD thesis, University of Cambridge, 2009.

Blake, Richard, *Evangelicals in the Navy, 1775–1815: Blue Lights and Psalm-Singers* (Woodbridge, 2008).

Brown, Ford K., *Fathers of the Victorians: The Age of Wilberforce* (Cambridge, 1961).

Carson, Penelope, *The East India Company and Religion, 1698–1858* (Woodbridge, 2012).

Carter, Grayson, *Anglican Evangelicals: Protestant Secessions from the Via Media, c.1800–1850* (Oxford, 2001).

Hilton, Boyd, *The Age of Atonement: The Influence of Evangelicalism on Social and Economic Thought* (Oxford, 1998).

Hindmarsh, D. Bruce, *John Newton and the English Evangelical Tradition: Between the Conversions of Wesley and Wilberforce* (Oxford, 1996).

Noll, Mark A., *The Rise of Evangelicalism: The Age of Edwards, Whitefield, and the Wesleys* (Leicester, 2004).

Rosman, Doreen M., *Evangelicals and Culture* (London, 1984).

Smith, Mark and Stephen Taylor (eds.), *Evangelicalism in the Church of England c.1790–c.1890* (Woodbridge, 2004).

Smyth, Charles, *Simeon & Church Order: A Study of the Origins of the Evangelical Revival in Cambridge in the Eighteenth Century* (Cambridge, 1940).

Stott, Anne, *Hannah More: The First Victorian* (Oxford, 2003).

Stott, Anne, *Wilberforce: Family and Friends* (Oxford, 2012).

Walsh, John D., 'The Yorkshire Evangelicals in the Eighteenth Century: With Especial Reference to Methodism', PhD thesis, University of Cambridge, 1956.

Wolffe, John R., *The Expansion of Evangelicalism: The Age of Wilberforce, More, Chalmers and Finney* (Nottingham, 2006).

---

[103] Gareth Atkins, 'Anglican Evangelical Theology, c.1820–1850: The Case of Edward Bickersteth', *Journal of Religious History*, 38 (2014): 1–19.

24

Anglicanism and Methodism

David R. Wilson

INTRODUCTION

During the decades immediately following John Wesley's death in 1791, study of the Wesleyan movement was dominated by the views of nineteenth-century Methodist historians by then separated from the Church of England and anxious to establish themselves in contradistinction from the Church they had left. Their conclusions were mirrored by nineteenth-century Evangelicals and Tractarians who were similarly prone to emphasize the shortcomings of the Hanoverian Church, now rectified—so the rhetoric went—by the more effective reforms of their own time, which were supposedly in continuity with unfulfilled efforts to revive the Church of England in the century following the Glorious Revolution. Subsequent generations of historians into the twentieth century generally maintained this teleological approach, seeing the eventual separation of Methodism from its mother Church as 'inevitable'.[1] Thus the default approach to studying Methodist history has been to see it as a *de facto* rival to the Established Church. Indeed, even the recent *Oxford Handbook of Methodist Studies*, for all that is very good in the volume, includes only scattered references to the Church of England, and only three pages directly addressing Methodism's Anglican context; nor does Part V, on Theology, include a chapter on Methodist ecclesiology.[2]

By contrast, this chapter looks at Methodism as it evolved *within* Anglicanism, both self-consciously and accidentally, and the ways in which even its apparent contradictions did at times spring from loyalty to the Church and its legacy, as well as from innovation. In addition, it has often been assumed that the status of the Church of England as the Established Church limited

---

[1] John Kent, *The Age of Disunity* (London, 1966), p. 182.
[2] William J. Abraham and James L. Kirby (eds.), *The Oxford Handbook of Methodist Studies* (Oxford, 2009).

significantly the ways it could draw upon at least some of the same cultural, economic, and religious trends, methods, and liberties of its Dissenting counterparts. David Hempton has observed that 'Religion . . . sinks its deepest roots into popular culture when it helps give expression to the social, economic, ethnic and cultural homogeneity of populations facing rapid change or oppression.'[3] It is worth asking whether and where Methodism might be seen as an Anglican manifestation of this dynamic. Were there ways in which the Church did compete in the religious marketplace in its relationship with, and even over against, Methodism?

Allowing Anglicanism to be a starting point rather than (from the perspective of hindsight) just a temporary encumbrance from which Methodism gradually freed itself,[4] this chapter is as much an examination of how John and Charles Wesley and their early Anglican colleagues could subscribe to Methodism *and* Anglicanism, to chapel *and* church, as of the ways in which they diverged. It explores briefly when, where, and how reforms took shape through the influence of Methodism within Anglicanism, first in England, but also through the missionary impulse already active within the Church.

Recent research has made the case that the English process of Reformation was as much a religious movement as its continental counterpart, and as such took far longer than historians have been wont to allow. Instead of seeing a Reformation that was fairly complete (or at least as complete as could be) by the time of the Toleration Act of 1689 that institutionalized an already existent Protestant pluralism of denominations, and that it was this at least nominally reformed Church that progressed little through the following century, recent work proposes that the Hanoverian Church continued to present some of the old challenges to pastoral and evangelistic efforts and plenty of new ones which required continued reform and enterprise.[5] As Gilbert Burnet wrote (*c.*1679): 'It cannot be denied . . . that our reformation is not yet arrived at that full perfection that is to be desired.'[6] In such a context, it might be expected that many eighteenth-century clergy understood their work as having continuity with that of earlier reformers.

---

[3] David Hempton, *Methodism: Empire of the Spirit* (New Haven, CT, 2005), p. 63.

[4] E.g. T. G. Williams, *Methodism and Anglicanism in the Light of Scripture and History* (Toronto, 1888).

[5] See Nicholas Tyacke (ed.), *England's Long Reformation 1500–1800* (London, 1998), chs. 10–12; cf. Jeremy Gregory, 'The Eighteenth-Century Reformation: The Pastoral Task of Anglican Clergy after 1689', in John D. Walsh, Colin Haydon, and Stephen Taylor (eds.), *The Church of England c.1689–c.1833: From Toleration to Tractarianism* (Cambridge, 1993), pp. 67–85.

[6] Quoted in Eamon Duffy, '*Correspondence Fraternelle*: The SPCK, the SPG, and the Churches of Switzerland in the War of the Spanish Succession', in Derek Baker (ed.), *Reform and Reformation: England and the Continent c.1500–c.1750: Dedicated and presented to Professor Clifford W. Dugmore to mark his Seventieth Birthday*, Studies in Church History, Subsidia, 2 (Oxford, 1979), pp. 251–80.

In several ways, this chapter ponders some of the same questions as Tyacke's volume regarding a continued Reformation in which Methodism had a role to play in catalysing exertions towards unreached ideals. In particular, how was Wesley's Anglican heritage important to the development of the reform emphases and organization of Methodism? These questions are not original, and this ground has in many ways been covered in the past quarter-century by revisionist rehabilitations of the Georgian Church that find their roots in the moderately more optimistic analysis of Norman Sykes. These early rehabilitations culminated in several key volumes offering a range of approaches, including looking not only at the institution at the upper levels, but at the Church in the localities—the dioceses, archdeaconries, and (importantly) the parishes.[7] It is hoped that this exploration of particular emphases of Methodism which drew strength from its Anglican context will contribute a clearer picture of the possibilities and liabilities of the Church of England in this period. In addition, although the question of allegiance has been a central topic of Wesleyan studies from the beginning and thus is not central to this chapter, it may throw some light on such concerns as a by-product.[8]

The following argument has three sections. The first revisits the ways in which Wesley was influenced by an Anglican religious stream. Part of what is remarkable in Wesley's Methodism is the way in which he maintained optimism regarding what could be accomplished within the Church, even though he was using methods considered 'irregular'. The second explores the implications of Wesley's experimental religion and the way it drew upon Anglican tradition and gave shape to his organization of preachers and societies.[9] In an age when the language of enlightenment was not instilled in a classroom but learned inductively as a native language, the precepts of empiricism were present in religious practice as much as anywhere. When one looks at Wesley's many explanations, rationalizations, and even what might be considered 'excuses' or 'arrogances' concerning his more substantial irregularities, it is apparent that his experimental approach led him to try things to see how they worked and to weigh them against the experiences of others. Wesley was one

---

[7] Norman Sykes, *Church and State in the XVIIIth Century* (Cambridge, 1934); Walsh et al. (eds.), *Church of England*; Jeremy Gregory and Jeffrey S. Chamberlain (eds.), *The National Church in Local Perspective* (Woodbridge, 2003).

[8] See Jeremy Gregory, '"In the Church I will Live and Die": John Wesley, the Church of England, and Methodism', in William Gibson and Robert G. Ingram (eds.), *Religious Identities in Britain, 1660-1832* (Aldershot, 2005), pp. 147–78; Frank Baker, *John Wesley and the Church of England* (London, 1970); Henry D. Rack, *Reasonable Enthusiast: John Wesley and the Rise of Methodism* (London, 2002 edn.).

[9] Cf. Rack, *Reasonable Enthusiast*, pp. 63, 385–7; Frederick Dreyer, 'Faith and Experience in the Thought of John Wesley', *American Historical Review*, 87 (1983): 12–30; Robert E. Cushman, *John Wesley's Experimental Divinity: Studies in Methodist Doctrinal Standards* (Nashville, TN, 1989); Isabel Rivers, *Reason, Grace, and Sentiment: A Study of the Language of Religion and Ethics in England, 1660-1780*, vol. I: *Whichcote to Wesley* (Cambridge, 1991).

of many who saw the value of both reason and practical, vital piety, and these came to the fore as he adopted and adapted, building a Methodist movement that was missiological and expansionist at its centre.

The final section addresses a specific example that illustrates how, for all the ways in which the relationship between Anglicanism and Methodism was conflicted, the irregularities, emphases, and structures of Methodism could function not simply as extra-establishment religion (outside the Church of England) but also as *extra* establishment (an extension or supplement to the Church of England).

How did the Church improve by deploying the same resources as Methodism and other 'chapel religion' to extend its reach and its level of pastoral care? Even if the Evangelical clergy found themselves retreating from some of the irregularities that Wesley sought to normalize and unify around them, in the latter part of the century particular instances of Anglican improvement are observable.

WESLEY, THE CHURCH, AND POSSIBILITIES OF REFORM

Methodism started as a possibility. It was a possibility for personal renewal, corporate revival, and institutional reform conceived and reconceived in the minds of the Wesleys, and eventually of the leaders with whom they came together to deliberate the actions of the 'United Societies' and to maintain a discipline within them. The way in which Methodism developed within Anglicanism was not in the sole control of the Wesleys nor any of the other Methodist leaders. However, there is broad agreement that for as long as John Wesley was alive, his authoritarian leadership might have been mitigated at times by his brother Charles (1707–88), his preachers, or circumstances, but was never more than partially and temporarily weakened, due to the voluntary contractual authority which he claimed.[10] Thus although it might make an interesting experiment to attempt to write a history of Methodism with deliberate inattention to John or Charles, the way in which Methodism and Anglicanism were related must ultimately include substantial reference to them. This section explores the context in which the very idea of the possibility of reform took shape and evolved in the form of Wesleyan Methodism.

Historians have found it difficult to take seriously Wesley's self-conscious and apologetic claims to be loyally devoted to the Church while diverging in so

---

[10] Cf. Frederick Dreyer, 'A "Religious Society Under Heaven": John Wesley and the Identity of Methodism', *Journal of British Studies*, 25 (1986): 62–83.

many ways from its order, even if such actions were portrayed as implements of reform.[11] Henry Rack, whose masterly biography of John Wesley presents the most even-handed approach to the apparent paradoxes and contradictions in Wesley's Methodism, still concludes that nearly 'everything about Methodism contradicted and cut across the existing Anglican system and seemed, if anything, to be an implicit, if not explicit, challenge to it and criticism of it'.[12] Similar criticisms of Wesley were not uncommon in his own time, coming from fellow clergy, bishops, and even former members of the earliest gathering of Oxford Methodists (e.g. Thomas Adam, rector of Wintringham; Bishops Lavington, Butler, and Warburton; and the former Oxford Methodist John Clayton). Indeed, the frequent tensions that arose around the Wesleys (John in particular) and the early Methodists in their relation to the Church are well rehearsed.[13] Yet the context surrounding his apparently contradictory claims to Anglican allegiance is generally unnoticed, scholars opting instead to address the contradictions themselves and issues of polity as they developed. However, Wesley's Church context is one of the keys to understanding these other issues.

It would be difficult to overestimate the degree to which the spread of religious ideas through publication and preaching during the English Reformation shaped the culture of Anglicanism up to the beginning of the eighteenth century. Following the Elizabethan Settlement, the possibility of holding differing opinions in tension while maintaining unity around a common liturgy (an inclination present in the sixteenth century), was given credence in the formularies of the Church.[14] Although different individuals would have had varying levels of exposure, the late seventeenth and early eighteenth centuries offered the personal and individualized faith of puritanism, the corporate and 'social religion' of Pietism, the spiritualized internal faith of the Moravians, and the moderated religion of Anglicanism (with its range of expressions) as filtered through the Homilies, the Thirty-Nine Articles, and the Book of Common Prayer, and latterly influenced by rationalism and empiricism, among others. Such an array was more accessible to those from families of

---

[11] But compare John Munsey Turner, *Conflict and Reconciliation: Studies in Methodism and Ecumenism in England 1740–1982* (London, 1985).

[12] John Wesley, *The Bicentennial Edition of the Works of John Wesley*, ed. Frank Baker and Richard P. Heitzenrater (Oxford, 1975–83; Nashville, TN, 1984–), 10, p. 17 [hereafter: *Works (BE)*].

[13] Baker, *John Wesley*; Joseph Wood, 'Tensions Between Evangelical Theology and the Established Church: John Wesley's Ecclesiology', PhD thesis, University of Manchester, 2012; Gregory, '"In the Church"'; Richard P. Heitzenrater, *Mirror and Memory: Reflections on Early Methodism* (Nashville, TN, 1989); Albert Brown-Lawson, *John Wesley and the Anglican Evangelicals of the Eighteenth Century* (Edinburgh, 1994); W. M. Jacob, 'John Wesley and the Church of England', *Bulletin of the John Rylands University Library of Manchester*, 85 (2003): 57–71.

[14] Cf. Christopher Marsh, 'Piety and Persuasion in Elizabethan England: The Church of England Meets the Family of Love', in Tyacke (ed.), *England's Long Reformation*, pp. 141–66, esp. pp. 159–61.

the clergy or those educated at the two universities, where they were exposed to the rising influence of empiricism, which celebrated the value of the integration of observable data into 'common sense'.[15]

In such a context, a modicum of eclecticism, for which John Wesley is often castigated, might be expected. Even if such eclecticism was uncommon, it was nevertheless formative for his conception of the Church and Methodism. As Gregory has pointed out, John Wesley's seemingly ambiguous religious affiliation or inconsistency ought to be seen in the light of this 'rich and varied inheritance he had in religious matters'.[16] Two factors (at least) made Charles and John Wesley's inheritance more abundant than that of some of their contemporaries.

Firstly, as is well known, a key aspect of their father's (Samuel Wesley, c.1662–1735) influence was a High Church emphasis on primitive Christianity,[17] a focus broadly shared within Anglicanism of the period.[18] Samuel, the son of a Nonconformist minister who was ejected in 1662, left Dissent for the Church of England as a young adult and after education at Oxford became the rector of Epworth in Lincolnshire, where John and Charles were born. Secondly, the systematic education they received from their mother, Susanna (1669–1742), provided not only a discipline that quite evidently shaped the highly organized scaffolding of Wesleyan Methodism, but also a legacy of borrowing ideas, not least Lockean ideas.[19] Susanna was the daughter of a puritan Nonconformist minister, Samuel Annesley, although she left nonconformity for the Church of England as a teenager after thoughtful consideration and comparison.[20] Not surprisingly, Charles and John were voracious readers, and John in particular had a keen ability to digest what he read and to assimilate a wide body of ideas into his personal understanding. His notable ability in this regard sometimes caused him to overestimate the capacity of his Methodist preachers and his broader constituency—including Anglican clergy—to do the same.[21] This parental and historical legacy fostered a practical approach to Christianity and ministerial practice that sprang from a deep well of Christian thought. The Wesleys were aware of historical revivals, which prompted a general optimism

---

[15] See Rack, *Reasonable Enthusiast*, pp. 47–53.

[16] Gregory, '"In the Church"', p. 159.

[17] Cf. Geordan Hammond, *John Wesley in America: Restoring Primitive Christianity* (Oxford, 2014), pp. 14–16.

[18] W. M. Jacob, *Lay People and Religion in the Early Eighteenth Century* (Cambridge, 1996); cf. David Manning, '"That is best, which was first": Christian Primitivism and the Reformation Church of England, 1548–1722', *Reformation & Renaissance Review*, 13 (2011): 153–93.

[19] Charles Wallace Jr (ed.), *Susanna Wesley: The Complete Writings* (Oxford, 1997), pp. 367–73; Dreyer, 'Faith and Experience'.

[20] Wallace (ed.), *Susanna Wesley*, pp. 367–73.

[21] On the books Wesley recommended and provided for Kingswood, see A. G. Ives, *Kingswood School in Wesley's Day and Since* (London, 1970); for his opinion of the limited learning experienced by those at the universities, see *Works (BE)*, 21, p. 248.

regarding the possibility of revival of true Christianity in the present age,[22] and John Wesley considered this to be eminently possible under the auspices of the Established Church, 'nearer the scriptural plan than any other in Europe'.[23]

John Wesley's view of the kind of reform and revival that was possible was shaped not only by history but by contemporary trends. Samuel had been part of the Anglican religious societies first formed in the 1670s under the leadership of the Church of England clergyman Anthony Horneck (1641–97). Horneck, preacher at the Savoy Chapel, advocated the founding of societies of Christians (led by their minister) in order 'to quicken each others [*sic*] Affection towards Spiritual things, and to advance their Preparations for another World...to live in all respects as it becometh the Gospel'.[24] Beside the innovation of the religious societies themselves, Horneck's particular trademark was the drawing up of 'rules' or 'regulations' for the systematic conduct of the meetings in order to achieve their purpose.[25] The early religious societies, as Eamon Duffy has observed, 'were an attempt to translate the ideal of "primitive Christianity" into a practical, above all, an [A]nglican reality'.[26] And, as Daniel Brunner has pointed out, these societies had both liturgical and experiential elements, as well as an 'intense and private devotion' which 'aroused considerable suspicion among the dignitaries of the Church'[27]— similar to the contestations over Wesley's societies sixty years later. John's own sense of identity is most observable in his 'interaction with others', where it appears that his 'highs came through contact with others rather than through inward soul-searching'.[28] This might have simply been a personality trait, but even so, the need for 'social prayer' and 'social religion' was nurtured in this revivalist movement. Wesley made a point of explaining 'that Christianity is essentially a social religion, and that to turn it into a solitary one is to destroy it'.[29] His main point was that the call of the gospel is to let one's 'light shine before men' and that reclusive religion obscured that light.

---

[22] Randy L. Maddox, 'John Wesley—Practical Theologian?', *Wesleyan Theological Journal*, 23 (1988): 122–47; cf. *Works (BE)*, 9, p. 310.

[23] John Wesley, *The Letters of John Wesley*, ed. John Telford, 8 vols. (London, 1931), VII, p. 28 [hereafter: *Letters*]; cf. *Works (BE)*, 9, pp. 340–1.

[24] Josiah Woodward, *An Account of the Rise and Progress of the Religious Societies in the City of London, &c. and of their Endeavours for Reformation of Manners* (3rd edn., London, 1701), p. 32.

[25] F. W. B. Bullock, *Voluntary Religious Societies, 1520–1799* (St Leonards, 1963), pp. 128–9.

[26] Eamon Duffy, 'Primitive Christianity Revived: Religious Renewal in Augustan England', in Derek Baker (ed.), *Renaissance and Renewal in Christian History*, Studies in Church History 14 (Oxford, 1977), pp. 287–300.

[27] Daniel L. Brunner, *Halle Pietists in England: Anthony William Boehm and the Society for Promoting Christian Knowledge*, Arbeiten zur Geschichte des Pietismus 29 (Göttingen, 1988), p. 21.

[28] Gregory, '"In the Church"', pp. 150–1.

[29] *Works (BE)*, 1, p. 533; cf. John Wesley, 'Preface', *Hymns and Sacred Poems* (London, 1739), pp. vi–viii.

The influence of his father and his sense that the essence of Christian devotion was missional (discussed later) came together in an age of associationalism of which Wesley took advantage and to which he contributed, drawing simultaneously upon the intellectual and systematic organizational rigour of his mother.[30] It is no surprise, then, that the primary framework within which Wesley sought to reform the Church was that of a network of religious societies.

John Wesley's sanguinity towards Methodism as a leaven within the Church was more than a naïve optimism or myopia of personality or temperament.[31] He and Charles both drew upon their Anglican background, suffused with an emphasis on the primitive Church and informed by examples of revival, most recently displayed in the work of the religious societies, and John, following on from the influence of his father, was influenced as well by his own reading of Horneck's works.[32] The associational culture within early Georgian society was the natural habitat of the social religion that the Wesleys considered central to true Christianity. Given the relative freedom offered by toleration (even if it offered less protection than has sometimes been suggested), if the picture of the eighteenth-century Church was as bleak as later historians would have us believe it seems odd that John Wesley, more prone to exceptional irregularities than his brother, would not have found the most expedient and judicious way of moving as fluidly into nonconformity as his parents had moved out of it. Certainly, his firm attachment to the Church can be explained in part by nurture and in part by political, social, and economic pressures (his early livelihood depended upon his Oxford income). Yet, as his behaviour over the course of more than eighty years demonstrates, he was not much inclined to cede his own will on the basis of any inducement other than the call of God as he understood it. There is undoubtedly merit in the idea that Wesley's affinity for social interaction and connectedness, particularly with his parents and his brother, but with also those he had come to know through religious friendship, probably provided the highest incentive for not leaving the Church. Even so, Wesley exhibited considerable fortitude in overcoming complaints against him, even when doing so risked disaffection from a close relation, as the later debates with Charles indicate.[33]

Two things repeat themselves in the narrative of his leadership of the Methodists. Firstly, John Wesley leant consistently on a call 'to obey God and not man'[34] as a justification for his divergences from Church order; and

---

[30] Cf. Peter Clark, *British Clubs and Societies, 1580–1800: The Origins of an Associational World* (Oxford, 2000); Bullock, *Voluntary Religious Societies*.

[31] *Letters*, VII, pp. 326–7; cf. E. P. Thompson, *The Making of the English Working Class* (New York, 1966).

[32] Hammond, *John Wesley*, pp. 33–4.

[33] Gareth Lloyd, *Charles Wesley and the Struggle for Methodist Identity* (Oxford, 2007).

[34] Cf. Acts 5:29.

secondly, despite his accusers, who viewed him suspiciously if not with complete incredulity, he consistently reasserted his love for the Church of England, whatever his animadversions on flaws in her doctrine or administration. Although later Methodists reinterpreting his attitudes after his death may have seen his statements of allegiance as idiosyncrasies, both he and Charles, when taken at their own word, maintained a genuine affection for the Church. This affection coalesced with the aforementioned aspects of their religious inheritance to foster a concept of the possibility of reform that existed pre-eminently *within* their Anglican faith.

John Wesley did not imagine reform to be a wholesale makeover, but rather an attempt to capitalize on assets present in the primitive ideals of early Christianity already commonly aspired to in the Church. Possibility combined with vocation could produce a sense of urgency and he easily became impatient with himself, with others, or with the process of reform mediated through Methodism. His expectations were not always met, and it was the fire of experimentation with its fits and starts that tempered his frustrations while creating new avenues of possibility. The following section examines this aspect of his thinking and practice.

WESLEY'S EXPERIMENTAL RELIGION, METHODISM, AND THE CHURCH

If Methodism was a possibility, it was also an experiment. It was an experiment in testing the claims of the gospel and thus a missionary endeavour. But it was also (and always, as far as Wesley was concerned), an Anglican endeavour. For all that has been observed regarding Methodism's persistent irregularities that always seemed to imply impending separation from the Church of England, held back only by Wesley's authority, Wesley's experimental approach was an extension of his Anglican heritage, despite moves that made it appear as if his allegiance was only superficial. The question of allegiance and the controversial moves that did in fact actually lead to *de facto* separation have been studied at great length elsewhere.[35] Less attention, however, has been given to the ways in which Wesley conceived that the Church of England provided an ecclesial setting in which his Evangelical ministry could be tested. Whatever Wesley's churchmanship and separatist

---

[35] Cf. note 14; also see John Munsey Turner, *John Wesley: The Evangelical Revival and the Rise of Methodism in England* (Peterborough, 2002), esp. pp. 96–111; A. W. Harrison, *The Separation of Methodism from the Church of England*, Wesley Historical Society Lectures 11 (London, 1945).

tendencies might have been, it remains that Methodism did, for all the apparent opportunities and inducements to leave, arise out of Anglicanism.

Anglicanism itself was eclectic in its foundations, having drawn upon a wide range of ideas from the continental Reformation as well as having its own variety of English divinity. The cloud of witnesses of the Church past and present represented for Wesley a body of experiences that could and should be tested for oneself. Wesley's context was shaped broadly by the empiricism of his day. In addition to the Lockean influence passed on by his mother, by the late 1720s Wesley had read Peter Browne's philosophy (an adaptation of Lockean ideas) at Oxford and abridged it, he was reading Locke in 1732, and he read Browne to his preachers in 1756. As Browne and Locke had, Wesley rejected deductive a priori reasoning, and although he never offered a truly systematic or speculative philosophy he championed experience as the means of certifying truth. Wesley also developed a spiritual empiricism (as did his coadjutor, John Fletcher), which Rack has rightly noted would have been seen by Locke and Browne as a sign of religious enthusiasm.[36]

Yet Wesley prioritized the revelatory witness of Scripture and the testimony of the earliest Christians—the primitive Church—whom he saw as being closer chronologically to Christ himself, and therefore as having more verity.[37] Subsequent to these, he saw the Church of England in which he was bred, and which was able to assimilate the puritan and Dissenting pieties which his parents had maintained after their conversion to Anglicanism, as an 'excellent... church; reformed after the true Scripture model; blessed with the purest doctrine, the most primitive liturgy, the most apostolical form of government'.[38] Even so— and importantly for understanding the apparent changes in Wesley's ideas of the Church and its epistemological authority—these were all only witnesses.[39] Wesley consistently, especially after his conversion experience in May 1738—though there were hints of it earlier—insisted that the key Evangelical doctrine of justification by faith must be tested in the laboratory of experience.[40] The preface to his *Sermons on Several Occasions* is a plain statement of his view: 'I have endeavoured to describe', he wrote, 'the true, the scriptural, experimental religion... it is more especially my desire... to guard those who are just setting their faces toward heaven... from formality, from mere outside religion, which has almost driven heart-religion out of the world'.[41] Salvation came, not only by believing the testimony

[36] Rack, *Reasonable Enthusiast*, pp. 386–7; cf. John Fletcher, *Six Letters on the Spiritual Manifestation of the Son of God* (Leeds, 1791).

[37] John Wesley, *The Works of John Wesley*, ed. Thomas Jackson, 14 vols. (Grand Rapids, MI, [1872 edn.], reprinted 1978), X, p. 484.

[38] *Works (BE)*, 1, p. 694.   [39] Cf. Baker, *John Wesley*, ch. 9.

[40] Randy L. Maddox (ed.), *Aldersgate Reconsidered* (Nashville, TN, 1990).

[41] *Works (BE)*, 1, p. 106.

of Scripture that one could truly become a 'child of God', or through mental assent to right ideas, or by being joined to an 'excellent Church', although these are all helps. Only through a complete reliance upon Christ and an inward change of the 'disposition of the heart' was salvation offered—the experience in the heart of a believer that one's sins are forgiven.[42]

For Wesley, the quest for salvation was intrinsically a missionary enterprise, first to seek after the lost state of one's own soul, and secondly to proclaim it to others. This dual emphasis had come together for him on the Georgia mission, for which he embarked with his brother and two others in 1735 under the auspices of the SPCK and SPG, recording that it was a journey undertaken 'to save our souls, to live wholly to the glory of God'.[43] Wesley and several others had already formed in Oxford a 'little company' of Christians, from the later 1720s, chiefly focused on prayer and learning for the purpose of practical piety. This little group was denominated by outside critics as a 'Holy Club', but developed under his leadership over the course of the next several years. A significant portion of the reading of this small company of 'Methodists', a term newly associated with them, was from the Fathers of the early Church. Geordan Hammond's important book expounds the way in which the Georgia mission was actually an experiment in reviving primitive Christianity in that John Wesley considered the pristine wilderness of the Georgia colony the best laboratory for applying the concerns of the earliest Christians to the mission of the Church there. Although the results of his mission were mixed, it was an incubator for his developing ecclesiology and subsequent experiments.[44]

Wesley thought of himself as somewhat independent as a missionary, appointed to the parish church in Savannah, but his connections with religious missionary societies should not be overlooked, for they were a part of the Anglican ethos that had shaped his understanding of voluntary societies. In particular, he could not have missed the organizational capacity of Thomas Bray, which, in a more limited but not dissimilar way as Wesley's Methodism, aimed 'to carry out missionary work and reinvigorate the work at home' through the means of Christian educational efforts in the parishes. This point, made by Craig Rose, emphasizes that Dissenters had already been drawing upon the voluntary nature of religious affiliation, particularly follow-ing the Toleration Act, and that Bray made the same point in his rationale for the forming of his own societies 'in order to promote the pure and primitive Christianity which we profess'.[45] Wesley, like his SPG and SPCK forebears, saw in Anglicanism the same potential for drawing on the practical piety and reasonableness of Christian faith represented by the Established Church, while

---

[42] *Works (BE)*, 1, pp. 120–1.   [43] *Works (BE)*, 18, pp. 136–7.

[44] Hammond, *John Wesley*.

[45] Craig Rose, 'The Origins of the SPCK 1699–1716', in Walsh et al. (eds.), *Church of England*, pp. 172–90 (p. 179).

adopting whatever methods experience indicated would be most useful for ushering in revival. Samuel Wesley, well acquainted with both, made a similar argument for the proliferation of Anglican religious societies designed to increase true piety.[46]

Wesley, for all the nurture he received as a child, only came latterly to what he considered saving faith. It was upon his return to England following his Georgia mission that he met the Moravian Peter Böhler, who, when Wesley thought that perhaps he should stop preaching because of his lack of faith, said to him: 'Preach faith *till* you have it, and then, *because* you have it, you *will* preach faith.' So began a new chapter in experimenting, as Wesley embarked again on itinerant preaching. Only a month later, in the home of a Mr Fox who had a society in Oxford, Wesley felt that his 'heart was so full' that he could not 'confine myself to the forms of prayer'. It was another key moment, for after praying extempore and finding it suitable, he resolved to pray either with or without forms of prayer, which would become a Methodist 'irregularity'. A month after that, Wesley was in the presence of two who shared their 'experiences . . . that God *can* (at least if he *does* not always) give that faith whereof cometh salvation in a moment'. Wesley's famous conversion at Aldersgate came later that month, on 24 May 1738.[47]

As Wesley had experienced, the shared experiences of others offered a means of grace not necessarily present in the forms of the Church outside the religious societies, and he was keen to establish societies as testing grounds for experimental religion. It should be noted that according to the empiricism of the day and common usage, 'experience' could be used to denote inward feeling, as Wesley certainly did, but even more commonly it referred to knowledge that comes by practice. Likewise, an 'experiencer' was '[o]ne who makes trials; a practiser of experiments'.[48] Wesley was eager to provide for what had been lacking in his own practice of religion, a place that not only affirmed that one could have an inward experience of God's saving work, but that provided a place to share and compare experiences. Wesley's idea was not original and clearly had knowledge of, if not direct links with, the Anglican religious societies of his father as well as with the SPCK and SPG, all of which were meant to be submitted to the authority of the Church of England. Wesley's aim, as Walsh has stated, was to offer in his societies 'what contemporary Anglicanism [otherwise] did not . . . a close-knit "Fellowship of Christian Brotherhood"'. Whatever clergymen assumed, the familiar forms of public liturgical worship, coupled with closet devotions, were not enough for some

---

[46] Samuel Wesley, 'A Letter Concerning the Religious Societies', in *The Pious Communicant Rightly Prepar'd* (London, 1700), unpaginated.

[47] *Works (BE)*, 18, pp. 228–36; cf. Maddox (ed.), *Aldersgate*.

[48] Samuel Johnson, *A Dictionary of the English Language*, 2 vols. (London, 1755), I, unpaginated.

sin-sick souls in search of spiritual growth and collective moral support.[49] Similarly, Brunner comments that the rise of the early religious societies was indicative of devotional needs of the laity that went beyond the 'formal, prescriptive ordinances of the Church . . . the Liturgy and Sacraments'.[50]

The experiment with societies expanded, and one of the differences between these and the earlier societies of Horneck and others was that they were not under the control or supervision of local clergy but under Wesley's direct authority. Wesley had a personal interest in managing the societies, which he 'united' in 1744 as a connexion, an offence in itself because it operated outside diocesan control, but also because it was a means of introducing other irregularities in the parishes of the local clergy, such as field preaching and extempore prayer. In addition, Wesley, on the basis of an experiment prompted by his mother,[51] approved lay preaching in his societies, a further offence to the clergy. Despite his early High Church views, Wesley increasingly became latitudinarian in his views of Church order and ecclesiology more generally, largely as a result of his experiences. If the methods produced the fruit of revival, and if they were either supported by, or at least not condemned by the testimony of Scripture, then they were worth using even if they flouted the canons of the Church.

The novelty of Methodist ways had certain advantages.[52] When Wesley and Whitefield first preached in the open air, the success they experienced offered experimental evidence that Providence had prompted the irregularity.[53] Similar experimental successes that seemed to prove the expediency of the gospel was more important than polity occurred in parish ministries too. John Fletcher, vicar of Madeley, together with Thomas Hatton, rector of a neighbouring parish, took to preaching outdoors in one of the Shropshire coal-mining villages with great results. 'If I had to do it again', Fletcher wrote, 'I would do it tomorrow.'[54] Wesley, as the movement's leader, chief traveller, and correspondent, well connected socially and politically, was better placed than the lonely circuit rider or resident society member to see these fruits. But he was not unaware that, while some of the fruit he saw might have come to maturity in his time, the seeds of revival had been planted by faithful Anglican

---

[49] John Walsh, 'Religious Societies: Methodist and Evangelical, 1738–1800', in W. J. Sheils and Diana Wood (eds.), *Voluntary Religion*, Studies in Church History 23 (Oxford, 1986), pp. 279–302 (p. 281).

[50] Brunner, *Halle Pietists in England*, p. 203.

[51] See Rack, *Reasonable Enthusiast*, pp. 210–11.

[52] D. Bruce Hindmarsh, *The Evangelical Conversion Narrative: Spiritual Autobiography in Early Modern England* (Oxford, 2005), pp. 135–6.

[53] J. Gillies (ed.), *Memoirs of the Life of the Reverend George Whitefield*, 7 vols. (London, 1772), VII, pp. 36–8; *Works (BE)*, 19, pp. 46–7; Rack, *Reasonable Enthusiast*, pp. 193–4.

[54] John Fletcher to Charles Wesley, 10 May 1765, Fletcher Volume Folios [hereafter: Fl.], 1: 65, Methodist Archives and Research Centre, John Rylands Library, Manchester [hereafter: MARC].

clergy. Similarly, William Grimshaw of Haworth managed his own societies in coordination with Wesley, and itinerated around his and surrounding parishes.[55] In a particularly ironic instance, in 1742 John Wesley preached in his father's former parish at Epworth, drawing a large crowd and apparently exhorting them for three hours. 'O let none think his labour of love is lost', he wrote in his journal, 'because the fruit does not immediately appear. Near forty years did my father labour here. But he saw little fruit of all his labour . . . But now the fruit appeared . . . the seed sown so long since now sprung up.'[56] As Wesley, perhaps more than anyone, would have been aware, this was the case for many of his Methodists. In a number of the conversion narratives collected by him and his brother, Methodism became a place of conversion or religious expression, but for many, their conversions came after a life in the parish church under faithful preaching.[57]

The story of Wesley's preachers desiring to serve the sacraments and his prohibition of this for a time until it could not be contained in certain parishes has been well studied, as has his ordination of preachers for America and subsequently for Scotland.[58] These ordinations proved no particular irregularity, given the exceptions of America's unique setting in which the Church had been displaced by war, and the fact that his move for Scotland was of no particular concern to contemporary High Churchmen, whose interest was in the polity of the Church of England. For obvious reasons, these breaches appeared to those outside, and many inside, Methodism as *de facto* separation if not *de jure* schism. This later anachronistic reading has prejudiced some historians against any kind of evolution or slow progression in Wesley's decisions, which were adaptations and experiments to situations in specific contexts rather than a pre-formulated plan to pave the way for a later separatist denomination. There was much more legitimacy than has typically been allowed to John Wesley's claims and Charles Wesley's attempts to minister to a multi-denominational constituency of Methodists while keeping the leadership of the Wesleyan Arminian part of the movement in faithful loyalty to the liturgy and canons of the Church. This has often been glossed over by references to John Wesley's irregularities, to impatient Methodist preachers (who, having neither ordination nor benefice, saw themselves as gospel reformers and thus pushed for authority to perform duties reserved for clergy), and to an overarching narrative that begins with a critique of the

---

[55] J. W. Laycock (ed.), *Methodist Heroes in the Great Haworth Round 1734-1784* (Keighley, 1909).

[56] *Works (BE)*, 19, p. 277.

[57] Hindmarsh, *Evangelical Conversion Narrative*, pp. 136–7; see MS Conversion Narratives: Early Methodist Volume (chiefly letters to Charles Wesley), *c*.1738–88, MARC.

[58] See Rack, *Reasonable Enthusiast*, pp. 230–1, 512–16; Russell E. Richey, 'Methodism in North America', in Charles Yrigoyen Jr (ed.), *T&T Clark Companion to Methodism* (London, 2010), pp. 89–111; Baker, *John Wesley*, pp. 254–81.

Church of England in the early eighteenth century as underserved, slothful, sometimes corrupt, and beyond hope of internal reform. Certainly, such criticisms occasionally came from John Wesley himself as well as from some of his revivalist contemporaries, both Anglican and Dissenting, but these must be viewed in context, in terms of the rhetorical function which critiques performed rather than the naïve assumption that critics of the Church simply related the facts.

The struggle to maintain pro-Anglican sentiment and practice amongst the Methodists was even more challenging in North America, where many gatherings of Methodists were interdenominational from their inception, having been built on the footings supplied by the work of Pietist revivalists like Otterbein and Boehm and having drawn from various religious groups, Anglican and Dissenting.[59] Furthermore, as Methodist leaders (and their constituents, apparently) complained, strictures upon the preachers preventing them from engaging in the full duties of the pastoral office, themselves unbeneficed, and the lack of a resident bishop to ordain or to implement parochial reform in the colonies, created an anxiety which Wesley had limited ability to ease. Despite what felt like 'extraordinary' circumstances (a term he sometimes used to bypass Anglican regularities), Wesley as well as many of his Anglican clerical colleagues were sternly resistant to the administering of the sacraments by any but clergy ordained in the Church. Where the irregularity of field preaching, itinerancy, and revival meetings fitted the missional landscape of the North American colonies and frontier, with its scatterings of Dissenting churches and Anglican parish churches, it was more difficult for Methodist leaders there to understand why similar exception could not be made for the use of the liturgy and particularly the sacraments. Wesley's answer of providing an edition of the Anglican liturgy and Articles as a sort of last measure was not enough to draw Francis Asbury (1745–1816) or his preachers back into a relationship that was neither desired nor particularly expedient.[60]

While there is plenty of evidence to show that Wesley was more optimistic regarding the role the Church of England could play in the revival than some of his preachers came to be,[61] and that there were quarters of the Church where his Evangelical irregularities and ostensible usurpation of authority provoked a welter of thoughtful as well as rash criticisms, his repeatedly stated priority was the task of Methodism '[t]o reform the nation, and in particular the Church'. Missionary enterprise implied entering 'foreign' territory, taking 'foreign' ideas, and it required 'extraordinary' measures. This was especially

---

[59] Richey, 'Methodism in North America'; Rowan Strong, *Anglicanism and the British Empire, c.1700–1850* (Oxford, 2007), pp. 81–3.

[60] Cf. Maddox, 'John Wesley'.

[61] See Rupert Davies, 'An Introductory Comment', and John Wesley, 'Reasons against a Separation from the Church of England', in *Works (BE)*, 9, pp. 332–3, 334–49 respectively.

true of America, where the circumstances, culture, and needs were indeed foreign and proved to require more nuance than the same Anglican–Methodist meld he tried to hold together in England. The events of the later 1780s, in which Asbury and Thomas Coke (1747–1814) and the Methodists in America separated into the Methodist Episcopal Church, proved more than Wesley could tolerate, but his displeasure was not enough to motivate them to recant. Ironically, when Asbury was ordained in America for the burgeoning denomination, Thomas Coke drew upon the primitive Church to defend the move. Even so, the organizational structure of American Methodism after separation reflected in its expansion to the frontier the inheritance of a missionary impetus, adapted the plan of itinerancy, and adopted Wesley's 'world is my parish' claim to develop itself as 'a church without boundaries'.[62] The pedigree of that missionary impulse is as eclectic as Wesley's own heritage, but there can be little doubt that his own early experience with missionary societies[63] and his missionary contacts with the Moravians were significant in the lineage.

Wesley's homeland had a 'foreign-ness' to the gospel as well and was thus missionary territory in a figurative sense. His occasional criticisms of the backwardness of the people were not the exceptional claims of an Evangelical fanatic, for such criticisms were shared by many clergy across England, like those who complained of the ignorance of basic Christian beliefs among their parishioners and embarked on their own initiatives to educate their parishes.[64] Indeed, these educational initiatives, missional in mindset and Anglican in origin, provided a significant body of evidence regarding the means which might effectively be used to reform the nation. If the cooperative relationship which Wesley expected to be possible between his Methodists and local parish ministries required more fortitude and commitment to mutual well-being than either party could muster, there were a variety of factors that contributed to the tension. Only some of his preachers seemed to be able vicariously to channel his Anglican allegiance, and sometimes they took umbrage at local clergy even before any offence had been committed. As early as 1753, Wesley had to urge his preachers at Conference to 'converse more with the clergy', and to avoid talking 'of persecution before it comes', a hint that Methodists could provoke hostility.[65] And he had to remind them periodically not to speak ill of

---

[62] See Russell E. Richey, *Methodism in the American Forest* (Oxford, 2015), pp. 90–2.

[63] On the missionary nature of these societies, see Brunner, *Halle Pietists in England*, esp. pp. 23–8, 101–19, 154–76; Hammond, *John Wesley*, pp. 44, 75, 110, 149; but see also Rack's note on the multiple motivations of the SPG and mission: *Reasonable Enthusiast*, p. 117.

[64] Gregory, 'The Eighteenth-Century Reformation', pp. 70–1, 75; cf. Jeremy Gregory, *Restoration, Reformation and Reform, 1660–1828: Archbishops of Canterbury and their Diocese* (Oxford, 2000), pp. 235–54; W. M. Jacob, *The Clerical Profession in the Long Eighteenth Century, 1680–1840* (Oxford, 2007), pp. 236–67.

[65] *Works (BE)*, 10, pp. 158–9.

the body of clergy. This could seem hypocritical when compared with his own complaints about opposition, yet it should be seen in the broader context of religious discourse, rather than as representing his general view of the establishment whose preaching and liturgy he often praised.[66] It also appears that Wesley had a higher tolerance level for dissonance between ideals and the practical concerns of Methodism, and his own actions were often the cause of bewilderment for others.

Because of the experimental nature of the movement, which relied upon adaptation rather than long-term planning, what its ideal might have been in Wesley's mind is a matter of inference. In particular, the marriage of the parish and the societies perhaps required more resources than were commonly available. Just as his Savannah parish of 'above two hundred miles' was too much for 'the labour of one man',[67] so some English parishes proved more than even diligent clergy could manage.[68] However, there were exceptions, and the next section looks at how Anglican and Methodist collaboration actually did become a reality.

CHURCH, METHODISM, AND CHURCH EXTENSION

How Methodism was supposed to function in tandem with the work of the Church has been a perennial question since Methodism first began. Yet for all of the challenges to maintaining a genuinely pro-Methodist Anglicanism (or pro-Anglican Methodism), there were a number of ways and places in which this did occur. In Bristol, for example, largely under the influence of Charles Wesley, Methodists reported sitting under Methodist preaching while continuing to receive the sacrament and attend services at their parish churches.[69] In addition, there were parishes where the relationship between the Church and Methodism ebbed and flowed, depending on the attitude and dutifulness of the incumbent as well as on affection (or disaffection) towards him.[70] It should also be noted that there were places where the Methodist people identified themselves with the Church even if the incumbent or fellow parishioners saw their participation in Methodist meetings as a form of Dissent.[71]

---

[66] E.g. *Letters*, VI, pp. 326–7.   [67] *Works (BE)*, 25, p. 474.

[68] Cf. Michael F. Snape, *The Church of England in Industrialising Society: The Lancashire Parish of Whalley in the Eighteenth Century* (Woodbridge, 2003), pp. 172–3.

[69] Jonathan Barry and Kenneth Morgan (eds.), *Reformation and Revival in Eighteenth-Century Bristol* (Bristol, 1994).

[70] Gregory, *Restoration, Reformation and Reform*, p. 229.

[71] Françoise Deconinck-Brossard, '"We live so far North": The Church in the North-East of England', in Gregory and Chamberlain (eds.), *The National Church*, pp. 233–42 (p. 238); Gregory, *Restoration, Reformation and Reform*, p. 227.

The Church had its own ideals of pastoral care, propagated in clergy manuals, in bishops' and archdeacons' visitation sermons and charges, and through clerical societies for mutual edification.[72]

The parish ideal for pastoral care was full duty in preaching (i.e. twice on Sundays), catechizing children in the parish (usually during Lent), reading prayers in church, observing fast days, and administering communion at least three times a year.[73] In addition, sufficient accommodation should be provided for all the parishioners to attend church and the building kept in good repair. Wesley's Methodism also had as its ideal that the gospel ministry would be supported by itinerant preachers (appointed by Wesley, or later, Conference), and that Methodist societies would be maintained, preferably with the full range of bands and class meetings, and ultimately that parish clergy would welcome Wesley and allow him to maintain authority over the societies in his connexion, although this latter expectation was cause for suspicion and at least a little resistance even amongst sympathetic Evangelical clergy like Samuel Walker of Truro and (as will be shown in the following) John Fletcher of Madeley. This section presents an instance in which these two ideals confronted one another.

Given Wesley's insistence that Methodism was conducive to Anglican religion, it is worth asking to what extent Methodism appears to have actually supported or extended the ministry of the Church: in what way was it actually a ministry of 'Church extension'? This is an attempt to reframe what has commonly been considered a practical rift between 'church' religion, institutionalized and unable by definition to be seen in any way as 'popular religion', and the 'chapel' religion of the early Methodists, adaptable, flexible, and more akin to Dissent, and generally uninterested in the Church's parochial concerns.[74] Recent research at the diocesan and parish level has revealed that religious participation was, in fact, much more fluid. As W. M. Jacob has observed, '[t]here is evidence that the relationship was often relaxed and that the boundary between the church and dissent was porous...Many dissenters attended their parish churches from time to time and...some Anglicans attended dissenting meeting houses.'[75] There were clearly parts of England where a lack of attention to duty by parochial clergy meant that

---

[72] Cf. Anon., 'A Society of Ministers of the Gospel in the Church of England', *Proceedings of the Wesley Historical Society*, 22 (1939–40): 52–7; John H. Pratt (ed.), *Eclectic Notes: or, Notes of Discussions on Religious Topics at the Meetings of the Eclectic Society, London, during the Years 1798–1814* (London, 1865 edn.); John Walsh, 'The Yorkshire Evangelicals in the Eighteenth Century', PhD thesis, University of Cambridge, 1956; Bullock, *Voluntary Religious Societies*, pp. 238–40.

[73] Cf. Rack, *Reasonable Enthusiast*, p. 16.

[74] A. D. Gilbert, *Religion and Society in Industrial England: Church, Chapel and Social Change 1740–1914* (London, 1976), pp. 8, 69.

[75] Jacob, *Lay People*, p. 6.

Methodism took on more of an ecclesial role, but there were many other instances where the relationship was negotiated with support of the parish church as a priority. It is difficult to generalize, for the boundaries were being negotiated throughout the century. To look at the situation from an Anglican starting point, Methodism often appears as part innovation, part adaptation, and part reliance upon traditional structures that could often be taken for granted. Complaint and conflict often ring loudest in historical accounts, but there is evidence of a quieter, more collaborative attitude in some quarters of a Church that was still reforming. These reforms took on different shapes, but a few examples highlight not only the variations but also the creative and industrious potential that existed within Anglicanism.

One of the most interesting cases of Church–Methodist relations during the eighteenth century is to be found in the parish of Madeley, Shropshire. At the heart of early industrializing England, Madeley presented most of the challenges to pastoral ministry to which the Church was supposedly unable to respond, yet it provided one of the clearest demonstrations of the way in which Methodism could serve as an augmentation of the ministry of the Church.[76] In 1760, John Fletcher, a Swiss émigré and acquaintance of John and Charles Wesley who experienced Evangelical conversion under their influence, was ordained three years previous to his induction as vicar of Madeley, where he served from 1760 until his death in 1785. He was closer to Charles Wesley, but was considered for a time by John Wesley to be the best choice to take over leadership of the Methodists, though Fletcher refused in favour of his parish ministry. Fletcher was married to the celebrated Mary Bosanquet (1739–1815), who in the 1770s had become the first woman preacher authorized by John Wesley to preach in his societies. Following her husband's death, she continued in the parish and expanded the ministry there.

Madeley had a single parish church (St Michael's), but no chapels of ease to serve the villages. Most of the two thousand inhabitants in 1760 lived in villages two to three miles from the church. This meant that there was a need for creative ministry to bring the cure of souls to parishioners. The old church, a Norman building seating six hundred, could accommodate just over half of the parish in two services. By 1815 the population had grown to over five thousand, presenting the church with a considerable challenge in providing for the parish's spiritual needs.

Church attendance was sparse when Fletcher arrived in 1760. Only about 160 people attended his first sermon and half as many attended his second. Yet only a month later he wrote to Charles Wesley that he had preached the gospel and that the seats of his church were now full.[77] From that point, attendance

---

[76] David R. Wilson, *Church and Chapel in Industrializing Society: Anglican Ministry and Methodism in Shropshire, 1760–1785* (New York, 2016).

[77] John Fletcher to Lady Huntingdon, 19 Nov. 1760, Fl. 2: 63–5.

generally remained high, so he began regularly preaching on Sunday evenings. After the morning service he catechized the children and any others who wished to attend, and the afternoon service followed. Subsequently, he instituted Friday evening lectures, which drew many more parishioners than he had anticipated: 'The number of hearers at that time,' he wrote, 'is generally larger than that which my predecessor had on a Sunday.'[78] In addition to daily prayers, Wednesdays (and some Fridays) were kept as fast days. Communion was administered monthly and on three feast days, thus surpassing the canonical minimum. Fletcher died in August 1785, conducting his full duty, including the administration of communion, on the Sunday before his death.[79] Fletcher vigorously performed his pastoral duty as an Anglican priest, but his exposure to the Methodists, as well as to the practice of forming religious societies for spiritual edification earlier in his life, prompted him to supplement his efforts.[80] This is the point at which Fletcher's Methodism joined with his Anglican identity to extend his ministry, demonstrating the Church's ability to adopt a more flexible approach to meeting the religious needs of the populace.

The Anglican ideal of pastoral care also had an administrative element, rooted in the medieval system of parishes seen as units 'of ecclesiastical administration and pastoral care ... large enough in population and resources to support a church and its priest, and yet small enough for its parishioners to gather at its focal church'.[81] This ideal has informed studies of church extension which have typically focused primarily upon church-building activity by the establishment. The term 'church extension' seems to have originated in the last decade of the eighteenth century.[82] The obvious association of the term might be with Thomas Chalmers, clergyman of the Church of Scotland, who chaired that Church's Committee for Church Extension and published numerous treatises on the subject, epitomizing the nineteenth-century critique of the Hanoverian Church for failing to reform itself in the light of an expanding population and changing demographic needs of industrial society by extending its reach via church-building.[83] This line of argument was taken up more recently by Peter Virgin, who asserted that it was 'just as well' that the masses did not 'show any great enthusiasm for the services of the Church of

---

[78] John Fletcher to Lady Huntingdon, 6 Jan. 1761, Fl. 2: 67–71.

[79] Anonymous Eulogies on John Fletcher, Fletcher-Tooth Collection, MAM Fl. 19/5/2, MARC.

[80] John Fletcher to Charles Wesley, 10 May 1757, Fl. 1: 65.

[81] N. J. G. Pounds, *A History of the English Parish: The Culture of Religion from Augustine to Victoria* (Cambridge, 2000), p. 3.

[82] See Robert Phillimore, *The Ecclesiastical Law of the Church of England* (London, 1895), pp. 1638–748.

[83] Thomas Chalmers, *The Christian and Civic Economy of Large Towns* (Glasgow, 1821), p. 129; D. King (ed.), *Two Lectures, in Reply to the Speeches of Dr Chalmers on Church Extension* (Glasgow, 1839).

England . . . [as] there would have been nowhere to put them', for this was one of the issues left 'largely untouched' until such reforms as the Church Building Act of 1818.[84] Alan Gilbert's conclusions that the established Church lost ground, largely to the chapel religion of new Dissent and Methodism, rely partially on this critique: 'Little was done between the reign of Queen Anne and the second quarter of the nineteenth century to enlarge the Church of England as a religious service organisation . . . The facilities at its disposal, measured in terms of personnel or in terms of accommodation for religious worship, increased only marginally, if at all.'[85]

The problems of a lack of accommodation and of unwieldy and expansive parishes in need of reform were real. However, as Arthur Burns has illustrated in his analysis of diocesan reform in the nineteenth century, critiques by historians of the lack of systematic reform before the Tractarians have overlooked the fact that throughout the eighteenth century reform was taking place at various levels, from the diocese to the parish itself.[86] One example is to be found in Mark Smith's examination of Anglican chapel-building and pastoral activity in Oldham and Saddleworth, in which he concluded that the 'Unreformed' establishment's 'failure to subdivide . . . may have helped to create a culture of church extension' as a foundation on which the nineteenth-century 'Reformed' establishment could build.[87] His conclusions are much more optimistic than the conventional view, asserting the Church's ability to rise 'to the challenge of its new circumstances with surprising vigour and imagination'.[88]

It was similar vigour and imagination which energized the Fletchers' efforts to extend the Church's reach. In Madeley, evidence for church extension is elusive if we think in terms of subdividing parishes or building new churches. There were other means, primarily represented in the realm of pastoral care. The fact that a new church was not built in Madeley until the 1790s hardly indicated that the Church was in decline or neglected. Rather, the situation prompted, and was met by, considerable pastoral vitality, augmenting both the range and effectiveness of the Church. Indeed, to look only to numbers of church buildings erected as a measure of the effectiveness of its outreach is to underestimate the creativity of local clergy in meeting parochial needs in spite of limited accommodation.

---

[84] Peter Virgin, *The Church in an Age of Negligence: Ecclesiastical Structure and Problems of Church Reform 1700–1840* (Cambridge, 1989), pp. 3, 5, 143.

[85] Gilbert, *Religion and Society*, pp. 27–8; cf. G. F. A. Best, *Temporal Pillars: Queen Anne's Bounty, the Ecclesiastical Commissioners, and the Church of England* (Cambridge, 1964), pp. 193–6.

[86] Arthur Burns, *The Diocesan Revival in the Church of England, c.1800–1870* (Oxford, 1999), pp. 16–17, 41–3, 76–8.

[87] Mark Smith, *Religion in Industrial Society: Oldham and Saddleworth, 1740–1865* (Oxford, 1994), pp. 41–2.

[88] Smith, *Religion*, p. 34.

Church extension in Madeley was accretive, building upon the canonically prescribed duties as opportunity presented or demanded, and then moving beyond the minimum. One of Fletcher's curates wrote: 'As often as a small congregation could be collected, which was usually every evening, [Fletcher] joyfully proclaimed to them the acceptable year of the Lord.'[89] Even though neither Wesley nor his preachers had spent any time in Madeley up to that point, Fletcher's association with Wesley was well known and it did not take long for his parishioners to associate Fletcher's zeal and evangelical doctrines with Methodism.[90] Already in November 1760, he wrote that parishioners had begun to call his 'meeting'—the Sunday church service—a 'Methodist one, I mean the Church'.[91]

In addition, Fletcher began holding Monday night services to counter the temptation to his coal-mining and iron-working parishioners to take their earnings to the alehouse on payday.[92] Fletcher seems to have overcome the considerable obstacles presented by industrialization, which, as Mather has shown, in some areas could only be 'solved by substituting informal evening gatherings—cottage lectures, schoolroom services and class meetings—for the regular worship of the parish church'.[93] When there were those who would not come to his church, Fletcher went to them: 'I preach every morning', he explained, 'to the colliers of Madeley Wood, a place that can vie with Kingswood for wildness.'[94]

Thus the first phase of church extension was represented by Fletcher's reputedly 'Methodist' zeal for declaring the gospel at every opportunity and in every place, that all would come to saving faith and worship God in 'spirit and in truth'.[95] This, however, raises the question: if every person was to attend divine worship, but the church would only contain half the parish in two services, how was this to be accomplished? The next phase required some innovation, albeit concordant with the long English tradition of gathering believers together into religious societies (outlined earlier).[96] Fletcher's answer to the need for accommodation was to look for the opportunity to take the

---

[89] Joshua Gilpin, *Short Account of the Life and Death of Rev. John Fletcher, Vicar of Madeley* (New York, 1805), pp. 185–6.

[90] John Fletcher to Charles Wesley, 12 Oct. 1761, Fl. 1: 84.

[91] John Fletcher to Lady Huntingdon, 19 Nov. 1760, Fl. 2: 4.

[92] *Works (BE)*, 21, p. 481; Barrie Trinder, *The Industrial Revolution in Shropshire* (London, 1973), p. 346; cf. E. P. Thompson, 'Time, Work-Discipline, and Industrial Capitalism', *Past & Present*, 38 (1967): 56–97 (pp. 72–5).

[93] F. C. Mather, 'Georgian Churchmanship Reconsidered: Some Variations in Anglican Public Worship 1714–1830', *Journal of Ecclesiastical History*, 36 (1985): 255–83 (pp. 278–9).

[94] John Fletcher to Lady Huntingdon, 10 Sept. 1763, Fl. 2: 9.

[95] John Fletcher, MS sermons, Matt. 25:40–6, Acts 5:42, MAM Fl. 20/14/2.

[96] John Fletcher, *The Nature and Rules of a Religious Society Submitted to the Consideration of the Serious Inhabitants of the Parish of Madeley*, ed. Melvill[e] Horne (Madeley, 1788), pp. 7–10; cf. John Spurr, 'The Church, the Societies, and the Moral Revolution of 1688', in Walsh et al. (eds.), *Church of England*, pp. 127–42.

Church to the people rather than trying to get people to the Church. The first such opportunity came in 1761. 'I have often had a desire,' he wrote, 'to exhort at Madeley Wood & the Dale... the door... is now opening, a little society of about 20 or 30 people has come together... in the 1st of those places, and another of some 20 in the second.'[97] In these meetings he realized the vision of 'social worship' commonly seen among Methodists.[98]

In some ways, the societies in Madeley reflected Wesley's Methodism, but there was an explicitly clerical and Anglican emphasis in Fletcher's societies more reminiscent of the early Anglican religious societies of Horneck and Woodward, of which he was well aware.[99] Fletcher drew up rules for his local societies, borrowing from Wesley's own *Rules*,[100] but amended them to reflect the Anglican nature of his gatherings, citing selections from the Thirty-Nine Articles.[101] As a parish incumbent, Fletcher was wise to indicate clearly that he convened the meetings as part of his clerical duty, noting that they were the means which the 'Church recommends, in the first Exhortation of the Communion Service... Such a Society then, is only a Company of People who... require, as says our Church, farther Counsel and Comfort for the quieting of their awakened Consciences, and meet to consult, read and pray with their Ministers.'[102] Fletcher maintained control of his societies, although from 1764 Wesley's itinerants preached among the Madeley societies regularly and these were thus incorporated into Wesley's connexion.

'Chapel' meetings, Gilbert claimed, were then the stronghold of Dissent or Methodism, the province of 'Extra-Establishment' religion. The establishment, on the other hand, was allegedly incapable of assimilating the currents of Evangelicalism and thus unable to compete in the market situation presented by 'chapel religion'.[103] In Madeley, however, the growth of Evangelical chapel communities was coterminous with the growth of the Church community itself. The societies provided Anglican worship in the local communities. Two met in homes of parishioners, and near the centre of the parish Fletcher built a preaching house at his own expense, where he could teach 'the children... to read and write in the day, and the grown up people might hear the word of God in the evening... and where the serious people might assemble for social worship'.[104] Following his marriage in 1781, he and his wife worked together, and in 1784 they commenced construction of a chapel in Coalbrookdale.

[97] John Fletcher to Charles Wesley, 27 Apr. 1761, Fl. 1: 13.

[98] John Fletcher, *Posthumous Pieces of the Late Rev. John William de la Flechère*, ed. Melvill[e] Horne (Madeley, 1791), pp. 31–3.

[99] Cf. John Fletcher to Lord Gower, undated, MAM Fl. 36/4/6.

[100] Cf. *Works (BE)*, 9, pp. 69–75.

[101] 'Of Works Before Justification', *Book of Common Prayer*.

[102] Fletcher, *Posthumous Pieces*, p. 10.

[103] Gilbert, *Religion and Society*, p. 51.   [104] Fletcher, *Posthumous Pieces*, pp. 31–2.

Between 1760 and 1785, Fletcher's ever-expanding ministry came to encompass all three parts of the parish (i.e. Madeley, Madeley Wood, and Coalbrookdale).

From the mid-1760s a Madeley parishioner would have been hard pressed to complain about a lack of church services or pastoral care. In 1793, Joseph Plymley, archdeacon of Salop (Hereford diocese), visited Madeley as part of an assessment. What impressed him was the pattern of worship: two services on Sundays, prayers on saints' days, and sermons 'twice every week on the evenings of working days in rooms appropriated for that purpose'. He had no scruples about the preaching in unconsecrated buildings established by the Fletchers, observing that it was in 'the most populous part of the parish and at a considerable distance from the Church'.[105] Aware of how the pattern of worship in the parish was established, he praised Fletcher's diligence and zeal. He also noticed a particular ecumenism, and not only among the Church Methodists: 'The people are much attached to their evening preachings, and the Quakers . . . encourage it very much, perceiving the good effects it has upon the Workmen, the persons who attend the meetings frequent the Church on Sundays.'

Nor was church extension diminished after Fletcher's death in 1785. By a series of providences, as she would claim, Mary Fletcher not only stayed in the parish, but was allowed to remain in the vicarage and continue managing the Madeley ministry plan, appointing curates who were amenable to the Methodist–Anglican system already in operation.[106] Under her leadership, the societies increased to four with up to seven meetings a week distributed among them.[107] In 1785 and 1789, she was instrumental in enlarging the Coalbrookdale chapel. In 1788, she had the tithe barn refitted as a preaching house, which came to be known as 'Mrs Fletcher's Room'.[108] When between 1788 and 1797 discussions regarding the poor state of the church fabric led to the demolition of the old church and the erection of a new and more commodious replacement, she opened her preaching rooms as *de facto* chapels of ease. At one point when there was a change of curates, a description was offered to one of the prospective candidates, which is worth quoting at length for the picture it provides of the extensiveness of the church's ministry:

> The constant inspection of 4000 people if you do it . . . will find you constant employment . . . Besides preaching 3 times on Sunday, & 2 every week, saints days

[105] J. Plymley and others, 'Ecclesiastical Notes and Descriptive Accounts of Parishes within the Archdeaconry of Salop', Add. MS 21018, pp. 187–90, British Library.

[106] 'Autobiography of Mrs Fletcher and Her Account of Her Husband', MAM Fl. 23/1; Draft letter of Mary Fletcher to Rev. [Samuel Walter], undated, MAM Fl. 13/1/73; Draft letters of Mary Fletcher to undisclosed recipients, MAM Fl. 13/1/106–7; Henry Moore, *The Life of Mrs Mary Fletcher, Consort and Relict of the Rev. John Fletcher, Vicar of Madeley, Salop*, 2 vols. (Birmingham, 1817), II, pp. 273–4.

[107] E.g. Draft letters of Mary Fletcher to undisclosed recipients, MAM Fl. 13/1/106–7.

[108] Mary Tooth to M. Davies, undated, MAM Fl. 2/9/1.

&c. an extensive & populous country lies round me . . . My Morning congregation on a fine day is between 3 & 600 w[hi]ch is as many as the Church can *conveniently* hold, & in the Evening not more than 200. At Colebrooke Dale at 7 o'Clock I frequently preach to between 2 & 300 & sometimes I have known as many as 400. On the week days however, I am seldom attended by more then 100 either at the Dale, Madeley Wood or Madeley. Near 200 people may be in Society.[109]

When the church was rebuilt, the regular Sunday services were held in rotation at the chapels in the respective villages, meeting in 'Mrs Fletcher's Room' when it was the week to worship in Madeley town. One of Mrs Fletcher's protégés who lived with her in the vicarage wrote that the parishioners were 'so well pleased with the arrangement that they are wishing the building of the Church did not go on so fast they do so well without it', illustrating that church extension should be considered as much at the ideological as at the material level.[110] The new church increased the seating capacity to 1,800. In addition, the chapels, though technically unconsecrated, were considered by both the archdeacon and the bishop as *de facto* Anglican chapels. By 1818 the population of the parish had risen by 253 per cent to 5,070, and the *Account of Benefices and Population* noted an increase in the accommodation of the parish in one church and three chapels—that is, the parish church and the society meeting houses in Coalport, Madeley Wood, and Coalbrookdale.[111]

While the ministerial work of John Fletcher at Madeley was exceptional in the extent to which church and chapel were not only collaborative but also coextensive, there were other examples of diligent pastoral care, preaching, and educational endeavours and a coordinate faithfulness of parishioners in their attendance at their parish churches. For all that Methodism offered in terms of social religion and novelty, parishioners were wont to rely upon the Anglican clergy for provision of pastoral needs. In an example highlighted by Jeremy Gregory, 'At St James', Dover, the rector observed that the Methodists had no meeting house, "and such of them as belong to Mr. Wesley's Society are not only punctual in their attendance at church, and at the sacrament, but in the course of twenty-three years I have often been called to visit them in sickness".'[112]

The picture which is developing from local parish studies[113] suggests that the work of the clergy in extending the reach of the church in the eighteenth century demonstrated considerable energy and creativity in a number of parishes.

---

[109] Melville Horne to Mary Fletcher, 11 Nov. 1791, Melville Horne Papers, PLP 56/9/2, MARC.
[110] Journal of Mary Tooth, MAM Fl. 14/1, p. 95.
[111] T. B. Clarke, *Account of Benefices and Population; Churches, Chapels, and Their Capacity* ([London], 1818), p. 95.
[112] Gregory, *Restoration, Reformation and Reform*, p. 229.
[113] Gregory and Chamberlain (eds.), *The National Church*; Jacob, *Lay Piety*; Gregory, *Restoration, Reformation and Reform*; Arthur Warne, *Church and Society in Eighteenth-Century Devon*

Thus, even though her examination of Oxfordshire in the eighteenth century confirmed the general picture of a church in need of reform, Diana McClatchey still noted: 'Herbert has had his companions in spirit in every age—men who attempted to meet the needs of their parishioners at every level, who scorned no by-way or bridle-path as being too humble a highway to the gates of Heaven... Such men were no monopoly of the nineteenth century.'[114] Walker of Truro and Grimshaw of Haworth were not the only instances of a Methodistic clerical devotion that were rooted in the parishes. An example remarkably similar to Fletcher's work at Madeley can be seen in the ministry of James Creighton (1739–1819). Like John Fletcher, he saw the need to work diligently to keep Methodism in the Church of England while practising some of its irregularities in his own parish as part of an extension strategy. Creighton's success in preaching throughout his parish, in fact, inspired the inhabitants to build a chapel of ease. Furthermore, in the 1780s Creighton established a preaching round in his parish, noting that it was his custom 'to meet [his parishioners] three times every Lord's-day; (not indeed the same congregation, for they could not all conveniently assemble at any one place, the parish being extensive, and the roads bad.) Some of them I met, exhorted, and prayed with early at my own house, or some other house most convenient for them: then I went to the Church; and afterwards returned, read the service and preached in the Chapel in the evening. The week days I spent... in preaching in other parts of the parish.'[115]

To these examples could be added the work of those like Vincent Perronet, John Crosse, Walter Sellon, James Stillingfleet, and Henry Venn, who like to Fletcher, held meetings in their vicarage kitchens.[116] Then there were those who extended their ministry by gathering to encourage their clerical brethren and joining in pulpit exchanges to bring freshness to church services, such as James Brown, Edward Stillingfleet, Edward Davies, and others who joined quarterly in conference at Worcester.[117] If John Wesley, as W. R. Ward has stated, 'not merely created a religious community, but

(Newton Abbot, 1969); Smith, *Religion*; Diana McClatchey, *Oxfordshire Clergy 1777–1869: A Study of the Established Church and the Role of its Clergy in Local Society* (Oxford, 1960).

[114] McClatchey, *Oxfordshire Clergy*, p. 91.

[115] James Creighton, 'A Short Account of the Experience of the Rev. James Creighton', *Arminian Magazine*, 8 (1785), pp. 241–4, 297–302, 354–9, 398–403, at 401; cf. Henry D. Rack, 'Creighton, James', *ODNB*.

[116] William Morgan, *The Parish Priest: Pourtrayed in the Life, Character, and Ministry of the Rev. John Crosse, A.M. late Vicar of Bradford, Yorkshire* (London, 1841), p. 99; Gerald Newman and Leslie E. Brown (eds.), *Britain in the Hanoverian Age* (New York, 1997), p. 732; George Russell, *A Short History of the Evangelical Movement* (London, 1915), pp. 63–4; Mark Smith, 'Crosse, John', *ODNB*; *Works (BE)*, 22, p. 211, n. 10.

[117] Cf. Peter S. Forsaith, 'An Eighteenth Century "Worcester Association"', in Paul Bolitho (ed.), *Silver Jubilee Miscellany, 1965–1990*, West Midlands Branch of the Wesley Historical Society, Occasional Publication 3 (Warwick, [1990]), pp. 44–51.

organised it rationally for purposes of pastoral oversight and evangelism', so these aforementioned evangelical and Methodist-leaning clergy accepted the confines of a pre-existing community formed by the bounds of an English parish and organized their own oversight by adapting what contemporaries considered Methodist impulses (e.g. extempore preaching, open-air preaching, focus on new birth and conversion, invitation of other preachers to their pulpits) to minister in their parishes.

CONCLUSION

It was Wesley's claim that Methodism was to be a spiritual leaven in the Church of England, but it has often been asserted that the establishment was too lethargic to either 'initiate pastoral developments',[118] or to incorporate the strengths of chapel religion. Wesley, however, was more optimistic, believing that the work of God was being revived and that Methodism had the potential to thrive within the Church of England (and beyond). Ecclesiologically, Wesley could see the Church as the body of all Christians and the Church of England as but one instance of the catholic body of believers. Under pressure from without, and prodding from within his movement, the obvious question to his contemporaries as well as to later observers was: 'Why not leave the Church?' It was a question that came up at conferences, in correspondence, and in publications. Wesley's responses always relied upon evidence that suggested that it simply would not be prudent.

Wesleyanism's structure of society, band, and class (and occasionally a select society), watch-nights, love-feasts, quarterly meetings, and circuits of itinerancy ridden by both lay and ordained preachers provided an assisted process of assimilation into Methodist culture for those who experienced conversion as well as for those prompted to consider their own spiritual state.[119] The simple condition for such exploration among the Methodists was 'the desire to flee the wrath to come', and the society offered a place where 'heart religion' could be moderated by a voluntary but bounded community, and experience tested in line with contemporary empiricism.[120] Furthermore, and demonstrating a continuity with the religious societies of the later seventeenth century, individual devotional needs engendered by the regular round of revivalist preachers (as well as evangelistic sermons from Anglican parish

---

[118] Gregory, 'The Eighteenth-Century Reformation', p. 79.

[119] On the Methodist structure and polity, see Wesley's 'Large' Minutes: *Works (BE)*, 10.

[120] Cf. Phyllis Mack, *Heart Religion in the British Enlightenment: Gender and Emotion in Early Methodism* (Cambridge, 2008).

pulpits) could find an outlet in Methodist meetings that the regular liturgical cycle of sermon, sacrament, and daily readings did not offer, meetings which were for Wesley true means of grace and aids to holiness.[121]

Although there were certainly a number of parishes where Evangelicalism in general and Methodism in particular were despised—specifically for their irregularities and infringements—this was not necessarily a sign that church reform was absent. Of course, Wesley's 'one thing needful', 'that inward universal change, that "birth from above"', that was central to Evangelical preaching was absent from many pulpits.[122] Yet Wesley sometimes found even moralistic sermons more profitable 'than . . . what are vulgarly called "gospel sermons"'.[123] The Established Church had its advantages, as Wesley's experience and the experience of his family and friends had taught him. Wesley, even when pressed, if sometimes frustrated or shaken, was able to note the advantages of maintaining Methodism within the Church, and there were warrants for this.

'Chapel religion' was not always in conflict or competition with Church ministry. Indeed, conflict and competition could signal Anglican success at reform in the parishes. That clergy did not always (or often) agree with Methodist irregularities and entered into debate about the best means of pastoral care (which always included concern for the gospel message and was not seen simply as an add-on to salvation once people 'believed') meant that there was a measure of shared engagement with common concerns.[124] Friction arising from Methodism's building of societies, using lay preachers, and sending itinerating preachers into Church parishes was not necessarily an indication of clerical laxity. In addition, historians often fail to see that Methodism in its sometimes odd relationship with the Church did in several places function either as a cooperative ministry, as Wesley claimed he always intended, or as an adjunct to the pastoral work of the clergy. Indeed, there is recorded evidence that even in some places where Methodists were numerous (suggesting enough of a critical mass to establish themselves separately), they still 'attend the Church and communicate regularly'.[125] There was also ambiguity over how to interpret the presence of Methodism in the parishes, especially when the preachers were ordained clergymen, who were sometimes

---

[121] On Anglican Evangelicals, see Ryan Nicholas Danker, *Wesley and the Anglicans: Political Division in Early Evangelicalism* (Downers Grove, IL, 2016).

[122] *Works (BE)*, 4, pp. 351–9.   [123] *Letters*, VI, pp. 326–7.

[124] Cf. Jeremy Gregory, 'Archbishops of Canterbury, their Diocese, and the Shaping of the National Church', in Gregory and Chamberlain (eds), *The National Church*, pp. 29–52 (p. 46); William Gibson, '"A happy fertile Soil which bringeth forth abundantly": The Diocese of Winchester 1689–1800', in Gregory and Chamberlain (eds.), *The National Church*, pp. 99–120 (pp. 105–6).

[125] W. R. Ward (ed.), *Parson and Parish in Eighteenth Century Hampshire: Replies to Bishops' Visitations*, Hampshire Records Series 13 (Winchester, 1995), quoted in Gibson, '"A happy fertile Soil"', p. 106.

held up as examples by their own parishes to less diligent clergy in neighbouring parishes.[126]

Even after the breach between Methodism and Anglicanism that took place in England following Wesley's death and the moves by the succeeding leaders of Conference, there were still churchpeople of an Evangelical and Methodist persuasion who refused to leave the Church of England. Indeed, as late as the 1840s there were those who had been nurtured under the likes of John and Charles Wesley and John Fletcher, and who wrote apologetics with the hopes that the cleavage between the Church and Methodists could yet be healed. The Evangelical William Morgan had served as curate to John Crosse, vicar of Bradford, and had close ties with the Wesleys and their preachers and was influenced by Fletcher's Evangelical network. He authored a life of Crosse in 1841 highlighting the way in which Evangelical pastoral ideals were embodied in the dutifulness of a parish priest in cooperation with the new forms and structures provided by Methodism.[127] Like the Church Methodists in Madeley who could still be found attending their parish church in the 1840s, Wesley's experiment was still a living Anglican possibility.

SELECT BIBLIOGRAPHY

Abraham, William J. and James E. Kirby (eds.), *The Oxford Handbook of Methodist Studies* (Oxford, 2009).

Baker, Frank, *John Wesley and the Church of England* (Peterborough, 2000 edn.).

Danker, Ryan Nicholas, *Wesley and the Anglicans: Political Division in Early Evangelicalism* (Downers Grove, IL, 2016).

Davies, Rupert, Ernest Rupp, and Alfred George (eds.), *A History of the Methodist Church in Great Britain*, 4 vols. (London, 1965–88).

Gregory, Jeremy, '"In the Church I will Live and Die": John Wesley, the Church of England, and Methodism', in William T. Gibson and Robert G. Ingram (eds.), *Religious Identities in Britain, 1660–1832* (Aldershot, 2005), pp. 147–78.

Harding, Alan, *The Countess of Huntingdon's Connexion* (Oxford, 2003).

Hempton, David, *Methodism: Empire of the Spirit* (New Haven, CT, 2005).

Lloyd, Gareth, *Charles Wesley and the Struggle for Methodist Identity* (Oxford, 2007).

Mack, Phyllis, *Heart Religion in the British Enlightenment: Gender and Emotion in Early Methodism* (Cambridge, 2008).

Maddox, Randy L. and Jason E. Vickers (eds.), *The Cambridge Companion to John Wesley* (Cambridge, 2010).

---

[126] Cf. Richard Hill, *Goliath Slain* (London, 1768), pp. 174–5; Donald Spaeth, '"The Enemy Within": The Failure of Reform in the Diocese of Salisbury in the Eighteenth Century', in Gregory and Chamberlain (eds.), *The National Church*, pp. 121–44 (pp. 142–3).

[127] Morgan, *The Parish Priest*, pp. vii, 204.

Rack, Henry D., *Reasonable Enthusiast: John Wesley and the Rise of Methodism* (Peterborough, 2002 edn.).

Richey, Russell E., Kenneth E. Rowe, and Jean Miller Schmidt (eds.), *The Methodist Experience in America* (Nashville, TN, 2010).

Walsh, John D., 'Religious Societies: Methodist and Evangelical, 1738–1800', in W. J. Sheils and Diana Wood (eds.), *Voluntary Religion*, Studies in Church History 23 (Oxford, 1986), pp. 279–302.

Walsh, John, Colin Haydon, and Stephen Taylor (eds.), *The Church of England c.1689–c.1833: From Toleration to Tractarianism* (Cambridge, 1993).

Wesley, John, *The Bicentennial Edition of the Works of John Wesley*, ed. Frank Baker and Richard P. Heitzenrater (Oxford, 1975–83; Nashville, TN, 1984–).

Wesley, John, *The Letters of John Wesley*, ed. John Telford, 8 vols. (London, 1931).

Wilson, David R., *Church and Chapel in Industrializing Society: Anglican Ministry and Methodism in Shropshire, 1760–1785* (New York, 2017).

Index

Page numbers in *italic* refer to illustrations

Index

Index